WHO ARE YOU:

WHO ARE YOU:

The Life Of

Pete Townshend

A Biography by
Mark Wilkerson

OMNIBUS PRESS

London/New York/Paris/Sydney/Copenhagen/Madrid/Tokyo

Cover designed by Chlöe Alexander
Picture research by Sarah Bacon

ISBN: 978.1.84772.704.6
Order No: OP52767

Exclusive Distributors
Music Sales Limited,
14/15 Berners Street,
London, W1T 3LJ.

Music Sales Corporation,
257 Park Avenue South,
New York, NY 10010, USA.

Macmillan Distribution Services,
53 Park West Drive,
Derrimut, Vic 3030,
Australia.

Every effort has been made to trace the copyright holders of the photographs in this book but one or two were unreachable. We would be grateful if the photographers concerned would contact us.

Printed by Gutenberg Press Ltd, Malta

A catalogue record for this book is available from the British Library.

Visit Omnibus Press on the web at www.omnibuspress.com

Contents

"*I think this 'honest' thing really comes from something else: it comes from an openness rather than honesty. I don't think I'm particularly honest. But there's nothing about me that I want to keep secret . . . I wanna be judged for what I am, and that's why I'm as open as I can possibly be . . .*

"*I don't really talk about my problems because I think people are interested in my problems. I talk about them because I think they might be archetypal, because they may be general, because they might be things that people can identify with, and that my thinking processes might actually allow people to get a look at themselves . . .*"

– Pete Townshend, 1982

Foreword

By Eddie Vedder

The overriding emotion that remains with me since I first read this tremendous book is one of extreme gratitude to Mark Ian Wilkerson who has painstakingly pieced together a fascinating puzzle, bringing into focus the life of Pete Townshend in all its complexity and glory. It cannot have been easy.

That it took ten years to complete surprises me not in the least, and Townshend himself should receive much of the credit for this since the extraordinary life he has led offers both generous and worthy opportunities for scrutiny. Through the ages Pete has offered his listeners huge doses of introspection, delivered both lyrically and in interviews, narrating his own story as it progressed in a way that is without parallel in rock. Within these pages both mediums are not only fully explored but braided together, creating a chronological fabric with a tight and intricate weave.

In many ways this book can be considered the ultimate collection of PT/Who information. And Mr Wilkerson shows the tenacity of a supreme collector, a biographer who understands that in order to have pride in the collection there can't be any holes in the cloth. I was perpetually amazed at how many new insights I gained from these pages, and this is coming from someone who thought he knew everything there was about the subject. I know there are many of you out there just like me, because we have met at shows and in late night bars where we have watched the sun come up fuelled by stories and experiences of all things Pete and The Who. As testimony to the revelations herein, there were things I discovered about nights when was I actually there, sometimes even onstage.

Pete's journey is remarkable not only in its exploration of music and spirituality (and a combination of the two), but because we as listeners have been privileged to join him for the ride. It is a unique relationship between artist and follower. In my case, looking back to adolescence from where I am now, it stands as perhaps the longest relationship I've ever had! So outside of Pete being an icon, legendary composer and fucking great guitar player, I will always see him as a teacher. And this book is full of lessons, a few I had forgotten, a few I won't forget again.

As someone who has dedicated a formidable amount of his energy to absorbing what an artist or group has to offer, this book offers a final unsuspected gift; not just a reminder, but a validation of that devotion. That of all the bands, authors and artists you could have attached yourself to, aligning with Pete Townshend and The Who instigated the greatest of rides; an incredible trip that was both visceral and intellectual, outwardly passionate and inwardly contemplative, a roadmap of peaks and valleys and destinations for which to aspire. It is with that realisation that I offer my final expression of gratitude, this time to Pete. For changing music, affecting minds, and giving love.

Enjoy your ride.

Eddie Vedder
Seattle
November, 2007

Prologue

To the groups of practicing mods who populated London in the early Sixties, life outside the local dance halls, clubs, clothes shops and other various gathering places was of minimal importance. They were consumed with their appearance, from their short, carefully styled hair down to their made-to-measure shoes. The fashions were quite specific: Fred Perry shirts, narrow trousers or Levi's shrink-to-fit jeans, custom-made suits with narrow ties, military parkas. Transportation was scooters, the most fashionable of which were Italian-made Lambretta and Vespa models fitted with as many gaudy accessories as possible, including whip antennas, extra lights and mirrors, and leopard skin seat covers.

Meticulous attention was paid to the smallest of details when it came to the mod lifestyle, all in the name of being cool. "The mod way of life consisted of total devotion to looking and being 'cool'," Richard Barnes wrote in his 1982 book *Maximum R&B*. "Spending practically all your money on clothes and all your after work hours in clubs and dance halls. To be part-time was really to miss the point."

The mod's favourite music centred around American soul, Tamla and R&B ('mod' is short for 'modernists', i.e. fans of the modern jazz music of artists such as Ray Charles, Jimmy Smith and Mose Allison) which was filtering slowly into Britain in the early Sixties. The favourites included Ben E. King, the Impressions, the Shirelles, and Muddy Waters. This music was far from mainstream, and it was decidedly difficult to obtain copies of the 'in' recordings, making it all the more appealing to the mod crowd.

London's West End, specifically Soho, became a hotbed of mod activity with clubs such as the Flamingo and the Scene setting many trends and featuring the most prominent and important proponents of mod, known as 'faces'. The atmosphere in these early R&B clubs was electric as these immaculately dressed, adolescents checked each other out. Amphetamine use was rampant – pills such as 'Purple Hearts' and 'French blues' maintained the requisite energy level. Many important groups played in London's R&B clubs at this time, including the Rolling Stones, the Animals, the Yardbirds, and a young Shepherd's Bush-based outfit called

The Who, formerly The Detours, who by mid-1964, had already attracted strong mod attention and thanks to the influence of their publicist Peter Meaden, had just changed their name to The High Numbers.

On June 30 that year, they began a 12-week residency in a small R&B club frequented by mods in Wealdstone, north west London. The Railway Hotel was a "very scruffy looking" place according to Kit Lambert, who would become their co-manager, and The High Numbers "were playing there in this room with just one red bulb glowing and an extraordinary audience that they had collected." Ambience management at the Railway fell to Richard Barnes, an Ealing Art School student who ran the club's entertainment bookings. Barnes had seen to it that the atmosphere was just right. "We turned off all the lights except two in which we had put pink bulbs," he wrote. "The radiators were deliberately turned up and all the windows blacked out . . . a capacity was fixed at 180 but there had been occasions when we had issued tickets for as many as 1,000, though a couple of hundred of those would have to content themselves with checking out the scooters in the courtyard."

The group, Roger Daltrey, 20, vocals, Pete Townshend, 19, guitar, John Entwistle, 19, bass, and newly acquired drummer Keith Moon, 17, played rock'n'roll, blues and R&B numbers – a fairly standard set for a local live act at the time – on a rather delicate stage made from beer crates and table tops. But what set The High Numbers apart from their contemporaries was the presence of Tamla-Motown songs in their repertoire (the Detroit-based label featured black soul artists such as the Miracles, the Marvelettes, Martha & the Vandellas, and Stevie Wonder) and their sheer volume. "They were the loudest group I'd ever heard," said Lambert. Townshend's Rickenbacker guitar, slung high, almost across his chest, responded with crushing volume to every gyration he made as he windmilled his arm, slashing his hand not across but *through* the strings, then facing his huge speaker cabinet and coaxing screeching feedback from the instrument. Moon's drumming left nobody unaffected; he bashed away with wild abandon as though his very life depended on it. The intense energy and power of his style often required the lashing down of his kit with rope prior to a gig. Entwistle, whose bass thundered through a cabinet similar in size to that of Townshend's, stood relatively still and expressionless as he observed the proceedings, with Daltrey fronting the ensemble, scowling, pacing, snarling into the microphone.

Before the end of their residency at the Railway, The High Numbers had drawn enough attention to warrant the construction of a proper wooden stage. The stage had a bit more room and was also slightly higher, something which the six-foot tall Townshend discovered during the show. "I started to knock the guitar about a lot, hitting it on the amps to get banging noises and things like that," Townshend described. ". . . It banged against the ceiling and smashed a hole in the plaster and the guitar head actually poked through the ceiling . . . When I brought it out, the top of the neck was left behind." Not really knowing what to do next, and noticing a few snickers from the crowd, which included a sizeable contingent of his Ealing Art College cohorts, Townshend smashed what was left of the Rickenbacker to pieces. "I had no recourse but to completely look as though I meant to do it, so I smashed the guitar and jumped all over the bits. It gave me a fantastic buzz. About a month earlier I'd managed to scrape together enough for a 12-string Rickenbacker, which I only used on two or three numbers. It was lying at the side of the stage so I just picked it up, plugged it in and gave them a sort of look and carried on playing, as if I'd meant to do it."

"This went down tremendously well with the audience," Lambert recalled in 1969, ". . . and that's how the whole thing started."

CHAPTER ONE

1945–1964

"Ever since I was in art college, I believed that the elegance of pop music is that it is reflective – it holds up a mirror; and that, in its most exotic and finest sense, it is deeply, deeply philosophically and spiritually reflective, rather than just societally."

– Pete Townshend, 2000

ON May 19, 1945 – just 11 days after Winston Churchill officially announced the end of the war with Germany to huge crowds in London – Peter Dennis Blandford Townshend (Dennis was his mother's maiden name, Blandford his father's middle name) was born in Nazareth House, an annex of West Middlesex Hospital, Isleworth, west London.

Pete was immersed in music from the very start. Parents Cliff and Betty were members of the entertainment corps of the Royal Air Force; Cliff an alto saxophonist, Betty a singer. They met in London when Cliff was a member of the RAF Dance Orchestra and Betty was a singer with the Sidney Torch Orchestra, which taped programmes to be sent to troops deployed overseas. The RAF Dance Orchestra (which became known as the Squadronaires) was immensely popular throughout Britain and during the war had played their brand of Benny Goodman/Glenn Miller-esque swing throughout Allied Europe.[1] After the war, when the band members left the RAF they went on the road to Britain's various coastal holiday resorts, maintaining a busy touring schedule up until the mid-Sixties, when they disbanded amid the surge of interest in contemporary popular music, led by The Beatles and The Rolling Stones.

In 1946, the Squadronaires began to accept extended summer bookings at holiday resorts in Britain, the first being in Clacton, a seaside town on

---

[1] When the Squadronaires played in Manchester, the opening act was the Ted Astley Orchestra, led by Pete's future father-in-law.

the east coast, then a more extended booking at the Isle of Man, an island off the coast of Lancashire in the north-west, which would last about 13 summers.[2] Pete accompanied his mother and father on these trips, soaking in the musical environment, watching rehearsals and shows, and playing on the beach. He travelled extensively with his parents until he reached school age, when his musical excursions were limited to the summer break.

"My father was a musician in a dance band, so I was brought up in two places," Pete said in a 1993 radio interview. "During the week we were in dance halls . . . This is as young as two or three years old, I was running around dance halls. My mother used to sing with my dad's band, I was kind of on the loose with guys that drank. I was a real kind of rock'n'roll baby . . . The other thing that they used to do at weekends was these Sunday concerts where there would be like variety shows. So there would be like girls, comedians, big stars from the USA . . . But my father also took me a little bit further, he took me into the orchestral writing of Duke Ellington which was very, very avant-garde in its time. He took me to see the Basie Band."

Pete's parents had settled in Acton, West London. The shadow of the recent war loomed large, as the area had sustained heavy damage from German bombs in recent years. "When I was four I lived in a house where 12 people had died," Pete told the *Daily Telegraph*'s Neil McCormick in 2006. "We played in bomb sites, we'd find bits of bodies, skeletons and watches every day." The Townshend family home, which occupied the lower floor of 22 Whitehall Gardens, was sparsely occupied much of the time since Pete's parents were often on the road, especially Cliff, as the Squadronaires were now known as the best swing outfit in the country.

Cliff and Betty Townshend separated for a protracted period when Pete was about five. Their son was sent to live in Kent with his maternal grandmother, Emma Dennis, known as 'Granny Denny'. "I was dumped with my grandmother for two years," Pete told *Rolling Stone*'s Anthony DeCurtis in 1993. "I was very lonely, never heard from my father at all. My mother used to come down on the weekend for an hour to see me,

---

[2] "Growing up around my father's band was wonderful," Pete told *The Desert Sun*'s Bruce Fessier in 2006. "The only regret I have was that, when my father invited me to play guitar with him in his afternoon band on the Isle of Man when I was about 14 or 15, I didn't have the confidence to join him. If I had, I would have side-stepped rock'n'roll and R&B and had a much quieter and no doubt more stable life."

dressed incredibly seductively. She was beautiful and I just longed to be with her. I just wanted to be with my fabulous, exciting, brilliant, beautiful parents. Instead I was with this bitter, crotchety, clinically insane grandmother."

Life at Grandma Denny's house was "hell", Pete recalled in 1993. "It was a fucking nightmare. My father used to send me five shillings a week, a fabulous amount of money in those days. And I would go to the shop with my grandmother and buy myself a toy and she would take the toy and put it in a cupboard. Then when my mother came to see me, my grandmother would make me get all the toys out as though I'd been playing with them. And then when my mother had gone, I'd have to put them all away again. She was a complete head case."

Pete again described his grandmother as "clinically insane" when he was interviewed in 1993. "It's kind of been the one ribbon that's run continually through my life," he told David Letterman, demonstrating the profound influence wrought by the two-year ordeal. "This is my cauldron," Pete told *Minstrel's Dilemma* author Larry David Smith in 1997. "If I go too deeply into this . . . opening it up . . . my relationship with my grandmother is something – which to date – I've not been able to make any sense of whatsoever. It's the only bit of my life that I haven't been able to make any sense of and, in a sense, I feel that if I was able to go into regressive hypnosis and either find some terrible trauma or nothing at all, it would be equally damaging to me as an artist." Pete's disturbing period of trauma and upheaval ended when Cliff and Betty Townshend reconciled and the small family was reunited, back in Acton.

While Pete had developed a strong distaste for his maternal grandmother, he enjoyed the company of his father's siblings and parents. As a young child, he used to visit his aunt Trilby's apartment, where he'd clumsily play the piano as she offered words of praise and encouragement, a childhood memory Pete later used in his novella *The Boy Who Heard Music*. "I spent very little time with her," Townshend told the author. "I was fond of her, but more fond of my paternal grandparents who lived below in the same duplex apartment, so I would always prefer their company if I could get it."

It was on the Isle of Man during the summer of 1956 that Cliff Townshend took Pete and his friend Graham 'Jimpy' Beard to see *Rock Around The Clock*, a film featuring music by Bill Haley & His Comets. "Well, they wanted to see it the next day and the next day and in the end we were giving them the money or getting passes for them," Betty told

Dave Marsh in 1983. "They were seeing this film daily – practically every rainy day, anyway. Peter really absolutely adored music, and when this Bill Haley and rock'n'roll thing started, he was right into it. He was very little; he was 10. And he loved it." Soon afterwards, Cliff took Pete to see Haley perform live – Pete's first concert. "I was 11 and-a-half-years old," Pete recalled in 1993, "and I remember once my friend ['Jimpy'] who came with me saying, 'Do you like this music Cliff?' He said, 'I like anything that swings.'"

From this point, Pete's interest in music began to focus on rock'n'roll rather than the swing music of his parents and their generation. As musicians themselves, Cliff and Betty were supportive of their son's tastes at a time when many disapproved of the direction that popular music was taking. Up to this point in his life the only musical instrument Pete had really showed an interest in had been the harmonica. "My father was essentially a pop musician in his day," Pete told the *NME*'s Richard Green. "I dread to think what would have happened if I had been brought up in a classical family. He promised me a harmonica which I never got and in the end I think I had to shoplift one a couple of years later." With the impact of *Rock Around The Clock* fresh in his mind, he began to show an interest in the guitar.

Guitars weren't new to the Townshend family. "My father had played the guitar when he was young and my uncle Jack had worked for Kalamazoo [a depression-era offshoot of Gibson], before the war, developing guitar pickups," Pete told *Guitarist* in 1990. "So there was a kind of a family thing about the guitar, although it was considered something of an anomaly then." Pete's original intention was to emulate his father and play saxophone, but ". . . I couldn't blow a note so he suggested the guitar," he said. "Chromatic harmonica was actually my first instrument and I got very good at it – not quite Stevie Wonder, but very good. Then I hit 11 and decided I did want to try the guitar . . ."

Pete's grandmother bought him his first guitar for Christmas in 1956, which he remembers as "a cheap Spanish thing", which again brought to the surface Pete's distaste for Granny Denny. "My father was going to buy me a guitar for my 11-year-old Christmas – and he would have bought me a fabulous instrument," Pete said in 1993. "But what fucking happened is that *she* bought it! She bought me a guitar like you see on the wall of a Spanish restaurant, a phony guitar. I was excited for a while, standing in front of the mirror, but I realised very quickly that I was never going to be able to play anything on it." Cliff taught his son some basic chords, but

Pete struggled mightily with the instrument, "just a really, really cheap guitar . . . I fought tooth and nail with it for a year and finally gave up because it was such a bad instrument."

In 1956, Pete was placed in Acton County Grammar School. As he entered adolescence and started to notice the opposite sex, Pete began to realise that the size of his nose was becoming an obstacle to his acceptance in the various social circles that existed at grammar school. His nose was often a topic of conversation both at school and at home and this unwanted attention affected Pete profoundly. "Grammar school was very painful for me," Pete told *Penthouse* in 1974. "I was very embarrassed and self-conscious about my nose for quite a while. I got obsessed with it. Music was my escape. My mother was no help, she seemed to think that anybody who wasn't beautiful couldn't be any good. She was gorgeous, of course. My father was very good-looking, too. How they spawned me I'll never know. Dad was kind to me about the nose, but in an unintentionally devastating manner. He used to say things like, 'Don't worry. Arthur Miller married Marilyn Monroe, didn't he?' I didn't want to look like fucking Arthur Miller, I wanted to look like James Dean."

Deciding against wallowing in self-pity, Pete grew defiant: the fact that people often bated him about his nose began to serve as personal motivation to succeed at something which would make them forget that his nose was ever there. ". . . I used to think, 'I'll bloody well show them,'" he told the *Evening Standard*. "'I'll push my huge hooter out at them from every newspaper in England – then they won't laugh at me.' And when I first started singing with a group, I used to go up onstage and forget that I was Pete Townshend who wasn't a success with the ladies, and all of a sudden I'd become aware that there were little girls giggling and pointing at my nose. And I'd think, "Sod 'em – they're not gonna laugh at me!" And I'd get angrier still. My whole absurdly demonstrative stage act was worked out to turn myself into a body instead of a face. Most pop singers were pretty, but I wanted people to look at my body, and not have to bother looking at my head if they didn't like the look of it."[3]

★   ★   ★

[3] Pete's physical appearance haunted him for years. When asked in 1986 to name the biggest obstacle he'd overcome in his life, 40-year-old Townshend replied, "Believing myself to be unattractive." But his nose was also recognised as a selling point. The Who's 1966 *Observer* magazine cover photo, with Townshend standing at the centre, was shot with a fish-eye lens – reportedly Chris Stamp's idea – which greatly exaggerated the size of Pete's nose.

Around this time, the Townshend family moved only a few hundred yards west of their Whitehall Gardens home to a spacious, two-floor terraced brick house just east of Ealing Common on Woodgrange Avenue. These larger confines welcomed additional family members, as Pete's brothers Paul and Simon were born in 1957 and 1960, respectively.[4]

Music was the common denominator around the household. "On a Sunday afternoon my Dad would come in and play his sax and all his mates would come in – Tommy Thompson with his bass, Billy Sharp playing the trumpet – and it was just like a fantastic house," Simon Townshend recalls. "It's quite extraordinary in some ways. A lot of drinking and a lot of partying and a lot of people around all the time, really."

But beyond the music and the gaiety, Cliff and Betty had a turbulent marriage – both had flinty tempers fuelled by frequent drinking (a trait which Pete would unfortunately inherit) and Betty had occasional affairs. Pete later referred to her as "unfaithful".

"It was a fiery household, without a doubt," Simon recalls, offering the following unsettling illustration of his parents' relationship: "If you've ever seen *Who's Afraid of Virginia Woolf* with Elizabeth Taylor and Richard Burton, you could literally put my mum and dad into those roles and they would slot in so perfectly."

Pete's grammar school friend and fellow guitarist Alan Pittaway, who lived in nearby Hart Grove, used to visit Pete at Woodgrange Avenue. Pittaway remembers a palpable tension between Townshend and his mother. "I think [Betty] obviously ruled the nest, because [Cliff] was away quite a lot as a professional musician," Pittaway says. "If I was round there and we were playing the guitar, Pete would become very anxious. She was quite physical, very strict. I never saw a nice side of her. I'm sure she had a nice side, but I never saw it. She always seemed to be very angry to me. I never worked out what it was she was angry about. I think that's why Pete was a quiet boy. He used to go to his room and play. Maybe that was his escape from it all – his own little world he created."

Pete had a complicated relationship with both parents. He offered some thoughts on the subject in an interview with the *San Diego Union* in 1989. "I wrote about my mother and the relationship we had," Pete said. "I've continued to write about it and it still hurts. She's still a very fiery,

---

[4] Simon Townshend was born at the Woodgrange Avenue home. Today, Simon and Paul Townshend both live there with their respective families. "It's hard to get away," says Simon, citing the house's family connections.

exciting, stimulating character, and she can hurt you very badly if she wants to. And I find myself doing the same back to her." Pete said that his relationship with his father "wasn't that intimate. He was very busy, and I think that in a Freudian sense, I'm doing the same thing; I don't see half enough of my family because I'm so wrapped up in my work. He was very simple, very loving, very uncomplicated, very straightforward and immensely proud that I was successful at anything. He really didn't like that it was rock because it wasn't really decent in his view; he hated the drugs. But he was an absolutely sterling supporter of anything I did." Pete added in a 1989 interview with *Guitar Player*, "I just wanted to be like my dad; you know, I worshipped him. He was a magnificent player and a fantastic man."

Meanwhile, Pete's difficulties learning to play his new guitar and his evolving taste in music soon saw his aspirations drift toward the banjo. "I started to examine what was happening, listening to Elvis Presley like all my friends," he said in 1990, "but to be honest I never really liked him, and also I think Scotty Moore was an aberration – it's not my idea of great playing," adding, "I know that's sacrilege to many people and I wouldn't want to slight him as an individual or as a player, because he's cited as a seminal influence by so many people, but for me it was more the sound of Nancy Whiskey. Yes, the sound of strumming guitars, such a glorious sound." Whiskey was a member of the Chas McDevitt Skiffle Group, which was riding the wave of the genre's new popularity with their single 'Freight Train', on which she sang lead vocals.

Both skiffle – a basic, uptempo variety of folk music – and trad jazz – a new form of swing – experienced considerable popularity during this period. Chief among skiffle musicians was Lonnie Donegan, who is credited with boosting the genre's profile with his 1956 hit 'Rock Island Line'. Pete was especially taken with the new wave of banjo players which emerged during the upswing of skiffle and trad. "The players I looked at were the guys with Acker Bilk, Ken Colyer and Kenny Ball," he said in 1990. "English banjo players really were a law unto themselves – you don't find that kind of brisk banjo playing on the original Louis Armstrong or Bix Beiderbecke records. But Acker Bilk's banjo player had this very vital, bright sound. He used a G banjo with a long scale and played it with lots of flourishes and I copied that until I went back to the guitar a couple of years later." Pete acquired a mandolin banjo, his sights firmly set on joining the Confederates – "quite a good trad band – we even had a tuba player," – at Pete's school featuring a trumpet player named John Entwistle.

The Confederates, who devoted more time to rehearsing than actually performing, played only at the local church youth club, the Congo Club (short for Congregational Club). "It was when I came closest to being part of a gang," Pete recalled to Richard Barnes. "I got caught up with a guy called Stewart Dodd. He and I both had big noses at school and he was nicknamed Oscar after some cartoon character with a big nose. He went through an incredible metamorphosis. We didn't see him for some time and I saw him rolling down the street drunk one day. I said 'Hello Oscar' and he smacked me in the teeth and threw a bottle at me. He had turned into a petty villain overnight and was caught up with a local bunch of hard nuts and just hated being called by his school nickname. I started to live in the real world after that.[5] I had shut myself away plunking away on the banjo at home and suddenly realised that the Congo wasn't just a place where we got together and entertained the troops, as it were. There was a lot of violence and sex and stuff going on."

The 14-year-old found being a member of The Confederates attractive for reasons other than music. Adult topics such as political activism and sex were vying for his attention. "We were all very left wing, or they were – I didn't know what politics was about, but I went on the Aldermaston march – or, again, they did," he said in 1990.[6] "And they were always disappearing into sleeping bags with girls . . ."

While initially excited about being in a group, Pete was rather self-conscious about his abilities as a musician. "I had to rush out and get a chord book," he recalled to Richard Green. "As I'd been buggering about playing guitar for nearly two years I wasn't getting anywhere. They expected me to play and were fairly impressed, which I couldn't work out. Perhaps they thought that if you could play three chords you could play the rest." At one time there were three banjo players – one of whom would eventually bump Pete out of the line-up. "This guy Alf Maynard had a Vega banjo and was very much the central figure of the band, so I got edged out. I was a better player than him but I didn't really fit and didn't push myself too much," Townshend told Richard Barnes.

---

[5] This rough encounter later formed the basis of an incident used in *Fish Shop,* an unrealised play Townshend was commissioned to write and record music for in 1978.

[6] The Aldermaston March was a Campaign For Nuclear Disarmament march from London to Aldermaston – the site of a new atomic weapons plant - the first of which took place on Good Friday, 1958, to protest Britain's initial atomic bomb tests on Christmas Island in the Pacific Ocean. The march, which covered over 50 miles in four days, attracted around 10,000 participants, according to the BBC.

Pete's brief tenure with The Confederates came to an end when an argument erupted with Chris Sherwin, the group's drummer. "We got into a fight and I hit him over the head with a bag and he had a concussion which I didn't realise," Pete recalled to Barnes in 1982. "As a result I was sort of ignored by our little school playground clique. They gave me the cold shoulder. I was a little disturbed by it and went more into my shell in a way and transferred it to the guitar. I just decided to use what was really a pretty bleak period for that."

This withdrawal from The Confederates, combined with a resurgence of an interest in rock'n'roll, saw Pete's banjo playing days come to a close in 1960. The recent success in Britain of Cliff Richard & the Shadows had brought the guitar to the forefront once again and Pete particularly admired their lead guitarist Hank Marvin. Chuck Berry, while enjoying immense popularity during this period in America, was yet to have an impact on him. "I never got much into roots rock apart from Bill Haley," Pete told *Sounds* in 1980. "I never liked Elvis very much or his band . . . I did like Jimmy Burton who played with Rick Nelson; he was a big influence."

Townshend bought a "reasonably good Czechoslovakian guitar" for £3 at 'Miscellania', his parents' antiques shop on Ealing Common and gave up playing his mandolin banjo, but the rapid strumming technique he had learned remained. "I also got myself a little amplifier and went electric," he recalled in 1993. Before long the amplifier became the first of many to suffer the Townshend treatment. "One day, I was about 14, John and I were sitting playing something together in the front room, not very loud, and Granny Denny came in and she said, 'Turn that bloody awful row down,'" Pete told H.P. Newquist of *Guitar* in 1996. And I said, 'Get out now or I'm going to kill you, you fucking old bag.' She yelled, 'How dare you talk to me like that!' So I picked up my amplifier and threw it at her. She ran to the other side of the door and the amplifier landed there in a big heap and it fizzed and went off. And I'd just bought it. I'd worked delivering newspapers for literally three years to buy it. And John looked at me and said in that low voice, 'That was good. Done it now, haven't you?' But I got it repaired."

Townshend and Entwistle soon formed another group with two school friends, with Pete playing guitar and John on bass. "We used to play Shadows numbers," Townshend told Green. "I was terribly happy with it and people quite liked us. It gave me a new confidence. I hadn't made it very well with chicks, and at the time when my mates started to get it

9

together with chicks I was getting into the guitar. It became quite an obsession." They called themselves The Aristocrats, then The Scorpions, and following the rehearsal-heavy tradition of The Confederates, they played only once, in front of an audience, at the Congo Club.

Pete's friend Alan Pittaway, whose first group, The Sulgrave Rebels, featured fellow grammar school pupil Roger Daltrey on rhythm guitar and vocals, later played guitar for The Mustangs, one of two popular local groups – the second being The Detours – whose members hailed from Acton County Grammar School. On October 21, 1961, Pete performed two gigs with The Mustangs. "We got him to join our band," Pittaway recalls, "'cause he was playing Shadows stuff and we were playing the same stuff [the centrepiece of The Mustangs' act was the Shadows' 1960 hit 'Apache']. We just needed an extra guitar so he did some gigs with us."

"They were the first gigs we had ever done," recalls Mustangs drummer Peter Amott. "The first one was at Shepherd's Bush Cricket Club, followed by probably Pete's first appearance at the White Hart hotel [in Acton]. The latter was actually a dinner dance for the BP Scout Guild, and we were most embarrassed as, after performing, we all stood in the middle of the dance floor whilst money was thrown to us by the audience."

Pete left school in the autumn of 1961 aged 16 and enrolled in a two-year introductory course at nearby Ealing Art College, which allowed him to pursue other interests.[7] "I did two years of foundation, when I was exposed to all the futuristic stuff," Townshend recalled to the author. "I went into graphic design rather begrudgingly because I had wanted to work on installation sculptures that involved small buildings and music. The sculpture school failed to get a diploma accreditation. I [later] used my talent for graphics in my early design work for The Who. Target T-shirts, T-shirts and jackets with medals and chevrons, The Who logo with the arrow based on the male symbol, etc. Strange that today most graphics is computer based which is probably what the ground-breaking tutors in my Foundation course were really predicting, not what I thought they meant – which was that computers would mean I could take my art to the world in a single bound one day."

The art school was less than a mile from the Townshend home on

---

[7] "It was probably the terrible noise I used to make on my first electric guitar that made my father suggest that I go to art school and concentrate on the graphic rather than the musical areas of education," Townshend told Andrew Motion in 1987.

Woodgrange Avenue. "It was such a great period for me. I had a natural artistic bent which was why I ended up at art school, but basically I should have done something to do with writing I suppose, but if I had I probably wouldn't have ended up sort of so open-endedly creative as I later became. The art side did get my brain going creatively and started me thinking."

Ealing Art College was a think-tank containing much local artistic talent that went on to musical careers, including future Faces/Rolling Stones guitarist Ronnie Wood and Queen frontman Freddie Mercury. Richard Barnes, who met Pete at the school in 1962 and has remained a close friend, recalled the atmosphere two decades later in his book *Maximum R&B*: "Ealing Art School was a very unusual art school. This normally staid institution had, in the same year that Pete enrolled, acquired a new head tutor, Roy Ascot. He had replaced most of the staff with young fresh Sixties designers and artists and was to begin a revolutionary experiment in art tuition based on the science of Cybernetics."

Cybernetics is defined, according to Webster's dictionary, as "the science dealing with the comparative study of human control systems, as the brain and nervous system, and complex electronic systems." Barnes recalled that Townshend, along with many "excited but confused students," jumped right in. "Printmaking, basic design, sculpture and colour theory," he added, "were all intermingled with feedback, noise-interference and automation principles," in the interests of studying and comparing the inner workings of man and machine.

One particular art school project involved each member of the class being assigned certain physical characteristics. Pete's rather debilitating scenario was to face life with no legs and an inability to communicate with others. To tackle the first problem, he and some fellow students fashioned a cart out of old orange boxes and the wheels from a baby carriage. "Not only did I have to push myself about on this cart," Pete said in 1982, "but I also had to communicate in a phonetic alphabet that my group had to think up. In a way it was like fucking acting school."

Prominent artists, designers and playwrights gave lectures at the school, including Larry Rivers, Robert Brownjohn, autodestructive art pioneer Gustav Metzger and American pop-artist R.B. Kitaj.[8] Metzger proved

---

[8] Pete told an interviewer in 1982 that ". . . artists like Jackson Pollock . . ." gave lectures while he was at Ealing Art School. In *Before I Get Old*, Dave Marsh pointed out that this was impossible since Pollock died five years before Pete enrolled.

particularly influential. Barnes wrote that the artist ". . . showed slides of paintings done in acid on sheets of metal showing the stages of 'beauty' as the acid slowly destroyed the metal and was later publicly acknowledged by Pete for his inspiration on autodestruction." Pete recalled that Metzger later, "turned up at some [Who] shows when we were smashing stuff up. He really got into it."

"In Britain . . . art colleges were intense, hothouse places, with brilliant, over-qualified teachers and pupils who left with a comprehensive avant-garde education and had to find a use for it in a deeply conservative society," wrote *The Guardian*'s Jonathan Jones in 2000. Artist and teacher Michael Craig-Martin told Jones, "I came to Britain in the Sixties, and was immediately teaching in a provincial art school and I couldn't believe how good the school was. They were sophisticated about art. What you often saw were extremely bright students who had failed in the conventional education system. At art college, the things that had been a disadvantage became an advantage. But when people came out of those institutions there was nothing for them. One of the reasons for them going into other fields, including pop music, was that there was nowhere for them to have a career in Britain."

Music was also a big part of life at art school. "There would be lessons where you sort of listened to jazz, or listened to classical music, or explored minimalism," Townshend said in 1982. "We had jazz musicians, film writers, playwrights as well as artists . . . to come and lecture. It was a clearing house and music was something that was very much considered to be okay and not something that you only did after hours. It was part of life. You could sit in a classroom with people painting *and* playing. I used to do it."

In 1962, Tom Wright, a photography student at Ealing Art School who hailed from Alabama, asked Pete to teach him some guitar licks after he'd overheard him playing in the common room.[9] Townshend visited the flat on nearby Sunnyside Road that Wright shared with his friend 'Cam' McLester and was blown away by the Americans' record collection, which had around 150 blues, R&B and jazz albums, many of which were very difficult to find in Britain. Townshend and Barnes became regular visitors to Sunnyside Road where Pete would teach Tom to play the guitar in exchange for access to the record collection. "I got my introduction to the blues and a lot of other stuff too like Mose Allison, Ray Charles, Jimmy

---

[9] Wright published a fascinating memoir, *Roadwork*, in 2007.

Smith, Jimmy Reed and [John Lee] Hooker," Townshend recalled in 1980.

"Hooker's chord work convinced me that pinning down a precise and solid chordal structure was far more important for me than learning by rote the solos of virtuosos like B. B. King and Buddy Guy," he elaborated in 1997.[10]

Chuck Berry, Howlin' Wolf, Little Walter, Bo Diddley, Booker T., Lonnie Mack and Jimmy Smith were just some of the artists in the collection that left an imprint on Townshend's memory, "and a few rather less obvious gems which none the less changed my head, the shape of my fingers, the way I walked and generally improved the appearance of the ladies I associated with," he told *Rolling Stone* in 1970.

Many evenings were spent listening to these important recordings while imbibing Wright's pot stash. "When I first got into pot I was involved in the environment more," Townshend told Richard Green. "There was a newness about art college, having beautiful girls around for the first time in my life, having all that music around me for the first time, and it was such a great period – with The Beatles exploding and all that all over the place. So it was very exciting, but although pot was important to me, it wasn't the biggest thing: the biggest thing was the fact that pot helped to make incredible things even more incredible."

Wright and McLester's stint at Ealing Art College ended when they were busted for possession of marijuana in late 1963 and deported from England. Wright asked Townshend and Barnes to move into the flat and keep an eye on the contents, an opportunity they both jumped at.

Meanwhile, in 1961, John Entwistle went on to join The Detours, the group fronted by Roger Daltrey, who'd left school to become a sheet metal worker and was earning a reputation for his abrasive manner. By mid-1962, the stage was set for Townshend's arrival.

"We brought in this guy on rhythm guitar because he'd come into a little bit of money and bought himself a Vox amp and a guitar," Entwistle recalled to Barnes in 1982. "We figured like if we had him in the group we'd be able to use his amplifier. He could sing a bit as well. The poor guy went on holiday with his fiancée and drowned, so we took over his amplifier. We figured he didn't need it any more. We still had this other rhythm guitarist called Reg Bowen, but he only knew about five chords so

---

[10] Pete saw Hooker perform at Soho's Flamingo Club in 1964.

eventually we started looking for a new rhythm guitarist and that's when I managed to persuade Pete to join. He didn't, however, want to join at first but I told him we had a real Vox amplifier, so he thought 'A Vox amplifier . . . well . . .' and he joined."

The five-piece Detours (with Pete playing rhythm guitar while Roger played lead) played numerous songs by Cliff Richard & the Shadows, with the group being "very much a singer with a backing band," according to Barnes. Townshend later complained that singer Colin Dawson (who used the stage name "Del Angelo") wiggled his backside too much while singing.

By late summer 1962, The Detours were playing at various company dances, bar mitzvahs and weddings, transportation being provided by drummer Harry Wilson's dad. The group secured their first residency around July, playing approximately five consecutive weeks at the Paradise Club in Peckham, south London. A key addition was made during this residency when Doug Sandom replaced Wilson as drummer.

Sandom, who was eight years older than the other members and brought stability and experience into the mix, recalls meeting The Detours for the first time on Acton High Street. "I thought they were a weird lot, I really did," Sandom recalls with a laugh. "They were younger than me, you know, I'd been playing for quite a while in different bands and they were really young. Anyhow, I got on fine with them. The guy I got on best with was John. Roger, he was a likeable bloke, you know, jolly . . . Peter was something different altogether. Hard to get on with. Peter was . . . very quiet. It was hard work trying to get to know him. I got on all right with him, it got better the longer I was there. He was just quiet. It was a love-hate [thing]. I loved his playing, I loved his music, but I didn't get on very well with him, you know."

Even at this early stage, the band members, especially Townshend and Daltrey, occasionally displayed a distinct distaste for each other, as Sandom told Barnes, "When we were practicing sometimes, it was nothing to see Roger smack Pete in the nose or something. They were always at each other's throats."

When asked about the previous quote, Sandom says. "Yeah, Peter reckoned I was overdoing it, but it's true. They used to fight, but they were mates the next minute. It was only a blow-up over something stupid. One I remember is that we were rehearsing in a working man's club and I think Peter was having a go at John who was such a quiet fellow, he wouldn't say nothing. I used to take [John's side] . . . he used to let Peter tell him off and shout and bully him. That time [Roger] did smack Peter, yeah."

In late 1962, The Detours played various venues, including a regular booking at Ealing's Jewish Youth Club and at dance halls and various company outings. The group generally played four or five nights a week, often driven to gigs by Betty Townshend, who carried the group and/or their equipment (there wasn't room for both) in the Ford van she used for her antiques shop. "It was my mother who actually gave us the most moral and vocal support in the early days," Pete told the *San Diego Union* in 1989. "She set up auditions, lent us her van and almost used to roadie for us."

Pete's supportive parents also provided a meeting place for The Detours. "We used to meet round at Betty's house, sit down and talk," Sandom recalls, pointing out that The Detours' equipment was stored at the house. "I used to see quite a lot of her. She was nice. She was good to us." Sandom recalls Cliff as "a really nice guy. I got on well with him," surmising that Cliff probably felt a particular affinity for Sandom since he was the eldest – and therefore most responsible – band member.

It was in November 1962 that Betty got The Detours their big break. Having gathered an impressive list of musical contacts and acquaintances over the years as a singer, she managed to get her son's group an audition with the area's leading booking agency Commercial Entertainments, which ran dances at numerous venues in west and south London. The nervous (Sandom told Richard Barnes that Pete was "white as a sheet") Detours auditioned by playing three songs at the Oldfield Hotel, in Greenford – an onstage affair during an intermission between sets by The Bel-Airs, one of the area's top groups at the time. "We went down there and they loved us, the crowd loved us, and that was it," Sandom recalls. "We had our foot on the bottom rung of the ladder." Gauging audience satisfaction as the deciding factor, Commercial Entertainments' manager Bob Druce signed The Detours to his books and within two weeks, they were regulars on Druce's pub and club circuit, which featured venues such as the Oldfield, the White Hart (Acton), and the Grand Ballroom in Broadstairs, Kent.

"[Druce] used to hire names like The Rolling Stones, The Hollies, The Searchers, all the top groups at that time, in the [early] Sixties and we used to open the night up, we used to play for an hour, then they'd go on, then we'd finish the night off," Sandom recalls. "And we never looked back then, you know what I mean? We were so busy, we'd work, work, all the time, very busy." Within a few months, Druce bought a van for the group, incrementally deducting the cost from their pay.

In late 1962, The Detours became a four-piece by bidding farewell to Colin Dawson, who was seemingly unable to juggle the commitments of an increasingly busy group, a full-time job, and a new fiancée. Soon after Dawson's departure, Cliff Townshend managed to land the group a regular Sunday booking at the Douglas House, Bayswater. "We used to do it Sunday lunchtimes from about two 'til about four," Sandom remembers, "and then we used to go on from there to one of Bob Druce's regular places to play at night."

Douglas House was a haunt of American servicemen so The Detours tailored their set-list accordingly, adding country and western songs, including a Johnny Cash medley. Doug Sandom: "They used to love it . . . a bit of Johnny Cash, of course, and every time we played anything they liked, they used to send us up a tray of scotch."

Ex-Bel Airs' bassist/singer Gabby Connolly was enlisted as a vocalist for the Douglas House residency. Doug Sandom: "The reason why we got Gabby there is because Roger couldn't fill a night out with vocals. So he used to help out with the vocals until Roger could fill a night, you know, do the whole night without anybody else. So he was there for a few months, maybe. But as soon as Roger felt like he was ready, Gabby went."

Roger's move to lead vocals paved the way for the group to truly develop a unique style. The event that precipitated this was a spring 1963 gig at St Mary's Hall in Putney, south-west London, where The Detours opened for Johnny Kidd & the Pirates, a tough, rockabilly-influenced combo whose stripped-down vocals/guitar/bass/drums formula and wild stage show (they dressed as pirates onstage) quickly earned them a reputation as one of the best rock'n'roll outfits in the country prior to the emergence of The Beatles. The sheer power and muscle of the Pirates' performance left a deep impression on The Detours, convincing Daltrey that a switch from lead guitar to vocals was necessary. "We thought they were great," recalls Sandom. "We thought, God, that *sound*. We loved the sound of that band."

After witnessing the Pirates' live, Townshend and Entwistle had a new appreciation for the power that could be elicited from their respective instruments. "If I'm going to hit a note or bend it, I really want to have to struggle for it, because I'm so physically wound up on the stage," Pete told *Guitar Player*'s Michael Brooks in 1972. "If I wanted to, I could pull the string up and break it with my hand. It's really weird, when I'm in the dressing room playing, I can hardly stretch the strings, and then when I go onstage I get a buzz and the strings feel slinky, they feel really slinky.

"The first guy that I met, my idol in England, was a guy named Mickey Green, who used to play with Johnny Kidd & the Pirates, and he was the first big note-bender, particularly on the G. And you'd freak over Jimmy Burton and you'd freak over Mickey Green and you wondered how they got that sound. Went to see a guy about it and he said it was the thin G, he uses like two 2nds instead of a G, right? So I got my guitar and I really got into it. I got to see Mickey play and I went backstage to see him and I asked him if I could play his guitar and he said, 'Sure, man.' I picked it up and he's got strings like bloody piano strings, they're huge! And the G isn't plain, it's wound, and he used to stretch it practically to the A string and beyond. Big hands and he would pull it down and tuck it under as well."

Townshend, Entwistle and Daltrey now had clearly defined roles into which they would grow into over the coming months, with each member finding his niche. Townshend's position as rhythm guitarist had now become simply *guitarist*.

Doug Sandom: "Peter, he was thrown in at the deep end there. He had to take over lead. And he got on quick, he's very sharp and that's where he got his style from – he's like, heavy chords . . . really heavy stuff, [because] he was copying Mick Green, the guitarist of the Pirates."

Aspiring to become a 'serious' band rather than simply a group of entertainers and since their personal tastes had evolved, the four-piece Detours progressed from playing Top 20 hits to R&B. Their set soon began to reflect the contents of Tom Wright's record collection and included songs by Chuck Berry, Jimmy Reed, Bo Diddley, Mose Allison, and Howlin' Wolf.

Financially strapped, The Detours stopped at nothing to keep up with those groups with better equipment. Handyman Daltrey told John Swenson, "When we first started, I used to make all the bloody guitars. We used to make our amplifiers as well . . . In them days it was all psychological warfare being in a group, so we hit on the idea of having the biggest cabinets you've ever seen in your life – yet inside we'd have this little 12-inch speaker. It looked like a bloody sideboard. It looked like me mum's front room onstage. People would come and see us and say, 'Hey, they must be good, look at the size of their gear.'"

Townshend and Entwistle shopped at Marshall's music shop on Uxbridge

Road, in search of new equipment. "Jim Marshall started manufacturing amplifiers and somebody in his store came up with the idea of building a 4 × 12 cabinet for bass," Townshend recalled in 1980. "John bought one of the speaker cabinets, and suddenly [he] doubled in volume. And so I bought one and then later on I bought another one and I stacked it on top of the other one. I was using a Rickenbacker at the time and because the pickup was right in line with the speakers I was instantly troubled by feedback. But I really used to like to hear the sound in my ears.

"I used to play at this place [the Oldfield] where I put my amp on the piano [at the back of the stage], so the speaker was right opposite my guitar. One day, I was hitting this note and I was going *ba-ba-bam* [hitting the guitar] and the amplifier was going *ur-ur-ur-ur* on its own. I said to myself, 'That's fun. I'll fool around with that.' And I started to pretend I was an aeroplane. Everyone went completely crazy."

Townshend's openness to new sounds was directly attributable to the environment he was exposed to in art school. "I was an arty little sod and I was actually experimenting," he told *Guitarist* in 1990. "I was . . . surrounded by real intellectuals, people that were experimenting all the time. I was greatly impressed by all this and wanted to please these people. A lot of it was posing, trying to drag something out of the band that it was resisting – this is pre-Keith Moon. . . . Marshall's were outraged and one day someone from Marshall's came and they were nagging me about the fact that the top cabinet was shifting and was going to fall off and get damaged, and I just said, 'So what?' and knocked it over! There was a tremendous kind of arrogance . . .

"Our experimentations were all to do with our irritation with the audience, who heckled if you played a rhythm and blues song that they didn't know. You'd get blokes in the back with their pints of beer shouting, 'What's all this rubbish? Play some Shane Fenton!'[11] And we just got louder as a result. Then the squeaks and farts did start to occur in the feedback . . .

"You could control it and it could be very musical – certainly that sort of thing where you hit an open A chord and then take your fingers off the strings . . . The A string is still banging away but you're hearing the finger-off harmonics in feedback. Then the vibrating A starts to stimulate

---

[11] Shane Fenton (with his backing band the Fentones) was a popular singer from the pre-Beatles era in England. Coincidentally, a young Keith Moon once tried joining the Fentones as their drummer.

harmonics in the other strings and it's just an extraordinary sound, like an enormous aeroplane. It's a wonderful, optimistic sound and that was something that happened because I was posing – I'd put my arms out, let go of the chord then find that the resulting noise was better."

In mid-1963, Pete attended a lunchtime music show in the Art School lecture theatre by an enigmatic post office telephone engineer whose strange demeanour and rumoured musical genius had the campus abuzz with gossip. The show, by Andy 'Thunderclap' Newman, playing mostly his own compositions on piano and kazoo, was, as Barnes described, "an incredible experience . . . Pete became slightly obsessed with [Newman]." Townshend obtained a home-made recording of some of Newman's work which was entitled *Ice and Essence*, ". . . an amazingly inventive album with all sorts of convoluted time changes." Barnes wrote in *Maximum R&B*. "It had an eerie, delicate, echoey quality about it and Pete played it constantly . . . [Once, Newman] visited Sunnyside Road and held forth about the valuable contribution Bix Beiderbecke made to jazz before he died. Pete went through a Bix Beiderbecke period for the next three or four weeks."

An important interest Townshend picked up from his friendship with Newman was in the methods the latter used to record music and other sound effects. Newman showed the young art student how he could multi-track instruments using two mono single-track tape players, skills which were invaluable to Townshend when he set about writing and recording songs in the coming years.

The Detours' first brush with recording occurred at about the same time that Townshend was learning the finer points of multi-tracking with Newman. The father of one of Pete and John's friends knew television composer Barry Gray, who had a home recording studio – something which impressed Pete greatly.[12] "[Gray] used to do music for a lot of space programmes for kids where they used . . . models [notably *Fireball XL5*, *Thunderbirds* and *Space: 1999*]," Pete told *Sounds* in 1980. "He did a lot of popular film music and he had his own studio and we did a demo there once." With Gray at the controls, The Detours recorded 'It Was You'[13]

---

[12] "I was struck by the fact that he used EMI equipment at home," Pete told Brian Carroll in an interview posted on www.ibcstudio.co.uk in 2005.

[13] Although The Detours never released 'It Was You', it was deemed worthy enough to be recorded by The Who the following year (which again, remains unreleased). It was later recorded and released by two other groups, The Naturals (1964) and Chaos & Co (1966).

and another Townshend composition entitled 'Please Don't Send Me Home' – the only songs he had penned to this point. The group also ran through a cover of Chuck Berry's 'Come On', based on The Rolling Stones' arrangement.

Pete had previously tried actively writing, but "it was always stories and things, never songs," he told *Beat Instrumental* in 1971. The next tangible step Townshend took towards song composition occurred after his exposure to the music and lyrics of Bob Dylan just after *The Freewheelin' Bob Dylan* was released in May, 1963.[14] The 18-year-old had heard the album at a fellow art school student's apartment and promptly bought the record, along with its predecessor *Bob Dylan* which had appeared the previous year. These albums, along with 1964's *The Times They Are A-Changin'* and *Another Side Of Bob Dylan*, cemented Dylan's position as an American music icon. Barnes remembered Dylan's effect on his flatmate: "When *Another Side Of Bob Dylan* was released Pete played it endlessly, especially the track 'All I Really Want To Do'. Dylan and particularly this track spurred him on with his own songwriting. After this he would sit down with a guitar and a notepad and play around with a few lines he'd written. He kept a book of odd bits of writing, possible lyrics, scribbles and doodles and general plans and ideas."

"As soon as I started to write," Townshend said in 1974, "I really came together in one piece for the first time."

On December 22, 1963, Bob Druce booked The Detours as support to The Rolling Stones at St Mary's Hall, the site of the explosive Johnny Kidd show earlier that year. The Stones, whose classic line-up had been together for less than a year, were already considered stars at this point with their second (and latest) single, 'I Wanna Be Your Man' heading into the Top 20. Townshend was awestruck.[15] Glyn Johns, then a singer for local group The Presidents as well as an apprentice recording engineer, was acquainted with the Stones and took the guitarist into their dressing room. "It was like going into a sacred place after the gig," recalled Pete,

---

[14] In 2000, when Pete was asked to name his number one musical influence, he said, "Bob Dylan. He told me . . . that a folk singer is simply a man with a very good memory. I very much appreciate his memory. But I also appreciate his courage and invention."

[15] "I remember when we were still playing 'Can't Buy Me Love' [sic] and maybe even the odd Shadows number thrown in when I saw the Stones on Ealing Broadway Station and thought, 'Christ almighty, what a motley crew – they should be shot, the lot of them,'" Pete told *Sounds'* Penny Valentine in 1972. "And every girl I fell in love with was in love with Jagger – no, come to think of it, my lot were always in love with Bill Wyman."

who was especially impressed with Brian Jones, who complimented The Detours and offered to help the group in any way he could. It was at this show that Pete saw Keith Richards warming up behind the curtain prior to the gig by swinging his arm in a circular motion, which Townshend would soon adopt himself for his famous 'windmill' strum which, over the years, would cause him to lose countless fingernails, among other injuries.

The Detours again opened for the Stones on January 3, this time at the Glenlyn Ballroom in Forest Hill, south-east London, during which Townshend suspended the use of the windmill in case Richards took exception. "I thought I was copying Keith Richards," Pete told *Sounds'* Steve Peacock, "so I didn't do it all night and I watched him and he didn't do it all night either. 'Swing me what?' Keith said. He must have got into it as a warming up thing . . . but he didn't remember and it developed into my sort of trademark."

The next month, a name change was necessitated when a group called Johnny Devlin and the Detours were spotted on the weekly Saturday night ITV show *Thank Your Lucky Stars*. A meeting was called shortly thereafter at the Sunnyside Road flat, attended by Townshend, Daltrey, Sandom, Entwistle and Barnes. ". . . we were kicking around names for a band," Pete told WNEW's Scott Muni in 1978, "and we were after something weird . . . and Richard Barnes, Barney I call him, came up with The Who."

"I finally thought 'The Who' worked best for many reasons," Barnes wrote in 1982. "It made people think twice when they saw it and it also worked well on posters because the name was so short and therefore would print up so big. Lou [Hunt, the announcer at the Oldfield] would have a field day with it, or a lot of problems."

The lengthy meeting ("We sat there all night trying to think of a name," Sandom remembers) adjourned without a decision being reached, but Daltrey, still acknowledged as the group's leader, supposedly made up his mind the following morning that they would be named The Who. "That was a Friday evening," Sandom remembers, "we all met again on the Saturday, and we said, 'Right, that's the name. That's our name now, yeah.'"

Sandom's sister-in-law, Rose, worked at a Shepherd's Bush brass foundry whose owner, Helmut Gorden, showed some interest in her brother-in-law's group. Perhaps entertaining thoughts of Brian Epstein's recent success with The Beatles and other Merseybeat groups, Gorden asked if he could watch the group perform.

Doug Sandom: "I said, 'Of course you can go.' I told the [group] he was going to come and they were over the moon, 'cause they thought, 'Oh, a backer, we've got somebody who's going to help us, like money-wise.'"

Impressed after seeing one of their Sunday night gigs at Acton's White Hart Hotel, Gorden met the group after the show and offered to manage The Detours and get them into the recording studio. This obviously delighted the members as financial backing would add a new legitimacy to their continued existence. A contract was drawn up and signed with Gorden, who solicited parental signatures for the three minors (Pete's parents chose not to sign, rendering the contract legally ineffective).

The Who remained on the Commercial Entertainments circuit, retaining Druce as agent while Gorden assumed the role of manager. The effects of Gorden's support soon became apparent in the form of a new van (to replace the Druce-financed Dormobile which had recently met its demise) and new clothes (including "long, light tan coloured leather waistcoats that came down to the knees" designed by Townshend, according to Barnes).[16] In the spring of 1964, Gorden showcased The Detours at the Stork Club, a central London showbiz hangout to which he invited booking agents, entrepreneurs and other potentially influential people along to evaluate the group. The result was The Detours securing a place on several theatre shows with the Arthur Howes Agency, considered one of the top booking agents in the country.

Around March 1964, Townshend and Barnes moved out of the Sunnyside Road flat. "They were forced to move," Dave Marsh noted in his Who biography *Before I Get Old*, presumably for some unforgivable transgression. Without any immediately available lodgings, the two began living in their van – an old ambulance bought from the father of a fellow art student.

"It had seats that folded down into two single beds and one double bed." Barnes described. "It had lights inside and sockets for shavers and was a very strange vehicle. We had a lot of fun with it. On lots of occasions we would be waved through traffic lights by policemen or waved down at accidents because, despite the fact that it was fairly dirty and had 'YARDBIRDS' written across the back in lipstick, they thought it was

---

[16] Entwistle later remarked that the arty coats made them look like "poof dustmen". "It was a leather coat, jacket," Sandom recalls. "It had no sleeves – it was disgusting. I don't think we wore it more than once or twice."

still an ambulance in service. For about three weeks we lived in this ambulance, parking it outside Sid's café opposite the college so that we could get up and go straight to the door and have breakfast."

Soon tiring of life in the back of a van, Townshend and Barnes settled into the two-room flat situated on the second floor of Pete's parents' house on Woodgrange Avenue.

"Barney, who I think would've made a great Who manager, had turned the room into a kind of silk screening lab making up posters and designs," recalls 'Irish' Jack Lyons, who first saw The Detours in 1962 and has been entangled in Who lore ever since. "It was almost a Pop Art workshop before Pop Art had come along. Lots and lots of pills were taken in that flat and lots and lots of creative ideas flowed. And all aided by the inspiration of a purple painted 40-watt bulb. I don't think they got many girls up there – that would have got in the way."

While Helmut Gorden's business acumen and financial position gave The Who a much-needed boost, his knowledge of the music business was questionable at best. Dozens of R&B groups were playing in the London area in 1964 following the chart success of the Stones and Manfred Mann, so staying afloat meant keeping at least one step ahead of the competition. In April, Gorden managed to arrange an audition with Fontana Records A&R man, Chris Parmenter who was impressed with The Who, but did not like Sandom's drumming and made this fact apparent.[17]

Doug Sandom: "It was brewing up . . . I was getting little hints here and there . . . You could feel it, that they wanted you out. It was so obvious . . ." Sandom recalls Parmenter "making life awkward straight away" at the audition, asking Sandom to use an unfamiliar kit rather than set up his own equipment. "I said, 'No, I want to use my own stuff,' and he insisted, and in the end I think I used it. You're not comfortable with somebody else's kit. And he just picked holes and I stood it for a little while . . ."

In a surprising outburst, Townshend, not particularly known as a leader at this point, told a surprised Sandom in full earshot of Parmenter and the others, "Get it together. What's wrong with you? If you can't get it right, then you're out of the group."

---

[17] "I knew it was coming," Sandom says. "John told me that I was being set up. . . . it was one of my birthdays or something, [Gorden] come round my house with my sister in law, Rosie, to the party, and he asked Rose, 'How old is Doug?' and she told him what my birthday was and that was my failure, then, being too old . . . They wanted me out. The image wasn't right."

The outburst humiliated Sandom, who recalled, "I just stood up and said, 'That's it. I'm finished with the band.' Peter said to me, 'You can't do that. We've got too much work.' I said, 'All right. I'll work for a month. If you haven't got anybody by then, hard luck.' The last job I done was at the 100 Club in Oxford Street."

Sandom's departure effectively ended what had always been an awkward relationship between the drummer and Townshend. "[Pete] was very clever. He never said anything really to your face. You'd get it from somebody else.[18] But, I loved him, really, it was the biggest part of my life, playing with The Who. And it completely . . . it wrecked me, when I left. I lost confidence in myself, I was murder to work with, I was murder to live with. I was like that for *ages*."

After bickering with Gorden over a suitable drummer and utilising both future Jimi Hendrix Experience drummer Mitch Mitchell and a session drummer from Marshall's for several gigs, The Who found their man one Thursday night in late April, at a gig at the Oldfield. Keith Moon, the 17-year-old drummer for local group The Beachcombers, approached the group and informed them that he could play better than the session drummer who was with them that night.[19] Moon was allowed to play during the second half of the gig and proceeded to bash and flail away with incredible energy and stamina, causing substantial damage to the session drummer's kit. Moon's violent thrashing of the drums impressed Townshend, Entwistle and Daltrey sufficiently for them to ask Moon to come along to the next show, which he did. "They never actually asked me to join [The Who]," Moon recalled in 1977. "I knew it by instinct . . ."

It was also in April that a freelance publicist and self-proclaimed 'taste master' named Peter Meaden met Gorden and arranged to see The Who. Meaden, a die-hard mod since 1961, operated an advertising company named 'Image' in partnership with Rolling Stones manager Andrew Loog Oldham, as well as serving stints as a publicist for Georgie Fame, Chuck

---

[18] "You couldn't help but like him, but Peter could be a pig, a pig of a man," Sandom told Dave Marsh. "He had a nasty thing about him – he could be so *sarcastic*, it was unbelievable. He could do things that you'd think, 'God, Pete, what are you *doing*?'"

[19] Moon's advances took place that evening despite the fact that he was intimidated by the band. "They were outrageous," he later remarked. "All the groups at that time were smart, but onstage the Detours had stage things made of leather. Pete looked very sullen. They were a bit frightening and I was scared of them. Obviously they had been playing together for a few years and it showed."

Berry, and the Crystals. Meaden possessed the music know-how that Gorden lacked and had a good grasp of which clubs were on the cutting edge, who the important music writers were (it helped he knew some of them) and precisely what styles of music and clothing were in vogue. Although Gorden had supported The Who with business savvy and money, the group did not identify with the middle-aged would-be entrepreneur at all.

Meaden, 22, belonged to the same generation as The Who, was full of ideas, and had the look of someone who knew exactly what he wanted and how he was going to get it. The Who's schedule was so busy that they were often playing up to five nights a week and were therefore unable to keep up with what was going on elsewhere in London's clubs. Meaden could fulfil the role of an important ideas man and provide a crucial contact with the press and the local scene. Although slightly mistrustful of this new figure, Gorden enlisted Meaden in promoting the group.

"As I recall, I think Pete regarded Peter Meaden's arrival as something entirely welcome after Helmut Gorden, who wanted to mould The Who into something like The Bachelors," recalls 'Irish' Jack, who saw the group regularly during this period. "Pete had a very healthy relationship with Meaden because he was really The Who's first manager [and] knew exactly where Pete was coming from. I didn't notice any particularly arresting difference in Townshend's behaviour except that he was now doing a lot more pills as in French blues and uppers like drynamil and having discovered he was entrenched in this mod pit via Meaden it was putting a lot of interesting ideas into Pete's head."

The mod movement hit its stride during the spring and summer of 1964. It had been brewing for a few years, with small factions cropping up in London's suburbs, but now it was spreading into the centre and beyond. Mod-oriented clothes shops and clubs began to emerge to cater to the growing demands of this highly selective subculture. Music writer Nik Cohn perfectly encapsulated the image: "The archetypal mod was male, 16 years old, rode a scooter, swallowed pep pills by the hundred, thought of women as a completely inferior race, was obsessed by cool and dug it. He was also 100 per cent hung up on himself, on his clothes and hair and image; in every way, he was a miserable, narcissistic little runt."

But mod was also the preferred means of many of saying 'up yours' to those in power at the time. "It was fashionable, it was clean and it was groovy," Pete told *Rolling Stone*'s Jann Wenner in 1968. "You could be a bank clerk, it was acceptable. You got them on your ground. They thought, 'Well, there's a smart young lad.' We made the establishment uptight, we made our parents uptight and our employers uptight, because although they didn't like the way we dressed, they couldn't accuse us of not being smart. We had short hair and were clean and tidy."

Meaden lived and breathed mod and Townshend became "fascinated by this almost invisible sect," Barnes recalled. "He was the first [of The Who] to start taking pills [notably drynamil]." The group soon realised that their publicist's eccentric behaviour – his fast, slick talking and non-stop energy – was down to an over-reliance on amphetamines. Meaden wanted The Who to cater to mod tastes by dressing in the appropriate fashions, getting the right haircuts, and basically flaunting a mod image. While Daltrey and Entwistle were hesitant, Townshend and Moon jumped right in. Soon, after trips to the barber shop and Carnaby Street (home to several stores which sold acceptable mod clothing), the members of The Who joined Meaden at "the high altar of mod", the Scene Club in London's Soho.[20] Since The Who's set was virtually all R&B, their tastes were already tailor-made for the mod audience. However, Meaden felt that the group name wasn't right. He persuaded The Who to adopt the more mod-friendly name, The High Numbers.

Now that The Who/High Numbers had found their drummer, Parmenter arranged a proper recording session in June 1964. Meaden brought along two 'originals' to record, which were really rewrites of two existing R&B numbers; 'I'm The Face' – a re-working of bluesman Slim Harpo's 'Got Love If You Want It' while 'Zoot Suit' was a new take on 'Misery' by US vocal group, The Dynamics. The group also recorded Bo Diddley's 'Here 'Tis', a part of The Who's live show at the time, as it was in such other London R&B groups as The Yardbirds (who recorded and released a live version on their *Five Live Yardbirds* album that year). While well performed and mod-friendly, the lyrics to both 'I'm The Face' and 'Zoot Suit' came across as contrived. The tracks were released as a single on July 3 but the record failed to make the UK charts, despite reports that Meaden purchased as many as 250 of the 1,000 copies available.

---

[20] "All I knew was I had to get [the group] established in the West End in a way that they would be recognised by the hardcore cult centre, which was the mods that used to hang out in the Scene Club, you know," said Meaden. "You can't get any more authentic than that. So I had to give them the golden seal of authenticity. If they could turn on these kids, then they could turn on the world. And so that's what the next move was."

By mid-1964, The High Numbers were in limbo. As The Detours and The Who, they had played hundreds of live shows over the past two years and, with the key addition of Keith Moon, they had improved immeasurably; they had also gained a manager and a publicist and released a record. But yet, the big break still hadn't happened.

CHAPTER TWO

1964–1965

"The guitar player was a skinny geezer with a big nose who twirled his arm like a windmill. He wrote some good songs about mods, but he didn't quite look like one."

– 'Jimmy', Quadrophenia, 1973

"[Gustav] Metzger had a profound effect on me. I was doing my first gig with The Who and took it as an excuse to smash my new Rickenbacker that I had just hocked myself to the eyebrows to buy. I really believed it was my responsibility to start a rock band that would last only three months, an auto-destructive group. The Who would have been the first punk band except that we had a hit."

– Pete Townshend, 2000

DESPITE the failure of their single, The High Numbers continued to look wide-eyed into the future. "Meaden maintained his unflagging energy," former *Melody Maker* writer Chris Charlesworth wrote in 1984. Helmut Gorden was persuaded to put the group on contract and pay them a weekly wage of £20 each. With this new steady income, Pete approached an art school instructor about the possibility of leaving college early.[1] "When he told the tutor of his intentions, the tutor was astonished to learn that Pete could make £20 a week playing guitar," Charlesworth wrote. "He advised Pete to become a professional musician right away."

The High Numbers (although they were still inadvertently being billed as The Who at some gigs almost a month after the name change) played a Tuesday night residency at the Railway Hotel, Wealdstone, near Harrow as well as appearing at mod strongholds, the Goldhawk Social Club,

---

[1] Pete's steady income also meant that he didn't need any further part-time jobs – while in art school, he'd reportedly supplemented his income with gigs delivering milk and working for a butcher.

Shepherd's Bush, and the Trade Union Hall in Watford during this period. Although reducing The Detours line-up from a five to a four-piece group had allowed the various members the freedom to settle into their respective roles, it was not until the arrival of Keith Moon that The Who/High Numbers had a distinctly unified stage attack and presence. Townshend's intensity onstage had found a match in Moon, who constantly wowed audiences with the speed and power of his drumming. Furthermore, he was not averse to kicking over his kit at the end of a show to complement Townshend's guitar bashing. The group were incredibly loud, violent and energetic and played with an abandon that consistently kept audiences on edge.

"I drifted into using bigger and bigger amps," Townshend recalled in 2000. "Bigger, more powerful, more distorted, more potent."

"Other people stumbled on feedback at the same time as me," he admitted to *Guitarist* in 1990. "Jeff Beck was using it when Roger went to see [Beck's then group] The Tridents rehearsing. He said, 'There's a shit-hot guitar player down the road and he's making sounds like you.' Then later, when we supported The Kinks, Dave Davies was adamant, 'I invented it, it wasn't John Lennon [referring to the intro of The Beatles' 1964 hit, 'I Feel Fine'] and it wasn't you!' I worshipped The Kinks and never let a bad word about them pass my lips, so I conceded. But I believe it was something people were discovering all over London. These big amps that Marshall were turning out – you couldn't stop the guitars feeding back!"

Daltrey added, "Smashing up the guitar was just one element of it: the other was the noise. The sound was just terrifying. It was a total cacophony. Before Pete wrecked his guitar he would jam it in the speaker cone. The noise was unbelievable! Even when the guitar was in a million pieces, it would still be letting out this unearthly, squealing, primeval howl."

It was at this point (July 1964) that Kit Lambert (or, as Richard Barnes referred to him, ". . . a man who confessed to having been the worst officer in the British Army") happened upon The High Numbers at the Railway Hotel. The group was playing to a packed house on the regular Tuesday night when Lambert walked in, surveying the scene like a building inspector rather than someone who had come to enjoy the show. "I was shit scared of him, because he looked so straight," Barnes told *Mojo* in 2000. "He was around 30 years old and was wearing a really expensive Savile Row suit. He looked trouble." When Lambert explained that he was a director looking for a group for his next film, Barnes breathed a sigh of relief and pointed out Peter Meaden. Following a conversation with Meaden and a typically blistering High Numbers performance which he would later describe as having "a satanic quality", Lambert telephoned his business and creative partner, Chris Stamp, about his discovery. Stamp was in Dublin, Ireland, working as an assistant director on *Young Cassidy*, a film based on the early life of Irish playwright Sean O'Casey.

Christopher "Kit" Lambert and Chris Stamp were an interesting pair. Lambert, 26, was the son of noted British composer and conductor Constant Lambert. A true eccentric, Kit's accent, dress and mannerisms were strictly upper class. Described as "an outrageous gay . . . arrogant, definitely, and very annoying" by future Who record producer Shel Talmy, Lambert had attended Trinity College, Oxford, and served for a short time as an officer in the British army in Hong Kong. In keeping with his keen sense of adventure, Lambert took part in an expedition to Brazil in 1961 to chart the course of the longest unexplored river in the world, the Iriri. After nearly seven months, the trip came to a horrific end when Lambert personally discovered his close friend and travelling companion Richard Mason had been ambushed, murdered and partially decapitated by a native hunting party.

With this harrowing experience fresh in his memory, Lambert spent six months studying cinematography in Paris, then took a position as a director's assistant at Shepperton film studios,[2] which was where he met Stamp. Five years younger than Lambert, coming from a working class background (his father worked as a Thames tugboatman), Chris had managed to acquire an assistant director's position by pursuing his brother, actor Terence Stamp, into the world of show business. Lambert and Stamp worked together on several movies (including *I Could Go On Singing* starring Judy Garland, Richard Attenborough's *The L-Shaped Room*, and a 1964 remake of the 1934 film *Of Human Bondage*) before deciding to make their own film about popular music. The two, who shared an apartment just west of London's Baker Street, were described by music writer Nik Cohn as dissimilar a pair as Laurel and Hardy.

"They were . . . are . . . as incongruous a team as [The Who] are," Keith Moon recalled in a 1972 *Rolling Stone* interview. "You got Chris on one hand [goes into unintelligible East London cockney]: 'Oh well, fuck it,

---

[2] Lambert worked on such films as *From Russia With Love* and *The Guns of Navarone* in this capacity.

jus, jus whack 'im in-a 'ead, 'it 'im in ee balls an' all.' And Kit says [slipping into a proper Oxbridge accent]: 'Well, I don't agree, Chris; the thing is . . . the whole thing needs to be thought out in damned fine detail.' These people were perfect for us, because there's me, bouncing about, full of pills, full of everything I could get me 'ands on . . . and there's Pete, very serious, never laughed, always cool, a grass 'ead. I was working at about 10 times the speed Pete was. And Kit and Chris were like the epitome of what we were."

Stamp flew back to London the following Saturday and joined Kit Lambert in time to catch the last part of a High Numbers' gig at Watford's Trade Union Hall. "I shall always remember that night we first saw them together," Stamp told George Tremlett. "I had never seen anything like it. The Who have a hypnotic effect on an audience. I realised that the first time I saw them. It was like a black mass. Even then Pete Townshend was doing all that electronic feedback stuff. Keith Moon was going wild on the drums. The effect on the audience was tremendous. It was as if they were in a trance. They just sat there watching or shuffled around the dance floor, awestruck."

Over the following month, Lambert and Stamp ousted Helmut Gorden and Peter Meaden, becoming managing partners of The High Numbers.[3] Pete and the others had mixed emotions about the change: the prospect of leaving the increasingly authoritarian Gorden raised few objections, if any, but parting with Meaden was more difficult. He had given the group an identity during the short time he was with them and certain members felt a distinct affinity towards him.

'Irish' Jack Lyons: "When Lambert and Stamp came along just after the beginning of August 1964, things were in a bit of a muddle. Because it seemed that in a very short while there had been four managers in succession. I know that Helmut Gorden had to go because all he wanted out of life was a short lived pop group. Meaden had been just right for The High Numbers and had connected in a big way with Pete through the mod ethic even though Pete still hadn't written a mod song despite Meaden's influences . . . But Kit Lambert and Chris Stamp were like loose cannons, unbelievably sharp. They were like a couple of hipsters who had the balls

---

[3] Lambert was informed by The Beatles' attorney, David Jacobs that The Who's contract with Gorden was legally invalid. Ironically, Gorden then asked Doug Sandom to help with legal action against Lambert and Stamp. "He's the one that got me out of the band," Sandom recalls, still incredulous. "He wanted *me* to help *him*! I said 'Leave it out. No way!'"

to stare down the barrel of a booking agent. Peter Meaden was becoming a pill-head and was having difficulty keeping himself together. So Lambert and Stamp arrived on the scene just at the right moment. I don't know what Pete thought (or thinks) about Peter Meaden's ousting. But I myself reckoned it was all done very shady, a bit like a bulging brown envelope handed over in the Intrepid Fox bar in Wardour Street.[4] He did complain that he'd been short changed. I think that looking back he could have been treated a lot better."

Ironically, just prior to their departure, Meaden and Gorden's work was beginning to pay off. Meaden arranged a five-week residency for the High Numbers at the Scene, London's hottest mod club. This Soho club featured DJ Guy Stevens, whose Stateside musical contacts enabled him to acquire many obscure recordings by black R&B, blues, and soul artists adored by the mod disciples. Townshend and Barnes used to visit Stevens' apartment and sift through his vast record collection, listening out for songs to add to The High Numbers' repertoire.[5]

Around the time of the change in management, Meaden also landed The High Numbers an audition with Rolling Stones manager Andrew 'Loog' Oldham at the New Carlton Irish Club, Shepherd's Bush. "Andrew was very excited by what he saw as we played R&B songs by Chuck Berry and Bo Diddley and a few Tamla Motown songs like 'Gotta Dance To Keep From Crying' and 'Motoring'," Townshend wrote in a 2001 web posting. "He predicted we would be successful . . . It was a magic day to have the manager of my favourite band tell us we were headed for great things." Despite his enthusiasm, Oldham, aware that Lambert and Stamp were manoeuvring to manage the group, decided to defer to them.[6]

---

[4] Meaden, who had no legal claim to the group, received a buyout for relinquishing control to Lambert and Stamp. He reportedly later boasted that Townshend sent him a thousand pounds every Christmas in a gesture of thanks for his early guidance of the band. "I was the fellow who saw the potential in modism, which is the greatest form of lifestyle you can imagine," Meaden told the *NME*'s Steve Turner in 1975. "I got The Who together because I loved the life so much. I got them together and I dressed them in mod clothes, gave them all the jingoism and all the paraphernalia of modism. It was right on the button. The timing was just right. And timing is where it's at."

[5] Stevens went on to produce recordings by Free, Mott The Hoople, and The Clash.

[6] Lambert appears to have always had a rather uneasy relationship with Oldham: "One day, to my horror, I saw Moon and Townshend stepping out of Andrew's [Rolls] with Brian Jones, all of them chatting conspiratorially," Lambert wrote in his unpublished memoir. "So when the boys got to my flat I drew my old service revolver, an enormous

Thanks to Gorden's Stork Club showcase, Arthur Howes' agency booked The High Numbers on five consecutive Sunday shows in the seaside resort towns Brighton and Blackpool throughout August and September, opening for major groups such as Gerry & the Pacemakers, The Kinks (who had just released 'You Really Got Me'), and The Beatles.[7]

Lambert and Stamp's first order of business as the group's co-managers was to get the members signed under a legal contract. Lambert had a music-savvy lawyer draw up an appropriate document which the individuals signed. Since the entire group consisted of minors being under 21, their parents also had to sign the document. This time, Pete's parents consented to the deal, after Cliff Townshend crossed out a clause which would have given Kit and Chris a percentage of any writing royalties due his son. The new document reportedly guaranteed the band members £1,000 each per year. Lambert would consume his savings and a significant inheritance in very short order keeping this promise.

Lambert and Stamp made a short documentary film, featuring The High Numbers and their mod audience at the Railway in August, before redirecting their energies into the group itself. The pair compensated for their distinct lack of knowledge of how the pop music scene worked with sheer intestinal fortitude. Mike Shaw, a friend of Stamp's, was brought in, pioneering his use of stage lighting. For the Arthur Howes dates, Lambert insisted to stage managers that The High Numbers be allowed their own lighting effects, which was largely unheard of in those days, especially at the bigger venues.

"We were the first group to have a Production Manager," Townshend said in 1987. "Mike ran a small light rig for us – just a couple of towers – but it made a hell of a difference. People were used to a single spot or a naked bulb."

Other Lambert and Stamp-inspired ideas involved sending the group to Max Factor on Bond Street for supplies and lessons on applying stage

Colt Special, lined the boys against the wall, and asked what's up . . . Andrew with his white Persian cat, tame joint roller and laced-up fly buttons was obviously impressing them, so I sort of cut in in no uncertain way. Next time I saw the Rolls arrive I jumped in, kicked the cat out of the way, and told him hands off or else."

[7] Beatles' fans certainly noticed The High Numbers after an August 16 support stint. "After the Blackpool show, The Beatles made a safe escape, but The High Numbers, who still moved their own equipment, were in the act of loading their van when a horde of Beatlemaniacs approached, screaming, tearing their hair and rending their garments at the sight of a pop group," Dave Marsh wrote in 1983. "Any pop group." The band emerged from the fray with the collars of their jackets ripped off, and Daltrey losing a sleeve.

makeup and trips to Carnaby Street for enough mod clothing for them to be able to maintain their image onstage and off. Work also began on the hunt for a recording contract as Kit and Chris proceeded to arrange for auditions for The High Numbers who made their television début, appearing on BBC2's *The Beat Room* in August.

The nucleus of Lambert & Stamp's empire, New Action Limited, was housed in a flat at Ivor Court, near Baker Street, which the pair had been renting since late-1963. New Action's environs were quite cramped, according to Anya Butler [later Forbes-Adam], Lambert's long-time assistant. "Chris slept on a bed in the hall," she told Andrew Motion in his fascinating biography *The Lamberts*, published in 1987. "I was on the sofa, and Kit was in the main bedroom. I got £8 a week, but Kit always borrowed it back. Theoretically I was doing publicity, but in fact I was cooking, sewing on Daltrey's symbols [to his mod sweaters], and consoling Moon for not being in The Beach Boys. We were a shambles, but we were a happy family."

Since Bob Druce was no longer acting as the group's agent, the management duo began searching for new areas in which to break The High Numbers, as Barnes recalled: "Kit had this Shell map of London on the wall and he had it covered all over with drawing pins and red and blue circles where The Who was going to play in different clubs."

Lambert and Stamp never seemed to rest. Kit, especially, was "thriving on sheer nerve," according to Barnes, and ". . . profligate and flamboyant in both his personal and business behaviour," as Dave Marsh put it. But Marsh also pointed out that while his management style may have seemed haphazard or ill-conceived, Lambert was not playing around. "Irrational as much of his behaviour undoubtedly was, it would be a mistake not to see Lambert as dead serious. He wanted and needed to make a giant pop success – and a small fortune – to prove himself to his father's memory and for his own satisfaction."

Around September, The High Numbers visited EMI Studios on Abbey Road for an audition. "That was an amazing session," Pete recalled in 1973. "We recorded it in the same room that The Beatles did their first album in [sic]. We were overawed by it and incredibly nervous. We did a tape which was bloody dynamite." EMI's John Burgess, who supervised the test, hedged his bets, as Kit received a letter dated October 22, asking if the group had any original material to offer.

An attempt at breaking the group in Greenwich, south-east London failed due to poor attendances. Just after The High Numbers played their last show at Greenwich Town Hall in late October 1964, Lambert decided to change the group name back to The Who. "The Who was easy to remember, made good conversation fuel, provided ready-made gags for the disc jockeys," Lambert said. "It was so corny it had to be good."

Stamp's gig enquiries resulted in a major coup – a weekly slot at the Marquee, a central London club located on Soho's Wardour Street. Originally situated on Oxford Street, the Marquee was a well-known, established venue for live R&B and jazz acts and a successful Tuesday night slot there would gain The Who the attention they sorely needed.

When Kit and Chris had sent The High Numbers to perform in London's East End, they enlisted Barnes to develop and print posters to attract an audience. The same method was employed for the Marquee show, this time a logo was designed by Brian Pike, a graphic artist hired by Kit, which featured the words 'The Who,' one above the other with the 'h' in the two words joined together. An arrow was drawn coming out of the top of the 'o' in 'Who', like the medical symbol for 'male'. A photograph of Pete windmilling his arm over a Rickenbacker guitar appeared in the upper left corner, while the words 'Maximum R&B' adorned the bottom of the poster. It was a defining image of The Who – one that has been used repeatedly over the four decades since its creation.

Although their first show at the Marquee on November 24, drew fewer than 30 hardcore fans from west London, by all accounts, The Who played a fantastic set and the numbers were more encouraging the following week, with a turnout of almost 300.[8] Soon the club was packed every Tuesday night, with The Who going on to break house attendance records set by Manfred Mann and The Yardbirds. The Marquee performances showcased The Who at a time when they were blossoming into an incredible live act. The effect these gigs had on the audiences was amazing. Dave Goodman, quoted in 1997's *The Who Concert File*, remembered:

> *"The first time I came out of my shell was when I saw The Who at the Marquee. I'd never seen anything like it. I couldn't imagine that people could do such things. I went straight out and broke a window, I was that impressed. It broke down so many barriers for me, just that one evening of seeing The*

---

[8] The first six weeks of the residency at the Marquee featured support band The Footprints, a later edition of The Mustangs, who hailed from Acton County Grammar School.

Who. The set was so fucking violent and the music so heady it hit you in the head as well as the guts, it did things to you. You'd never heard anything like it. 'Maximum R&B' said the poster . . . and fuck me, was it!"

In 1994, *NME* writer Keith Altham remembered his first encounter with The Who, which occurred at the Marquee:

"I arrived late and heard what sounded like someone sawing through an aluminum dustbin with a chainsaw to the accompaniment of a drummer who was obviously in time with another group on another planet and the most deafening bass guitar in the world. The vocalist was virtually inaudible amidst the cacophony. I turned on my heel to leave but Kit [Lambert] came up behind me with a brandy, promising in his beautifully fruity public school accent that, 'This will be a moment you will remember all your life.' He pulled me into the sweaty, smelly confines of the Marquee where a large number of mods in their vented jackets and Fred Perry shirts leapt about in delight. I was astonished.

"The long lanky guitarist with the big hooter was doing a passing impression of a malfunctioning windmill, all the while extracting a torturous scream from his guitar which sounded as though several Siamese cats were being electrocuted inside his speaker cabinet. This, I was reliably informed, was 'feedback'. Then the surly looking blond thug up front screaming 'I'm A Man' threw his microphone at the drummer who retaliated by hurling sticks at his head and thrashing around his kit like a whirling dervish. The bass player's hair was dyed jet black (his tribute to Elvis) and in his black clothes on a very dark stage was almost invisible. He made up for this by turning his volume control up so high he could be heard in the next world.

"Finally the apocalypse arrived on cue when the guitarist raised his guitar above his head and smashed it to splinters on the stage while the drummer kicked his drums in the general direction of the vocalist who made a determined effort to hit him over the head with one of his cymbals. When the dust finally settled and the cheers subsided, Kit turned to me. 'Wasn't that wonderful, dear boy?' he asked."

A typical set-list of the time might feature songs such as Mose Allison's 'Young Man Blues', Howlin' Wolf's 'Smokestack Lightning', Bo Diddley's 'I'm A Man', 'Here 'Tis' and 'Pretty Thing', and lengthy improvisations based on the riff from The Kinks' 'You Really Got Me', and Booker T. and the MG's' instrumentals 'Green Onions' and 'Plum Nellie' (Townshend told Jann Wenner in 1968 that MG's guitarist Steve Cropper ". . . really turned me on to aggressive guitar playing") and the Phil Upchurch Combo instrumental, 'You Can't Sit Down', which featured Townshend's overdriven guitar.

Back in the days of his early groups, a friend of Pete's had sparked an interest in tape recording. "The guy had a tape recorder and we used to have such fun with it, doing spoof radio shows and stuff like that, and I set my heart on getting one," Townshend told *Guitarist* in 1990. "My mum and dad had a junk shop, in which I worked, and inevitably a tape recorder came in – it was a Grundig or something. I couldn't dub on it but I rapidly realised that all I needed was another tape machine and I'd be able to."

Still sharing the flat on the top floor of his parents' house with Barney, Pete set about converting one of the front bedrooms into his first home recording studio. Barnes remembered the logistics involved in *Maximum R&B*:

> *"A friend of ours from art school . . . undertook the task of laying down a one-inch thick cement floor all over the existing floorboards of this room. It had a layer of chicken wire in to strengthen it. We bought some very expensive sheets of sound-proofing material. These were eight by four sheets of about three-inch thick compressed straw or something. Each sheet weighed about a ton. We had to get six volunteers from Art School to help lift each one."*

Pete's equipment at the time consisted of two mono tape machines which Lambert bought for Townshend to use for composing, a single microphone and a makeshift metronome he'd fashioned out of a variable-speed turntable. One of the tape machines may have ultimately met its demise at the hands of Pete's youngest brother. "I remember him bringing over a tape machine when I was about four or five," Simon recalls. "I think he brought it over for [my brother] Paul and I absolutely took it completely apart – every screw, everything I could undo – a proper tape machine, you know? And I had it all over the floor of my room." Young Simon's predilection for dismantling items around the house – including door handles – earned him the nickname 'Screw Loose'. "I do remember Pete having a terrible go at me about that tape machine," he says. "I even got a smack for that."

One of the first songs that Pete recorded using his new setup (in winter 1964) was entitled 'Call Me Lightning'. "One of the oldest demos I have,"

Townshend wrote in 1982.[9] "Recorded with another song called 'You Don't Have To Jerk'[10] at the flat my art school pal Barney shared with me. The song is a very clear example of how difficult it was for me to reconcile what I took to be Roger's need for macho, chauvinist lyrics and Keith Moon's appetite for surf music and fantasy sports car love affairs." The recording (released on the 1987 collection *Another Scoop*) is interesting because it demonstrates both Pete's abilities as a musician at the time and the demo's remarkable quality, a crisp, clean sound, featuring multi-tracked acoustic and electric guitar and harmony vocals. Townshend remains impressed with these demo recordings, ". . . although [they] are a little brittle-sounding," he told *Guitarist* in 1990, "they were the first things I ever did and they sound really good." The Who eventually recorded 'Call Me Lightning' in 1968.

Lambert managed to sign The Who with an American record producer named Shel Talmy who had recently produced the Kinks' hits 'You Really Got Me'[11] and 'All Day And All Of The Night'. The contract gave Talmy, using his considerable clout, the authority to choose a label. Furthermore, under the terms of the contract, Talmy stood to make more money than all four members of The Who and their management team combined. However, the deal got the group in the studio, something which they had been trying to do for months.

'I Can't Explain' was recorded at Pye Studios, London, in early November 1964. The group's first recording session with Talmy was by no means a pleasant experience, as Townshend revealed in 1971, "Shel Talmy was a great believer in making groups who were nothing into stars. He was also a great believer in pretending the group didn't exist when they were in a recording studio. Despite the fact that our first few records are among our best, they were the least fun to make . . . However, dear Shel got us our first single hits. So he was as close to being God for a week as any other unworthy soul has been."

On hearing the demo of 'I Can't Explain', Talmy added a few choruses

---

[9] In 1996, Pete mentioned a song entitled *Silver Stingray* "and a couple of other mock-Jan and Dean things" as other very early examples of his writings in his first demo studio.
[10] The 'Jerk' was a popular dance of the time.
[11] In a 2000 interview with *Mojo*, Ray Davies stated that Shel Talmy's role in recording 'You Really Got Me' was minimal. Talmy's recording of the song was "swamped in echo. It was horrible," Davies said. The Kinks re-recorded the song (at their own expense), "and we bashed it out with no echo." Talmy "had to be there", Davies said, but his input was minimal. ". . . he was happy to be named producer."

to extend the length of the song and rearranged a few lines. He was not impressed with the group's backing vocals and enlisted all-male trio the Ivy League to do the job. Likewise, Townshend's abilities as a lead guitarist were brought into question when local session player Jimmy Page, who went on to forge his own legendary career with Led Zeppelin, was brought in to lend a hand. Pete was not impressed with this turn of events and insisted that he play lead on the song. He reportedly won the battle since Page did not have a 12-string Rickenbacker, considered key to the song's sound. For the B-side, Page wouldn't let Townshend use his fuzzbox so he ended up playing on 'Bald Headed Woman', which was recorded in about two hours.[12]

"It can't be beat for straightforward Kink copying," Pete said of 'I Can't Explain' in 1971. "It seems to be about the frustrations of a young person who is so incoherent and uneducated that he can't state his case to the bourgeois intellectual blah blah blah. Or, of course, it might be about drugs." Like The Kinks' early singles, The Who's début single was short, sweet and to the point. Its timelessness and sheer staying power is demonstrated by the fact that the song would be used as the opener for the vast majority of Who live shows over the next four decades.

In *The Complete Guide To The Music Of The Who*, Chris Charlesworth assessed 'I Can't Explain' as capturing the sentiments of youth: ". . . an explosive debut, a song about the frustration of being unable to express yourself, not just to the girl of your dreams but, in a broader sense, to the world as a whole."

Charlesworth touched here on the essence of the song and in plenty of examples of Townshend's future writing, a tremendous amount of depth lay beneath what was immediately apparent in the lyrics. This phenomenon escaped even the writer himself.

"I wrote 'I Can't Explain' about a kid who couldn't explain to a girl that he loved her – that was all it was about," Townshend later commented. "A couple of months later it was on the charts, and I started to look at it closely . . . and I realised that the song was on the chart not because it was a little love song, but because it openly paraded a sort of weakness."

'I Can't Explain' ". . . was a *desperate* copy of the Kinks," Pete told *Uncut's*

---

12 ". . . I was there for the whole session but I wasn't needed," Page told *Mojo* in 2004. "I actually play on 'Bald Headed Woman': just a few fuzzbox phrases. We played it live in the studio but I was just there to augment things. It was such a thrill to suddenly find myself doing a session that was so totally dynamic. Straight after that, I went to see The Who live at the Marquee and we got to know each other better."

Simon Goddard in 2004. "I just thought, 'This'll pay the rent for a while and then I'll go back and be an artist.' I had no idea. This deputation of kids came up and said, 'This really means something.' I was kind of going [uninterested] 'Yeah, yeah, yeah' and they went, 'No, you don't understand, this really means something.' And I still went, yeah, whatever, but then they got hold of me [shakes fists] and said, 'No! You don't understand!' And I thought, 'No, I *don't* understand.' I remember walking away and thinking, 'This is really significant, I think I'm going to be an artist in the modern world, I've just found that I have an audience, I've just found that I have a role which is that I can reflect this group of people immediately.' Admittedly it was a bunch of pilled-up mods but it was better than nothing."

In an effort to make 'I Can't Explain' a hit in the US because, as he said, "the big bread was in America, not England", Talmy sold the record to Decca's American subsidiary, who released the single in England on their Brunswick label[13] on January 15, 1965. Competition that month included The Kinks' 'Tired Of Waiting For You', Tom Jones' 'It's Not Unusual', and The Righteous Brothers' 'You've Lost That Lovin' Feeling'. The single failed to make an impact in the US (American Decca was not particularly receptive to rock'n'roll), reaching only number 93.

Shortly after the release of 'I Can't Explain', while Stamp was working in Norway on the Kirk Douglas movie *The Heroes Of Telemark*, Lambert put Pete up in a room above his own flat, which doubled as the company's new offices in Eaton Place, Belgravia.[14] "Kit dragged me out of that environment because he thought it was decadent," Townshend told Barnes. "He took me away from the decadence that was ours to the decadence that was his."

An additional factor that led to Pete's change of residence was the

---

[13] UK Decca turned Talmy down, according to Andy Neill and Matt Kent's exhaustive 2002 Who chronicle *Anyway Anyhow Anywhere*. Brunswick, incidentally, was the label to which Bill Haley was signed.

[14] The move to upper-class Belgravia was at least partly motivated by Lambert's wish to project an impression that New Action was a thriving, profitable outfit. An additional ploy was his reported insistence on using a hired Rolls-Royce as his preferred mode of travel. The company was actually at least £60,000 in debt at the time, according to Andrew Motion. "At Eaton Place," Lambert later said, "the bailiffs kept coming and going. I used to have a bust of my father's head which I used to put down the loo and make Anya sit on top of it. She would have to sit there for ages. I used to say to her, 'No. No. Make it look authentic. Take your knickers down.'"

attitude of his parents who were far from happy about his attempts at transforming the upstairs flat into a recording studio.

"It didn't have the effect of soundproofing at all, it had the opposite effect," Simon Townshend recalls, laughing. "It sort of amplified the problem." "They had egg boxes everywhere on the walls," Paul Townshend told Marsh in 1983. "and they knocked a hole in one wall to put in a window. And they didn't put the window in; they didn't get round to that. Then the cement made the ceiling start to bow in downstairs. There was a blazing row, and my mum and dad kicked 'em out."

Life at Eaton Place saw Townshend's introduction to the ways of the upper classes. "Kit's grooming started with etiquette and showing Keith and me the right wines and so on," he told *Mojo* in 2000. "Up to the last years of his life, Keith was still ordering the vintage of Dom Perignon that Kit said was the best." Lambert also introduced Townshend to a record collection markedly different from that of Tom Wright in that it included "Sinatra, Ellington . . ." Pete described to Motion in 1987, "and a fair amount of baroque music including [17th century British composer Henry] Purcell's 'Gordian Knot Untied', which he played all the time. But not much pop."

Lambert gave Townshend an album of works by Purcell. "It was just full of Baroque suspensions and I was deeply, deeply influenced by it," Pete told *Guitar Player* in 1989. "I remember I'd just written 'I Can't Explain' . . . I was on my way, but I was just copying. Then I sat down and wrote all the demos for The Who's first album and it's just covered in those suspensions: 'The Kids Are Alright' [and later] 'I'm A Boy', they're full of them. And ['Gordian Knot Untied'] is still one of my favourite pieces of music. In that sense, it was another very, very important thing that I got from Kit, because he wasn't just a manager and he wasn't just a record producer; he was a fantastic, extraordinary friend. I remember I was staying at his flat in Belgravia once and he put it on for the first time. I heard it and went into the room and there were tears streaming down his face, because it was his father's favourite piece of music and it reminded him of his dad."

Lambert also introduced the pop guitarist to opera. "I became interested in opera because Kit was the son of Constant Lambert, the music director of Covent Garden and the Royal Ballet in the Fifties," Townshend told the Austrian newspaper *Kurier* in 2007. "Kit had a private box at Covent Garden that I often used. I saw all kinds of opera. My favourite classical opera composer is Verdi. For an Englishman there perhaps is no more deeply affecting opera composer than Benjamin Britten. His *Silas Marner* is superb. My favourite modern opera composer is Philip Glass. I remember one of my toughest nights at the opera in the Sixties was sitting through a particularly dark production of *Boris Gudonov*, today one of my favourites. I drank champagne in the box, lay on the floor and fell asleep."[15]

Life with Lambert, who was essentially homosexual, although Townshend prefers to describe him as bisexual, also meant that Pete witnessed first-hand London's covert gay scene. "We used to eat at all the gay restaurants . . . and dine out with Quentin Crisp and all that," Townshend revealed in 1982. "I didn't care." He was careful to point out that Lambert's motives were purely professional. "Just for the record," Townshend told *Rolling Stone*'s Kurt Loder in 1982, "if Kit Lambert was gettin' into rock music 'cause he was looking for boys, there was certainly no approach made to any individual in The Who – *ever*, under any circumstances. Maybe we weren't his type."[16] Motion pointed out that ". . . the truth is that Kit's friendship with Townshend was charged less by sexual attraction than by the appeal of shaping and directing an as yet unrealised talent. He regularly pointed out how remarkably unattractive the band were and agreed with a friend who, on first seeing them, pronounced them 'the ugliest in London'."

'Irish' Jack Lyons: "Kit had grown up as the only son of Constant Lambert. You can't get any more aristocratic than having the ballet dancer Dame Margot Fonteyn as your godmother. So while Pete was introducing Kit to the murky world of Soho clubs and mods riding around on scooters, Kit took Pete under his wing taking him to the best restaurants [hoping the cheque didn't bounce!] fine wines and baroque music. And it was Kit who first planted the idea of rock opera into Pete's head. All of these strains of opposing cultures was not lost on both of them. I remember we were somewhere once and Pete made some comment about the service in a restaurant and I remember thinking at the time 'Good God, that's exactly what Kit would say. Pete's becoming Kit.' I think that Pete certainly picked up a lot of his sarcasm by listening to Kit."

★ ★ ★

---

[15] A decade later, Townshend introduced his brother-in-law, Jon Astley, to the world of opera. "[Jon's sister and Pete's future wife] Karen and he took me to see Benjamin Britten, which was staggering," Astley recalls.
[16] In a *Mojo* interview from 2000, Shel Talmy's view was that Lambert was "hot after Townshend." This statement must be weighed against Talmy's stated dislike of The Who's co-manager.

On January 29, The Who landed a major television appearance when the editor of ITV's *Ready, Steady, Go!* attended one of the group's Marquee shows and was sufficiently impressed to book The Who for the Friday early evening programme – considered the hippest music showcase in England and an important trendsetter – which currently boasted a viewership of nearly three million.

NME writer Roy Carr described the group's appearance that evening: "As it transpired, Lambert discovered that the one person responsible for assembling the weekly studio audience was ill, and so Lambert *kindly* volunteered to supply a ready-made crowd of *typical teens*. What the *RSG* producers didn't know was that Lambert had herded together the entire audience from the Goldhawk Social Club in Shepherd's Bush and that each one was both bona fide mod and diehard Who fan. That night, the other acts on the show really didn't stand a chance. But The Who and, in particular their audience, were sensational. In just under three action-packed minutes, the mod movement had spread the word right across the British Isles, and the word was The Who."

The audience consisted of the '100 Faces',[17] a large contingent of The Who's most rabid mod fans. Lambert had even supplied them with scarves to shower at the group at the song's climax.

A further television plug arrived in March when The Who were asked to perform on *Top Of The Pops* (with an average viewing audience of around 5.5 million at the time) as the replacement for a group who had cancelled at the last minute.

"It was exciting," Townshend wrote in a *Melody Maker* column in 1970. "You only got on the show, apart from the plug spot, if your record was in the charts, so it was instant status, and the doors of the studio were always surrounded by lots of pretty young fans who were always waiting for some other band, it seemed. In those days we had to mime to our record, thus, it was a cinch. No worries about throats or atmosphere, or getting in tune, just about what colour pants to wear, or what silly outfit to put on to attract the camera's attention. Keith would get about 80 per cent

---

[17] "You know, The Who had an army," Pete told *Mojo*'s Pat Gilbert in 2006. "When we played our residency at the Marquee we had a following called 'the 100 Faces' who were not just people we gave free tickets to, these were fucking frontline Shepherd's Bush faces, White City faces. One of them was Roger's cousin . . . Another guy, Winston, a black guy, was without question the most beautiful, best-dressed Jamaican guy that I'd ever seen, and he had the courage to speak in almost an Oxford University accent . . . incredible eccentrics and personalities."

of the camera time, simply because the director was convinced it was a drummer-led group. Every time the camera swung to me I would swing my arm like a maniac."

Two more appearances on *Top Of The Pops* followed within the next month, pushing *I Can't Explain* to number eight – its highest UK chart position. With a hit record, The Who now had more live bookings than they could handle, usually performing onstage 20 or more times a month during this period. Now that they had the attention of the public, the challenge was for the group to remain there.

In April, The Who began work on their debut album at London's IBC studios, with Talmy producing and Glyn Johns engineering. The album was to contain mostly covers with 10 staples from their live set: 'I'm A Man', 'Heat Wave', 'I Don't Mind', 'Lubie (Come Back Home)', 'Please Please Please', 'Leaving Here', 'Motoring', 'Shout And Shimmy', 'Daddy Rolling Stone' and 'Anytime You Want Me' mixed with only two Townshend compositions, 'Out In The Street' (a.k.a. 'You're Going To Know Me') and 'Anyway Anyhow Anywhere', The Who's second single.

As a follow-up to 'I Can't Explain', 'Anyway Anyhow Anywhere' was an important record in that it was more Who than Talmy. The single effectively reflected the group's biggest strength – their live firepower – complete with screeching feedback and Moon's now standard anarchic percussion assault. "Kit realised that we had to be seen before people would begin to buy our records," Entwistle told Dave Marsh. "The intention was to encapsulate The Who's entire stage act on just one side of a single, to illustrate the arrogance of the mod movement and then, through the feedback, the smashing of the instruments."

"We recorded it at IBC Studios in next to no time," says Talmy. "After doing the basic backing track, we set up Townshend's stack and let him do the various whooshing, smashing, Morse code and feedback effects as overdubs. It was as simple as that."

"I was laying on my mattress on the floor listening to a Charlie Parker record when I thought up the title," Pete wrote in *Rolling Stone* in 1971. "I just felt the guy was so free when he was playing. He was a soul without a body, riding, flying, on music . . . The freedom suggested by the title became restricted by the aggression of our tightly defined image when I came to write the words. In fact, Roger was really a hard nut then, and he changed quite a few words himself to toughen the song up to suit his temperament. It is the most excitingly pigheaded of our songs."

At the time, Daltrey told the *NME*'s Alan Smith that 'Anyway Anyhow Anywhere' was written at 3 a.m., the day before it was recorded, "when he and Pete were locked in a room to make them concentrate on songwriting." Daltrey was given a co-writing credit on the song, which became the opening music for *Ready, Steady, Go!* for a time.

The song also was one of the first to feature feedback; in fact, Decca initially returned the master to Talmy, believing it to be defective due to the various roaring and screeching noises. Released in May, 'Anyway Anyhow Anywhere' reached number 10 in the UK charts.

By mid-1965, the original mod movement began to cool considerably in the London area (due in part to media commercialisation). "[The Who] think the mod thing is dying," Pete said. "We don't plan to go down with it, which is why we've become individualists." 'Anyway Anyhow Anywhere' was described as the 'first pop-art single'. The style represented "something the public is familiar with in a different form," Pete was quoted at the time. "Like clothes. Union Jacks are supposed to be flown. We have a jacket made of one.[18] Keith Moon, our drummer has a jersey with the RAF insignia on it. I have a white jacket, covered in medals."

As an ex-art student, Townshend was best qualified to espouse the virtues of Pop Art to anyone who would listen, telling the *Observer*: "From valueless objects – a guitar, a microphone, a hackneyed pop tune, we extract a new value. We take objects with one function and give them another. And the auto-destructive element – the way we destroy our instruments – adds immediacy to it all."

"We stand for Pop Art clothes, Pop Art music and Pop Art behaviour," Pete further elaborated to *Melody Maker*'s Nick Jones in July. "This is what everybody seems to forget – we don't change offstage. We live Pop Art. I bang my guitar on my speaker because of the visual effect. It is very artistic. One gets a tremendous sound, and the effect is great . . . If guitars exploded and went up in a puff of smoke, I'd be happy. The visual effect would be complete . . . Well, our next single is really Pop Art. I wrote it with that intention. Not only is the number Pop Art, the lyrics are 'young and rebellious.' It's anti-middle class, anti-boss class, and anti young

---

[18] "Kit came up with the idea for that jacket – he should be posthumously knighted for it," Daltrey said in 2000. "Prior to that, the Union Jack had only ever been flown on buildings as the national flag. When we walked into a Savile Row tailor and said, 'Will you make a jacket out of this?' They said, 'No.' They thought they'd go to jail."

marrieds! I've nothing against these people really – just making a positive statement."

"Kit Lambert described 'Anyway Anyhow Anywhere' to reporters as, 'A pop art record, containing pop art music,'" Townshend wrote in a 1971 *Rolling Stone* essay. "'The sounds of war and chaos and frustration expressed musically without the use of sound effects.' A bored and then cynical Nik Cohn – Christ he was even more cynical than me – said calmly, 'That's impressionism, not pop art.' I repeated what Kit had briefed me to say, mumbling something about Peter Blake and Lichtenstein and went red. Completely out of order while your record is screaming in the background: '*I can go anyway, way I choose, I can live anyhow, win or lose, I can go anywhere, for something new, Anyway, anyhow, anywhere.*'"

The Who's Tuesday night residency at the Marquee Club ended on April 27 – although they would return to the club on several occasions over the next few years. This booking – combined with a series of important television appearances to promote their first singles – had brought the group the reputation and press attention they needed to become a successful, nationally recognised act. While they still played regularly throughout the London area, The Who began to travel further afield as word of their live act spread across the country.

In March, The Who had performed at a Leicester University Rag Rave. Film student Richard Stanley was present, as was his friend Roger Ford,[19] who filmed the group that evening. Although Stanley recalls the B&W short 8-mm film was ". . . very minimalistic", he remembers that "it was enough to see what was going on, it was really quite amazing. [Roger Ford] rushed, actually, into the bar where I was and said, 'Good grief, there's a guy in white trousers, and he's bleeding all over his trousers, because he's playing the guitar like crazy!'"

On May 1, The Who returned to Leicester to play a Saturday night hop at the College of Art and Technology. That evening, Stanley augmented The Who's spare lighting rig (which he recalls as "these two 1K bulbs and that's all") by projecting his films from the balcony onto the group and the white wall behind them.

Richard Stanley: "They were really strange [films]. I mean I'd made one called 'Sleeping And Digging' which was just a series of very surreal things with people asleep while bicycles were passed over them . . . very, very

---

[19] Ford later earned an Oscar nomination for art direction on the 1995 hit film *Babe*.

bizarre, and I think that's why Pete was intrigued, he kept turning round as he was playing to look at what it was – he couldn't work out what the hell was going on. And at that time it was quite a radical thing to do and I suppose that was his interest . . . [During the mid-Sixties] there was all of this technology that was making it possible for people to do things themselves, not within the studio system, if you know what I mean. And when I was working on that side in film, Pete was doing the same thing in music."

Townshend sought out Stanley after the show and the pair struck up a friendship. "I'm not sure why we became friends as we were a lot different," Stanley points out, "but there was a shared enthusiasm for ideas, and I also treated him as I would any other art school colleague. This was at a time when there were soon to be a lot of hangers-on and business people moving in to Pete's life, and I believe he was/is always loyal to those he knew from 'before'. I also got on with his other friends – and he got on with mine, and my parties for instance were ones where he could come and just be 'ordinary' – I think it was quite a luxury for him at that period."

In June, *Melody Maker* ran an article with the heading, "Every So Often A Group Is Poised On The Brink Of A Breakthrough. Word Has It It's The Who." The article provides an interesting account of The Who's stage show during this period, penned by their champion on the paper, young mod Nick Jones. "Their music is defiant, and so is their attitude. Their sound is vicious. This is no note-perfect 'showbiz' group, singing in harmony and playing clean guitar runs. The Who lay down a heavy beat . . . Moon thunders round the drums. Townshend swings full circles with his right arm. He bangs out Morse code by switching the guitar pick-ups on and off. Notes bend and whine. He turns suddenly and rams the end of his guitar into the speaker. A chord shudders on the impact. The speaker rocks. Townshend strikes again on the rebound. He rips the canvas covering, tears into the speaker cone, and the distorted solo splutters from a demolished speaker. The crowds watch this violent display spellbound . . . it's an exhausting act to watch. But also highly original and full of tremendous pace."

The Who's first trip overseas, a three-day stint to Paris in early June, drove home the pathetic state of New Action's finances. "When the time came to leave, Kit had not even got the money for the fare home and had to be bailed out by [Chris] Parmenter," Motion wrote in 1987. "When they got back they found that the bailiffs had become so insistent that Kit was forced to shift offices from Eaton Place back to Ivor Court.[20] His stay there was a brief one; in November he uprooted himself again, this time to an even posher address: Cavendish Square, just north of Oxford Circus. The move had commercial as well as domestic advantages: Robert Stigwood, the successful Australian booking agent, had a flat in the same building. He agreed – for £2,000 – to act for the band."

The uprooting of New Action meant that Townshend had to relocate; moving into his own flat in Chesham Place, Belgravia. According to Dave Marsh, Pete "decorated the place with pages torn from a book on pop art which he'd swiped from the Ealing Art School library." The 20-year-old musician equipped the spare room with his second home recording studio, including (eventually) a Vortexion CBL stereo tape machine, several microphones (as opposed to the single mike which graced his Ealing studio) and guitars. *Melody Maker* reported that Pete owned nine guitars during this period, all on hire-purchase, and that he was receiving unemployment benefit at the time. In 1975, biographer George Tremlett illustrated the young bachelor's lifestyle during this period:

> "Whereas in those days Roger, Keith and occasionally John were to be found late most evenings at the clubs that then mattered, the Ad Lib and the Cromwellian, Pete Townshend began living an almost reclusive life up in his Belgravia flat. At first he had just a mattress on the floor to sleep on, his clothes hung from coat hooks, and furniture consisted mainly of a loaded bookshelf, a pile of albums, a telephone, most of the group's cast-off equipment (mended guitars, microphones, amplifiers, etc.). There, once his day's work with the group was done, Townshend would while away the night hours, writing, experimenting with sounds."

Pete was in the middle of producing ". . . a crop of songs," Townshend said in 1971, "which I was, by then, writing using a tape recorder. Kit Lambert had bought me two good quality tape decks and suggested I do this. It appealed to me as I had always attempted it using lesser machines and been encouraged by results . . . Anyway, ensconced in my Belgravia two-room tape recorder and hi-fi showroom, I proceeded to enjoy myself writing ditties with which I could later amuse myself over-dubbing, multi-tracking, and adding extra parts. It was the way I practised. I learnt

---

[20] Film-maker Tony Palmer recalls, "I knew Kit very, very well and many's the time that Kit told me, 'The bailiffs came and took the furniture away,' or, 'We were trying to set up a tour and we didn't have a phone.'"

to play with myself. Masturbation comes to mind and, as a concept, making demos is not far off."

In addition to Andy Newman and Barry Gray, Joe Meek also influenced Pete when it came to the the art of home recording.

Richard Stanley: "[Meek] was one of the first people in London that had sort of his own little studio, and made his own records there, and he didn't use the kind of studio system at all. And Pete was like that also, he wanted to – well, it was mainly for demos, but I think he always had the dream that he would be able to do the things himself . . ."

With a growing confidence that two self-composed hit songs inevitably brought (and a simultaneous wariness brought on by an unfavourable review in *Beat Instrumental* which criticised the unoriginal results of The Who's initial album recording sessions), it was announced in the July 17 edition of *Melody Maker* that the group had delayed the release of their first LP due to a last minute musical policy change and that more Townshend (and Daltrey) originals would be included.

"I took the band over when they asked me to write for them," Townshend told Motion in 1987, "and used them as a mouthpiece, hitting out at anyone who tried to have a say in what the group [mainly Roger] said and then grumbling when they didn't appreciate my dictatorship."

Among The Who's endless TV shows and live appearances throughout England over the summer was a notable appearance at the 5th Richmond Jazz and Blues Festival on August 6. Sharing the bill with The Yardbirds and The Moody Blues, The Who played a five-song set which included 'Anyway Anyhow Anywhere', during which Pete smashed a Ricken-backer into his Vox speakers, tossing it to the back of the stage, and a new number entitled 'My Generation', which at that point, still lacked the trademark stuttering vocals and thundering climax, which made the final product so memorable.[21]

The Who's first European tour, which consisted of two shows in the Netherlands followed by four gigs in just two days in Denmark, began in late September. Pete found himself with a few days of free time prior to the beginning of a Danish stint on September 25: "I got drinking with a

---

[21] In early September, members of The Who's road crew visited London's Battersea Dogs' Home in search of a guard dog. Unfortunately, while they were inside, the van, packed with their equipment, was stolen. The following day, the group received a consignment of new amplifiers from Vox.

crowd of blokes and they invited me back to their flat for the night. But when I woke up next morning there was a policeman standing by the bed – and it was then that I discovered they'd all gone, and it wasn't their place at all. It was somebody else's house and that was why the police had been called. At first it was a bit sticky. But after I had shown them my passport and explained who I was and how I happened to be there, they let me off. But it was all still a bit of a shock."

The Who might have actually met their match for outright raucousness in the crowd present for the first show that following day. "In Aarhus, they got completely out of hand," Pete told Tremlett. "That's a farming area, and the hall was packed with 4 to 5,000 young farmers, a rather rough audience . . . the group that went onstage before us had had bottles thrown at them and we'd lost some of our equipment. When this other group came off, they told us we could use some of their equipment . . . but then we went out onstage, and the bottles started flying again, then the lads started to storm the stage, and this other group dashed back on to rescue their equipment . . . we had only been onstage for four minutes before the show was stopped, and of course things got worse after that. The fans stormed out of the hall and started to wreck the town . . . we heard afterwards that they had done £10,000 worth of damage, and that made the front page of all the Danish papers."

The various arguments between the individual members which had been simmering since virtually The Who's inception – and which had intensified as Townshend's leadership role grew – reached boiling point. All except Roger had been popping pills during the European tour (Daltrey couldn't partake since the pills affected his voice) and backstage in Aarhus, Daltrey dumped Moon's supply of French Blues down the toilet. When Moon tried to retaliate, "Roger badly beat Keith up, knocking him out," Barnes wrote in 1982. "When Keith was revived, they had to go on and do their second show of the evening [in Aalborg], which was understandably tense."

When the group returned to London, Townshend, Entwistle, and Moon demanded that Daltrey should leave The Who after finishing their work promoting 'My Generation'. "Originally the group was run by the iron glove of Roger," Townshend told *Record World* in 1974. "He used to be very tough in getting his own way. If he didn't he'd shout and scream and stamp and in the end he'd punch you in the mouth. We'd all got big egos in the group and none of us liked [him]. We all got together and politely asked Roger to leave." Daltrey stewed over this during recording sessions destined for The Who's debut album, produced by Shel Talmy, at IBC studios in October and November, 1965.

With the release of 'My Generation' in October 1965, The Who cemented their reputation as a hard-nosed group who reflected the feelings of thousands of pissed-off adolescents. The song was the complete package containing all the commercial appeal of 'I Can't Explain', combined with the aggressive feedback and live aura of 'Anyway Anyhow Anywhere'.

" 'My Generation' was written as a talking blues thing, something like Jimmy Reed's 'Talkin' New York Blues'," Townshend told Nick Logan. "In fact, 'Generation' started off as my folk song single. Dylan affected me a lot. Then it went through six or seven changes." According to Pete, it was Chris Stamp who saw the song's potential when Townshend played him the original demo. "[Stamp] was convinced it could be the biggest Who record yet," Pete wrote in 1971. "Bearing in mind the state of the demo, it shows an astuteness beyond the call. It sounded like Jimmy Reed at 10 years old suffering from nervous indigestion. Kit made suggestion after suggestion to improve the song. He later said that it was because he was unsure of it. I went on to make two more demos . . . the first introduced the stutter. The second had several key changes, pinched, again, from The Kinks."

In an era of innocence, 'My Generation' was an all-out kick up the rear for anyone who wasn't happy with their lot in life. The bite of lyrics such as *why don't you all f-f-f-fade away*, with its threat of the harsher 'F' word, seemed to sum up the frustration of countless youths across the nation. The song simply *dripped* attitude. "If 'My Generation' was the only record The Who had ever recorded, they would still deserve an honourable mention in any history of rock," wrote Chris Charlesworth in 1995. "['My Generation'] is still the best known song in their entire catalogue. Pete Townshend has often regretted penning the memorable lines '*Hope I die before I get old*' but 'My Generation' remains the hardest hitting single released by any UK pop group in 1965. The Beatles [and most of their contemporaries], remember, were still mostly writing love songs at the time this was released."

After being released on October 29, 'My Generation' reached number two in the UK, selling around 300,000 copies despite the fact that it was at first banned by the BBC who considered Daltrey's stuttering an insult to those suffering from the affliction. The song was quaintly reviewed by the *NME*'s Derek Johnson as: "A storming, raving shake-beat, with crashing cymbals, raucous guitar, reverberating bass and hand-claps throughout – and that's just the backing."

"'My Generation' was very much about trying to find a place in society," Pete reflected to *Rolling Stone*'s David Fricke in 1987. "I was very, very lost. The band was young then. It was believed that its career would be incredibly brief. The privilege that I had at the time was to be plucked out of bed-sitter land and put in a flat in the middle of Belgravia with two tape machines. It was private, and I could look out at these people who seemed to me to be from another planet. I remember one of the things I bought when The Who first became successful was a 1963 Lincoln Continental. I was driving with the top down through London, and a woman in a car going in the other direction looked at me. She was wearing a string of pearls, blonde hair, very beautiful, about 35. She kind of looked at me as if admiring me in my car. Then her lip curled, and she said, "Driving Mummy's car, are we?" That one incident, among a series of other key incidents, made me hate those people.

"I really started to respond to that. 'All right, you motherfuckers, I am going to have you. I am going to be bigger and richer, and I'm going to move into your neighbourhood. I'm going to buy that house next to you, Lord So-and-So.' . . . *Hope I die before I get old* is something I still have to live with, but not for the reason many people think. I have to be very, very vigilant not to become one of those people I despised."

Another incident which fuelled Townshend's anger towards the establishment at the time involved a run-in with the Queen Mother. "Even though I was young and smashing guitars, I still loved the Queen Mother," he told *Q*'s David Cavanagh in January 2000. "Fucking stopped, though. It was in 1964 [sic]. My manager Kit Lambert felt that I was unduly held down by my art school friends, so he moved me into Chesham Place, the road between Clarence House and Buckingham Palace. I had this Packard hearse parked outside my house. One day I came back and it was gone. It turned out that she'd had it moved, because her husband had been buried in a similar vehicle and it reminded her of him. When I went to collect it, they wanted 250 quid. I'd only paid 30 for it in the first place."

Following the release of the immensely popular 'My Generation', any story concerning The Who was considered newsworthy. In November, some rather belated rumours arose that they had fired their singer as a result of friction within the group. Although Daltrey's altercation with Moon had taken place almost two months earlier, all had been quiet in the pop press until now. The November 20 edition of *Melody Maker* ran a front-page story entitled 'The Who Split Mystery'. "Wild tales in London's in-clubs flashed the news that 20-year-old singer Roger Daltrey would be leaving the group," the article announced.[22] "It was said that young singer Boz, of the Boz People, would be Daltrey's replacement.[23] It was also thought another drummer would be brought into the group so that Keith Moon could 'explore other fields of percussion.'"

Chris Stamp was quoted in the piece: "This is absolute c-c-crap! Quite seriously I've never heard such a lot of rubbish. Does anybody in their right mind think The Who would split at a time like this? Everybody knows there is conflict within the group, and there have been some hefty rows lately, but this doesn't mean that the group will bust up. They just argue about their 'sound' and talk about all the things they want to achieve sound-wise . . . We hear rumours that Roger is leaving everywhere we go . . . it's just crap. The Who once and for all, are not 'breaking up'."

Daltrey was indeed on his way out of The Who just prior to the release of 'My Generation', but the success of the single threw a wrench in The Who's plans. As the single shot up the charts, it became apparent that the group could be a successful proposition – provided they could stay together. "[Roger] was quickly reinstated when 'My Generation' leapt up the charts," Charlesworth later wrote, "and its success undoubtedly saved Roger from a life as a tearaway – and The Who from extinction."

When *Fabulous* writer (and future Who publicity agent) Nancy Lewis first interviewed the group in early 1965, she predicted they'd split within six months. "They didn't seem to like each other very much and they were such different people, I just could never see them lasting," she told John Swenson.

"Our personalities clash, but we argue and get it all out of our system," Townshend admitted to *Melody Maker* that June. "There's a lot of friction, and offstage we're not particularly matey. But it doesn't matter. If we were not like this it would destroy our stage performance. We play how we feel."

He went one further when telling *Disc*: "We get on badly . . . Roger is

[22] "There were actually periods when Roger left the group for several weeks and I was The Who's singer," Pete told *Guitarist* in 1990. "Robert Plant talks about the fact that when he first saw us I was the singer. He came to see us three nights in a row and offered himself for the job . . . as did Steve Gibbons when he came to see us and Roger wasn't there. Obviously none of them thought I was any good!"
[23] Boz Burrell went on to stints with King Crimson and Bad Company.

not a very good singer at all in my opinion. He has got a good act, but I think he expects a backing group more than an integrated group. I don't think he will ever understand that he will never have The Who as a backing group."

After a meeting was held and the other three were persuaded to let him stay, Daltrey promised that he would attempt to curb his anger. "It was an amazing sort of transformation he went through," Townshend told Barnes, ". . . from being one of the most aggressive, violent people I knew, to being one of the most peaceful. He had to learn to live with a lot of things he didn't like and what I always admired about him was the fact that he managed to do it, because knowing the kind of power he had as a young man that he gave up in a sense, for the sake of the group, took a lot of guts."

A song The Who would record six years later put things into perspective for Daltrey. "'Behind Blue Eyes' for me, really speaks volumes," he said in 1999. "'*When my fist clenches, crack it open*', it just all made sense. That's the only way we used to deal with anything in the part of England where I grew up. Everything was solved with a fight, whoever won the fight, that's the way you went, simple as that. But obviously it didn't quite work that way in a band, and they slung me out for fighting, and the band was everything, it was my band, and it meant . . . it was my whole life, so I had two choices, give up the fighting or give up the band. There's no choice whatsoever."

Looking back, Townshend says more has been made of The Who's violent past than is necessary. "You have to remember that The Who's period initially was the mod thing where there would be fights in the dance halls," he told *Mojo's* Pat Gilbert in 2006. "Roger would have allies in the hall and you'd often see him jump offstage. But the friction within the band was overstated and very rarely fell into actual physical encounters – there were maybe two or three in the whole history of The Who."

The group's debut album, *My Generation*, released in early December 1965, reached number five in the UK charts but flopped in the US on its release four months later in altered form as *The Who Sings My Generation*. Of the original recording sessions, only three songs – 'Please Please Please' and 'I Don't Mind', both written by James Brown, and Bo Diddley's 'I'm A Man' – made it on to the final track listing. Townshend penned the remaining tracks, including 'The Kids Are Alright', which remain among his most memorable Who compositions. Of the rest, there was 'Out In The Street' – a tight, heavy R&B song which suffers somewhat from the introductory guitar flourish being quite similar to that of 'Anyway Anyhow Anywhere'. Townshend's guitar prowess is demonstrated on 'The Good's Gone',[24] while 'La La La Lies' and 'It's Not True' exhibit the characteristics of a prototypical Who song. The wacky lyrics of the latter provided a glimpse of Townshend's penchant for weird, humour-tinged compositions which would eventually spawn titles such as 'I'm A Boy', 'Happy Jack' and 'Little Billy'.

'A Legal Matter', a twangy, country-tinged number which featured Townshend singing lead vocals on a Who record for the first time was, as he described in his 1971 *Rolling Stone* essay, ". . . about a guy on the run from a chick about to pin him down for breach of promise. What this song was screaming from behind lines like, '*It's a legal matter baby, marrying's no fun, it's a legal matter baby, you got me on the run,*' was 'I'm lonely, I'm hungry, and the bed needs making.' I wanted a maid I suppose. It's terrible feeling like an eligible bachelor but with no women seeming to agree with you."

The album was rounded out with a thunderous instrumental entitled 'The Ox', Entwistle's nickname. "In the studio it was possible – with a bit of frigging around – to get the sound and energy we had onstage, and this is the first Who record where we really caught that," Townshend recalled. "Because this is an instrumental, what you get is *the band*, the sound of this tremendous machine working almost by itself . . ." The song features a thrilling performance by Moon, who as Marsh described in 1983, ". . . simply eclipses every surf drummer in history on a song that is nothing so much as an Anglo 'Wipe Out'."

---

[24] Pete explained his early tendency of avoiding guitar solos to *Guitarist* in 1990: ". . . I knew Jimmy Page – Led Zeppelin weren't formed then but I'd seen him in various bands and if anything his playing slowed down as he got older! He was an extraordinary player, arrogant, flash . . . And Eric, with The Yardbirds, used to play absolutely beautifully and he'd only been playing a year! And Jeff Beck, who always had that quality of making the guitar sound like a voice . . . That was the kind of marketplace I was in, and although I hadn't been belted round the chops by Jimi Hendrix yet, I definitely didn't want to be competing with those players . . . I was very embarrassed playing on The Who's first album because I tried to play solos and I could hear the jazz creeping in. So I made a conscious effort to keep away from feature solos. And it did feel very much like a competitive area . . ."

CHAPTER THREE

1966–1967

"This 'being angry at the adult world' bit is not all of us. It's not me and it's not John. It's only half Roger, but it is Pete."

– Keith Moon, 1966

B Y early 1966, Pete had left the Belgravia flat and moved to Old Church Street, Chelsea. In her 1974 book, *The Who . . . Through The Eyes Of Pete Townshend*, author Caroline Silver described his new abode as, ". . . a penthouse apartment in the middle of London's smart Chelsea district. Far below, charming grey-roofed houses stretch away, interspersed with neat, green squares, to the River Thames. Tugboats and barges come and go all day on the river; on the far banks are the flashing coloured lights of the Battersea Fun Fair. It is the kind of place anyone would envy Townshend for living in, which makes him feel self-conscious and anxious to move somewhere else." A recording studio occupied one room, while broken guitars adorned the walls of another.

Having penned three consecutive UK hit singles, Townshend was emerging as a bright young figure on the British music scene. As he gave an increasing number of interviews to the music media, he came to be regarded as an interesting, articulate spokesman for his generation with an often unflinching regard for the truth. On January 5, when The Who appeared on the television show *A Whole Scene Going*, Pete publicly admitted in a solo interview that he was an active drug user.

More controversy appeared in the March 26 issue of *Melody Maker*. The paper's weekly feature, 'Pop Think-In' canvassed a pop star's opinions on various subjects, especially on popular music and cultural issues; opinions which weren't previously thought of as particularly important by the general media. When the subject of Vietnam came up, Pete commented, "Actually it's turned into a bit of a bore, one of those questions like Korea. That war was never won was it? There will always be teenagers ready to throw themselves under tanks. I wonder what I would do if we were in the same position. I always stand by Young Communist principles. If I was in Russia and in some harsh five-year plan – if it was for the good of the country – I wouldn't mind. I would get joy out of seeing something being done, like new libraries being built. But for a youngster to face foreign troops blasting away about something they don't even understand . . . well really they all ought to get out." The principles of the Young Communist league had been familiar to Townshend for a few years now – he had joined the organisation while at art school.

Pete was on more solid ground with Pop Art. "It's still my favourite form of art. My favourite artists are Barry Fantoni and Peter Blake. What I like most of all is it's English. Foreign Pop Art I hate. I don't think you can enjoy it unless it's relevant to your own country. It has no relevance to The Who except we used its ideas . . . I think we did a lot for it in this country. If we hadn't have done it, it might have taken another year to catch on. The number of journalists I had to explain it to, especially on local papers. Pop Art encompasses performances, what are called 'happenings' and auto-destructive performances, including smashing guitars. I used to talk to Kit about Pop Art a lot and suddenly he came out with this idea. He told us: 'Keith is going to have a bull's-eye on his T-shirt, Pete is going to wear badges' – all these were his ideas. At the beginning it took a lot of guts to wear them."

'Irish' Jack Lyons: "Around '66, Pete had built up a reputation as one of the most brilliant interviewees for any magazine and the more highbrow the magazine the better. At the time there was only two people who gave the best interviews anywhere [in my opinion] and that was Bob Dylan and Pete Townshend. Right then I lived, ate and dreamed Townshend. He was my hero. My fucking idol."

Townshend's declaration of his adherence to Young Communist principles particularly floored Lyons. "Nobody ever said that," he recalls. "It was reckless, brave and it made my hair stand on end even if the communists had frightened the fuck out of me circa 1963. I still have that original interview from *Melody Maker*. For months I was walking around with it folded in my inside pocket like a travelling companion."

Several months later, Pete appeared as a guest in *Melody Maker*'s 'Blind Date' weekly segment, where various celebrities gave their often acerbic opinions on the latest releases. The selections (chosen by the paper and played to Pete as he reviewed them) included Cliff Richard's 'Time Drags By' ("What a load of crap"), Nancy Sinatra's 'In Due Time' ("This must have been written by some C&W writer who doesn't know the modern lyrics scene"), The Temptations' 'Beauty Is Only Skin Deep' ("Nice sound. I like this sort of thing"), and Oscar performing 'Join My Gang', a song written by Pete ("I like it, I think it's good. I'm still waiting for the money from this.")

Meanwhile, in January, Chris Stamp visited New York to attempt to re-negotiate The Who's recording contract. The group's lack of success in the US stemmed from American Decca's unwillingness to promote their records. 'I Can't Explain' had reached an unimpressive number 93 in America, while 'Anyway Anyhow Anywhere' didn't even make the charts. 'My Generation' stalled at 74, while *The Who Sings My Generation* (released in April '66) would also fail to reach the charts. It seemed that Decca, who dealt mainly in country music and light pop, and were staffed mostly with older, conservative types, weren't ready for an unorthodox act like The Who. "American Decca was sort of archaic," Stamp confirmed to Richard Barnes. "I realised that we would never break The Who with this company." Thus the battle lines were drawn between The Who, their record label and Shel Talmy.

Frustrated with Talmy's dictatorial style of producing, The Who's financially poor recording deal and Decca's ineptitude in getting the group noticed in America, Lambert and Stamp consulted an attorney in an effort to find a way out of Talmy's contract. While in America, Stamp had been offered an advance from Atlantic Records and was eager to begin a relationship with the company. Lambert wrote to Talmy to inform the producer that The Who no longer wanted to be associated with him and that their contract (which had four years remaining) was no longer valid. "I received a letter in the post saying something to the effect that my services were no longer required," Talmy told *Record World*. "I don't think I ever fell out with the group at any stage but they were very young and they were very influenced, possibly unduly influenced, by their managers. Kit Lambert is not one of my favourite people and I was happy in one way because it meant I would not have to be associated with him. We came very close to blows at one point."

When Talmy baulked at the prospect of losing The Who, Lambert decided to force the issue by releasing their next single on a different label. The follow-up to 'My Generation' was supposed to be 'Circles', a Townshend song which the group had recorded with Talmy and was scheduled for release on Brunswick/Decca. However, in mid-February, without Talmy's knowledge, The Who recorded 'Substitute', a new Townshend composition. A few weeks earlier, they had also self-produced a new version of 'Circles', which became the B-side of 'Substitute', when released in March on Reaction,[1] a label specially set up by The Who's agent Robert Stigwood, through Polydor Records.[2] (Atco, a subsidiary of Atlantic, issued the single in the US a month later.)

'Substitute', about which Townshend later commented he'd made "... after hearing a rough mix of '19th Nervous Breakdown' by the Stones," wasn't a difficult song for him to write. "The lyric, so applauded by rock critics, was thrown together very quickly," he revealed in 1987. "Smokey Robinson sang the word 'substitute' so perfectly in '[The] Tracks Of My Tears' – my favourite song at the time – that I decided to celebrate the word itself with a song all its own."

Regardless of its apparent simplicity, 'Substitute' was a successful release. "The lyric has come to be the most quoted Who lyric ever," Townshend wrote in 1971. "... it somehow goes to show that the 'trust the art, not the artist' tag that people put on [Bob] Dylan's silence about his work could be a good idea. 'Substitute' makes me recall writing a song to fit a clever and rhythmic sounding title. A play on words. Again it could mean a lot more to me now than it did when I wrote it. If I told you what it meant to me now, you'd think I take myself too seriously.

"The stock, down-beat riff used in the verses I pinched from a record played to me in 'Blind Date', a feature in *Melody Maker*. It was by a group who later wrote to thank me for saying nice things about their record in the feature. The record I said nice things about ['Where Is My Girl' by Robb Storme & the Whispers] wasn't a hit, despite an electrifying riff. I pinched it, we did it, you bought it."

'Substitute' also marked Townshend's first lesson in production, as he confirmed in his 1971 *Rolling Stone* essay: "Kit wasn't really in a position to steam in and produce. A blond chap called Chris at Olympic Studios got the sound, set up a kinky echo, did the mix, etc. I looked on and have

---

[1] To confuse things, two pressings of 'Substitute' were released simultaneously on the Reaction label; one of which titled the re-recorded version of 'Circles' as 'Instant Party'. Further complicating matters is the fact that The Who recorded an unrelated song of Pete's entitled 'Instant Party Mixture' (produced by Talmy) in January, 1966.

[2] "Shel Talmy had to be got rid of," Townshend told *Zigzag* in 1971, "and the only guy who was really powerful enough, who was concerned with The Who in any way whatsoever at the time and who wouldn't suffer by it was Robert Stigwood. So we were temporarily on his label."

taken the credit whenever the opportunity has presented itself ever since."

After 'Substitute' appeared on the Reaction label, Talmy immediately countered, obtaining a court injunction within four days of the single's release which prevented Reaction from pressing any more recordings of the 'Circles'/'Instant Party' B-side since he'd already recorded the song with The Who. UK Decca issued their own Who single, the aptly named 'A Legal Matter', with the B-side, 'Instant Party', actually the version of 'Circles' which Talmy had intended as The Who's fourth single prior to the contract squabble. The group now had two singles released in Britain within days of each other on two different record labels.

"The pop world is evenly split over the promotion of the two Who singles presently on the market," read the March 19 edition of *Melody Maker*. "Their single on Polydor's Reaction label, 'Substitute', climbed to number 20 in this week's *MM* chart, but their other release taken from the *My Generation* LP, titled 'Legal Matter', on Brunswick hasn't yet hit the Pop 50.[3] The High Court battle over The Who's recording contract with Shel Talmy, their ex-recording manager, still goes on, but will not now effect the distribution of 'Substitute'. The disc now has a completely new B-side, called 'Waltz For A Pig' by The Who Orchestra." 'The Who Orchestra' was actually the Graham Bond Organisation – a jazz-pop quartet managed by Stigwood, featuring bassist Jack Bruce and drummer Ginger Baker (soon to form Cream) – who recorded the instrumental (the 'pig' reportedly being Talmy) for Reaction since The Who were legally bound not to record until at least after the court hearing set for April 4.

Pete described the hearing to *Zigzag* in 1971: "Shel took [the case] to the High Court judge and said things like, 'And then on bar 36 I suggested to the lead guitarist that he play an innuendo, forget the adagio, and play 36 bars modulating to the key of E flat,' which was all total rubbish since he used to fall asleep at his desk while a bloke called Glyn Johns did everything.[4] Eventually we found ourselves in court and we dreamed up even more preposterous replies. 'Shel Talmy certainly did *not* tell us at the 36th bar to play an innuendo,' we said. 'He told us to do such and such, and we suggested blah, blah, blah.' All this in incredible, grand, grandiose musical terms."

Talmy, represented by Quentin Hogg, distinguished QC and future

---

[3] 'Substitute' reached number five while 'A Legal Matter' reached only 32.
[4] Johns went on to produce *The Who By Numbers*, *Who Are You* and *It's Hard*. He was also named associate producer of *Who's Next* and several 1971/72 Who single releases.

Conservative peer Lord Hailsham, gained the upper hand in the court-room. "It just looked like the judge was going to go with Quentin Hogg because he was making him laugh and all that," Stamp claimed. "You suddenly saw British justice." When the case was described to the elderly judge, he mistook "Who" as an acronym for the World Health Organisation.

While the legal battle with Talmy dragged on, The Who were forced to maintain a hectic – but increasingly lucrative – touring schedule. With the recent European popularity of 'My Generation' and 'Substitute', the group were now commanding live fees of up to £500 per show. They embarked on their first package show theatre tours in the winter and spring, in addition to gigs all over Britain, the most prestigious of which was the *New Musical Express'* Poll Winners Concert at the Wembley Empire Pool, north London on May 1, alongside such heavyweights as The Beatles, The Rolling Stones, The Yardbirds, The Small Faces, and Roy Orbison. In their review, *NME* regarded The Who's two-song act as the most notable of the evening. "The screaming was deafening for The Who. I don't know that it was music; it was more like watching violence put to rhythm."

"The Who by this time were very into their Union Jack period and looking incredible," Chris Stamp told Tony Fletcher, the author of *Dear Boy: The Life Of Keith Moon* in 1999. "Pete did his feedback thing and we had smoke bombs going off. And we did this destructive ending with Pete's guitar. And Keith, who had knocked over a few drums here and there, really went for it. He did a huge thing with the drums, I think they even fell off the stage, he made a huge mess. He did it to be with Pete, to top Pete, and to also make The Who's presence felt, make sure the Stones and The Beatles had to follow *this*."

The Who were now using 'My Generation' as the final number in their live act. Richard Barnes described a typical rendition of their most powerful song in *Maximum R&B*: "It was the climax of a powerful, loud, uncompromising set and it was at the end of 'My Generation' that Pete would start hitting his Rickenbacker on the floor to get strange electronic noises and effects from it. He would set up a feedback pattern and then run the mike stand down the strings to get a screeching loud electronic scraping noise . . . Then, with a mean look he'd start poking the speaker cabinet with the guitar and ripping holes in the fabric covering. The tension and drama of their act was intense. Snarling and scowling, Townshend would unleash his fury on his equipment. He would attack the speaker cabinets with the guitar, swinging it above his head and smashing the cabinet, using the guitar as an axe. The Who were the most outrageous and stunning live act to hit the British scene. They were sheer violence and frustration set to music."

Townshend's penchant for flailing his equipment about during live shows caught up with him at a May 20 performance at the Ricky Tick Club in Newbury, Berkshire. As the group performed 'My Generation', one of Keith's drums fell over, knocking a cymbal onto Pete. "I wasn't hurt, just annoyed and upset," Townshend later told an interviewer. "Keith and John had been over two hours late. Then I swung out with my guitar not really meaning to hit Keith. I lost my grip on the instrument and it just caught him on the head." Moon, who sustained a badly bruised face, a black eye and a cut on his leg, refused to play with the group for a week, during which time they used a temporary replacement. Townshend visited Moon's home to offer an apology, but the drummer wouldn't come to the door. According to Barnes, "Things were not well within the group and several fights and arguments later there was a possible break-away from the group by Keith and John, who were planning to combine with two members of The Yardbirds to form a new group to be called Led Zeppelin – a name invented by John."[5]

Relationships within The Who were once again nearing breaking point and Moon and Entwistle weren't the only disgruntled band members. "Roger was gonna leave the group," Townshend told *Zigzag*. "It was just an amazing time in The Who's career.[6] We were more or less about to break up. Nobody really cared about the group. It was just a political thing. Kit and I used to go for long walks in Hyde Park and talk about combining what was gonna be left of The Who with Paddy, Klaus, and Gibson."[7]

---

[5] In May 1966, Moon recorded 'Beck's Bolero' with Jeff Beck, Nicky Hopkins, and two future members of Led Zeppelin. "I remember Townshend looking daggers at me when he heard it," Beck later told Tony Fletcher, "because it was a bit near the mark. He didn't want anyone meddling with that territory at all."

"The thing is that when Keith did 'Beck's Bolero', that wasn't just a session, that was a political move," Townshend told *Zigzag*. "It was at a point when the group was very close to breaking up. Keith was very paranoid and going through a heavy pills thing. He wanted to make the group plead for him because he'd joined Beck."

[6] Andy Neill and Matt Kent's 2002 definitive Moon-era Who chronology *Anyway Anyhow Anywhere* lists four May 1966 Daltrey-less Who gigs featuring Pete and John sharing vocal responsibilities.

[7] A trio, originally from Liverpool and Hamburg, who were managed by Brian Epstein.

With the group on the verge of disintegration, Pete entertained the possibility of signing with new management. Rolling Stones' manager Andrew Oldham offered his services. "Andrew found out that Kit Lambert and Chris Stamp were losing control of The Who and he stepped in and suggested he pay for me to fly to meet Allen Klein [Oldham's business advisor, who wined and dined Pete on a yacht on the Hudson River] in New York," Townshend said in Oldham's 2002 autobiography *2Stoned*.[8]

Klein offered to assist in extricating The Who from their contract with Talmy, in addition to dangling the promise of a hefty advance if they signed with MGM (the label to whom some of Klein's clients, among them Herman's Hermits, were signed). Townshend made a return trip to New York to discuss matters further, this time accompanied by Lambert, Stamp, their attorney Edward Oldman, and Keith Moon. "[Oldman] just took two looks at Klein and said, 'We're leaving,'" Pete told *Zigzag*, "so we ate his caviar, had a look at the Statue of Liberty from his yacht, shat in his toilet, and went back to England."

The young guitarist-composer developed a distinct distaste for Klein, perhaps due to his overbearing business demeanour.[9] "It was all around that time I was having trouble with Kit and Chris," Townshend explained in *2Stoned*. "Then Guy Stevens stepped in and got me to have another meeting with Chris Blackwell at Island, which came to nothing. During a meeting at my house Kit Lambert arrived and sat down and wept and wept and wept; he just couldn't believe I was going to dump him. I told him, 'Listen, if you can get the band back in shape again everything will be fine.' Somehow Kit managed to pull it back together. [Kit and Chris] blamed Andrew for driving me to walk away, but in actual fact I felt that Kit and Chris did not know how to take The Who to the next level."

Apparently having regained their charge's confidence, but fighting a

---

[8] Oldham says that he never intended to oust Lambert and Stamp, despite the pair's impressions to the contrary. "My Who agenda was very simple," Oldham maintained in *2Stoned*. "Pick up the mantra of 'fuck Shel Talmy', for whom, from my snob-driven lack of an ethical position, I had no feelings one way or the other. Insert Lambert and Stamp as producers, myself as Executive Producer on the art and hustle, and Allen [Klein] as the financial manager over the whole lot of us."

[9] Pete wrote a song called 'Lazy Fat People' during this period. "That song was about Allen Klein," he told *Zigzag* in 1971. "Allen Klein tried to get hold of The Who as being the first of his purge on rock. I mean, he shat all over The Beatles and the Stones. Fuck knows how we managed to get out of it." Townshend has since played down Klein as being the song's inspiration.

losing battle in the courts, Lambert and Stamp settled with Talmy. The Who ended up staying with American Decca on a renegotiated deal which gave them three times the royalties they had previously made. Polydor assumed rights to the group's European releases. With Shel Talmy out of the picture, this meant that The Who could choose their own producer. Talmy received a favourable settlement: a five per cent royalty on The Who's recordings through 1971, which would end up including their two best selling albums, *Tommy*, and *Who's Next*. This was the price The Who paid for artistic freedom in the recording studio.

One of The Who's opening acts during a show at Blackpool's South Pier on May 28 (which marked Moon's return to drumming duties after his fall-out with Townshend) was the Rockin' Vickers, featuring guitarist Ian 'Lemmy' Kilmister, the future Motörhead bassist/frontman. To the apparent irritation of Townshend, the Rockin' Vickers recorded 'It's Alright', a blatant steal of 'The Kids Are Alright', produced by Talmy. "They were playing it before I joined the band, pinched it, added half and Townshend threatened to sue," Kilmister claimed in a 2006 *Mojo* interview. "The Who became good mates later . . ."

In July, another Townshend song, 'So Sad About Us', was recorded by the Merseys, a duo managed by Kit Lambert, as the follow-up to their UK hit single, 'Sorrow'. Townshend, who served as producer, considered the song "did quite well", in his 1983 liner notes to the *Scoop* demo collection. The Who went on to record and release it on *A Quick One* later in the year. He'd written the song at the home of his friend John 'Speedy' Keen. Keen (nicknamed Speedy for his motorcycling prowess) was ". . . a talented drummer and emerged as a great writer as soon as I opened my ears to him properly." During this period, Keen (who would later emerge as the drummer/lyricist for Thunderclap Newman) chauffered Townshend to Who gigs all over Britain for a reported £15 per week.[10] Keen later shared the upstairs flat in Wardour Street that Pete moved into that summer. "We had a lot of things in common," Keen told Dave Marsh in 1983. "We liked really good cars, big cars with big engines. We liked high-energy music . . . At that time, you couldn't get a long paper between us. We were close."

---

[10] Pete's hiring of Speedy may have been an act of self-preservation: on May 29, 1966, Townshend was involved in a car accident and was later fined after being found guilty of dangerous driving. He suffered another car accident on June 29, while jet-lagged from his first trip to New York.

On June 2, The Who commenced a six-day Scandinavian tour, playing to an audience of 11,000 in Stockholm. A few days later, the show in Orebro began late and fans rushed the stage. Just a few songs in, police cut the power. "With the stage lighting and amplifiers now dead, Pete Townshend furiously stormed over to the power supply room of the building ready to tackle both the police and stagehands," Joe McMichael and 'Irish' Jack Lyons reported in 1997's *The Who Concert File*. "The power was soon restored, however, and the concert continued with Who roadies defending the mains power switch. But the police once more intervened, cut the electricity for a second time and the concert continued with Keith Moon offering an improvised drum solo. Soon tiring of the solo, Moon joined Townshend and threatened the policemen guarding the power switch but they soon realised that nothing more could be done and The Who withdrew after an aborted set."

Townshend's short fuse onstage was becoming increasingly evident. Later in the year at another Swedish show, he ripped the stage curtain down in a rage after it had been lowered during The Who's performance. Some of the group's equipment smashing during this period was so violent that it provoked complaints from fans who feared for their own safety. An example of this occurred at the newly renamed Windsor Jazz & Blues Festival, which took place at Windsor Racecourse on July 30. The annual event had been moved from Richmond, its original location, due to noise complaints. Pete, dressed in a dinner suit complete with bow tie and with girlfriend Karen Astley in tow, led The Who through a powerful set which opened with their high-octane interpretation of the *Batman* theme. However, as eyewitness Richard Barnes recalled: "[The Who] thought that they weren't getting across very well and so finished with 'My Generation' where Pete smashed his guitar into his amps and ripped all the fabric off the front and started laying into the speakers inside. The guitar split and then split again, the head was ripped off and then the neck snapped. He continued until the guitar was smashed to small pieces. Keith kicked all his drums over and they were rolling around the stage while Roger smashed the cymbals with his fists, hurled mikes at the back of the stage. Not content with this, Roger then started to kick out all the footlights at the front of the stage. Keith then got a bucket of water and threw it into the audience. The whole stage was covered in yellow smoke from smoke bombs which were being hurled onstage by Kit Lambert and Chris Stamp as they encouraged the onstage demolition. The crowd went absolutely wild. Keith said, 'After that show, the roadies came on in little white coats and shovelled the equipment into buckets. The audience had smashed up all their seats and the whole place looked like Attila the Hun had ridden through it.'"

One of the songs featured in The Who's set at the Windsor Jazz & Blues Festival was their forthcoming single, 'I'm A Boy', which got completed the following day at IBC studios. At the time, Pete had been working on an idea he named *Quads*, set in 1999, which told of a world where prospective parents were able to choose the sex of their children. One such couple chose four girls, but were mistakenly given three girls and a boy. Undaunted, the couple raised their children as if they had four girls, dressing their frustrated little boy in girls' clothes and denying him involvement in any boyish activities. "The song, of course, is about a boy whose mother dresses him up as a girl," Townshend wrote in 1971, "and won't let him enjoy all the normal boyish pranks like slitting lizards' tummies and throwing rocks at passing cars. 'I'm A Boy' was my first attempt at Rock Opera."

'I'm A Boy' appears to be the only song which materialised from the *Quads* idea, but 'Disguises', a song from the same time, features similarly idiosyncratic lyrics and confused subject matter. Pete apparently had ideas for the project which went beyond 'I'm A Boy'. "[*Quads*] goes on in later life where the three girls become a singing group, and I had amazing visions of Keith, John and I pretending to be The Beverly Sisters," Pete said in 1971. "There was a lot of comedy in it . . . but I think at the same time it was a heavily serious thing as well because it had these flashbacks to childhood, which I was very into at the time."

Released on August 26, just two weeks after Decca issued 'The Kids Are Alright' on 45 (the legal settlement allowed the company to continue releasing singles from *My Generation*), 'I'm A Boy' reached number one on the *Melody Maker* chart but stalled at number two in *NME* and the other charts including the BBC's *Top Of The Pops*. The recording sessions in late August from which the single emerged marked the beginning of a period of prolific recording by The Who at IBC studios for their second album. With Talmy out of the picture, the group, with Lambert still learning the ropes of production, now had carte blanche in the studio and Townshend recalled the album as being enjoyable to record. "It was a wonderful and unrestrained creative period," Chris Stamp wrote in 1995, "during which my partner Kit Lambert, The Who and myself were all discovering how to make records for ourselves, and trying out all kinds of ideas, no matter how far out and crazy they seemed to be."

After *Quads* failed to come to fruition, Pete continued in his quest to write thematically linked music. 'A Quick One (While He's Away)' proved to be the next incarnation of this desire. Recorded at IBC, Pye, and Regent Sound studios in autumn 1966, this six-song medley clocked in at over nine minutes and was Townshend's most ambitious effort yet.[11] "Pete and Kit had been talking for a while about extended themes and ideas in rock'n'roll," Stamp recalled in 1995, "and they both felt it could be done in an operatic way without renouncing the basic balls of rock. ['A Quick One'] was the first shot at that idea, with its themes of love, betrayal and forgiveness." Through its six phases, the mini-opera tells the story of a lonely woman whose lover is far away ('Her Man's Gone', 'Crying Town') and the arrival of several suitors, one of whom is a Welsh train driver ('We Have A Remedy', 'Ivor The Engine Driver'). The girl becomes involved with Ivor but confesses all upon the return of her lover, who forgives her ('Soon Be Home', 'You Are Forgiven').

Despite its admittedly light subject matter, 'A Quick One' was an effective song and typified this period of The Who, a phase during which they recorded a wide variety of material; everything from an unlikely medley of 'My Generation' and Edward Elgar's 'Land Of Hope and Glory' (intended for a special edition of *Ready, Steady, Go!*) to 'Run Run Run', which would become the first composition on The Who's new album. The song had previously been recorded that year (but unreleased) by two fellow west London mod groups, The Birds (who featured Ronnie Wood as their guitarist) and The Cat, the latter version produced by Pete.[12] The effects of Talmy's absence are quite noticeable on The Who's version of the song; Entwistle's loud bass acting very much like a lead instrument, sharing the spotlight with Townshend's guitar. Pete's musicianship had markedly improved since the previous album, thanks to a year packed with live shows.

'Whiskey Man' and 'Boris The Spider', Entwistle's first Who compositions, were recorded in early October. "Politics or my own shaky vanity might be the reason, but 'Boris The Spider' was never released as a

---

11 "['A Quick One'] was inspired by an obscene spoof baroque opera my friend Ray Tolliday and I had written and recorded at my Wardour Street home studio for Kit Lambert's birthday in early 1967 [sic]," Pete wrote in a 2001 article in Q. "That was called *Gratis Amatis* and featured – among others – Titania, who had to be 'disowned', because she 'let her knickers down'." Another leftover Townshend idea from this period, which went unrecorded by The Who, was entitled 'King Rabbit'.
12 The Cat featured John 'Speedy' Keen on drums and guitarist Chris Thomas, who went on to an illustrious music production career.

single and could have been a hit," Townshend wrote in 1971. "It was *the* most requested song we ever played onstage, and if this really means anything to you guitar players, it was [Jimi] Hendrix's favourite Who song. Which rubbed me up well the wrong way, I can tell you. John introduced us to 'Boris' in much the same way as I introduced us to 'My Generation' – through a tape recorder. We assembled in John's three feet by 10 feet bedroom and listened incredulously as the strange and haunting chords emerged. Faced with words about the slightly gruesome death of a spider, the song had enough charm to send me back to my pad writing hits furiously."

Daltrey's composition, 'See My Way' was demoed, with Townshend's assistance, at the latter's Wardour Street flat. The silly *Addams Family*-esque harpsichord of 'I Need You' marked the arrival of the first of Moon's two compositions for the album. The second, which more than eclipsed the first in silliness and, more importantly, sheer drumming brilliance, was an instrumental entitled 'Cobwebs And Strange'. Stamp recalled that the recording of the song, which was based on an Ara-besque tune released in 1960 by Tony Crombie entitled 'Eastern Journey', ". . . involved marching up and down past a mono mike because Kit Lambert, years ahead of his time, thought this might create a 'stereo' effect. Keith played orchestral cymbals, Pete was on penny whistle, Roger blew a trombone, and John played the trumpet."[13] If any instrumental could ever give an accurate portrayal of what was going on inside Keith Moon's head, this might have been it. Townshend blew the dust off 'Cobwebs And Strange' in 1993, when using it as the opener during his *Psychoderelict* solo tour.

Recording resumed in November on The Who's return from dates on the Continent, with the group taping their required Xmas single at CBS studios. The subject matter of 'Happy Jack', a hermit who lived on the Isle of Man, was dredged from Pete's childhood memories during the Squadronaires' residency on the island. "There was no character called 'Happy Jack'," he wrote in 1971, "but I played on the beach a lot and it's just my memories of some of the weirdos who lived on the sand." As the final note to 'Happy Jack' fades out, Townshend can be heard shouting

[13] In addition to telling John Swenson "our manager was completely nuts", Entwistle said that 'Cobwebs And Strange' was ultimately recorded with the band members standing still because as they marched they lost time with the backing track which was being played on a monitor at one end of the studio. "If we'd worn cans we could have gotten tangled up, so we finally had to track it standing still . . ." Entwistle told Swenson.

'I saw ya!' at Keith Moon, who'd been asked not to distract the others as they sang backing vocals, but was spotted larking about in the control room. Released in December, the single reached number three in the UK and proved to be the first Who single to break the US singles charts, climbing to number 24 on its release there the following spring.

Townshend referred to *A Quick One,* also released in December, as The Who's first real album, ignoring the Talmy-produced *My Generation* in the process. Apart from the album's title, renamed *Happy Jack* for the American market (*A Quick One* was deemed too suggestive), the only difference between the UK and US releases was the omission of 'Heat Wave' to make room for 'Happy Jack' due to its success in the States. *A Quick One* reached number four while *Happy Jack* only got to 67 on the *Billboard* album listings.

A Quick One was well received in the music press – *Melody Maker* called it "An incredible new album . . . at last it fulfils the promise of The Who."

"The Who of *Happy Jack* are clearly not The Who of *The Who Sings My Generation*," Jon Landau wrote in the July/August 1967 issue of *Crawdaddy!* "They have metamorphosed with the best of them, and the changes are vast. In fact, the new Who are really a contradiction of the first order. Onstage the group is still famed for its uninhibited exhibitionism and its instrument destruction tactics in which, via various gimmicks, one is led to believe that the world is coming to an end. But listening to *Happy Jack* after being familiar with The Who's live antics, and the first album, one is apt to be surprised. *Happy Jack* is an almost arty, and for The Who, restrained affair. It emphasises the group's rare talents, in the areas of self-editing [a lost art if ever there was one], humour, lyricism, and other things which one generally expects to find in the wilder groups. The more extroverted side of the group is, in fact, played down.

"They're sharp, sarcastic, cynical, but never weighed down with their own self-importance. They are a life-force on a rock scene in which too many people are hiding behind facile, slogan songs about how all the world needs is for everyone to love everyone else. Nor do they have to rely on psychedelic lyrics, or pseudo-poetry, or meaningless attempts at the recreation of the beauty of the Eastern pattern completely out of its natural context, to create music. Rather, they are much more influenced by the Western classical tradition, both instrumentally and lyrically, than that of any other culture. The Who don't pretend. Their music is them and they don't have to defend it by coming on too arrogantly, or freaky, within the context of the music itself. They say what they have to say in a manner that is perfectly natural for them, and therein lies their magic and their charm. We would all do well to listen, and to learn."

"Just after we'd finished *A Quick One* [The Who] became a big clubbing band; we used to go down to the clubs a lot," Townshend recalled in 1975. "I got to know [Paul] McCartney pretty well, and he was really raving over the album and saying that track 'A Quick One' was exactly the sort of thing that The Beatles were working towards. He said they'd been really inspired by it. And when *Sgt Pepper* came out [June 1967] I remember very smugly thinking, 'It's all because of *A Quick One*.'"[14]

In the summer of 1966, Pete was filmed in his new flat at 87 Wardour Street for the American TV programme *Where The Action Is*. The segment – which ultimately wasn't screened – featured Townshend extolling the virtues of loud music, explaining, "One of the reasons for having music fantastically loud is because you get so many people that'll just turn a deaf ear to what you do, you know, just won't listen to what you do. It doesn't matter how good or bad it is. In fact, the bigger it is normally, the more they'll close their ears to it, so the louder you've got to work. Volume is a fantastic thing. Power and volume!"

Pete's apartment lay a little to the south and across the street from the Marquee Club. "[He] was now living in a very big room with a kitchen attached on the top floor of a building on the corner of Wardour Street and Brewer Street, in the heart of London's Soho," Barnes described in 1982. "He'd got a carpenter to build a whole wooden environment into the room. There was a raised platform and a sort of wooden DJ's booth, where he could sit and play records and tapes surrounded by electronic toys and gadgets. [Pete had upgraded his equipment to two Revox 15 tape decks, a "rough patch bay", a limiter and a mixer.] His bed was raised up seven foot from the ground and the underneath was used for seating. The whole thing was built as one continuous structure from the same wood, even the floor. Little steps led up to the raised stage area and built-up seats. It looked very strange – something like a modern lecture theatre. Not particularly homely.

"In the centre of Pete's pad was a large stone garden pedestal about

---

[14] In a January 1967 interview, Pete said, "The only Beatle I've ever suspected of having anything in common with was Paul McCartney . . . I like all the things he says, and all the songs he writes . . . They are basically my main source of inspiration – and everyone else's for that matter. I think 'Eleanor Rigby' was a very important musical move forward. It certainly inspired me to write and listen to things in that vein."

three foot in diameter for holding a small shrub or bush. This served as Pete's rubbish bin and ashtray. One day as we were sitting there he suddenly realised that it was getting quite full. He picked it up – it was quite heavy – and simply tossed the contents out of the window on to busy Wardour Street five floors below. He didn't even look to see where it had all gone."

Pete recalled life in the apartment in 1970: "Listening to records on a giant system at 200 watts. Making love in the bed built up near the ceiling, watching *Alice In Wonderland* on the telly, eating baked beans straight out of the tin."

In mid-December, Bob Pridden started his long tenure with The Who. "I was forced to take over as head road manager straight away which was a bit scaring at first," he told *Record World* in 1974. "I'd been working with the John Barry Seven before that – a very placid crowd – but I knew what The Who were up to, like smashing their equipment. On that first night [at Streatham Mecca] it was all fine. The gear went up and it was really nice and then when they went onstage I was so scared. It was the most amazing experience I've ever had. Something clicked, like with Pete, the aggressiveness, the whole thing, the dynamics, the music, everything, and I was quite stunned. At the end of the act everything got smashed to pieces. Roger just walked off and he said to me: 'Get it fixed for the next gig' and I'm just looking at all those bits and that was when I made my mind up to get into it and do it. I really liked it funnily enough. It was a challenge."

On December 20, The Who guested on the final episode of the music show which had helped to establish them in Britain, *Ready, Steady, Go!* With a tip of the hat to one of their most important influences, the group played 'Please Don't Touch' by Johnny Kidd & the Pirates (Kidd was killed in a car accident back in October) along with a short version of 'I'm A Boy'. The following night, The Who opened a new club, the Upper Cut.

'Irish' Jack Lyons: "It was a trendy type place in Forest Gate in east London. The owner was a man called Billy Walker who had been the British heavyweight champion boxer, hence the name. I went to the show with Pete in his car but I can't recall any more discussions or arguments about religion or interview devices or why my hair would never be like George Harrison's. At the outset of most of our journeys Pete would come across very pissed off as if giving you a lift to the show was the biggest thing in your life and you should be extremely grateful. Afterwards, some-where in the middle of a debate on style or mod songs, he would lighten up and actually be pleased you were with him. He could be, how shall I say, 'difficult'. I remember the gig wasn't exactly full that night even though the band were great. I'll always remember years later [future Who, then Small Faces drummer] Kenney Jones told me that gig was where he first met his wife. When I went into the dressing room it was obvious there had been a verbal argument and I think Pete or Roger was laying down the law how doing these celebrity type gigs was a waste of time.

"Anyway we trooped out of the dressing room and headed for the car. A painter chap who had gotten on Pete's nerves in their dressing room stuck his head through the car window and asked for a lift. Pete was about to say, 'Sorry, we're full,' when I suddenly said something like, 'Come on in, there's plenty of room.' Pete got angry with me and told me to mind my own fucking business when it came to who could get a lift and who couldn't. Pete wanted to go to a night club and when I said I couldn't go because I had work in the morning he got very pissed off and tore me off a strip in front of the others, saying things like, 'I don't know why you bother coming to these shows if you're not up to it.' I was certainly very red faced. I phoned him a week later and he accepted my 'apology' for being *rude* to him. Did I mention difficult?"[15]

The public saw yet another episode of Townshend's explosive temperament at the New Year's Eve 'Psychedelicamania' (billed as a 'Giant Freak-Out All Night Rave', and with lighting courtesy of Gustav Metzger) show at the Roundhouse, north London.[16] After three consecutive power outages, he lost it and commenced to destroy his equipment in a rage. "Pop stars are renowned for their moody temperament but Pete Townshend went too far at the excessively violent climax to The Who's act," wrote onlooker Bill Montgomery in a letter to *Melody Maker*. "He went into [an] unparalleled frenzy and using the guitar as a sledge hammer sent amplifiers toppling across the stage amidst clouds of smoke, sending hangers-on scurrying for cover. The whole audience reared back from the

[15] With the benefit of hindsight, Lyons may wish that he'd stayed in the car that night. According to *Anyway Anyhow Anywhere: The Complete Chronicle Of The Who*, Pete and company went on to Blaise's in Queens Gate, Kensington to witness the Jimi Hendrix Experience for the first time.

[16] "I had one of my very few acid trips when I went to the Roundhouse once to watch Pink Floyd," Townshend told the *Radio Times* in late 2006. "I walked all the way from Portobello Road to the Roundhouse [four miles], and by the time I got there the trip had worn off. It was quite strange watching Syd Barrett stone cold sober and realising actually that he wasn't very good. But it would have been brilliant if you were on acid."

stage in absolute terror. Excitement onstage, yes, but violence which threatens to involve fans – no thanks!"

"We've got to the stage when we end the night by destroying everything – which is expensive," Townshend told an interviewer in early 1967. "I think in pop though, it's good because it has big impact and personally, we find it a great laugh. I smash guitars because I like them. I usually smash a guitar when it's at its best. What I do isn't sadistic. It's aggression. I think aggression has a place in society today – whereas sadism and masochism hasn't."

In January, 1967, Pete was once again a featured guest for *Melody Maker*'s 'Pop Think-In' column. On fashion, he declared, "I used to dress soberly but I've found that colour has become more important in my life than it was ever before."

This rediscovered love for colourful clothing could perhaps be attributed to his girlfriend, 20-year-old Karen Astley, formerly a dress design student at Ealing Art School. "The story was that she was the cloakroom attendant at the Railway Hotel in Harrow," says Karen's younger brother, Jon. "She was very much into west London gigs. She probably went to the Oldfield Hotel." Although only an acquaintance of Pete's at the time, Karen had brought home a copy of 'I Can't Explain' in early 1965.

Jon Astley: "I thought, 'Oh, this is great! And I was really quite hooked into The Who quite early on." When his sister became the guitarist's girlfriend, Astley was finally able to see The Who perform live. "Pete, bless him, took me to a gig. I was quite young, but my parents seemed quite happy to let me go. I must have been 14 or 15. I can't remember where it was, somewhere like Luton. I just remember being completely blown away."

"I found some other hobbies outside of tape recording: cooking, kissing Karen, restaurants, making love to Karen," Pete would later write in 1983. "In fact my life with Karen enriched my output as a writer. We made lots of friends and as a couple were more social than I had ever been on my own, my demos had a bigger audience."

One of the stops on the couple's social circuit was the UFO club, an important congregation point for London's burgeoning underground scene in the mid-Sixties. UFO (standing for either 'Unidentified Flying Object,' or 'Underground Freak Out') stayed open all night, hosted psychedelic groups (the early Pink Floyd were regulars) in addition to offering various films. "We showed Marilyn Monroe movies, Kenneth Anger's films, William Burroughs' Cut-Ups – all of which in those days were regarded as very interesting and experimental," Sixties' chronicler Barry Miles told Pink Floyd biographer Nicholas Shaffner in 1981. "You could get fruit juice and sandwiches, but no alcohol – which, looking back, seems extraordinary." The social scene at UFO brought together many like-minded souls and it was here that Townshend met such people as producer Joe Boyd and artist Mike McInnerney for the first time.[17]

Pete had already experimented with acid and he had access to high quality LSD from the Sandoz laboratory. If his lysergically tinged memories of events at UFO are to be relied upon, all was not well at times. "I remember being in the UFO club with my girlfriend, dancing under the effect of acid," Townshend told *Q*'s John Harris in 1996. "My girlfriend used to go out with no knickers and no bra on, in a dress that looked like it had been made out of a cake wrapper, and I remember a bunch of mod boys, still doing leapers, going up to her, and literally touching her up while she was dancing, and she didn't know that they were doing it. I was just totally lost."

The Who's first important show of the year took place in late January at London's Saville Theatre. To coincide with the recent release of *A Quick One*, the group decided to dramatically alter their stage show. "They talked of a completely new act," Barnes wrote in *Maximum R&B*. "The act they had been doing for 18 months would be entirely changed. The Who played better than they had done for months. The group whose trademark was the destruction of their instruments had stopped smashing up their gear. There was no ritualistic guitar and drum obliteration in this show. No smoke bombs. The Who had replaced these ingredients with even better playing and singing. It was the only way to drop part of their act and improve their show." It's possible that another reason for the drastic alteration of the stage show was the presence of the Jimi Hendrix Experience as support act.

"I was completely unaware of what [Jimi] was about," Townshend told *Q*'s David Cavanagh in 2000. "All he had was his guitar and a little road amp, and [Hendrix's manager, ex-Animals bassist] Chas Chandler brought him to talk to me about amplifiers. He looked scruffy and unassuming. I thought, 'I must help this poor' – I'm going to get politically incorrect now – 'badly dressed idiot negro because he's obviously going to die of

---

[17] Featured on the poster for the first December '66 UFO/Nite Tripper club event, designed by Michael English, was the face of Karen Astley.

starvation.' I told him I'd been using Marshalls, but that I felt that a new amp called Sound City was better. He turned to Chas and said, 'We'll have one of each.' Then I went to see him play and I fucking wished I'd kept my mouth shut."

"I had a very reverent attitude toward him," Townshend later confessed, "but I don't think he took us [The Who] very seriously."[18]

On February 12, 'Irish' Jack telephoned Pete and asked for a lift to The Who gig that evening at Greenford's Starlite Ballroom.

"He didn't sound too happy but said 'OK'. He picked me up at the corner of the Lyric cinema in King Street and of course we were back arguing about religion and a strange oddity this: how sometimes a song can be more powerful than the band playing it. Ah! I had got through at last! But it was a short-lived profundity because no sooner was there a gleam of self-realisation in Pete's eyes when the car slowed to a stop and he said, 'I think we've run out of fucking petrol, Jack.' We walked to the nearest service station which was about a mile down the road. Then we walked back to the car with a can of petrol and continued on to the Starlite. That night for some odd reason Pete decided to play in a pullover and dark shades. As I watched him from the wings it occurred to me that Pete [might be] putting my philosophy to the test. It seemed to me that by dumbing down his usual stage clothes Pete had risen above them and if anything now he and 'I Can't Explain' had become bigger in stage presence than usual. It worked!"

One evening after a gig around this time, Jack invited Pete back to his lodgings for supper. "I was sharing a three-roomed flat with my landlady, this woman called Mrs Boyle who let's just say did not take too kindly to coloured people. She was quite racist. When we got back to the flat she was watching the *Eamonn Andrews Show* which was a popular Sunday night talk show. Muhammad Ali was one of the guests and Mrs Boyle let it be known to me and Pete as we sat on the settee that she hated 'niggers'. Pete was appalled. He came out to the kitchen where I was cooking some soup for us and asked me how could I possibly live with this woman. Pete was beside himself with anger. He finished the soup avoiding my attempts to food poison him and stormed out of the flat. I had a big row later with Mrs Boyle."

On March 21, The Who left for their first trip to America, arriving in

---

[18] In 2004, when Pete was asked why *Tommy* featured very little electric guitar, he said, "The reason for that is Jimi Hendrix – he just made me stop playing, really."

New York, according to Andrew Motion, ". . . to be greeted by 1,000 screaming teenagers who had been rounded up by Stamp and grouped under a 10-foot banner saying 'I LOVE THE WHO'." Along with Cream, The Blues Project, Wilson Pickett, Smokey Robinson and the Miracles, and several other performers (with Mitch Ryder and the Detroit Wheels headlining), The Who were scheduled to perform five shows a day for nine consecutive days from March 25 to April 2 on the Murray the K Show at the RKO 58th Street Theater. Pete tried to make a big impression at the press reception, wearing, as he told the NME's Keith Altham the following month, "an electric jacket with flashing light bulbs.[19] We worked hard on propaganda for the first three days and I had two stock quotes everyone wrote down. They were 'we want to leave a wound' and 'we won't let our music stand in the way of our visual act!'"

One of the methods The Who used to ensure that Pete's "stock quotes" held true was to reintroduce their destructive stage habits.

"They were chosen to close the show [sic] and wisely so," Al Kooper, who was a member of The Blues Project, wrote in his book *Backstage Passes*. "The first day everyone in the cast stood in the wings to see what all the talk was about. They launched into 'My Generation' and you could feel it coming. Keith Moon flailed away on those clear plastic drums, and it seemed like he had about 20 of them. It was the first time any of us colonists had seen the typical English drumkit. He had huge double bass drums, one of which said THE, and the other of course, WHO. Moon just beat the shit out of them for 15 minutes non-stop.

"Pete Townshend leaped in the air, spinning his arms wildly and just being the most generally uninhibited guitar player ever seen in these parts. Roger Daltrey broke a total of 18 microphones over the full run of the show. And John Entwistle would just lean up against his amp taking it all in. They reached the modulation part of the instrumental and Townshend spun his guitar in the air, caught it, and smashed it into a placebo amp. No cracks in his Stratocaster so he aimed for the mike stand. Whackkkkk! Crack number one. Then the floor. Whommmmmmmpppp! The guitar is in three or four pieces and he's still got a signal coming out of it. All of a sudden Moon kicks his entire drum kit over and the curtain rings down in

---

[19] The jacket "proved to be something of an anticlimax, because a girl had appeared on TV recently with a dress working on the same principle," Pete told Altham. "Reporters kept asking me where I had got my copy from and I said, 'It's psychedelic and it cost $200 and it's supposed to blow yer mind!'"

a cloud of artificial smoke. I realised my heart was beating three times its normal speed. I figure, as a critic of that show, my electrocardiogram was the best testimonial I could have offered."

"We were smashing our instruments up five times a day," Townshend told *Musician* in 1982. "We got two songs – the act was 12 minutes long – and we used to play 'Substitute' and 'My Generation' with the gear-smashing at the end, and then spend the 20 minutes between shows trying to rebuild everything so we could smash it up again. Or we'd run around pawn shops trying to buy stuff on the cheap."

With perhaps a nod to Hendrix, Townshend developed an affinity for Fender guitars due to their low cost and durability, preferring them to the less sturdy Rickenbackers he had used until now. "I discovered Fender guitars are very strong and cheap out in the US," Pete said a few months later. "Telecasters and Stratocasters are just too tough," he added in 1982, "Once on the Murray the K Show, I chopped a Vox Super Beatle amplifier in two. They're made out of chipboard . . . and I chopped right through the whole thing. It was a 4 × 12 cabinet, and it fell into two bits. I picked up the Stratocaster and carried on playing, *and it was still perfectly in tune!* Now *that's* a guitar for you! I think they're the most beautiful guitars ever designed."

The Who's act cost them a fortune,[20] but this first exposure in America was critical to their future success. The British contingent were also terribly irreverent to the show's other performers, including their host, the popular New York DJ, Murray Kaufman, as Townshend told *Musician* in 1982.

"[Murray] used to complain because he had what he called his personal microphone for doing the introductions with, and we were fairly irreverent towards it . . .[after destroying their own equipment], when we ran out of microphones, his used to come in for a bit of a bashin'. And so we used to actually get daily lectures from him about abusing his personal microphone, which we thought was pretty funny. Then the last thing was when Wilson Pickett called a meeting because we were using smoke bombs as well, and he felt that we were very unprofessional, and that the smoke was affecting everybody else's act. Actually, I think he didn't like following us. But they were all on a different *planet*, basically. We didn't really know

---

[20] The trip's expense was significantly enlarged by Moon and Entwistle's profligate room service bills at the Drake Hotel, which reportedly alone exceeded the payment the band received for their Murray the K Show performances.

what was going on and we didn't take it very seriously. And when it got to the last day we all put funny masks on and went in and sat and listened to [Murray the K] with these masks on. I remember, he asked us to take them off, demanded we remove them." (They didn't.)

The Who returned to London in early April. Pete sensed the dawning of a new phase for The Who. "Every member of the group is beginning to come into his own," he told *Melody Maker's* Nick Jones that month. "We're having no internal setbacks, and we've started to break into the American scene. The American tour was like it was in London when we first started to get really big. It's like starting again all over."

The first business to attend to was recording The Who's next single, 'Pictures Of Lily', a song about a young man admiring naked pictures of a Twenties-era actress ("an old vaudeville star, Lily Bayliss," according to Pete).

"Merely a ditty about masturbation and the importance of it to a young man," Townshend wrote in 1971. "It's all about a boy who can't sleep at night, so his dad gives him some dirty pictures to look at. Then he falls in love with the girl in the pictures which is too bad because she is dead. John and I used to exchange pictures like that when we were at school. We used to go into grubby little shops to buy them . . . looking at dirty pictures is a normal part of adolescence."

"The Who are moving into a class of their own," *Melody Maker's* review announced and this was confirmed by a high chart placing of number four in Britain (but only a disappointing 51 in the States, where it was reportedly banned by many radio stations).

'Pictures Of Lily' was also the first Who record to appear on Track Records, Lambert and Stamp's latest venture,[21] for which they enlisted the band members as talent scouts. With two of the most unpredictable and explosive acts leading the way in The Who and the Jimi Hendrix Experience, and with the similarly quirky Lambert at the helm, Track soon established a reputation for frequently veering off the beaten path but the approach proved fruitful: within the company's first nine months, the label boasted several Top 10 records, and a six per cent share of the total

---

[21] The tactics used to launch Track Records were vintage Lambert and Stamp. They observed "the methods of biscuit and washing powder firms that marketed goods roughly the same size as a box of records," Lambert told John Heilpern in 1969, ". . . and [then] marched into the boardroom at Polydor – one of the biggest companies in the business . . . and offered them a partnership."

British market. After the first year, Lambert's venture showed a £30,000 profit. However, the continuing success of Track meant that Lambert and Stamp's time away from The Who increased.

On April 7, The Who embarked on a two-week tour of Germany, for which Lambert invited Townshend's friends Richard Stanley and Chris Morphet – now both studying at the Royal College of Art – along to shoot a promotional film and photographs.[22] Track labelmates, John's Children, featuring young lyricist/ guitarist Marc Bolan were booked as a support group.

Richard Stanley: "John's Children had a pretty wild act at the time involving slashing up pillows and feathers flying all over the stage, so they were a pretty amazing warm-up act, and when the guys came on, you know, they had quite a lot of wildness to beat, so they were fantastic shows in my opinion."

During the tour, Pete often ate with the two art students; on one occasion at an Indian restaurant. "That was the first time actually I heard about acid," Stanley recalls. "We were in, like, Ludwigshafen or somewhere, and [Pete] was talking about how LSD was just, '*Really, really, really, really, really* fantastic,' and that if we were on acid then the flock wallpaper – you know, the type you find in Indian restaurants – would've been kind of moving and floating around, and so forth. He was describing this incredible experience he'd had and we as two good, middle-class boys, we were quite astounded by it, but not intending to get involved. We were just amazed at these experiences he'd had . . . and was having."

On another occasion, Townshend claimed that Lambert had introduced him to a dentist who practiced hypnosis.

Richard Stanley: "Apparently under the hypnosis, the doctor had said, 'Whenever you get on the stage, you will always give the very best performance that you possibly can,' and Pete sort of swore at that meeting that he was not quite sure whether he was ever de-hypnotised, 'cause he always had this thing with going onstage and something else taking over

---

[22] Lambert reportedly hired the pair, although Morphet doesn't recall ever receiving any money. "I took all of my photos of The Who for love really, you know," he says. "I can't remember whether I ever got paid any money by anybody for taking any. . . . me and Richard Stanley did a little bit of filming in Germany of The Who on tour, and I kind of took stills, but I never remember much of it being sort of like a commercial kind of thing [laughs]. And all the pictures I ever took of The Who really, it's just 'cause I loved the band."

but whether that's true or not or whether he was just enhancing the narrative, I don't know."

While Townshend often preferred the company of Morphet and Stanley during the tour, he still didn't hesitate to defend his bandmates when the need arose.

Richard Stanley: "German authorities, or so-called 'jobsworths' as Keith would call them – anybody in petty authority, and the police and so forth – were really kind of against The Who and I remember in Ludwigshafen, the police were mistreating the boys. We were sitting in the dressing room backstage, and Pete just smashed a beer bottle on the table and went out, eager to defend his mates, he wasn't going to take any shit, you know? Police or security guys."

Morphet recalls Ludwigshafen because Bob Pridden was "beaten up by the German police" when "the fans kind of wrecked the stadium and things."

Some light relief was provided with a break in the Black Forest. Richard Stanley: "We just stopped the cars and the [group] went up into the mountain streams and were splashing around with their guitars, they were absolutely frozen. They were all raving mad, and I had them rolling down mountains of grass and stuff."

Following a week-long Scandinavian tour, The Who slotted in recording sessions for their third album. However, Entwistle broke a finger on his right hand backstage at a gig in Stevenage on May 17, rendering him unable to play properly despite limping through a few shows, while Moon badly strained his stomach muscles at CBS studios two weeks later. Recording was put on hold while both recuperated, although a handful of live gigs went ahead, with guest drummers Julian Covey and Chris Townson (of John's Children) filling in.

In mid-June, The Who flew back to the US, playing two small club dates, one each in Michigan (Ann Arbor's Fifth Dimension club held only 250 people) and Illinois, prior to heading to the West Coast; firstly for two weekend shows at Bill Graham's Fillmore Auditorium. Pete thoroughly enjoyed the Fillmore performances, both of which featured the Carlos Santana Blues Band as support act. "It was a gas," Townshend told *Melody Maker*'s Nick Jones on his return to England. "It was like going back to the Marquee club . . . And the amplification at the Fillmore is too much. It's a great pity that England doesn't take pop as seriously as those American guys do. The bloke who runs the Fillmore really worried about what we thought of his place and whether the amps were OK. They're really conscientious."

Townshend was also impressed with the audiences: "Oh man, they are too much. The vibrations you pick up are incredible. They want to hear what you're playing . . . now I understand why every group comes away from there saying 'That's the best gig we've ever played.' I'd really like to get something going like that in England. The PA system is fantastic. The whole place is very well built for sound and acoustics. It's a rock group's paradise. And the audience! You've just got to play well. You can't help it. They just love music. That's what it's all about. That's why a place like the Fillmore is open seven nights a week with top bands there all the time because the people really understand and dig pop music."

The audiences' demands meant a major change in The Who's live set, since their standard performance currently lasted around 45 minutes. "Playing for the Fillmore, which had the first great sound system, forced us to explore all the old and new repertoire we had," Chris Stamp explained in 1995. "We rehearsed any material we could, including 'A Quick One'. We only had one afternoon to do this but that night was magnificent. The band had found their enthusiasm for playing again with the longer, less structured sets and 'A Quick One' sounded fabulous."

Next on the schedule was the Monterey International Pop Festival, attended by over 200,000 people, which for many was the apex of the Summer of Love. The Who's slot took place on the evening of June 18, the third and final evening of the festival, following an afternoon which featured a performance by Indian sitar player Ravi Shankar. Also on the bill that evening were Jimi Hendrix, The Grateful Dead, Big Brother & the Holding Company, and the Mamas and the Papas.[23]

"This is a group that will destroy you completely in more ways than one," Eric Burdon said by way of introduction.

"The Who were in a dangerous mood from the first chords of 'Substitute'," said journalist Keith Altham, who was there to cover the event for the *New Musical Express*. Apprehension built as the group moved up a gear to tackle Eddie Cochran's 'Summertime Blues'. Suddenly, The Who clicked and found that gestalt quality which made them unique. Against all expectations, the beautiful people began to stir. As the set climaxed with a frantically paced version of 'My Generation', all hell broke loose. Townshend went berserk, smashing his Stratocaster on the

---

[23] Pete reflected on what he considered a lack of "big names" at the Monterey show in a *Melody Maker* article two weeks later. "The Beatles should have been there," he wrote, "the Stones should have been there."

stage before attempting to fell a stack of amps with it. Splinters and sparks flew as the road crew descended, desperate to save the festival's PA system from being destroyed. This well-meaning attempt at a salvage operation was seen by Moon as a personal affront. The drummer booted the best part of his kit across the stage and exited stage left.

There was a momentary stunned silence before the crowd rose in waves to applaud. The Who had experienced their first breakthrough in the New World although they were displeased with their sound, as they hadn't brought their own Marshall equipment over from England, having to settle for inferior hired Vox amplifiers.

Only one act could have followed that. Townshend, concerned about rumours that Hendrix was going to smash his guitar, went to see Jimi Hendrix prior to his set. "I had it out with him," Pete told Barnes in 1982. "I said, 'You're not going to go out there and smash your guitar, are you?' He got very nasty about it . . . He varied between being very nice to me and being a bit arrogant." After The Who's set, Townshend watched the Jimi Hendrix Experience's performance and Jimi's subsequent guitar pyrotechnics. "I was sitting next to Mama Cass and she turned to me and said, 'Isn't this guy stealing your act?' and I said, 'Yeah, but, you see, he's so fucking great, who cares?' "[24]

Backstage at Monterey, Pete and Karen met Owsley Stanley, who had recently synthesised a powerful hallucinogen named STP. "We took some on the plane coming home, thinking it was acid," Townshend said later. "It turned out to be STP, something that I would never ever take. It was bloody terrible. I mean, you wouldn't believe it. You know when they say under Japanese torture, sometimes, if it's horrible enough the person actually gets the feeling that they're leaving their body? In this case, I had to do just that, abandon my body.

"It was actually about a four-hour hump, whereas a normal acid hump is about 25 or 30 minutes . . . you have a hump and then plane off into a nice trip. Well, on this STP trip, the hump was about four to five hours, and it was on an aeroplane over the Atlantic. I said, 'Fuck this, I can't stand it any more.' And I was free of the trip. And I was just like floating in mid-air looking at myself in a chair, for about an hour and a half. And then

---

[24] Townshend was apparently jealous of the press attention Hendrix was drawing. "Why are you spending so much time with Hendrix," he snarled at Altham at the airport after Monterey, according to Altham's 2004 *Mojo* article. "We're paying your fucking fare home. I hope we're going to get something out of this in *NME*."

I would go back in again and it would be the same. And I was just like, zap, completely unconscious as far as the outside world was concerned. But I was very much alive, crawling alive . . . It was like a hundred years on the aeroplane across the Atlantic. I never realised what a fragile mind I had. Eventually it tailed off and . . . then you need a week to repiece your ego, remember who you are and what you are."

Such a "terrifying trip", as he described it, led Townshend to abandon psychedelic drugs immediately.[25] "It really did make me push the whole thing away," Pete said in 1977. "If I hadn't had that really awful trip on that plane back from Monterey, I probably would still be into drugs . . . I actually felt physically damaged by it. That's why I never really feel I'm doing anything courageous or selfless by not involving myself in [the drug scene]. It was very easy to do."

[25] "I didn't even smoke a cigarette again for four years," Pete claimed to Andy Neill and Matt Kent.

CHAPTER FOUR

1967–1968

"Baba washed the religious preconceptions from my heart with my own tears. I love Jesus far more now than I ever did at infant school as I sang, 'Yes, Jesus loves me.' Now I know he really was the Christ. . . . Only one person on this earth is capable of an absolutely perfect love for all and everything, and that is, when earth is fortunate enough to be his illusory host, the Messiah. The Avatar. He just came and went. Meher Baba."

– Pete Townshend, 1970

"I was 22 years old, The Who had begun to fail, we hadn't made it in America, we hadn't had a big hit in the UK with 'I Can See For Miles', which was unquestionably the best thing I was ever gonna write in my life. And I thought: 'It's over. I started when I was 18, and four years later, it's finished. And as a last gasp, I sat down and started to write something wild and pretentious and mad and dangerous."

– Pete Townshend, 1977

BY mid-1967, Pete had moved out of his Wardour Street digs into Karen Astley's flat in Eccleston Square, Pimlico. Shortly thereafter the couple moved to a top floor apartment on nearby Ebury Street in lower Belgravia, where Pete installed a home studio. "The most fascinating thing about this recording studio in particular, was that it was the room in which . . . the first few songs from *Tommy* were born," Townshend wrote in 1977's *The Story Of Tommy*. "I worked pretty much when I liked and the sound didn't seem to disturb any neighbours. In the same house, down in the basement, lived an elderly but quiet couple who didn't ever complain. In my studio I had a drum kit, an organ, an electric piano, two old Revox stereo tape recorders, a rather ancient but well made microphone mixer, and some odd effects that I used to use to enhance my recordings."

The fact that the "elderly couple" didn't complain is quite remarkable considering that, "[Pete] had two four-by-twelve [speakers] up against each wall and a club amp driving it," as 'Speedy' Keen described, "and to sit and listen to music that loud and powerful, it was a bit too instant. That was the trouble."

Pete brought his brothers Paul and Simon, both budding guitarists, to the studio to mess about in. With The Who frequently on tour, the Townshend family saw less and less of Pete, which made the occasions that he did visit Woodgrange Avenue all the more special. During this period, Simon recalls he and Paul were playing in the street with friends, when their elder brother triumphantly cruised by in a massive black Lincoln Continental convertible, with the electric top retracting.

Simon Townshend: "It was the height of summer, with people hanging out of their windows . . . when Pete drove down the road. For Paul and I, it was a big moment, because we were so proud of him. But we didn't see a great deal of Pete . . . From year to year, we'd see him at Christmas, we'd see him between tours if he was touring."

On June 28, The Who hastily recorded and released as a single cover versions of two Rolling Stones' songs, 'The Last Time' and 'Under My Thumb' to protest against the savage prison sentences imposed that week on Mick Jagger and Keith Richards for drug charges. With Entwistle away on his honeymoon, Townshend played bass (along with keyboards and backing vocals) on both songs.[1]

In early July, The Who (along with Al Kooper, who was enlisted to play organ) were at New York's Talentmasters Studio on 42nd Street, recording tracks for their next album prior to embarking on a full-scale American tour. The group returned to Talentmasters during a break in the tour in early August for further recording work, including completing a track they had started in London, 'I Can See For Miles'.

"I always feel that the best constructed early song that I ever wrote was 'I Can See For Miles'," Pete said in a 1978 radio interview. "I put about two solid days into that and when it actually worked . . . I think the lyrics are great, they create a great sort of impression of images and the music is harmonically exciting."

Released in September (a month later in the UK), the single reached number nine in America (The Who's highest single chart placing in the

---

[1] It was reported The Who intended to record more Stones songs to keep the group in the public eye but Jagger and Richards were soon released on bail and freed on appeal.

US) and a respectable tenth place in the British charts. However, Pete was thoroughly disappointed at the song's failure to climb any higher. "That was a real heartbreaker for me," he said. "It was a number we'd been saving, thinking that if The Who ever got into trouble this one would pull us out. On the day I saw it go down [the charts] I spat on the British record buyer. To me this was the ultimate Who record and yet it didn't sell."[2]

"The real production masterpiece in The Who/Lambert coalition was, of course, 'I Can See For Miles'," Townshend wrote in his 1971 *Rolling Stone* article. "We cut the track in London at CBS studios and brought the tapes to Gold Star studios in Hollywood to mix and master them. Gold Star owns the nicest sounding echo chamber in the world . . . I swoon when I hear the sound. The words, which ageing senators have called 'Drug Oriented', are about a jealous man with exceptionally good eyesight. Honest."

On July 13, The Who kicked off their first full-scale North American tour – an eight-week package affair involving 40-plus shows in 28 states. In an unlikely pairing, The Who supported Herman's Hermits,[3] a harmless yet tremendously successful British pop outfit, thanks to the two groups being signed to the same entertainment agency, Premier Talent.

"We have just left New York and are flying to our first concert with Herman,"[4] Pete wrote in a letter to *Melody Maker*, published the following month. "I haven't seen Herman's own plane yet but have heard it's amazing – with 'Herman's Hermits' and 'The Who' painted in dayglo paint along the sides. We're all looking forward to the tour in general excepting a few crisis points we would rather avoid, like Dallas and Houston, etc. The New York groups have told us such amazing tales of the effect long hair has on shotgun carrying farmers there!"

According to *The Who Concert File*, The Who played around 40 minutes most nights, listing the group's basic set, which they raced through with little or no delay between songs, as 'Substitute', 'Pictures Of Lily',

---

[2] Kit Lambert's godfather, composer William Walton, heard 'I Can See For Miles' and passed word through Kit that the song "indicated real greatness", Townshend told the *Washington Times* in 1992. Pete said that Walton's words encouraged him to begin work in earnest on his rock opera *Tommy*.

[3] ". . . I said [to *16* magazine in a 1966 interview], 'Listen, you know these Herman's Hermits guys are the biggest band in America . . . you know, I have a mission, it is to rid the world of this shit!' Pete said in a 1989 radio interview ". . . And we did it, right out from under Herman's Hermits' noses. We went out with them and undermined them and just made sure they never, ever came back."

[4] The first shows on the tour were actually in Calgary, Canada, on July 13.

'Summertime Blues', 'Barbara Ann', 'Boris The Spider', 'A Quick One', 'Happy Jack', 'I'm A Boy', and, with its customary auto-destructive finale, 'My Generation'. "It was spellbinding," Tom Wright (Pete's former art school crony, who was recruited mid-tour as The Who's photographer before being appointed tour manager) told Richard Barnes in 1982. "A lot of times there was no clapping whatsoever, just dead silence. People in the front rows were just sitting there with their mouths opened – stunned."

"America was very good for us," Pete informed *Melody Maker* following the tour, "because we had to re-think and start again. They were fresh audiences who hadn't heard us live." The American audiences' reactions to his guitar smashing were different, too. "In England I used to get people asking me for my guitars and calling me terrible names because I smashed equipment up. They said I wasn't worthy of having such expensive guitars just to wreck them, so why didn't I give them away. But in the States it was the other way round. They thought it was a gas. They loved it. I became a kind of hero. I was presented with beautiful guitars – just to smash them up. It became ludicrous."

The Who also sounded much better on this tour than on previous visits since they finally brought their own Marshall amplification over, along with Keith Moon's new custom made Premier 'Pictures Of Lily' drum kit. It was during this tour that Moon's destructive habits first took hold.

"Keith feels he has to be involved in some sort of entertainment," Townshend told John Swenson. "And the first really big thing ever was on the Herman's Hermits tour. We went to Georgia, where they sell fireworks, and they sell these things called cherry bombs, and one day I was in his room and his door knocker was all black like he'd been putting these things in and I said, 'Could I use your bog?' and he smiled and said, 'Sure.' I went in there and there was no toilet, just sort of an S bend, and I thought 'Christ, what happened?' He said, 'Well this cherry bomb was about to go off in me hand and I threw it down the toilet to stop it going off.' So I said, 'Are they that powerful?' and he said, 'Yeah, it's incredible.' So I said, 'How many of 'em have you got?' with fear in me eyes. He said 'Five hundred,' and opened up a case full to the top with cherry bombs. And of course from that moment on we got thrown out of every hotel we ever stayed in. The Holiday Inns were phoning round saying, 'Don't let this group in – they blow up the hotels.'"

A more public demonstration of Moon's love for explosives occurred on September 15, when The Who appeared on the *Smothers Brothers Comedy Hour* to plug 'I Can See For Miles'. Each member was on top form during the introductions, with all involved making co-host Tommy Smothers feel as uncomfortable as possible. Following a mimed run through 'My Generation', complete with smoke bombs, Townshend proceeded to smash his guitar in front of Moon's drum riser, unaware that one of the bass drums contained a mammoth dose of explosive powder – an estimated three times the accepted load for such a stunt – that Moon was about to detonate. The ensuing explosion, which, so legend has it, caused fellow guest Bette Davis to pass out as she watched from the wings, knocked Townshend down, singeing his hair and badly damaging his eardrums. Smothers told *Mojo* in 2004: "I was looking around and Townshend comes staggering over, as was scripted, but I'm looking at him for injuries. He wandered over and grabbed my guitar and smashed it, too. But I'll bet you his head was ringing. It must have sounded like a siren inside his skull."

On their return to England, The Who continued recording their next album. "I write a lot of songs on aeroplanes," Pete said in 1968, "but they sound just like songs written in aeroplanes. Let me see: 'I Can't Reach You' – 'our love was flowing, our life was soaring' and 'I can't reach you; I'm a billion ages past you and a billion years behind you.' It's all spacy, cloudy, you know; sun glinting on the wings, big massive jet engines silently soaring through the quiet skies, you know all this stuff is great for lyrics."

Six months later, The Who recorded 'Glow Girl', a song with an aeroplane crash theme. "I never regarded myself as a person afraid of travelling by air," Pete told *Rolling Stone* in 1968. "When we did the Herman's Hermit tour in an old charter plane, I wrote so many songs about plane crashes, it was incredible.[5] I did a song called 'Glow Girl'. I wrote it because we were taking off in a plane which I seriously thought was going to crash . . . and as I was going up I was writing a list, I thought, that if I was a chick and I was in a plane that was diving for the ground and I had my boyfriend next to me and we were on our honeymoon or we were about to get married, I know what I'd think of. I'd think about him and I'd think about what I am going to be missing.

"I just went through a big list of what was in this chick's purse – cigarettes, Tampax, a whole lyrical list and then holding his hand and what he felt and what he was gonna say to her . . . The man, he's trying to have

---

[5] The band's mid-August flight to Tennessee ended with an emergency landing onto a foam-covered runway.

some romantic and soaring last thoughts. Eventually what happens is that they crash and they are reincarnated at a very instant musically. What I wanted was the list getting [more and more frantic], she's going through her handbag, ballpoint pen, cigarettes, book matches, lipstick and Excedrin and he's going, 'We will be this and we will do this and we will be together in heaven and don't worry little one, you're safe with me,' and all this kind of bullshit.

"What happens is The Who do an incredible destruction as the plane hits the ground, explosions . . . then 'It's a girl, Mrs Walker, it's a girl . . .' That was supposed to be the end of the thing and you suss out that they've been reincarnated as this girl."

While The Who had spent a great deal of time in the studio, plans for how their third album should be presented (especially in the wake of *Sgt Pepper's Lonely Hearts Club Band*) had not been forthcoming. During a visit to Track Records' offices in Old Compton Street, Pete found Chris Stamp poring over a list. "I said to him, 'What's that?'" Townshend told Chris Charlesworth. "'Oh, just a list of songs that I thought might make up the next album.' 'Album? What album?' 'Well, you've got to have an album out.' 'But *that* and *that* and *that*.' 'You're joking. What a boring old album.'"

Faced with the prospect of issuing an album of songs, most of which, with the exception of 'I Can See For Miles', Townshend considered weak, he pleaded with Stamp to consider delaying the album's release. "Chris was insistent on its release," Townshend wrote in a 2001 *Q* magazine article, feeling Stamp's desire for a quality album was secondary to his goal of getting more Track product on the market.

"I panicked. I can remember pacing around [Stamp's] office, wildly brainstorming, Chris, with a bemused expression on his face, waiting for me to come up with something. I needed an idea that would transform what I regarded as a weak collection of occasionally 'cheesy' songs into something with teeth. Suddenly I hit on it: we would turn the entire album into a pirate radio segment and actually sell advertising space to manufacturers and fashion houses. My intention was not only to lampoon corporate advertising, but also to get our share of the revenue. Chris immediately got to work and fixed up two art directors for the sleeve and attempted to sell the space between songs on the album to advertisers. With an anticipated sale of less than 50,000 copies companies like Coca-Cola were unwilling to take space and pay for it. They sent a case of 20 cans of their beverage instead.

No matter, by now I was away. . . .

"I came up with 'Odorono', which turned out to be a fully rounded and rather plaintive song about a singer who, because she has B.O., fails an audition with the impresario Harold Davison . . . We spent an additional two weeks on this effort and wrote and recorded a dozen or so jingles. When the brilliant Kit Lambert finally played me the album cut together I was very happy with the result. What made it fly was, of course, the proper radio jingles he had managed to get hold of. A dedicated American jingles company made these, but they were not properly licensed and Track released the album under the threat of a lawsuit."

Among The Who's own jingles were 'Heinz Baked Beans', 'Rotosound Strings', 'Charles Atlas' and 'Track Records' – the majority of which were thought up by Entwistle and Moon in a pub near to where the group were recording at De Lane Lea studios, in Kingsway, London. Townshend's idea to use commercials between songs on *The Who Sell Out* was both a satire of and a tip of the hat to the pirate radio stations to whom he credited much of The Who's initial success,[6] and which had been rendered illegal as a result of the Marine Broadcasting Act enacted in August, 1967. "You don't realise how good something like the pirates are until they've gone," Pete said at the time.

Among the Townshend material gathered on *The Who Sell Out* were tongue-in-cheek character ditties ('Mary Anne With The Shaky Hands') yearning love songs ('Our Love Was', 'I Can't Reach You'), psychedelia ('Relax') and a memorable first person account of an adolescent rite of passage ('Tattoo'). Also included was 'Armenia City In The Sky', written by Speedy Keen in a boost to his burgeoning songwriting ability, which featured various studio effects and backwards guitar.

Also recorded during the sessions was a powerful, mainly instrumental jingle extolling the "grace, space and pace" of Jaguar cars. "I wrote a long-winded instrumental called 'Jaguar' which was not included on the finished record though The Who made a good job of it," Pete wrote in *Q*. A last-minute inclusion, 'Sunrise', recorded at IBC studios in early November, featured only Pete singing and playing acoustic guitar. This jazzy, romantically oriented song provided a glimpse of his future inclinations in his solo career.

---

[6] Ronan O'Rahilly, who owned the Scene club in Soho, was also the owner of the first pirate radio station, Radio Caroline.

"Keith didn't want ['Sunrise'] on the record,"[7] Townshend revealed to *Sounds* in 1980. "See in a way that's a bit of a giveaway to the fact that at the time I was studying a bit of this jazz thing . . . I was studying Mickey Baker methods and I had two of his tutors, both of which were magnificent. And it's all that I've ever needed to get into slightly more complex chord work. And that song I wrote for my mother to show her that I could write real music."

In defining his lifelong passion for jazz, Townshend told the author, "I didn't take things much further than the Mickey Baker books, but I copied a lot of Kenny Burrell solos note for note. Wes Montgomery was a favourite too, and someone I could copy. But my great jazz idols were Miles [Davis], John Coltrane, [Charles] Mingus, [Thelonius] Monk, [Charlie] Bird [Parker], etc. I could never be anything but inspired by them. I could never play what they play. I discovered Keith Jarrett before the masses too [when he was working with Charles Lloyd] and he still raises my heart. Music like this is as powerful as Bach to me. It's rare a rock tune has the same potential for uplift and transport. It happens, but not often."

The *Sell Out* album's final piece, 'Rael 1 & 2', demonstrated a distinct step forward from 'A Quick One' in two key areas: firstly, unlike the mini-opera, 'Rael' was not at all meant to be humorous – the overall feeling was far 'heavier' and, secondly, the quality of the writing (and consequently, the performance) was far superior. The tangible step forward which took place between these two works can be traced to several factors. Since Kit Lambert had introduced him to classical music back in 1965, Pete had developed an appreciation for the genre and his girlfriend's father was composer Edwin 'Ted' Astley – best known for scoring film and television themes, including the Sixties television series *The Saint* and who, like his future son-in-law, multi-tracked demos in his home studio. "I was studying orchestrations and stuff like that, and I'd bought a piano," Townshend said in 1975, "and then I did a lot of orchestrations and I bought lots of books about it and I used to speak a lot to Karen's dad about orchestrations and stuff like that." Like Lambert, Ted had no time for musical snobbery. "Musically, anything went as far as he was concerned," says Jon Astley.

Pete had "dithered tremendously" with 'Rael', which he "intended . . .

---

[7] This was probably because both of his vocal contributions to the album, 'Girl's Eyes' and 'Jaguar', were left on the studio floor.

to be written for full orchestra and to be a genuine opera. Looking back, I can't quite remember where The Who fitted in, because I had Arthur Brown lined up as the hero." Townshend entertained further thoughts of using the eccentric singer while he was writing *Tommy* the following year.

From a 10-year perspective, Townshend described the plot of 'Rael' in *The Story Of Tommy*:[8] "The story was about 1999 [not as cliched as 2000 you see] and the emergence of the Red Chinese [the Redchins] as world leaders. The only spiritual note was that the Redchins were regarded as being fairly evil because they were crushing the old established religions as they conquered . . . In 1966, at my studio in Wardour Street I wrote this [one of the first idea sheets for *Rael*]:

> "*Opening is set at sea. In order to create a wide linear feeling in the opening of the opera. The sound of the sea in deep echo is heard. It must be fairly artificial so as not to start too heavily.*
>
> "*NARRATOR SINGING. Someone, a man, is leaving home (thoughts of home). He is wealthy. He has broken many ties. It is a time of indecision. He is on a boat that recently left harbour and is heading out to sea. He wonders if he is doing right.*

"Basically the story was running into about 20 scenes when Kit Lambert reminded me that while I was pretending to be Wagner, The Who needed a new single. What did I have? I had 'Rael'. Thus 'Rael' was edited to four minutes [too long for a single in those days ironically] and recorded in New York for that purpose . . . No one will ever know what it means, it has been squeezed up too tightly to make sense. Musically it is interesting because it contains a theme which I later used in *Tommy* for 'Sparks' and the 'Underture'."

When released in December, 1967, *The Who Sell Out* was well received by critics, but didn't fare any better than The Who's previous two albums, reaching number 13 in the British charts (48 in America, where it was released in January).

"*The Who Sell Out* has become a truer account of the Sixties than any other document," Dave Marsh overstated in his essay accompanying the album's reissue in 1995, "not only because it captures the form in which

---

[8] Rael was ". . . all about 'overspill' when the world population becomes so great in years ahead that everyone is assigned to their one square foot of earth," Pete told the *NME*'s Keith Altham. "We played it onstage in Manchester and Scotland and everyone just looked at us with their mouths open – the complication was just too much."

our passions played out, but because in the very triviality of lyrics like 'Tattoo', 'Mary Anne With The Shaky Hand' and 'Odorono' it captures the sad state of our generation's internal affairs that leads inexorably to the smashing revelation of the album's masterpiece, 'I Can See For Miles'. *The Who Sell Out* holds a mirror up to reality, and the great part is, it turns out to be a rock'n'roll mirror, something that gives you a totally distorted picture while revealing the truth. If you can't get your mind around that paradox, two things are true: you aren't gonna have nearly as much fun with this album as it has to offer, and you must have missed the Sixties."

"As Dave Marsh wrote, what the entire album seemed to be about was setting up 'I Can See For Miles', one of the best songs I had written by that time," Townshend wrote in his 2001 *Q* essay. "But there are some really good songs on the album, and they are a bit cheesy. The format delivers them in a way that allows the 'weaker' songs to work."

Nik Cohn, who reviewed the album for *Queen*, wasn't happy that the advertising concept was only applied to one side of the album. "The trouble is that the idea hasn't been carried right the way through; it has only been half-heartedly sketched in," Cohn wrote. "This, of course, is a traditional Who fault – Pete Townshend works something out, the group half completes it and then everyone sits back until another group walks in and steals the whole thing. In a way, it's an attractive fault, it shows a nice lack of intensity towards success. In this case, however, it's a disaster.

"What this album should really have been is a total ad explosion, incredibly fast, loud, brash and vulgar, stuffed full of the wildest jingles, insane commercials, snippets from your man [DJ Emperor] Rosko, plus anything else that came to hand – a holocaust, and utter wipe-out, a monster rotor whirl of everything that pop and advertising really are."

"*Sell Out* sounded radically different from the [Who's] stage sound at the time," John Swenson wrote in his 1979 Who biography, "a fact that may have had something to do with the record's poor commercial showing. While *Sell Out* was a clever statement about the basic pop medium, radio, The Who's stage show continued to be all guts and glory, rock on the cutting edge . . . onstage 'Relax' became a fiery hard-rock extravaganza with an extended solo spot for Townshend. During the solo he would experiment with feedback, playing Hendrix-style licks on occasion, and build long, hypnotic statements out of a simple melodic idea, often working out patterns which would eventually emerge as part of the overall structure of *Tommy*."

★   ★   ★

Following Pete's abandonment of mind expanding drugs, his spiritual investigations had led him to believe in the existence of extraterrestrial beings and UFOs.

"I was heavily into flying saucers," Townshend wrote in *Rolling Stone* in 1970, "believing them to hold a key somehow to the future of humanity. At the time I sincerely believed I had seen several in the Florida area, today I don't really care." He had read the Spaceship sagas of author George Adamski, who wrote, "that on another planet in our system existed a race of people who were spiritually perfect," Townshend recalled in 1977. "He claimed that he was in contact with them. While reading the books I believed this, somehow this man taught me to open my mind. In other words he taught me faith."

A visit to his friend Mike McInnerney's house helped realign Townshend's spiritual inclinations, as the pair sat down for a philosophical conversation. McInnerney, art director for the underground paper *International Times*, was one of the UFO club crowd and Karen Astley had designed the clothes for his wedding to girlfriend Katie. "I had an immediate strong feeling for Pete," McInnerney told Dave Marsh in 1983, "and felt that I would like to give him some books on Meher Baba. Baba has a way of grabbing you fundamentally and then hanging on. There was a lot of Baba activity in London at the time, and Pete just picked up on it."

"I was ranting and raving about," Townshend wrote in his 1970 *Rolling Stone* essay entitled *In Love With Meher Baba*, "talking too much and finding in Mike someone who talked just as much as I did. Every time I came up with a world-wise theory that had taken me years of thought to get clear he would say, 'That's such a coincidence man, this guy Meher Baba said something similar to that in this book, *The God Man*.' After I had heard my very last precious revelation hit the dust at the sound of Mike's voice declaring that Baba had already said it I just had to look at the book. What I saw, apart from a photo in the front cover of a strange and elderly man, was shattering."[9]

Townshend's discovery of Meher Baba (Persian for 'compassionate father'), a spiritual master born in Poona, India, in 1894, came at a time when it was fashionable to look to the East for divine inspiration, most notably The Beatles' dalliance with the Maharishi Mahesh Yogi. However, unlike their gradual disillusionment with the Indian guru, Pete had discovered a spiritual entity whose teachings grasped his imagination and

---

[9] *The God Man* by C.B. Purdom is currently available through Sheriar Press.

would affect him and his work profoundly from this point forward.

"What was so sneaky about the whole affair was the way Baba crept into my life," Townshend wrote in 1970. "At first his words were encouraging, his state of consciousness and his claims to be the Christ exciting and daring, later they became scary. I began to read his words, read of his astoundingly simple relationship with his disciples . . . and of his silence for 40 years [Baba took a vow of silence in 1925, which lasted until his death in early 1969. He communicated by pointing to letters on an alphabet board]. It became clear that the party was over. If I read any more lines like 'What I want from my lovers is real unadulterated love, and from my genuine workers I expect real work done,' I would have to decide once and for all whether the whole thing was really for me or not."

An outline of Baba's life and message was provided inside the original pressing of Townshend's 1972 solo album, *Who Came First*, from which the following is extracted:

> *"Baba's appeal extends to people of every background. His followers include Protestants, Catholics and Jews in the West, Hindus, Muslims, Zoroastrians and Buddhists in the East, and even many who have considered themselves agnostics or atheists. In a word, Baba and what he teaches are universal. He can be understood in terms of the context of every broad religious tradition, yet he is clear in pointing out that he belongs exclusively to none of them . . . Baba gives no rituals or ceremonies, no particular diets or exercises, no specific form of meditation to his followers. There are no 'churches', no designated teachers. There is no fee. True religion, in Baba's eyes, is not a card-carrying affair but rather a matter of 'the heart', the degree to which one lives an honest and loving life. Baba regards the avowed atheist who faithfully carries out his work in the world as far more blest than the man who, claiming to be devoutly religious, shirks his practical, everyday responsibilities. 'The greatest sin,' he said, 'is hypocrisy.'*
>
> *"Baba said he was God Almighty on earth or the God Man. He claimed, 'In the world, there are countless Sadhus, Mahatmas, Mahapurushas, Saints, Yogis, and Walis, though the number of genuine ones is very, very limited. I am neither a Mahatma nor a Mahapurush, neither a Sadhu nor a Saint, neither a Yogi nor a Wali. I am the Ancient One. The Highest of the High!' "*

Townshend further explained his relationship with the Avatar in a 1980 *Trouser Press* interview. "It's a hard thing to explain, but if you live your life according to the guidelines set down by Meher Baba, you don't need anyone else to tell you how to do things. It's about living a better life and a more loving life in a traditional humanitarian [way], which we are all born with the potential to achieve anyway. But having a focus, someone you really respect but don't necessarily think is a super-being, someone you respect above anyone else demonstrating a real love for you when you think that you're a lump of shit – that's all it needs. It just needs someone to give you back your self-respect, and then it's *your* job from there."

"I never met Baba," Pete admitted in the 1970 *Rolling Stone* article. "Never wrote him a letter or received one. How am I hanging on? I'm not hanging on, I'm *stuck* on. People could easily get the idea that I'm an unwilling Baba lover, or 'Baba Tryer' as I prefer to call myself. No, it's just that I was unwilling to let go of that incredible piece of happiness, that unqualified stab of love that I didn't even ask for, didn't expect, and it's made my life, which I know to be as colourful as any, grey in comparison. The key is that knowledge of his awesome power, awesome knowledge and bliss he enjoys; that flash, is the basis for the search for my true self.

"Baba did not come to teach. He came to awaken. He did not come to form a religion, nor organise any cult, creed, sect or movement in his name. He did not take steps to do so . . . I feel that never will I be able to stand back from myself and pretend anymore that God is a myth. That Christ was just another man. That Baba was simply a hypnotic personality. The facts are coming home to me like sledgehammers, not through the words I read in books about Baba, not through even his own words. But through my ordinary daily existence. Meher Baba is the Avatar, God Incarnate on our planet. The Awakener."

On October 22, The Who played two shows at the Saville Theatre, supported by Vanilla Fudge – one of the new wave of American underground groups. By now The Who's stature in their homeland was dangerously slipping thanks to their absence in America and the British habit of thirsting for the next musical trend, which left all but a hardcore tending to view them as yesterday's men, remnants from the mod era that was now almost a memory. With this in mind, for the Saville shows, The Who displayed appropriate over-the-top showmanship with Pete playing a double-necked Gibson guitar bought in America while sporting a sparkling 'Pearly King' suit (made by Karen), covered with hundreds of buttons. Significantly, the group didn't destroy their equipment even though the shows were pre-billed as presenting the same show that American audiences had witnessed on the Herman's Hermits tour.

An ensuing 18-date British theatre tour – billed with Traffic, The Herd, The Marmalade, and The Tremeloes – began with a disastrous show in Sheffield on October 28. Because the show overran, The Who were left with only enough time to perform three songs. "The band's tempers were pushed to the limit," reported 'Irish' Jack Lyons and Joe McMichael in *The Who Concert File*, "and Roger Daltrey and Pete Townshend had a disagreement onstage that ended in a scuffle. The concert finished with Pete kicking his speaker cabinets over onto the theatre manager who had ordered the act to be curtailed. Pete then grabbed the manager by the throat and dragged him across the stage."

The following night in Coventry was no better: "The first performance ended in the destruction of the theatre's footlights as well as Pete's guitar when the curtain was lowered during The Who's set. Amplification problems had delayed the show by about 20 minutes with only 10 minutes before the second show was due to start. As a result, the tour manager ordered the curtain be brought down. Pete and Roger were left in front of the curtain and 'God Save The Queen' was played over the house PA system. Pete shouted for the curtain to be raised, threw his guitar on the stage and began his assault on the footlights."

A brief, 11-show American visit followed in November, contrasted by gigs at a school gymnasium in Southfield, Michigan[10] to larger shows at the Cow Palace, San Francisco, and the Hollywood Bowl, Los Angeles where The Who appeared on a bill with the Animals, the Association and the Everly Brothers. The tour also included two shows at New York's Village Theater, which would later reopen as the Fillmore East. The Vagrants, featuring guitarist Leslie West, opened these concerts, showcasing their own auto-destruction routine at the end of their version of Tim Hardin's 'If I Were A Carpenter'.

"In New York each successive appearance grew wilder and more apocalyptic," John Swenson wrote. "At the Village Theater . . . the hostile audience threw shoes and other objects at a hapless Tiny Tim as he bravely tried to entertain the bloodthirsty throng of Who fans with 'Tiptoe Through The Tulips', while the sounds of The Who's road crew nailing

---

[10] The Who used the PA of opening act, the Amboy Dukes. "I really wasn't that worried that they'd trash the speakers," Ted Nugent told *Mojo* in 2004, "but I did have a moment when I saw Townshend kick one of my stacks."

Keith Moon's drum kit to the stage came hammering out from behind the curtains. When the band finally played, a near riot broke out in front of the stage."

These shows helped to consolidate The Who's burgeoning reputation in America as a spectacular live act. It was a different story in Australasia where the group ventured in January 1968 on a problematic, eight-date package tour with The Small Faces and ex-Manfred Mann singer, Paul Jones. The local PA systems were not of the calibre The Who were used to using overseas. In *A Fortnight Of Furore*, a publication chronicling the visit, Andy Neill wrote that "the [Who] had already started to drop the equipment smashing antics in Britain, but felt obliged to resurrect them, to win over new audiences, particularly here in Australia where their reputation for this preceded them. Besides this, there was good reason for the band smashing their equipment on this tour as it was, quite simply, piss poor."

As the tour wore on, Pete's impression of Australia worsened, as Neill recounted: "Townshend found how backward Australian hotel room service was when, phoning down for breakfast one morning, at what he considered a reasonable hour, he was laughed at by the desk: 'This is Orstraylia mate, we get out of bed in the morning here.' Pissed off, he decided to take matters into his own hands. Visiting a local supermarket he purchased a large box of cornflakes and a gallon of milk. Returning to his room he poured the contents into the sink and after sampling a few mouthfuls of his breakfast delicacy, he left the rest to solidify into the sink like concrete before checking out of the hotel."

It wasn't all bad vibes. In Melbourne, a girl who had been hanging around The Small Faces created enough of an impression on Pete for him to compose a jubilant song entitled 'She's A Sensation' (later amended to 'Sensation', for *Tommy*), while his friendship with Small Faces' bassist/songwriter Ronnie Lane intensified after they discovered a mutual interest in Baba's teachings and Sufi mysticism.

The incident that proved the last straw between The Who and Australia occurred on an internal flight from Adelaide to Sydney on January 28, when an exchange of views with an air hostess over refreshments resulted in the entire entourage being herded off into a holding room at Melbourne airport by Commonwealth police. The Australian papers, who had already filled columns with negative press towards both groups, had a field day and the story was picked up back home in Britain.

"Australia, the nation, was up in arms at what these long-haired monsters were supposedly up to," Neill wrote, "so much so, that the then Prime Minister, Senator John Gorton [apparently] sent a telegram requesting they never set foot in Australia again."

In 2000, *Q*'s David Cavanaugh asked Townshend what response he gave to Gorton's telegram. "I suppose my reply was to never go back to Australia again. What was actually more insulting was that the telegram said we couldn't go back. We've never seen a copy of it, but I know someone who says he's got it. They also created an extraordinary taxation event for us as well, which meant that they took all our money. It was terribly humiliating and I've never really quite recovered from it, I must say."

Over three decades on from the tour, Townshend still hadn't returned. "The Who won't come here, I'm afraid," Daltrey told Australia's *Undercover News* during a February 2000 visit. "You Aussies upset Townshend. He's got a very long memory . . . your bloody Prime Minister said, 'Get out you Pommy bastards and don't come back' . . . We've had heaps of offers but Pete just will not come." It wasn't until 2004 that he finally changed his mind.

Safely back in London, in mid-February, Pete was filmed by his friend Richard Stanley for *Lone Ranger*, a film which served as Stanley's Royal College of Art diploma work.

Richard Stanley: "I'd been working on a movie called *Burd* which was kind of modelled after Pete himself, and that eventually kind of subsumed into *Lone Ranger*, and some fellow students came on board."

One of these was graphic designer Storm Thorgerson, who as co-founder of the design group Hipgnosis went on to design dozens of famous album covers, notably those for Pink Floyd.

Richard Stanley: "Actually there was a very funny connection between Pink Floyd and The Who because Storm and [fellow designer] Dave Gale and these other people were kind of in the Floyd camp, and I was in The Who camp, and they were often sort of negotiating to try and get them to play together. In fact at one other dance – at the Royal College of Art – Pete was there as my guest, not playing, just as a friend and they were trying to get him to play, to jam with the Floyd. It didn't happen, but there was always these things going on."

Lone Ranger told the story of two brothers, "one of whom", as Stanley explains, "is this rock star and the other is totally mad. [The film] actually focuses on the guy who's totally mad and wild and kind of dances and waltzes and dreams through reality, and there's a scene at breakfast where they talk about the day ahead, which Pete and this guy, Matthew Scurfield did."[11]

Footage was shot of Townshend and Scurfield driving in the former's Lincoln Continental convertible.[12] Richard Stanley: "They go out for a drive, and Matthew, the brother, is standing up in the car pretending to be Hitler and Mussolini and looking at people and then at some point, he jumps out of the car and after that we just focus on the Matthew character, or the Lone Ranger."

In the weeks following filming, Pete wrote and recorded the soundtrack music in his Ebury Street flat. Stanley: "I stayed there for a while in the summer when I hadn't got a place to stay. We spent some time experimenting with different things up in the studio."

Stanley describes the *Lone Ranger* music as "very, very un-Who like, and very kind of personal. There was quite a lot of Hammond organ in it and there's a sort of pastiche of a country song – [in a country drawl] '*I'm the L-o-o-o-n-n-e R-a-a-a-n-n-ger* . . .' Apart from the sequence where the car drives [around], the [film] music's quite hard, heavy stuff, but none of it sounds like The Who. It's more jokey, music hall type of music."

The 22-minute film was initially banned by the Royal College of Art "because it didn't conform to old-style film-making," says Stanley. "It looked more like a crazy music promo. However, there was a huge protest and they had to show it." *Lone Ranger* went on to win several awards.

Three weeks after their return from Australia, The Who embarked on a nine-week tour of North America and Canada, their first as a headlining act. The tour, which mostly featured shows in ballrooms and colleges, began on the West Coast on February 21 with a date at San Jose's Civic Auditorium. Three shows in San Francisco followed, during which recordings were made for a proposed live album.

During a week-long break prior to heading up to Canada, Kit Lambert took The Who into Gold Star recording studios in Hollywood to finish off 'Call Me Lightning' and 'Little Billy's Doing Fine', which had been started a few weeks earlier in London. The latter, an anti-smoking song recorded

---

[11] Scurfield went on to perform dozens of roles both on screen and onstage, including several roles with Shakespeare's Globe Theatre.

[12] Stanley says the black Lincoln II had its mechanical problems, recalling that the reverse gear didn't exactly work as normal. "If you wanted to reverse, you had to go under with a wrench . . . but it was a beautiful car."

for the American Cancer Society, was ultimately rejected for being too long to use as a jingle.

After dates in Vancouver and Edmonton, the tour swung back down through the Northeast with dates in Minnesota, Michigan and Illinois before the group's coach drove all the way to San Antonio five days later. Footage of The Who performing at the Opera House in Peoria, Illinois was shot by BBC producer Tony Palmer for his documentary film on pop, *All My Loving*.

Tony Palmer: "The Opera House in Peoria, Illinois [was] a great big wooden barn. [Pete] hated it because the backstage facilities were so appalling. He kept saying, 'Where the *hell* is Peoria, Illinois?' And although the audience was fantastic, the acoustics were absolutely dreadful – and he said to me, 'The only solution is to burn this place to the ground. Do you want to help?'" Palmer managed to talk him out of it.

The tour then wound back up the East Coast as far north as Canada prior to heading to New York to appear at Bill Graham's newly opened Fillmore East on April 5 and 6. The nationwide civic unrest which resulted from Dr. Martin Luther King Jr.'s assassination on April 4 dissuaded many from attending, so the intended two shows were reduced to one per night. Like the concerts promoted by Graham on the West Coast, both were recorded.

John Swenson floridly described the finale of one of the Fillmore gigs in his Who biography: "Townshend led the band into 'My Generation' with all the blind fury of a general leading his troops to certain death. His gaunt, haggard figure looked especially menacing in front of his stack of buzzing, crackling amplifiers with their torn coverings and splintered cabinets. Leaping high to accent certain chords visually, then angling toward Moon for his solos, Townshend played his heart out on this song and Moon responded with a tremendous drum accompaniment. The performance closed on the frenetic note after Townshend had hurled his guitar in the air, smashed it against the amplifiers, the stage, Moon's drum kit, and his own body until it was a barely recognisable mash of wood and wire. Moon's drum kit also went, just for good measure."

"I gotta admit I'm kinda down tonight," Townshend had told the audience, "because of several things. Most of it is being kicked out of three hotels in one day." While in the Big Apple, Moon had managed to get The Who entourage ejected from the Gorham and Waldorf-Astoria hotels after blowing up his toilet, throwing cherry bombs from a ninth floor window and blowing a door off its hinges. The following morning the group had a scheduled photo shoot for *Life* magazine. When the group's

US publicist Nancy Lewis found them, they were in a dour mood. According to Tony Fletcher's account in *Dear Boy*, "Pete, citing his lack of sleep, made it quite clear that he 'wasn't going to go for any fucking picture for any fucking *Life* magazine.' That Townshend had his fiancée Karen Astley with him, and that she too had suffered because of this extreme example of Moon's behavioural swings, only added to the guitarist's aggravation . . . Finally, sharing their frustration but with the additional burden of her own responsibilities, Nancy Lewis burst into tears. Only then did Townshend agree to the photo shoot."[13]

On May 20, the day after his 23rd birthday, Pete and Karen married at Didcot Registry Office in Oxfordshire. "Like most men I thought I'd never get married," Townshend told *Disc & Music Echo* in 1969. "I just never felt it was necessary. Karen and I had been living together for about two years and it was OK. But then I realised there were so many problems if you didn't get married. Actually I went to make out my will, because I wanted to leave some things to Karen, and then I thought, 'Well, why not get married? Then she would get everything anyway if anything happened to me.'"

Shortly thereafter the newlyweds moved from Belgravia into an 18th century Georgian house on the Thames embankment in the west London suburb of Twickenham. The £16,500, three-storey house – restored years earlier after sustaining damage from German bombs in World War II – stood on half an acre of ground facing Eel Pie Island, on which was located the Eel Pie Island hotel, an established venue which played host to trad jazz in the early Sixties prior to becoming one of London's better known R&B strongholds.

Pete added an £8,000 home recording studio upstairs which included a separate control room/studio in two tiny adjacent rooms and a light hooked up to a switch in the kitchen so Karen could call him for dinner. Assisting as a handyman during this period was her younger brother Jon, as he recalled, "I used to come and lay floors and stuff . . . doing odd jobs, because I was just a student, a poor student, at the time."

The only problem with the studio, which soon became apparent, was the fact that it was "slap bang in the middle of the building," as Townshend described in 1977. While he could play guitar to excessive

---

[13] The resulting photographs included one of the most familiar images ever taken of The Who – draped in a Union Jack against the Carl Schurz Memorial in Morningside Park, New York City.

volume levels through earphones (a major factor in his eventual hearing damage), the drums and piano meant that "when I worked nobody slept."

During the approximately 14 years that Pete lived in the house, the home studio was occasionally relocated. Jon Astley: "He did have different studios . . . for different projects, he tended to move around . . . the studio for the *Who's Next* demos was in a little bathroom on the second floor, while for a time the studio was located in another second floor room at the front of the house, facing the river. He also had a studio upstairs on the top floor for a short period and he used to use the basement as an echo chamber."

In addition to containing his home studio, the Townshend home was often a gathering place for friends to socialise. Richard Stanley: "I would be out there fairly regularly and [so was] Mike McInnerney, he lived out in Richmond as well, so that wasn't far away – five minutes by car – and then a lot of Baba friends lived in the Richmond/Twickenham area . . . Pete would sort of meet people in fairly relaxed surroundings, you know, sitting in the kitchen or something."

Richard Barnes recalled visiting the Townshends not long after they'd moved in. "I was very surprised by them," he wrote in 1982. "They were both incredibly warm and genuine and down-to-earth. Pete had lost all his sneering unpleasantness and the 'I'm A Big Shot Pop Star' ego trip had disappeared. He was relaxed, interesting and for the first time in years, very, very happy. I didn't know what to put it down to. I thought that it must have been a combination of being married and fairly wealthy and successful. And more importantly their new found relationship with Meher Baba, pictures of whose smiling face with twinkling eyes were hanging around the house."

Another impressed observer was *Disc & Music Echo* reporter Hugh Nolan, who visited the house for an interview. Nolan noted the Baba pictures weren't only on the walls but also in Pete's car. "Baba has made an incredible amount of difference in my life," he told Nolan. "Not so much outwardly – I still shout at cars which get in my way, I still talk too much and I still smash up guitars when I can't afford to. Baba is the Avatar of the Age – the Messiah. He can't do anything but good. He has completely and utterly changed my whole life and, through me, the group as a whole."

Townshend's about-turn with regard to his religious beliefs struck some of his friends as quite ironic.

'Irish' Jack Lyons: "I remember that Pete used to treat with a measure of disdain the fact that I used to go to mass, this was around '65–'66. He would sneer and harp on about why he was an advocate of the Young

Communists. I mean, communists scared the shit out of me because to my mind back then Castro had brought us to the brink of World War III and the 1962 Cuban missile crisis scared me to fuck. Of course, the whole irony about all of this is that when I got married [in 1970] and went to London for our honeymoon, Pete came round to my aunt's to drive my wife and I out to his house in Twickenham to have dinner. As we drove along leafy Richmond, Pete cracked a joke about my moustache. 'That's my Che Guevara moustache,' I said. Pete practically brought the car to a halt and turned to me saying, 'But I thought you were a devout Roman Catholic?' 'And now I'm a communist,' I replied. When we got to the house he started telling me all about Meher Baba and how he had changed Pete's life around for the good. I was dumbfounded."

The change in Townshend's outlook actually had an adverse effect on some of his professional relationships. "It was very difficult for the people around me to accept that I was living a very different kind of life," he told Q's John Harris in 1996. "Roger and Keith didn't take the piss, John Entwistle would. I think he was embarrassed by it. And I lost Kit Lambert and Chris Stamp. I remember Kit Lambert calling me and Karen, Lord and Lady Townshend: 'Oh, Lord and Lady Townshend in their house in Twickenham with their babies.'"

Townshend told the author that it was a combination of factors which led to a distancing between himself and Lambert. "I think Kit also had problems with the intensity of my relationship with Karen . . . She was my first full-time girlfriend. It was rather black and white. We moved away from London to the suburbs, and I suppose that happened partly so we could be closer to the little Meher Baba group we had found that gathered there – but it was also expediency. We could not afford to buy a house in central London where we had both lived close to Kit and Chris and seen a lot of them until 1967."

There was no time for the Townshends to honeymoon. The Who needed a new single out as it had been almost nine months since 'I Can See For Miles', so just two days after his wedding Pete was back at work, recording a comical ode reflecting the working classes' fondness for beer and greyhounds.

Townshend became interested in greyhound racing through his friends Chris Morphet and Richard Stanley. "I used to go to the greyhounds all the time," Morphet recalls, "and I made a film of my own about greyhound racing as well."

Richard Stanley: "Chris was always fascinated by these kinds of relics of English society, being a Yorkshireman himself, and I started going regularly with him. This was just something we would do, like going to the football, or going to see basketball or something, because it was actually a bigger spectator sport per week than football . . . it was just a great atmosphere and we were always having fun there, and it was nice to go to the East End of London – to Romford or Catford, or somewhere, and be involved in this kind of . . . men in flat caps and people in loud waistcoats atmosphere. We invited Pete to come along, because he quite liked these things where he wasn't exposed to the fame, the hangers-on, and so forth. Going to somewhere like Romford Dog Racing Stadium was an absolute guarantee that he would be totally anonymous, and I think that was very nice for him. We went several times, and the song 'Dogs' kind of came out of that but it was a bone of contention with The Who. It was in a way connected with this *Lone Ranger* music hall type of music."

'Dogs' limped to a poorly number 25 when released in the UK in June (for obvious reasons, the single was felt to be too abstruse for the American market). The fact that this eccentric ditty was favoured over 'Melancholia', a superior song Townshend wrote and recorded in demo form the previous year (and The Who recorded just a few days after 'Dogs') suggested that his supply of appropriate material was dwindling. Townshend wrote in 1983 that 'Melancholia' "was obviously totally wrong for the band at a time when we had just failed to get a hit with the glorious 'I Can See For Miles'. I suppose I was really melancholic when I wrote it."

In desperation, 'Magic Bus', a song written back in 1965, and which had already been recorded by a group named The Pudding in April, 1967, was dug out of mothballs. Despite the fact that it went on to become the "most requested live song for The Who along with 'Boris The Spider'," according to Townshend (who would later describe the lyrics as "garbage"), 'Magic Bus' fared even worse than 'Dogs' in the British charts, reaching 26, while attaining one place higher in the States.

Being considered neither underground rock nor commercial pop, The Who's standing in Britain was fading; their last three singles had all been commercial disappointments, their overseas touring commitments had kept them out of sight while new groups like Cream, the Jimi Hendrix Experience, and Pink Floyd emerged to challenge their position. Their survival now depended on America keeping them afloat on a sea of fiscal liability.

"They were too much in debt," George Tremlett wrote in 1975. "In one interview with me, Daltrey had said [I thought at the time, almost despairingly] that their total debts had risen to around £100,000 – more recently, in . . . *The Observer*, he said: 'When we got our first hit, 'I Can't Explain', we started earning what was then pretty good money, say £300 a night. But after the first year we were £60,000 in debt. The next year, after working our balls off, we were still £40,000 down. And the biggest choke of all came the year after that when we found we were back up to £60,000 again. Every accountant's meeting was ridiculous. We always owed so much money that we ended up rolling around the office laughing ourselves silly.' "

"I was petrified that the band was going to finish," Townshend recalled in 1977. "I felt strongly that I was being tied down too much to single records. I felt that if I had to say everything on a record in three minutes flat then I wasn't ever going to say very much. I wanted to find a way to stretch it a bit more without making it pretentious or pompous and without making it sound like classical music."

Townshend's inclinations towards coming up with a new direction for The Who coincided directly with his discovery of Meher Baba's teachings. He thought of writing a series of thematically linked pieces of music focusing on man's spiritual quest. "In my first notes," Pete later recalled, "I talked of an opera that would tell a spiritual story in a parallel way, from the inside and from the outside . . . but the solid undercurrent riding through all the material was the fact that I was in a 'new-found spiritual mood'."

'The Amazing Journey' – which formed the nucleus of Townshend's new project – started life as a poem of epic proportions, clocking in at over 230 lines. It began with the narrator describing his 'illness', and the 'amazing journey', a spiritual adventure which he'd experienced in a dream.

> *. . . The master gravely shook his head and I*
> *Knew that despite his infinite wisdom, infinite power, infinite*
> *awareness*
> *That he would not, could not tell me where to look.*
> *Or even what to look for. I had to find the answer myself.*
>
> *Sickness will surely take the mind*
> *Where minds can't usually go*
> *Come on the amazing journey*
> *And learn all you should know*

This initial segment brought to mind a phase in Baba's spiritual development, referred to by biographer C.B. Purdom as the opening of his "inner eye", which began when Baba met a Perfect Master named Hazrat Babajan in 1913, an elderly woman (reportedly 122 years old at the time) who kissed him on the forehead. He subsequently fell into a catatonic state, a trance that would, according to Purdom, leave him almost totally oblivious to his surroundings for nearly nine months. This was the beginning of Baba's transformation into a Spiritual Master.

"['The Amazing Journey'] is poetry, sometimes good, often terrible," Townshend wrote in *The Story Of Tommy*. "It was all stream of consciousness stuff, but when I read it back then, it staggered me. I realised that I had described a story that I could never have dreamed of myself let alone put to music. But the strangest part of all is that there was no development stage between this Hesse-like tale of mystery and spiritual intrigue, and what we today see to be *Tommy*. I just lived with the story, invented a name for my hero, Tommy, and started to write songs."

CHAPTER FIVE

1968–1970

"I lost touch with The Who's mod audience, and I decided that what I actually had to do was I had to write something for me. And where I was at the time was in a very strange place. I had had a couple of acid trips and hated it – everybody else in the world was wearing funny clothes and blowing their heads off and wearing flares with flowers in their hair, and I felt very out of step with it, but I was interested in the mysticism. I was interested in the spiritual side of it. So I thought maybe what I could try to do was marry the pop single with this idea of this mystical journey, and that's when I started to work on Tommy.*"*

– Pete Townshend, 1999

WITH 'Amazing Journey' forming his new project's foundation, in mid-1968, Pete began to incorporate several songs he'd recently written such as 'Sensation', 'I'm Free', 'Welcome' and 'We're Not Gonna Take It' into the story.

Throughout The Who's 41-date North American tour (which commenced on June 28 at the Shrine Auditorium, Los Angeles), Pete laboured over his grand idea (which went under various working titles including *Journey Into Space* and *The Brain Opera*) whenever the inspiration took him, as well as entering into many discussions with the rest of The Who between shows. "I used to rush back to the hotel room to work," he wrote in *The Story Of Tommy*, "writing songs or collating lyrics, or scribbling out ideas . . ."

On August 2, The Who played a memorable concert at the Singer Bowl in Flushing, New York, supporting the Doors. "'Sally Simpson' was about a rock star and it was based on Jim Morrison," Townshend told Barnes in a 1975 interview for *The Story Of Tommy*. "I met him in New York and he just absolutely amazed me – some bird went up to talk to him or something, one of his bodyguards just punched her in the midriff and she doubled up and he just carried on talking, he didn't see her. Then the same afternoon at this club he actually tried to pull this chick . . . I wrote that thing and then realised that in a way he was exactly like what Tommy was, and I just re-wrote it."

Reaching San Francisco during The Who's three-night run at the Fillmore West, Pete sat down at 2 a.m. with *Rolling Stone*'s Jann Wenner for a lengthy interview which featured a detailed description of his work-in-progress that included many integral elements of the finished product. The fact that Townshend went into such great detail may be partly due to the fact that he was, as he admitted the following year, "very hyped up on coke".[1]

The in-depth conversation was a prime example of an artist using the interview process to broach ideas, in a sense putting themselves on the spot and creating expectations among their audience. "What I do is force myself to do [projects] by announcing things up front . . ." Pete said in 1975. "I said so much [about *Tommy*] that it just *had* to be finished – I had to get it done."

"I'm working on the lyrics now for the next album," he told Wenner, explaining the idea was provisionally titled *The Deaf, Dumb And Blind Boy*. "It's a story about a kid that's born deaf, dumb and blind and what happens to him throughout his life . . . he's seeing things basically as vibrations which we translate as music . . . That's really what we want to do. Create this feeling that when you listen to the music you can actually become aware of the boy, and aware of what he is all about, because we are creating him as we play."

The plan was to switch from reality to fantasy using musical interludes between the more conventional songs which described Tommy's experiences. "You've got a double-barrelled plot," Townshend explained in 1975, "one minute you'd see him from one angle objectively, and the other minute you'd see him from the other angle subjectively, so one song followed another song, followed another song, followed another song . . . each one was going to be followed by sort of an impressionistic dream-sequence-type piece of music."

The idea for these "dream sequences", some of which were to feature

---

[1] "We'd been drinking orange juice and in the middle of a long and wandering answer [Pete] asked if I had spiked his drink," Wenner said. ". . . when I asked him what he meant by 'spiked', he said he felt as though he were beginning an LSD trip. I hadn't slipped him anything."

sound effects (for example, battle sounds following 'Overture' and assorted pinball machine sounds where appropriate), proved too difficult to execute, possibly due to recording constraints, and ended up in consolidated form within the tracks 'Sparks'[2] and 'Underture'.

Townshend didn't feel comfortable writing the more sleazy elements of the story so he delegated that responsibility to Entwistle, who came up with 'Cousin Kevin' and 'Fiddle About'. "I didn't think I could be cruel enough," Pete told *Rolling Stone* in 1969. "[Both are] ruthlessly brilliant songs because they are just as cruel as people can be. I wanted to show that the boy was being dealt with very cruelly and it was because he was being dismissed as a freak."

'The Acid Queen' dealt with the adolescent Tommy's encounter with a woman who claimed she could cure his affliction. "The song's not just about acid," Townshend told *Rolling Stone* in 1969, "it's the whole drug thing, the drink thing, the sex thing, wrapped into one big ball. It's about how you get it laid on you that you haven't lived if you haven't fucked 40 birds, taken 60 trips, drunk 14 pints of beer – or whatever. Society – people – force you. [The Acid Queen] represents this force."

One of the initial concerns elicited from Wenner's interview regarded Townshend's choice of subject being severely disabled. "Tommy became deaf, dumb and blind when I realised that there was no way to get across, musically or dramatically, the idea of our ignorance of reality, as I had learned it to be, from reading Meher Baba," he wrote in 1977.[3] This statement underlined the theme of *Tommy*, the foundation of 'The Amazing Journey' poem.

"We have our five senses, and we have our emotions . . . but there are whole chunks of life, including the whole concept of reality, which escapes us. We don't really know who we are, we don't really know how we got here, and we don't really know what our aim is, we don't understand the concept of infinity, and our minds are unable to accept it. We don't understand suffering or what causes it, we don't understand life itself or what motivates it, we can't accept death and we feel it to be unjust [although it is part of the wheel of life]. So I decided that the hero had to be deaf, dumb and blind, so that, seen from our already limited

---

[2] In 1962, English Baba devotee Delia DeLeon, a friend of Pete's, compiled a booklet of Meher Baba's sayings, entitled *Sparks*.

[3] Pete also wrote "letters to different organisations, including a foundation in Los Angeles that put on concerts for the psychosomatically impaired," according to Andy Neill and Matt Kent's *Anyway Anyhow Anywhere*.

point of view, his limitations would be symbolic of our own.' "

The day after the *Rolling Stone* interview, Pete ran into fellow Baba follower Rick Chapman in San Francisco. "He was talking about drugs and things," Townshend wrote in 1970, "and what Baba says about it, and he says, 'Of course you're not still smoking dope, are you?' So I said, 'Yes, sure. What's Baba said about dope?' 'Didn't you know that it's been proved now that pot's a hallucinogenic drug, so it falls into Baba's teachings?' he said . . .

"And then as it started to go down I started to realise how much I credited to drugs. I used to think, 'Well, man, I can't play the guitar unless I'm stoned, I can't write a song unless I'm stoned, I can't be happy unless I'm stoned, I can't listen to records unless I'm stoned, I can't do anything unless I'm stoned. Because if I'm not stoned it's not as good.' Well, I've . . . kind of just got out of that, and I get just as much now out of everything perpetually 24 hours a day as I used to out of that high . . .

"Baba did emphasise to a young devotee going to see him in about 1966 that the biggest single gesture a man could make for youth, would be to spend his life trying to show the dangers of dope. Remember, Baba was concerned with a set of people that felt the psychedelics held the key to religious experience, to Universal consciousness. God in a pill."

At this stage, the lyrical imagery throughout *The Deaf, Dumb And Blind Boy* was soaked in Baba references. "The process of writing was controlled by my direct involvement with Baba," Townshend confirmed. "His stuff is completely self-contained, and it's a good point to start fucking-up from." However, Pete was quick to point out that his work wasn't coming from above. "I don't mean divinely inspired," he asserted. "You get a lot of crap from the close devotees of Baba, stories about people rushing up to him and saying, 'My daughter was dying in Poona and I said a prayer to you and you came in a vision and she was well again.' Baba says, 'I'm sorry mate. I don't know anything about that.' It's obviously their faith, their love for him that did the trick. It's like Jesus saying, 'It's your faith that made you whole.'"

While the story's concept grew, Townshend's ambitions increased in tandem, as he recalled in 1979. "At one time, I was studying orchestrations and listening to Wagner and all kinds of amazing things trying to get into full scale grand opera and I was going to enlist Arthur Brown whose voice I thought was somewhere between a Wagnerian tenor and Screaming Jay Hawkins and have him as the lead singer." (It's worth remembering that Townshend had considered using Brown for 'Rael' the previous year).

Brown, the flamboyant leader of the Crazy World of Arthur Brown, one of Track Records' stable of artists, had achieved a number one UK hit single with 'Fire', produced by Townshend and Kit Lambert, that summer.[4]

"I didn't believe I could do [*Tommy*] in the framework of The Who," Townshend later explained. "I'd had the idea of rock opera way before, but when I met Arthur Brown, I was convinced that he was the perfect foil for it, he was a great rock singer with an operatic range and all that. I thought about writing an opera for him but it was something outside of The Who – I was hedging my bets. It was Kit that kept pushing me back to the band. He seemed to have greater foresight than we did as to the level that The Who would reach."

Within a few weeks of the conclusion of the North American tour at the end of August, the first recording session for what became *Tommy* took place at IBC studios in Portland Place, London. The Who worked in between gigs to bring in money, a necessary evil due to their dire financial situation. This intermixing, however, was beneficial as songs were often first played live, resulting in well-rehearsed, high quality takes for the actual recording.

When it came time to tape 'Smash The Mirror', with its high-register "*rise, rise, rise, rise*" vocals, Pete recruited his younger brothers, Simon and Paul to help out.

Simon Townshend: "Pete had taken us to the studio . . . just for a night out. We were enjoying going up and down in these lifts and God knows what, getting chocolate out of the machines and stuff . . . and then about 2 a.m., we got the call to go in the studio and sing – that was amazing. 'Speedy' Keen was there in the studio that day as well, playing drums, messing around on the drums."

As the sessions continued, the story evolved into the unlikely notion of the central character of the rock opera becoming the Messiah. "My sort of cameo was that Tommy started off deaf, dumb, and blind, and his coming to know what it was like to be normal was for him what it would be for you and me to become infinitely conscious," Townshend elaborated in 1974. "It was a big step for him – equivalent to the biggest step anyone can take, which is to stop living in illusion and see reality, infinite reality, for

---

[4] 'Fire' was later recorded by The Who for inclusion on Townshend's *Iron Man* album in 1989.

the first time. This is why I originally used it. I had this double story in my mind and then I made him jump. He became a double person, so that not only did he become normal like you and me but he jumped beyond that into what I was paralleling with it – into being a universally conscious person.

"Tommy's awareness of the world is completely unjaded. He gets everything in a very pure, filtered, unadulterated, unfucked-up manner. Like when his uncle rapes him – he is incredibly elated, not disgusted, at being homosexually raped. He takes it as a move of total affection, not feeling the reasons why. Lust is a lower form of love, like atomic attraction is a lower form of love. He gets an incredible spiritual push from it where most people would get a spiritual retardment, constantly thinking about this terrible thing that's happened to them. In Tommy's mind, everything is incredible, meaningless beauty."

'Sensation' was, ". . . the song Tommy sings after he's regained his senses. He realises who he is and becomes totally aware . . . the moment is that of divinity. Tommy is worshipping himself, knowing what he is and speaking the truth . . . I used all the sensation stuff because after all this time where Tommy's just been getting vibrations, now he's turned the tables. Now you're going to feel *me*! I'm in everything; I'm the explosion; I'm a sensation."

"The institution of the church comes up in *Welcome*," Townshend told *Rolling Stone* in 1969, "The followers want to know how to follow [Tommy] and he tells them very simply what to do. He's telling them what they want to hear – 'It's going to be all smooth and fun and we're never going to speak, we're going to drink all night and have the time of our life. You can do good things, go out and get new people, and for this you'll win gold stars.' He knows they're completely off the track and is trying by his very presence to make them aware of what they should be doing – coming in to the house and then getting out again. Instead of that they want more action."

"Rama Krishna, Buddha, Zarathustra, Jesus and Meher Baba are all divine figures on earth," Pete said in 1969. "They all said the same thing; yet *still* we trundle on. This is basically what Tommy is saying [this was also, of course, what Baba had said]. But his followers ask how to follow him and disregard his teaching. They want rules and regulations; going to church on Sundays – but he just says 'live life'."

Which leads to 'We're Not Gonna Take It': "All the time they demand more and so he starts to get hard: 'Well if you *really* want to know what to do, you've got to stop drinking for a start. You've got to stop smoking pot.' And he starts to lay down hard moral facts – like Jesus did – but nobody wants to know."

While Tommy's new-found universal consciousness provided some clarification as to the story's ending, the work as a whole was in danger of foundering due to its lack of a clear plot. "We had been in the studios making it for eight months," Entwistle told *The Observer*. "We had terrible trouble with the story, in fact, at first it just didn't make sense. It was only because Pete had to keep adding bits that it became a double album."

"[*Tommy*] was falling all over the place," Stamp confirmed to Barnes in 1982. "It was just not coming together and that's when Kit wrote a script." Lambert's input at this point was invaluable – he managed to clarify what was a rather abstract storyline and set the group on course to complete the task. "He was working all through the night on the script," Stamp said, "and when it was finished we went straight round to the printers. We had it printed up as a script to impress the group and had 20 copies made up. It was going to be the first Lambert/Stamp production."

"Kit's real contribution will never, ever be known, because, of course, it wasn't production at all, it was far deeper," Townshend told *Zigzag* in 1971. "The word *producer* is, I think, an absurdly misused word anyway. Kit was much more involved in the overall concept of the thing – much more than people imagine. Not all that much, in fact, with the overall sound, although he did produce it and mix it and he did make us work at it."

It was also Lambert who led to the work becoming known as a 'rock opera' as Townshend explained in 1999: "I wasn't aware of the minefield that I was getting into when I playfully called this piece that I was working on a rock opera, but Kit was just fantastic, he kind of took me the other way . . . I'd say, 'Are you sure it's OK to call this a rock opera,' and . . . he'd say, 'Well, yeah of course it is,' and I'd say, 'Well the story's a bit dodgy at the moment," and he'd go, 'Yeah, but all opera's got a stupid story,' and I realised later actually that some of his ambitions of course were to usurp the musical establishment."

In the autumn of 1968, The Who's American record label Decca lost patience with the lack of new product while the group were busy working on *Tommy*. "We kept telling them it would be ready next week, it would be ready next week, it would be ready next week," Townshend told the *LA Free Press*' Chris Van Ness in December 1971. "And it never was."

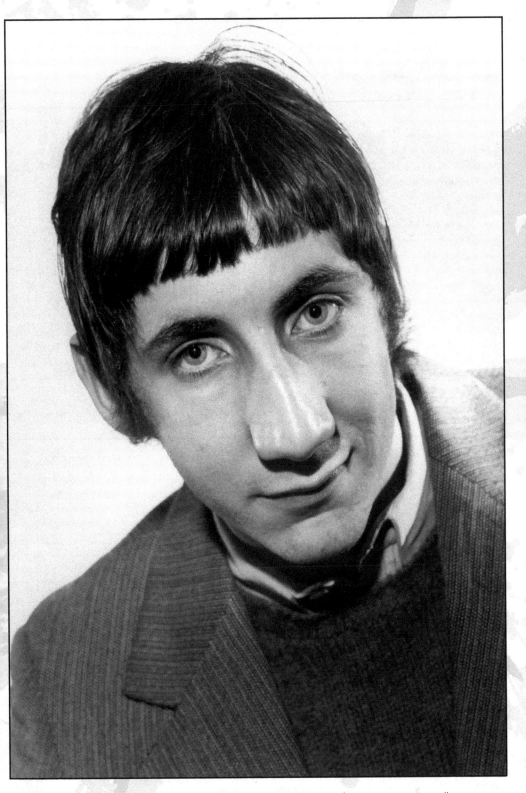

Pete in 1967, the year he discovered Meher Baba. "[It's about] having a focus, someone you really respect but don't necessarily think is a super-being, someone you respect above anyone else demonstrating a real love for you when you think that you're a lump of shit – that's all it needs." **(HARRY GOODWIN)**

Pete's father, Cliff Townshend (third from left) in The Squadronaires, the RAF dance band.

Pete's childhood family home in West London, 20 Woodgrange Avenue, Ealing. (PICTORIALPRESS.COM)

CERTIFIED COPY OF AN ENTRY OF BIRTH

GIVEN AT THE **GENERAL REGISTER OFFICE**

Application Number W154739

	REGISTRATION DISTRICT			Brentford					
1945	BIRTH in the Sub-district of			Chiswick		in the County of Middlesex			
Columns:-	1	2	3	4	5	6	7	8	9	10
No.	When and where born	Name, if any	Sex	Name and surname of father	Name, surname and maiden surname of mother	Occupation of father	Signature, description and residence of informant	When registered	Signature of registrar	Name entered after registration
30	Nineteenth May 1945 Chiswick Hospital Chiswick U.D.	Peter Dennis Blandford	Boy	Clifford Blandford Townshend	Betty Veronica Townshend formerly Dennis	L·A·C· 923804 R·A·F· (musician) of 1B Grosvenor Parade Ealing	B·V·Townshend mother 1B Grosvenor Parade Ealing	Twenty ninth June 1945	F·G·Bond Deputy Interim Registrar	—

CERTIFIED to be a true copy of an entry in the certified copy of a Register of Births in the District above mentioned.

Given at the GENERAL REGISTER OFFICE, under the Seal of the said Office, the _____22nd_____ day of _____March_____ _____2004_____

BCAZ 187687

CAUTION: THERE ARE OFFENCES RELATING TO FALSIFYING OR ALTERING A CERTIFICATE AND USING OR POSSESSING A FALSE CERTIFICATE ©CROWN COPYRIGHT

WARNING: A CERTIFICATE IS NOT EVIDENCE OF IDENTITY

Pete's birth certificate.

Pete as a boy on a trip to a Butlin's Holiday camp with his parents.

German performance artist Gustav Metzger, founder of the Auto-Destructive school of art, and inspiration for the young Townshend, pictured in July 1961.
(KEYSTONE/STRINGER/GETTY IMAGES)

The Detours (l-r) Pete, John Entwistle and Roger Daltrey, on stage at the White Hart Hotel, Acton, in 1963.

The High Numbers on stage at the Scene Club, London, summer 1964. **(DEZO HOFFMAN/REX FEATURES)**

The early Who at a photo session in Westminster, March 1965.

(DAVID WEDGBURY© NOT FADE AWAY ARCHIVE/SNAP GALLERIES)

Pete on stage wearing
Union Jack jacket with
Rickenbacker guitar, 1965.

(KING COLLECTION/RETNA)

The Who in Amsterdam for a Dutch TV show recording, September 20, 1965. **(PICTORIALPRESS.COM)**

Pete in his mother's antique shop, Ealing Common, 1966. **(PICTORIALPRESS.COM)**

Pete at work at his Wardour Street home studio. The Who's second album, *A Quick One*, is visible in the background. **(LFI)**

Pete smashing his guitar at the climax of the Who's performance at the Windsor Jazz and Blues festival, July 30, 1966. **(PICTORIALPRESS.COM)**

The Who mime for Dick Clark's *Where The Action Is!* TV show, London, March 1966

(MICHAEL OCHS ARCHIVES/GETTY IMAGES)

Pete enjoys breakfast during the Who's spring 1966 UK tour. (HUGH VANES/REX FEATURES)

Chris Stamp and Kit Lambert, the Who's managers. (JAN OLOFSSON/REDFERNS)

Kit Lambert with Pete, 1966. (PICTORIALPRESS.COM)

The company took matters into their own hands by releasing a concoction of previously released material titled *Magic Bus – The Who On Tour*. "Decca Records really smarmed all over this one," Pete vented in his 1971 *Rolling Stone* article. "Buses painted like Mickey Mouse's last trip. Album covers featuring an unsuspecting Who endorsing it like it was *our* idea . . . Decca's answer to an overdue *Tommy*: *The Who – Magic Bus, On Tour*. Great title, swinging presentation. Also a swindle as far as insinuating that the record was live. Bastards."

"[The album] was a culmination of all the most terrible things American record companies ever get up to. Just exploitation," Townshend told Van Ness. "They didn't care about *Tommy* ever coming out; they just wanted to exploit The Who while The Who were big – though we weren't that big then, really – and make a few bucks, because who knows what may happen tomorrow . . . I mean that's the worst thing that's ever gone down, and there are a few people in the LA part of Decca that I won't even look at, because they were there at the photo session, knowing it was for an album cover."

In December, The Who took part in an elaborate TV special *The Rolling Stones' Rock'n'Roll Circus* alongside fellow guests including John Lennon, Yoko Ono, Eric Clapton, Mitch Mitchell, Jethro Tull, Taj Mahal and Marianne Faithfull. The spectacular "was, in fact, the most exciting pop show I have ever seen," Keith Altham reported in *NME*, "and one in which I was involved alongside those 'maniacs' Keith Moon and Pete Townshend, who organised compulsory audience participation until 5 o'clock Thursday morning . . . clowns, a fire-eater and cowboy on horseback led to The Who. They performed their mini-opera, in which Keith Moon regaled us with his latest impersonation of a human fountain by having beer spilled onto his snare drums while in top gear. Although he might smile at the thought, Townshend is now almost a piece of pop folklore, with his Catherine Wheel arm movements and aggressive leaps. He must make great TV."

It's often been said that the reason the Stones never released the film (at the time) was because they were upstaged by The Who's blistering performance of 'A Quick One',[5] a far superior rendition to that which was

---

[5] "You know why it was never shown, right?" *The Kids Are Alright* producer Jeff Stein asked *The Hollywood Reporter*'s John Burman in 2003 of the *Rock'n'Roll Circus* footage. "The [Who] kicked [the Stones'] fucking arse. So brilliant. The energy at the end of that piece. It feels like the roof is going to come off – Pete and Keith flailing away."

played at Monterey 18 months earlier which can be attributed to The Who's non-stop touring since.[6]

By the end of the year, *Tommy* was ostensibly complete until Townshend let his friend, music writer/author Nik Cohn, listen to an early preview tape of some of the tracks. "Nik and I used to go all over Soho playing pinball all the time," Pete told *Uncut*'s Simon Goddard in 2004. "He was fucking obsessed by it. He'd written a novel called *Arfur: Teenage Pinball Queen* about this girl who he introduced me to one time. She was this podgy little girl who used to hang around Soho, probably a prostitute, about 15, but she was a fantastic pinball player. At that time, the setting for the end of *Tommy* was going to be a church, so we played it to a few people, including Nik Cohn. He kind of liked it but he said, 'It's all a bit *dark*, isn't it!' I just remember saying to him, with maybe an element of sarcasm, 'So if it had pinball in it, would you give it a decent review?' He went, 'Of course I would, anything with pinball in it's fantastic.' And so I wrote 'Pinball Wizard', purely as a scam.

"I knocked it off," Townshend commented in 1996. "I thought 'This is awful, the most clumsy piece of writing I've ever done': "*Ever since I was a young boy, I played the silver ball, from Soho down to Brighton, I must have played them all.*" Oh my god. I'm embarrassed. This sounds like a music hall song.' "*Sure plays a mean pinball.*" I scribbled it out and all the verses were the same length and there was no kind of middle eight. It was going to be a complete dud, but I carried on. I attempted the same mock baroque guitar beginning that's on 'I'm A Boy' and then a bit of vigorous kind of flamenco guitar. I was just grabbing at ideas, I knocked a demo together and took it to the studio and everyone loved it."

'Pinball Wizard' shifted *Tommy*'s focus back from religion to rock, or, as Barnes put it in 1996, "'Pinball Wizard' made it more Rock Opera than God Opera." At a point when perhaps the whole theme had become bogged down in its own deeper meaning, 'Pinball Wizard' introduced some levity. The song also provided a means of demonstrating Tommy's first real taste of success in life.

"The whole point of 'Pinball Wizard' was to let the boy have some sort of colourful event and excitement," Pete told *Rolling Stone* in 1969. "'Pinball Wizard' is about life's games. Tommy's games aren't games. They're like the first real thing he's done in his life . . . this is Tommy's first

---

[6] The performance was first seen in the 1979 Who biopic *The Kids Are Alright* and eventually released on video in 1996.

big triumph. He's got results. A big score. He doesn't know all this; he stumbled on a machine, started to pull levers and so on, got things going, and suddenly started getting incredible affection – like pats on the back. This hasn't happened to him before, and the kids are his first disciples. It's supposed to capsule the later events, a sort of teasing preview. It's meant to be a play off of early discipleship and the later real disciples. In a funny sort of way, the disciples in the pinball days were more sincere, less greedy than later on, when they demand a religion – anything to be like him and escape from their own dreary lives, do things his way and get there quicker."

The 'Holiday Camp' setting at the end of *Tommy* was added to make the pinball theme more palatable.

"There may have been some embarrassment because what I felt was that I'd been selling this thing to the band as being really quite deep and then suddenly I felt as though I was losing my nerve," Townshend told Goddard. "I remember saying to Keith one day, 'It doesn't feel right any more, this Pinball Wizard thing. Suddenly he's a fucking pinball player!' I didn't think we needed to nail down what Tommy was: he could have been a guitarist or a singer or a preacher or anything – a charismatic individual. But suddenly he was a pinball player and I felt uncomfortable with it being placed in this idea of a pseudo-church. Then Keith said, 'Well, what about a holiday camp?'[7] because I was always going on about holiday camps, I was almost brought up in Butlins. So I ran off, wrote 'Tommy's Holiday Camp' and then wrote a couple of lyrical changes to bring pinball and the holiday camp into the story, so it felt as if this was being lightened up towards the end. But it also seemed more radical, there being more of a sense of commercialism brought in at the end, that he's selling shades and T-shirts and everything in a very absurd, comical, cartoon-y marketplace. Which, of course, pop is! So it all suddenly started to feel natural, that we were on safe ground because we were satirising our own industry."

★　　★　　★

---

[7] "Keith said, 'Well I've been thinking that it would be a good idea to set the whole thing in a Holiday Camp,'" Pete said in 1975. "I said, 'What a great idea' and Keith said, 'Well OK I'll write that tonight.' I thought, 'God Almighty, if Keith goes off and gets into writing songs about Holiday Camps, I don't know how they're ever going to fit in.' So I said to him, 'Don't worry Keith, I've already written it' . . . when I got home I wrote the short piece called 'Ernie's Holiday Camp'. Keith got the credit for it because it was his idea, and also I felt, it turned out just as he himself would have written it."

At the same time as The Who were working on *Tommy*, Pete had his own side project; producing an unorthodox musical trio Thunderclap Newman, which comprised his art school muse Andy Newman, ex-chauffeur/flatmate 'Speedy' Keen and 16-year-old Scottish guitarist, Jimmy McCulloch.

"Independently all three of them came to me, or I got involved with them with a view to helping them," Townshend told *Zigzag* in 1971, "and then suddenly I realised – or rather, it was Kit Lambert again who said to me, 'You haven't got time for all of them; why not try them together?' I thought, 'Impossible, three more unlikely people you couldn't get,' but they got in a room together, they played together on some film music for a friend of mine, and they were really great, and I played them back the tapes and they said, 'Yeah, seems to work,' and they liked it and they were all enthusiastic about it as a concept."

Thunderclap Newman recorded an album, *Hollywood Dream*, at IBC and Pete's home studio over the course of a year, starting in early 1969. In addition to producing, Townshend played bass under the pseudonym Bijou Drains (presumably for contractual reasons) and contributed pedal steel guitar to the instrumental title track. Chris Morphet recalls playing harmonica on two tracks while Richard Stanley was also present at the odd session.

Richard Stanley: "[Thunderclap Newman] were going through a sticky patch – creatively – and one experiment that I persuaded Pete to carry out was where I suggested that we should do some sessions at [Pete's] house, in which Thunderclap, who was just this amazing jazz improvisational pianist, would play and I would put photographs in front of him on the piano that I had chosen, which were meant to replace musical notes, and to change his playing, as it were. So I had pictures of crocodiles, or whatever, and . . . it was just a kind of a Rorschach test, to see what happened, and it was quite effective. I think it sort of freed up the [mental] block a bit."

The first single from the sessions, 'Something In The Air'[8] (formerly known as 'Revolution') was number one in the UK charts for three weeks when released in mid-'69 and also cracked the US Top 40. Riding the momentum of their surprise hit, Thunderclap Newman went on an ill-fated tour. "I had to go away to America with The Who in the middle of it

---

[8] By coincidence, the Squadronaires had a popular tune entitled 'There's Something In The Air'.

all and that number one was so unexpected," Townshend lamented to *Melody Maker* the following year. "I never even got to see them play a gig, although I hear it was a disaster and the audiences were fantastically disappointed.[9] Andy enjoyed the tour, but people thought they were going to be a rock group, which wasn't the idea . . . financially it didn't do them any good at all, despite having a number one single. There was nothing to follow it up and I feel very guilty about it." Apparently not all audiences were disappointed. "It's a shame, because they did a European tour with Deep Purple, and in some of the places they actually went down better than Purple," recalls former Track Records' employee Dana Wiffen. "I used to go along to where they were rehearsing and they were great to watch and listen to."[10]

Returning home from a Who gig in northern England, Pete learned that Meher Baba had died. "Avatar Meher Baba dropped his physical body at 12 noon on 31st January 1969, to live eternally in the hearts of all his lovers," read the cable released by Baba's secretary in India. Townshend was especially saddened by the fact that he hadn't become closer to Baba during his lifetime.[11] "When I got home and the news was broken to me," Pete said, "I felt as if I hadn't had enough time to really make myself ready, to learn to love Baba and hang tightly to his apron strings as the whirlwind of spiritual events around the closing of his manifestation speeded up." Baba's death prompted Townshend to record Cole Porter's 'Begin The

[9] "Speedy, for a start, should never, ever, ever have got on the stage because he's not constitutionally built for it, he's incredibly nervous." Pete told *Zigzag*. "The first gig we did was really strange," Keen told *Melody Maker*'s Chris Welch in July 1969. "Because I was busy playing the drums, I couldn't get my breath to sing . . . I was just squeaking." The situation was remedied by shifting Keen to rhythm guitar, while Jimmy McCulloch's brother Jack took his place on drums.

[10] Newman released a solo album, *Rainbow*, in 1972. While Townshend didn't actually produce the album, he told *Zigzag*, "I've edited it and done some mixing and stuff like that . . . sort of 'creative production'." Keen wound up working for Track, releasing various solo recordings and later producing albums such as *L.A.M.F.* by the Heartbreakers and Motorhead's self-titled debut in 1977. He died in March 2002, aged 56. McCulloch joined Stone The Crows and in 1974, Paul McCartney's Wings. He died in 1979 of heart failure from a mixture of morphine and alcohol, aged 26.

[11] While the two never met, Baba was reportedly aware of Townshend. "I sent [Baba's sister] Mani the *Observer* colour magazine which one week carried the story of The Who and had a photograph of Pete and the others on the cover," London Baba devotee Delia DeLeon wrote in 1991. "While Mani was looking at it, Baba came into the room and put his hand on Pete's face. Subsequently Mani gave Pete this photograph when he visited India."

Beguine' (the Avatar's favourite song) at his home recording studio that month, which would ultimately appear on the Baba tribute album *Happy Birthday*, released on Baba's birthday the following year.

The first taste of *Tommy*, 'Pinball Wizard', was released in March, the same month that Pete's first daughter, Emma Kate, was born. The single did well on both sides of the Atlantic, reaching number four in the UK, while attaining 19 in the US. Regarded as by far The Who's best effort since 'I Can See For Miles', the single was met with a great deal of praise,[12] but some critics were concerned with *Tommy*'s overall moral message even before hearing the finished product. Articles started appearing in the British music press under such headings as "Is This Man Sick?" Townshend responded by sending out a press release to the music critics and DJs he felt were sympathetic, pleading for them to hold their judgement until the album proper was released.

Following a short series of gigs through Scotland in late April, The Who previewed *Tommy* in a high profile showcase at Ronnie Scott's club in Soho on May 1. The group had dedicated much of the previous two months to rehearsing their overhauled live show and invited an audience of mostly journalists to witness the result. "As enormous speaker cabinets were piled high along the walls of the club and hummed ominously at the assembled throng, Pete dryly explained the storyline," *Melody Maker* reported. "The band soon launched into a non-stop rendition of *Tommy* followed by 'Shakin' All Over' and 'Summertime Blues' thrown in for good measure.

"In the confined space of Ronnie Scott's club which is more accustomed to the refined rhythms of jazz, the overwhelming intensity of The Who's performance left scores of people literally deaf," *Melody Maker* explained. "Despite the discomfort of those nearest the speakers, nobody wanted to miss a minute of the group's riveting rave-up . . ."

Tommy, The Who's fourth album – wrapped in a triple fold-out sleeve designed by Mike McInnerney, containing a lavishly illustrated libretto – was released in late May and eventually became a resounding success, reaching number two in the UK and four in the States, where the album stayed on the charts for a total 47 weeks.

"*Tommy* is a milestone in rock music, a milestone in the career of The

---

[12] "I didn't think 'Pinball Wizard' would be a hit," Pete told *Melody Maker*'s Chris Welch in April, "especially as it's an uptempo, swinging rockaboogie about a deaf, dumb and blind person."

Who and a milestone in Pete Townshend's development as a composer," Chris Charlesworth wrote in *The Complete Guide*. . . . "Despite its faults – muddy production, misleading story line, some flawed songs – the double LP incorporates intriguing ideas and musical devices that Pete had been experimenting with for most of his professional career . . . Whatever confusion is thrown up by the lyrics, the music – a textbook lesson in rock construction – carries the whole."

Tommy was met with mostly ecstatic reviews; *Rolling Stone* called the album "probably the most important milestone in pop since Beatlemania", while the *New York Times'* Nik Cohn stated: "*Tommy* is just possibly the most important work that anyone has yet done in rock." However, the *NME*'s Richard Green wasn't impressed. "I really was looking forward to this 'pop opera', which has occupied Pete Townshend's mind for so long. But what a disappointment. Running for over an hour, it goes on and on and isn't totally representative of The Who; maybe it's time for a change in style, but if this is it, I long for a return to the old days . . . Pretentious is too strong a word; maybe over-ambitious is the right term, but sick certainly does apply."

Townshend had previously responded to such an accusation in a *Disc And Music Echo* interview, explaining, "What I was out to show is that someone who suffers terribly at the hands of society has the ability to turn all these experiences into a tremendous musical awareness. Sickness is in the mind of the listener and I don't give a damn what people think. I'm very pleased with the way the album has turned out . . . Sure, the boy is raped and suffers, but we show that instead of being repulsed and sickened, he has the means to turn all these experiences to his own good."

Pete expressed several regrets regarding *Tommy* following the album's release, one of which concerned the ending, as he later explained. "My whole idea was that Tommy was left behind, poignant, you know, 'See Me, Feel Me' and you didn't get enough of it. That should be the last thing you hear, whereas the last thing you actually hear is 'Listening To You'. I felt that was one mistake. There were lots and lots of others. We could have gone on forever and still not got it right." On another occasion, he added, "It's definitely not a total success. I've had a lot of kids come up to me and say, 'Well, look man, you've spent two years on it, why didn't you spend three years on it and tighten up some of the bad things about it?'"

Townshend outlined further misgivings in a 1987 interview with *Rolling Stone*'s David Fricke. "One of the ironies of *Tommy* was that because of the Woodstock movie the 'See Me, Feel Me' chorus in the finale became a real anthem for the hippie dream, a theme for the gathering of the tribes. Yet the whole point of *Tommy* was that Utopia was not around the corner, that this explosion of positive youth energy was already being co-opted – in this case by a deaf dumb and blind 'guru'. Why is it that rock songwriters are not allowed to be ironic? Why is it that satire can only be comedic? Why can't rock satire be real satire, real irony? I know that a lot of people heard *Tommy*, listened to certain tracks and completely misread them. What people went for in *Tommy* was the celebration, not the denouement. The sad thing is I continue to live with the finale, not the bit in the middle. What was important at the time, and continues to be important, is that the human individual accepts the fact that he or she is capable of being spiritually swayed. And in order to make the best of that, they really have to listen to what's being said. It's no point being carried away by the uplift.

"I suppose the mistake I made in *Tommy* was instead of having the guts to take what Meher Baba said – which was 'Don't worry, be happy, leave the results to God' – and repeating that to people, I decided the people weren't capable of hearing that directly. They've got to have it served in this entertainment package. And I gave them *Tommy* instead, in which some of Meher Baba's wonderfully explicit truths were presented to them half-baked in lyric form and diluted as a result. In fact, if there was any warning in *Tommy*, it was 'Don't make any more records like that.'"

However, the ever contradictory Townshend ultimately conceded that the album was something special.[13] "*Tommy* was very arduously put together, and very clumsily put together. Yet it's got a grace that I just can't account for." He also admitted that he may not have been particularly easy to work with. "What other three musicians would have put up with all my bullshit in order to get this album out?" Pete said in 1969. "It's *my* apple, right. It's my whole trip, coming from Baba, and they just sat there, let it come out, and then leapt upon it and gave it an extra boot."

"There's this amazing letter I've got from a kid in Chicago," Townshend told *Sounds'* Penny Valentine in August, 1972. "We played

---

[13] Pete reviewed the original recording of *Tommy* in 2003 while preparing to remix the album. "When I heard these tracks again last year, for the first time in years," he told *Uncut's* Simon Goddard in 2004, "I thought, 'Fuck! This was a *band*, a really *good* band.' *Tommy* is probably Keith at the height of his studio powers and John, too, before he got into [impersonates frenetic bass scales] – all that. It was good, straightforward, powerful, innovative bass playing."

there and this kid came up and said, 'Hey Mr Townshend, I've got to tell you what happened when I first heard *Tommy*, I was like listening and Baba came to me . . . I became Tommy and ever since I've been in this amazing spiritual trance.' And he wrote this letter about how Baba came out of *Tommy* and how it was all planned and then how upset he's been when he'd found his friends weren't getting the same thing happening. So I thought, 'Fuck it, maybe one or two people have got that hit so it's worth doing for that reason.' But on the other hand at the same time it's working on a number of other levels – it's entertaining, you know.

While *Tommy* received plenty of praise, the rock opera made an even greater impact on the stage. The group discovered this when rehearsing their new live set at the Community Centre in Hanwell, west London. "We did one day's rehearsal, did the whole thing from start to finish and that was when we realised we had something cohesive and playable," Townshend told Chris Welch. "Keith and I went to a pub on the way back and sat there, both incredulous at how quickly it had come together. Roger had become something else and we discussed what would happen and how it would change everything. We knew we had something that was magic and that magic wasn't as clear on the album as it would have been in live performance.

"It made Roger a singer, it made Roger an icon, it made Roger like Jim Morrison or like Robert Plant, or like 'The Lead Singer'. It gave him the right to grow his hair and wear the tassel jacket and swing his mic around instead of just posing and looking angry and, like, 'Don't fuck with me,' which isn't who he is by any means, but it gave him a vehicle, it gave him a part that he could play."

Pete also revealed to Welch that Kit Lambert was "furious when he spent months capturing our dynamics on *Tommy* then we went out and played it six times better than we had in the studios."

Three dates in Detroit at the Grande Ballroom (the venue was now being managed by Tom Wright) kicked off The Who's tremendously successful US *Tommy* tour in early May 1969.[14] Townshend took the stage wearing conventional "work clothes", complete with Meher Baba button,

---

[14] On their arrival in the US, Pete and Bob Pridden dropped by Manny's Music store in New York for supplies. "Pete Townshend would come into the store and just take a guitar off the wall and shout, 'Pay you later, see ya!'" wrote Manny's owner Henry Goldrich in his 2007 book, *The Wall of Fame: New York City's Legendary Manny's Music*.

playing a Gibson SG.[15] Following openers such as 'Heaven And Hell' (written and sung by Entwistle), 'I Can't Explain' and a dynamic cover of Benny Spellman's 'Fortune Teller', The Who performed parts of *Tommy* before ending with numbers such as 'Summertime Blues', 'Substitute', 'Shakin' All Over', and 'Magic Bus'. Audiences were consistently blown away. "So strong was the new material," wrote Chris Charlesworth in 1984, "that Pete abandoned smashing his guitars on American stages as he had continued to do long after breaking the habit in England. Occasionally, when the mood took him, a Gibson SG bit the dust for old times' sake, as if to emphasise that these really were the same four who toured America with Herman's Hermits two years earlier."

During the first of a three night stand at New York's Fillmore East on May 16, a plain-clothes police officer took to the stage in an attempt to warn the crowd of a raging fire adjacent to the hall, which had already consumed a supermarket and a five storey apartment building. Before he could get the words out, Pete kicked the cop off the stage and ended up being charged with third degree assault.

Townshend described his onstage tendency to fly off the handle at a moment's notice to BBC interviewer Jeremy Paxman in 1977: "When I'm on the stage I'm not in control of myself at all. I don't even know who I am . . . I'm not this rational person that can sit here now and talk to you. If you walked onstage with a microphone in the middle of a concert, I'd probably come close to killing you. I have come close to killing people that walked onstage . . . A policeman came on when the bloody building at the Fillmore in New York was burning down and I kicked him in the balls and sent him off . . . I'm just not there. It's not like being possessed, it's just, I do my job and I know I have to get into a certain state of mind to do it."[16]

The Who's most successful American tour to date reached its conclusion on June 19 at the Fillmore West. "I will never forget that tour, the finale of *Tommy* never failed to mesmerise me along with the audience," Townshend wrote in 1977. "It always felt to me like a prayer, I always felt myself full of Meher Baba when we performed it."

---

[15] "The first time I started to use the Gibson SG model guitar is when I got fed up with Fenders," Pete told *Guitar Player*'s Michael Brooks in 1972. ". . . So I went to the manager and said I really need an alternative to this and he said I think you'd like the newest SG and I looked at it. I played it and it rang, it sang to me. . . ."

[16] Townshend was eventually fined $75 for this incident after a June court appearance in New York.

The Who took it relatively easy upon their return to British soil, performing 10 dates over a six-week period, most of which took place during the last week of July and the first week of August. On July 5, during two prestigious Pop Proms shows at the Royal Albert Hall, sharing the bill with Chuck Berry, some disorderly rockers in the crowd tried to disrupt proceedings by throwing sharpened pennies at the stage. The Who returned to the States in mid-August for two appearances: Bill Graham's Tanglewood Music Shed in Lenox, Massachusetts (sharing the bill with B.B. King and Jefferson Airplane) and the Woodstock Music and Arts, held on Max Yasgur's sprawling farm near Bethel, New York State.

After the month long US tour, Pete had not wanted to play any more shows in America for the foreseeable future. The Woodstock promoters, however, had other plans in store. "We needed one more key act," production coordinator John Morris recalled in 1989. "To get The Who for Woodstock, Frank [Barsalona, of Premier Talent, The Who's US agents] and I had Peter Townshend to dinner at Frank Barsalona's house. Frank's an insomniac and I was pretty good at staying awake in those days because I was almost as much of an insomniac. And we wore Peter down to the point where he agreed to do it. Finally. This is after him saying for hours and hours and hours, 'No, no, no. I'm not going to do it, I'm not going to do it,' because they didn't want to stay in the US that long. They wanted to get back to their families. Or he wanted to. . . . He was sitting in a corner and finally he said, 'Okay, all right. But it will have to be $15,000.' And I had to look him straight in the face at six o'clock in the morning and say, 'We only have $11,000 left. That's all that's left in the budget.' And I thought he was going to kill me, but he was just too tired. He just said, 'Oh, all right, if you let me go to bed. Whatever you say.'"

The Who's appearance was due to take place on Saturday, August 16, sandwiched between Sly & the Family Stone and Jefferson Airplane. Townshend felt at odds with Woodstock's 'peace and love' philosophy.

"All those hippies wandering about thinking the world was going to be different from that day," he recalled in 1982. "As a cynical English arsehole I walked through it all and felt like spitting on the lot of them and shaking them and trying to make them realise that nothing had changed and nothing was going to change. Not only that, what they thought was an alternative society was basically a field full of six foot deep mud and laced with LSD. If that was the world they wanted to live in, then fuck the lot of them."

"My impressions of [the festival] were quite bad," he told the *San Diego*

Union's George Varga in 1989. "A lot of mud, polluted water, polluted drugs. A moment of pleasure at seeing a picture of my guru, Meher Baba, up on a telephone pole, and then a horrifying scene where a guy high on acid shimmied up the pole, touched the picture, screamed, 'It's on fire,' fell and broke his back on an ambulance below. A terrible irony . . ."

"That was the worst gig we ever played," Roger Daltrey told the *New Yorker*. "We waited in a field of mud for 14 hours, sitting on some boards, doing nothing, and doing nothing is the most exhausting thing in the world."

The notoriously short Townshend fuse was burning quickly. "I immediately got into an incredible state and rejected everyone," he later recalled. "And I was telling really nice people like Richie Havens to fuck off and things like that."

Backstage, matters weren't improved when, thanks to all the liquids being spiked with acid, the band members had to endure tripping against their will. When The Who took the stage at around 3.30 a.m. on Sunday, they were none too happy about the ridiculously long delay they'd endured (Karen and baby Emma Townshend were waiting in a hotel room in nearby Liberty) and not particularly enamoured of the idea of playing in front of the estimated 500,000 people in attendance. "We were more arrogant than nervous before we went on," Pete told Dave Marsh.

The Who began their set in the dark with 'Heaven And Hell' and 'I Can't Explain' before heading into *Tommy*. Just after the group finished playing 'Pinball Wizard' political activist Abbie Hoffman decided to make his grand entrance. "I remember standing on the stage," Woodstock photographer Henry Diltz recalled in 1989, "and Abbie Hoffman suddenly ran out and grabbed the microphone and said, "Remember John Sinclair and the guy's in prison for smoking pot," or something like that . . . suddenly Peter Townshend was standing there with his guitar and I saw him raise it up, kind of holding it over his shoulder, and walk up behind Abbie Hoffman and just go *boink!* right in the back of the neck. It was almost like a bayonet thrust . . . one quick little jab right in the back of Abbie Hoffman – who fell down, I remember. It looked like a fatal blow. He was really pissed at this guy taking over the microphone."

Townshend's swat sent Hoffman sprawling into the photographers' pit, a good 10-foot drop. "Hoffman screamed unheard curses into the gale of the music," Marsh wrote in *Before I Get Old*, "then ran over a hill and out of sight." While tuning his guitar, an incensed Townshend issued a brief warning to the audience: "The next fucking person who walks across this stage is going to get fucking killed!" The audience seemed initially amused at this, leading Pete to follow with, "You can laugh. I mean it!" No further demonstration was needed to show how far removed The Who were from the peace and love vibe. "The Who sliced through the flower power like a chain saw in a daisy garden," wrote *Time* magazine's Jay Cocks in 1979, and "played with an intensity that took the show away from such Mallomar bands as the Jefferson Airplane."

"What Abbie was saying was politically correct in many ways," Townshend wrote in his essay that accompanied The Who's 1994 boxed set, *Thirty Years Of Maximum R&B*. "The people at Woodstock really were a bunch of hypocrites claiming a cosmic revolution simply because they took over a field, broke down some fences, imbibed bad acid and then tried to run out without paying the band. All while [ex-MC5 manager and Hoffman crony] John Sinclair rotted in jail after a trumped-up drug bust. My response was reflexive rather than considered. Later I realised his humiliation on that occasion was fatal to his political credibility."

The Who's Woodstock appearance took a turn for the better at sunrise.

"*Tommy* wasn't getting to anyone," Townshend recalled in 1982. "By this time I was just about awake, we were just listening to the music when all of a sudden, bang! The fucking sun comes up! It was just incredible. I really felt we didn't deserve it, in a way. We put out such bad vibes . . . and as we finished it was daytime. We walked off, got in the car, and went back to the hotel. It was fucking fantastic."[17]

On their return to England, The Who appeared in front of 200,000 at the second Isle of Wight Festival, headlining the afternoon of August 30 with a powerful sound system which carried a warning to spectators to keep 15 feet away from the speakers.

"The Who made their usual spectacular entrance – this time by helicopter," reported the *NME*'s Richard Green. "All of us backstage got covered in all sorts of flying muck, and *NME*'s intrepid photographer, Stuart Richman, was almost decapitated by a sheet of hardboard that suddenly took flight! The group went straight onstage to be greeted by a roaring welcome. The first number, 'I Can't Explain' [sic – actually it was

---

[17] However, Townshend continued to view The Who's Woodstock set as subpar and in 1994, he reportedly blocked MCA's attempt to release a 25th anniversary CD of the band's entire Woodstock set.

'Heaven And Hell'] began. Roger's long-fringed jacket was open revealing a bare torso; Pete Townshend's outfit consisted of a white boiler suit ["I used to go on wearing a boiler suit and Dr Martens in defiance of fashion," Townshend told the *NME* in 1980]; John Entwistle maintained a serious expression and Keith Moon had a look on his face as though he was suffering the ultimate torture. 'Young Man Blues', which was written [by] Mose Allison, began quietly and became a roar-up. Then came the inevitable long selection from *Tommy* – very clever and intricate, but it tended to go on a bit. Eddie Cochran's 'Summertime Blues' was great, as was 'My Generation'. 'Shakin' All Over' was obviously dedicated to the bird I was with, as she didn't stop shivering all weekend.

"I was very glad to have seen The Who – they were right on form and must be rated as one of the world's best groups. Their loud sound does not detract from their performance, which is as visually exciting as it is musically together."

The Who were probably the act that stole the entire festival despite Bob Dylan making his first stage appearance in several years the following evening. "It was a great concert for us because we felt so in control of the whole situation," Townshend told Barnes. "We were able to just come in, do it and not need to know anything about what was going on. In other words, we didn't spend time at the festival getting into the vibrations, didn't stay to see Bob Dylan, didn't care what was going on. We knew that the stage act we had, with *Tommy* in it, would work under any circumstances because it had worked many times on tour."

"Pete was a powerhouse to listen to and watch," Barnes wrote in 1982. "Jumping, leaping, twisting, swerving, swinging his arm like a rotor, punishing his guitar and forcing everything he could out of it."

A month later, following short visits to Scotland[18] and Amsterdam, The Who were back in North America on a 30-date tour with opening acts including The Kinks and The James Gang. The tour featured a six-night stand at New York City's Fillmore East, where Pete met Leonard Bernstein backstage. "He shook me and said, 'Do you know what you've done?!'" Townshend recalled in 1994. "Of course, what he was talking about was that I was going the next step in what he had done with *West Side Story*, which was creating a popular song cycle, a musical that was really rooted in street culture."

---

[18] During which, three-quarters of the group, barring Entwistle, attended the screening of Richard Stanley's *Lone Ranger* for the Edinburgh Film Festival.

By December, The Who could look back on 1969 as the year that had finally propelled them to rock superstardom. "[*Tommy*] not only sold in vast numbers but also put The Who in the position where they could negotiate huge advances on the renewal of their US and other overseas contracts," wrote George Tremlett. "This they did, and by the stroke of a pen they each became dollar millionaires . . . With *Tommy*, The Who arrived. They never lost money after that."

While the group's financial situation changed things overnight, Townshend sought to put his sudden wealth to good use. As well as generously contributing to various charities, he helped keep afloat the Meher Baba Information Centre, the first of which was located at his old flat on Wardour Street. About 70 people had attended the centre's opening in August 1968, including Baba's youngest brother, Adi, his wife, Frenee, and Miss Delia DeLeon. "[Delia] is an actress who is now in her seventies, who met Baba when he looked like the most exciting thing to hit Hollywood," Townshend wrote in 1970. "She has the heart of a young girl, and Baba has said that she is very spiritually advanced. Her flippancy and impetuosity are more likenable to a mischievous child than an illusion-wise worker for the Avatar.

About a year later, Townshend's desire to get rid of the lease on the flat necessitated a hunt for a new site for the Baba centre. Karen allowed the group the use of her old flat in Eccleston Square and the move took place in December 1969. "It's cool and fairly light for a basement," Townshend wrote in describing the new headquarters, "and it's small. A hundred people have been known to squeeze in there. Only about 20 of them got served with tea. The centre is run and financed by a committee which includes myself. The committee sees to it that it is open a couple of days a week, and keeps the bills paid and the library full. It also drinks a lot of tea."

A hung-over Townshend spent New Year's Day morning 1970 at his Twickenham home being interviewed by *Melody Maker*'s Chris Welch over breakfast. *Tommy* had proved a huge critical and commercial success, but there was a danger that its success might become marred by overkill.

"So much has been written, said and done about it, that it is beginning to be a pain in everybody's arse . . ." Townshend opined to Welch. "There are still people who want to hear about it in Europe, but we definitely won't exploit it any further than that and the film we are making which is based on the ideas that went into *Tommy*." Pete explained that the contents of the film were still up in the air. "The question is – what is the film going to be about, now that the album has been milked to death already?"

Townshend also discussed plans for a new Who project. "I've got ideas for one. But a lot of my ideas will be channelled into the film. We'd like to do an album of songs next – other people's songs. Then there are plans for a 'live' album. Bob [Pridden], our roadie, has been recording us on gigs . . . and he has been getting some incredible results. A lull is inevitable. There will be a quiet period for the group as far as the public will be concerned. But the success we have had will make us work harder. We will be taking our stage show to a higher standard of professionalism. We'll use more dynamics and not just put on two hours of noise."

Pete also promised that "there is a single coming. We're going to record it next week and probably have it out in January." The record in question, 'The Seeker', recorded on 19 January at IBC studios and self-produced by the group, reached number 19 in Britain and 44 in America.

"I wrote it when I was drunk in Florida," Pete explained to *Rolling Stone* that May. "Quite loosely, 'The Seeker' was just a thing about what I call Divine Desperation, or just Desperation. And what it does to people."

Conspicuously absent in the producer's role was Kit Lambert. As the year progressed, it became apparent that Townshend and Lambert's relationship was cooling considerably. A key factor revolved around the proposed *Tommy* movie, the content and viability for which the pair reached stalemate over.

Despite his growing distance from The Who, Lambert achieved his ambition of taking the rock opera into the most important opera houses of Europe. "The idea was an adaptation of [Kit's] original intention to launch *Tommy* by having it performed at the opera houses in Moscow, first, then New York," wrote Andrew Motion in 1987. "This scheme had fallen through because the director of the Metropolitan Opera House in New York, Rudolph Bing, could not easily be convinced of *Tommy*'s merits. Once it had been performed and acclaimed at the Coliseum in London, other cities followed suit, and the band eventually performed in opera houses in Paris [the Champs-Elysees Theatre], Copenhagen [Det Kunglige Teater], Cologne, Hamburg, Berlin [each at the cities' Stadt Opera House], Amsterdam [Concertgebouw] . . . It was a triumph of organisation and a graphic illustration of the distance that the [Who] – and rock'and'roll – had travelled since its beginnings."

Pete soon grew tired of the amount of VIPs present at these upper class establishments. "Thousands and thousands of kids were coming to see us and then only about a hundredth of the kids who wanted to see us could," Townshend told *Rolling Stone*. "And we'd go in and play and like the first 20 rows would be Polydor people. Or Prince Rainier and his royal family and honestly it was such a bad scene. We were going to play the opera houses in Vienna, Moscow and the New York Metropolitan, but I just thought that was the biggest hype bullshit I'd ever heard of. We blew it out . . ." until June, when The Who actually played two shows at the venue – America's largest classical music organisation.

"The thing I didn't dig about it is that we didn't play big enough places. The opera houses are very small. There are 1,500 people usually and you could see every face. But you can't win them over. Say there's an old guy in a bow tie out there, he's come up to write a review in some opera paper or some serious music paper and most of the night he sits there with his fingers in his ears. It's just impossible to work when someone's doing that." Keith Moon later told *Rolling Stone*'s Jerry Hopkins that performing in front of such audiences was ". . . rather like playing to an oil painting."

In February (Baba's birth month), a tribute album entitled *Happy Birthday* was released. "Unaccustomed as I am to making my affection, devotion, love, interest, obsession or whatever you like to call it KNOWN to someone like Baba – who is now after all in the abstract, R.I.P. – the way I know best is music," Townshend told *Sounds*' Penny Valentine in 1972. "And also I do feel the need to display my affection and commitment to Baba."

Happy Birthday ". . . emerged from the spirited group of young people who I met when I first came to Richmond," Townshend recalled in the essay which accompanied his limited edition boxed set *Avatar* in 1999. "This was a group who seemed to me to gather around Michael McInnerney and his then wife Katie . . . At the time they lived in part of a beautiful Victorian villa called Willoughby House situated very near Richmond Bridge. There was a large garden and on warm summer days a motley gathering was usual . . . Not everyone that was attracted to the teachings of Meher Baba was artistic, but enough were to inspire me to suggest that we all get together to make a record."

The album featured a 28-page book containing "poems, religious essays, photo and newspaper collages ['All Britain Duped by Sham Messiah' proclaimed a 1932 headline] and a couple of paintings by Mike McInnerney," *Rolling Stone* reported. "Like the record, the book radiates friendliness and warmth. Even more than the record, it reflects the fact that Meher Baba excluded no one: many different human types are recognisable among the contributors, stupid and smart, complicated and direct."

A limited edition of 2,500, *Happy Birthday* was available only from the Universal Spiritual League in London and from Rick Chapman's Meher Baba Information office in Berkeley, California, with proceeds benefiting the Baba Foundation. The songs included Pete's demo version of 'The Seeker' ("which I still dig more than the version done by The Who," he confessed), a poem by Maud Kennedy set to song entitled 'Content', and 'Day Of Silence'. The latter two were described by *Rolling Stone* as "peaceful ballads with acoustic guitar and buzzing mandolin." "I wrote 'Day Of Silence' on July 10," Townshend later explained, "which is the day that followers of Baba choose to spend without speaking, they communicate by using pencil and paper. I wrote the lyrics the day after so I wouldn't break my silence."[19]

Townshend's other contributions were 'Mary Jane', a catchy, banjo-led farewell to marijuana in response to Baba's anti-drug stance, 'The Love Man', and the year-old demo of Cole Porter's 'Begin The Beguine'. Townshend also played on an excellent Ronnie Lane song entitled 'Evolution'.[20] Two strange songs, the Ron Geesin instrumental 'With A Smile Up His Nose They Entered'[21] and the very weird spoken-word 'Meditation' by Mike da Costa rounded out the album. *Rolling Stone* described the latter as "a poetic freakout . . . which will surprise anyone who has never tried to meditate . . . It's a track that can strike you as comic or painful, or both."

Having contemplated issuing a live album for some time, virtually every show from The Who's 30-date US tour the previous autumn, plus five

---

[19] *The Who Concert File* pointed out that the following year The Who played Dunstable Civic Hall on July 10, "a clear case of silence breaking!"

[20] *Evolution* was a different arrangement of The Faces' 'The Stone'.

[21] Geesin, a Scottish composer and musician, worked mostly with film music. He and his friend, Pink Floyd bassist Roger Waters, scored a film version of Anthony Smith's 1968 book *The Body* in 1970. 'With A Smile Up His Nose They Entered' was written for Floyd drummer Nick Mason's wife, Lindy. "She was quite a good flautist – but not quite good enough to actually get around it," Geesin told Floyd biographer Nicholas Shaffner. "So then I got a professional to record it on Pete's album." Andy Neill and Matt Kent documented in *Anyway Anyhow Anywhere* that Geesin "opened three unpublicised university shows for The Who" in October 1971. "He did two test gigs with us, and to put it mildly, he wiped the floor with The Who – just him and his bits of paper and his piano playing," Townshend told *Zigzag*. "He's so far ahead of his time as a performer that people just can't pick up on it."

additional English dates in December, had been recorded but none of the results had proved totally satisfactory. Following the American dates, Townshend had intended to review the tapes to assemble a live compilation, but, "Suddenly someone realises there are 240 hours of tape to be listened to," he told *Rolling Stone*. "So I said, 'Well, fuck that, I'm not gonna sit through and listen,' you'd get brainwashed, let's face it! So we just fucking scrapped the lot, and to reduce the risk of pirating we put the lot on a bonfire and just watched it all go and we said, 'Right, let's get an eight-track.'"

The Who's only two live dates in February were recorded on Pye's eight-track mobile recording unit with the specific intention of the results being issued as a live album. Both the venues were small (the university refectory at Leeds held 1,500, while Hull City Hall held 1,800) and the band were fresh, coming off a two-week break since their European opera house tour, although Townshend, in an interview on the day of the Leeds show, said they were "exhausted physically and mentally." The Valentine's Day show at Leeds, in particular, found The Who in top form. The Who's set still featured *Tommy* in its entirety preceded by a mixture of the group's most successful singles and numbers that worked well live: 'Heaven And Hell', 'Fortune Teller', 'Tattoo', 'Young Man Blues', 'Summertime Blues', and 'Shakin' All Over'.

A few months later, Townshend commented that "[Leeds] just happened to be a good show and it just happened to be like one of the greatest audiences we've ever played to in our whole career, just by chance. They were incredible and although you can't hear a lot of kind of shouting and screaming in the background, they're civilised but they're crazy . . . it's a good atmosphere."

The Hull gig the following night featured a set list identical to that played at Leeds but the general consensus was that the show simply did not measure up to the previous night's pyrotechnics which were released in truncated form as *Live At Leeds*. In 1995, MCA (Polydor in the UK) issued an expanded version – and in 2001, virtually the whole concert – on CD.

Jon Astley, who remixed and remastered the original tapes for both releases, later told Who fanzine *Generations*, "Pete wanted me to listen to Hull but it's really not as good a show."[22] Technically, the recording of

---

[22] It turned out that the decision as to which show would make the cut was made easier when it was discovered that parts of the bass track during the Hull gig did not record due to a faulty microphone.

both shows was flawed as the high end on Townshend's guitar often distorted. Pete, who mixed *Live At Leeds* in his home studio, was not impressed with Pye's unit nor their engineers. "They did a terrible job on the recording," he complained to *Rolling Stone*. "They fucked it up incredibly . . . they got crackles all the way through, horrible crackles. But I'm just going to put it out anyway." (The record labels for *Live At Leeds* carried the information "Crackling Noises OK – Do Not Correct!")

Released in May, *Live At Leeds* reached a most satisfactory number four in the US, while attaining one notch higher in Britain. The album's plain brown cover – intended to look like a bootleg – doubled as a folder complete with a replica of the original 1964 Maximum R&B Marquee poster and facsimiles of other assorted pieces of Who paperwork from the early years.

"That was just a brilliant idea by some designer who used to work at Track at the time, always coming up with nutty album sleeves," Townshend told *Trouser Press* in 1980. "The first super-controversial album sleeve was the one with Lennon and Yoko naked on the front [*Two Virgins*], and Track distributed that; and then they brought out the Hendrix one [*Electric Ladyland*] with all the naked birds on the front, and they were really into album covers and we weren't. We didn't really give a shit, despite the resident art school member."

The record received a great deal of praise, becoming commonly regarded as one of the finest live representations ever of a rock band. In his *New York Times* review, Nik Cohn called *Leeds* "the definitive hard-rock holocaust. It is the best live rock album ever made."

"*Live At Leeds* was specifically designed to prick the pomposity of *Tommy*," Chris Charlesworth wrote in 1983, "and display instead The Who's original tough edge, a side of the band that had become submerged amid the grandiloquence of the [rock] opera. Many newer fans could be excused for assuming The Who to be art rock dilettantes but *Live At Leeds* put matters back into perspective. It was gut-wrenching hard rock from start to finish, a timely reminder that The Who were first and foremost rockers at heart."

Live At Leeds was the first Who recording that managed to come close to replicating the power and volume of their live performance. As Townshend commented, "The first thing that struck me on hearing it was how much you need to see The Who live." It also showcased The Who's unique onstage chemistry in several examples of mid-song improvisation; the 14-minute extension of 'My Generation', which included a reprise of sections from *Tommy* is a prime example. "I still feel that the 'Sparks' section that we did onstage in *Live At Leeds* gets close to what's possible for that classical rock thing," Townshend said in 1974. "I always imagine a classical conductor with his hair flying. The Who, and Keith especially, are capable of those classical flourishes – the expressive Wagnerian dynamics stuff."

The heavily distorted, full-throttle style of guitar work featured in *Live At Leeds* is viewed by some as the foundation of the heavy metal genre, an opinion which particularly horrified Townshend, who later told *Guitar Player* that he'd trade "150 Def Leppards for one R.E.M."

"The Who are not Led Zeppelin and we're not Deep Purple and we weren't responsible for heavy metal but a lot of people kind of draw that kind of line from *Live At Leeds* onwards," he told Simon Goddard in 2004. "I used to see Ritchie Blackmore carrying his guitar up and down my street when I was 14 or 15. *He* invented heavy metal. I didn't. He was doing it years before us and probably invented power chords as well. So I dunno why he's such a sullen, dark, evil motherfucker . . . We did *Tommy* on the road all over the world, we did *Live At Leeds* and then it was, 'Oh, The Who have invented heavy metal.' And then we were tied into this fucking thing of every show having to be more of a virtuoso explosion of energy than the one before. And after that, I believe The Who were just ruined."

CHAPTER SIX

1970–1971

"CHANGE. Is it really possible to change anything with music, or to even ease society into a position where what they listen to can change what they feel? Rock is capable of doing amazing things . . . The only time I am spurred to action is when I feel that I can change the world through Rock, via The Who, via music. We want to change people by taking them UP."

– Pete Townshend, 1971

"For me, what's important about Lifehouse *is . . . the whole business, the whole process, the whole story, is about what makes this whole thing about pop music, rock music and a rock band, different from the music that went before, different from the art that went before, different from popular art of today . . . what makes it stand out and, in fact, what makes it the vertebrae of modern life . . ."*

– Pete Townshend, 1999

FOLLOWING the Yorkshire gigs in February 1970, The Who broke from playing live shows for nearly two months and tried reworking their live set. "We're doing rehearsals and recordings to get some new numbers into the stage act and record them for a new album at the same time," Townshend told *Rolling Stone* in April. "We'll probably keep some of our numbers from *Tommy* like 'Pinball Wizard' and stuff like that. We're doing some shows in England during this period, the next couple of months, to try it all out."

They also commenced recording what was planned as the next Who album in Townshend's 8-track studio, located in his garage in Twickenham. At one point, Pete even had curtains hung across the middle of the studio, "for when Keith came over and played, because Keith liked to be behind curtains as if he was appearing onstage," Jon Astley recalls. Tracks recorded there included a John Entwistle song, 'Postcard', 'Now I'm A Farmer' (which Pete had written roughly two years earlier) and some of his newest compositions, 'I Don't Even Know Myself', 'Water' (" 'Water' is one of the heaviest things The Who have ever done," Townshend said in October. "It's relaxed and fantastically solid, not screaming and wailing guitars.") and 'Naked Eye', the coda for which came out of the band's onstage jams.

The Who re-took the stage on April 18 at Leicester University in a continuing trend of playing British colleges. However, the show, before an audience of about 1,600, soon turned ugly. "There were a load of Hell's Angels idiot-dancing all over everyone," Townshend recounted. "It got to the point where they were causing such uproar we had to stop playing *Tommy*. It wasn't worth it, so to give the rest of the crowd some enjoyment we went into 'Shakin' All Over'. The Angels tried to get onstage and one threw a bottle of Newcastle Brown which hit me in the head." Pete left the stage bleeding and received eight stitches at a local hospital.

"I think that if I had not been quite so pissed and quite so bloody," he told *Zigzag* in 1971, "I would have got stuck in a lot further and probably got a lot more badly hurt. Because I got hit on the head, and it bled a lot, I thought I'd better get to a hospital, but I was really wild; I broke my guitar across some geezer's collarbone but it didn't seem to do much to him – he had a ring in his nose, I remember."

The Who resumed their gigging itinerary on April 25 at Nottingham, travelling to Dunstable, Exeter, Sheffield, Kent, Manchester and Lancaster before ending on May 16 at York. On June 7, the year's only US tour – a four week affair – began with two performances at New York's Metropolitan Opera House.[1] The Met's Opera Company Director, Rudolph Bing, was persuaded to put aside his initial reservations and accept The Who's booking after he listened to the *Tommy* album and was suitably impressed. As Richard Barnes pointed out in *Maximum R&B*, "It must have been the first time that the Metropolitan Opera House had the smell of pot smoke drifting around its gold chandeliers."

---

[1] "[Kit Lambert's] proudest moment, he liked to boast, was when in 1970 *Tommy* became the first work of contemporary popular music to be performed to a capacity audience in the Metropolitan Opera House, New York," wrote Tony Palmer in Lambert's 1981 obituary, published in *The Times*. "His father would have savoured the occasion."

The matinee show received a particularly flattering appraisal from an unlikely source – *Life* magazine: "Rock music may have reached its all-time peak with the recent performance at the Metropolitan Opera of *Tommy*, The Who's opera about a deaf, dumb and blind pinball wizard who becomes a pop hero and martyr. A great leap across the gaps of generation, class and culture, the performance installed rock as a maturely rounded art in the shrine of the great European classics. It demonstrated the willingness of the Establishment in its most uptight organisation to cooperate with the youth culture in its most drastic and uncompromising medium. Best of all, it afforded The Who – a great musical organisation long in coming to fame – the opportunity to do brilliantly what no other rock group ever dreamed of doing.

"From the moment the boys walked onstage, it was obvious they were determined to give their greatest performance. Flashing their delightfully tawdry show tricks, they worked the Met as if it were a grind house in Yorkshire . . . Pete Townshend, a gawky, goony airplane mechanic in a white coverall, pogoed across the stage like Bugs Bunny riding an electric broom . . . Though the boys used every trick in the book to keep the crowd riveted on them, there was no gimmickry in their music. Of all rock groups, The Who has delved the deepest into the rock essence. They have reached now a level of accomplishment in their idiom directly comparable to the attainments of jazz musicians in theirs. Every song is grasped with authority, charged with energy, performed with flawless ensemble and fascinating solo work. It was just these gifts that forged the 20-odd numbers of *Tommy* into a compelling art work. They have been even more impressively evidenced by The Who's recent concerts, of which *Tommy* is the principal part . . .

"The instant they hit the final chord, the entire audience, thousands of freaks in fringes and tie-dyes, leaped to its feet in a stunning ovation. Townshend stammered a few words of gratitude, Moon and Entwistle engaged in a brief water battle, then the whole group jumped into a cycle of scorching encores. Whipped half-dead from this two-and-a-quarter-hour performance, as well as an equally long matinee, Pete Townshend gathered his last energies to improvise an elaborate and moving coda, based on melodies from *Tommy*. As the audience sat spellbound, the concert resolved itself as a huge symphonic fantasia. When the gold curtain came looping down and the crystal chandeliers glimmered into light, 4,000 people had become one gargantuan child, stamping and chanting, 'More! More! More!' "

The audience's demands for more still poured forth even after the day's second show. "We did two shows each two-and-a-half hours long," Pete told *Trouser Press* in 1980. "That's the longest I've ever played; they were pretty close together and it was five hours of solid rock, not Grateful Dead stuff but heavy, exhausting stuff. We never did encores anyway, and I was told that we didn't have to do an encore if we didn't want to, but I should at least go on and thank the audience for their 15 minutes of spontaneous applause. Of course, their 15 minutes of spontaneous applause was about as spontaneous as an orgasm. It was extremely worked-on . . . I went to speak and someone threw a can of Coke at me."

This prompted Townshend to throw the mike stand into the crowd and bark, "After two fucking hours, boo to you too!"

Despite the Met posters touting the New York gig as the opera's last run-through and Pete's recent comments in *Rolling Stone* to the contrary, The Who played *Tommy* at the next stop – two shows at the Mammoth Gardens in Denver, Colorado – and onwards throughout the rest of the tour. An experience during his stay in Denver gave Townshend the initial inspiration for a new song.

"I had lost my temper with a groupie, who on my arrival presented me with a bottle of C.C. [Courvoisier Cognac] and maybe even herself [I should be so lucky]," he recalled in 1977. "But I threw her out. I got a little worried that that wasn't the way to do things and wrote the above prayer [*Baba – when my fist clenches . . . crack it open*] which I later used in the bridge of *Behind Blue Eyes* . . . later that night in the same hotel, I was awakened by a small group of White Panthers who had come to violently avenge Abbie Hoffman, whom I threw offstage at Woodstock. I came very, very close to getting my head cracked open when I lost my temper with them [they were quite small people], then a giant emerged from the shadows in the hallway. He was big, black, hated me and he called me chicken shit. Such is life that I ran for it."

"After I got into San Francisco and had comfortably settled into the hotel," Pete wrote in a 1970 *Rolling Stone* article, "the first person I met to cheer me up was John Sebastian. With his lady, they sparkled through the coffee shop, Mr And Mrs Tie Dye. They came to both shows in Berkeley and tie dyed a boiler suit for me . . . The show at Berkeley that night [16 June] was the best we did in the States that tour. The sound was great, if a little loud for such a small place, and the crowd just super-aware and alive . . . After the show, I met a lot of Baba-friends . . . They were cool, and it goes without saying that they allowed me my pop star exhilaration that night as Keith and I and the gang destroyed what was left of our minds and bodies and hotel rooms.

"In the morning I visited Murshida [Ivy Duce, leader of San Francisco-based Baba group, Sufism Reoriented]. Her presence always astonishes me, it's easy to tell just how much high level work Baba is doing through her. Her eyes are calm and tired, but her life frantic and ordered. We talked about her work and my desire to make a film, of the special *Happy Birthday* record/magazine we had made in London to celebrate Baba's birthday. Murshida had not taken to it with unqualified praise to say the least. I think she forgave me and my pals in the end for allowing our egos to breathe using Baba's name as an umbrella. He is so much like a father, like a friend, that it's easy to forget that he is also God Almighty. Being with Murshida reminded me of the fact, it always does. Next day Rick [Chapman] called me and took me in his '60 Continental into the 30-mile queue into Berkeley from S.F. There was a bus strike, I think.

"First stop was a house called Meherstan which is the "light" centre for young Berkeley Baba lovers . . . I talked a bit about *Tommy*, how it had all come about. I compared their centre to our own in London, and we talked pretty formally about life with Baba in general. I talked about dope and my [1967 STP] trip, why and how I had stopped using it and watched knowing smiles from young people flash as I spoke of the new high that I was getting from being with Baba . . . After Meherstan we went to the home of Robert Dreyfuss, the guy Baba told to tell the West about dope, and I met several Baba lovers of the 20-year-oldish variety who seemed obsessed with chiropractry and small Indian cigarettes rolled out of a single tobacco leaf called Beedies, that smell just like dope."

Pete left the following morning to catch up with The Who in Texas where the tour continued through Dallas and Houston, before The Who's first performance in Memphis. When leaving the city on board an Eastern Airlines airplane, an innocent remark from Townshend to Peter Rudge, The Who's US tour manager about their record "going a bomb" led to unexpected consequences when a passing stewardess overheard the remark and thought Pete was talking about a bomb on the plane. She informed the pilot who radioed the control tower and taxied the plane to a secluded part of the airport where all 69 passengers were taken off and searched along with their luggage by police. Nearly an hour and a half later the plane left but Townshend and Rudge were detained to be questioned by police and FBI representatives.[2] They finally arrived in Atlanta at 10.30 p.m., only to find that the equipment truck had suffered a delay en route. The show finally started around midnight, nearly four hours late.

The James Gang – who opened for The Who in Pittsburgh on the previous American tour – were support act on several shows during the tour. Townshend was duly impressed with their guitarist, Joe Walsh and the two developed a friendship. "[The James Gang] got thrown on a Who show as the opening act," Walsh told Mark Brown of the *Rocky Mountain News* in 2006. "The Who were premiering *Tommy*. It just happened that Pete came early that day and stood by the side of the stage and watched the show . . . We've always been on the same wavelength . . . After that, he kinda took me under his wing, and that's really where I learned my style of how to sing and play."

"Joe Walsh is definitely one of the best guitarists in rock that I've come across," Pete wrote later that year, adding that "[Walsh's] playing makes my neck tingle like only Jimi Hendrix has affected it before."

With the success of *Tommy*, *Live At Leeds*, and The Who's legendary live performances, Townshend's confidence in mid-1970 was at an all-time high.

"As well as being a major milestone for The Who, *Tommy* was also very much Pete Townshend's own personal achievement," George Tremlett assessed five years on, "it was recognition of this which confirmed his reputation as a creative musician and brought him to the very forefront of rock music, not only in Britain but internationally. Like Bob Dylan and John Lennon, he was mentally and intellectually prepared for it – a tough, determined, ambitious, even ruthless person on the surface, but articulate and idealistic, possessing a conscience, intensely political, well-read, classically aware, and content in his private life."

However, Townshend was also aware that he was responsible for continuing The Who's momentum. "Until we made *Tommy* we had largely

---

[2] John Entwistle's account of the incident, given to George Tremlett in his 1975 book *The Who* and to Andy Neill & Matt Kent in 2002's *Anyway Anyhow Anywhere*, is somewhat different. "The Who were waiting at the airport for a plane at a time when hijackings were becoming frequent," Tremlett described. "An announcement was broadcast over the public address system that the plane would be delayed, and the loudspeaker nearby started to make a humming noise. As a gag, Townshend dropped to his knees in front of the speaker and said with mock tears: 'OK . . . OK . . . Turn it off . . . I confess . . . I'll tell you where I put the bomb.' A passing stewardess thought this was a real hi-jacker – and at once the airport was sealed off, the plane was cancelled and Pete was hauled away for two hours' questioning by the F.B.I."

been our own bosses," he said in 1974. "Suddenly all that changed – for the first time in our lives we were really successful, really taken over by the audience, and we had to do as we were told. America, the great consumer nation, told us, 'There are 50 million kids over here that want to see you perform. What are you going to do about it – stay in Twickenham and work on your next album, or come on over here and perform?' So we went on over and got involved in the standing ovations and the inter-views, the 19-page *Rolling Stone* article, the presentations of the Gold Albums, all that. It took two years to work on anything new."

In the latter half of 1970, Pete began a monthly *Melody Maker* column entitled The Pete Townshend Page which ran for nine months. The column, which often displayed his refreshing humility, also became a veritable posting of ideas which were whirling around inside Townshend's head, some of which were soon to become the next major project intended for The Who. "I went to pick up his columns on two or three occasions," *Melody Maker*'s Chris Charlesworth recalls, "and each time I'd be invited in for a cup of tea or coffee. The house was very lived-in, a bit untidy and plenty of activity, just a scene of happy domesticity. I do remember his daughter was only quite little then. Pete had a little studio upstairs, rather cramped, and I would go up there with him. He'd always have finished his column, typed out on a typewriter, only about 1,500 words or so, and they were never edited, not that I knew of anyway. I don't think he overwrote but even if he did I suspect that [*Melody Maker*] editor, Ray Coleman, would have been unwilling to cut Pete's text."

In the first instalment, printed in the August 22 issue of the paper, Townshend explained, "I'm beginning my first page of this bulky journal in particularly strange surroundings. On holiday I am, far away from the sounds of London's traffic and Keith Moon on an island in the Blackwater Estuary called Osea. The most exciting thing about Osea Island is probably the causeway that you have to drive over to reach it. It's over a mile long and is just about revealed for a few hours each low tide for the milkman and postman to make a mad dash across, make their rounds and get back again. As you drive over, the sea splashes over the front of the car and you feel a bit like a sea captain at the bridge as starfish and crabs come hurtling through the windows. I'm hoping that the messenger who comes all the way from *Melody Maker* to collect this trivia doesn't throttle me when he realises he'll have to spend 12 hours looking at a 10 acre caravan site before he can get back home again . . ."

Despite the levity of the column, Townshend was merely limbering up prior to conveying his latest ideas. With the recent success of *Tommy*, he had witnessed firsthand the power of rock music and his faith in the medium was boundless. "Rock," Pete wrote, "follows with alarming accuracy the moods and whims, the ups and downs of its listening age group. It REFLECTS, like a rather dusty mirror, the changes that are going on, many of which escape the conscious minds of even the men who write the music." However, ". . . whatever rock causes or excites in men, it is only catalysing emotions and actions around what is already in them."

"[Rock] can face up to trouble without giving a hint that it really is affected," he commented in early 1971, "and exhibits carefree attitudes on the surface, or maybe even deep down inside, at the same time it is CHANGING things. Usually for the better, unlike most political change."

Townshend's observations regarding the power of rock and its effect on an audience (and vice versa) lay at the root of his next project. He spent the next few months gathering his thoughts and ideas as he pondered how to execute them.

"From the cab of Maxine the Motor Home I begin this month's essay," Pete wrote in the September instalment of his monthly column. "Maxine is a large and lovely meat wagon with blood red striping. She comes from the US of A and is what we British would call a motor caravan.[3] I bought the thing to ride in at the Isle of Wight [Festival]. You know, ask in the other groups for tea and cakes . . .

The Who were scheduled to co-headline the third Isle Of Wight festival, with the Doors, on August 29. "When we first arrived backstage at the IOW there was a good, low class mood in the air. It was easy though to detect that it would have little to do with what was going on out in the audience. Before we left our cosy hotel the barmaid had noticed Keith's white clothes and said, 'You're not going to wear those nice clean things OUT THERE are you?' As though he was off into battle. The press had ruined a lot of people's potential happy weekend by exaggerating reports of water shortage and security trouble . . . I read the papers too and got nervous and we didn't take the baby. When I got there I realised what a fool I was. This wasn't a battle, or an invasion. It wasn't a gathering of anarchists, nor even really a running gamut of tired Rock Artists in the usual festival tradition. It was a weekend on an island for a lot of young

---

[3] A Chris Morphet photograph of Pete driving 'Maxine' is featured on the cover of Townshend's 2000 release, *Lifehouse Elements*.

HUMAN BEINGS . . . The fact that the young people of today do things together in large numbers without the organisation of a field marshal is regarded suspiciously by all these days."

The Who provided part of their huge PA system[4] to be used for the event, taking the stage at about 2 a.m. on Sunday morning. "At the Isle of Wight festival I met Mike Wadleigh, the director and innovator of the *Woodstock* movie," Pete wrote. "It was greatly embarrassing for me to hear him announce that the cameraman's bum I had kicked off the stage during our show at Woodstock had belonged to him. Bearing in mind that we have some great work done for us in The Who sequence in the film I figure he cannot be a man that holds a grudge. Lesson for Abbie [Hoffman]."

The festival was being documented by Newport Folk Festival director, Murray Lerner. Richard Stanley manned one of the cameras during The Who's set. "I was out on a crane in front of the stage at 3 o'clock in the morning," Stanley recalls. "It was quite a heavy experience, about 20 metres above the ground, you know, with The Who's full million watts blaring at me . . ."

The Who gave a memorable performance to the estimated audience of 600,000 although Townshend wasn't happy with how it went. "Our performance dwindled quietly and ineffectually away at the IOW," he wrote. "We had played far too long, nearly three hours, making it hard for Sly [& the Family Stone] to follow playing to such a weary audience and leaving the stage on an anticlimactic note rather than an excited one . . . We have deliberately cut down our act to leave us more energy to cope with the most important part of the show. The finale. It doesn't matter how well you play, if you don't leave on the right foot you may as well not bother."

The Who followed the Isle of Wight with several mid-September dates in Germany, the Netherlands and Denmark prior to returning to Britain for a 23-date tour over two months. "Our show at Purley Orchid Ballroom [on October 8] was quite an experience," Pete reported in The Pete Townshend Page. "I came closer to complete physical exhaustion than I ever have before at a performance and yet we are playing a slightly shorter show on this tour . . . The last time we played there was so long ago I can't remember, and as we walked through the audience to the stage,

---

[4] "Their PA alone takes up one gigantic truck – and the guitar amps occupy another," Chris Charlesworth wrote in a November 1970 *Melody Maker* article entitled 'Whole Lotta Who Gear'. Townshend was now using four 4 × 12 cabinets topped with two 100-watt Hiwatt amplifiers. The entire PA system, which Bob Pridden estimated at costing £5,000, had an output of up to 2,000 watts.

surrounded by bouncers, I heard elderly mods asking for 'I Can't Explain' and 'Substitute' with such zest that I began to believe they were new releases.

"The first two days of the tour were an education for me. I took my motor caravan and attempted to gypsy the gigs at Cardiff and Manchester ... After taking six hours to reach Cardiff I looked in at the Sophia Gardens where we were to perform to find out what time we were due on. Finding out I had three hours to spare I decided to look for an AA [Automobile Association] approved caravan park that was close to the city centre according to my map. Off I went, driving for nearly an hour with no success. Eventually I dropped into a friendly cop shop where they gave me complicated but explicit directions. I followed them carefully and eventually arrived at the site. Checking in, paying my seven and six and getting a set of keys to the bog I enquired how to get to the Sophia Gardens as I would be getting back late – and would the gates be open? 'Oh, there's no need to worry about the gates,' the smiling warden said as I contemplated the last 90 minutes driving. "Sophia Gardens is right next door, in fact you can see it from here.

"Despite this terrible indignity I hurriedly walked off to the gig with me boiler suit under me arm feeling like a local Welsh lad made good, and checked in. The James Gang were about to play and I went to watch. I got as far as their first few bars. The bass player's amp stopped working after he'd played only three notes and the impact of their incredible opener, 'Funk 49', was dampened. I didn't watch anymore, feeling like maybe I was a jinx, and waited till they came offstage a little disenchanted with the equipment we had lent them (BLUSH).

"The crowd in Cardiff were incredible. It was the first airing of the now shortened *Tommy* in Wales and we enjoyed the show as much as we have ever."

The tour drew typically rave reviews. "When Chelsea play at Stamford Bridge, the cheers filter up into the skies like nowhere else. So it was with The Who at Hammersmith Palais on Thursday [October 29]," began Chris Charlesworth's *Melody Maker* review. "Playing on their home ground for the first time in years, the world's most exciting stage act finished their tour with all the stops out."

Townshend was now ready to move forward after 18 months of playing *Tommy* live. "After the James Gang tour," Pete told *Disc and Music Echo* in October, "we'll only be doing occasional gigs, just to keep a hand in. To be very, very honest we're getting a little bit bored with our current material. The first few gigs of the tour were really nice to play. They were such good halls and sympathetic audiences. But the gigs are getting almost like nine to five. And *Tommy* is becoming a bit thin . . . we are always very conscious of what we are doing and we are beginning to wonder whether people are bored with it. So we are getting off the road to concentrate on other things."

The Who's last performance of *Tommy* in its entirety (until it was revived in 1989) took place at the Roundhouse in Chalk Farm, north London on December 20. Among the opening acts was Elton John, to whom Townshend dedicated the final performance of *Tommy*.

Meanwhile, Pete's new concept – what became known as *Lifehouse* – was taking shape. Having written a script,[5] he approached Universal Studios regarding financing a movie based on the idea. Matt Kent, who interviewed Townshend about the project in August 1999, described it as "a rock film which encompassed a fictional story melded together with live concert footage of The Who. The result [Pete] felt would move rock away from the commercial excesses it was only really just beginning to find itself exposed to and place it back firmly in the hands of the audience, where he felt it belonged."

The proposed album The Who had been working on at Pete's home studio since earlier in the year was shelved as was the idea of an EP containing four of the tracks ('Postcard', 'Water', 'I Don't Even Know Myself' and either 'Now I'm A Farmer' or 'Naked Eye'). "We've pulled it out because of other ideas floating around," Townshend confirmed. "We've done six tracks, about one and a half sides. But when we started work on it, Kit was ill. Since then Kit's come up with the idea for an album with a film. I've got an LP of music but I don't know if the structure of the story is strong enough to hold a film. We won't get back together until next year, but there's definitely an album there."

"What I want to do," he said at the time, "is to attempt a follow-through and achieve something which will have as big an impact as *Tommy* did."

The central theme to *Lifehouse* was first outlined in the September instalment of The Pete Townshend Page:

> *"There's a note, a musical note, that builds the basis of existence somehow . . . This note pervades everything, it's an extremely wide note, more of*

---

[5] Daltrey recalled in 1999 that the script "didn't make any sense, none of us could grasp it, but it had some good ideas in it."

a hiss than a note as we normally know them. The hiss of the air, of activity, of the wind and of the breathing of someone near. You can always hear it. Andy Newman told me once how people cannot bear to spend too much time in anechoic chambers because of the horror of complete silence. Anechoic chambers are not only completely silent but all sound that is produced within them is sort of swallowed up by absolutely non reflective walls and ceilings. You shout but you hardly hear yourself! At midnight when you lay in bed, gently falling into sleep, it gets louder not quieter. It doesn't seem to come through the ears and the air, but it is made up of elements that are. Finally, when it reaches deafening proportions you are asleep, drowned in sound . . . The key to this unexciting adventure that I'm leading you on is that everybody hears it. Moreover, I think everybody hears the same note or noise. It's an amazing thing to think of any common ground between all men that isn't directly a reflection of spiritual awareness . . . It's a note, it's notes, it's music – the most beautiful there is to hear."

Townshend's elucidation of this theory was relatively easy to comprehend. However, the more he elaborated, the murkier the definition became. "I've got kind of a pivot idea," he told *Disc and Music Echo*'s Roy Shipston in October 1970, "basically based on physics, closely linked with the things mystics have been saying for a long time about vibrations in music. It's a cyclic idea, a bit lame at the moment. But I've got some songs which are similar in potential, just like 'Amazing Journey', 'Sensation', 'Pinball Wizard' and 'I'm Free' were to *Tommy*. From those songs, the whole thing evolved. It's about a set of musicians, a group who look like The Who, and behave remarkably like The Who, and they have a roadie who is desperately interested in ideals for humanity. It's basically a science-fiction fantasy idea.

"This roadie is wrapped up in electronics and synthesisers. He is fantastically serious about finding 'The Note' and spends all his time converting Egyptian charts and musical mysticism into an electronic circuitry – and discovers all these wonderful and weird oscillations . . . Anyway, this group find a note which, basically, creates complete devastation. And when everything is destroyed, only the real note, the true note that they have been looking for, is left. Of course, there is no one left to hear it, except the audience, of course, who are in a rather privileged position."

"It's a sort of futuristic fantasy, a bit science fiction," Pete told the *New York Times* the following February. "It takes place in about 20 years, when everybody has been boarded up inside their houses and put in special garments, called experience suits, through which the government feed them programmes to keep them entertained.[6] Then Bobby comes along. He's an electronics wizard and takes over a disused rock theatre, renames it the Lifehouse and sets it up as an alternative to the government programmes. Next, he chooses a basic audience of about 300 people and prepares a chart for each of them, based on astrology and their personalities and other data; and from their charts he arrives at a sound for each of them – a single note or a series, a cycle or something electronic – anything that best expresses each individual . . . I don't want to go into incredible detail, because I'll probably change it all; but the basic idea is that Bobby takes these sounds and builds on them and through them the audience begins to develop. First they attain a state of harmony, then a state of enlightenment and they keep growing all the time.

"On the Lifehouse stage there is a rock group, which will be The Who, to comment on the sounds and celebrate them. But they aren't the heroes and neither is Bobby. The real centre is the equipment itself, the amps and tapes and synthesisers, all the machines, because they transmit the sounds; the hardware is the hero. Anyhow, the Lifehouse gets more and more intense, until Bobby takes over the government programmes and replaces them with the new sounds, so that everyone wearing the experience suits gets plugged into them and shares them, and it goes on – the sounds keep developing, the audience keeps attaining higher states and, in the end, all the sounds merge into one, like a massive square dance. And everyone starts bouncing up and down together, faster and faster, wilder and wilder, closer and closer and closer. And finally it gets too much, the energy, and they actually leave their bodies. They disappear."

An additional and more detailed Townshend description, entitled 'An Introduction To *Lifehouse*,' appeared as a 1999 article in *The Richmond Review* (it also served as the introduction to the booklet accompanying the 2000 boxed set *Lifehouse Chronicles*), which outlined the story "as it was presented to The Who in 1971":

A self-sufficient, drop-out family group farming in a remote part of Scotland decide to return south to investigate rumours of a subversive concert event that

---

[6] "In *Tommy*, I achieved the hero's spiritual isolation by making him deaf, dumb and blind," Pete wrote during an online chat on www.barnesandnoble.com in May, 2000. "In *Lifehouse*, I achieved the same isolation for the entire human race by placing the majority of them on a worldwide grid [through] which they experienced all their entertainment and important educational life experiences."

promises to shake and wake up apathetic, fearful British society. Ray is married to Sally, they hope to link up with their daughter Mary who has run away from home to attend the concert. They travel through the scarred waste-land of middle England in a motor caravan, running an air-conditioner they hope will protect them from pollution. They listen, furtively, to old rock records which they call 'Trad'. Up to this time they have survived as farmers, tolerated by the government who are glad to buy most of their produce. Those who have remained in urban areas suffer repressive curfews and are more-or-less forced to survive in special suits, like space-suits, to avoid the extremes of pollution that the government reports.

These suits are interconnected in a universal grid, a little like the modern Internet, but combined with gas-company pipelines and cable-television-company wiring. The grid is operated by an imperious media conglomerate headed by a dictatorial figure called Jumbo who appears to be more powerful than the government that first appointed him. The grid delivers its clients' food, medicine and sleeping gas. But it also keeps them entertained with lavish programming so highly compressed that the subject can 'live out' thousands of virtual lifetimes in a short space of time. The effect of this dense exposure to the myriad dream-like experiences provided by the controllers of the grid is that certain subjects begin to fall apart emotionally. Either they believe they have become spiritually advanced, or they feel suffocated by what feels like the shallowness of the programming, or its repetitiveness. A vital side-issue is that the producers responsible for the programming have ended up concentrating almost entirely on the story-driven narrative form, ignoring all the arts unrestrained by 'plot' as too complex and unpredictable, especially music. Effectively, these arts appear to be banned. In fact, they are merely proscribed, ignored, forgotten, no longer of use.

A young composer called Bobby hacks into the grid and offers a festival-like music concert – called the lifehouse – which he hopes will impel the audience to throw off their suits (which are in fact no longer necessary for physical sur-vival) and attend in person. 'Come to the lifehouse, your song is here.' The family arrive at the concert venue early and take part in an experiment Bobby conducts in which each participant is both blueprint and inspiration for a unique piece of music or song which will feature largely in the first event to be hacked onto the grid.

When the day of the concert arrives a small army force gathers to try to stop the show. They are prevented from entering for a while, the concert begins, and indeed many of those 'watching at home' are inspired to leave their suits. But eventually the army break in. As they do so, Bobby's musical experiment reaches its zenith and everyone in the building, dancing in a huge dervish circle, suddenly disappears. It emerges that many of the audience at home, participating in their suits, have also disappeared.

"There is no dramatic corollary," he advised in 1999. "I didn't try to explain where the [audience] may have gone, or whether they were meant to be dead or alive. I simply wanted to demonstrate my belief that music could set the soul free, both of the restrictions of the body, and the isolating impediments and encumbrances of the modern world."

Over the next three months Pete went into a creative frenzy, writing and recording at his home studio which now contained an impressive array of equipment, including what he described to *Beat Instrumental*'s Steve Turner in a 1971 article as "a Terry Riley type Lowry organ," an ARP 2500 synthesiser, a VCS3 analog synthesiser ["when I'm drunk I can still operate it!"], a set of Ludwig drums, and a 1947 Fender amp, given to Pete by Mountain's Leslie West.

Townshend's musical arsenal was rounded out with several guitars and a Wurlitzer electric piano. The studio's control room contained an upright piano, a Shobud pedal steel guitar, and shelves of demo tapes. The recording equipment included "a 3M eight-track and an Ampex four track which [Pete] uses for mixing down to stereo but which he hopes to use for quadraphonic mixing," Turner explained. "With these he incorporates a Neve mixer and Dolby noise reduction units. The output from the mixer is fed through a SEA power amp which he said he rated incredibly high. Finally, he said there are Tannoy speakers fitted into oversized Lockwood cabinets."

The set of approximately 20 demos Townshend came up with were of exceptional quality, with much of his original synthesiser work being retained for use on the finished Who recordings. "The demos I made to accompany the *Lifehouse* film script I wrote in '71 are among the best I have ever produced," Pete rated in 1983.[7] "I had come fully to grips with working multi-track . . . I had managed to get a good tight drum sound in a room only 10 feet by 15 that was crammed with synthesisers, organs and a seven foot grand piano," although he admitted he had trouble "coming to grips with the incredibly rich harmonics" of the ARP.

---

[7] Glyn Johns agreed with this assertion. "Pete's demos were always fantastic and were always a challenge," he told an interviewer in 1999. "Very often I'd listen to the song that we were about to cut and I'd go, 'How the hell am I going to compete with that?' Really, really brilliant demos . . ."

Coincidentally, Ted Astley also shared his son-in-law's enthusiasm for this new technology. "My mum and dad always had Sunday lunch and Pete and Karen would come down," Jon Astley recalled. "Sundays were quite sacred in that way. My dad at the time was getting into synthesisers as well, which is quite interesting. They'd disappear and have a chat about the latest toy and dad would play him pieces."

Part of Townshend's plan regarding interaction between band and audience was tied up with the mechanics of the synthesiser which Pete considered the perfect tool for translating an individual's personality into music. His experiments with the instrument aimed to "mechanically reflect the basic information about an individual, like height, weight or astrological detail, in music," he informed *Rolling Stone*.

"While I was working on the *Lifehouse* script I actually did a lot of experiments with sounds that were produced from natural body rhythms," Townshend further elaborated to *Penthouse* in 1983. "I was working with the musical bursar of Cambridge University at the time. What we did was ask some individuals a lot of questions about themselves and then subject them to the sort of test a GP might undertake. We measured their heartbeat and the alpha and beta rhythms of the brain; we even took down astrological details and other kinds of shit. Then we took all the data we'd collected on paper or charts and converted them into music, and the end result was sometimes quite amazing. In fact, one of the pulse-modulated frequencies we generated was eventually used as the background beat to 'Won't Get Fooled Again'. Later I used another one of the pulse-modulated frequencies as the foundation for 'Baba O'Riley'."

The use of synthesisers in 1971 was a huge step for The Who and one that wasn't without considerable risk for a band who'd been known as a straight ahead, no-frills four-piece and an instrument that was still seen by many as a novelty device.

"Someone once said that when you play around with synthesisers you end up suffering from a disease called 'synthesiseritis', Townshend later wrote in 1982. "I suffer happily." Daltrey claimed in October 1971 that at one point, "it was in the air for Pete not to play guitar anymore, and just play keyboards . . ."

Aware that his initial draft of *Lifehouse* might be deemed too "abstract", Townshend acknowledged to *Record World* that his ideas required "physical testing". He planned to develop the concept by performing several experimental shows in front of a small audience and set about searching for a suitable venue. After looking at an old cinema, a closed gaming and billiards club, and even considering purchasing and converting a house, Pete settled on the Young Vic Theatre in London, which had opened the previous September.[8]

"It really doesn't seem to be worth doing anything to me," Townshend wrote in the February 13 instalment of The Pete Townshend Page, "unless it can either do something for Rock or do something for its audience. The Who's coming performances and film work at the Young Vic will do both. Nothing can't happen. Basically what we do could change our audience, our music, our status, and even the way we walk. If it all doesn't change anything else it will change me."

Record Mirror described the Young Vic as having an "almost Shakespearian-styled stage area and audience tiers. The room is octagonal, built from roughly scored concrete blocks." The fact that the stage ran down the centre of the venue, which only held 450 people, appealed to Townshend.

"Pete came along here some months ago to see *Waiting For Godot*," the Young Vic's artistic director Frank Dunlop told *Record Mirror* in January, "and then he brought the rest of The Who and they were enthusiastic too. It was this that prompted them to give a concert and we threw the doors open and let anyone come who wanted to dance to the music."

This first show on January 4[9] attracted, "a completely mixed up crowd, part theatrical hangers-on, part freaks, part Who fans," as Townsend told the *New York Times* a month later.

"I knew what I needed and I was just waiting for the money to come," Pete told Matt Kent in 1999, referring to the two million dollars Universal Pictures were prepared to stump up for a *Lifehouse* film to be produced by Lambert and Stamp. Townshend further revealed that, as one of the repertory theatre's board members, he could have bought the Young Vic out with a portion of the funds from Universal, or provided money for the theatre to stage productions.

---

[8] Kit Lambert introduced Townshend to the Young Vic's director, Frank Dunlop. "Through our meeting at AD8, a gay restaurant in Kensington frequented by Rudolf Nureyev, I became a patron [of the Young Vic]," Pete wrote in 1999. "I give this snapshot not to deepen the impression that I enjoyed a bisexual life with ballet dancers, but rather to show that I moved in exalted circles of wildly wilful, imaginative and creative people, and when I spoke to anyone about *Lifehouse* socially, they were encouraging and enthused."

[9] According to *Anyway Anyhow Anywhere: The Complete Chronicle Of The Who 1958–1978*, the first *Lifehouse* rehearsal took place at the Young Vic on November 15, 1970.

"I knew exactly what was going on and I knew that they couldn't mount productions without money. I said to Frank Dunlop if you give us this theatre for a couple of months, so we'd get to the point where we'd have a bit of a daily thing going here . . . we'd written some songs and we'd play to people who were coming in every day because they want to see how their music was coming on . . . we could take a portion of money from the budget and put it in the grant for them and you could use it for your first production of *Waiting For Godot* or whatever it is you want to do. That side of it was very, very clear. My problem with the artistic director then, Frank Dunlop, was that he thought, by holding a press conference when he did the first couple of days, that he could push forward the creative side of the production. What it actually did was to really put me on the spot and it confused the band."

That press conference took place at the Young Vic on January 13. "We are intending to produce a fiction, or a play or an opera and create a completely different kind of performance in rock," Townshend announced. "We are writing a story and we aim to perform it on the first day we start work in this theatre. Tied in with the whole idea is the use of quadrophonic sound and pre-recorded tapes. About 400 people will be involved with us and we aim to play music which represents them . . . Rock's real power as a liberational force is completely untapped . . . so a new type of theatre, a new type of performance has to be devised to present it . . . If a film of this is made, it will become the first real rock film . . . because it will reflect a reality."

"The press conference was the beginning of the end," Townshend lamented in his 1999 *Richmond Review* article. "I was portrayed by some as confused when I was merely tired and by some as arrogant when I was merely deeply committed to the idea that the story would work, that The Who could pull it off."

For the Young Vic shows, The Who invested in a new quadrophonic PA system reportedly costing £30,000 and a complex pre-recorded tape rig, all of which were in keeping with the project's forward-thinking theme.[10]

"We developed an amazing set of hardware," Townshend told *Rolling*

[10] Pete's view of the future as presented in *Lifehouse* included some eerily sharp observations regarding the use of computers. His "grid" was an almost dead-on portrayal of the internet. "I saw it all coming," Townshend told the *New York Post*'s Dan Aquilante in July 2000, tongue lodged firmly in cheek. "I mustn't take credit for it. In college in the 1960s, I took a course in cybernetic theory taught by Roy Ascot. It was he who gave me my grip on what the future was."

Stone at the time. "I spent £12,000 on synthesisers alone. You know in FM radio they have cartridges where, as soon as you hit the button, out comes music? We've got this system where I've got this row of foot pedals, and when I hit one something just comes out. It might be a brass band, a full orchestra, a plane going by, an explosion, whatever."

As happened with *Tommy*, Townshend talked up *Lifehouse* to such an extent, he now had to deliver but despite the ambitious melding of songs, technology and a movie script, exactly what The Who expected to achieve at the Young Vic still remained unclear. Townshend certainly wanted an unprecedented level of interaction and commitment from his audience.

"I don't mean that I seriously expect people to leave their bodies but I think we might go further than rock concerts have gone before," a hopeful Townshend told the *New York Times* in February. "I know that when live rock is at its best, which often means The Who, it stops being just a band playing up front and the audience sitting there like dummies. It's an interaction which goes beyond performance. We aren't like superstars, we're only reflective surfaces. We might catch an energy and transmit it, but the audience doesn't take more from us than we take from them, not when the gig really works. That's what we want to take further at the Young Vic: we want to see how far the interaction can be taken. At first we will be playing there every Monday, but if the experiment works, if people keep coming back and going along with it, we might step it up to two or three or four nights a week, whatever is necessary. By the end of six months, anything might happen."

"We were most passionate about the audience," Pete said in a 1985 radio interview, "and the audience's role, particularly in concerts, that a good audience has to be one in which everybody loses themselves. You don't go onstage to *find* something, you go onstage to *lose* something. You don't go to a concert in order to be *given* something, you go to a concert in order to become abandoned, to lose yourself."

"The aim is change," he wrote in February's Pete Townshend Page, "a change of lifestyle for the band, a change of focus for our audience and a change in the balance of power that Rock wields. The music we play has to be tomorrow's, the things we say have to be today, and the reason for bothering is yesterday. The idea is to make the first real superstar. The first real star who can really stand and say that he deserves the name. That star would be us all.

"The Young Vic becomes the 'Life House', The Who become musicians and the audience become part of a fantasy. We have invented the fantasy in our minds, the ideal, and now we want to make it happen for real. We want to hear the music we have dreamed about, see the harmony we have experienced temporarily in Rock become permanent, and feel the things we are doing CHANGE the face of Rock and then maybe even people.

"There is a story connected with each person that will walk into the Life House, but for now we have made one up for them, until we know the real one. We have music that will stimulate them to stay with us through lengthy marathon concerts, and perhaps even boring filming. We have sounds ready that will push us a lot further than we have ever gone before, but what the result will be is still unknown. Our hero is Bobby, the mystic-cum-roadie that puts all the fantasies in our heads into action, and gets results . . .

"The efforts of the super roadie and their astonishing outcome can be watched, and augmented by your own efforts at the Young Vic. I'll tell you when."

"I was hoping for, at a maximum, to have gone in there [the Young Vic] for a couple of months," Townshend explained, "but I thought I would get a couple of weeks out of it, particularly if I could pay for it. What happened was that no money came, I sat and waited and waited and no money came."

By the time The Who decided to begin the Young Vic shows without financial backing, the selection of available evenings was limited. "We had the Young Vic for as long as we wanted before it opened, as long as we wanted," Townshend claimed. "I used to go down there every day, it was empty for week after week after week . . ."

Pete felt that the one-show-a-week schedule didn't provide enough continuity for the audiences to feel the necessary level of involvement.

"My intention was to use the place for as long as I could get it and was really bitterly disappointed when Frank Dunlop announced we could only have it for two days a week," Townshend told Kent. "What I needed was a daily experience, to be able to say to somebody that came in, 'What's your name, where do you live and do you know anything about The Who?' I did actually say to one of them, 'If I write you a song will you come back tomorrow to listen to it?' and he said, 'Yeah, I'll bring my mum and dad.'

"That was the kind of scenario that I was hoping for, something where we would start to build up what, I felt, would be a real mirror of what was going on already in the best pop music which was, that I write a song about you guys as a generality and then other 'you guys' type people identify with that process. If I did it 'one to one', what would be the difference? I think it would be more special, more acute, more intimate and in a sense, more involving and, maybe, make each one of those people who got a song written about them the centre of their own group of a hundred or hundred thousand faces. They would become figureheads in their own right. What I'd end up with is a single man PR campaign, who consolidates a lot of interest, particularly in younger fans in The Who, who without them there wouldn't be a band."

After a preview show the night before, The Who began a Monday night residency at the Young Vic on February 15. However, several factors combined to derail *Lifehouse* in short order.

"I had no hope of producing anything like the expansive music I had envisioned and attempted to describe in my fiction," Townshend recalled in 1999, "but certain people around me believed that was my target. Whispers of 'madness' fluttered backstage like moths eating at the very fabric of my project."

Among the mutterers were the rest of the band who still didn't appear sold on the idea. "I could explain it to Roger and John and Keith, and they'd say, 'Oh I get it, you put these suits on and you put a penny in the slot and you get wanked off,'" Pete told *Q*'s John Harris in 1996. "I'd go, 'No, no, it's much bigger than that.' 'Oh, I get it, you get wanked off *and* you get a Mars bar shoved up your bum. I get it.' 'No, no, no, it's bigger than that, man . . .' When I delivered the first draft of the script, Roger said, 'This'll never work, this film.' I said, 'Why?' and he said, 'You could never get that much wire.' That kind of thing did send me over the edge."

Daltrey also wasn't particularly enamoured of Townshend's technological infatuation. "Roger wanted to go back to what was safe. The fact of the matter was that we had done *Live At Leeds* and we had done guitar, bass and drums," Pete contended in 1999. "Cream had done it and Jimi Hendrix had done it . . . Nobody wanted it, everyone was fed up with four-hour guitar solos, so I was really trying to do something new and innovative and also, in a sense, give [The Who] something which would honour the fact that we were one of the few bands that could go into a film company and get a budget."

The scepticism surrounding Pete's ideas also stretched to those working around The Who. "It wasn't an idea I can clearly remember everyone thinking 'Yeah' about," Chris Stamp said in 1999, while publicist Keith

Altham commented, "It always worried me that I couldn't grasp fully what the impact of *Lifehouse* was, because of my job as the Who's press agent, and I felt that I should make an effort to understand and comprehend this very complex idea. And I felt a lot less bad about it when I realised so many other people who were exceptionally brighter than I was couldn't grasp it either."

Rather than interacting enthusiastically with the band, the Young Vic audiences seemed content in their traditional roles as mere spectators, happy to enjoy the music, but not particularly willing to participate in the proceedings. "People were quite happy to sit and listen to what we were doing," Townshend recalled in 1999. "In the end it was we who said, 'Ah, fuck it. Let's get this place rocking.'"

The indifference crushed Townshend as *Zigzag* later described: "It was clearly too much for a random selection of skinheads who, despite being told that the event was experimental, expected The Who to perform as they always had." Or, as John Entwistle put it, "They wanted us to play 'My Generation' and smash guitars."

Townshend disagrees with this common view. "They were so little they didn't know who The Who were," he stated in 1999. "The idea that we played a bunch of Who hits to keep them quiet is bollocks because they wouldn't have known us from Adam, they were schoolchildren."

Meanwhile, the press continued to file reports on the projected *Lifehouse* movie. "The Who are about to make their first film," the *New York Times* reported in early February. "It is called *Bobby* . . .[11] Shooting will start this summer with an American release expected by November . . . Townshend has gone into retreat, holed up inside his house and private studios in Twickenham, where he's hammering out a storyline. Bearded and bleary, he works 15 hours a day . . . and can still hardly believe that a film is really, truly happening."

Townshend's plan was to intersperse the *Lifehouse* storyline with Young Vic live footage but from the outset, the film idea was sabotaged by Kit Lambert's refusal to let go of his idea for a *Tommy* movie. Ever since he'd written a script during the album's recording sessions, Lambert visualised the rock opera being transferred to celluloid.

"We've spent a year trying to get a film together for *Tommy* and it's so long gone now that we've dropped it," Pete told *Disc and Music Echo* back in late 1970. "I think Warner Brothers have the film rights and they can make

[11] The *New York Times* reported that Andy Newman had been cast as Bobby.

a film whenever they want, with whoever they want . . . Kit and Chris are really keen to get some sort of musical film together for The Who. Really, it's the only step we can take to keep us moving forward . . ."

Lambert had talked Universal into backing both a *Lifehouse* film and a *Tommy* film but with the latter holding far more importance in his eyes.

"[Kit] told me we would all three together [Lambert, Townshend and Frank Dunlop] develop the script I'd written," Townshend wrote in An Introduction to *Lifehouse*. "We never did, and for a while I wondered why. Recently Frank explained that behind my back Kit had confused him, saying my idea was unworkable, that Frank should go through the motions, then let it fade and move on to the more important project, a movie of *Tommy* which Kit hoped to direct as his first feature."

"I had written a script, which Universal Pictures had read and apparently understood," Pete recalled almost three decades later. "Then there was silence. I came up against my first real brick wall since I had started writing and acting as spokesman for The Who and many in their audience. Until then I had felt omnipotent, I hope not arrogantly. But that wall that rose up between me and my *Lifehouse* film stood up to every energetic idea I threw at it. I could not work out what to do."

Although the relationship between Townshend and Lambert had cooled considerably, sometime around early March, the latter called Pete with an idea. As a means of finding a way forward, Lambert suggested The Who fly to New York to record the *Lifehouse* material as it currently stood at the newly opened Record Plant.

"I remember being sceptical," Townshend wrote in 1995. "Kit had been doing hard drugs . . . But he convinced me that he would co-produce with Jack Adams – a solid engineer I had worked with myself in New York."

"The idea itself wasn't going anywhere . . . we weren't tackling the storyline," Stamp recalled in 1999, "so Kit's idea as their producer was to move to the most sophisticated recording studio, to try and record these songs . . . He knew about the Record Plant in New York – he'd actually worked there a few times – and so the band flew over to New York to record some tracks . . . I think probably that what Kit envisioned doing was the same as he had done with *Tommy*, trying to get more and more into Pete's idea and working it out that way."

By mid-March, The Who were recording at the Record Plant. "The New York sessions were great fun," Townshend recalled. "We were the first band to use the revolutionary new Studio One . . . which opened during our sessions. It was a great experience but very stressful. I remember drinking very heavily and Kit was out of control . . . He was also disappearing to shoot up all the time . . . I just drank bottle after bottle of brandy as usual – probably imagining I was showing great self-restraint."

Their location was also not exactly a distraction-free setting for a band trying to focus on the task at hand, as Stamp described, "New York is the hedonistic town, so everyone was getting more loaded. The more halcyon hallucinogenic days had passed on now to the more sort of neurotic, narcotic days. And there's the night life of New York with after-hours bars, the clubs, the sex, the everything. It's just a little bit more un-intimate for sitting down and getting seriously creative as a group of people. So the recordings didn't really work in the Record Plant."

After recording 'Won't Get Fooled Again', 'Love Ain't For Keeping', 'Getting In Tune', a cover of Marvin Gaye's 'Baby Don't You Do It' (which featured Leslie West guesting on lead guitar), 'Pure And Easy' and 'Behind Blue Eyes' (with Al Kooper on keyboards) over a span of six days, Townshend reached the end of his tether.

"When I got to New York I found that Kit had changed, and not entirely because he had become a heroin user," Pete wrote in his *Richmond Review* essay. "I realised later he had been deeply hurt by my failure to see how desperately he wanted to produce and direct a movie of *Tommy* and I had blocked him, fearing I would lose my mentor and friend to Hollywood. I lost him anyway. At the time, in New York, I was still obsessed with my own problems and was unaware of all this. He had completely lost all affection for me and began calling me not 'Pete', but 'Townshend', or 'Pete Townshend'."

Having called a group meeting, he entered Lambert's room at the Navarro Hotel. "I heard him raging to his assistant Anya Butler: 'Townshend has blocked me at every front. I will not allow him to do it this time . . .' Something inside me snapped. I suppose it was hearing this man that I loved so much calling me by surname and with such anger. Perhaps I deserved it but it devastated me.

"During the subsequent meeting, as Kit stamped around the room pontificating and cajoling, shouting and laughing, I began to have what I now know to be a classic New York Alcoholic Anxiety Attack Grade One," Townshend wrote in 1995. "Everyone in the room transmogrified into huge frogs, and I slowly moved toward the open tenth floor window with the intention of jumping out. Anya spotted me and gently took my arm. There is no question in my mind that she saved my life. I was by that time a kook."[12]

"I had the first nervous breakdown of my life," he told *Rolling Stone* in 1974. "And I'm just not the sort to have nervous breakdowns. What'd happen is I'd spend a week explaining something to somebody and it'd be all very clear to me, then they'd go, 'Right, that's OK – now can you just explain it again.' There were about 50 people involved and I didn't have the stamina to see it through. A creative person has to work in isolation."

"Over the next year, Pete was in a maudlin state," Frank Dunlop told *Mojo* in 2004. "I remember him bursting into tears for no apparent reason on more than one occasion. My regret is that with the job I had I couldn't help him as a freelance director would have. I couldn't just go off and get it done. *Lifehouse* was a gigantic effort. I always felt I wasn't useful enough to him."

Townshend's frustration regarding the evident inability of all but himself to understand *Lifehouse* lingered.[13] "I was at my most brilliant and I was at my most effective," Pete said in 1999, "and when people say I didn't know what the fuck I was talking about what they're actually doing is revealing their own complete idiocy, because the idea was *so fucking simple!* It is not complicated. The only thing that's complicated about it is the fact that it was talked about too early by people who didn't know what they were fucking talking about."

"I've worked myself on something you'll never see to the point of nervous breakdown," Townshend revealed in 1971. "We've worked probably harder in the last year than ever before. I've never come across something like this before – I've always felt an abundance of energy; particularly if it's one of my projects; I've always thought I've got to push it through, put more energy into it than other people. In this particular case it went on and on and after about six months with no product, only

---

[12] An article in the fall 2000 issue of *Revolver* reported that Pete was on the 24th floor of the building. "I thought, 'I must get some air,'" Townshend told *Revolver*. "And I stumbled towards the window. I was about to jump out, when Kit's secretary grabbed me – just like that! I nearly killed myself. *That* is when I gave up on *Lifehouse*."

[13] A great deal of this frustration must have been lifted upon the release of the 1999 *Lifehouse* radio play, which Townshend has described as "the definitive version" of the fictional aspect of the project and also by the advent of the *Method* in 2007, which represented the reality.

problems, and only me involved in it and the rest of the group getting bored, John getting involved in making his own album, Roger ringing me up every day trying to dissuade me from doing the project, saying that what we really needed to do was go out on the road, we eventually gave up and to put it frankly we just went back into the old mould."

CHAPTER SEVEN

1971–1972

"We're all very similar as physical bodies, we enjoy the same degree of self-punishment, the same music, and we enjoy playing together, but we have different basic ethics on how to live our lives and they don't cross. Deeply written into Who philosophy is the fact that each member thinks the other guy's way is total bullshit but it's all right by me. I may be putting words in people's mouths but that's probably true. So let's say I'm tolerated in my mystical beliefs although I should imagine there's a bit of fear in the group that I might grow my hair down my back and start putting solo albums out . . . do a George Harrison basically."

— Pete Townshend, 1972

"I think the idea people have of us now – or at least our present image – is that people are starting to talk of us as a band that are changing. Which is nice. But what they'll realise in time is that we have changed before. I remember that sort of thing was said when we did 'Magic Bus' for some peculiar reason. People said, 'What the fuck's going on here, lots of acoustic guitars and clicking noises.' And I feel 'Join Together' is today's 'Magic Bus', and I think when we go on and do some more Who then they'll see it in that light."

— Pete Townshend, 1972

AFTER the abortive sessions at the Record Plant and with Townshend's stalemate with Lambert precluding any further collaboration on *Lifehouse*, it became necessary to involve another creative soundboard. Pete contacted Glyn Johns, a highly regarded professional engineer whose résumé included five Rolling Stones albums, four by Steve Miller, Led Zeppelin's first album and the Beatles' *Get Back* project (released in altered form as *Let It Be*) to name a few. The selection of

162

Johns, who was Shel Talmy's engineer during The Who's early recording sessions, did nothing to ease the tension between the band and Lambert. Johns clearly disliked Lambert, and since Johns had taken Talmy's side during The Who's contractual dispute, the feeling was mutual.

Johns was no fan of Lambert's abilities as a producer, telling Dave Marsh, "I thought they were atrocious," referring to The Who's Lambert-produced recordings, "absolutely atrocious – amateur night. I think *Tommy* is absolutely atrocious from a sound point of view. Embarrassing. I mean, Kit Lambert didn't have any idea whatsoever about how to make a record – none. The band would dispute that, and more power to 'em. But I mean from an engineering point of view, from a sound point of view. I'm sure he had wonderful ideas and he was a very explosive character. And I know, because Pete's told me on numerous occasions – they all have – that he did come up with great ideas and he was a great influence on the band. But he didn't know how to make records – not from an engineering point of view, at any rate."

Johns was initially brought on board simply to mix the Record Plant recordings but impressed by the songs, he successfully persuaded Townshend that it would be worthwhile to start from scratch at Johns' regular workplace, Olympic Studios, to record what would become *Who's Next*. First, they did a test run at Stargroves, Mick Jagger's Berkshire home, using the Stones mobile studio, recording 'Won't Get Fooled Again', which yielded remarkable results (indeed, the recording was of sufficient quality that, with a few overdubs, the Stargroves version of the song was retained for use on the finished album).

The sessions at Olympic began on April 9, with final recording being wrapped up in June. "We just went in there for four days," Pete said in 1983, "just a casual thing, to try out what we wanted to do. We did six numbers in four days – finished. Went in a week later and did another six. Went in a week later, did another six. We were just churning the stuff out. We had enough for two albums when we were finished."

As recording got under way, a double album was mooted of the *Lifehouse* songs with the film project to follow later in the year after the new material had reached a satisfactory performance level onstage. However, over the next month, the double concept gave way to a single disc. "Just before Glyn programmed *Who's Next*," Pete told *Revolver* in 2000, "he took me out to a pub. He said, 'Pete, tell me just once more about this *Lifehouse*.' I thought, Oh God! So I told him the story. And he sat there thinking. I thought he was going to say, 'Now I get it!' And instead he said, 'I don't understand a *fucking* word that you said.'"[1]

"We could have put together a really tight concept album I think," Townshend told *Zigzag* in 1971. "Roger thought so too at the time but Glyn Johns was very adamant that from his view as an observer he couldn't see any concept. And I think maybe he could have been wrong. I don't really know. I think that as a producer he perhaps stands a little too much away from the ethereal concepts that a group gets involved in because it's active, it's working and it's exciting and tends to just listen to what comes out of the speakers and take it at its face value without realising, of course, that a whole lot of people who are interested in The Who are very deeply into everything that we're doing, all of the time."

On April 26, the band took the Rolling Stones' mobile set-up to the Young Vic as planned and recorded the performance, which proved to be their last at the venue. Pete's daughter, Aminta Alice,[2] was born just two nights before the show, prompting him to smoke a cigar during the performance and announce to the crowd that he was a "proud father for the second time."

The material Johns selected from Townshend's *Lifehouse* tapes formed the tightest, most consistent Who album to date. Pete's experimentation with synthesisers is immediately apparent with the shower of notes that begin 'Baba O'Riley', which he named after Meher Baba and composer Terry Riley, whose innovative use of synthesiser loops – particularly on his 1969 album *A Rainbow In Curved Air* – had proved an inspiration. The song's complex backing track was a result of Townshend's experiment in entering an individual's personal data into a synthesiser in the hopes of discovering a melody, or pattern.

"The whole thing about [*Who's Next*] is the two tracks, 'Baba O'Riley' and 'Won't Get Fooled Again', use a synthesiser in a completely different way than anyone had ever used one before", Johns said in 1999, "where it actually provides a rhythm, it's not just a sound, but it's a rhythm as well. It's to the best of my knowledge the first time anybody had used synthesiser like this. First of all nobody I knew anyway knew how to work

---

[1] "I found it very difficult to understand the script," Johns told Dave Marsh in 1983. "I mean, I could not get a grip on it. In fact, I don't think it's possible for anybody to understand it. I was incredibly impressed with the fact that he had written it. I was incredibly impressed with the professional manner in which it was written. But I didn't understand it. And I told him so."

[2] It may be significant to note that Delia DeLeon's sister was named Minta.

them. They were really difficult to programme and get any kind of sound out of."

However, in 1982, Townshend gave a different account of how he arrived at the arrangement for 'Baba O'Riley' to *Musician*.

"I went out, bought a Larry Berkshire organ, pushed the marimba button, and *played*. And people kept saying, 'That's incredible synthesiser work on that,' and I'd say, 'OK, sure, you're telling me, right?'"

When reminded of his previous interpretation of programming people's personal statistics into the instrument, he said, "Oh that was totally misconstrued. What I was actually doing was collating all kinds of detail about six subjects for the *Lifehouse* film. One was Arthur Brown, the other was Meher Baba, and the rest were the four members of the band. I took astrological details and I was going to take heart rates, pulse rates – everything that I could find out about people – to use as controlling parameters for synthesiser music. Now this was back in '72 [sic], and the synthesiser, even then, was still pretty much of an unexplored instrument. I realised I was pushing the technology a bit hard, so I backed off. What I did do in the end was create the musical equivalent of a found poem – like taking a few lines out of a newspaper and calling it a poem."

'Bargain' featured lyrics which mirrored a 1950 Meher Baba quote: "We must lose ourselves in order to find ourselves; thus loss itself is gain."

"The song is about the spiritual search, so written about my relationship to Meher Baba, not about him," Townshend wrote in a November 2006 web posting. "In *Lifehouse* it was a love song, but a love song about a higher love, a love between disciple and master."

'Love Ain't For Keeping, originally recorded and later played live in an electric format, was a simple, acoustic homage to the pastoral lifestyle that the main characters Ray and Sally enjoyed, complete with an uplifting melody and soaring three-part harmonies.

'The Song Is Over' filled an important role in the *Lifehouse* script. "This would originally have come at the end of the film," Pete told *NME* in August 1971. "I had a rough script where all the Young Vic audience would dance and dance and all freak out, and then disappear. Then you would have heard this song." In 1999, he added that the song signified "the end of a lifetime, the end of an experience."

The final uplifting lines were taken from 'Pure And Easy', recorded during the sessions but which Johns surprisingly omitted from the album.[3]

---

[3] It was eventually released in 1974 on *Odds And Sods*.

Originally titled 'The Note', 'Pure And Easy' summarised the theme of the entire work. " 'Pure And Easy' is a very pivotal track for the *Lifehouse* project," Townshend said in 1996, "and it begins, '*There once was a note, pure and easy,*' and this was inspired by a piece of writing by the Sufi teacher Inayat Kahn, who was also a musician, so a lot of his writing was about vibration and music, about the spiritual search being wrapped up in the idea that we're looking for a note which suits us all. And at some point this got misinterpreted by people that what I was writing about was the lost chord. I don't know what the lost chord is," he laughed.

In 1999, Pete stated that 'Pure And Easy' was "the 'Amazing Journey' of *Lifehouse*" and "essential to any look at the atmosphere of the story."

"It's a song about reflecting creation musically, i.e. there being one infinite consciousness – everything in infinity being one note and lots of other consciousnesses being us and vaguer consciousness being gas and grass and space," he told *Zigzag* in 1971. "I just wrote a lyric about all this – talking about it as music. That is really one of my favourite songs, it really should have been on *Who's Next* . . ."[4]

'Getting In Tune' was "a straight pinch from Inayat Khan's discourse of mysticism of sound," Townshend informed *Zigzag* in September, "where he says music is one way of individuals getting in tune with one another and I just picked up on that."

Originally "a song about driving in America," as Pete recalled in 2000, "in *Lifehouse* ['Going Mobile'] is a song about escape from duty and responsibility, about being able to run away."

In 1971, Townshend referred to 'Behind Blue Eyes' as a "throwaway". Some 35 years later, it's among The Who's best-known songs. It's also regarded by many as one of Pete's most autobiographical songs, despite the fact that it wasn't written as such. "I remember my wife saying she liked this one from the kitchen below after I had finished the harmony vocals," he recalled in his 1983 *Scoop* sleevenotes. "The band later added a passion and a fire that really made it blossom from the sad song it appears to be into the proud self exposé it became on *Who's Next*. Not a personal song at all, or at least not intended to be. It's about the villain in the [*Lifehouse*] story feeling he is forced into playing a two-faced role."

"['Behind Blue Eyes'] was written about a man who actually was a villain and he seemed to be a villain; he's accused of being a liar and a

---

[4] "Glyn played us the album the way he thought it should be and we said, 'Great. Put it out,'" Townshend told Dave Marsh in 1983.

cheat, when in fact his motives are absolutely pure," Townshend elaborated to *Musician* in 1982. "So I tried to capture this character that I'd written and then realised it was me afterwards, and about a part of me that I hadn't considered: the inability to be taken literally because of the way people take you to be. You can never define, you can never control how people react to you, however much of a star you think you are. You can never hide what you really are."

'Won't Get Fooled Again' rounded out the album. " 'Won't Get Fooled Again' was a refutation of the value of revolution," Pete told *Musician* in 1982. "I don't believe in revolution and war. Revolution is the ultimate betrayal . . . every revolution, even the necessary revolutions, or the Russian or Chinese revolutions; they are betrayals because they equalise, without recognising other people's aspirations."

"I wrote 'Won't Get Fooled Again' as a statement against the new politicians, that they weren't gonna fool me with their claim that they had a new way of doing things," he said in radio interview three years later. "The original song wasn't a very aggressive song, but again as usual when Roger started to sing it, he sounded like he certainly *wasn't* gonna get fooled."

The song's lethal power chord riffing was perhaps executed with an extra edge due to the anger which Townshend cites at the song's core. "['Won't Get Fooled Again'] was a song, really, about telling people who were telling me what to do to fuck off!" he told *Hit Parader* in 1975. "It was a time when I was incredibly exposed . . . I refused to change my telephone number, and I refused to not open the door. I thought, 'Well, fuck it, if I can't deal with things that come along, then I might as well fucking give up.' So I tried to deal with everything logically and intelligently, tried to handle people.

"And about halfway along, I got fed up with being lectured, and I got fed up with people telling me what rock'n'roll was all about, and what rock musicians were supposed to do now, and how rock'n'roll musicians were supposed to help overthrow the capitalist regime, and how rock'n' roll was supposed to sort of finance co-ops and communes and do this and that, and how because you were a rock'n'roll star and everybody looked to you for guidance and inspiration, that your responsibility was a political responsibility and a liberationist responsibility.

"I felt, all of a sudden, 'I quit,' and I thought, 'Well, no, all right, if I do have any kind of responsibility, let's not give it any kind of low level. Let's go to the fucking top of the building, let's call it a spiritual responsibility.

Let's say that I am responsible for the spiritual well-being of my patients. So fuck off the lot of you. And I take great pleasure in saying it now. It's one of the songs I enjoy most on the stage, because I still feel that way."

When Pete reviewed the song in a 1987 *Rolling Stone* interview, he dubbed 'Won't Get Fooled Again' "the dumbest song I've ever written. It was dumb to deny the political role of the individual, the political responsibility of the individual. Burning your draft card is a political act. Throwing your vote away is an apolitical act. And 'Won't Get Fooled Again' was an apolitical song. Luckily, most people didn't listen to the verses. *There's nothing in the street/ Looks any different to me/ And the slogans are all replaced, by the by . . .* They just listened to the catch.

"It was an irresponsible song. It was quite clear during that period that rock musicians had the ear of the people. And people were saying to me then, 'Pete, you've got to use The Who. You've got to get this message across.' It was like Abbie Hoffman said on the stage of Woodstock that John Sinclair was in jail for one lousy joint [sic] and I kicked him off the stage. I deeply regret that. If I was given the opportunity again, I would stop the show. Because I don't think rock'n'roll is that important. Then I did. The show had to go on . . . I greatly regret that it's one of the most powerful songs that I've ever written. The Labour party asked me if they could use it in their election campaign. And I said, 'Yeah, but please let me rewrite the verses.'"

While *Who's Next* arguably remains the most powerful album of the band's career, the songs which were set aside following the decision to edit the record to a single disc were equally impressive.

"I think that if 'Pure And Easy' had been in the original mix people would have understood what the other songs were about so much better," considered Townshend in 1999. "They would have known, so much better, what songs like 'Won't Get Fooled Again' were about. If you'd heard 'Pure And Easy' you would have known why I was so angry about revolution. What was happening was that my sacred heart, which was the music, was being used for political purposes and that made me angry."

Another high quality leftover was 'Too Much Of Anything', "which if I'd done as a really great rock song would have been a killer," Pete said. "It's about excess and living your vices. I deliberately did it in a southerly drawly twang to keep it much lower. I put much more energy into 'Love Ain't For Keeping' . . . I had a few failures, such as 'Teenage Wasteland', which was supposed to have been the overture and didn't quite land and some of the musical experiments which didn't quite land until many years later when I got them to land with *Psychoderelict*."

'Mary' was "a song intended to bring some romance into the sci-fi plot [of *Lifehouse*]. Mary was a character in the script. The song wasn't recorded for *Who's Next* by The Who as we decided to make it a single album rather than a double."

"What we have to do now is rebuild ourselves because we were so heavily involved in the film idea," Pete told *Melody Maker* in early July. "We have been doing gigs without any advance publicity here and there, not because we were testing out a new stage act and didn't want any publicity but because we always do gigs like that. They are not very big gigs and they will sell out instantly. If we advertise them in the press there will be lots of people turning up who can't get in. We like playing these small gigs. We did four shows before we started recording to try the new act out onstage . . . We are doing another three this weekend. We had to go back to gigging and find our feet again after the film business before we could start moving anywhere."

The Who presented most of this new material during the run of low-key gigs throughout April and May, including 'Love Ain't For Keeping', 'Pure And Easy', 'Time Is Passing', 'Behind Blue Eyes', 'Bargain', 'Getting In Tune', 'Too Much Of Anything', 'Baby Don't You Do It', and 'Won't Get Fooled Again'. However, the *Lifehouse* material didn't seem to gel onstage as *Tommy* had done so admirably.

"Indeed, two of the most important songs, 'Song Is Over' and 'Baba O'Riley', seemed technically impossible without a much-expanded line-up," Lyons and McMichael wrote in *The Who Concert File*. "The synthesiser backing tape was mastered on 'Won't Get Fooled Again' only and it was some months before The Who actually attempted 'Baba O'Riley' on the stage."

The fact that the band experienced difficulty in getting *Lifehouse* across onstage effectively ended any hopes of a film. However, Townshend still held out hope for his beloved project. "I still feel that the group should be making the film," he told the *NME* in July. "There is so much that the whole Who organisation, our whole team could do in a film. This may sound like blowing our own trumpets but I don't think there are very many other groups who have the knowledge of stage rock theatre but at the same time the necessary lack of ego to carry it off. At the moment we are leaning heavily on the fact that we are good experienced musicians and can put on a good stage act. But . . . and I hate to rub it in . . . what we really need is a film."

Although the band was disappointed with the new material's lack of fire onstage, they could still bring the house down. "In a climax that only The Who can generate," *Melody Maker*'s Chris Charlesworth said when reviewing the band's July 10 show in Dunstable, "Pete smashed one of his current three Gibsons into fragments to the obvious approval of the capacity crowd. While Keith knocked his drum kit off the platform, Pete hurled the remains of the guitar in the audience bent on rushing the stage for souvenirs . . . The Who will always be with us. And while they are they continue to wear the crown of the most exciting live band in existence."

It was during this run of shows that the cover photo for *Who's Next* was taken when the band pulled over en route between Sheffield and Leicester to relieve themselves on a slag heap. The 'pissing on the obelisk' shot was also a jab at director Stanley Kubrick. "Yeah, it was meant to be a sort of gag when we pissed up against the monument," Townshend confirmed to *Oui*'s David Rothman in 1980. "It meant that when we asked Stanley Kubrick to direct *Tommy*, he said, 'Fuck you.'"

"I just think the mechanics of [*Lifehouse*] could have been realised in a film that would've been bigger than *2001*," Pete told *Q* in 1996. "It would have been the musical *2001*. That's why on the cover we're pissing on the obelisk. The band didn't get it, but that was the idea. I thought this was a huge technical magnum opus that could have been absolutely extraordinary. It would have been *Fahrenheit 451*, *Lawnmower Man* and many other films rolled into one. *Woodstock*, even. I couldn't understand how it hadn't happened. This was an extraordinary moment of visionary imagination for me, and it seemed to have been wasted. Now I understand that not everything you imagine is necessarily at the appropriate time. We were incapable of doing it. We could write songs, make albums, tour. That was about it."

Released on August 14 in the US, *Who's Next*, the band's fifth studio album, reached number four and ascended to the top in Britain when issued two weeks later. Praise poured forth with reviewers calling it "superb" and "brilliant".

"*Who's Next*, regardless of what you may have been led to believe to the contrary, is neither the soundtrack to the realisation of Pete Townshend's apparently aborted Hollywood dream, the greatest live album in the history of the universe, nor a, shudder, rock opera, but rather an old-fashioned long-player containing intelligently conceived, superbly performed, brilliantly produced, and sometimes even exciting rock 'n' roll," wrote *Rolling Stone*'s John Mendelsohn, who went on to call the album "one of the most masterfully recorded rock records in recent memory."

Who's Next was also praised for its overall sound, particularly since *Tommy* was generally regarded as inferior in this area. "For the first time The Who were recorded by someone who was more interested in the *sound* than in the image of the group," Townshend told *Sounds'* Penny Valentine in 1972. "Glyn's not particularly interested in Who image, whereas when Kit was producing us that was all he cared about . . . I don't think Glyn produced. I think he engineered. I mean this is why in the end, when it came to the crunch about what to put on the little label, we put co-produced. Because Glyn had done something that was different to what Kit did but Kit definitely *produced* The Who. He would produce material out of a band that had nothing to offer. Glyn couldn't do that."

"I still think that *Who's Next* is one of the best sounding Who albums because the demos for that record were so good," Townshend said in 1983. "There were good songs, and good ideas, but Glyn Johns our producer stuck his neck out to enhance and evolve not just the songs, but also the *sounds* I had produced at home." Another reason for the album's great tone is Pete's use of a guitar sent to him as a gift from Joe Walsh.

"[Walsh said] 'I've got something for you . . . a 1957 Gretsch,'" Townshend told *Guitar Player* in 1972. "I said, 'Great, cheers, man,' and it turned out to be a real knockout. I was being polite. I opened the case and it was bright orange and I thought, 'Ugh! It's horrible, I hate it.' I went home and went into my studio and plugged it in and it totally wrecked me out, it's the best guitar I've got now. It's the Chet Atkins model, with double pickups, f-holes and single cut-away . . . I used that guitar on every track on *Who's Next*, it's the best guitar I've ever had. It won't stay in tune onstage but if it did, I would use it. It's the finest guitar I've ever owned, it's the loudest guitar I've ever owned. It is so loud, man, it whips any pickup that I've ever come across . . . If I plugged it in my amp tonight, normally I'd be working on volume six or seven, but I would work this guitar on one."

The Who's 1971 summer visit to North America marked their biggest tour to date for which a new, state-of-the-art, £20,000 PA system was unveiled. With the band playing to increasingly larger crowds, the venues used on previous tours simply proved too small to accommodate ticket demand. However, The Who gave their audiences value for money, playing a long but disciplined set (unlike others in their status bracket) and rarely played an encore.

Alongside such familiar standbys as 'I Can't Explain', and 'Substitute', their set opened with new songs 'Love Ain't For Keeping', 'Pure And Easy', Entwistle's 'My Wife' (from *Who's Next*), 'Bargain', 'Behind Blue Eyes', and 'Won't Get Fooled Again', which the band reproduced by playing along to a pre-recorded synthesiser tape. ('Baba O'Riley' was performed in the same fashion when it was added to the set later in the year.) 'I Don't Even Know Myself' (recently released as the B-side to a single edit of 'Won't Get Fooled Again') and, in a nod back to their Marquee past, an elongated take on Marvin Gaye's 'Baby Don't You Do It' followed before a selection of songs from *Tommy*. The show's homeward stretch started with 'My Generation' with either 'Magic Bus', the still-unreleased 'Naked Eye' and a jam on 'Road Runner' or another chestnut from The Who's past bringing the show to an exhilarating close.

Kicking off in heavy rain in Forest Hills, New York, on Thursday, July 29, the band members and crew attached rubber blocks to their shoes in order to avoid electrocution on the wet stage. John Swenson recalled Pete's antics that evening: "At the end of 'Magic Bus', Townshend broke the neck off his guitar and flung it into the photographers' pit. When a jittery roadie scuttled out to retrieve the body, Townshend threatened him with menacing gestures to stand aside . . . Townshend then took a second guitar and, grabbing it like a paddle, picked up the body of the broken first guitar, tossed it into the air, and slammed it with the second guitar as it came down. Both guitars broke into pieces at Townshend's feet. He then picked up a microphone stand and beat the mangled guitar bodies into splinters. The audience could hardly believe it and Townshend walked off the stage with the certain knowledge that he had successfully revived a legend."

In a rare display of onstage destruction, Entwistle joined the fray, demolishing his Gibson bass. The Who's second Forest Hills show took place two nights later, this time in hot, humid weather which sent countless cockroaches scurrying across the stage with many meeting their fate under Townshend's Doctor Martens boots. Following shows at 20,000-seat-plus arenas at Saratoga Springs and Philadelphia, The Who found that their new PA system was painfully loud (even by their standards) when they played four early August dates at Boston's relatively tiny 4,500-seat Music Hall.

"I'm terribly sorry about you with your fingers in your ears," Townshend told one beleaguered punter on the second night, "a very sad sight to see. We have slight problems adjusting from a 4,000 seat hall to a

30,000 seat hall. We're trying to bridge the gap. We're playing four nights. If we're a bit loud in Boston, it's because we're not loud enough in other places. Just don't put your fingers in your ears, otherwise I'll throw me guitar at you!" The excessive volume even wore on Daltrey, who knocked Townshend's amplifiers over the following night and stormed offstage after his pleas to turn down were ignored.

Sound problems plagued the entire tour and the tension onstage was palpable. Townshend smashed a guitar at almost every show. In Chicago, he hammered his Gibson SG into the stage lights in a rage when the electricity cut out after yet another problem with the PA. Two nights later, the tour was over. "The Who ended their *Who's Next* tour in a hailstorm of furious sound," wrote Swenson, "leaving yet another American audience dazed in their wake."

A year on from his initial idea, Townshend was faced with the fact that his hopes for a *Lifehouse* film were fading. "To go into it at any length, it gets more and more confused, and that's why [The Who] broke down," he said in August. "I could see the finished product, but I couldn't explain how I thought we could get there . . . With songs, I outline the idea to them and then make a demo. That's where this experiment fell down. You can't make a demo of a film. I wrote a script, but I'm not a scriptwriter so that wasn't overly well received. We got very, very close to what would have been a revolution in rock'n'roll, but we didn't really have the fodder to carry it off. We had to stop being The Who for so long we realised it was going to take months to rebuild ourselves. So here we are with no film. And I want to get a film done more than anything else . . ."

In an effort to spark some momentum towards the development of a celluloid vehicle, The Who assembled at Roger Daltrey's new manor house in Burwash the following month to engage in some creative discussions. On hand to film the proceedings were Richard Stanley and Chris Morphet.

"Pete and I had been talking about this idea of not only just producing an idea, but in a sense recording the process of producing [that idea], so we talked about this whole thing of what is *Lifehouse* about," Stanley recalls. "Part of it was about the relationship between the band and so forth, and how they got on with each other, so there was this idea to film some conversations, to do some interviews with each person, talk about what they were interested in and it was totally experimental, it was not meant in any way to be necessarily part of anything, but it was a way to get the ball rolling, and that's what Pete wanted, you know – to start the ball rolling . . ."

Ultimately, Morphet and Stanley's footage of the conversations served to reinforce the reason that *Lifehouse* failed to reach fruition. "It revealed that Keith was still just interested in entertaining, and Roger was, you know, still confused about everything and so forth," says Stanley. "It was all extremely tentative, but it did expose, I think, some things between the band, and it was quite interesting to have them all together in one place, but when it was done, I didn't see that it was going to do very much really."

The upheaval experienced during the struggle to come up with a film almost signalled the end of The Who. "There have been lots of breakups threatened . . . one fairly recently when we were trying to get the *Lifehouse* film together," Pete revealed to the *NME* in 1972. "It sort of ended up me against the world – that sort of thing. In that particular case, I had one idea about what the group should be doing, and the group had another idea." Ultimately, The Who realised that their new material had proved an enormous success and that their live shows were consistently garnering rave reviews. "I mean we came out of the whole film problem with a fantastic amount of energy and zest just to play and just to have fun," Townshend said in early 1972. "We got so brought down by the problem of what we were trying to get into that we ran back and picked up the guitars and banged away – as if to say 'Fuck everybody.'"

In September, The Who (along with The Faces, Mott The Hoople, The Grease Band, Lindisfarne and America) participated in a Bangladesh benefit concert at the Oval Cricket Ground in South London.[5]

Chris Charlesworth, who was there to cover the event for *Melody Maker,* recalls, "Afterwards I went for a meal with the band and Kit Lambert, and I brought along my sister Anne who was visiting London from Yorkshire. This was the first rock concert she'd ever been to, so it was a pretty good introduction – ringside seats for The Who playing for 35,000 on a warm evening. For some reason she ended up sitting next to Pete at the restaurant and they talked together for a long time. Anne was not part of the music business, and although she enjoyed the show, she wasn't at all in awe, she treated Pete like any other bloke. I think he really

---

[5] "Though it received far less attention than the George Harrison benefits staged at Madison Square Garden earlier that summer," Marsh noted in *Before I Get Old*, "The Who and their comrades raised as much or more money for the cause – and theirs got into the hands of the UNICEF officials and to Bangladesh itself much more swiftly."

appreciated that because he told me afterwards how great it was to sit and talk with someone who wasn't fawning over him and trying to impress. For years afterward, whenever I saw Pete, he'd ask after Anne and would ask me to pass on his regards. Unlike so many rock stars Pete wanted to stay in touch with normal people, as it helped him keep his feet on the ground."

In early October, The Who played at colleges in Reading, Guildford and Canterbury, with crowds of only a few hundred at each. This latest batch of small gigs with minimal publicity served as warm-ups for The Who's first British tour in over a year, which officially began with an October 18 performance at Southampton's Guildhall. *Melody Maker* supplied a typically enthusiastic review of the show:

> *"[The Who] used the best combination of songs to whip up the excitement to an awe inspiring climax as huge searchlights beamed down on delirious fans drunk with ecstasy at the group's new finale. A 'Magic Bus' / 'Naked Eye' medley runs into 20 minutes of material from* Tommy *finishing with the 'See Me, Feel Me' reprise. An instant to catch breath and 'My Generation' closes – surely the best combination they could pick. Whining feedback foiled the two openers, 'I Can't Explain' and 'Substitute', but from then on the group clicked into top gear. 'Behind Blue Eyes', with its strong vocal lines, showed just how good The Who's new PA system can sound, while 'Baba O'Reilly' [sic] and 'Won't Get Fooled Again' brought the audience to their feet on each occasion."*

Also that month 'Let's See Action', one of the *Lifehouse* songs left off *Who's Next*, was released in the UK and Europe and reached number 16.

Early November saw The Who open a new 3,500-seat venue, the Rainbow Theatre (formerly the Finsbury Park Astoria) by playing three nights, and being brought on by a troupe of dancing girls. Pete marked the occasion by wearing a silver lame boiler suit with the Rainbow's logo sewn on the back.

Next The Who returned to America, playing large arenas across the country on an 18-date tour which ended in mid-December. A full crew of sound and lighting men accompanied them alongside tour manager Peter Rudge, who was in charge of ensuring the operation ran like clockwork. Offstage the band members rarely mixed, with Daltrey retiring early to bed, Townshend withdrawing to his hotel suite to read or write, while Moon hit the town (often with Entwistle in tow), sometimes destroying his hotel room. The rock'n'roll temptations were ever present on the road as Charlesworth, along to cover the opening show in North Carolina, recalls.

"Pete and I were sat next to each other on the flight to Charlotte and the conversation got round to the subject of women. Apparently he'd been staying at some rich man's house somewhere in Florida and all these beautiful women had come on to him and he didn't really want to know because he loved his wife. He was talking about how difficult it was to resist them. Later on on that flight he got a terrible nosebleed and I ended up cradling him in my arms, holding his head back."

Townshend found time to devote to more spiritual matters during the tour when visiting the Meher Spiritual Center in Myrtle Beach, South Carolina, which Baba had set up during the Fifties. "It's made up of lots of lakes, kind of an inland Hawaii-type situation with lakes and fairly easy jungles leading down to the Atlantic coast," he described to *Penthouse* in 1974. "There are three or four thousand acres there that were a gift for an American Baba centre.[6] There are lots of little cottages and places where you can go and stay. Baba loved the place. I went there for one day, in the middle of the tour, and spent the night in this cabin, a place where Baba had lived. All of a sudden, for the first time in my life, I felt that I was in his presence . . . I put my head on the bed and fucking thought the most incredibly . . . unthinkable, unrepeatable, and unspeakable thoughts I've ever had. It was so awful, it was like being in hell. I completely broke up. I finally went out with fucking tears streaming down my face. Tears of self-pity. And I thought that I'd blown it. There I was, in the presence of the Master for the first time, and all that bullshit, all that filth."

Townshend believed that what he had experienced in the cabin was, "me fighting like mad not to surrender and using the most subtle, most subconscious way that I knew how. It was very, very spooky."

The Who's greatly anticipated December 9 concert at Los Angeles' 18,000-seat Forum sold out in less than 90 minutes, with fans camping out overnight to secure front row seats, which had been left available for public sale at the band's behest rather than being reserved for corporate guests. The show, the band's first in the city for 18 months, eclipsed previous sell-out records set by the Rolling Stones and the *LA Times* reviewer was moved enough to describe The Who as "the greatest show on earth". Pete took to the stage wearing a tie-dyed jumpsuit and when

---

[6] The Meher Spiritual Center remains an active spiritual retreat. Visit www.mehercenter.org for further information.

introducing the *Tommy* section, an ornate fake crown on his head, which he tossed into the crowd.

While in Los Angeles, Townshend followed Moon's penchant for wacky toys by purchasing a hovercraft as a Christmas present for his two younger brothers.

"It was my Dad's toy, really, more than Paul and I," Simon Townshend recalls, "'cause my Dad would start it – it was out on our front garden . . . we used to park cars on there. And the hovercraft was there, yeah . . . *mental!* Keith Moon bought one as well and crashed his. We bashed ours up at Pete's house in Goring . . . and Paul had a bit of an accident with it. Smashed part of it off, which had to be fixed up and . . . that was one of the few times that it got used . . . I remember, on that day as well, Paul went up the river on it, through a load of fishing rods while all these people were fishing."

The hovercraft was perhaps the most outlandish example of the many gifts Townshend brought back from abroad. "There was always anticipation in the air when he was finishing a tour, because the first thing he would do is stop by with presents," Simon recalls. "A really loving brother in that way, without a doubt and he would always make a big issue, a big deal of it and try and impress everybody as much as he could."

The US tour ended on December 15 in Seattle, The Who's last show in America for two years. Nik Cohn had accompanied the band on part of the trip, on a fact-finding mission to form the basis of a film script he was set to write, as Townshend recalled to the author: "Nik was supposed to be working on a script for *Rock Is Dead: Long Live Rock.* This was something of a part fiction rock documentary, I suppose, a precursor to *Spinal Tap.* If it had happened our version would have been ironic rather than comedic. My idea was to write songs about how rock had developed, but then how it had been co-opted by various factions not entirely artistic. Nik's heart was not in it."

An alternative celluloid project was also mooted, announced by Chris Welch in a *Melody Maker* interview with Roger in late 1971. "We start in January, and Pete is writing the music," said Daltrey. "The film should have been *Tommy* when the LP came out. That's when there should have been a film. In the film we do what we are good at – and that's playing. We'll get more involved as it progresses. It's going to be called *Guitar Farm* but I don't want to say too much about the story."

Townshend described *Guitar Farm* to the author as "a Utopian rock music idyll based partly on an update of *The Wizard Of Oz*," adding that it was "an extramural project in which I had little interest, written by Denis Postle, and partly driven by the film-maker Richard Stanley, both of whom were principals in the film-makers cooperative Tattooist International of which I was a member."

Tattooist International was "a group of directors and camera people who were quite radical – politically radical – but they were all established names," recalls Richard Stanley. "People like Mike Hodges who did *Get Carter*, and Nic Knowland and Chris Menges and people like that. But Tattooist became quite famous for doing rather radical political films and we also serviced John Lennon's movies, like provided the equipment and the editing and so forth. So we worked quite a lot with Lennon, and also with the other Beatles as well. Tattooist was mainly a documentary company and it sort of had this connection with the music business."[7]

Stanley recounts that *Guitar Farm* was based on the idea "that there was an island somewhere – which would later prove to be an aircraft carrier, but it was so overgrown that it was not noticeable – and on this island, all the people who had ever gone missing but never found, lived. So Glenn Miller was there with Hitler and Amy Johnson, etc., etc. It was meant to be a magical island in which all the trees and nature produced sounds so whenever you brushed through some undergrowth, it made sound, or you touched a tree and it made sound. And there was a guitar farm on the island where they actually grew guitars. It was a very bizarre thing – whether it was ever makeable I don't know."

MGM producer Herb Solow – executive producer of *Star Trek* – became interested in the concept, and the project gained momentum. "I talked it over with Pete," says Stanley, "and Pete was extremely interested in a guy called Mike Myers' basic idea . . . it got to the full script stage and Pete was involved in script conferences, he came down, we were staying in a castle for a while in Banbury, or a big old house, working on scripts and talking it through, and we had many communications about it. But in the end it got to be quite big, and MGM were actually, you know,

---

[7] In 1969, Townshend composed the title music for a Tattooist International documentary about the European Council for Nuclear Research, written by Denis Postle and broadcast on BBC2. The following year, he contributed music for another Tattooist effort, this time an experimental film called *Double Pisces*. According to Neill and Kent's *Anyway Anyhow Anywhere*, Pete contributed his demo of 'I Don't Even Know Myself' and played organ and guitar on an instrumental entitled 'Piledriver', accompanied by 'Speedy' Keen on drums and percussion.

wanting to take it a stage further, from a script to actually a screenplay, and develop it and see what could be done, and Pete was going to do some demos and at that time it just became perhaps too much of a threat to Kit Lambert's own plans. He brought in the heavy guys – lawyers and so forth. Denis Postle, who was the leading writer at Tattooist, and I went to see these people and got threatened . . . drop the project. Pete in a way had to make this decision, you know, does he go with this film that might never happen, or does he stick with a machine that works."

Townshend's earlier recollection that he had "little interest" in *Guitar Farm* jars with Stanley's memory of Townshend presenting the idea of "a river of consciousness, flowing through the countryside, gathering all the streams from either side, from left and right, and then flowing out into the ocean.[8]

"Pete certainly attended a lot of meetings, and contributed a lot to it . . . but certainly his enthusiasm slackened as the thing went on. But I don't think he was uninterested, certainly at the beginning when we got the money together to do it." Whatever the extent of Townshend's involvement, it appears that he didn't produce any new music for the project.

In 1972, The Who decided to take it easy following their recent hectic touring schedule. "We have plans for avoiding what we feel is going to be a very political year," Townshend told *Guitar Player* magazine.[9] "No schedule, no gigs, there's a rumour that we might play in Moscow one day. We're not planning to come back to America until 1973, and that's about it."

Pete took advantage of his open schedule and travelled to India on a Baba sabbatical in February.[10] "India was an absolutely, totally mind-blowing

---

[8] The imagery was probably inspired by one of Baba's teachings and would be addressed again in 'The Sea Refuses No River' on Townshend's 1982 solo album, *All The Best Cowboys* . . .

[9] The Nixon-McGovern presidential race took place in 1972.

[10] Pete relayed a humorous (and perhaps apocryphal) anecdote about his trip to India during a radio interview with Scott Muni in 1978: "You travel 11, 13 hours on the aeroplane and arrive in India and there's women in sheets and they look at you and they go 'Sahib, Sahib,' and beggars come up and people with no legs and no eyes. I figured at least I'm alone. I get my bags and I walk over to the hotel in Bombay and I walk in and I check my bags and go off to the room to catch some sleep and some guy comes up to me and says, 'Hello dere. Are you . . . you're not, eh . . . you're not Peter Townshend?' So I said 'Yes.' 'Oh, Peter Townshend of The Who. Oh, please give me your autograph, I'd be most, most grateful. Give me your autograph! Ah, The Who, most wonderful, wonderful music. You know they reflect the feeling on the streets of Bombay!'"

experience," Pete told *Penthouse* two years later. "I went over there and the first thing that hit me was that India was a fantastically beautiful country. It's the only place where poverty is almost pure. I mean *I* felt like the fucking peasant with my 20 suitcases and my first-class ticket and my charcoal-grey suit. I felt like a pig, I really did. So to cut a long story short, I ended up in the tomb where Baba was buried. There's a ritual that goes on there in which you walk in, put your head down to the ground, and walk out again. It's a kind of sacred procedure. Awful in a sense. It's just what Baba would never, ever have wanted . . . a ritualistic thing. The first time I went in there, I put my head down and tried to really feel like I was in Baba's presence. And I had the same thoughts that I had when I was in the bedroom at [the Meher Spiritual Center in] Myrtle Beach. And the same thing happened once again, when I went around the second time.

"By this time I'm really starting to know what I'm going to think as soon as I get in there. So the third time I go inside, I'm standing there thinking, 'Well, I'm washed up. I'm never, ever going to be in the presence of God, so I might as well fucking enjoy being with all these people and have a good time during my unhappy years on earth.' And suddenly this young guy walks in and he's obviously got dysentery very bad. He's small and fragile, his face is white, and he's shaking like a leaf. Somebody kind of ushers him forward and he looks like . . . well, he brought out all my maternal instincts, if that's possible for a man. I just felt so much compassion for him . . . so much sorrow for him . . . and I see him get down, put his head to the ground, and tears begin to stream down my face. I'm so wrapped up in this kid that by the time I get my head down, I've forgotten about what it was that was in my head. I forgot that whole trip. So I get up after realising that this guy was just a device to get me out of the way, you know what I mean? It was Baba's compassion that had arranged it. It was nothing else. I felt so insignificant that I might as well have been a speck of dust. It was the most incredible feeling I've ever felt in my entire life. And I went out afterwards and collapsed in thanks. That's what happened in India."

Pete's stay lasted about a month, during which he lived with a group of Baba's close followers and visited the Avatar's tomb on an almost daily basis. "There is a ritual there, when all his followers stand around the tomb and sing 'Begin The Beguine' which was one of his favourite songs," Townshend told *Creem* in 1980. "It totally zapped me out when I was there. I stood up after all this and was crying and everything."

Pete remarked that his spiritual experience in India made him reluctant to return. "I'm kind of nervous about going back again," he said. "I mean, I've had my little zap. I don't know how much more I could handle. It's like a door was opened for an instant, just so you could quickly glance inside. Then it slammed shut again. And you think, 'Christ, is that where we're all going?' Because if it is, we're all right. I'll tell you that right now." He did make a return visit exactly four years later.

Five years of following Baba's teachings had brought a certain amount of composure to Townshend's life. "I don't use dope, for instance, but I'm often with people who do," Pete told *Rolling Stone*. "Baba changed my life in that respect. I don't normally get involved in the usual group road scenes, dirty parties . . . but it goes on around me. I mean, Baba lovers in the States are incredulous. They walk into my room and go 'Jai Baba,' which means 'victory to Baba,' and there's a room full of people . . . broken guitars on the floor, piles of whiskey bottles, television sets out in the street, lemon curd all over the wall – they just can't equate the two things. I'm not saying I'm sitting there aloof, like the bloody lighthouse in the middle of the stormy sea – I'm affected, I'm involved, and part of the time I'm doing it – it's just that Baba is strong enough to keep hold of you, and it's possible for you to keep hold of him whatever you're doing."

"Previous to being involved with Baba I tended to weigh things up very carefully whereas now I'm much more impulsive," Townshend told Charlesworth. "I just sort of chase my Karma around with the feeling that Baba's got his thumb on my head, so everything's all right. At the same time I haven't changed all that much. I've still got a bad temper and I'm fairly aggressive as a musician. Quite simply, I write more honestly now."

Pete shared his feelings about Baba on his return from India, appearing on a religious television show *How Can You Be So Sure?* in late March. He also set about creating the second Meher Baba tribute album, *I Am,* at his home recording studio in Twickenham, distributing the 1,500 copies among its intended audience. The album, which, like its predecessor, featured music written and performed by a group of Baba followers variously augmented by Townshend, who played such instruments as drums, guitar, synthesiser, and even synthesised flute.

Along with an edit of Pete's original lengthy instrumental demo of 'Baba O'Riley', the record included Meher Baba's Universal Prayer,

'Parvardigar' ("Distant God").[11] "I don't actually say this prayer, I just happened to put it to music, but a lot of other people do say it," Pete told *Rolling Stone*. "I think it's an important one, which Baba dictated; it's like the replacement for the Lord's Prayer that he had dictated as the New Messiah. Preposterous as it may sound, I thought that by putting it to music a lot of people would just be saying it without thinking about it. It's an amazing piece of music, and the words are pretty amazing – as a prayer, it is the most unbigoted, unbiased prayer, it is praising everything in a very abstract way, so that anybody can get off on it. Even if you're an atheist you could still dig this, because it's in praise of life."

Because both *I Am* and *Happy Birthday* were very limited releases, pirate copies began to emerge in the US labelled *The Pete Townshend Meher Baba Album,* but with poor sound quality and no accompanying information. In addition, the title misled listeners into believing that Townshend wrote and performed on all of the tracks. "On the second one, I only did two bloody songs," Pete told the *NME*'s Nick Logan. "I was getting credited, in some cases, with doing really strange songs . . . songs I had bugger all to do with apart from the fact that I edited the album together."[12]

To remedy this, Townshend broached the idea of letting Decca release *I Am* on a larger scale. "What Decca said to me, indirectly, was 'These albums are selling at $11.98 in stores, and there's nothing we can do about it under the Piracy Act because it's not a legitimate record,'" he told *NME*. "They didn't make any contract pressure or anything. In fact nobody has. Everybody in the business . . . I don't know for fuck's sake why . . . but everyone in the business – Track, Decca, Polydor – they've all been so respectful. It's almost as if I was a fucking monk, y'know, and that they regard making these albums as part of my therapy or something. The record companies are giving up incredible amounts of percentages. I think it's because [George Harrison's] *Bangla Desh* set certain traditions that the industry are very proud of, and rightly so, and they are anxious to

---

[11] A German language version of 'Parvardigar' was also recorded. "When I recorded the 'Parvardigar' prayer on 31 August 1971 for the album *Who Came First*, someone suggested I should do versions in several languages," Townshend wrote in the *Scoop 3* liner notes in 2001. "An Austrian follower of Meher Baba, Hilde Halpern, did the translation, working literally from my own free adaptation of Meher Baba's Universal Prayer. There was no official release of the result."

[12] It has been difficult to verify the accuracy of this story, as bootlegged copies of Townshend's Baba albums are difficult, if not impossible, to find. Rick Chapman of Meher Baba Info does not specifically recall seeing a bootlegged Baba album, but does not doubt that they exist.

perpetuate this. Anyway, they said to me, 'We'll put this out, we'll give you a dollar an album' – which is an incredible amount of money – 'and we'll make sure the thing is done in good taste.' I thought, 'Well why not? How many copies do you want?' They said, 'Well we'll take 25,000 to start with.' So I nearly fell through the fucking roof. I said, 'How many? Christ, that's a lot of albums.' So I said, 'Listen if we're going to go into it on this scale, why don't I just do a completely fresh album?'"

Decca and Track agreed to donate 15 per cent of the retail price for Baba-related activities,[13] and Pete selected songs from *Happy Birthday* and *I Am* including work by other Baba devotees, alongside other material, most notably Billy Nicholls' 'Forever's No Time At All'.[14] The resultant album, *Who Came First*, released in September, contained an eclectic mix of performances, including Ronnie Lane's song 'Evolution', featuring Townshend on acoustic guitar, which was first recorded by The Faces as 'The Stone' on their 1970 debut album *First Step*.

"This version has got something about it theirs hadn't and I think they're quite happy about us doing it," Townshend told *Sounds* in 1972.

"We recorded ['Evolution'] in my home studio, and I felt very much a part of it," Pete told the *Austin Chronicle*'s Jody Denberg in 2007. "[Lane] was very much a part of what I was doing in those days. Our relationship was very intimate, kind, thoughtful, very constructive, and quite spiritual in quality. He brought out something in me. He broke me down, I suppose, with his humour. But when we did that song, I was just stunned. What he had actually done is taken Meher Baba's very complicated description of the universe and the way that consciousness travels and grows and evolves and turned it into a really amusing, light-hearted, and funky song. That was Ronnie's way: he was a real storyteller."

Also included were the *Lifehouse* demos of 'Pure And Easy', 'Time Is Passing' ("Another track The Who recorded for *Who's Next* that was rejected," Townshend told *Rolling Stone*) and 'Nothing Is Everything' (a.k.a. 'Let's See Action') offering a glimpse of Townshend's oft-vaunted home recording technique.

"This record hasn't let me do things musically that I hadn't done before,

---

[13] "They offered $150,000 advance, tax free, to donate to various charities connected with Meher Baba," Townshend said in 2005. "It was an offer I couldn't refuse."

[14] Singer/songwriter Nicholls was signed to Immediate Records in 1966 and sang on the Small Faces' *Ogden's Nut Gone Flake* album among some of the label's releases. He had gotten to know Townshend in 1970. Billy's son Morgan, also a musician, is Townshend's godson.

because it's music that was already in existence," he said at the time. "If I were doing a proper solo album, I would probably show off more – how well I can engineer, or how well I can play the piano. In a way we're using chuck-outs. But then, I do like the idea of people hearing what I do at home."

Pete included 'Let's See Action' "because I felt it said more about Baba than it did about the revolution," he told *Sounds*. "It was written about the revolution but somehow, in retrospect, I felt it was more about the action here [hits his chest] than here [raises his fist in the air]. And also I felt The Who's version was a bit joggy, a bit casual."

Jim Reeves' 'There's A Heartache Following Me' proved an interesting selection. "The sort of thing I'd never do, though I really enjoyed doing it," Townshend explained in 1972. "It was one of Baba's favourite songs. He heard someone playing it outside where all the disciples were, and he said that song, that guy's voice, are really amazing . . . he said that the words of it were very much the words that the Messiah would sing."

Written on The Who's 1970 tour while in Pittsburgh, 'Sheraton Gibson' "grew out of a really interesting writing session that I had," Townshend recalled in 1996. "I was in a hotel – I don't think it was the Sheraton Gibson, but it might have been[15] – and I'd been out and bought Bob Dylan's *Self Portrait,* which was a double album, and it was a bit of a dip in and see record, lots of different styles, and I was inspired by it. And I thought, 'This guy is a great genius, no question about it, but he's incredibly prolific and humorous and mischievous, and what would happen if I just sat down, put on a tape machine – I had an early, primitive cassette machine with me – and just put myself on the spot and made songs up as I went along? How many could I come up with?' And I came up with eight, and I totally made them up, start to finish, every detail, nothing added, nothing taken away, and what you hear is what I wrote. So it uses the kind of chords that fall under the fingers, but what the song actually does evoke is how I felt at the time."

Who Came First was largely viewed as a Meher Baba tribute rather than a bona fide Pete Townshend solo album. "[The album is] in a way dedicated to Baba, but mainly dedicated to the people who want to know the way I

[15] The song referenced a barbecue Townshend attended with the James Gang and their manager Mike Belkin during the 1970 US tour. "It was written in the Sheraton Gibson Hotel," Townshend said during a live chat on barnesandnoble.com in May 2000. "One of the most important songs [completed during the same session] was an early version of 'Bargain'."

feel about him," Townshend told *Rolling Stone* in 1972. "I find that when I try to talk about Meher Baba . . . I can't put it into words. So I thought maybe I should use my talent – with a small 't' – as a musician and try to put the feeling and the mood across that way."

"Meher Baba is an amazing man," Townshend praised to *Crawdaddy* in 1973. "He's dead now, three years since, but one still gets the feeling of a *now* presence. No single thing that has ever happened to me has changed the way I see and do things in this world so much. This album is meant to reflect these changes." The album is ". . . not for [Baba] to listen to, his ears aren't around, but so that he will be around whenever it's played."

While *Rolling Stone* called *Who Came First* "a brilliant and moving album . . . the music manages to fuse high devotional feeling with commercial mastery resulting in powerful music," Dave Marsh's review, published in *Creem*, was more dismissive. "Baba books and such have always seemed trite to me, without a whole lot to add to the body of cosmic aphorisms, but since he spent most of his life in silence, one doesn't expect much . . . It's inconsequential stuff . . . *Who Came First* is there, if you want it, which I don't suppose I do, particularly. It's a curiosity, more than anything, or an idiosyncrasy."

In May 1972, The Who booked time at Olympic Studios, working again with Glyn Johns, for the projected follow-up to *Who's Next*. Songs recorded during these sessions included 'Join Together', 'Relay', 'Long Live Rock', 'Put The Money Down', 'Love Reign O'er Me', and 'Is It In My Head?' (the latter two being held over for The Who's next project). Pete also came to the studio armed with demos for songs entitled 'Get Inside', 'Women's Liberation' (alternately titled 'Riot In The Female Jail') and 'Can't You See I'm Easy?'

While much of the work completed at Olympic was of excellent quality, the general consensus was that it sounded too much like an extension of the previous album. "We finished an album with Glyn Johns working at Olympic," Townshend said later. "We put a rough assembly together, and it sounded like a shadow, if this is possible, of *Who's Next*."

"So I said, 'Fuck this,' . . . well, everybody did unanimously," he told *Rolling Stone* in October. "We decided to have one side of the album just good tracks, and the other side a mini-opera. So I went off and started working on that, and got really excited about an idea I had, put about 14 or 15 songs together, and went rushing back and said, 'Listen, I'm not going to play this stuff, but I can tell you that what I've got knocks shit out of what we have already done, so let's shelve all that, put a couple out as singles, and I'll incorporate some others and we could do a new opera.' So that's basically what I'm working on at the moment."

This shift of focus precipitated a change in working methods as Townshend recalled. "I thought at the time, and Glyn was courteous enough to agree, although it did mean scrapping all his work, which was pretty amazing, to scrap the album as such and put out odd singles. However, he didn't stop there. I also thought it would be better to work in another studio with another engineer and again Glyn was very nice about that. We'd put in a fantastic amount of work together and it was pretty much an exhausted relationship at that time."

"When [the work done at Olympic] fell through in May '72, I said we needed an album, and couldn't put off doing something that was going to last. You know, we couldn't keep treading water and I had this idea for a project for a long time, and it really came out of The Who been going for 10 years and lots of backward looking and I thought it would be nice to have an album that encapsulated everything The Who had ever done, with a big sort of flourish, so we could really start afresh."

This retrospective idea – named *Rock Is Dead: Long Live Rock* – was represented by its key song 'Long Live Rock', which was eventually given to Billy Fury to record for his cameo in the film *That'll Be The Day* later that year (and which featured Keith Moon among the cast). The Who's version first appeared on 1974's *Odds And Sods* compilation.

'Join Together' and 'Relay' – both remnants from the *Lifehouse* experiment – were released as interest-maintaining singles in June and November, reaching numbers 9 and 21, respectively.[16]

In August, Pete used a suite at Brown's Hotel in Mayfair for the purpose of conducting interviews regarding his latest activities, including a new European Who tour (rehearsals for which were taking place at that time) and the upcoming release of *Who Came First*. "In the suite there are comfortable armchairs, sandwiches, drinks, coffee, a nicely relaxed atmosphere," described *Sounds'* writer Penny Valentine. "Townshend, with a newly grown small beard, looks splendid in his usual day attire of well cut trousers and tight knitted French sweater. He's back from holiday [in the South of France] and – as usual – raring to go."

---

[16] "I thought we might do a Marc Bolan and get this one ['Relay'] out quickly before 'Join Together' gets cold," Townshend said in August, "also, because 'Join Together' wasn't a huge success."

"The really interesting thing about the rehearsals is that we've been stuck in the studios and it's this thing about not playing together for seven months," Townshend told Valentine. "So for our own benefit – aside from the numbers from *Who's Next* which Europe hasn't seen us do and will be new numbers to them – we're doing a couple of numbers from the new album ['Long Live Rock' and 'The Relay'] we recorded in June."

On August 11, The Who went back on the road with a 15-date European tour which stretched into mid-September. The band used backing tapes for the *Who's Next* material and for 'Relay'. Pete, dressed in cheesecloth white, a Baba pendant around his neck, was now playing a Gibson Les Paul guitar rather than the SG model he'd been playing since the Woodstock era.

The switch from Gibson's SG model to the much heavier Les Paul was borne out of necessity. "They took the old SG off the market like about a year ago, so we used up every old SG in the country," Townshend told *Guitar Player*'s Michael Brooks. "I don't break them deliberately any more, but when I spin them around, when I've had a few drinks, I bang them and they crack and they break. They're made out of really light wood, it's a light guitar. The factory stopped making those particular SG's. So we said, 'You're going to have to make 'em for us, you're going to have to customise them for us,' and they said OK but it's going to be about $3,000 a guitar. So anyway, we had four of them made for the beginning of the tour. They brought them up to us but the guitars were totally different. The pickups were in a different position, and on and on, so I said, 'Forget it.' So I raided every music store in the country practically, looking for old SG's. My favourite guitar now for the stage is the Les Paul Deluxe with the small Epiphone pickups that you can buy off the shelf for $50.00."

The tour wound through Germany, Belgium (Pete greeted the crowd with "Hello Brussels sprouts!") and Scandinavia. An eyewitness account of the August 24 Gothenburg show was translated in *The Who Concert File*:

"The well-behaved Swedish audience was quietly watching as The Who appeared onstage with their gear. Pete Townshend approached the microphone and asked the audience not to panic. The Who was obviously used to a different reaction. Anyway, Pete backed up a few steps and made an enormous standing jump straight up into the air and landed on his knees on the stage floor with a great crash. The music started, extremely loud. After the song,

Townshend grinned and pulled up his trouser legs revealing a pair of enormous knee-pads.

The following day, The Who entourage checked into their hotel in Copenhagen. Ominously, Keith Moon found that select rooms contained waterbeds. "We were having coffee in his room and I said how great it would be if we could get the mattress in the lift and send it down to flood the lobby," Townshend told Charles Young of *Musician* in 1989. "Of course, it wouldn't move, but Keith tried to lever it out of the frame, and it burst. The water was a foot high, flooding out into the hallway and down several floors." Moon unbelievably bluffed the hotel management into believing it was not his fault, resulting in an upgrade to the Presidential Suite. The suite's expensive furniture was reduced to firewood after the show, with Moon and Townshend playing major roles in the destruction.

On September 9, The Who played before a daunting 400,000 fans in Paris at the French Communist Party's annual festival. "Actually, I didn't know it was for the Communists until we got here," Townshend told *Rolling Stone*. "Well, it's our first chance to exploit the Communists, eh?" At Pete's invitation, Eric Clapton attended this show, at which *Sounds* filed a report. "Mid-set, The Who reached their peak with 'Won't Get Fooled Again' and 'Magic Bus', Townshend vacillating hideously between a resigned poker face and an evil grimace. 'Get on board . . . come on,' he urged, and then lurched to the front of the stage, dripping with perspiration, and went through the motions of taking the stalk [of one of the many red roses which had been thrown on the stage] between his teeth and hurling a grenade into the crowd gesticulating a mighty explosion. It was a positive allusion to the large Vietnam banner that hung over the fete and a clear mnemonic of Pete Townshend, revolutionary."

The September 14 show in Rome – the final concert on the tour – was The Who's first in the city since 1967.[17] Chris Charlesworth was there on behalf of *Melody Maker*.

"Pete, Roger and John flew out to the gig from London and went back next morning on the same flight as me," says Charlesworth. "I do remember there was a press conference where journalists were asking questions in Italian and there was a translator. The Italian press were asking political

---

[17] The Who had a poor following in Italy: *Who's Next* had sold only 7,000 copies there in over a year.

questions and Pete didn't want to get involved so he just said 'Next question!'"

The atmosphere at the gig was electric despite the audience's muted reception as Charlesworth's review reported:

> *"Despite the long absence the audience sat impassively throughout the kind of set that most groups would swap their PAs for . . . It seems an almost unbelievable situation: fans are unable to demonstrate their appreciation of an act for fear of arrest and future banning of rock shows . . . Townshend is the most fluid mover I've seen since [that year's Munich] Olympic gymnasts. He twists and turns and spirals around, leaping from one side of the stage to another, spinning his arm like a propeller from start to finish. He falls over, somersaults and crashes to his knees like a man on a trampoline. Some day he'll go head first into his stack of speakers, break both legs and an arm, but that's his style and he couldn't change it if he tried . . . Townshend smashed his guitar into fragments – the first break of the tour – at the end and the Italian fans didn't know what had hit them. He swung it wildly at Moon's kit, and took three heavy blows against the stage floor before the instrument succumbed. The body left the neck and the whole mangled mess arrived in the front row. The police moved in and the ovation was stifled as a result."*

Plans for further touring in early 1973 (including a visit to Japan) were put on hold indefinitely. Townshend revealed to *Disc* that he was working on "something big . . . we are after something for the main body of the stage act – something like *Tommy* but not an opera – just a theme to run through it."

CHAPTER EIGHT

1972–1974

"Quadrophenia was really a grand flourish to tie up all the loose ends of The Who's obsessive thing with adolescence and rock'n'roll, which with people like Roger is still not dead, you know, but it's dead in me. I'm just not interested in punks on the street anymore, I'm not interested in baggy white trousers, and kids with their hair cut off. I'm too old for it, and I just wanted to – in one big fell swoop – build Jimmy up into this big sort of super-hero and then flop him down and leave him where we are today, fully illustrating the complete emptiness of the whole thing. And that's why it's not a particularly pleasant trip, in a way it's a very miserable sort of frustrated story. But I think it was important to do. I now feel good about the possibilities of future albums."

– Pete Townshend, 1975

"A lot of The Who has been lost in volume since we left *Tommy* out of the live show," Roger Daltrey told *Record Mirror* in December. "[The stage show has] lost some of the light and shade, and I've found it a lot less rewarding without the character of Tommy."

In November, a version of *Tommy* featuring the 104-piece London Symphony Orchestra, along with a 60-voice choir, was released. Produced by American producer Lou Reizner, the album featured a prestigious cast of singers including Steve Winwood, Rod Stewart, Ringo Starr, and Richie Havens, among others. While Reizner wished for Townshend's involvement from the beginning, he was initially hesitant to oblige. "Normally I wouldn't have got drawn into it," Pete commented during the recording, "but because Lou Reizner's such a persuasive fellow, I just found myself getting involved. It's simply a matter of me coming along to the sessions, listening to what's happening, and then approving the various tracks. I've got no control over anything anyway." Ultimately Townshend was flattered. "It's great to just sit here and hear the London Symphony Orchestra playing a piece of my music. And that someone like Lou has enough enthusiasm to spend money [reportedly about £60,000] and gather together all these amazing people, just knocks me out."

Reizner, who produced Rod Stewart's early solo albums, had lined up The Faces' singer for the lead role. "Well, I thought, for Christ's sake, it's gonna look super-competitive, with people comparing Rod's interpretations to Roger's," Townshend told the *NME*. "I spoke to Kit and Chris about it, and they felt that there wasn't too much chance of it actually happening. Nevertheless, I asked Lou if he would use Roger, because he's heard the backing tracks and was extremely keen to get involved." Reizner complied; Stewart's role was reduced to singing 'Pinball Wizard' while Daltrey got the opportunity to take another shot at *Tommy* in the recording studio.

"When The Who originally did it – as with most recordings – it was a little hurried towards the end," Townshend informed the *NME*, "so the vocals weren't perfect – plus the undeniable fact that as a singer Roger has improved a fantastic amount."

Director Tony Palmer was approached to film a documentary about the recording. "I said I would love to," Palmer recalls, "but I was doing something else at that moment which was somewhat preoccupying me. So I had to pass on that one, to my regret, because I think that would have been interesting, to see how that particular album was put together."

While the edge of the original got lost in translation, the reworking features some fine vocal performances. Roger's singing was arguably at its peak during this period, and Merry Clayton's take on 'The Acid Queen' was testament to what a female vocal showcase the song was, something which would be proven again by Tina Turner and Cheryl Freeman. Pete, as the Narrator, sang on 'Overture', and lead vocal on 'Amazing Journey' and 'Sally Simpson'.

"This is one mighty beautiful package," wrote *Melody Maker*'s Chris Welch. "Townshend's masterpiece has finally got the treatment it deserves with an all-star cast, a full symphony orchestra and a presentation that ranks among the best in the history of rock albums . . . Missing, of course, is the driving beat of The Who and the overall power that comes with having a rhythm section with Moon and Entwistle at the head, but instead we have a character for each part, each bringing his own style to the thoughts of Townshend . . ."

Dave Marsh held the opposite view: "It was fatuous and bombastic Camp, a betrayal of the spirit of the original – and of The Who."

On December 9, the London Symphony Orchestra and featured guests (as on the recording, apart from Peter Sellers deputising for Richard Harris and Keith Moon in place of Ringo Starr) performed *Tommy* at the Rainbow, whose stage was transformed into a giant pinball machine for the occasion.[1] The two shows caused Townshend (who revealed to Dave Marsh that he had grown "disenchanted" with the project by the time of the concerts) a great deal of anxiety, which he duly treated by ingesting copious amounts of brandy, and his performance suffered because of it. Dave Marsh recalled events as follows: "Townshend, who, as narrator, was supposed to help make the story flow, was dead drunk, missed cues, blew lines. Pete was particularly horrible during 'Sally Simpson'. In the course of the evening, he insulted the audience, Reizner, orchestra conductor David Measham and, at the end, wiped his arse with the libretto and staggered off the stage."[2]

"*Tommy* will pay my pension all right, as my Dad keeps telling me," Pete told *Melody Maker*'s Mark Plummer the following month, "but on that stage I felt very open. It was me, Pete Townshend, having to answer all the criticisms levelled at *Tommy*. I'm not a nervous person, I don't usually feel nervous; when I'm onstage with The Who I can forget I'm Pete Townshend. I'm able to become part of The Who and go crazy without having to be me."

A repeat performance of Lou Reizner's *Tommy* was held at the same venue the following year, with Daltrey and Moon reprising their roles. "I was very excited about that event but, having fucked it up the first time around, I didn't do it again," Townshend told *Uncut* in 2004. "What was interesting about that second time was that I was sat with my wife Karen and it was the first time I'd ever seen Roger from the audience. I remember turning to her and saying, 'He's fucking good, isn't he?' And he was great. I'd always thought Roger was a bit naff, I'd always thought he was a bit of a nuisance – y'know, swinging his microphone around and getting in the way of my guitar sound. That was the moment I realised

---

[1] The event was originally planned to take place at the Royal Albert Hall, but was deemed "improper" by the venue's management. The Rainbow concert raised almost £10,000 for the Stars Organisation for Spastics charity.

[2] "The story behind that is, unfortunately, a lot more shallow," Townshend told *Uncut*'s Simon Goddard in 2004. "I was drinking quite a lot at that time and I forgot to paste the words into this book which I was reading from. I'd only pasted in the first half of it, so what actually happened was I was wiping my arse on the basis that the book was no good. I thought somebody had ripped some pages out. I'd had too much to think about so up to that point I'd been narrating and when I got to that page and there was nothing there I thought, 'Oh, fuck.' I just arsed about, basically."

that, through *Tommy*, Roger had made this connection to the audience and become a theatrical performer. I had much greater respect for him after that."

During the initial preparations for *Quadrophenia*, Pete was spending what he described as "a tremendous amount of time" with Eric Clapton in an effort to help him overcome a crippling heroin addiction.

"I was having to answer hysterical phone calls from [Clapton's girl-friend] Alice Ormsby-Gore practically every night," Townshend said later. "She always wanted me to go over there. It was an hour and a half's drive, and always at awkward hours of the night . . . When I got there, usually she just wanted to explain what was happening. Eric would be asleep somewhere and she would be running around hysterically. What was worrying her, what she needed to talk about, was that she was giving Eric all of her heroin supply, most unselfishly. And then she was having to deal with Eric's extremely selfish outbursts, accusing her of doing the reverse.

"It was a typical junkie scene. It was despicable. But even through all that, you know, I got to like and love them both very much. It was the first encounter I'd had with heroin addicts. I wasn't prepared for the lies, I wasn't prepared for the duplicity."

The Townshends' marriage began to feel the strain. "[Karen] measured it all against time spent with her," Pete later wrote, "fairly minimal at the best of times, and very minimal during this period."

Townshend's support for his old friend culminated with two all-star concerts at the Rainbow Theatre on January 13, Clapton's first per-formances in over a year. "It wasn't my idea to do the show, it was Eric's idea," Townshend claimed. "It came about through Bob Pridden, our main road manager, who lives near Eric, and sees him quite a lot. We've exchanged 'hellos' and 'goodbyes', but never ever got together. So I decided to go down and see Eric to revive an old friendship really. I had a look at his home studio, which I really liked, and he started to talk about these tapes. I asked him what had happened to his last album, and he said, 'There it is, over there.' And there was this pile of tapes on the floor, and I said, 'What's become of it?' and he said he was waiting for Andy Johns to come back to finish it off. But Andy was working for the Stones and con-sequently inundated, and I started to get down to helping Eric finish it off.

"The real point is I don't think Eric really wanted to finish it off. And a lot of work I did on it was kind of wasted. But he's now talking about getting it finished. There's some good material there . . . I think it was recorded at a period when Eric was doing sessions for Stevie Wonder and it was at a time when although the band was about to split they were playing particularly well. If it was finished it would make a fine album.

"Eventually I got worried about it ever getting done and Eric seemed so lethargic about the whole idea, and one day he just rang up and said, 'I'm going to do this gig at the Rainbow, do you fancy helping out?' He more or less said, 'I'll do it if you'll do it.' It was a schizophrenic turn-around that is so typical of Eric. One minute he can be completely down on something, and then he'll put in a year's work. He worked hard on the concert, and although he was surrounded by good, eager, sympathetic musicians, it was still all his songs, and he had to teach us them all. It was two weeks solid rehearsals at Ronnie Wood's place ['The Wick', a historic home on Richmond Hill.]

"I just don't know why [Pete] picked on me to do the Rainbow concert," Clapton told *Conversations With Eric Clapton* author Steve Turner in 1976. "It could have been anybody but I'm grateful he chose me. I was just pleased to be doing it because I wouldn't have made up my mind to do it on my own. It had to be someone dragging me around by the scruff of my collar and making me do this and that."[3]

Alice Ormsby-Gore was the daughter of Lord Harlech, who in turn was close friends with world-renowned violinist Yehudi Menuhin. Menuhin referred Clapton and Ormsby-Gore to Dr Margaret "Meg" Patterson, a Scottish surgeon, to undergo her unorthodox therapy in an attempt to terminate their addiction.

The treatment, which had originated as 'electro-acupuncture' in Hong Kong's 850-bed Tung Wah hospital in the early Seventies, was initially intended to create analgesia in surgery patients. Dr Patterson (the hospital's head of surgery) and neurosurgical consultant Dr H.L. Wen soon discovered an unintended side effect: the treatment proved a reliable means of virtually eliminating the patient's desire for heroin.[4] Patterson and Wen soon set about locating patients who were willing to be treated for their dependency. After 40 addicts underwent the electro-acupuncture technique, Dr Wen reported in the *Asian Journal Of Medicine* that a

---

[3] There was talk of a tour to follow the concerts but the idea never made it past the planning stage.

[4] During this period, Hong Kong was a hotbed of drug abuse and Patterson estimated that approximately 15 per cent of the hospital's surgical patients were opiate addicts.

40-minute treatment "consistently stopped all withdrawal symptoms for a period of time," and that "repeated treatments over a 10-day period, according to the addicts, completely removed the desire of the addicts to take their drug of addiction." After witnessing over a hundred patients undergo the treatment, in a 1976 report to the United Nations Office for Drug Control and Crime Prevention, Patterson emphasised that despite the encouraging results, the procedure had been performed in less than ideal conditions.

Therefore she returned to England to refine the electro-acupuncture technique into what became known as Neuro-Electric Therapy (NET). Over the years, the use of acupuncture needles gave way to ear clips containing tiny needles, and eventually to flat electrodes pressed against the skin behind each ear through the use of a headset. In addition to reducing discomfort and the risk of infection, this also enabled Patterson's patients to move around freely, and even sleep, during their treatment. The electrical current, less than two milli-amps, was provided by a portable battery-operated box which enabled the physician to adjust the frequency and wave settings of the stimulus received by the patient depending on withdrawal symptoms and the type of chemical dependency being addressed. The discomfort experienced was minimal, as Patterson wrote: "the patient can wear the electrodes quite comfortably on a continual basis for as long as the treatment period lasts, typically five to ten days."

Clapton underwent the procedure for five weeks, sleeping on a fold-down bed in the Patterson family's crowded Harley Street flat. Townshend, who was a regular visitor, was especially impressed with the treatment and word of Patterson's innovative procedure soon spread throughout the music industry.

Pete also worked with other musicians during this period, including playing bass harmonica on Gallagher & Lyle's 'Give A Boy A Break' (produced at Olympic by Glyn Johns and included on the duo's 1973 album, *Willie And The Lapdog*), producing and performing on several tracks by the eccentric characters John Otway and Wild Willy Barrett and making a guest appearance on *Jesus Christ Superstar* singer Yvonne Elliman's cover version of 'I Can't Explain'.

Townshend had first encountered Otway the previous year. "I'd recorded a track with Willy – or a couple of tracks – and we'd pressed them up as a single which I was selling locally," Otway recalled to the author. "Willy had some involvement with some management in London, a chap called Ian King who was involved in, as I understand it, a charity for homeless people and things, for which Pete Townshend helped out. Ian King played Pete a copy of this single, and Pete offered to produce it, so subsequently me and Willy went down to Twickenham to meet him. I was only about 19 or 20 years old . . .

"I was actually convinced that Willy was pulling my leg about Pete Townshend producing the tracks. All the way there, in the van, I was sort of saying, 'Look, I'm only going 'cause my friends have told me to come.' I was really quite convinced, and it wasn't until he opened the door that it suddenly dawned on me . . . '*Oh*, there's Pete Townshend.' And there we were sitting in his living room, and suddenly I realised I was going to have to play guitar in front of him which was daunting to say the least.

"It was a song called 'Misty Mountain' with me playing guitar and Willy playing fiddle. I think Pete was actually quite fascinated by Willy's fiddle playing. Willy's pretty much as near a genius multi-instrumentalist that I've ever worked with. I know that word is overused, but he was really quite phenomenal at playing banjo, fiddle, steel guitar – an array of instruments, in pretty much an unusual way, with various mixtures of bluegrass and blues and stuff, which was quite unusual for a guitarist from somewhere like Aylesbury in Buckinghamshire, or wherever he came from."

Duly impressed, Pete booked time for Otway and Barrett at Olympic studios in October 1972, where, according to Otway, the duo recorded 'Misty Mountain' and 'Gypsy', with Townshend playing bass and Speedy Keen on drums. While these tracks went unreleased, the experience provided Otway and Barrett with sufficient inspiration to hole themselves up at Otway's house and record a new batch of demos. In early 1973, the duo reconvened at Pete's home studio to record 'Murder Man', 'If I Did', 'Louisa On A Horse', and another version of 'Misty Mountain'.[5] The first two of these tracks were coupled together and released as a Track single in April with the credit: 'Recorded at Eel Pie Sound for Community Music'.

In addition to producing the tracks in his second-floor home studio, Townshend also contributed bass, guitar, and synthesiser. Otway recalls Pete "spent *ages* working on getting that [whooshing synthesiser] part on 'Louisa On A Horse' right." The percussive rhythm running throughout the drum-less 'Murder Man' is "actually Pete doing that with his mouth,

[5] While it has been documented that Townshend was involved in the recording of only these four songs, Otway also recalls recording the song 'Bluey Green' with Townshend. "We might have re-recorded that for the album, but I know he did do a version of 'Bluey Green'," he says today.

which is great," Otway enthuses. "It was a really creative thing – I mean, he taught Willy and I loads . . . he was stunning to work with. He put in *hours* . . . he really knocked us into shape. I mean, I'd hardly done any recording before and at that time recording was outrageously expensive anyway. So to actually record in a serious recording studio like Olympic with the Stones wafting around . . . and even just working in Pete Townshend's house . . .

"I know I can remember him playing the rhythm guitar part on 'Louisa On A Horse', and being like three feet away while he actually put his guitar part down. There was something quite wonderful about just being that close to somebody that good and actually just watching how they work – 'Ah . . . *that*'s why they're that good' . . . what an experience."[6]

'Louisa On A Horse' b/w 'Misty Mountain' weren't released until August 1976 on a Track single, with the self-titled *John Otway & Wild Willy Barrett* album, which included all four songs, following (on the Extracked and Polydor labels) in 1977.

The 'I Can't Explain' session with Yvonne Elliman took place on April 17, 1973 at London's Air Studios. "I was just invited to play because she was covering one of my songs, and I didn't mind, although I don't think I added anything new," Townshend recalled to John Tobler and Stuart Grundy in 1983. However, Elliman recalls the experience as far more meaningful and had talked to producers Rupert Hine and David McIver about including a cover of the song on her second album, being recorded for Deep Purple's label, Purple Records.

"I remember them mumbling about the possibility of getting Pete to come in and lay the guitar part down. Surely, they were kidding. I was a young, inexperienced, rock'n'roll wannabe . . . I think they thought they were kidding too, because when they announced that he *would* come by, they were bubbling over the top with giddiness, like a child's excitement over the news about the circus coming to town. So, you could imagine the awe we all felt as the *man* walked into the room. While trying to be cool, we stumbled and bumbled around trying too hard to make him comfortable, when all he needed, it seemed, was his guitar and the bottle of brandy he carried in."

Apparently Townshends's demands for more volume drew on more

---

[6] Several years later, Pete gave Otway and Barrett some time at his studio in Goring. "He just contributed a bit of studio time – he wasn't involved with the recording," Otway recalls.

electricity than was available, as Elliman floridly recalls, "While he was filling the air with unreal notes connecting several octaves at a time, the room at Air Studios suddenly went dark. It was instantaneous. There were no sparks or flashes of fire; just a rumbling buzz a half of a second long, then pitch black. Pete mumbled, 'Wot's 'appened?' . . ." The session ground to a halt while Townshend, Elliman and the other musicians headed to a nearby pub until the power was restored. 'I Can't Explain' was released as a single in August and included on Elliman's *Food Of Love* album released two months later.[7]

Meanwhile, Pete's new project had grown in the wake of the original *Rock Is Dead: Long Live Rock* idea. While still faithful to the retrospective angle of its predecessor, the new story focused on the central character's youth. "At the moment I'm pretty excited about it," Townshend had told Penny Valentine back in August. "It'll be a decade of The Who in January . . . What's happened to the individual members of the group, how they've changed? So I thought a nice way of doing it was to have a hero who, instead of being schizophrenic, has got a split personality four ways and each side of this is represented by a particular theme and a particular type of song.

"I'm the good part of the character needless to say – the choir boy who doesn't make good, the sea scout who gets assaulted by the scout master. Then there's the bad part, which is Roger, breaking the windows in coloured people's houses, turning over Ford Populars and things of that nature. Then there's the romantic part which is John Entwistle, falling in love with the girl next door, everything really going well until her mother catches them one day in a compromising situation and flings him out and he goes off frustrated, despairing. Then there's like Keith – totally, irresponsibly, insane. Playing jokes on his girlfriends, telling terrible lies, blowing up the place where he works. And joining all these moods and songs together.

"I've written a lot of stuff about this period and it's all come out sounding like old Who material – quite unconsciously. And it gave me the idea to consciously do that. To start off with early Who sound and come

[7] In 1996 Elliman's little-known version of 'I Can't Explain' was given unexpected exposure when DJ Fatboy Slim (a.k.a. Norman Cook, formerly of the Housemartins) sampled Pete's riff for 'Going Out Of My Head', included on Slim's 1996 album *Better Living Through Chemistry* and released as a single the following year.

through – more and more synthesiser, more and more snazzy recording until you get to the point where he finds himself coming together, fitting together like a jigsaw. Going from that period of sort of fucked up amazing spiritual and social desperation, despair with politics and everything – to come together as one piece of music which is The Who."[8]

Townshend offered a further description of some of the specific events in the protagonist's life: "I was writing one song about being kicked out of home and eventually he has this final row with his dad about cutting his hair, his mother finds dirty books, gradually their son is being eroded before their eyes, turning into something they can't relate to any more, and I used a bit from 'Zoot Suit' and I sort of glorified it into a big thing – *Zoot suit with white jacket and side vents five inches long.*

"At the end I wrote this song where the kid is really fucked up with drugs and chicks and his family, not getting on at school, identifying himself with a militant group, tries to help workers' causes and finds that not only is he powerless but they resent it. And I started to feel that when you write about somebody that has *everything* happening to them you somehow realise how everything does affect everybody."

Quadrophenia, as the work became known, was the story of a young mod in Sixties London, although the connection – other than the 'Zoot Suit' reference – wasn't immediately apparent in Townshend's August '72 description. Pete had been reminded of The Who's mod connections when he and 'Irish' Jack Lyons started corresponding.

"At the time – this would be around mid-1972 – we were writing regularly to each other and I used to pen him some amazingly long letters," Lyons recalls. "They were something like 16 or 17 handwritten pages of stream of consciousness.[9] In one of my letters I remember telling him how I had just become the first bus conductor in Cork to wear the celebrated Doctor Marten boots. Whether he was tickled pink to hear this or not, I don't know . . . but his reply was to the effect that he was elated in the knowledge that one of his oldest friends had embraced Seventies youth culture . . . even if I was 29 at the time and he only a couple of years behind! He could be much more gracious in his letters than sometimes in

---

[8] "When writing *Quadrophenia* I was inspired by the acquisition of a splendid new Bosendorfer 7' 4" grand piano which I still have today," Pete wrote in the *Scoop 3* liner notes in 2001. "It was squeezed into the tiny room I used then, but it sounded extraordinary, still does."

[9] Not surprisingly, Lyons soon got writer's cramp. To remedy this, Townshend sent him an old portable typewriter.

his physical presence. Fuelled by this response, I then sent Pete my old Goldhawk Club membership card through the post for him to look at, and requested that he return it to me by registered letter so it wouldn't get lost, which he did. And then his letter opened with something like 'Memories . . .' etc. So the next few letters between us consisted of me reminding him of some of the stuff we did when we were mods down at the Goldhawk Club in Shepherd's Bush. He never actually consulted me about *Quadrophenia* but he obviously had me in the back of his head because of our correspondence."

While Townshend's decision to make the central character Jimmy (whose name did little to quell numerous *Tommy* parallels) a mod was widely viewed as an affectionate look back to The Who's roots, it also provided an apt stereotype for his screwed-up hero.

"There are so many tragic things involved with the mods," Pete explained in April 1973, "the fact that they grew up and became respectable – that's a miserable situation. The fact that they turn into middle aged pop stars, that's miserable. The fact that they're badly educated kids, deprived, and the only things they have are kicking people and dancing, that's miserable. But at the same time it's got this incredible triumph in that this kid's an individual in the midst of a world where the individual doesn't exist."

An essay penned by Townshend through the eyes of the protagonist, which appeared inside the sleeve of the finished *Quadrophenia* album, set the scene. Jimmy suffers from a severe identity crisis which is further complicated by the problems he encounters at home, at work, with friends and in his love life.

He ends up out at sea, stranded on a rock:

> ". . . *the bleeding boat drifted off and I'm stuck here in the pissing rain with my life flashing before me. Only it isn't flashing, it's crawling. Slowly. Now it's just the bare bones of what I am.*
>
> *A tough guy, a helpless dancer.*
> *A romantic, is it me for a moment?*
> *A bloody lunatic, I'll even carry your bags.*
> *A beggar, a hypocrite, love reign over me.*
> *Schizophrenic? I'm Bleeding Quadrophenic.*

Several songs on *Quadrophenia* successfully articulated Jimmy's various internal struggles, from identity crisis ('The Real Me', 'Is It In My Head?',

'Dr. Jimmy') frustration with his peers ('Cut My Hair') to spiritual desperation ('Helpless Dancer', 'Drowned', 'Love, Reign O'er Me'). While
'The Dirty Jobs' and 'I've Had Enough' expressed Jimmy's dissatisfaction,
songs, such as 'Drowned', demonstrated a yearning for a higher level of
understanding.[10] "Mixed up in *Quadrophenia* was a study of the divine
desperation that is at the root of every punk's scream for blood and
vengeance," Townshend wrote in 1977. This desperation becomes more
evident as the album progresses, ending with an impassioned plea for love
('Love, Reign O'er Me').

After the Olympic sessions the previous summer, Pete had hinted that The
Who needed a change of surroundings to start afresh. The problem was
they couldn't find a satisfactory studio. "We tried everywhere," said
Townshend, "test recorded at every studio but nothing came of it." This
resulted in the purchase of an old church in Battersea, south-west London,
and converting it into a recording studio, which ultimately became known
as Ramport. When recording was ready to start on *Quadrophenia*, the
studio, referred to as 'The Kitchen', was still under construction.

"The [Who] decided to start the new album at Ramport studios even
though it wasn't finished," Richard Barnes wrote in *Maximum R&B*.
"They were determined that Ramport was going to be a top rate studio
and had been dissatisfied with the control room so had ripped out all their
work and were rebuilding it. The studio itself, however, was finished. So
they brought in Ronnie Lane's mobile, parked it outside, and ran cables
out from the studios across the pavement and into the mobile, which was
used as the control room. A video camera gave the engineer, Ron
Nevison, a view of the studio and two way mike link-ups were installed
for communication."

While this was not the perfect environment in which to record, it paled
in comparison to other distractions which faced The Who during this
period – the most important involving the band's management affairs, as
Chris Charlesworth described, "The style of management provided by Kit
Lambert and Chris Stamp, the stretching of cheques, the snappy ideas, the
full tilt promotional thrust that characterised the workings of New Action

---

[10] "Because I record at home I have often knocked songs together quickly simply so I can
enjoy some recording, or to try out a new gadget or technique," Townshend told *France
Metro* in 2007. "My song 'Drowned' happened that way, and yet it is one of the most
powerful songs I've written about spiritual longing, and the desire to submerge into the
nothingness of the universe."

Ltd, were ideal for the Sixties, but in the climate of the Seventies, when The Who no longer needed promoting through outrage, when logistical professionalism and sound financial advice was required, the management team was largely redundant."

Peter Rudge now looked after The Who's touring affairs in America while Bill Curbishley had risen through the ranks to look after day-to-day matters in London. A school friend of Chris Stamp's, Curbishley began as a Track Records employee in 1971 after serving a gaol term for armed robbery. "Bill's a tough cookie and was able to handle the egos within the band," says former Track employee Dana Wiffen. Curbishley was officially appointed The Who's manager in 1976, a position he still retains.

Around 1972, Daltrey ordered an independent audit of New Action's books and found that large sums were unaccounted for. Adding further fuel to the fire, Lambert and Stamp had dismissed Daltrey's first solo album (released in April '73). Because they had invariably sided with Townshend on group policy, Daltrey's distrust of the pair only increased. Meanwhile he asked Curbishley to manage his affairs and brought Entwistle over to his side against the management.

Townshend and Daltrey remained at odds on the subject during the following year. "I know Roger's very conscious all the time of the money set up," Townshend told Chris Charlesworth. "I think it's quite simply because he can't sleep at night unless he does actually know what we're earning. But that's probably because he's never spent the way Keith and I have – which is why we don't care how much we've got. We spend what we want to spend and never ask questions later. I've never got into the red because my writing money has kept me a wee bit ahead of the group but Keith has occasionally gone into the red through overspending. But in the end you just say, 'We're just going to have to do a few more tours or something.'"

An incident involving monies owed in back royalties proved to be the final nail in the management's coffin. When the band requested money to complete construction work on Ramport, Lambert, by all accounts, sanctioned a substantially smaller amount than they'd requested, then went off to Venice, where he promptly stopped payment on the cheque. "The band went absolutely fucking crazy," Curbishley told Marsh. Lambert had been living in Venice since late 1971 in the Palazzo Dario, an elaborate 15th-century house with a marble façade. "A lot of the pop sycophants went, but none of the band," Townshend told Andrew Motion in 1987. "He desperately wanted us to go, but we were not interested, or too busy." Lambert's young boyfriend, Tito, was another reason why Townshend stayed away. "They really loved each other," he told Motion, "but the boy hated me."

Meanwhile, *Quadrophenia* wasn't coming together as quickly as Pete would have liked and he expressed his frustration at the album's slow progress to *Melody Maker*'s Mark Plummer in February. "I've got to get a new act together for The Who," Townshend declared, "and I don't care if it takes me two years before you see The Who again, we've got to get something fresh." He lamented his inability to "write a strong plot" and reiterated that the band needed new material to rejuvenate The Who's stage show. "We've tried going through all the hits, basing a show on that, but that doesn't work. It's all in the past now; people don't really want to sit and listen to all our past."

Pete spent much time on recording the various sound effects heard on *Quadrophenia*. Water being a central theme throughout, various recordings of rainfall, thunder, and crashing waves were made to facilitate the idea. Townshend used a portable Nagra tape recorder and Ronnie Lane's mobile recording studio housed in an Airstream trailer.

"Pete took it down to the south coast once when he was talking about *Quadrophenia* and was doing recordings on the beach," recalls Richard Stanley. "He got into this whole idea of location recording in stereo . . . I think partly my interest in film also led to his own interest in film and such things like location recordings . . . certainly there was a kind of interest in the filmic aspects of the music, in much the same way that maybe people write books today, thinking that they might be made into a film, which kind of affects the way they write the book."

The intricacies of capturing these sounds were recounted by Richard Barnes in *Maximum R&B*: "Pete and his driver, Rod, did much of the recording for the effects. Rod bribed a train driver with £5 to blow his whistle as he was leaving Waterloo station – strictly against British Rail regulations – for the beginning of '5:15'. Pete drove down to Cornwall and [*Quadrophenia* engineer] Ron Nevison towed the mobile there to record the sea, wading along the shore, flocks of mallard ducks taking off and so on. Nevison was stopped and questioned by the police when he was trying to secretly record crowd noises at Speaker's Corner in Hyde Park. He sent his girlfriend to ask the brass band on the Kensington Gardens bandstand to play a Souza march which he recorded with his hidden Nagra."

The Who finally entered the studio in May to begin recording the project, which was now being acknowledged as a double album due to the amount of material Pete had written. "In the last couple of years, Townshend, Daltrey, Moon and Entwistle have become involved in various solo projects and seemed in danger of drifting apart," wrote *Melody Maker*'s Chris Welch. "It's as if they have taken faltering steps away from the parent body, with varying degrees of success now to return to their alma mater, and get down to the hard business of making Who music."

Townshend brought in Lambert in an effort to consolidate and clarify the storyline as he had done with *Tommy*, and at the same time, perhaps rekindle their collaborative flame, which had been all but extinguished during *Lifehouse*, but things unravelled fairly quickly. Lambert, who continued to abuse drugs and alcohol, "didn't make out very well," according to Townshend, "and argued with Daltrey. I felt let down and took over despite the fact that I had more than enough on my plate." "[Kit] left me holding the baby for the production, which was bloody difficult," Pete added in 1987.[11]

For the *Quadrophenia* sessions, instead of presenting finished demos to the studio for the band to hear, Townshend brought in what he described as "rough sketches on tape".

"It was a very ambitious cooperative project," he told John Swenson. "I wanted everybody in the group to write their own songs and stuff. Everybody was supposed to engineer their own image, as it were. I wanted the group to go in and play a piece of music which was completely spontaneous and then give people their respective segment of the track. Let's take 'Can You See The Real Me', for example. It's a semi-spontaneous backing track with loose words which I structured later on. So you get that real sort of vital Who backing track sound with some words over the top, and then I'd take the guitar part away and build it into something: Keith, the drum part, that kind of thing. What we could do is take all these individual things down and strip them away and get down to the basic backing track as though that was the result of the stuff instead of

[11] Track's Dana Wiffen recalls that eventually the band did their best to keep Lambert away from Ramport during the recording of *Quadrophenia*. "They didn't tell Kit when they were there because they didn't want Kit to come along and muck it up, basically," he recalls. "Because he would turn up and he would not do what they wanted, because he was so out of it himself. And unfortunately that's the way they did it in the end, they tried to keep quiet, unless they wanted him to come along for any reason, they didn't tell him when they were there. They were trying to avoid him basically."

the starting point. As always the band just looked at me like I was crazy and walked away. I've explained it to a lot of people and everybody seems to be able to understand it but them. Then John wrote a song which he wouldn't play for me because he thought it summed up the whole album in one song."

As a result of the other members' lukewarm response to his cooperative approach, Townshend took on the entire project as his own – not only writing the entire album and playing guitar and keyboards,[12] but also assuming the role of producer in Lambert's absence.

He was clearly overcommitted. The others, however, responded positively to his rough demos with The Who's rhythm section giving some of their best performances to date. Moon's drumming was "free and fluid", according to Townshend, while Entwistle felt that "I really let myself go on playing bass. I played very easy on [the album]." Townshend was impressed with Entwistle's efforts in recording the album's various layered horn parts, telling John Swenson, "In the past John's always been as much a quiet one in the studio as he is onstage. The experience he's had in arranging stuff on his own albums and zest and energy at the recording sessions was incredible. He worked like 14 hours at a stretch on each number, multi-tracking horns. His attitude to Who music has really matured. And that's why there aren't any Entwistle compositions on this album as such because his energies went elsewhere."

During the sessions it was agreed that Ken Russell would direct a cinematic version of *Tommy* the following year. Russell, who was often at various *Quadrophenia* sessions for script consultations with Townshend, offered David Litchfield of *The Image* the following fanciful account of one such session for 'Drowned'.

"We were there [at Ramport] the night they recorded a number called *Rain* [sic] and there was a cloudburst and they wanted a stereo rain effect. We were in this caravan outside and bit by bit the playing stopped except for the piano and I went in and the floor and the roof had caved in as they were singing and the rain had really deluged them. They were soaking wet and there were firemen with a hose pumping it out except for the actual man in the cubicle playing the piano and he was gamely playing on and he

---

[12] Chris Stainton, of the Grease Band, played piano on '5:15', 'The Dirty Jobs', and 'Drowned' when Who regular Nicky Hopkins was committed to other work. Townshend reportedly wanted Stainton to tour with The Who post-*Quadrophenia*, but Daltrey, keen on maintaining a four-piece Who, talked him out of it.

was up to his neck in water and when they opened the door it poured like a waterfall, which was very funny."

Recording wrapped up in late summer, whereupon Townshend and Nevison retreated to Pete's new studio at his Goring-On-Thames cottage to complete and mix the album. "It took much, much longer to mix and blend than it did to record the backing tracks," Townshend said. "Stuff like 'The Rock' and 'Quadrophenia' were all recorded here at the house, all John Entwistle's horn parts."

Some pieces of music intended for *Quadrophenia* didn't make it onto the finished product. "One or two of them were incorporated into the film soundtrack album," Pete wrote in his 1983 liner notes for *Scoop*. "This theme ['Unused Piano'] was never finished, yet somehow it still captures the atmosphere of triumph and futility attempting to co-exist in the heart of the hero I created. Part of this theme was eventually used as a chorus on 'Cut My Hair'." The instrumental 'Bank Holiday Bash' and a Townshend-composed piece sung by Entwistle entitled 'We Close Tonight' were also left off the finished product, the latter resurfacing on the expanded edition of *Odds And Sods* in 1998. Another composition, 'Recorders' was "intended as an atmosphere merely to link a couple of tracks on *Quadrophenia*," he wrote in 1983. "It was never used. I borrowed one of my children's plastic whirling tubes – it was a popular toy for a few months in England, like the hoola hoop. I also strummed away on some cello strings."

A chief reason for the protracted mixing period was Townshend's intention to use quadraphonic sound. "You see, the whole conception of *Quadrophenia* was geared to quadraphonic, but in a creative sort of way," he told *Hit Parader* in May 1974. "I mean I wanted themes to sort of emerge from corners. So you start to get the sense of the fourness being literally speaker for speaker. And also in the rock parts the musical thing would sort of jell together up to the thunder clap, then everything would turn slowly from quad into mono and you'd have this solid sort of rock mono . . . then a thunder clap and back out again . . . When we came to mix it we spent months mixing it and then found out that MCA was using the CBS quad system and . . . you might as well forget it."

Even after the release of *Quadrophenia*, for a time, he planned on releasing a quadraphonic version of the album: "For a while we'll see our records as two editions . . . one in a stereo mix, one in a quad mix. That has to be the way it has to be because stereo at the moment is so much more mature and advanced than quad is. Everyday they make an improvement in the quad set-up; you know everyday I get a piece of mail through from CBS telling me that they've got another dB of separation from front to back and that, you know, if we buy the new modified encoder-decoder we'll get better results."

During that period, Pete invited 'Irish' Jack and his wife to the studio for an advance airing of the new album. "We went to a small spooky studio somewhere in Soho as far as I can remember," Lyons recalls. "I think we actually went back to the Ship pub for another couple of drinks and he gave me the cab fare to get back to my wife's auntie's house in Dagenham. I remember that in the bar we had this brilliant conversation whereby he was telling me and Ron Nevison how some guy had absolutely conned him into buying his American Thunderbird. The guy had a silver tongue apparently and saw Townshend coming a mile off. Pete used to park it outside his flat in Brewer Street."

In September, Pete flew to Los Angeles with the *Quadrophenia* tapes to personally oversee the mastering with Arnie Acosta at The Mastering Lab and the album was released in October (US) and November (UK). From the opening image of waves breaking on the beach to Moon's crashing finale to 'Love, Reign O'er Me', *Quadrophenia* presented the story of an archetypal adolescent's internal anguish in remarkably clear and cohesive fashion. The storyline was much clearer than that of *Tommy* (for British audiences, at least) and flowed in a linear fashion. Townshend's guitar was much more subdued in the mix on this relatively keyboard-heavy album, which, with the addition of Entwistle's horns, made it a distinctly different sounding proposition.

"It's not really a story as such," Pete told the *NME* in November. "There's a big difference between this and something like *Jesus Christ Superstar* or *Tommy*. It's not a story, more a series of impressions of memories. The real action in this is that you see a kid on a rock in the middle of the sea and this whole thing explains how he got there."

Townshend is immensely proud of the album. When asked by the author as to which of his artistic accomplishments he's most proud, he replied, "*Quadrophenia*. This drew together all my skills, long before I had the affirmation of my creative roles in either the movie or the Broadway shows of *Tommy*. I am still pleased with its spiritual common sense. A boy has a bad day, goes off to the beach, takes drugs, his day gets worse, he rows out to a rock, it rains."

Quadrophenia reached number two in both the US and UK. "Prime cut Who," wrote Charles Shaar Murray in *NME*'s October review. "You realise that Pete hasn't blown it after all. Face it, he very rarely does . . . if you're genuinely prepared to work at getting into it and let it work at getting into you, then you just might find it the most rewarding musical experience of the year."

Melody Maker was similarly complimentary. "*Quadrophenia*, The Who's new double album, is better than *Tommy*," gushed Chris Welch. "Pete Townshend's brainchild, a year in the making, sets new standards for British rock music, and will undoubtedly prove as big a worldwide success as the famed 'rock opera'. Released next week, it is a massive project . . . that tells the story of the life of a Who fan during the mod era of the mid-Sixties. In a series of brilliant performances, The Who capture the aggression, frustration and inherent romanticism of youth, with each member of the band representing a facet of the mythical hero – this time called Jimmy – and his 'quadrophrenic' [sic] personality."

Lenny Kaye's *Rolling Stone* review gave the album a less ecstatic reception: "*Quadrophenia* is The Who at their most symmetrical, their most cinematic, ultimately their most maddening . . . they have put together a beautifully performed and magnificently recorded essay of a British youth mentality in which they played no little part . . . Tea kettles whistle over the ominous voicings of the BBC, hints of The Who in concert cut in and out of Jimmy's fragmented dreamings, slim and checked jackets mingle with seersucker and neatly cut hair. To the American mind, *Quadrophenia* might thus seem as strange as portions of *American Graffiti* could appear to English experience, but it's to be assured that the appeal of semi-nostalgic shared memories must perforce work as well for one as the other . . .

"Pete, for better or worse, is possessed of a logic riveting in its linearity, and if in effect we are being placed in the mind of an emotionally distressed adolescent, neither the texture of the music nor the album's outlook is able to rise to this challenge of portraiture. Despite the varied themes, Jimmy is only seen through Townshend's eyes, geared through Townshend's perceptions, and the aftermath as carried through four sides becomes a crisis of concept, the album straining to break out of its enclosed boundaries and faltering badly.

"This is reflected in the songs themselves, vastly similar in mode and construction, running together with little differential to separate them. Only a few stand on their own as among the best The Who have ever done ('The Real Me', 'Is It In My Head?', '5:15', the Townshend theme of 'Love, Reign O'er Me') and of those it's interesting to note that several are holdovers from the lost Who album Glyn Johns and the band worked on before the onset of *Quadrophenia*. Also, given the inordinately complex personalities that make up the group, little is sensed of any Moon, Entwistle or Daltrey contributions to the whole. Their roles are subdued, backing tracks when they should rise to shoulder the lead, pressed on all fronts by the sweep of Townshend's imagination . . .

"Pete has been The Who's guiding force, their hindsight and hellbound inspiration. It is his mastermind that has created the tour de force recording breakthroughs of the album, the realistic and panoramic landscape of pre-Carnaby Street England, arranged the setting so that each member of the band could give full vent to his vaunted and highly unique instrumental prowess. Indeed, it might easily be said that The Who as a whole have never sounded better, both ensemble and solo, proving unalterable worth and relevance in an age that has long passed others of their band's generation into fragments of history. But on its own terms, *Quadrophenia* falls short of the mark . . ."

Kaye's point about the subdued roles of Moon, Entwistle or Daltrey was to resonate when Entwistle and Daltrey both voiced their dissatisfaction at Townshend's labours.[13] "When the album was completed, it took only a few days for Roger to express his disgust at the result," Pete later wrote in *Rolling Stone*. "I had spent my summer vacation mixing it, and he had popped in once to hear mixes, making a couple of negative comments about the sound but seeming quite keen to let me 'have my head', as it were, in production. Fundamentally, I had taken on too much, as always, and couldn't handle the strain when things went wrong and people blamed me. I felt I was perfectly entitled to gamble and lose, as no one else seemed prepared to, either with *Quadrophenia* or even The Who's career. So, I felt angry at Roger for not realising how much work I had done on the album – apart from writing it – and angry that he dismissed my production as garbage."

On October 4, The Who appeared on BBC-TV's *Top Of The Pops* to plug '5.15', the preview single from the album. Having to satisfy the Musicians Union that the band would not be simply miming, and being kept waiting to tape their spot, Townshend was not in the best of moods.

---

[13] Glyn Johns was not impressed with the final mix of *Quadrophenia*, either, calling the album "totally unimaginative from the point of view of sound – every track sounded exactly like the last one, and the last one didn't sound very good . . . Not only did these tracks sound similar from a literal sound point of view, but there wasn't nearly enough imagination in the arrangements."

At the end of the song, out of frustration, he smashed the Gretsch guitar Joe Walsh had given him (he later had it repaired).

The next challenge facing Townshend was The Who performing *Quadrophenia* live. Backing tapes were used for the various synthesiser tracks and sound effects on the album, requiring a great deal of rehearsal time at Shepperton Studios for the band to work the album into their act. The tension between Townshend and Daltrey boiled over during one run-through.

"I've only ever had one fight with Pete and that was during *Quadrophenia*," Daltrey recalled in 1975. "It was a bit of a shame because it was a non–argument, and the last thing I wanted to do in the world was to have a fist fight with Pete Townshend. Unfortunately, he hit me first with a guitar. I felt terrible about it afterwards, but what can you say? Pete should never try to be a fighter. But when he was being held back by two roadies and he's spitting and calling me a dirty little cunt and hits me with his guitar I become very angry. And I was forced to lay one on him. But it was only one."

One punch was all Daltrey needed, as it knocked Pete out. He was taken to hospital and reportedly suffered temporary amnesia.[14] The rift between the two men ran unchecked for two years before the pair showed any signs of burying their differences.

Quadrophenia hit the stage on October 28 in Stoke-on-Trent as The Who kicked off a 10-date tour of England prior to a 12-date American and Canadian jaunt scheduled to end in mid–December. The band used a quadraphonic PA system and a sophisticated array of backing tapes to accommodate the various sound effects and additional instrumentation featured on the album. Moon wore headphones on certain tracks, synchronising his playing to the tapes. Up to 20 guitar changes were necessary for Pete during the first night's full run-through of the album. *Melody Maker* offered a review of the second night's performance in Wolverhampton:

---

[14] Some of the *Quadrophenia* rehearsals were filmed for use on screens behind the band during the upcoming tour, but footage of the altercation between Townshend and Daltrey has never surfaced. "That was one of the pieces I was most broken-hearted actually didn't exist," *The Kids Are Alright* film-maker Jeff Stein recalled in September, 2003, "where Pete and Roger were going at it and Roger decked Pete and knocked him out. And Keith was over Pete's prone body, and he's kind of crying, saying, 'Pete! Pete! If you're still alive we'll do anything you say from now on.' That kind of thing . . ."

"Musically, [Quadrophenia] wasn't as effective as the record, but when it gets worked in it should prove fairly phenomenal. Monday night could have benefited by trimming it down. Pre-recorded tapes of seagulls, sea and thunder echoed effectively around the hall and helped create a suitable atmosphere."

This complex, somewhat mechanical method was anathema to The Who's basic three instrument assault and Townshend's discomfort soon reached breaking point. "We were exhausted from making the record and all kinds of things by the time we started touring," he recalled in 1996. "I got very wrecked emotionally."

His emotions weren't the only things to be wrecked on the fifth night of the tour in Newcastle. "During '5.15', Townshend flipped out completely when the tape synch came in 15 seconds slow," Dave Marsh wrote in 1983. "He stepped to the side of the stage, grabbed Bobby Pridden by the scruff of his neck and pulled the poor road manager bodily over the mixing desk, then tossed him toward centre stage. As Pridden sprawled in front of the crowd, Townshend began pulling at the soundboard, yanking out wires, demolishing many of the pre-recorded tapes it had taken so many weeks work to piece together."

"The Who rock band lived up to its reputation for violence onstage with an expensive display of guitar and amplifier-smashing at the Odeon Cinema last night," Steve Hughes wrote in the November 6 edition of the *Newcastle Evening Chronicle*. "The concert was stopped in chaos when guitarist Pete Townshend bawled out sound engineers, destroyed pre-recorded backing tapes and smashed equipment during the group's presentation of its latest rock opera. It was a ridiculous display of un-warranted violence witnessed by thousands of easily influenced teenage pop fans. Townshend, a temperamental but brilliant guitarist, is quite notorious for sudden fits of violence onstage which have almost become accepted as part of the act by his many followers. But this time stage hands rushed to disconnect electric amplifiers and Townshend's electric guitar after he swiped it into the stage floor.

"Tempers flared after drummer Keith Moon had trouble with head-phones. He let the drumsticks fly as the sound engineers battled to fix them. Then Townshend intervened, yelling at the engineers behind control panels on the side of the stage. He ripped out backing tapes and heaved over equipment into the side curtains. The three other members of the band just stared. The safety net was lowered to the stage but the lights stayed out. Fans sat, quietly at first in total darkness and usherettes –

obviously quite frightened – frantically flashed torchlights across the audience. After 10 minutes, with absolutely no trouble from the audience, the curtain was raised and Daltrey launched the band into a medley of 'oldies'. Then he yelled four-letter words at the audience, calling them – among many other derogatory terms – bastards and tried to explain everything by singing 'My Generation', a song about the generation gap and how no one understands the younger generation.

"Then Townshend hurled his guitar against the upstanding microphone and smashed it into a score of pieces by banging it against the stage floor. He then turned on a row of piled amplifiers at the back of the stage and hurled a top one to the floor. Moon waded through his range of drums, spilling them across the stage and Daltrey took a last kick at his microphone. They all left to thunderous applause."

While Hughes referred to Townshend's antics as an "extremely childish publicity stunt", he added, "Otherwise, [The Who] were musically immaculate, as always."

Pridden, who had to be persuaded not to jack in his job that night, spent the next morning repairing the equipment Townshend had damaged. "We had no money and I had to buy a guitar out of my own pocket to keep the flag flying," Pridden told Barnes. "And [Pete] is on the phone, 'Do you need a hand down there Bob?' I understand it, if I didn't, I wouldn't have been with them all those years."

In *Before I Get Old*, Dave Marsh suggested that Townshend was perhaps distressed by the backstage arrival of 'Irish' Jack, who hadn't seen the band in "some time". Lyons announced that he was now 30. "Incredible," Pete said. "I couldn't believe it. I always thought he was younger than me, for a start. You always think the audience is younger."

Jack's version of events is somewhat different. "What happened in Newcastle is that there had been a lot of tension even before I arrived," he recalls. "Back then, everyone shared the one dressing room. Pete and I had dinner before the show and I had some very expensive wine. I was getting slightly sloshed by the glass . . . and cheeky. After the meal we were standing up trying to out talk each other and I resorted back to an old favourite of mine . . . 'Pete, why wasn't 'Boris The Spider' a single?' This annoyed him and he made some retort. I was half serious, half play acting and I grabbed him by the lapels and I said, 'Why didn't you say in the song 'Happy Jack wasn't tall but he was a man, *and he lived in the Republic of Ireland.*' And Pete grabbed me back and pushed me up against the restaurant partition and growled, '*Cos I couldn't make it fucking rhyme!*' We didn't get on too well after that on this particular night. I think what broke the camel's back was when he saw me getting into Roger's car to go to the gig. He gave me a kind of look that said 'Judas'. Although afterwards when I collapsed backstage after drinking a pint glass of Southern Comfort he was gracious enough to give his room to me to recover in. And then he welcomed me back to his house with open arms to drive to the London Lyceum a few nights later."[15]

While Pete's playing was considered excellent during this tour (*NME*'s Roy Carr wrote "Townshend is 101 per cent pure raw nervous energy; his licks are as fresh and aggressive as in his old auto-destruct days."), *Quadrophenia* onstage simply wasn't working. As the tour wound on, the album segment steadily diminished as individual songs were dropped.

"We had to play in time to the pre-recorded tapes," Entwistle explained to John Swenson, "and we found that if we couldn't hear them, even though Keith had the backing track on his earphones and could continue drumming in time, the rest of us would be completely lost. It turned out that we weren't able to hear the tapes most of the time, and we started to play sloppily and got bored and we noticed the kids were getting bored too. It's one thing to play to the sort of metronomic backing track of 'Won't Get Fooled Again', but with the complex time changes of *Quadrophenia* we got crossed up too easily. We had to play it perfectly to make it work each time, we had to play it with an incredible amount of energy or it sounded bad, whereas our normal act is set up with songs that even if we play badly will still sound good, so we can afford to have a bad night and still get away with it."

The Who's 1973 North American tour (with supporting act Lynyrd Skynyrd) began in typically chaotic fashion at San Francisco's Cow Palace on November 20. This time it was Moon, not Townshend, who provided the theatrics, as he gradually stopped playing and sprawled over his drum kit. Moon had faltered earlier in the show and was apparently temporarily revived by a cold shower from the road crew while Townshend bought time by talking to the audience. This time, however, there was no

---

[15] At the Lyceum, there were more than twice as many fans as available tickets, which obviously resulted in less than ideal conditions. Crowd surges during The Who's set on November 11 nearly sent the PA tumbling into the crowd. "Luckily, people like me noticed and held [the speakers] in place for five to 10 minutes until the roadies realised what was going on and helped secure them again," photographer Robert Ellis told *Mojo* in 2004. "The Who were oblivious and kept playing – never realising that a disaster was so narrowly averted."

reviving Keith, who was clearly done for the night.[16] The Who managed to continue the show that night after enlisting a drummer from the audience for the last few numbers.

"Moon slept solidly for 10 hours afterwards, and stayed in the following evening watching telly on The Who's night off in Los Angeles [a very unusual pastime for Keith Moon, especially in LA], determined to rest his tired frame and be on top form for the opening Forum show," Chris Charlesworth reported in *Melody Maker*. Charlesworth joined the band in the dressing room following the first LA Forum show, shortly after Keith Moon had taken it upon himself to hurl chocolate cake at his band mates . . . Townshend, who was on the receiving end of most of Moon's cake, looked tired but happy . . . About an hour earlier, 19,500 fans had stomped and cheered for over 15 minutes in the Forum, refusing to leave even though the house lights had been raised and probably well aware that The Who rarely do encores. But tonight their enthusiasm was rewarded with just that . . .

"Incredible? The Who doing an encore. So on they came again, weary, exhausted, Moon in particular must have been feeling the strain as 'Baby Don't You Do It' is a number with much emphasis on the drumming. But they blasted through the song, climaxing with Townshend unstrapping the Gibson and, gripping the fretboard as if it were an axe, bringing it down on to the stage with a resounding crash time and time again until it cracked around the 12th fret."

The tour wound through Texas, Georgia, Missouri, Illinois and Michigan, but after a show in Montreal on December 2 the entire entourage was jailed for seven hours as a result of a particularly enthusiastic bout of hotel room demolition. Townshend got glass in his eye when he and Moon heaved a marble coffee table through a window. The Canadian police were not amused by the band's antics – according to Charlesworth, Pete was "shoved into the back of a police car and he was terrified the cops were going to beat him up." The hotel-smashing incident did nothing to ease the tension between Townshend and Daltrey, "who was furious because he'd retired to bed early and hadn't been involved in the demolition," Charlesworth wrote. The entire party of 16 were released

---

[16] The official explanation was that Moon was suffering from 'jet lag', while Keith was reportedly actually suffering from the effects of PCP, an animal tranquiliser which had been slipped into one of his pre-show drinks. "Keith had been drinking with two girls before the show and somebody had spiked their drinks . . ." Richard Barnes wrote. "They were taken to hospital and apparently one of the girls very nearly died from it."

following payment of damages totalling $6,000 and only just made Boston in time for that night's show.

In response to a rabid demand for tickets for their three Lyceum shows, The Who played an additional four shows in their home city just before Christmas. Townshend was especially pleased with these dates at the Sundown Theatre in Edmonton, north London, feeling that the shows "broke down the barriers between performers and audience. I felt like a member of the 'Oo an' all that," Pete told *Melody Maker*, "but I also felt like one of the crowd."

With the enjoyable, intimate Sundown shows fresh in his mind, Townshend experienced the polar opposite at the cavernous Palais des Sports in Paris, the second concert on a six-date tour of France in February 1974.

"Speeding from the Palais des Sports in a chauffer-driven limousine, Pete Townshend expressed bitter reservations," reported *Melody Maker*'s Steve Lake in his account of the show the following week. "It was too big, he said, far too big. It felt impersonal. He was disgusted, too, with the French lighting crew, who had apparently bungled the explicitly simple instructions Townshend had given them." After just three songs, a transformer blew, shutting down power to The Who's PA system, and emitting a cloud of smoke ("I thought Roger's make-up was burning off," Moon quipped). Fifteen minutes later, power to the PA was restored and the concert resumed.

"They determined to compensate the crowd for the electronic misdemeanour," Lake continued, "and delivered a set so packed with visual action that it was astounding that they were able to sustain the pace they set for themselves . . . 'Drowned' from *Quadrophenia* was the absolute killer, reaching a crescendo with Townshend demolishing another $350 guitar, bouncing it twice off the stage, and finally snapping it at the base of the neck with a sledgehammer swipe at his speaker stack. Sparks flew from the jack-plug socket . . . 'See Me, Feel Me' wound up the show proper, following hard on the heels of 'Pinball Wizard', and the lighting crew again upped the house lights to reveal 26,000 pairs of upraised arms waving, and flapping back and forth in approximate time. It was a magnificent and moving sight from the stage. Whoever said that rock'n'roll is essentially about the transference of raw energy was exactly right. The Who were giving it all away and the kids were sending it right back at them . . .

"The Who huddled stage centre, arms entwined, sweating profusely.

They grinned their appreciation and staggered off, carrying the triumphant Moon aloft. Paris won't forget for a long time."

For the French dates, The Who decided to drop their highly touted quadraphonic PA system due to the amount of complaints that had surfaced from fans whose view was either partially or completely obstructed by the two speaker towers that were positioned among the audience seating. Another change took place at the tour's conclusion – Townshend had finally tired of the problematical *Quadrophenia* backing tapes: they were either too slow, too fast, or came in at the wrong time, providing more in the way of artistic frustration than audience enjoyment. *Quadrophenia* itself was not played again until The Who showcased it on their 1996/97 tour.

CHAPTER NINE

1974–1976

"Why we haven't foundered, obviously, is that we have a tradition in the band which nobody dares to transgress. If anybody mentions breaking up they literally have to wash their mouth out with soap and water . . . it's like swearing in church. It just doesn't come into the picture."

— Pete Townshend, 1974

"If I had ever dug in my heels about Tommy *and said no-one has the right to change my conception, it would have killed* Tommy *dead as a concept. A dead classic. I felt it was still evolving, still unfinished and still alive . . . With Ken Russell I was prepared to make concessions and compromise some points in order to have Ken make his alterations — it just meant another evolution in the concept. I told him I didn't care if he altered all the words if he needed to: "Listening to you I get the porridge" — whatever he wanted."*

— Pete Townshend, 1975

AS the recording of *Quadrophenia* had commenced, talks concerning the prospect of *Tommy* becoming a feature film took a positive turn when Robert Stigwood became involved. Stigwood, who had produced the 1973 film version of *Jesus Christ Superstar*, negotiated a deal with Columbia Pictures, stepped in as producer and provided the leadership and financial wherewithal to land such stars as Jack Nicholson, Tina Turner and Ann-Margret. Ken Russell had been Pete Townshend's original choice as director of a *Tommy* movie just after the album was released in 1969, but, according to Townshend, Russell had told him that he was "booked up for the next couple of years."

Over the intervening four years, Townshend was approached by several prospective directors, but nothing had materialised. "Everyone wanted to do the film – everyone thought they had the rights," Russell recalled in

1994, "and there were hundreds of scripts as well, and probably dozens of directors for all I know, but none of the scripts or directors had apparently pleased Townshend."

"What has happened in the past," Pete told *Rolling Stone* in June 1974, "is that an American director has come over and taken me to lunch, sat me down and said, 'You know, Pete, we're talking about a million-dollar movie here, and er, what we wanna know is your thoughts, we wanna know how you wanna make the movie, Pete.' They were saying, 'OK, you little English poof, you make the film and please make it gross six times as much as the album did.' And I'd sit there and tell them how to make it. They'd go away and decide, 'Well, maybe we were wrong about wanting to make it.' A week later another mogul comes over, takes me out to lunch, and says, 'Pete, we wanna know how you wanna make the movie . . .'"

"On the day I met Ken Russell I was strolling around London recording street noises in stereo for the *Quadrophenia* album," Townshend recalled in *The Story Of Tommy*. "I had my tape machine in a suitcase and the mikes concealed in a holdall. At the time I was after 'casual conversation'. I saw an interesting group and sidled sideways up to them pointing my holdall into their midst. The conversation I heard was fascinating. In the group were Ken Russell, Chris Stamp and Mike Carrearas, who were all unhappy that they hadn't been able to locate me that afternoon for a meeting they were about to have. As you can imagine, I just felt all this meant that the film *had to be*."

Townshend started preparation on the soundtrack for the film in December 1973. "The great thing about Russell," Pete said, "was it was his idea to do [the film]. He came up with suggestions, and I realised I was in the presence of the 'Guv'nor.' So all I have to do is run off when he tells me he needs a new song and just do it. It's great working under somebody rather than always having to do the pushing and leading."

The first 12 weeks of 1974 were occupied largely with recording the soundtrack at Ramport. Shortly after The Who went into the studio to begin re-recording the score, Keith Moon "fell ill" and couldn't work.[1] "In a way it was a blessing in disguise," said Townshend. "I mean we were

---

[1] Recent events finally caught up with Moon. His father had died the previous October, while that same month, his long-suffering wife of seven years, Kim, left him, taking their daughter Mandy. Moon largely absented himself from the Russell *Tommy* sessions – filming *Stardust* (the sequel to *That'll Be The Day*).

terrified as to how it was going to work out without him, because we only had two months to do the whole thing. So I thought rather than try and replace him with *a* drummer, I'd choose an ideal bunch of musicians for each song." An illustrious cast of musicians, including guitarists Eric Clapton, Ron Wood and Mick Ralphs were called upon to lend their services, along with pianists such as Chris Stainton and Nicky Hopkins, and drummers Kenney Jones and Mike Kellie. "Yes, most people were happy to come and work on the album," Pete recalled. "*Tommy* might be a bit of a cliched old hag but he commands respect."

Other stars were considered for major parts in the film, including Stevie Wonder. "Well, this is a really awful story," Townshend told Richard Barnes in 1975, "because Stevie Wonder was offered the part of the Pinball Wizard by Robert Stigwood and I think was interested in doing it. Then Ken said you can't have a blind Negro being beaten by a deaf dumb and blind white kid, because, well, it's just racially wrong. When the news got back to Stevie Wonder he was incredibly annoyed. When he came over to England [to play the Rainbow Theatre], Eric Clapton and I went to see him and he wouldn't talk to us. He wouldn't talk to Eric at all because I was with Eric, and Eric couldn't work out what was going on. But when Eric saw him again in America he was really nice to him."

Other notables mentioned in connection with the roles of the Acid Queen and Pinball Wizard included Mick Jagger, David Bowie, Lou Reed and David Essex.[2] Townshend had apparently envisioned the unlikely figure of Tiny Tim as the Pinball Wizard ("I imagined that [the song] would sound really great on a hundred ukeleles," Pete said), Arthur Brown as the Doctor, and "a sort of older jazz singer who could sing rock, like Cleo Laine or Georgia Brown or somebody of that ilk, or maybe even somebody like Joan Baez," in the mother's role of Nora Walker.

"I resisted all the legitimate actors," Townshend said in 1975. "I resisted them all. I didn't want Ann-Margret in it. I didn't want Jack Nicholson and I didn't want Oliver Reed in it, because none of them were rock people and I wanted people that could sing rock – it was Ken who said that he had to have those people."

A week before the film shoot commenced, Pete played his first ever solo

---

[2] "Ken Russell wanted David Essex in it [as the Pinball Wizard], which was very weird because everyone else was against it," Townshend told Barnes. "I like him as a bloke and I really feel bad about the fact that he was ever suggested and did the work that he did and was then turned down, because I don't like the way it reflects on me. Because we are good friends."

concert – an unnerving but successful experience at the Roundhouse, Chalk Farm, north London on April 14. His appearance was part of an Easter benefit show (featuring Coast Road Drive, Byzantium, and the headliner, American folk singer Tim Hardin) organised to raise funds for the Camden Square Community Play Centre. "While we were recording the music for the *Tommy* film with Ken Russell, a couple of the backing singers were trying to buy a bus for some orphanage or something and I said that I'd do a concert to raise the money," Townshend told *Radio Times* in late 2006.

When the unpredictable Hardin withdrew from the bill, Pete was faced with headliner status and a much longer set than he'd anticipated. "I thought it was going to be a very small thing but it turned out to be bloody massive," Townshend told Barnes, "and people were ringing me up and saying, 'I hear you're doing a solo gig at the Roundhouse' and I thought, 'Hold on, this is getting out of control.'" Under pressure, Townshend spent the week prior to the show feverishly rehearsing his set. While he had played solo at private Meher Baba gatherings, this was his first public appearance without The Who. "When I met Pete on the day of his solo concert he was as white as a sheet," Barnes recalled in 1982. "He told me that he hadn't been able to eat for the last three days."

Townshend practically brought his entire home studio to the Roundhouse, performing amid tape recorders, effects boxes, several guitars and microphones and miscellaneous other equipment, including a table with a lamp for his set list and lyric sheets. Included in his performance were Who staples such as 'Substitute', 'Pinball Wizard' and 'Behind Blue Eyes', and even the original demo tape of 'My Generation' was played. Pete also included 'Girl From The North Country' and 'Corrina, Corrina' (both recorded by Bob Dylan on 1963's *The Freewheelin' Bob Dylan*), and Tim Hardin's 'If I Were A Carpenter' among his eclectic set. The show was well received, apart from an obnoxious fan who repeatedly screamed out his unlikely request for 'Underture'. After repeated verbal warnings, Townshend went into the crowd and threatened the man. Once the heavy mood had lightened, Townshend added his own self-deprecating lines to the 'Magic Bus'/'My Generation' finale: "I'm so nervous I guess it shows/don't say a thing about my great big nose."

Tommy filming began on April 22. The movie contained no dialogue, consisting purely of music from beginning to end and while the soundtrack recording was completed prior to filming, any changes which needed to be made during production would dictate a corresponding adjustment to the soundtrack. Having accepted the role of musical director, reportedly after his fee was increased by a considerable amount from $100,000 to £100,000, Townshend's responsibilities multiplied as the schedule progressed. "Pete had his own caravan on the set, closely monitoring scene alterations that required changes to the incidental music," Andy Neill and Matt Kent noted in *Anyway Anyhow Anywhere*.

Originally budgeted at £1 million with filming set to take up to 12 weeks, the movie wound up costing twice that amount with shooting occupying a total 18 weeks. Therefore, one can well imagine the many adjustments and rewrites that occurred.

"Had I known how much time is involved in making a feature I think I would have stopped fantasising about films altogether," Townshend remarked in June. "People talk to me – 'How can you spend two years making an album like *Quadrophenia?*' – but it's nothing like this."

"A lot of what I was dealing with was incredibly complex and time-consuming and a bit of an education," Townshend told *Uncut* in 2004. "I could go and do a film score tomorrow. I won't. I've been offered many. I turned down *Blade Runner* because I thought, 'Fuck, I'm not going to go there again.' As a composer you believe you're king, but even when you compose for a movie, even if the movie is your composition, as it was, Ken Russell was the king. So what would actually happen is we'd go into the studio, he'd sit with his eyes shut, we'd play and he'd say, 'No, this bit needs to be longer,' and I'd say, 'Well, what do you want us to do?' and he'd say, 'Just make it longer, I need more time.' So we'd play a longer track and you'd find that would be Ronnie Wood pissing about on slide guitar for 15 or 16 bars and then you'd find that when it's finished, the editor decides that it's not enough music to cut to so he'd loop up stuff, and then I would have to work on these loops.

"I just felt like a dogsbody. I thought, 'Where's the music?' There are bits of the *Tommy* film, in the 'Acid Queen' bit, for example, where you see Tina Turner doing all her stuff and you hear this loop going round with some sound effects chucked on top of it in a hurry to try and make it sound a bit different. I didn't feel that I would ever, ever, *ever* be able to work with a director again, and I never have. I loved working with Ken and I loved doing the *Tommy* movie, but once is enough."

One scene required footage of The Who onstage. Naturally, the shooting didn't take place without incident. "There was only one real injury [during the *Tommy* filming]," Barnes wrote in *The Story Of Tommy*. "It was when The Who are playing and the crowd had to storm the stage. The signal for this was Townshend smashing his guitar and throwing the neck up in the air, but one take he threw it a bit high, and it came down on a girl's head."

"There was blood everywhere," remembers Townshend, "and she was carried off to hospital. But she came back a few hours later and told us she was 'very honoured' to have been smashed over the head by Pete Townshend's guitar. I gave her the guitar."

Barnes also described a scene featuring Eric Clapton strolling down the aisle of a church in Portsmouth miming to 'Eyesight To The Blind' flanked by a slightly uncomfortable-looking Townshend and Entwistle. "Everyone was pissed out of their brains that day," according to Townshend, who told Barnes, "I've piddled about with acting but I don't feel comfortable doing it."

On May 6, The Who played a low-key warm-up gig in Oxford before headlining an ambitious day-long concert on the 18th at south London's Charlton Athletic Football Ground (one of the first occasions a British football stadium had been used for such an event) in front of a crowd officially set at 50,000, but estimated to be closer to 80,000 due to gate-crashers. Supporting acts included Montrose, Lindisfarne, Bad Company, Lou Reed and Humble Pie. What should have been a triumph was less so thanks to a lack of camaraderie between the band members. Now that the bulk of *Quadrophenia* had been jettisoned from their stage repertoire, the set largely consisted of a retrospective look back over The Who's history. Townshend, who was drunk as a lord on brandy, was disappointed at the crowd's easy acceptance of what he considered to be a lacklustre per-formance and began to question the validity of continuing with what he continued to regard as "a circus act".

Once filming on *Tommy* wrapped up at the end of the summer, the tedious and painstaking process of dubbing and synchronising the film music took place. Townshend claimed to have spent six weeks in "total seclusion" in his studio, a period of "manic involvement" during which he claimed to have put in as many as 23 hours a day. A number of mixes had to be constructed to suit various film formats, which saw Pete and a team of technicians working all the way up to Christmas.[3] Exhausted from his self-imposed workaholic schedules, Townshend concluded that his home

---

[3] Townshend was later nominated for a 'Best Score Adaptation' Oscar for his work on the soundtrack.

studio was partly to blame and "tore it all out", leaving the cottage in Goring as his sole recording locale.

The *Tommy* soundtrack was released in the US in February 1975 (a month later in Britain) and charted at numbers two and 21 respectively. The double album featured three new Townshend compositions, namely 'Champagne', 'Mother And Son', and 'TV Studio' while several of the original compositions were revamped ('Bernie's Holiday Camp, '1951'). Highlights included Tina Turner's 'Acid Queen' and Elton John's rendition of 'Pinball Wizard'. Oliver Reed and Jack Nicholson's shared inability to sing[4] was somewhat relieved by the extensive use of choir-like backing vocals, which Townshend, Billy Nicholls and a host of others overdubbed at Ramport.

When the movie premiered in March,[5] it predictably received a harsh reception from music critics who regarded it as camp and farcical, or as Dave Marsh pointed out, "a fairy tale for new initiates." Townshend tended to vacillate, generally regarding the enterprise with serious intent. "Many Who fans feel the *Tommy* film is not what The Who is about," he wrote in *Rolling Stone* in 1977, "or even what *Tommy* is about. In truth, it is exactly what it is about. It is the prime example of rock'n'roll throwing off its three-chord musical structure, discarding its attachment to the three-minute single, openly taking on the unfashionable questions about spirituality and religion and yet hanging grimly on to the old ways at the same time."

"The people that didn't understand it or didn't run with it were the people that had preconceptions to the way it was going to look," Pete told Scott Muni in 1978. "They'd spent too long living with that album, they had got their own film in their head and they didn't like somebody like Ken Russell coming along and making pictures which didn't fit in. I had to extinguish in my own mind the film which I had for *Tommy*, before I could even begin to talk to Ken about the way it should look. You know, when you're working with a director that's going to be any good at all,

[4] "Robert Stigwood rang up and said he'd got Jack Nicholson," Townshend recalled in *The Story Of Tommy*, "and I said 'Who's Jack Nicholson?' and he said he was one of the biggest stars in America at the moment. So I said 'Can he sing?' and he said no." Pete quickly responded, 'I'm not having another fucker in this film who can't sing. Oliver Reed's giving me nightmares as it is.' Reed later said, "I sang a few notes and Townshend fell about laughing in the studio."
[5] Chris Stamp received an Executive Producer credit for the *Tommy* film; Kit Lambert was credited only as 'original album producer'.

you've got to let the man do it . . . And so I decided, 'Right, let Ken do it his way,' and I had to let go of my own ideas and consequently, I really enjoyed it and it really came to me afresh but to a lot of people who hadn't let go their own ideas about it, it was sometimes disappointing and sometimes shocking."

Some 15 years on, Townshend continued to defend the movie in a 1993 interview with the *New York Post*. "I still love it. I don't know whether I did the right thing by the piece or Who fans, but Ken Russell is, in my eyes, still one of the great British directors, and a great eccentric. As it recedes further into the distance, you realise that it's a great movie; the cameos in it were great, and whether it's the best thing or not, we probably have him to thank for MTV." Russell, incidentally, called *Tommy* "one of the easiest and most pleasurable films I've ever made."

Townshend's exhausting experience in assembling and producing the *Tommy* soundtrack pushed him to the brink of a nervous breakdown not unlike the one he'd experienced at the New York *Lifehouse* sessions. His initial enthusiasm had been replaced by one of sheer resignation. "I have resisted all conventional movie work since the enormous strain of working on Ken Russell's *Tommy*," he told the author. "I thought rock was tough. Making movies is exciting but there is never a moment's break."

Burned out, experiencing marital problems and prematurely balding,[6] Pete was on the brink of a breakdown by mid-1974. As a result, his alcohol consumption dramatically increased.

At a private Who concert for the *Tommy* extras in Portsmouth in May, Townshend recalled signing "several managerial and recording contracts in a complete fog.[7] The only event I remember is quietly screaming for help deep inside," he wrote in 1977. "I got very scared by memory blackouts, as scared as I had ever been on bad LSD trips eight years before. Once in July 1974 – just after the *Tommy* filming – I sort of 'came to' in the back of my own car. Keith and John were with me [we were probably going to a club], but although I knew who they were, I didn't recognise either my car or my driver, who had been working for me for over two months. The shock that hit me as the pieces fell into place was even more

---

[6] Townshend's hair loss, according to Dave Marsh, "terrified him. He still wasn't 30. He had scalp treatments, which restored most of the loss, but these were painful, time-consuming and, while he underwent them, disfiguring."

[7] Townshend didn't realise he'd signed anything until a legal problem arose several months later.

frightening than the black holes in my head as the memory lapses began. Eight drug-free years and still this mental demise."

In addition, Townshend discovered that a large amount of his publishing money couldn't be accounted for, roughly half a million pounds. This tipped the scales in favour of Daltrey over the management dispute with Kit Lambert and Chris Stamp, and Townshend reluctantly joined in the litigation. With The Who's recording revenues effectively frozen due to the pending legal action, the band had to tour to make money. It was under these conditions that The Who played four shows at New York's Madison Square Garden between June 10–14 (the 12th being a day off). The shows sold out after a 60-second commercial aired at the end of a Who radio special on March 31.

"Pete was in a depressed state when he arrived in New York," described Chris Charlesworth, now based in the city as *Melody Maker*'s US editor. "He'd been on the wagon for a few days and was sober at the Garden rehearsals but on the opening night things started to go wrong."

Townshend was staying at a separate hotel, opting for the luxurious Pierre on Fifth Avenue while the others lodged at their regular New York digs, the Navarro on Central Park South.

"I was supposed to interview Pete in his room at the Pierre Hotel on the Wednesday afternoon," Charlesworth recalls, "but when I went up there and knocked on the door of his room there was no reply, so I kept on knocking and eventually he opened the door. It was obvious I'd woken him and he was a bit rough, had a bad hangover. I think I offered to come back later, which I did. I gave him an hour to get himself together. He was quite gracious even though he was in a bit of a state. I think he made the effort for me because he knew I was a Who supporter, a friend of the band."

Charlesworth noted that after the interview, "it dawned on me how much responsibility Pete had to everyone, that the band and the film makers and his family all relied on him and that it probably was a huge strain. People always imagined rock stars to have this gilded life of luxury, but in the mid-Seventies Pete was obviously under a lot of pressure to provide for everyone – write songs [for the band], perform [for the fans], earn money [for his family], work on the film [for everyone] and there can't have been much time left for himself."

The Madison Square Garden shows, substandard performances by general consensus, demonstrated to Townshend that he was in no shape to be onstage with a band whose reputation lay on being the finest live act in the world.

"For the remainder of the week," Charlesworth wrote, "Pete submerged himself in brandy, stayed out most of the night clubbing with Keith and John and joined in heated disputes backstage."

"In all the years I'd been with The Who I'd never had to force myself," he told Nik Cohn. "All the leaping about and guitar smashing, even though I'd done it a thousand times, it was always totally natural. And then, on the first night at the Garden, I suddenly lost it. I didn't know what I was doing there, stuck up onstage in front of all these people. I had no instinct left; I had to do it from memory. So I looked down into the front row and all these kids were squealing, 'Jump, jump, jump.' And I panicked . . . I was lost . . . The other three shows I was terrified."

Pete began drinking Remy Martin straight from the bottle onstage. "I got smashed or I couldn't have gone on," he told Cohn, "my drunken legs gave way under me as I tried to do a basic cliche leap and shuffle."

A frustrating week ended with the final show on June 14, when Townshend smashed three Gibson Les Paul Deluxes. Not content to be left out of any wanton destruction, Keith Moon smashed Pete's only remaining Les Paul. Upon his return to London, an admittedly "mixed up" Townshend told Bill Curbishley that he would never work on the road with The Who again. "I might even have said that I felt The Who was finished," Pete revealed in 1977.

Following the disappointing Madison Square Garden performances, Townshend continued to fret over the "mind-bending and complex" *Tommy* soundtrack, although he (and Moon) found time to appear onstage at three Eric Clapton shows towards the end of Clapton's US 'comeback' tour in August.

Yvonne Elliman, who was a vocalist in the band (and had sung on Clapton's current, commercially successful album, *461 Ocean Boulevard*) recalls that Townshend was "very different from how I remember him [from the 'I Can't Explain' session the previous year]. The alcohol was missing and he was dressed all in white."[8]

Elliman was "trying to be 'one of the boys' on the tour. I did what they did, which included drinking outrageous amounts of alcohol . . . at one point, I was trying to keep up with Eric, which meant drinking from the time you got up. Pete did a small, personal 'intervention' on me during one of those lost periods, and I'm so glad my mind was lucid enough to

[8] It should be noted that other observers recall Townshend being far from sober during the three shows in which he guested at Atlanta, Greensboro, and West Palm Beach.

grasp and hold on to this memory. It was the next morning after a gig, and the band were scattered here and there in what was a circular hotel that featured visual access to all floors and doors, which opened out to the centre of the hotel. I sat on a bench and waited for the signal to board the vehicle bound for the airport. I felt pretty lousy and was openly drinking 'the hair of the dog that bit me' from a whiskey bottle (same as I had seen Pete do).

"Pete walked out of his door, right next to mine, sees the state I'm in and says, as he slowly walks by, 'You know, you shouldn't be drinking like that. You're a pretty lady – you don't need to do that.' Then he got in the lift. I looked at that bottle, put it down, and didn't drink a drop for a few days." Although she ultimately did resume drinking, "one lasting change did occur – I never did drag a bottle around with me in public again."

Meanwhile, with Daltrey still required for *Tommy* filming and dubbing work, Entwistle addressed the need for the release of a new Who album by scouring through the band's tape archive at Track Records' offices in Soho.

The album, released in October as *Odds And Sods*, comprised three *Lifehouse* songs left off *Who's Next* ('Pure And Easy', 'Put The Money Down', and 'Too Much Of Anything'), tracks intended for the scrapped 1970 EP ('Postcard', 'Now I'm A Farmer'), three unreleased tracks from 1968 ('Glow Girl', 'Faith In Something Bigger' and the unused American Cancer Society jingle, 'Little Billy'), The High Numbers' 'I'm The Face' (the only previously released track but included for its obscurity), long-time stage finale 'Naked Eye', and the *Quadrophenia* predecessor, 'Long Live Rock', which rounded out an interesting collection proving how great a band The Who were to have such quality leftovers.[9]

In the autumn of '74, Murshida Ivy Duce visited London. Duce was "head of the Sufi movement in the States, as reoriented under Meher Baba's directives," Townshend explained.

"Murshida Duce is a remarkable woman," he wrote in 1977. "She heads a group of about 300 initiates, all committed to total honesty and respect for her authority. She has Meher Baba's sanction as the legitimate Murshid along with 'in line' decree from her own deceased Murshid,

---

[9] The photo used on the cover of *Odds And Sods* was taken by Graham Hughes backstage in Chicago in November 1973. "Pete didn't like it and ripped it up," Hughes told *Mojo* in 2004. "Then he realised that shot was the one, so we stuck it back together and that was it – all tears and Sellotape."

Murshida Martin. Murshida Martin herself took over under the instructions of the famous Inayat Khan, a spiritual teacher and master musician whose books on Sufism present a poetic system for modern life . . . Meher Baba gave an explicit charter to Murshida Duce and it is under the limitations of this charter that she works today. I am not a Sufi initiate, but her spontaneous help in my life has always touched me."

"Pete arranged a large reception [for the initiates]," wrote fellow devotee Delia DeLeon in 1991. A leading British Baba follower, DeLeon frequently encountered and corresponded with Meher Baba from 1931 until his death in 1969. She first met Townshend back in 1967 through Mike McInnerney and the two developed a close friendship. In his January 1990 introduction to *The Ocean Of Love*, the book (published in 1991) in which Delia described her experiences with Baba, Townshend wrote:

> *"Delia DeLeon was a follower of long standing when she influenced me and others who looked for spiritual truth during the Sixties. It appeared that apart from her love for Him, her spiritual Master, she possessed and wanted nothing. He was her obsession. He was her absolute and singular focus. As I enjoyed a wonderful family and successful career when I first heard about Meher Baba such total devotion was impossible for me, but Delia DeLeon became an example and inspiration for me."*

One evening during Murshida Duce's visit, "as he drove me home, Pete broached the idea of my making a film telling stories of my experiences with Baba," DeLeon recounted in *The Ocean Of Love*. She agreed, somewhat hesitantly, to go ahead with the idea, but was shocked at how quickly the idea became a reality, as she wrote, "To my horror, within four days, I was told the film crew would come to my flat to start – no preparations, no scenario, no discussion of questions. They turned up, plus Pete, Billy Nicholls, Richard Barnes, and John Annunziato, a photographer who had arrived in London with his wife, Linda. I was recovering from an angina attack but managed to pull myself together, though how I stood up for two days to seven hours of interviewing I will never know."[10]

At the start of 1975, 'Irish' Jack Lyons left his wife and two children, and moved back to London. "I was living in a fucking 10′ × 8′ cell in Notting Hill Gate, Clanricarde Gardens and working as a porter at Brompton Hospital," Lyons recalls. "I was never so miserable, so lonely, so truly

---

[10] The film, *Delia*, was eventually finished for the opening of Meher Baba Oceanic in July 1976.

fucked up in my life." Jack had been in the UK for some weeks before he mustered enough courage to see Pete as "probably in the back of my mind I was ashamed that my marriage had fallen apart." One Sunday in March, Lyons made the trip to Twickenham and walked down Water Lane to the Townshend home.

"It was early evening and there was nobody in," he recalls. "I went up to The Swan pub and had a few half glasses, careful not to arrive at Pete's house drunk. At about 11, I strolled down and found him taking some stuff out of the back of his car. He had obviously just come back from Goring . . . When Pete saw me he put on this big smile and I hugged him. He actually thought I was over on holiday and couldn't work out why I hadn't written in such a while. Once we got inside and I told him the news he changed completely. Whereas I was expecting him to say something like, 'Separated? That's rock'n'roll, man. Have a cigar,' he actually gave me a first class bollocking, telling me I had walked away from a beautiful woman and small children and had left a steady job on the buses. He went on and on and was very fucking angry with me.

"I slept on the settee downstairs and he drove me to the station the next morning. It was that day that I realised that Pete Townshend was a bigger friend to me than I had ever bargained for. He really cared about me. He could be a bloody curmudgeon but inside he had a heart of gold. And yes, he did suffer fools gladly because I was one for leaving my wife and children and fucking things up. In April my wife came to London for her birthday and we decided to get back together again."

That same month, and just a few weeks prior to his 30th birthday, Pete gave a long interview to Roy Carr, a friend and journalist with the *NME*. Carr found Townshend in a bitter state of mind, questioning his place in music. "I really hate feeling too old to be doing what I'm doing. I recently went to do a BBC-TV interview and when I arrived at the studios there were all these young kids waiting outside for the Bay City Rollers. As I passed them by, one of the kids recognised me and said, 'Ooo look, it's Pete Townshend,' and a couple of them chirped 'Ello Pete.' And that was it. Yet the first time The Who appeared at those same studios on *Top Of The Pops*, a gang of little girls smashed in the plate glass front door on the building."

He described the emotions that began to take hold of him at the Madison Square Garden shows, feeling that perhaps The Who had become a nostalgia act.

"To some extent The Who have become a golden oldies band . . . it's just that when I'm standing up there onstage playing rock'n'roll,"

Townshend explained to Carr. "I often feel that I'm too old for it . . . When Roger speaks out about 'We'll all be rockin' in our wheelchairs' he might be but you won't catch me rockin' in no wheelchair . . .

"I can tell you that when we were gigging at the early part of last year I was thoroughly depressed. I honestly felt that The Who were going onstage every night and, for the sake of the diehard fans, copying what The Who used to be. I dunno what's happening sometimes. All I know is that when we last played Madison Square Garden I felt acute shades of nostalgia. All The Who freaks had crowded around the front of the stage and when I gazed out into the audience all I could see were those same sad faces that I'd seen at every New York Who gig. There was about a thousand of 'em and they turned up for every bloody show at the Garden, as if it were some Big Event – 'The Who triumph over New York' . . . it was dreadful. They were telling us what to play. Every time I tried to make an announcement they all yelled out 'Shhrrruppp Townshend and let Entwistle play 'Boris The Spider' and, if that wasn't bad enough, during the other songs they'd all start chanting 'Jump . . . jump . . . jump . . . jump . . . jump.' I was so brought down by it all! I mean is this what it had all degenerated into?"

Townshend's frustrations weren't limited to The Who as a live act. "I've been working on tracks for [a] solo album. Invariably what will happen is that once we all get into the studio, I'll think, 'Oh fuck it,' and I'll play Roger, John and Keith the tracks I've been keeping for my own album and they'll pick the best. So as long as The Who exists, I'll never get the pick of my own material . . . and that's what I dream of. But if The Who ever broke up because the material was substandard then I'd really kick myself . . . they are the people who put the pressures on me. Let me make this clear. I don't put pressures on them. I don't say, 'We've got to get into the studio this very minute because I've got these songs that I've just gotta get off my chest.' It's always the other way around. They always rush up to me and insist that we've got to cut a new album and get back on the road. Believe me, there have been times in The Who's career when I would have gladly relinquished the responsibilities of coming up with our next single or album to another writer. There've been a lot of people who said they would have a go but somehow it never quite worked out."

The interview was published in America as well as Britain and Townshend later regretted having been so open, not the only time in his career he would feel this way. "After my total downward spiral during the filming of *Tommy*," he wrote in 1977, "and after living with the desperate fear of further humiliation of the Madison Square Garden variety, I did a few interviews with the London-based rock press. My final undoing was to see among them a face I knew and to imagine that it belonged to someone who cared about me more as a person than as a rock performer. I should never have expected that. Blaming the group, I blurted out my tears, my depressions and woe to a couple of writers whose sympathies were, to put it mildly, a little to the left wing of rock journalism. When they appeared in print, the results were catastrophic. Roger was understandably outraged, and retaliated to my abject misery in his own interviews published a few weeks later . . . I feel now as though we were both, to an extent, manipulated by a skilful and opportunistic reporting chain, that the derision handed out to me by Roger for my weakness and indulgence did me a lot of good. It hurt me at the time, but when you're so far down, so the saying goes, the gutter looks up. I had, after all, been derisive of Roger in print many times."

Townshend's response to his perceived manipulation by the press was to stop granting interviews, a major step for someone who communicated so much through the medium. However, the long, heartfelt interview with Carr and Townshend's songwriting process proved cathartic. "I got my head down to try to write a bit for the coming album and came up with some reality tinged with bitterness," he wrote in 1977. "It was hard for me to admit what I knew as I was composing; that what was happening to me was an exorcism. Suicide notes tend to flush out the trouble felt by the potential ledge jumpers. But once the truth is out, there's no need to leap."

During this time, several meetings were held to discuss The Who's direction. "For two years I was anticipating the punk thing," Pete told *Trouser Press* in 1980, "wondering how it was going to happen and getting really frustrated when it didn't. I spent a lot of time personally forcing the band, especially Roger, into conversations about it and around the time of *The Who By Numbers* we used to have really quite heavy conversations about where music was going to go – particularly in this country – and whether we should be involved in it, and the problem with Moon living in America and living that Hollywood lifestyle and whether we should try to force him to come back to England – all those kind of things.[11] Whether our music should change, whether we should let The Who tradition just bash on until it got really boring, whether we should try to force change

---

[11] Keith Moon had moved to the fast lane of Los Angeles, with his new girlfriend Annette Walter-Lax, in August 1974. They lived there until September 1977.

by starting labels and working with other bands. Before the emergence of punk, The Who was the only band who actually sat 'round a table to decide, 'Should we go on or not?' Would we be doing music a favour if we just fucking stopped? We actually considered that."

One idea, which had been announced during the Madison Square Garden shows the previous summer, had The Who recording an album of songs written by other songwriters, such as Ray Davies and Frank Zappa. Townshend told the *New York Times* that he planned a television show to complement the album, with one scene featuring "The Who and 100 topless lady accordionists."

In April, Townshend began recording demos of new material at Goring. Along with his nine songs which appeared on *The Who By Numbers*, Pete recorded demos of 'Girl In A Suitcase' (later released on 1987's *Another Scoop*) and 'To Barney Kessell', a jazz-oriented composition which Townshend dedicated to the popular jazz guitarist. "I play a lot like this," Pete wrote in his liner notes to 1983's *Scoop*, "it isn't really exploratory jazz as I work with fairly well tried chords, but it's a style of guitar I enjoy."

Later that month, recording began on *The Who By Numbers*, using Ronnie Lane's mobile set-up for recording on the Shepperton Sound Stage – a location the band chose over their own Ramport studio.[12] Townshend's decision to rehire Glyn Johns as producer as well as recording the album without any synthesisers gave *The Who By Numbers* a back-to-basics feel.

"I remember seeing quite a lot of Pete here at the time," recalls Jon Astley, sitting in a second floor room in Townshend's former Twickenham home, "and he was really into string instruments. He'd bought ukeleles, mandolins, and he picked up a banjo. He'd hardly played banjo but he worked at it for about a week, and when I saw him, say, a week later, he's like, *completely*, able to play a banjo. Maybe only one picking pattern but he's got it down, and you kind of think, 'Wow! He can actually pick up any stringed instrument and he *had* it.' I think that was the thrill of when he did *The Who By Numbers*. He was just grabbing hold of all sorts."

For the sessions, Townshend and Moon both (temporarily at least) curbed their substantial alcohol intakes, and Daltrey managed to remain

---

[12] "There's a strong chance we'll never record [at Ramport] again because it's always booked," Townshend told *Hit Parader* in 1974. "And we can't get the time. There just aren't any studios in London, there are only about 10."

silent about Townshend's recent derision of The Who in the press, although he was inwardly seething. In the singer's opinion, the friction improved the quality of the work. "Pete was incredibly down when he first played us those songs, and very cynical about what he had written," Daltrey later revealed. "When I first heard them it made me unbelievably angry. His cynicism and my anger combined made *The Who By Numbers* a good Who album, although I didn't think so at the time. Without the anger it would have been unbearable."

Townshend appeared genuinely excited about the record, saying, "Track by track, the new album that The Who are making is going to be the best thing we've ever done. But if people expect another grandiose epic then they ain't gonna get it. 'Cause this time we're going for a superb singles album."

The sessions continued into May, with the bulk of the material being completed within just a few days in the month's final week. Overdubs were added in June, and the final product was mixed in July and August at Island's Basing Street Studios in Notting Hill, west London.

"Recording the album seemed to take me nowhere," Townshend wrote in 1977. "Roger was angry with the world at the time. Keith seemed as impetuous as ever, on the wagon one minute, off it the next. John was obviously gathering strength throughout the whole period; the great thing about it was that he seemed to know we were going to need him more than ever before in the coming year. Glyn Johns was going through the most fantastic traumas at home with his marriage. I felt partly responsible because The Who recording schedule had, as usual, dragged on and on, sweeping all individuals and their needs aside. Glyn worked harder on *The Who By Numbers* than I've ever seen him. He had to, not because the tracks were weak or the music poor (though I'll admit it's not a definitive Who album) but because the group was so useless. We played cricket between takes or went to the pub. I personally had never done that before. I felt detached from my own songs, from the whole record; although I did discover some terrific sportsmen in our road crew."

While the album was being mixed, Daltrey's response to Townshend's recent negative comments to the press arrived in the August 9 issue of the same journal.

"I never read such a load of bullshit in all my life," he told the *NME*'s Tony Stewart. "To be perfectly honest, it really took a lot of my Who energy out reading that. Because I don't feel that way about The Who, about our audiences or anything in that way. It was an unbelievably down interview. And I still haven't come out of it properly yet. I've talked to fans and I think Townshend lost a lot of respect from that article. He's talked himself up his own arse. And there are quite a lot of disillusioned and disenchanted kids about now.

"My main criticism was the generalisation of saying The Who were bad. The Who *weren't* bad. I think we've had a few gigs where Townshend was bad . . . and I'll go on record as saying that. I think we had a few gigs where under normal circumstances we could have waltzed it. We could have done Madison Square Garden with our eyes closed, only the group was running on three cylinders. Especially the last night.

"I can understand [Pete's] musical frustration. He must be so far ahead now with just writing songs for The Who. But surely if The Who isn't a vehicle to get those frustrations out he should find another vehicle. But use The Who for what it is. A good rock'n'roll band, that's all. And one that *was* progressing. I say *was* because we haven't done anything for such a long time. Hopefully when we get back on the road we'll still progress. But if we have any more statements like that I don't see how we can. 'Cos I know it's taken a lot of steam out of me and I'm sure it did with the others."

The Who By Numbers was released in October on Polydor – not Track Records thanks to the management litigation[13] – reaching number seven in Britain and eight in the US. The album was well received in the music press, with none other than Roy Carr concluding his review that he thought it no less than "brilliant". A few years after its release, Townshend admitted to Scott Muni, "I really liked a lot of the stuff on that album."

Many fans viewed *The Who By Numbers* more as a Townshend solo album than a true Who outing, and the introspective 'However Much I Booze' was a case in point. Daltrey refused to sing this intensely personal song, leaving Townshend to sing his own words:

> *I see myself on TV, I'm a faker, a paper clown*
> *It's clear to all my friends that I habitually lie, I just bring them down*
> *I claim proneness to exaggeration, but the truth lies in my frustration*
> *The children of the night, they all pass me by*
> *Got to dress myself in brandy, and sleep while high*
> *But however much I booze, there ain't no way out*

---

[13] Track finally went into liquidation in 1978.

The other track featuring Pete on lead vocals was 'Blue, Red And Grey', a sparse arrangement consisting of Townshend strumming a ukelele accompanied only by Entwistle's horn arrangement.[14]

"Glyn wanted it on the album," he told *Trouser Press*. "I cringed when he picked it. He heard in on a cassette and said, 'What's that?' I said, 'Nothing.' He said, 'No. Play it.' I said, 'Really, it's nothing. Just me playing a ukulele.' But he insisted on doing it. I said, 'What? That fucking thing. Here's me, wanting to commit suicide, and you're going to put that thing on the record!"

"All the songs [on *The Who By Numbers*] were different, some more aggressive than others, but they were all somehow negative in direction. I felt empty," Townshend wrote in 1977. 'Slip Kid', "came across as a warning to young kids getting into music that it would hurt them, it was almost parental in its assumed wisdom." 'Squeeze Box' was "obviously recorded for fun and intended as a poorly aimed dirty joke," Pete recalled in his 1983 *Scoop* sleevenotes. "I had bought myself an accordion and learned to play it one afternoon. (That is not meant to be flash, I don't mean I learned to play it properly, just to manage to work it without falling over!) The polka-esque rhythm I managed to produce from it brought forth this song. Amazingly recorded by The Who to my disbelief. Further incredulity was caused when it became a hit for us in the USA."[15]

'How Many Friends' was about "what was happening to quite a few people around us," Townshend told Matt Kent in 1999, "about what was happening to Kit Lambert and to Keith Moon, Eric Clapton, who we were seeing a lot of at the time, Viv Stanshall, Legs Larry Smith. A number of people who I could see, and myself as well, who were having a lot of problems with hangers on."

Townshend described one such problem in detail to *Goldmine*'s Ken Sharp in 2006: "Going onstage once at the Fillmore in San Francisco I felt the hand of the boy behind me touching my butt. I looked back and saw someone I had come to like a lot, and didn't want to hurt his feelings. I said nothing to encourage or discourage him, but I steered clear of him from

---

[14] The Townshend solo version was reportedly chosen over a full band recording done at Shepperton.

[15] 'Squeeze Box' became The Who's first Top 20 single since 'Won't Get Fooled Again' in 1971. *Q*'s David Cavanaugh asked Townshend in January 2000 which song he wished he'd never recorded. " 'Squeeze Box', he replied. "I loved my demo of it, but I find it excruciating listening to Roger singing it." In 1982, Pete told *The Record* that the song "was as bad as [Paul McCartney & Stevie Wonder's] 'Ebony And Ivory'."

then on. But it stayed in my mind for a long time. When that happens as a man you sense a little of what it might be like to be a woman who has to tell a man she really likes that he can't sleep with her. As a performer we feel the rules are set out by our fans. One by one we discover that they each have conditions we can never live up to. So we end up with a few, we can count on one hand, that take us as we are. This song is about fans, not friends."

'In A Hand Or A Face' was "cynical and tried to cut down the growing dependence I had on mysticism and psychic phenomena," Townshend wrote in 1977. Even Entwistle's humorous 'Success Story', a sardonic song about a band's rise to stardom, featured some of the "reality tinged with bitterness" which Townshend described, as Entwistle sang, "Take 276, you know this used to be fun."

"*The Who By Numbers* isn't what it seems," Dave Marsh wrote in his *Rolling Stone* review. "Without broadcasting it, in fact while denying it, Townshend has written a series of songs which hang together as well as separately. The time is somewhere in the middle of the night, the setting a dishevelled room with a TV set that seems to show only rock programmes. The protagonist is an ageing, still successful rock star, staring drunkenly at the tube with a bottle of gin perched on his head, contemplating his career, his love for the music and his fear that it's all slipping away. Every song here, even the one non-Townshend composition, John Entwistle's 'Success Story', fits in. Always a sort of musical practical joker, Townshend has now pulled the fastest one of all, disguising his best concept album as a mere 10-track throwaway . . .

"From *My Generation* to *The Who By Numbers*, time and ageing have been Townshend's obsession, as if he were trying to live down the statement that made him famous: 'Hope I die before I get old.' If this is his most mature work, that's because he has finally admitted that there is no way out, which is a darker and deeper part of the same thing. Typically, The Who face the fact without flinching. Indeed, they may have made their greatest album in the face of it. But only time will tell."

After the completion of *The Who By Numbers*, Pete used the subsequent time off to recharge his batteries. "I decided to try to get some spiritual energy from friends in the USA," he wrote in 1977. "My family [particularly of course my wife, who as a matter of personal policy tries to avoid the aspects of the music world that I still find exciting] had suffered a lot from my pathetic behaviour of the previous year, but they would naturally be by my side on any trip other than Who tours."

Among the reasons for the visit was an idea he'd been nurturing. "For a few years, I had toyed with the idea of opening a London house dedicated to Meher Baba," Townshend recalled in the same *Rolling Stone* essay. "In the eight years I had followed him, I had donated only coppers to foundations set up around the world to carry out the Master's wishes and decided it was about time I put myself on the line. The Who had set up a strong charitable trust of its own which appeased, to an extent, the feeling I had that Meher Baba would rather have seen me give to the poor than to the establishment of yet another so-called 'spiritual centre.'

"I was genuinely unprepared for the unfolding that transpired in that six weeks. My mind was clouded with the idea of trying to run a 'centre' for Avatar Meher Baba; with the difficulties I would have trying to deal with people's whims and complaints; but most of all, with the hypocrisy of trying to do such a contentiously idealistic thing while enjoying the kind of life I had been living."

Before leaving for America, Pete set about reviewing his difficulties with The Who's singer. "In early August, I had written Roger a note, telling him that I felt there had been a lot of unnecessary strife between us, and that I hoped I could earn his respect again." A few weeks later, Townshend again wrote to Daltrey. "I told him I would support him in whatever he did. I felt it a strange thing to say.

"Roger often sang songs I'd written that he didn't care for with complete commitment, and I took him for granted. I said what I wanted to say, often ignoring or being terribly patronising about the rest of the group's suggestions, then sulked when they didn't worship me for making life financially viable . . . In New York, a good friend of mine gave me some advice. I tried to explain that I felt the problems in The Who were mainly about me and Roger, not the myriad business problems that seemed so manifestly cancerous. I was counselled quite simply: 'Let Roger win.'

"The statement isn't as cruel or flippant as it sounds. This person knew The Who and its history and cared about all of us deeply. The advice meant that I should demonstrate to Roger that my letters were sincere by not hanging on to past grievances or differences. Most of all, I should bow to the changing status quo within the group, created by the fans' new identification with Roger as front man, rather than with me as its mouthpiece."

The Townshends first stop was the Baba retreat in Myrtle Beach, South Carolina.

"As our party [my wife, my two little daughters and a few friends who travelled with us] crossed the threshold onto Meher Baba's home ground, we were all staggered by the impact of the love that literally filled the air," Townshend described in 1977. "Despite the strength I felt growing within me, I think I can speak for our whole party when I say I felt exhausted by Myrtle Beach. God's endlessly present love isn't to be taken lightly. It's great to be forgiven, but it hurts to admit you were wrong in the first place. I realised that I would not be reaping such fantastic emotional and mental rewards had I not been in pretty bad shape; a condition for which I had no one to blame but myself . . .

"We spent an unbelievable 10 days. I talked to the older devotees of Meher Baba about my plans for a new place in London and they were naturally encouraging. The sun shone, the children enjoyed themselves, we relaxed and relished rejuvenation at the Master's command. The fears I had that I would not be strong enough to see through the imminent testing rehearsals and tour with The Who receded."

The Townshends then travelled on to Walnut Creek, California to visit Murshida Duce, who invited Pete over when she'd visited England the previous year.

"In California," he continued, "we were well looked after, taken into the bosom of the Sufi family there, provided with a furnished house, picnics, swimming pool, outings to state parks, camping trips to the Sierras and all kinds of straight-laced relaxation. You are probably as mystified as I am as to where the spiritually beneficial work was being done in this kind of programme, but spirit was what was needed, and spirit was what I got, even if it didn't fit preconceived notions.

"On arrival in California, I went for a talk with [the Murshida], to gossip, to bring her up-to-date on events at home, to ask her advice about the colour of the walls at the newly planned Baba house in London. Instead, to my amazement, I sat and poured out my very soul. I couldn't for a second have anticipated this happening. She sat and listened as I told her every grisly detail: the paranoia, the drunken orgies, the financial chaos, the indulgent self-analysis [continued herein, I'm afraid] and, of course, the dreamy hopes for the future.

"Without batting an eyelid she listened to stuff that was making me recoil within myself, then went on to talk a little about her own youth, her life with her husband, the trouble some of her students were having at the time. In short, she got me right in perspective. At the end of this month with her, we packed our bags, said our farewells and headed home, my wife and the kids to school, me to rehearsals with the band."

★   ★   ★

It was late September, and The Who began rehearsals for their first extensive tour in two years. Daltrey had filmed his starring role in another Ken Russell vehicle, *Lisztomania* while promoting his second solo album, *Ride A Rock Horse*, Entwistle toured and recorded with his band Ox, and even Moon had released a solo album *Two Sides Of The Moon* earlier in the year.

"Keith later told me I walked into the rehearsal hall smiling," Townshend wrote in *Rolling Stone*. "He related this because he had found it remarkable. Something positive had happened to me."

Entwistle, however, remembers the band's reunification differently. "When we got together to work on our act before touring again Pete was obviously not into it. So we went down to Shepperton for two days to rehearse without Roger singing, just Pete, Keith and myself playing instrumentals, all those old things. We had such a good time that we turned around completely and found ourselves playing better than we had in years."

Following some initial teething troubles (*Rolling Stone* described the opening October 3 show in Stafford as "sloppy"), The Who had hit their stride by the time they returned home to London for a three-night stand at Wembley's Empire Pool in late October. Support act on all tour dates was the Steve Gibbons Band.[16]

As a result of tightening up their stage act, the band settled into a set list which would remain virtually unchanged over the next year. In addition to a sample of early singles and a handful of songs from *Who's Next*, a nine-song *Tommy* medley became the centerpiece due to the massive popularity of Ken Russell's movie. The repertoire was nowhere near as progressive as Townshend had hoped when composing *Quadrophenia*; in fact, most shows during the year-long tour featured no songs from that album, while only two were included from *The Who By Numbers*, much to Polydor's chagrin. Despite this retrogressive step, The Who's live show during this period was regarded as unbeatable. "They played with renewed energy," stated *The Who Concert File*, "easily reclaiming their crown as the world's greatest live rock'n'roll band. Pete rediscovered his mastery of the electric guitar, playing searing solos and slashing rhythm,

---

[16] The Steve Gibbons Band were discovered in 1974 by none other than Peter Meaden, who co-managed them with Who manager, Bill Curbishley. A decade after being out-manoeuvred by Kit Lambert and Chris Stamp, Meaden was back in The Who circle. He was an adviser during initial production on the *Quadrophenia* movie just prior to his death on July 30, 1978 from barbiturate poisoning.

jumping and windmilling in his inimitable style, all with new found vigour. Overjoyed at his enthusiasm, Roger, John and Keith performed as if their lives depended on it. Many fans still consider that The Who's rebirth in 1975/76 represented some of their finest moments . . ."

Following a nine-show trek through the Netherlands, Austria, and Germany,[17] The Who kicked off their North American tour – a month-long, 20-date affair which took in over $3 million – at Houston's new 18,000-seat basketball arena, the Summit, on November 20. Reggae band Toots & the Maytals opened all shows. The tour was an operation of mammoth proportions, the band travelling with 14 tons of equipment, including a PA system consisting of 72 speakers. "This tour was the first time they used their $36,000 lasers in the act," wrote Richard Barnes.[18] "They were employed during the *Tommy* section which . . . consistently brought the house down."

Townshend was in good spirits at the opening of the tour, telling Nik Cohn, "I've stopped drinking and I haven't lost my nerve onstage, not yet. Keith Moon has started smashing up his hotel rooms again, which is always a good sign." All the shows – including a sold-out date at Pontiac, Michigan's enormous 78,000-seat Silverdome, which The Who were the first band to play at – drew rave reviews, with adjectives such as "stunning, phenomenal, awesome, devastating, magnificent, glorious," and "explosive" appearing in almost every review covering the shows. At the final show in Philadelphia on December 15, Pete smashed his Les Paul to climax a successful two months of touring, during which The Who single-handedly reclaimed their position as the greatest rock'n'roll band in the world.

The year ended with three shows at London's Hammersmith Odeon on December 21, 22, and 23. "The Odeon was transformed into a huge

---

[17] Moon resumed his antics on the band's private plane during the European tour. "The toilet was in the back of the plane," Bill Curbishley told Tony Fletcher in 1999. "And on the way back Pete Townshend went in there and Moon locked him in, so Townshend kicked the door off. Moon carried the door down to the cockpit and said, 'I believe this is yours, old chap,' and gave it to the pilot and put it on his shoulders. So the pilot's trying to fly this plane with a fucking door on him!"

[18] The Who's stage lighting became an important facet after The Rolling Stones US summer tour in 1972. "Bobby [Pridden] and our lights man went over there and came back saying we'd got to get our lights together because theirs were amazing," Townshend told *Sounds*' Penny Valentine that August. "To which I said, 'Look what have I been saying?' because our lights are expensive but pathetic – which is not the case with the sound because that's expensive and worth it."

Christmas party with a Who Christmas Pack left on every seat, containing Who balloons, streamers, masks and a badge," Matt Kent wrote in a 2004 *Mojo* article. "Monty Python's Graham Chapman [a friend of Moon's] compered the shows and was promptly booed offstage every night. Moon made his grand entrance descending to the stage on a winch." *NME*'s Steve Clark commented, "If you thought rock was dead at that moment in time [during the shows], you must have been born in the wrong age. Easily the year's best display of rock'n'roll."

During a two-month break at the start of the year, Townshend took the opportunity to follow up on some of the things he and Murshida Duce had discussed the previous year. Pete spent the month of January looking for a suitable location for his planned Meher Baba centre. "After viewing several places, he took me to see the Boathouse in Twickenham," Delia DeLeon wrote in 1991. "It was in such a very dilapidated condition that we had to climb ladders to view it. His deep instinct was to buy it and rebuild it according to his idea of a Baba centre/workshop which would have living accommodations and a theatre. Encouragement came from India and America, and I was happy to know this dream could at last come true." Once restored, the building later became known as Meher Baba Oceanic.

Later that month Pete and Delia travelled to India just prior to the seventh anniversary of Baba's entombment, known as the Amartithi. Townshend had planned to visit India during a break from touring the previous October, but changed his mind not long before leaving.

"It was a joyful two weeks," DeLeon recalled. "We arrived the day before [Amartithi] and so were able to take part in this very special day and its prayers and songs . . . There in that lovely, peaceful place one feels strongly enfolded by Baba's love . . . All were interested in the progress of Meher Baba Oceanic and gave Pete their wholehearted support . . . As Pete and I sat alone in the Tomb that last morning to pay our final respects to Baba, he sang his own arrangement of the Master's Prayer, 'Parvardigar', and it seemed to draw the two of us together in a karmic bond, a moment that lingered in my mind many weeks after my return."[19]

At the same time, the third Meher Baba Association album, *With Love,*

---

[19] Townshend also played for other Baba lovers during his stay. His performance of 'Pinball Wizard' and 'Drowned' in front of a handful of seated onlookers was captured on film and released as part of a Baba documentary, *The God Man*.

was released, featuring two Townshend-penned instrumentals, 'His Hands' and 'Lantern Cabin', along with a song entitled 'Sleeping Dog'. Other musical disciples featured on the limited edition release of 4,000 included Billy Nicholls, Ronnie Lane, and Medicine Head's Peter Hope-Evans.

By late February, The Who were back on the road, performing in Zurich, Munich and Paris prior to heading to the US in early March. The American leg (with the Steve Gibbons Band again opening all dates) got off to a bad start when only two songs into the band's set in Boston, Moon collapsed and the remainder of the concert was cancelled while the next show at New York's Madison Square Garden was moved back a day to March 11. A 'flu bug' was blamed and a security guard was posted outside Moon's hotel room at the Navarro to prevent the drummer going out on the town.[20] This didn't sit well with Moon, who had sufficiently recovered enough to destroy the entire contents of his suite. He cut his foot so badly during the rampage that, according to Bill Curbishley, he almost bled to death.

While in New York, Chris Charlesworth, *Melody Maker's* US editor, caught up with the band. "Pete was interested in going downtown to rock clubs to check out the beginnings of the city's punk scene and for some reason I took him to the 82 Club and not CBGBs. Maybe no one was on at CBGBs that night. Anyway, it was in his limousine on the way there that the Boston record ['More Than A Feeling'] started playing and Pete listened to it quite intently. It was the first time he'd heard it as it probably hadn't been released in the UK and he turned to me afterwards and said something like, 'That record will sell five million copies.' I already knew it because it had been out a while and done very well and I thought to myself, 'What a great A&R man he could have been.'"

The tour continued through the central US and on to the West Coast, finishing at Boston Garden on April 1 to make up for the cancelled gig. Following two dates in France, The Who launched their 'Who Put The Boot In' tour of three British football stadiums with opening acts the Sensational Alex Harvey Band, Little Feat, the Outlaws, and Chapman-Whitney's Streetwalkers. The first a return to Charlton Athletic Football Ground in front of 60,000 on May 31, put The Who in the *Guinness Book*

---

[20] Pete had led an effort to get Moon seen by Meg Patterson prior to this next round of touring. Moon was abusing alcohol and cocaine. After receiving counselling from George Patterson (Meg's husband), Moon played his first concert sober in a decade at Zurich. However, three days later in Paris, he was off the wagon and destroyed his hotel room after the show.

Of Records as the 'World's Loudest Pop Group'. The band's mammoth PA system spewed forth 120 decibels at 50 metres, enough to permanently damage the hearing of those who were close enough to the speakers.

"Although loud, the sound was clear and sharp," Barnes wrote in *Maximum R&B*. "The sound system specially built for the show by Tasco, and costing £7,000 just for that night alone, had never before been used in England. The long throw bass speakers ensured that even people at the back got high quality sound . . . At the climax of 'Listening To You', all the £100,000 lights including the huge arc lights set up behind the group, facing out into the audience, were switched on, and the effect from this simple piece of theatrics produced one of rock's greatest and most climactic moments . . ."

NME called the show's climax "a masterstroke. The [Who] put the proverbial boot in." Despite the heavy rain, crowd violence, long delays and The Who's traditional refusal to do an encore, the second Charlton concert was considered a great performance, as were The Who's shows at Glasgow, in front of 35,000 and Swansea, where 25,000 attended.

During a break from touring, Pete's vision of a London Meher Baba Centre was finally realised. "Oceanic was a Meher Baba Centre for 5 years with 16-mm film dubbing and editing suites, a cinema and four-track studio," Townshend recalled in 1982. The complex also served as a regular meeting venue for devotees and, with Pete offering upstairs rooms at £1 a night, a very economical source of shelter for a number of American Baba lovers who needed an overnight stay on their pilgrimages to India. "Meher Baba Oceanic was opened on July 3, 1976 with 10 days of music, drama, films, and food," recalled Delia DeLeon, who held regular Tuesday night meetings at Oceanic throughout its existence. Adi Irani, Baba's secretary and a disciple, attended the opening, and Mehera, Baba's leading female disciple, gave her blessing to the proceedings.

"She sent a beautiful pink silk coat once worn by Meher Baba which became the centrepiece of a small collection of precious artefacts that were touched, used or worn by the Master," Townshend wrote in a July 2001 web posting. "Everything began well, and I greatly enjoyed being a part of the constant ebb and flow of international visitors. I also enjoyed hosting musical concerts, plays and film shows as well as the more usual talks and devotional gatherings . . . From 1976 until the middle of 1979 I was [blessed by all but self-appointed] very much in the forefront of all activity in the UK surrounding Meher Baba."

The films shown at the opening of the Baba centre had been sponsored by Pete and produced at Oceanic. They included *The East/West Gathering* and *O, Parvardigar*.[21] "Pete loves Baba deeply and in my view his greatest achievement is probably his beautiful setting of 'Master's Prayer' to music and later the production of the film *O, Parvardigar*, with this as the sound-track," DeLeon wrote in 1991. "This film is most important as it shows Baba at different stages of His life, with the lepers, masts, at darshan programmes, and with His devotees in different parts of the world."

The *Delia* film, which Townshend wrote, directed and narrated, also premiered during the opening of Oceanic. "Pete promised me the film would be shown," DeLeon recalled. "With so much to do, this meant he and John [Annunziato] had to work sometimes all night to get it finished."

During The Who's mini-tour of the eastern US in early August, Pete managed to grab a few days' relaxation at Myrtle Beach. The Who played four shows, beginning with two in Largo, Maryland, followed by big outdoor concerts in Jacksonville and Miami. Chris Charlesworth provided the following report in *The Who Concert File*:

> "*[The Who] were closing an open air all-dayer in a big stadium in muggy, unpleasant weather after an ill-judged, weak supporting cast had limped on and offstage to little purpose. A greedy promoter had overcharged and Florida was never Who territory, so the crowd numbered 35,000 instead of a poten-tial 60,000. This hurt their pride and they were angry at what had hap-pened, furious in fact, and having watched The Who at close quarters scores of times by then I knew all too well that anger could bring out the best or the worst in them. Sharp words were exchanged backstage and I kept my distance; only Keith, fuelled as ever by Remy Martin brandy, seemed sociable. But come showtime there was an extraordinary transformation and all their fury, all the frustration and pent-up rage that spilled out of Pete and Roger, was channelled into the music, and they played an absolute blinder, as powerful as any show in the classic '69–'71 era. The Who at their almighty best came flooding over everyone in that stadium that night. At the end they smashed their equipment in an orgy of gleeful destruction and the crowd exploded with endless ovations because they'd never seen or heard anything like it before, nor would they ever again.*
>
> "*Afterwards, backstage, in the calm of the caravan that served as a dressing room, I clearly remember sitting down next to Pete and remarking to him on how good this show had been. Exhausted, slumped in a corner, his fingers*

---

[21] Both are still available through Sheriar Press.

shredded and covered in blood, his skinny, loose limbed body wrapped in a towel, he knocked back a huge plastic beaker of brandy in one gulp. There was a strange, faraway look in those deep blue eyes of his as he looked up at me. He thought for a minute, fingered the Meher Baba badge that hung from his neck, then managed a wry smile. 'We were playing for the people who weren't there,' he said."

The final nine date leg of the year-long tour opened in Arizona on October 6 and featured stops along the West Coast (The Grateful Dead opened up two open-air stadium shows in Oakland on October 9 and 10), winding up at Maple Leaf Gardens in Toronto on October 21.

"A lot of things came to a 'glorious' head in Toronto," Townshend wrote the following year. "The road crew threw a party for us, and it was the first party I had been to for at least five years which meant anything to me. I don't go to a lot of parties, but I'm glad that I made this one. I suddenly realised that behind every Who show are people who care as much as, or more than, we do. Talking to the individuals who help get the show together enabled me to remember that audiences care, too.

"When I sit in an audience, one of the things that makes it enjoyable is the energy I spend *willing* it to be the best thing I have ever seen. I get to see some great concerts that way. Ask any Who fan if they care how well we are playing on any single date. The Who don't count as much as people might imagine, but as performers their response to the audience's energy is vital."

The Toronto show was to take on an even deeper significance. Though no one knew it at the time, it proved to be Keith Moon's last performance before a paying audience.

CHAPTER TEN

1976–1978

"We used to think we were rebels, but what did we do? We went out and we rampaged around like a small commando troop, you know, we went over to America, to Europe, to Australia, we smashed up the hotel rooms, we shagged all the women, and we collected all the money and we came back, and we expected to be heroes, not just heroes in rock'n'roll but we expected to be heroes in the world, you know, in society as it stood. Of course, it doesn't happen that way."

– Pete Townshend, 1985

FOLLOWING The Who's hugely successful 1976 tours of Europe and America (which reportedly grossed in excess of $8 million), Townshend looked forward to arriving back home to his family, of whom he had seen very little over the previous year.

"I wanted to return as a conquering hero because it had been a marvellous tour for us," he recalled in 1984. "But when I got to the front door steps I wasn't the hero. I walked back to the kids who didn't even know who I was. They were very cagey and intimidated by me. They were even more perplexed because I wore an American sea captain's uniform which I'd bought in Chicago.[1] I can see their faces still."

The weeks following his return provided a timely reality check to a man who'd neglected his responsibilities as a husband and father while being consumed by his role as a famous musician and songwriter.

"Our marriage staggered on for a while but then came a showdown," Townshend wrote the following year. "My old lady just broke down one day and said she'd run out of energy and that was it. It dawned on me that what she was really saying was, 'I don't really love you. I don't care

---

[1] In October 1978, Townshend told *Melody Maker*'s Michael Watts that he'd worn the uniform "quite happily for two months every day; in fact, I used to walk about playing this Wagner tape 'Overture to *Tristan Und Isolde*', walking around like a Nazi."

whether you go away or whether you stay. I don't give a damn about you or your life, or the way you don't think about us.' I went away for two days and thought about all she had said. I saw the truth . . . that if I lost Karen and the family I wouldn't be able to face life at all. What's more, I wouldn't be able to do anything for The Who either."

"I just felt burnt-out, clap-ridden and alcoholic," Pete told *Melody Maker*'s Michael Watts in 1978. "I made up my mind then. 'I've gotta get my priorities right.' And one priority that I sorted out was that I needed stability and I needed my family, and I needed that more than anything else."

"I made a conscious decision that my first love, The Who, would in future take second place to my real love – my wife and my daughters," he wrote. "There were things I got from The Who that nobody could ever get from a marriage partnership. But on the other hand what really made me a human being was my relationship with my old lady. I knew that's what I needed to preserve most. From that point of view my family became my first priority . . . Some people who are heavily into The Who felt this was a great snub on my part because, in effect, I was telling them, 'Listen, you're not as important as my family.' Fortunately others understood my predicament."

One of those who understood was Dave Marsh: "Because they're a Sixties band, The Who feel a special sense of responsibility [shared, perhaps, only by the ex-Beatles, Bob Dylan and The Rolling Stones] not only about musical matters but about questions of lifestyle, image and ethics," Marsh wrote in 1978. "For Townshend, these are especially weighty concerns; rock is not just a livelihood and a fantastic source of energy, it is so much a cornerstone of belief that he sees his spiritual master, Meher Baba, 'through two slits, R & R.'

"This sense of responsibility is at the core of Townshend's determination to avoid a lengthy tour . . . the responsibility he feels for his audience and the rock ideal is outweighed, at least for now, by the responsibility he feels to his family."

"I don't want to do the American tour again," Townshend told John Swenson in 1977. "My kids are getting pretty old now – eight and seven. When I have an extended period at home, they get noticeably happier. It makes me think about those four months away from home every year, to end up with a lot of American tax bills and maybe nothing else. I love being onstage. It's a great kick, but I think I can live without it. Are we really making the fans happy? Every time we go into a town we get complaints we're not playing long enough. If we play at a big stadium we get complaints it's too big and they can't see us. The only answer is to play in small halls for years at a time. I've got other things to do."

Another important reason for Townshend's decision was the alarming condition of his hearing. According to Pete, the first tangible evidence of his hearing loss came following The Who's concert at Anaheim Stadium on March 21, 1976. The size of the audience (55,000) demanded the use of a larger-than-normal sound system, as Townshend told Scott Muni in 1978.

"We had an enormous PA system and a very, very large monitor PA system and we started up, I played a chord, Roger sang one note, and the sound hit my left ear, and I've never really been able to hear properly out of it since. I had really lousy earaches for about three or four months afterwards . . . then I realised that my hearing overall had sort of dropped. I discovered this in the most alarming way: I couldn't stand the sound of my kids' voices . . . So I went to this ear shrink . . . and he said, 'You really should be careful. If you're careful, you'll still have your hearing when you're 40.' And I said, 'When I'm *what*? . . .Well, I'm 33 now – that's *seven years*.'

"Then I went to another guy. He was a little bit less pessimistic. He said, 'Well, if you conserve your hearing, if you wear earplugs on the stage, if you don't listen to music loud at other times, if you keep away from rock concerts, if you don't go to shows, if you don't listen to loud bands, and . . . this kind of thing, your hearing will tail off at the normal age.' I just started to think very seriously about a life without music. I mean, even without me being a musician, a life without music, and I decided, and I say this before God, that I'd rather go blind than go deaf. It's my life, music. I'm a writer, I'm a composer, my greatest moments are to sit at a piano or pick up a guitar and *fly*, you know. I communicate with people through music, through what I write . . . After the third meeting with a separate doctor, I got three separate opinions, and he said exactly the same thing, he said you've really got to be careful otherwise you're going to go deaf very soon. I just went back to the band, and I said, 'Jesus Christ, you know, what do I do?'"

The revelation that his hearing problems could be potentially debilitating was a sobering wake-up call to Townshend. "I wish it was a rumour," he told Muni. "I'm going deaf, and I really don't like the sensation. I have to struggle to hear what people are saying a lot of the time."

It also led him to consider what The Who's enormous PA system was doing to their audiences' hearing. "Listen, if I choose to put an amplifier up and blow my own head off, that's *my* business," Townshend declared. "But the thing that makes me wake up in a cold sweat is the fact that the sound intensity measured six rows back at an average Who concert has been measured as high as like, 126db, which somebody has told me is enough, practically, to physically blow your eardrum into the ear cavity . . . I just think about . . . the kids that have to be out in the front. I mean, I'm like that. If I go to a concert, I want to be flattened, and I get lost, I lose myself . . . You *fly*, and one of the things that helps you to fly, I think, is that thing that your brain is being shaken like a walnut inside your skull. But if, while it's making you fly, it's making you deaf, then what the hell? And what really makes me, as I say, lay awake at night is the thought that while people are listening to my music, I'm taking away their capacity to listen to it for more than a short period of time. My younger brothers are both about to go and get their ears tested."

While live decibels undoubtedly contributed to his hearing problems, Townshend later contended that, prior to the Anaheim show, a substantial amount of damage had already been inflicted – not from years of playing in front of a literally deafening PA system, or listening to extremely loud music at home or in his car, but from the use of headphones.[2]

"That's where my problem started," he informed *Musician* in 1989. "It's very important to make this point. It was *earphones! Earphones! Earphones!* It was going home after gigs, to my own studio, and playing guitar through the earphones. My sound was an electric sound. You couldn't reproduce it on acoustic guitar. It had to be with earphones. Obviously I couldn't have a Marshall stack in my living room and practice with the babies upstairs. I used earphones for 20 years. That's what caused the damage . . . It's also a different situation when your head is clear and you're not drunk. Wearing earphones when you're drunk can increase damage by a factor of 10, I think. Some of the muscles that operate the eardrum are disabled by alcohol."

When Pete broke the news of his desire to cease touring, he expected a great deal of resistance but the other band members, on the face of it, at least, respected his decision with the strongest backing, to Townshend's considerable surprise, coming from Roger. "He said to me, 'I don't care

[2] "Even with a relatively small amplifier, you know, if you hook the earphones up to the speaker terminals, you can blow your own head off," Townshend told Muni in April. "On the stage once, I saw Keith Moon, who uses earphones to follow a drum track, I saw his earphones *catch fire*, on God's honour, *catch fire* on his head there was so much level . . . and he's still going, louder, *louder!*"

whether we tour or make records or don't make records. I just always want to be able to work with you, always be able to sing your songs and, above everything else, I want you to be happy.' This was Roger Daltrey, right? The person I was seeing as a competitor. It was a revelation. Nobody has ever talked like that to me. Nobody. Not my mother, not my father, not my kids, not my wife. Nobody ever said things like that and meant them."

With The Who effectively on ice, Pete entertained thoughts of a solo project. "Last year after the US tour I was sick of working with The Who," Townshend told the *Los Angeles Times* in 1977. "I suppose it would have been just as easy for me to have rung up Roger Daltrey and arranged to have done an album with him. But I couldn't even conceive of the idea of writing songs. The last Who album, I barely wrote enough songs. *The Who By Numbers* had no leftover songs at all, I'd stopped dead. But I was eager to do something in the studio with Glyn Johns, our producer, without the heavy pressure of a Who gig."

The answer arrived when his old friend Ronnie Lane came up to London from his Welsh farm to visit Townshend.

"Basically the [*Rough Mix*] album came about because I was in financial trouble,"[3] Lane told Dave Marsh in 1983, "and I went to see Pete, not to ask for anything, just to see him socially. Obviously, we talked about each other's state. Mine came up and he said, 'Well, we've talked about working together in the past. Why don't we get an album together?' I said, 'That would solve my problem.' It did."

By the time the *Rough Mix* sessions started in a loose fashion in the summer of '76, Lane and Townshend had known each other for over a decade. Jon Astley, Johns' engineer on the project, recalls that they "had a lot in common, from the end of the Sixties to the early Seventies in that they were both in pop bands, but also they had wives who knew each other and saw quite a lot of each other, and they all lived locally. So socially they knew each other and got on."[4]

---

[3] Lane had been left virtually bankrupt after mounting a money-draining tour with his band Slim Chance known as the Passing Show ("life is only a passing show" was another of Baba's teachings), a traveling roadshow in which the musicians lived together in tents and performed along with jugglers, dancers, and circus artistes.

[4] In addition to the work the pair did together on the Baba-related albums, in 1972, Townshend guested on two songs on Ronnie Lane and Ron Wood's soundtrack to Alexis Kanner's *Mahoney's Last Stand*. The album's release was delayed until 1976.

After laying down demos using Lane's mobile studio in September, recording sessions for the project began at Olympic Studios in early November 1976, concluding in early summer 1977. Providing additional instrumentation were a host of guests, including Eric Clapton, Charlie Watts, Peter Hope-Evans, Billy Nicholls and session keyboardist John 'Rabbit' Bundrick.[5] Astley recalls his brother-in-law as "actually quite relaxed in the studio and really enjoying it," a marked difference from the last Who recording experience which took place at the height of Townshend's disagreements with Daltrey. This lighter mood translated into the songs, which were generally relaxed and upbeat in nature.

"I suppose that if you're working just down the road from home at Olympic, beautiful drive across Richmond Park to get to the studio, nice people to work with, great musicians, you know, two or three takes and you'd have what you wanted, Glyn Johns, great sound, of course – then it's going to be a doddle," Astley opines.

The sessions were generally scheduled from noon to around 8 p.m., as both Townshend and Johns wanted to spend the evenings with their families. "Glyn really hated going beyond eight o'clock with all the bands I worked with . . . he liked to get in his car and go home and see his wife as much as Pete did," Astley recalls, adding that the schedule didn't work for Lane, as "Ronnie sort of came alive about four or five o'clock in the afternoon."

A quota of five Townshend compositions ended up on *Rough Mix*: 'My Baby Gives It Away', 'Misunderstood', 'Street In The City', 'Keep Me Turning', and 'Heart To Hang Onto', a song Pete described in 2005 as "one of the most special songs in my solo repertoire," adding, "I'm stunned we rejected it as a Who song, but we did."[6]

'Misunderstood' was "a song which I expect was flown past The Who at some point, and probably Roger said something like, 'Well, it's great, Pete, but it's obviously yours, isn't it? I don't know that I can sing that,'" Townshend said in 1996. "It's not actually a song about how I felt

---

[5] Bundrick, whose buck-teeth inspired his nickname, had previously worked on Johnny Nash's *I Can See Clearly Now* and Bob Marley's *Catch A Fire* albums, as well as playing keyboards in Free and Back Street Crawler.

[6] Three tracks – 'Only You', 'Good Question' and 'Silly Little Man' – were included in the 2006 reissue of the album, representing the balance of the recorded work from the *Rough Mix* sessions. 'Good Question' had a working title of 'Brrr' and was included under that name on Townshend's 1983 *Scoop* collection of demos.

particularly. I was just writing a song about that kind of James Dean syndrome – you know, I would much prefer to be confused and gorgeous than as I really am, which is, as I think I say in the song, fairly easy to penetrate, but that's another kind of sub-teenage angst all of its own."

'Street In The City' was "a song about walking through a city and picking up paranoia everywhere," Pete revealed, "[The song was written by] deliberately going to somewhere like Oxford Street and picking up feelings from people and writing them down quickly . . . looking up at people on buildings and looking at people in office blocks, and trying to get a sense of, you know, "That man over there painting that wall – I wonder what he's like in bed with his wife," and "That priest – I wonder what his childhood was like," trying to project and create characters.

The song also made reference to an experience Townshend had while waiting for an appointment outside the Wig & Pen, a popular Fleet Street haunt of lawyers and journalists. A man stepped out on a high window ledge, and a crowd began to gather. "Two journalists were standing nearby and I heard one say, 'If he falls, we're in the money,'" Pete told *Melody Maker*'s Chris Welch in 1977. "Then the bloke on the ledge started cleaning the windows, and the crowd melted away."

Although *Rough Mix* was a combined effort, it contained no joint Townshend/Lane compositions. "I've never really been able to co-write comfortably," Pete told the *Austin Chronicle* in 2007. "I suppose for me it's probably about control. When I sit down with somebody else, I find it quite tricky to get past the fact that there's a kind of creative negotiation going on, which I don't know that I've got the generosity of spirit to deal with. Ronnie was extraordinary in that respect; he could work with anyone. He was so adorable but such an underestimated musician in those early days. He wasn't a real Who fan. He wasn't into the punk rock that The Who was into. He loved coming around and listening to my demos, the little things that I did that The Who never recorded."

Lane had another take on the situation. "I couldn't make out why we didn't spend an hour or two or an evening or two to write a song together," he told Dave Marsh. "I've got a few ideas. Pete had a few ideas. My ideas weren't finished, and with his help they could have been finished – things like that. And vice versa. So I said, 'Why don't we get together and write some things?' He turned around and said, 'What? And split the publishing?' I was floored. I never brought it up to him again."

The pair only sang together on two songs, 'Heart To Hang Onto' and a cover of Don Williams' 'Till The Rivers All Run Dry'[7] and didn't appear on every song. "I didn't play on 'Annie' and Ronnie didn't play on 'Street In The City'," Townshend told Chris Welch in 1977, "but everything else . . . yeah. We generally made room for each other." Pete was particularly proud of his work on Lane's 'Nowhere To Run', telling Welch, "I did a hell of a lot on that . . . I felt I had achieved something as an arranger on that one.

"As far as Ronnie's stuff was concerned I really enjoyed working on them. But Ronnie's contribution to my stuff was much, much deeper. It's hard to explain. For a start, I don't think I would have done the album or the kind of material I did, if it were not for Ronnie's encouragement. And that hasn't just started with this album. It has been constant. Ronnie's been one of the few people that I've played demos to, and he has always encouraged me to do stuff away from the mainstream of Who clichés."

Rough Mix was a punning but appropriate choice of title – the wistful folk of Lane's 'Annie' shared very little in common with Townshend's quirky, percussive 'Misunderstood', for example.

"You wouldn't think they were recorded in the same studio, or practically on the same day at all," says Astley. "I found it strange that they didn't sing together more, and Ronnie didn't do back-ups on Pete, and Pete didn't do back-ups on Ronnie. Although it did happen; Pete did have Ronnie sing back-ups on 'Misunderstood'. So they were involved . . . it didn't strike you at the time, but afterwards I thought, 'I wonder why they didn't work more on each other's songs.' It was a bit *his* songs and *his* songs."

The musicians' schedule and compositional styles weren't the only things that clashed. Despite their long-time friendship and mutual respect, Townshend and Lane frequently rubbed each other the wrong way. "The abuse [between Townshend and Lane] was unbelievable," Astley confirms.

"Sometimes Ronnie and I would talk about life," Townshend later recalled. "That would mean Ronnie insulting me and me hitting him. Sometimes Eric Clapton would come to play. That would mean Ronnie insulting him, Eric hitting him, and then falling over. Glyn and Ronnie often discussed Ronnie's songs. That consisted of Ronnie trying to keep

---

[7] During the *Rough Mix* sessions, Townshend and Lane attended Don Williams' September 30, 1976 concert at the Hammersmith Odeon, at which Eric Clapton appeared as a guest. Musically incestuous, Townshend appeared as a surprise guest during Clapton's Rainbow Theatre show on April 29, 1977.

Glyn in the studio till three or four in the morning while he insulted him."

"I can remember it was the first time when I realised that Ronnie was getting sick," Pete told the *Austin Chronicle* in 2007. "We had a little argument about something; he accused me of treating my wife very badly and said something a bit indecent about me. I pushed him or punched him, and he just went flying. I thought, "Well, he's a little guy, but God, this is a bit strange." He really went flying. I helped him up, and I said, 'What's up?' And he said, 'Oh, I just lost my balance.' And I said, 'You look like you are drunk.' I went back, and somebody else in his circle said to me, 'We think Ronnie might have MS.' That was the very first time I realised that was happening."

While Astley recalls that the altercation was exacerbated by the copious quantities of brandy consumed during the sessions ("Ronnie, certainly, was falling-down drunk"), he points out that it wasn't particularly out of character for Townshend to flare up. "Usually he'd do it verbally. He could cut you down but someone like Ronnie he couldn't cut down; he'd just say, 'You load of shit!' Some people would stand up to Pete; most people defer. And if they defer, Pete's won and he's fine and he's happy, but when someone does stand up to Pete and he is in a temper, then you're in trouble."

Released in September 1977, *Rough Mix* broke the Top 50 on both sides of the Atlantic and received unanimously favourable reviews. "The Who's Townshend and former Face Lane come by their rock'n'roll inclinations honestly, and obviously, but spiritual inclination is their long suit here," Marsh wrote in his *Rolling Stone* review. "Both men are followers of Meher Baba, the Indian spiritual master who died in 1969, and this has given the album a sort of humility – not to say modesty – which is its special virtue . . .

" 'Keep Me Turning' is a spiritual parable that is undoubtedly much clearer to its author than to any other listener. The organ, guitar and drum interplay makes the song exciting, but what draws me back time and again is the yearning and vulnerable quality of Townshend's vocal. This is spiritual rock'n'roll in the very best sense: it doesn't always make sense except in the heart, which won't ignore it. Its wit and charm strike beyond the confusion of its verses to the heart of the chorus, where the devotional imagery is most complete, and the guitar part at the bridge, which is among the most supple and liquid Townshend has ever done . . .

"Don Williams' 'Till The Rivers All Run Dry' is a country love song, but in this context – and considering Baba's love for Jim Reeves' 'There's

A Heartache Following Me', which Townshend did on his first solo album – it's clearly a tribute to the master. 'Heart To Hang Onto', written by Townshend but on which Lane sings the verses and Townshend the choruses, wears an even thinner veil. There's a brutal war going on in the song's mid section between Townshend's *Tommy*-like guitar and John Entwistle's brass arrangement. This is the perfect musical expression of the cosmic quest – this is the real 'The Seeker' . . .

"The glory of this album and of the work of Pete Townshend and Ronnie Lane throughout their careers is that art and the deepest spiritual aspiration are completely intertwined. Often, of course, that makes for a rough mix, and a rougher life. But it's worth the turbulence, for it touches closer to the heart of the rock'n'roll experience than almost anything I know."

Townshend felt that *Rough Mix* "gave me confidence to do something on my own . . ." as he explained to Scott Muni in 1978. "When you know that every album that you do is going to be measured against the band that I believe is the best in the world, it makes you a bit reticent about going and doing it, you know. I did the album with Ronnie because I wanted to get my head going again, you know, and it really did, it wasn't meant to be a big deal. It really got me writing. And it was good for him, too, 'cause he was just forgotten."

"For me, that album was a divine collaboration, a life-changing record," Pete further elaborated to the *Austin Chronicle* in 2007. "1976 was a very critical and intense year for me in a whole number of different ways. I did a lot of stuff with The Who and a lot of extramural stuff, too . . . The other thing was that the record was critically acclaimed. It made me confident that I could pursue a solo career. It may also have been the record that sowed the seed of doom for The Who. I think already by '76, I was running out of ideas as to how to get The Who to move to the next level, if there was one."

Also that year, Pete worked with two of his most important inspirational mentors on an unrealised project. Kit Lambert had wanted to re-record his father's version of *Rio Grande*, which had never been released in stereo.

"It was my idea to do *Rio Grande*," Townshend told the author. "Kit's mother was extremely excited by the project. We also hoped to do orchestral recordings of all kinds of new and old pieces in the British catalogue, including pieces by his Godfather William Walton. In the end Kit faded, as he mostly did at this time . . . [Lambert] had no money, and was borrowing from me all the time, large amounts I could ill afford. Money that should have been spent on the recording project was instead spent on Kit's living expenses, always lavish. I still adored him, and felt bad to see him fading, but we all knew he was doomed."[8]

In 1996, Townshend told John Pidgeon, "[Kit Lambert and I] were talking about doing a project which would eventually embrace his father Constant Lambert's unrecorded catalogue of compositions, and we wanted an orchestral collaborator for that. The way that we thought we would start was with a series of experiments orchestrating compositions of mine, and I suggested my father-in-law Ted Astley, who had done film music."

The stillborn *Rio Grande* idea led to several Townshend compositions featuring Astley-arranged orchestrations, beginning with 'Street In The City' (on *Rough Mix*), followed by 'Brooklyn Kids' (which Pete demoed at his house in Goring), 'Football Fugue' (recorded at Olympic Studios), and 'The Ferryman' and 'Praying The Game' (both done at Abbey Road Studios) during September 1978 and eventually released on *Another Scoop*.[9]

"The idea was for Pete and my father to do an album together," says Jon Astley, "and those were the first pieces that were recorded by Glyn and myself as trials."

Of 'Street In The City', Astley says, "It's string-led. It's not like overdubbing strings – it's a string *piece*. Pete recorded the guitar track live along with the string orchestra. I think Glyn wanted him to actually sing at the same time, but that was going to be too much . . . Dad and he worked quite close together on the arrangement – I think Pete would visit my father in the studio. I remember my father trying to make demos as well, sometimes, of the string arrangements, which was quite funny. But he'd certainly sit down and play Pete arrangement ideas on the piano. So there was a collaboration there, they didn't go in cold. I don't think [Pete and

[8] By 1976, Lambert had returned to London from Italy and was deeply in debt. "He was living in unbelievable squalor in his house in Egerton Crescent," a Lambert associate told Andrew Motion in 1987. "There had been a fire, and he was virtually living under a tarpaulin over the fire damage. He had his two dogs and seven puppies with him, and there was dog shit everywhere. You had to hold your nose when you went in. And it was terribly hot – he had to have heaters on all the time because of his druggy state."

[9] Another song to feature Ted Astley's strings, 'I Like It The Way It Is' was also recorded at Olympic in 1978. It was ultimately included in the 2001 collection *Scoop 3*, admittedly "suppressed for many years" because of its subject matter: Townshend's inability to curb his alcoholism.

Glyn Johns] realised that my dad was that off the wall, though, which was great, 'cause they all went 'Wow!' " Astley recalls with a laugh.

Astley, who noted that "another three or four [songs] and they could have produced an album," posits that perhaps there was little record label interest in such a project. "That would be my guess, otherwise they would've probably gone on and finished it."

Townshend praised his father-in-law to Hugh Foley in 1989 as being "very much a mentor and a prime influence in my life. He's an extremely brilliant, gifted man, a wonderful friend, as well, to me. He has what I think all great musicians have, and that is absolutely no snobbery whatsoever about music . . . One thing that Kit aways used to say about his father was that the main thing is that he would have loved not only the music of Purcell and Stravinsky and Prokofiev and all the other great ballet composers, but he would have loved the music of The Who, and that musical snobbery was something which he despised."

In January 1977, The Who's legal wranglings with Lambert and Chris Stamp came to a close following a six-month series of negotiations. The final, interminably long meeting involved Townshend, his accountant, Stamp, and businessman Allen Klein, who'd become entangled in the situation when David Platz, who owned Essex Music, had sold him shares, apparently unbeknownst to Pete. "Klein apparently produced sheets of figures, totally confused everbody, haggled over his cut for collecting the monies, and after 12 hours presented Townshend with a cheque," *NME*'s Tony Stewart reported in 1978.[10]

Townshend later told Chris Welch that he "had two whiskies" and, along with Stamp, headed for the Speakeasy Club where his protégés John Otway and Wild Willy Barrett were performing. "I burst in, ignored John and Willy who were on their last number, smashed a few glasses, trod on a few toes and hit a few people, all friends of mine," Pete told the *NME* in 1978. "I dunno why I went. I should have just gone and banged me 'ead against a wall. Then I thought I saw Johnny Rotten. Then I said to Chris, 'Oo's that there?' An' he said, 'It's one of the Sex Pistols. It's . . .' And I'd already gone and I'd got him and cornered him against the bar. I said something like, 'What the fuck are *you* doing here?' And he said, 'Well, what the fuck are *you* doing here?'

"I thought he was Johnny Rotten for about the first five minutes I was

---

[10] In *Before I Get Old*, Dave Marsh reported that Pete received $1 million "in full settlement of his US copyrights to date" and "several hundred thousand dollars in back royalties."

talking to him. Then I suddenly realised it was somebody else. It turned out to be Paul [Cook], the Pistols' drummer. And I sat him down and I was really preaching at the poor little sod. Then Steve Jones, the guitar player, came and sat down and I went, 'rock'n'roll's gone down the fuckin' pan!' and I tore up the royalty cheque.

"About half way through the tirade Paul looked at me really confused. He didn't really know what I was talking about. And he said, 'The Who aren't going to break up are they?' 'Break up?!' I said. 'We're fuckin' finished! It's a disaster!' And he said, 'Ahhh, but we like The Who.' I went, '*you like the 'oo? Ahhhhhhhhhhh!*'"

Townshend was "disgusted" at Cook and Jones' lack of interest in picking up the mantle. "I was telling Paul Cook about the shit that I'd been through and The Who were fucking finished and rock'n'roll was finished, if this was what it was down to," he later told *Rolling Stone*. "[The Sex Pistols] were the only band that had a chance. And that they had to fuckin' pick up the banner. And they weren't interested in rock ideals. I mean, all Paul Cook and Steve Jones were into was going around the world and making money and fucking birds. Really! To that extent. I've met them since and I've said that publicly and they haven't come up and sort of said, 'Hey no! It's not true. We do care about our music.' They just wanted to be in a band and be successful."[11]

Townshend continued his account of that memorable night. "I stormed out of the place and the next thing I knew I was being woken up in a doorway in Soho . . .

"And I got in and me old lady was waiting for me . . . sitting there with the rolling pin, but too tired to use it. She said, 'Where have you been?' I said, 'I've been to hell.' And I really did feel that I'd actually been to hell, and that's what the song 'Who Are You' is about."

The Punk movement in England provided a major, albeit temporary, upheaval in the music business and Townshend contended that it provided rock music with an overdue catharsis. "One of the reasons I'm really pleased that The Who kept going is because if we hadn't carried on, and had the Stones not carried on, The Sex Pistols would never have existed, and I think The Sex Pistols were incredibly vital," he explained to *Musician* in 1982.

---

[11] Although he was disappointed by Cook and Jones' fan-style adoration, Townshend was most impressed by the Sex Pistols' singer John Lydon. "Since then, I've met Johnny Rotten and *he* is completely different," he said. "He's such a great guy – sort of like meeting a white Jimi Hendrix. I can't explain it. Just the feeling of being in the presence of someone that's really great. And who isn't gonna compromise."

"I think we've suggested some kind of analogy of rock'n'roll being like a river, and what's interesting is that it doesn't matter whether you join that river when it's massive and wide, or when it's a tiny, trickly stream. You're still joining the river, and travelling at the same speed as every other drop of water in that river. Whether you're nearer the source, or still have a long way to go, none of that matters. In fact, you can even make your presence felt initially by jumping in with a big splash and swimming aggressively the wrong way for some time or even building a dam which will hold that river up for a while. And that's, to some extent, what The Sex Pistols did. They made a big splash, and in a sense, they held it up for a little while. And then when they stood back – it *rushed* forward. The nicest analogy I think of is a tap that is kept stopped for a long time, and when it's opened for the first time for a long time, a whole lot of rust comes out. And then, water starts to run very pure again. And the punk movement, ostensibly, was that rust. But it was also, strangely enough, the first flow of fresh water for a long time."

"[Punk] freed me," Townshend told *Rolling Stone*'s David Fricke in December 1987. "It allowed me to be myself. It dignified me, in a way, to be cast to one side. I felt very uneasy with the way The Who were inevitably on the road to mega-stardom. I believed that the punk movement would free me from that. It did. It freed me from it, that it was all crap and that the bottom line was we were all flesh and blood. But The Who as a band didn't believe it. I ultimately had to stop using the band as a vehicle for my songwriting. In a way, I've got the punk explosion to thank for making that decision."

Sufficiently inspired to write new material, Pete spent a great deal of 1977 preparing songs for The Who's next album. In September, Townshend told Chris Welch that "The Who were going to go into the studio – I don't know if we are still going. I talked to Roger about it yesterday. But I don't want to do another album. I'd rather make a film which Roger seemed keen to do . . . I dunno what we're going to do." The following month Townshend revealed to the *Los Angeles Times* that he had "40 songs ready for the next Who thing."

"I'm keen on trying to steer The Who in the direction of doing grandiose projects of some sort," Townshend said, in view of the straightforward, non-concept element of the band's last album *The Who By Numbers*. "It would be easy pickings to stick out a hard-edged rock album which would sell a couple of million in the States but, frankly, I'd prefer to make a film, despite the fact that my hair fell out when we did *Tommy*."

The Lifehouse film project, dormant since 1972, returned to the drawing board. Townshend was at least partially motivated to pursue the idea by his desire to stay off the road. "For the band to do a big film instead of an album – and reach fantastic amounts of people – would mean we wouldn't have to play so many concerts," he told the *NME* in 1978. "The band went along with it, so I've developed the *Lifehouse* script."

Townshend regarded this second script as "pretty interesting. It was more landed and more grounded than the first one" he said in 1999. "It was more about music." The storyline was fleshed out, including more details of the original characters' futuristic environment. The new screenplay "was about music, machines and people changing colour, the effect of how you could work out what people's karma was without psychic powers, what would happen if psychic power became part of the instrument of government. A lot of those type of things, for example a policeman could come and know whether you are a good man or a bad man without needing evidence. There were also statements about what had gone wrong with rock'n'roll, in other words the people that were in power at the time used big weapons, big machines, loud noise, whereas the people that were really nice, the good people, used acoustic instruments and played in little clubs!"

"[The new Who album is] not a concept as such, but some of the material was written for a film idea which I had way, way back in 1971 which was called *The Lifehouse*," Pete told Scott Muni in 1978. He was still keen to develop *Lifehouse* as a film, he said. "Quite how long it would take, it could take a couple of years, you know, I mean, films, in that respect, in rock terms are very frustrating 'cause they're so slow, but then you know, so are Who albums for God's sake! A couple of songs I think we'll put in just as a taster, there's a song called 'The Music Must Change' which will probably be on the album, there's another song called 'Guitar And Pen' which is about the way I write basically, how precious the guitar and pen are, and just several songs about music but hopefully we would include some of the stuff which was originally intended for the film like 'Song Is Over', 'Won't Get Fooled Again', 'Baba O'Riley', 'Getting In Tune', 'Pure And Easy', all these songs were written for *Lifehouse* originally.

"So with that material to jump off from, rework, brought up-to-date, plus a good body of new stuff I think it could be the great Who film, hopefully. 'Cause although *Tommy* was a great event in The Who's career, the film wasn't really a Who film. I'd like to see the *Lifehouse* film be a Who film from start to finish, a Who production."

Also included in this second incarnation of *Lifehouse* were post-*Who's Next* compositions such as 'Relay' and 'Join Together'. As well as 'Music Must Change' and 'Guitar And Pen', newer Townshend tracks slated for the project included 'Who Are You' and 'Sister Disco', while John Entwistle contributed '905', a song from his long-planned but recently scrapped science fiction concept album.

Townshend was upbeat regarding the prospects of this second attempt at *Lifehouse*. "Seven years later a lot of what I wrote about has since become accepted," he crowed to the *NME*, "particularly in America, where they're into metaphysics, the connection between your mood and the way you live your life and the vibrations in the air. It was all spacey talk when I first started. The rest of the band thought I was insane . . ."

Before the *Who Are You* sessions commenced, the newly named Who Group Ltd purchased a stake in their regular rehearsal location, Shepperton Film Studios, Middlesex. When not in use, the three sound stages and the rehearsal space were often rented out to other name bands, while the numerous buildings housed The Who's impressive array of state-of-the-art equipment. As well as this, Polydor boasted that The Who had the most advanced laser and lighting displays in the world. Space was provided for lighting engineer John Wolff and sound man Bobby Pridden to experiment and develop new ideas in their respective areas of expertise.

With Keith Moon returning to Britain from Los Angeles, The Who began recording at Ramport in late September, with Glyn Johns at the helm and Jon Astley engineering. From the outset, the band's schedule caused problems. Townshend's family life had improved considerably since he resolved to change his habits once The Who were off the road. "For me, the last three years have been the happiest of my life as far as my family go," he told *Good Morning America* interviewer David Hartman in August 1978. Hartman had asked Townshend how he kept a happy marriage and family life going when he was away so much. "You don't," Pete shot back, "after every tour you run home and you try to put it back together again . . . I've had three years at home, taking the kids to school, taking flowers home after a day at the office, and so on, and then you start to build a relationship."

As with the *Rough Mix* sessions, Townshend and Johns preferred working normal daytime hours, then returning home to their families.

"Roger didn't like to do lead vocals until the evenings," Astley recalls. "Understandably, his voice certainly wouldn't warm up until evening, and his brain, too. And Pete didn't like working evenings, so that was that."

This disjointed working process meant that Townshend and Daltrey hardly saw each other during the *Who Are You* sessions, a situation which did little to alleviate the palpable tension between the two. "[Pete] was going home before Roger worked, so it was like shift work," recalls Astley. "Pete would disappear and Roger would come in through the door. And as Pete was going, quite early on, he said to me one day, 'Make sure he sings the melody, 'cause he tends to really fuck it up,' or something like that. And I realised that there was a strain there between Roger and Pete, in that Pete would write these songs, and then have to hand them over, and Roger would have to interpret them and sometimes Roger's interpretation took him away melodically from what Pete had in mind."

In addition to Daltrey and Townshend's differing schedules, another factor which precluded much from being accomplished during the *Who Are You* sessions was that Moon, Townshend and Entwistle were all drinking heavily.

"I remember the port coming out at six o'clock every evening," Astley recalls. "Pete sometimes would be there, but generally, he used to go home to pick up the kids and go and do some family stuff. I think Pete was beginning to question his drinking problem around about *Who Are You*, especially when he had to drive home."

Astley recalls that Townshend had recently begun "going up and down the Thames by boat, so he could drink. That was one of the reasons – he probably got banned from driving at some point, he thought, 'How do I get to the studio? I'll buy a boat.' He used to get to Ramport by boat. It isn't close to the river, but I suppose they just sent a car down to where he'd moored his boat and he'd come back."

Having worked with his father-in-law during *Rough Mix*, Pete utilised Astley-arranged strings for two songs on the *Who Are You* album: 'Had Enough' and 'Love Is Coming Down'. Another track, 'Sister Disco', featured synthesised string recorded at Townshend's Goring studio. "Pete hadn't written all the songs and he asked me to go with him to Goring and work on some string embellishments and stuff for some of his demos, to play to the band," recalls Jon Astley. "So we went down there and we worked on 'Sister Disco' . . . Came back from there, and Pete and I very proudly played what we'd been working on, we only had a few days down there, and then it went off between Roger and Glyn."

In late October, less than a month into the recording sessions, Daltrey thumped Johns following a heated argument – apparently over the string accompaniments. Astley says that he didn't see the fight, as "it was out in the corridor outside, but I remember Glyn coming in, a bit tearful and just saying, 'I'm going.' And Roger's screaming and shouting and doors were crashing and that was it."

Astley points out that up to this point in the sessions, Johns had "made it very obvious that he adored and loved Pete and didn't think much of Roger." He also had a problem with Moon's drumming, which also didn't help matters. Added to this, Johns hadn't expected *Who Are You* to take so long as he was committed to producing Joan Armatrading's next album.[12] Johns was also "bored rotten" so Astley became producer by default. Ultimately, the pair shared a production credit on the album.

Townshend addressed his hearing problems by experimenting with earplugs during the sessions ("That's great until you try and sing," he told Muni, "it really is a bit strange") and staying clear of loud noises. "When the band go back to goof off on the loud playbacks, I have to stay outside . . . I've got things like an earphone kit with a lamp in the line, so when you're listening to music, if it goes over the peak, this light lights up, and I use that when I'm working in the studio, I use that when I'm doing overdubs, and that's working OK. I'm finding that I'm getting used to the lower levels that I'm working at."

"I remember Bob [Pridden] being very proud about that [special head-phone set-up]," Astley recalls. "He'd commissioned this thing to be made for Pete."

In December, The Who performed live for the first time in over a year, at the Gaumont State Theatre in Kilburn, north London, in front of only 500 fans. The show was set up specifically because there were no definitive, in concert film renderings of 'Baba O' Riley' and 'Won't Get Fooled Again' for *The Kids Are Alright*, a biographical film on The Who that was currently in production. "I thought we needed something to bring the film full circle," Jeff Stein, the film's producer, told *The Hollywood Reporter*'s John Burman in 2003. "Basically, I was lobbying, pleading, begging, cajoling, to get them to do a show and finally they acquiesced and we put on a show at Kilburn . . . It was a fairly small theatre. I thought it would be a great, intimate, powerful show and it was just a disaster . . . it was a train wreck."

---

[12] The album was *To The Limit*, one of four Armatrading albums Johns produced between 1976 and 1979. Among the musicians who played on her records with future links to Townshend and The Who were percussionist Jody Linscott and bassist Pino Palladino.

The Who stumbled along between takes, stopping and starting, a pale shadow of their once staggering selves, with Moon especially misfiring. Townshend perceptively commented from the stage that the show was a waste of film, and ultimately the footage was deemed unworthy for use in the movie.

"Pete was in a bad mood, which sometimes fuelled their finer performances," Stein told Burman, "but the only two things we ended up with after shooting that whole show was a little bit where Pete issues that challenge from the stage, which is basically, 'Any of you in the audience want to come up here and take away my badge, come up and try it.' I used that bit. And there's a moment during 'Long Live Rock' in the final bows/end credits where they are all coming up the stairs and they are kind of not very happy and . . . John throws a punch at the cameraman and Keith is about to throw a chair at us and actually did, but we slammed the door in time."

An avid fan from New York since the Sixties, Stein had met The Who after hanging out backstage after concerts, travelled to England to participate in the aborted Young Vic *Lifehouse* sessions and assembled a book of live photographs in the early Seventies as a teenager.[13] Stein approached Townshend about the possibility of a Who biopic when the band was in New York in March 1975 for the *Tommy* film premiere.

"Pete was staying at the Pierre and I think I went up and knocked on the door to his room and he wasn't there," Stein told Burman. "So, I knock on this other door and Yoko Ono opened it, because John and Yoko were staying there. So, I thought, 'Whoops. Wrong room,' but I think he was visiting him. So, I finally found him and I remember this most distinctly, I was pitching Pete while he was brushing his teeth before he goes to the premiere. So I was like, giving him my impassioned plea and he's brushing his teeth, going, 'Mmph rrorrog mmmph' and foaming at the mouth, which should have been an omen!

"And at that moment, I thought, 'OK. That was good enough for me. I think I got Pete's backing. We're getting traction. Let's go.'"

After approving a 17-minute sampler a year later, The Who's company provided financial support for Stein's movie and helped him locate

---

[13] "I still have the guitar Pete's breaking on the last page of the book," Stein told *The Hollywood Reporter*'s John Burman in 2003. "By then I knew him well enough that he spotted me in the front row or two and flung this big chunk of the broken guitar at me and, I'm like, bloodied because it had jagged edges. And my brother was standing there, like punching people out who were trying to grab it from me. It was a beautiful moment."

footage. Townshend, "the only person in The Who who actually was tracking stuff and had gotten some stuff together and had stored it," according to Stein, was especially helpful. "Pete was always behind the scenes," Stein told Burman. "He was the man behind the curtain. I could always go to him to help resolve conflicts, whatever."

One capacity in which Townshend wasn't willing to provide help, however, was that of interviewee. "Pete did not want to do any new interviews [for the film]," Stein said. "He thought there was enough material on him – that he was always the one who was their spokesman . . . He thought, 'You know, equal time for the other members of the band.'"[14]

In the New Year of 1978, the recording of *Who Are You* suffered further setbacks. Pete was visiting his parents' home on Woodgrange Avenue in February when an argument between his mother and father erupted in the kitchen. After several futile attempts to intervene, Pete smashed a window with his hand in frustration.

"Yeah, I was there," Simon Townshend recalls. "Mum and dad were arguing, and Pete was just trying to get some attention, I guess, because he rarely saw them, and . . . I think he just basically was like sitting there, listening to this *constant* bickering and arguing and fighting and yelling – and they'd all had a good old drink – and Pete just went, 'For fuck's sake!' *PSSHHH* [imitates punching fist through window] like that. And just looked at them. And he's got a hand all covered in blood, he's put his fist through the window, could have lost the use of his hand forever . . . I think it was just a sign – 'For fuck's sake, just shut up!'[15]

The injuries, although not serious, would render Pete incapable of playing guitar until early March. "We're about three-quarters of the way through, and . . . it's been so slow, you can't imagine," Townshend told Scott Muni the following month. "I look with great jealousy at these young bands that are going in and knocking out albums in eight hours, the way we did our first, but it's good. It's really good and we're all happy. We're . . . relieved to still be together and working and we're enjoying doing it and the music is coming out just great."

The band's first rehearsal following Townshend's injury at Shepperton

---

[14] Townshend's position didn't budge 25 years later when a spruced-up version of the film was released on DVD – he again declined to be interviewed, leaving Daltrey as the only member appearing on the Bonus Extras disc.
[15] Just prior to the window-smashing incident, "I got drunk . . . when I went out on the boat with my dad and granddad," Townshend told *Melody Maker.*

Studios on March 6, also served as an audition for keyboardist John Rabbit Bundrick.[16] "We played and jammed for hours on end," Bundrick said later. "Then at the end of it, I was told by Pete, 'You've got the job if you want it.'" In the early hours of the following morning, Bundrick broke his hand when he fell out of a taxi after celebrating his new job with The Who.

He had been carousing with Keith Moon who caused problems at the sessions from day one, both in his usual mischievous way – he walked straight through his kit which Jon Astley had spent an entire day setting up and miking, in addition to setting fire to a notice board in the studio – and also due to his poor physical condition. Moon's ill health – he was overweight and battling alcoholism – took its toll on his physical ability to play during these sessions. While drumming is an inherently physically demanding occupation, Keith's ability required nothing less than superhuman stamina.

"Pete was definitely worried about Keith at the time," Astley recalls. "Keith started to really go off the rails in the mid-Seventies. His playing [during *Who Are You*] was dreadful, actually."

Townshend recalled the situation to *Musician* in 1989: "About halfway through the recording of *Who Are You*, [Keith] was showing up late and not playing very well and I got into this mood: 'I'm not taking any more of his shit.' So I rang him up and told him to get the fuck down here. He came running down, babbling excuses. I got him behind the drums and he could not keep the song together. He couldn't play. He'd obviously been out the night before to some club. He'd put his work second. Again. But before I could say anything, he went [imitates chaotic drum solo]. 'See?' he said. 'I'm still the best Keith Moon-type drummer in the world.'

"There was nobody to top him doing that. But unless you wanted that, you were fucked. It happened that on that [particular] song, we didn't want that. Keith wrestling himself. He was funny, but he was capable of so much more. He was such a wonderful drummer, not just an apeshit drummer. But he had reduced himself to that in the eyes of the world and in his own eyes. A couple of days after that, he started to call me up just to say good night and I love you. He did that about 10 times, and you

---

[16] The previous month, Bundrick had undergone Meg Patterson's Neuro Electric Therapy at Patterson's house in Kent, in an attempt to rid himself of alcoholism. While the treatment successfully curbed Rabbit's appetite for liquor, he maintained that he compensated for this by simply drinking more wine and beer.

could tell he was crying a little bit. He'd say, 'You do believe me, don't you?' I'd say, 'Yes, but you're still an arsehole.'"[17]

Townshend wasn't in the best position to be lecturing about Moon's overindulgence at this point. "A friend from AA came in to talk to Keith [during the *Who Are You* sessions], worked with him for two or three weeks. He said Keith was a heavy drinker with a strange emotional makeup. Then he said *I* was an alcoholic. I wondered how he'd worked that out, because I hadn't had a drink in three or four weeks. I went back in the studio and I said to Glyn Johns, 'Do you believe it? Keith's been coming in here every morning for weeks, vomiting on the mixing desk, taking pills for this and that, and I'm supporting Keith by not drinking, and I could use a drink, but I haven't had a drink, and this guy thinks I'm alcoholic.' Glyn kind of looked at me. Keith's driver was there, and I took him outside, and I asked, 'I haven't had anything to drink, have I?' He said, 'No, no.' I said, 'Listen, you don't have to defend my position. Have I had anything to drink?' 'Not apart from when you go home.' 'What do you mean?' 'Well, every night after work you go off to the bar and drink a bottle of vodka. Everyone thought you all were just not drinking while you were working. At the end of the session, you drink a bottle of vodka like water.' And I suddenly remembered what I'd been doing. I was drinking alcoholically, but I didn't deal with it until several years later."

By mid-March, Glyn Johns was once again involved with the recording of *Who Are You*, and booked two weeks of time at Mickie Most's RAK studios in St John's Wood, north London. Astley recalls that "the idea was a change of scenery might be good," and that Johns had concerns about the sound in the control room at Ramport, while he was "a big fan of the desk" at RAK.[18] Johns brought in two extra musicians for the RAK sessions, bassist Dave Marquee (who had played on *Rough Mix*) and keyboardist Rod Argent.

"The idea was, this was a big, big room that you could divide in two, we could put a drum kit in there and everyone could play together live, this is how Glyn wanted to work," Astley recalls. "Up until then, what was happening was Pete was coming in with the demo which was so fantastic and absolutely rigid time-wise, because everything was done to a

---

[17] When Moon announced plans to marry his girlfriend Annette Walter-Lax in late 1976, Townshend was named best man.

[18] "The sound in the control room at Ramport wasn't what you took out with you," says Astley. "It sounded great in the control room, but when you took a cassette out and listened to it, it wasn't right."

drum machine or a click, so we used that as a base . . . we kind of worked with Pete's demos becoming the backing tracks, and Glyn always liked to work with the band playing together, that's how he made records. He felt that it was a perfect opportunity in a new studio to do that, and he liked John's playing, but he wanted a bass player to hold down the bottom end, so he had both bass players playing at the same time. The idea was for John to be able to go [imitates frenetic lead bass playing] or whatever, and at the same time to have a boom going on down at the bottom end at the same time, which of course doesn't really work. It was a nice try."

The RAK sessions ended abruptly after a week, one of the major factors being Moon's inability to deliver. The situation reached boiling point when Pete, Roger, Jon Astley and Keith went to dinner one night and Moon was given an ultimatum.

"It was a bit of a shock, because I thought everything was going swimmingly well," says Astley. "Here I am, I'm having dinner with The Who, in a restaurant in north London, fantastic, and suddenly they all rounded on Keith. I don't know if Glyn was there or not, three or four of them anyway, rounded on Keith and said, 'Listen, this is it. If you don't get your shit together, you're out of the band.' So he did get himself back into shape, and he was great until he finished all the drumming when there was nothing else for him to do . . . I didn't see much of him after that. He got back into clubbing again. I know he was clubbing. He was always getting into trouble."

After Townshend and Astley returned to Goring for a couple of weeks' work, The Who returned to Ramport and the recording of *Who Are You* was finally wrapped up in May. The album was released in August.[19] While the *Lifehouse* link was difficult, if not impossible, to detect, the most obvious theme prevalent throughout *Who Are You* is Townshend's dissatisfaction with the state of contemporary popular music and The Who's fear of stagnation – most obviously represented in 'New Song' and 'Music Must Change'.[20] 'Sister Disco', which followed a similar thematic line, also featured some impressive synthesiser work. "It isn't quite Kraftwerk," Townshend later wrote, "but in 1976 I don't think they were doing it much better."

[19] The final mixing was undertaken by Astley after Johns' mix was rejected by The Who's management.
[20] After discovering that Moon couldn't handle the difficult time signature of 'Music Must Change', Townshend left the original percussion track from his demo intact: namely the sound of his footsteps walking across the tiled floor of his Goring studio.

While the song had been played in an embryonic form onstage at the end of 1976, 'Who Are You' was completed shortly after Townshend's encounter with the Sex Pistols at the Speakeasy. "['Who Are You'] is very misunderstood," Pete confessed in a radio interview eight years later. "It's actually a prayer, believe it or not, I think, scuppered for once by Roger's overkill. In fact what I was doing was trying to sort of ask who and where, what God was, you know. That's what the song was really about, about the hell of living on the street and going through money trouble and all that stuff, and continually looking up to the sky and saying, 'Who are you, who are you, who are you?'"

Astley recalls that Townshend "turned up with this very long demo" for the track, "with this guitar going [imitates the 'Who Are You' backing track sound] and all this stuff happening on it, and a drum kit and backing vocals and handclaps and guitars. And we all went, 'Great, fantastic but it's a bit long.'" After consulting with Townshend, Astley cut "five minutes out of the middle, which went into kind of all that *ooh ahh ooh ahh ooh ahh* . . . kept all the good bits out of that and chopped out the bits where not a lot was happening. I also took a verse out of it as well . . ."

Who Are You, which reached number six in the UK and two in the US, garnered a reasonably complimentary review from *Rolling Stone*'s Greil Marcus:

> "*This is by no means a great record, but despite the doubt, guilt, worry and self-laceration in almost every song, it's a strangely confident one. Again and again, the persona is that of the cripple, the victim of disaster, but* Who Are You *is not the work of cripples, no matter how many breakdowns and bottles The Who have left on their 14-year-old trail . . .* Who Are You *is an LP The Who have been working toward all through the Seventies. The fears of ageing, irrelevancy and the dissolution of one's self, one's band or one's audience that peeked out of* Who's Next *and* The Who By Numbers *have finally surfaced whole . . .*
>
> "*It will be a real disappointment if another three years pass before the next Who album: this one seems to have left them ready for the new music they claim they can't make – a claim that's obviated by what is new and, more importantly, compelling on* Who Are You. *I said this was, despite its claims to oblivion, a confident record: what makes it so is The Who's refusal to settle for mere 'survival', for automatic applause and meaningless* pro forma *hits. Pete Townshend recognises the fact that, after a decade which seemed happy with its own dead end, bands like The Clash have broken*

through limits he had half-accepted. In this case, the child really is father to the man, and that means the chance to start all over again is at Townshend's fingertips."

In *Before I Get Old*, Dave Marsh pointed out that "the music doesn't reinforce the message: There is nothing truly new here [on *Who Are You*], no real departures." Marcus agreed: "'Music Must Change' might be announcing the need for a New Wave, but it's quite consciously two years out of date, and, what's more, the music itself sounds old and stiff – there's not a single musical concession to punk, reggae or even hard-nosed rock."[21]

"I've got so used to playing guitars so loud, that when I try and play them soft, I can't," Townshend told Muni. "So a couple of the guitar solos on the latest album, they're almost like jazz solos. I'm a big fan of jazz guitar players. I particularly like people like Pat Martino and people like that, and Kenny Burrell. And I've always liked that kind of playing. So I'm starting to play a little bit more like that. Because that doesn't have to be loud. And so my whole sort of musical perspective is changing."

Although Marsh pointed out that "the playing [on *Who Are You*] is grand in the way that *Who's Next* was, which makes it ideal for onstage interpretation", Townshend remained adamantly against touring.

"The problem really with the group at the moment is . . . we're in middle age as a group, I mean not just as human beings," he had told Muni towards the end of the album sessions, "and you have to completely review the way you work, you have to review your lifestyle, your energy level is different, and touring in the USA is something which requires more than just a manager to lay the gigs out and an aeroplane to ride around in. It requires a whole energetic burst. You can goof off in a studio, but you can't goof off on the road. If you goof off on the road, you miss the date. Without going into it too deeply, last time we were on tour, we missed a couple of dates. And this is the first time it's ever happened to us, and I don't like it . . .

"The road is a place where you can only afford to be 100 per cent professional. If you're sick, or if you're tired, or if . . . emotionally, you just can't handle it, then you shouldn't be there. So The Who will tour if they're in shape to tour. And if they're not in shape to tour, they won't.

---

[21] "The *Who Are You* period should have been a really good period for The Who," Townshend later commented. "What kind of upset it was Punk."

It's as simple as that. That's why there's a certain conflict in the air at the moment, because what I want to do is I want to get the album done, I feel so confident that the album is going to create a new surge of energy in the band, and hopefully that will give us all the confidence to get out and do it with vigour."

CHAPTER ELEVEN

1978–1980

"The Who have gone through a fucking hell of a period of crisis . . . I became terribly self-conscious and self-obsessed with the band and the band's past . . . I don't know quite what it is, but it's something like a great expunging of problems has occurred with Keith's death. Obviously, we all need to see a purpose in his death or use a positive result from it. But even if we were reading things into what was really just a tragic event, I still don't think we should have got quite the kind of result we've got at the moment. We seem to have a clean break, and I feel I can just go on the stage and do what the fuck I like. Still a little tied down to the old stuff, but I think we can get over that, get past it – get past the history."

– Pete Townshend, 1980

"You know, I think The Who stopped two albums too late. I think if I'd stopped two albums earlier, when Keith died, I would never have ended up with a drinking problem, and I would have never ended up creating the kind of emotional havoc that I played not only in my family's life but in the life of others."

– Pete Townshend, 1989

IN 1978, Townshend started his own music and literary publishing ventures under the name of the Eel Pie Group. The book-publishing arm specialised in children's titles, music books and several Meher Baba-related publications. A bookstore named Magic Bus was opened in Richmond, not far from Townshend's home, and in April, office space in New York was opened in preparation for the mail-order release of one of Eel Pie Books' titles, *The Story Of Tommy*. Written by Townshend in conjunction with Richard Barnes, the book chronicled the writing of the original album and also the making of the film.

"What I tried to do with this book is to try to cover the areas that haven't been covered before," Pete told Scott Muni. "You know when we did the album way, way back, I did something like 120 interviews in one tour on the subject of *Tommy*, I talked it right out of myself. I explained it, I explored it, I tried to reason it out and tried to justify bits of it that didn't work and celebrate bits of it that did. When we started to do the film with Ken Russell, I decided at that point that I would make a book about the making of a film. I'm fascinated with films and I do make films, and I thought it would be great to have a book, right from the inception to show how a film is made, everything. We did that, we drew all the material together, but the book wasn't really ready to go out, it didn't feel quite right. So I started to add more material to it. I added a large section which I wrote myself on the actual ideas that brought *Tommy* forth as a story, I'd written pages and pages of notes in 1966 and '67 about, really about also the concept of rock opera, whether it would work, whether or not it would survive, whether or not it was reasonable. And I've included all that early stuff in the book, and there's a long interview in the book with this mate of mine, Richard Barnes, who did the artwork, which really I can't take any credit for, but I think it is fantastic. It's a full colour book right the way through . . ."

Eel Pie's other venture focused on offering recording facilities, equipment and guidance to new acts. Townshend leased a building in Berwick Street, Soho, and "equipped it with some of the stuff from my country studio which had a leaky roof," he wrote in 1982. The services offered by the company included allowing bands to use the PA system, transportation, or even small loans to pay for recording time. "To press 2,000 singles costs nothing," Pete said. "We'll tell you where to go, give you $500 and that's it. Pay us back off the top. Anyone can make a record now for $20 an hour which – by 1965 standards – would be of exceptionally high quality." The first of these was by a London band called The Skunks, whom Townshend saw perform at punk venue, the Vortex Club. Their single, 'Good From The Bad' was released in June '78.

"What fucks bands up now is [the] PA, because the standard of PA that people are used to now, even from small bands, is so high. You can go on with a Telecaster copy, but you can't go on with a shitty PA and unless the club or the other group have a good one, you've got to spend $350 to hire one. In my company, we try to cut across that by forming a co-op, allowing the bands to use the PA and the van free, and if they got a deal they'd put money back in."

Townshend was cautious to point out that Eel Pie should not be mistaken for a charitable organisation, despite the fact that it undoubtedly provided many bands with an otherwise unattainable opportunity. "I'm often called altruistic in the press, but that's not entirely true. There's a side to that that's exploitative, if you like. Whereas The Who deals with superstars and upwards, my company starts from street level. The reason is: I'm keeping my nose to the ground. In the world of million-pound movies you can lose sight of what's springing up in the city suburbs."

Townshend also had plans to launch his own label, Propellor Records, commemorating the launch with a fly-by featuring World War II-era Spitfire aircraft. "I tried to form the company last year and it's proved to be much harder than I thought," Townshend told Chris Welch in 1979. "I thought it would be a breeze, but it's very difficult to provide the kind of money that's required. To pay a young band today, just a silly retainer and to pay for them to perform and record and supply their equipment, you need £50,000 a year. And they'll never earn that money from their first album or concerts. It's . . . finished. But I'm hoping The Who will start a record company, because I'm very keen to continue being involved with bands from the ground up."

Other activities occupying Townshend's time during this period included assisting John Annunziato's New York-based film-production company, Nunzi Productions and a musical film called *Fish Shop*.

Melvyn Bragg, the presenter of ITV's arts programme *The South Bank Show*, who knew Townshend through Ken Russell and had interviewed Pete in 1974 while a presenter of the BBC arts flagship *2nd House*, initially commissioned Townshend to write a television play with music.

"I had this idea about a kid," Townshend told *Melody Maker*'s Michael Watts in October 1978. "It's purely autobiographical. I thought I'd actually do something that's outfront autobiographical for a change rather than try not to do something autobiographical which ends up that way. So it's about a kid who's learning to play the guitar and is in a band, and he gets involved in a relationship with an old guy who has given up a tremendous musical career to do some menial task and is absolutely fascinated by this. And then he also gets tied up in a relationship with his best friend, who becomes a villain, and there's a terrible fight between his best friend and the old man. It's set in London, and there's a sequence in Spain in the life of the old boy. I've written four songs for it."

"[*Fish Shop*] was to be directed by one of the *South Bank* team." Townshend recalled to the author. "I wrote the script, and a number of songs, and was very excited about it, but I had far too much on my plate at the time and I couldn't find time to commit to the six week schedule of shooting they required. I used the story as the basis for one of the short stories in my *Horse's Neck* collection. This story, like most of the shorts in that book, was pinned on one or two autobiographical memories that I elaborated enormously to create fiction."

On May 25, The Who played a specially arranged gig to complete production on *The Kids Are Alright*, after the subpar results of the Kilburn show the previous December. Persuading Townshend to play again proved a monumental task for Jeff Stein.

"I think there were two issues," Stein told *The Hollywood Reporter* in 2003. "One, I know he was afraid he would totally lose his hearing. And two . . . he said, 'Don't make me play live. Because if you make me play live for this film, I'll get that taste of blood in my mouth and I am like Pavlov's Dog. When I get the taste of blood I can't stop. And I'll hit the road again and I can't do it.' I think he thought it would kill him. I think [it was] dealing with Keith, dealing with the band, dealing with their place, dealing with, you know, again as I said, were they an endangered species? It was the middle of the punk movement. He didn't want to be perceived as a dinosaur. It must have been devastating."

Despite the long odds, Stein, who admitted he "was probably a total pain in the arse", pulled it off. The decision was made to perform at Shepperton because of its location outside London's city limits – the Greater London Council wouldn't let the band use its laser show which Stein wanted to capture on film. An invited audience of 500 was bussed in from London, with an assortment of alcoholic beverages on board to ensure there was an appropriate mood for the show.

Although Stein was only specifically looking for definitive versions of 'Baba O'Riley' and 'Won't Get Fooled Again', The Who played around eight songs prior to heading offstage. "They ended with 'Won't Get Fooled Again'," said Stein, "and it was weak. And I was beside myself. I thought, 'OK. Here's the moment of truth. You live with this and this is the end of the movie or you go and beg for them to do it again.' Besides the fact The Who didn't much like encores, which was why they smashed their shit up at the end of the show. Now, they have to play the same song twice, which wasn't going to go over well. I knew it. I can't even tell you how I felt going backstage, walking through the minefield."

Again, in spite of the odds against him, Stein made his way to the dressing room and managed to cajole the band back onstage to perform a more dynamic rendition of 'Won't Get Fooled Again' which was used for the finale of *The Kids Are Alright*.

Four months later, a *Rolling Stone* article by Dave Marsh indicated a brighter future for The Who. "The conflicts between Daltrey and Townshend have been resolved – they speak of each other as friends rather than as enemies enjoying a temporary truce," Marsh wrote. "Keith Moon seems on the way to recovery from whatever physical and mental demons have plagued him."

Townshend and Daltrey's relationship benefited from a band meeting at a local pub during the Shepperton filming, where it was decided, "'Look, this is a band. Let's not be afraid of being a band. Let's not be afraid of being The Who. Let's not be afraid to be different. Let's not be afraid to take stances. Let's not be afraid to be affected.' That was a conscious decision that we took after a talk 'round the table', Townshend told Marsh, "and it was most effective in my relationship with Roger. We decided not so much to stop fighting as to stop deliberately getting in each others' way and giving each other a lot more space."

Within days of its publication, Marsh's report, entitled 'The Who Come To A Fork In The Road', took on a much more ironic meaning after Keith Moon died on September 7 from an accidental overdose of Heminevrin – a sedative he'd been prescribed in an effort to curb his alcoholism. Townshend, holidaying with his family on Alderney, a tiny island in the English Channel,[1] was understandably devastated by the news. "Pete just went into a shell," Jon Astley told *Generations*. "He was in complete shock." It didn't help matters that it was Townshend who, after receiving the news of Moon's death from Bill's wife Jackie Curbishley, had to call Entwistle and Daltrey, and toughest of all, Moon's mother. Astley remembers Pete receiving the news. "He was, 'Oh God, he's bloody gone and done it,' and then dashing off to the airport to get on a plane. And that was it."

"I helped get [Keith] a flat in London because he was broke after his stay in California," Townshend told *Musician* in 1989. "I helped him get back on his feet by getting this flat. And a couple of days later [*sic*] he died in it."[2] The sheer abruptness of Moon's death took the band by surprise,

---

[1] Alderney held a sentimental value for the Astley family, who had holidayed there frequently. "We used to stay at this old hotel when we were kids," recalls Jon Astley, explaining that the Townshends carried on the tradition. "Pete and Karen took a house on the island that we used to go to quite regularly."

[2] "Poor old Keith couldn't get a flat in London," Townshend told Scott Muni five months prior to Moon's death. "Nobody would give him a flat anywhere . . . So I said, 'Listen, Keith. *I'll* get you an apartment. So I go out and I get this apartment for him

although he had spent most of his life abusing his body to the absolute limits. "The worst thing is that none of us were there when he died," Entwistle told *Time* in 1979. "We must have saved his life 30 times in the past, picking him up when he was unconscious and walking him around, getting him to a doctor."

The remaining members gathered at Shepperton Studios the day after Moon's death for a long meeting, but the dominant subject was Moon's estate, not the future of The Who. Following the meeting, Townshend issued an official statement:

> "Our first thoughts as a band are for those people who were closest to Keith: his mother; his ex-wife, Kim and daughter, Mandy; and his fiancee, Annette, whom he was due to marry shortly. Next, we think about the fans of The Who. We are poised with an album in the charts, and films in the making, and although there have always been questions, the future looked better prior to Keith's death than ever before.
>
> "Next, we think about ourselves and I have to admit that it's now we cry the tears that just can't be held back. We have lost our great comedian, the supreme melodramatist, the man who apart from being the most unpredictable and spontaneous drummer in rock, would have set himself alight if he thought it would make an audience laugh or jump out of its seats. We have lost our drummer but also our alter-ego. He drove us hard many times but his love for every one of us always ultimately came through.
>
> "The Who? We are more determined than ever to carry on and we want the spirit of the group to which Keith contributed so much to go on, although no human being can ever take his place. We loved him and he's gone.
>
> "I have always complained that up until now when I have walked into a pub, someone has slid next to me, nudged me, and said, 'Hey, that Keith Moon, what is he really like?' For the first time in my life I will know what to answer. I wish I didn't."

In the weeks following Moon's death, Townshend engaged in a flurry of activity, including becoming a consultant for the *Quadrophenia* film, recording demos, and continuing work on the *Fish Shop* television play.

[which turned out to be owned by Harry Nilsson] . . . The day after, the *day after* he moves in, I get this letter from the woman downstairs. 'Dear Sir . . .', and the complaints list, they run 14 or 15 pages of complaints. All of a sudden I wake up and I'm like, 'Jesus Christ, do you know what's happened?' I said to my old lady, 'I'm Keith Moon's landlord!' I've put myself in this situation where I'm Keith Moon's landlord. It's a great experience, I can tell you."

Pete also assisted his friend, fellow Baba-follower and musician Raphael Rudd in recording his first solo album.

"In June 1978, I was a 19-year-old studying for my masters at the Manhattan School of Music in New York City when I received a phone call that changed my life," Rudd wrote in 2001. "It was Pete Townshend of The Who. He'd heard my music and was inviting me to record professionally at his Eel Pie Studios in London. I couldn't believe it . . . By September I was recording my first solo album, *The Boy*, with Pete keeping an eye on things. It was he who came up with the title, an affirmation of the importance of the artist remaining young at heart."

"Raphael Rudd and I met because of our mutual interest in the Indian spiritual master Avatar Meher Baba," Townshend wrote in a brief essay on the sleeve of Rudd's 1996 release *The Awakening – Chronicles*. "When about five years old Raphael met Meher Baba, who took the child's hands in his own and gazed into his eyes. Later, when Raphael became a musician and dedicated his work to his master, it became clear to everyone that Meher Baba had inspired the child forever. I didn't meet Meher Baba in the flesh. But I was pleased to be able to work with Raphael on this recording project that was to be dedicated to Meher Baba . . . I regarded myself as Raphael's musical mentor during that period. Today, we inspire each other on a more equal footing. I am greatly influenced by Raphael's piano style."

Rudd arranged and conducted members of the London Philharmonic and London Symphony Orchestra for a block of the *Quadrophenia* movie soundtrack. "Raphael orchestrated the final scene of the film and conducted the orchestra with great authority despite being only 21 years old at the time," Townshend wrote in 1996.[3]

"To this day Raphael and I regard ourselves as fellow voyagers on the path to God – who we see manifested clearly in the perfect life and continuing compassionate spiritual presence of Avatar Meher Baba. This might seem romantic, and it is of course. But whatever we like to believe as spiritual seekers, and however lost or vain we might become in our pursuit of art and fame, we are both utterly certain that we are merely channels for the will of God."

Tragically, Rudd was involved in a car accident in Los Angeles in

---

[3] In December 1979, Townshend and Rudd also performed together at Oceanic for a gathering of Baba followers, and again the following December. Both shows were recorded and an 18-song CD, *The Oceanic Concerts*, was released in October 2001.

February 2002 and lay in a coma for five weeks. He died that April at the age of 45.

On October 3, Pete participated in a recording session at Abbey Road Studios for Paul McCartney's all-star Rockestra (included on Wings' 1979 album *Back To The Egg*). Also taking part were Townshend's boyhood hero, Hank Marvin of The Shadows ("that was a weird one", Pete later commented), Ronnie Lane, Kenney Jones, John Paul Jones, John Bonham, and Dave Gilmour – the latter described as having "an enormous beer gut" as Townshend told *Melody Maker*. Bonham "had a big beer gut as well. He played amazingly, incredible." Eric Clapton and Jimmy Page were also scheduled to participate, but failed to show, prompting Townshend to cheekily comment, "I think they were both scared."

The nine hour session – in which the aggregation recorded two McCartney songs, 'Rockestra Theme' and 'So Glad To See You Here' – was also filmed, something which, according to Linda McCartney, Pete was initially edgy about. In an interview with Michael Watts a week later, Townshend described the session as "amazing, absolutely amazing. My dad is a saxophone player and used to be in the Squadronaires, and it reminded me of their old reunions where you get a Scotsman and a guy from Newcastle and they talk about, 'Oh, that's a great band, and what a player, what a bloody player!' It was really like that, boring old farts forever. Great fun."

Further activity on Townshend's already full agenda consisted of readying material for the *FREE Charity Album*, released to benefit Meg Patterson's Pharmakon Clinic, a 30-room experimental drug rehab facility which was due to open in Sussex in January. Others who'd been approached for material were George Harrison, Keith Richards, Jack Bruce and "members of Led Zeppelin", according to *Melody Maker*. Originally the record was due to feature new material from Townshend and Eric Clapton, but because of scheduling problems, a "previously unreleased Who track" – namely Pete's demo of 'Relay' – was included.

Also in that month of October, Townshend visited the set of *Quadrophenia* in Brighton, where filming for the $2.5 million movie, lasted just under two months commencing on September 30. Pete was joined by 2,000 extras (a mix of unemployed youths and mods recruited from a nearby scooter rally) for the recreation of a Bank Holiday beach fight between mods and rockers. Some interesting candidates were originally up for the part of Jimmy Cooper.

"Johnny Rotten and Sham 69's Jimmy Pursey are being considered for the leading role in the movie *Quadrophenia*," Tony Stewart reported in the August 12 edition of *NME*. "He asked to talk to me about it," Townshend said of Rotten, "but I don't see how it'll change anything. I don't think he'll do it. In fact I'm 100 per cent certain he won't." Pete saw Pursey on television and "thought he looked right for Jimmy" according to Stewart. Pursey was also reportedly keen to do it. However, the leading part was awarded to Phil Daniels, and a supporting role given to Leslie Ash, neither of whom had much acting experience. The character of the ace face was initially offered to Stuart Goddard, better known as Adam Ant, but was ultimately played by Sting, of The Police.

Meanwhile, questions concerning the future of The Who were mounting. Although Townshend had announced that they would continue, observers wondered what form the 'New Who' would take. Would one drummer be chosen to replace Moon or would the band use session musicians? Would they ever perform live again? "Roger and I have really got to get together and thrash out . . . not a compromise, but what is really gonna work," Townshend told Watts, "and if we can't do it so that it will work, then we should knock it on the head."

A chief concern of Townshend's inevitably concerned his hearing. "The amplifier levels that we use at the moment, John and I, are really deafening and my ears are at a critical stage at the moment," he told Watts. "If I'm careful now I'll only go deaf when I'm 50, but if I'm not careful it'll be when I'm 40. There's no option, unless they dream up something in the next couple of years."

Ironically, Moon's death enabled The Who to experiment beyond the confines of their traditional four-man line-up. Rabbit Bundrick had already been enlisted as an auxiliary keyboard player and the addition of a brass section was also being considered. "For a long time I felt inhibited by being a rhythm player, and what I'd really like is to see the band have a keyboard player on piano and organ, and another guitar player so that I'd be free to do synthesiser work onstage and play various styles of guitar," Townshend told Chris Welch the following January. "Then we could do some of the more complex material from The Who's history."

A line of illustrious drummers including Ginger Baker, Carl Palmer, Aynsley Dunbar, Tony Newman and Phil Collins offered their services. "When Keith Moon died, I rang Townshend up and said, 'If ever you need a drummer, I would love to do that job,'" Collins revealed in 1994.

"He said, 'Yeah, that would be great, man,' but . . . Kenney Jones was always gonna be the guy that took over. But I just kind of knew that you had to have *fire* to play with The Who and although I don't look it now, I've got *fire*. And I would have loved to have done that job . . . played with that band – playing that stuff is what I used to do in front of the mirror when I was learning to play the drums."

In November, Townshend offered the job to old friend and ex-Small Faces/Faces drummer Kenney Jones. In 1974, after The Faces had gone their separate ways, Jones had played on the *Tommy* movie soundtrack and had musically gelled well with Entwistle and Townshend. Jones had also played with Pete in the Rockestra, where one imagines the subject of the drumming position with The Who was broached.

"There was nobody else in my opinion," Townshend told Welch. "It's not a question of Keith being replaced, either. Kenney would be the first to say that Keith was irreplaceable and that nobody could copy him and nobody would want to. Kenney was a much bigger part of The Who, anyway, than most people realise. We've always had this incredible link with The Faces . . .

"Keith was very responsive. He'd play off you. Kenney is a much more formal drummer who lays it down. But he's awake, he's alert and the feeling is we are starting up a new band . . . People have got to live with the fact that The Who they knew has gone, and that they'll never see it again."

Also under consideration to join The Who was Jones' former Faces bandmate, keyboardist Ian McLagan. "I wanted him," Townshend told Welch. "He's a good guitar player too. I was very keen to get him." Hiring McLagan would have perhaps created an uncomfortable situation for all involved, since he married Moon's ex-wife, Kim, that October.

The lone dissenting voice in the hiring of Jones appears to have been that of Roger Daltrey. "Roger really resisted Kenney being brought as a quarter member," Townshend told *Musician*'s Charles Young in 1989. "He wanted Kenney on salary. I said, 'No, I'm not ready for that.' It means we're still running The Who. It's like we're on a pilgrimage to find Keith. To be really unpleasant about it, I'm kind of glad Keith is gone. He was a pain in the arse. The band wasn't functioning. This is a chance to do something new.' "

"I had terrible fights with Pete over [Jones]," Daltrey told *Music Connection*'s John Lappen in 1994. "Kenney was a good drummer and a nice guy, but nowhere near the drummer for The Who. His wasn't the right style. But no one would listen to me. I used to go home in tears over that. It came to a point where I told Pete that either Kenney goes or I go. Pete looked at me, square in the eyes and said, 'I guess that's no choice at all,' basically telling me I could leave the band. I was devastated. We patched things up but it was me who had to swallow my pride and go back to Pete. He'd never apologise for anything if there was a fight. I've had to eat a lot of shit over the years to help keep it all together."

The new Who began rehearsals at Shepperton Studios in late 1978, beginning the process of learning to play with not only a new drummer, but one whose formal approach was the polar opposite of Moon's. Townshend publicly expressed a great deal of optimism, his comments occasionally bordering on the inappropriate considering that Moon had been dead for just a few months.

"We're finding ourselves in a way," he told *Melody Maker* in January 1979. "Ironically, Keith's passing was a positive thing. It meant that it was impossible to continue to be bound by Who traditions . . . I feel very excited about the fact that The Who is a well-established band with a tremendous history, but suddenly we're in the middle of nowhere – a new band. I'm really excited about it."

Jones' baptism of fire with The Who before an audience took place on May 2, 1979 at the Rainbow Theatre, virtually a year after Moon's last stand at Shepperton. The show was originally intended to be a final rehearsal prior to The Who leaving for the Cannes film festival in France, but it was agreed that the new line-up, including Rabbit Bundrick ("our all-new British Texan keyboard player", Townshend announced from the stage) should be introduced on home turf as a gesture of goodwill to British fans. Despite the show being announced at only 48 hours' notice, all 3,000 tickets sold out in well under an hour. A large contingent of the crowd were mods, part of the so-called Mod Revival, which, thanks to the *Quadrophenia* film and new bands like the Jam whose sound and image paid homage to the early Who, had gained popularity in Britain.

"Outside the Rainbow where we did our first [post-Moon] concert," Townshend said in 1980, "I couldn't resist going up to a row of kids in parkas that all had 'The Who' on and I said, "Have you ever seen The Who play before?" And this kid turned 'round and he didn't know who I was. He was queueing up for tickets and I don't think he cared. He gave me a look like, 'Fuck off, cunt,' and I suddenly realised that that symbol is just a symbol, just like the bloody swastika was to the Hell's Angels. It meant nothing to them. The people most responsible for the mod fashion thing coming back are the Jam. They started it, and we were just lucky that the film was there . . ."[4]

"Five shadowy figures loped onstage at 8.35 and cut into a wilful, almost irreverent execution of 'Substitute' that had the entire audience on its feet from the first bar," reported *Melody Maker* on the Rainbow show. "Relatively adventurous arrangements of material both obscure and well-worn, irresistibly urgent treatments of their simpler stuff, and a new found enthusiasm for performance suggest that the new Who might prove to be even better than the old Who."

A more adventurous set list featured selections from almost every phase of the band's career, from 'I Can't Explain' to 'Who Are You', 'Pinball Wizard' to 'Won't Get Fooled Again'.

"The Who are making a new beginning – in one sense a beginning from scratch," wrote *NME*'s Paul Du Noyer. "In a strange and magical way, The Who are not reliving their history tonight but remaking it afresh. What *could* have taken place was an act of homage to the past 15 years: a celebration of affection and nostalgia, maybe tinged with a little sadness; an occasion for reverence or ritual, for the outward preservation and the inward destruction of everything Pete Townshend ever meant to rock'n'roll. What did happen was a fine, great and gorgeous rock'n'roll gig: no more and no less; as superb a show as The Who can ever have produced.

"Townshend bounds from one side to another, executes the legendary windmill chord-smash and generally performs like a man tasting freedom for the first time in years."

The following week, the band entertained the press and prospective distributors on board a rented boat at the Cannes Film Festival where *The Kids Are Alright* and *Quadrophenia* were being premiered. On May 12, The Who played before 10,000 fans in a Roman amphitheatre in Frejus, 25 miles west of Cannes. Impressed with the turnout, they agreed to play an additional performance the following night, despite the fact that the first screening of *The Kids Are Alright* coincided on that same night. "We did have discussions about the sanity of that gig," Townshend recalled, "but we're up to our necks in investment and emotional commitment,

---

[4] Kenney Jones, incidentally, backed a *Quadrophenia* clothing line. "It's the last thing on earth I would want to do, be involved in clothing lines," Townshend remarked. "I never even saw the clothes. I wouldn't mind a Sting suit, mind you, but the suit Sting wore in the film must've cost about 300 quid. But you can get anything you need to be a mod at the shop at the top of the road."

and it's important to get across that we're still very much a live band. The films aren't a tombstone to Keith Moon."

Although completed prior to Moon's death, *The Kids Are Alright* naturally took on a whole new significance due to the timing of its release. As well as the footage of Moon's final Who show at Shepperton, the film also featured many humorous snippets and examples of his antics over the years.

"The movie is good," Townshend told *Sounds* in 1980. "It's not exactly a documentary of The Who or its history or anything like that, it's just a collection of whatever was available. Some of it is TV trash and some of it is very good live footage and some of it is very bad live footage. Kind of a bit of everything. It's fun though, I think. It's a film about the group, not me."

The double album soundtrack maintained the random theme, consisting of various live, studio and television performances from throughout The Who's career, with the glaring omission of *Quadrophenia*. It reached number 8 in the US; 26 in Britain.

"*Quadrophenia* is a powerful film," Townshend later declared. "We don't appear in it and there's not a hell of a lot of music, but we're proud of it." Desiring a realistic portrayal rather than the fantasy route taken by Ken Russell for *Tommy*, Townshend considered Alan Parker or Nicolas Roeg as the movie's producers, but when Franc Roddam's name was thrown into the mix by Who associate (and *Quadrophenia* co-producer) Roy Baird, the search was essentially over. Pete had seen Roddam's enormously successful television play *Dummy*, about a deaf and dumb prostitute, and "liked it a lot," Roddam told the *NME*. The admiration was mutual with Roddam describing Townshend as "extremely bright, aware and well-informed . . . a very rich man, but still in touch."

Roddam collaborated with two writers in drafting a script for the film, which, he promised, "remains true to the spirit of the album, of The Who and the mods, and of revolt itself."

"The idea of *Quadrophenia* is that someone is not being allowed to be themselves," Roddam told Michael Watts. "There are pressures from family, school and work, and if you want to move on you have to resist those pressures . . . What I'm doing is a translation of the album, if you like . . ."

"It's very difficult when you make a film – when you *produce* a film – because in the last analysis you have to hand it over to the director," Townshend told *Rolling Stone* in mid-1980. "I wrote the script, originally

– the first draft screenplay I wrote with Chris Stamp – and there was no riot scene at all. Not at all. For me, *Quadrophenia* was about the fights, and the riots, happening in the kid's *head*. The *threat*: 'I'll do anything, I'll go anywhere' – and what you're dealing with is a little wimp. Who's fucking *useless*. Who couldn't fight anybody. He had his few pills, and his bottle of gin, and he *felt* like he could. It was a study in spiritual desperation: the fact that all that desperation and frustration leads somebody to the point where for the first time in their life they realise that the only important thing is to open their heart. It wasn't about blood and guts and thunder – in the way that the film turned out to be . . . I suppose the director, Franc Roddam, thought it would make good cinema. And I think to some extent it's possible [the film] has sharpened [the violence] up, but I think it runs a bit deeper."

Roddam confirmed that Townshend was very supportive during the making of *Quadrophenia*. "Townshend, of course, was like a sort of guiding light," he told *NME*. "He was very gracious – gracious enough to say, 'I made the album, the film is yours. I trust you to go away and make it.'

"In *Tommy* the music dominates the film and is the central driving force behind it, it controls the narrative. In *Quadrophenia*, the music contributes to the narrative and supports it but very rarely takes over from it. That's quite a difficult decision because it's putting the music in second place, so it's a very different kind of film."

Predictably, the movie, much like the album, fared better in Britain. "In America, the film is slow," Townshend explained to *Trouser Press* in 1980. "It does good business in the cities, but when it goes out on the road it stays in a cinema for a week and then moves on. Probably because it's a music film it'll make its money back over a period of years, like *Monterey Pop* did. The reason that it's doing incredible business in England is that we were lucky that the mod movement was having its renaissance around the time that the film came out. In fact, it was already well-established, as I understand they certainly didn't have any trouble getting people for the film. A lot of the kids in the film were actually existing mods from Sheffield, Stafford and a few other places, and they had scooters and they had parkas and they had all the kit."

The *Quadrophenia* soundtrack – another double – featured key songs from the original work, plus three newly recorded Townshend compositions, 'Four Faces', 'Joker James' and 'Get Out And Stay Out', which all fitted neatly (perhaps too neatly) into the *Quadrophenia* theme. Side

Four of the album consisted of songs which fit the time period with selections from artists such as The Kingsmen, Booker T & the MGs, The Ronettes and James Brown. "The soundtrack, remixed by Entwistle, sounds even better than the recorded original," wrote *Time*'s Jay Cocks. (The album reached 23 in Britain; 46 in the US.)

The production of *The Kids Are Alright* and *Quadrophenia* "greatly postponed" any planned filming of *Lifehouse*, the *NME* reported in May. "I think it's probably killed [*Lifehouse*] stone dead, to be quite frank," Townshend stated, explaining that the film would probably take two years, with an estimated budget of at least £12 to £15 million. "But I don't know whether it would be possible to make it as a British film, and I wouldn't be interested in making it as an American film, 'cause I live here. Also, I no longer care that much about it, in fact. When I wrote it I was absolutely passionate about it. It was bound up in that period of The Who when Kit Lambert was still involved in my writing and in a managerial sense. And I felt then was the time The Who should've gone in and made a film. The idea was really to hit *Tommy*, to meet that audience head-on.

"Now the only reason I've revived *Lifehouse* was because at one point I figured it was the one way The Who was gonna be able to continue working and communicating at the level that we had as a performing band and reaching a very wide audience."

"I'd done a couple of scripts for [*Lifehouse*], but I can't see the wood for the fucking trees anymore . . . *Lifehouse* was . . . kind of a nutty idea at the time, but I've since brought it a little bit down to earth, rationalised it a bit. What still excites me about it is that it does contain a concert and a story, and it does contain a lot of my feelings about what rock is and what music is, why music has a spiritual value and why the effect of rock music has a spiritual value."

While the latest attempt at reviving *Lifehouse* stalled, The Who had produced two successful films dealing with their history, while a third, *McVicar*, went into production in 1979 with Roger Daltrey cast as convicted jailbird John McVicar. Its success the following year proved greatly pleasing to Pete.

"We're just proud of the fact that we managed to make a film in England," he said. "It wasn't entirely English money, but *McVicar* was made with a lot of English money and the *The Kids Are Alright* was made with all our money and it'll make it back. It's great to be able to cock a snook at all the Americans who say that we're finished as a nation of film-makers. Most film-makers don't have the first fucking idea of what gets kids into the cinema, and it's not just tagging music onto something. It's making films in the British tradition, which is the only kind of film that I think we can make well, which is the kind of *Saturday Night And Sunday Morning* thing. I know it's depressing, but that's our *cinéma vérité*, if we ever had one."

"What these two films do is tie up, once and for all – fully, totally exploit, wring out and wring dry – everything that The Who ever did," Townshend told *Oui's* David Rothman in 1980. "We're almost at the point at which The Who are going to produce their next major creative piece. All this stuff will be gone and done, and the old Who will be – dare I say it? – buried. So, in a way, it's a good thing. We're up against the wall again."

While the year 1979 signalled a new beginning for The Who, demonstrating that they had the ability to surmount the previous year's upheaval, Townshend's personal battle with alcohol intensified. The situation, he recalled in *The Courage To Change*, Dennis Wholey's 1984 book on alcoholism, began around 1974.

"My wife, Karen, began feeling that there was a potential problem, while I felt it was just the way I was and the way I lived. So we'd have lots of conversations. I would try to justify the way that I ingested alcohol by saying it was part of being a successful person. She didn't buy that at all. What's really peculiar is that I did . . . I always felt that drinking and work were tied together in a totally appropriate and proper way. This was despite the fact that my great partner, Roger Daltrey, never drank to excess, not from the beginning of our career to the end, and still doesn't . . . But I felt that I had a bigger responsibility because I was writing songs and was the spokesman for the band. And I wasn't allowed to bring those pressures home. This was the conspiracy that my wife and I carried together. We were accomplices. When I got home, family life was sacrosanct, but it got to the point where that charade could go on no longer."

After Moon's death, Townshend's alcohol consumption began to affect his ability to perform, a development which although surprisingly uncommon at this point, would seriously affect The Who's live shows over the coming months. An early instance of his deterioration occurred on June 27, when he took part in the opening show of the Secret Policeman's Ball, Amnesty International's four-night fund raising event at Her Majesty's

Theatre in London. In his first solo performance in five years, Pete capably performed 'Pinball Wizard' and 'Drowned', solo with his Gibson acoustic guitar, but his duet performance of 'Won't Get Fooled Again' with classical guitarist John Williams was noticeably flawed. He seriously lagged at the beginning of the song, mixed up some of the words, and generally looked disorientated.

"The first day of that [event] went on for ever, and seriously, I think I fell asleep onstage in the middle of the song and actually came round," Townshend told Stuart Grundy and John Tobler for their 1983 book *The Guitar Greats*, adding the rather feeble excuse, "but everybody in the audience was doing it too, because the show went on for nearly four hours, and everybody was sitting there after their big dinners and two bottles of wine . . ."

A second solo appearance took place on July 13 at the Rainbow. This time, the occasion was a Rock Against Racism benefit concert, organised to raise money to pay the legal costs of those arrested in a London area anti-racism demonstration. Townshend had become personally involved through one of his business ventures.

"I've got this recording studio called Musician's Co-Op, which people use in a community way," he told *Oui*'s David Rothman in March 1980. "Sometimes they pay me money, but usually it's free, because I like their music or what's involved or whatever. There was a band called Mystic, a British reggae band, and they have a community of their own called People Unite. They were based in Southall, which has a lot of Asians, Africans and West Indians mixed in with the whites. There's a lot of tension there – occasional fights and things like that.

"Mystic came to my studio and worked for about two weeks. They're Rastafarians and smoke joints like this long [spreading his arms about three feet wide]. This one guy in the band really impressed me – a guy called Clarence. See, when they'd come into the studio, they wouldn't just have the band record; they'd have apprentices there as well. About five guitar players picking away. I was deeply impressed with the way they lived. My spiritual principles prohibit the dope, but at the same time, they seemed to respect my spiritual stance, and I had to respect theirs. Then I hear that one of the group is in the hospital with brain damage, that somebody had put an iron bar through his skull during a riot against the fascist National Front. I thought, 'Please, God, may it not be Clarence.' Because without him, this whole group of two or three hundred people in the area – young kids and families, who all depended on this band for a living and a raise on debts and everything – would be fucked. It was him. So I've decided that I'm going to stand up and get counted. I think fascism stinks. And I'm going to go onstage and say so. And I'm a bit scared. Not for me. I'm scared for my family, and the people around me."

Pete helped organise the show and was impressed with the fact that "everybody I rang in the music business was right there. Their position was quite clear. With rock, you're on the front line. You represent the sharp edge of a lot of people's ideas. Ten years ago, I had a stand-up row with Abbie Hoffman about politics and rock. I said, 'No way am I ever going to let politics get on the stage of a rock'n'roll concert. It's got fuck-all to do with it'. Now I'm starting to think maybe I was wrong."[5]

As well as supplying the event's lighting and equipment through his Eel Pie recording company, Townshend topped the bill backed by Kenney Jones, Rabbit Bundrick, Tony Butler and Peter Hope-Evans (all of whom appeared on Pete's solo album *Empty Glass*, which was being recorded at the time). The band played 'Won't Get Fooled Again', 'The Real Me', 'Cat's In The Cupboard' (which Pete announced from the stage he'd written the previous week "and recorded on Monday for my solo album"), 'Bargain', 'Drowned', 'Let's See Action', 'My Generation' and 'Tattoo' in a performance which also included a cover of 'Blue Suede Shoes' and concluded with Townshend smashing his Les Paul.

Pete's involvement in the Rock Against Racism benefit motivated him to become more publicly involved in politics. "For a long time, I just stood back and whenever a political issue came up, I tried to keep out of it, because [the Abbie Hoffman incident] really tainted it for me," he told Grundy and Tobler. "I don't think I became more open again until the Rock Against Racism thing – it seemed that fascism was getting a foothold against a backcloth of unease in this country, and I didn't like the look of that at all . . . So I've changed quite a bit, and the band's attitude to playing for charity has changed, because initially, we played charity shows, but didn't let anyone know we were doing it. It's our business whether or not we give our money away, so for a long time The Who ran a charity, the Double O Charity, which still gives a lot of its earnings away to charity . . . we were giving away quite phenomenal amounts of money, and nobody knew, which I suppose made us feel fairly smug, but when somebody says,

---

[5] When asked by Rothman if he'd like to say anything to Abbie Hoffman regarding the Woodstock incident, Townshend replied, "No, no. I don't want him coming up onstage again. I'd still kick the fucker off."

'Why don't you do a charity concert, you filthy rich pig?' you eventually have to tell them what you've been doing . . ."[6]

The Who were back onstage in late August, playing to a crowd of over 50,000 at Wembley Stadium. AC/DC, Nils Lofgren and The Stranglers opened the show. Two weeks later AC/DC followed The Who to Germany, where, along with Cheap Trick and the Scorpions, they played to 65,000 fans in Nuremburg.

Within a fortnight, The Who played their first US concerts since October 1976 with two shows at a small theatre in Passaic, New Jersey as a warm-up to five consecutive nights at Madison Square Garden, which restored the band's confidence in themselves.

"We needed to be reminded of all the promise and possibility of rock," *Time* magazine's Jay Cocks wrote in an article entitled 'A New Triumph for The Who'. "Of its dangers, and the reasons for facing them down. Of its limits, and the necessity of testing them, trampling them and resetting them still higher. Whether there's a question of age, relevance and survival, or a more general concern about definition and direction, all doubts were settled, and all bets were off, when The Who played five sold-out dates at Madison Square Garden . . . The Who set new standards, redeemed old promises and put a few ghosts to rest. These concerts may become not only one of the seminal rock events of 1979 but a route dynamited into the new decade . . .

"The Who endure partly on their own wild momentum, partly on the strength of Townshend's compositions – some of the most brilliant, adventurous and lacerating in all rock – and partly on the indestructibility of the covenant with the fans, who will never let their band off easy . . . This kind of rock'n'roll communion is strictly hardcore. The limousine crowd does not turn out in force for a Who date . . . The Who still play for the kids, an audience that has nothing to do with age. These kids are anyone for whom rock'n'roll is far from entertainment and closer to a matter of life and death."

During the Garden run, on the fourth night, Pete cut the palm of his right hand on his guitar, left the stage to receive stitches, and returned to finish the gig, while the final show on September 18 ended in an onstage pie fight. The band, who were augmented by a four-piece horn section

---

[6] The Who started the Double O charity back in 1976 – an early, primary recipient of funds was the Chiswick Women's Refuge (formerly known as Chiswick Women's Aid), which provided shelter for women and children who were victims of domestic violence.

throughout the tour, left New York triumphant after entertaining over 100,000 fans during their seven-day stay in the area.

Two months later, following four UK warm-up shows – two apiece in Brighton and Stafford – the band returned to the States for a lengthy tour, with the first stop at Detroit's Masonic Auditorium on November 30. The fact that Townshend was prepared to commit to spending time away on the road demonstrated a drastic about-face in his attitude to touring. Only back in May, he had remained emphatic in his stance, earnestly telling reporters, "I don't want to [tour], I really don't. It would kill me."

"Before Keith died," Pete told *Rolling Stone*'s Greil Marcus the following year, "I decided that practically all the personal problems I had – whatever they were, whether it was boozing, or difficulty at home with my family – was because of The Who on the road. When we came off the road, I spent two and a half years not touring – under great pressure from the band to tour, but I resisted, and said, 'No, I want to try it, and see what happens.' I got to the end of that period, and all my problems were still there. Some of them were worse."

Townshend had also reversed his position regarding the band's set list, finally coming to terms with the fact that audiences wanted to hear The Who's older songs. Dating back to his depressing experience at Madison Square Garden five years earlier, Pete had recoiled at the thought of simply churning out 'Who classics' in a ritualistic manner which reeked of a complete lack of spontaneity. Initially, he simply didn't know how to deal with it. "For ages, my reaction to that was just to stop," he told *Trouser Press* in 1980. "For two and a half years we didn't do any shows because I just refused to play, but then I started to hang with a few bands and it was probably Steve and Paul from the Pistols who told me, 'Why the fuck do you worry about it? Just get up and play. All right, it's ritualised. Who gives a shit? Just play!' . . .

"Bits of The Who's show are still rooted in tradition, and we go through the motions to a certain extent because people do wanna hear the old stuff. What you've got to watch is the hypocrisy of pretending that you're not proud of what you've done, and the hypocrisy of pretending that you don't enjoy and are able to lean on the value of those gestures."

The standard set list on this tour featured only two songs – 'Who Are You' and 'Sister Disco' – from the band's last album *Who Are You*, leaning heavily on the back catalogue including 'I Can't Explain', 'Baba O'Riley', 'The Punk And The Godfather', 'Behind Blue Eyes', 'Bargain', 'Drowned',

'Pinball Wizard', 'My Generation', 'Won't Get Fooled Again', 'Magic Bus', 'Long Live Rock', and 'Summertime Blues'.

Perhaps seeking an escape from what was rapidly becoming a miserable experience, Townshend developed an obsessive passion for playing the popular Space Invaders arcade game while on tour. "Pete was addicted, and we were constantly looking out for machines," Richard Barnes recalled in *Maximum R&B*. "We nearly missed every flight that took off from an airport that had one in the coffee shop. When we arrived in one new town, before he'd even got his cases brought up, Pete was on the phone to the lobby asking about Space Invaders machines. He even got Yellow Pages and rung around all the bars to discover if any had one." Townshend was eventually given his own Space Invaders machine later during the tour. "At each gig it would be set up in the hospitality room," wrote Barnes, "and Pete would challenge the roadies to games. However, if it was therapeutic for Pete, it was the opposite for Roger. He hated the noise and it was agreed that at the end of the tour he would be allowed to smash it up with an axe."

Only two shows into the tour, and a little over a year since the death of Keith Moon, The Who were shaken by a further tragedy. In a frenzied crush to enter Cincinnati's Riverfront Coliseum for the concert on December 3, 11 fans were trampled, the news of which was kept from the band until the show was over. The deaths were blamed on several factors: poor security, a first-come, first-served general admission ticket policy, and the fact that only four doors were opened into the venue to allow the crowd of several thousand waiting outside in the frigid weather to enter.

The band members were shattered by the news. "If it had happened inside I would never have played again," Townshend told *Time* a few weeks later. With Pete already experiencing marital discord, still inwardly grieving Moon's death and facing alcoholism, the Cincinnati catastrophe tipped him over the edge. "What made me stop thinking the show had to go on was obviously Cincinnati," he later told *Rolling Stone*'s David Fricke in 1987. "It was a terrible lesson to have to learn. For a long time, I couldn't live with that. It was directly responsible for me literally, emotionally falling apart."

"I just want to work and be happy," a distraught Townshend told a Detroit disc jockey a few days after the incident. "We didn't know anything about the accident. But everything in my life tells me to stop – my two little girls, my brain, body, everything tells me to stop. I'm not going to stop. I just don't care, really. I really don't care what happens anymore."

Throughout his career Townshend had used the interview medium almost as a confessional, rashly stating what was on his mind without reflection on the consequences. Unfortunately, this tendency was to land him in hot water in early 1980 during an interview with *Rolling Stone's* Greil Marcus: "The amazing thing, for us, is the fact that – when we were told about what happened at that gig, that 11 kids had died – for a second, our guard dropped. Just for a second. Then it was back up again . . . it was, fuck it! We're not gonna let a *little thing* like this stop us. That was the way we *had* to think. We had to reduce it, because if we'd actually *admitted* to ourselves the *true* significance of the event . . . we could not have gone on and worked. And we had a tour to do. We're a rock'n'roll band. You know, we *don't fuck around*, worrying about 11 people dying. We *care* about it, but there is a particular attitude I call the "tour armour": when you go on the road you throw up an armour around yourself, you almost go into a trance.

"We did go home . . . and we talked about it with our families and our friends," he said, but then added, "If I could dare say it, I'd say that Cincinnati was a very, very positive event for The Who. I think it changed the way we feel about people. It's changed the way we feel about our audience."

Townshend's attempts to describe The Who's tour rationale and to try and find a positive aspect to the tragedy, no matter how well-intentioned they were, appeared heartless on the printed page.

"I watched Roger Daltrey cry his eyes out after that show," Townshend told Marcus. "I didn't, but he did. But now, whenever a fucking journalist – sorry – asks you about Cincinnati, they expect you to come up with a fucking theatrical tear in your eye! You know: 'Have you got anything to say about Cincinnati?' 'Oh, we were *deeply* moved, terrible tragedy, the horror, loss of life,' *arrrghh* – what do you do? We did all the things we thought were right to do at the time: sent flowers to the fucking funerals. All . . . *wasted*. I think when people are dead they're dead."

Townshend later told Dave Marsh that he regretted the "unfortunate" outburst, claiming that his comments had been "sensationally framed, without vocal inflections; it actually looks like I actually mean what I'm saying or at least, that I believe what I'm saying is worth saying. When I spoke to Greil Marcus, I was sarcastic and – I thought – self-detrimental about the group's bloodyminded determination to carry on after the tragedy. I was simply trying to illustrate how absurd show-business thinking is. It didn't come off and hurt the feelings of the relatives."

The decision was made to continue the tour but Townshend later wished he'd had the courage of his convictions and called time on The Who. "I had a big, big problem because I had been the big rock idealist and now it was all letting me down," he told Dennis Wholey in 1984. "The industry hadn't fulfilled its promise. Rock'n'roll had changed the length of men's hair and very little else. I felt like a fool because I'd waved the banner so aggressively. And what was really worse, I felt that I was being used by journalists.

"I hated the feeling that I was in a band on the downward slide that was killing people in Cincinnati, killing off its own members . . . We were into making big money and anybody who got in the way or had a problem, we dropped. Nobody seemed to notice. Nobody seemed to think this was a particularly bad thing, or we pretended it wasn't, anyway. I felt it start to kill me. Something was getting its teeth into me . . . I should have stopped working with the band. I should have stopped and had another look at rock'n'roll, the thing that I loved and cared about so much, which I held above all other things.

"I had so many great hopes. I could see that the band wasn't doing what I wanted it to do. I cared about doing it for all the wrong reasons. I carried on doing it for Roger. I carried on doing it for John Entwistle. I carried on doing it for the fans. I carried on doing it because I had a contract. I carried on doing it because I had 30 employees. I carried on doing it, and I shouldn't have. I should have stopped and taken a hard, hard look at the music business and myself and come to the conclusion, which a lot of other people had come to, that the best years of The Who were the early years."

The show after Cincinnati in Buffalo, New York went ahead as scheduled, with several precautionary measures: The Who did away with their soundcheck (it was reported that the Cincinnati melee reached boiling point when fans heard the band performing a soundcheck, mistakenly believing that they were missing the beginning of the show), and the start time was pushed back by 90 minutes to give the audience extra time to enter the venue. Roger announced from the stage, "You all heard what happened yesterday, there's nothing we can do, we feel totally shattered, but life goes on. We all lost a lot of family yesterday. This show's for them."

By a strange quirk of fate, the Cincinnati tragedy served only to increase The Who's popularity, making headlines worldwide while *Time* magazine made the band their cover story. The band's shows on the '79 US tour were drawing their own press attention in the form of rave reviews and massive attendances. Following a sold-out concert in Cleveland and a performance in front of 41,000 at Pontiac's Silverdome, The Who played the International Amphitheatre, Chicago on December 8, which was simulcast to nine area movie theatres, all of which sold out. Townshend and Daltrey appeared to thoroughly enjoy themeselves, hamming it up for the expanded audience, and Chicago was widely regarded as the best show of the tour.

"At the end of a two-hour show the lasers were fucking helpful, because then you could stand still and let them do the stuff," Townshend said in 1980. "Or if I was having a problem playing a decent guitar solo, I could whirl my arm a couple of times and it would have the same effects as a well played guitar solo. And that *da-da-rrraaanggg* gesture that I do: every now and then I do it and I think, 'Christ, I'm fucking glad that belongs to me. It gets me out of so much trouble!'"

Following two shows in Philadelphia on December 10 and 11, Pete decided to travel to the Meher Spiritual Center in Myrtle Beach for a few days' rest and relaxation prior to the next show, which was in Maryland on the 13th. Townshend and Barnes, along with a friend from San Francisco, chartered a Learjet for the trip to South Carolina.

"Pete told them to take off vertically," Barnes recalled in *Maximum R&B*. "Pete had experienced this before and warned us to be ready. As soon as the jet had taken off, the pilot pulled the stick back and we climbed almost vertically up to 40,000 feet. It was so exciting that we asked if they would land and take off again but they couldn't. After spending so much time and $5,000 arranging to get to South Carolina, Pete never set foot in the Baba Center. He spent the whole time trying to catch up on sleep in the Myrtle Beach Hilton a half a mile up the coast from the Baba Center."

This anecdote, while perhaps simply illustrating Townshend's exhausted state at this point of the tour, also provides a glimpse that his personal beliefs were being compromised as a result of his increasing alcohol abuse.

"I'm very heavily into Meher Baba, but I also drink like a fish," he confessed to *Trouser Press* in 1980. "I'm still not the most honest person in the world. It's difficult, but I do at least know what's happening to me. I accept that there is a larger reason for me being alive than just being a rock star."

"I was living against a lot of the principles of Meher Baba that I initially found enriching," Pete later told *Time Out*. "Meher Baba came down very heavily against drugs, for example. So for a while I pushed him out of my life because I wouldn't live within those principles."

On their return to London, on December 28, The Who played a charity concert at the Hammersmith Odeon to aid starving refugees in Kampuchea (Cambodia) – part of a series of shows held over four nights headlined by such acts as The Clash, Wings, Queen and Ian Dury, organised by U.N. Secretary General Kurt Waldheim and promoter Harvey Goldsmith.

"The Who's evening was both exhausting and exhilarating," *Rolling Stone* correspondent Paul Gambaccini wrote of the event. "Two of Britain's best new groups – The Pretenders and the ska-revivalist Specials – played powerful sets, followed by a marathon Who performance that lasted almost three hours."

While the show was well-received, it further spotlighted Townshend's worsening state. He was clearly drunk, contributing erratic and often out of tune guitar work, at times forgetting to play, substituting wild, embarrassing dancing in its place and providing such less-than-inspiring onstage asides as "Aren't you glad you were born in London and not in poxy Kampuchea?"

Townshend returned to the venue the following evening to perform as part of Paul McCartney's all-star Rockestra (as he had done on the studio recording). The sold-out crowd "reached near-hysterical pitch," according to *Rolling Stone*, when "reports of a Beatles reunion in the *Daily Mirror* and similar speculation in the *Evening News* brought out fans who were willing to pay scalpers up to $440 for the sold-out show . . . an hour before Wings were to perform, ABC-TV sent word that it would pay $2,000 for two minutes of film of a Beatles reunion, and rumours spread through the audience that John Lennon had arrived." The much-trumpeted reunion, of course, did not occur.

Townshend and Lane were confused about the time they were due to report to the venue for rehearsals and, finding nobody there, they decided to visit several pubs in the Hammersmith area. By the time they turned up at showtime, both were plastered and Townshend was in an uncompromising mood, taking delight in refusing to wear the tacky gold top hat and gold lamé jacket that McCartney had insisted all the musicians should wear for the occasion.[7] Townshend took the stage, rather worse for wear, in a faded suit as part of the 19-piece Rockestra finale alongside the likes of Lane, Kenney Jones, John Bonham, John Paul Jones and James Honeyman-Scott of The Pretenders. The band performed Little Richard's 'Lucille', The Beatles' 'Let It Be' and the Rockestra theme.

"Up onstage [Townshend] appeared disheveled," Chris Charlesworth wrote, "his unkempt hair a tangled mess, baggy trousers bunched at his ankles, swaying drunkenly as if to taunt the prim and proper ex-Beatle."

Back at the family home, The Who's first protracted touring in years was taking its toll and Pete's strained relationship with his wife had reached breaking point. "Karen finally said, 'Listen, the drinking is starting to affect the family. I won't have that,'" he wrote in *The Courage To Change*. "I said, 'Karen, I can't stop drinking. I can't. Particularly when I'm working.' So she said, 'Well, then, when you work, you stay away.' That sounded reasonable, so I started to do that. If I was recording I'd check into a hotel, do some work, or maybe go to the States for a couple of weeks. I'd come back home and dry out completely, maybe just a glass of wine with a meal on Sunday. Then I'd go away again for a couple of months and do some work and then come back."

He moved to an apartment located above a shoe shop on London's Kings Road, and also spent time at his country home in Berkshire. "That was a weird year," Townshend recalled. "Some weird things happened to me. My wife and I became estranged . . . Eventually, I started to find social solace elsewhere. I dropped a lot of our mutual friends. I found a few others. I started to get involved with temporary girlfriends. I could go into a nightclub anywhere in London and everybody in the building would know who I was. I spent very little time at home. That's when it all began. Around that time, Karen and I decided that it would be best if I took my problems elsewhere, permanently."

In addition to frequenting clubs, Townshend was a regular concert attendee and saw many bands over the next two years.[8] One of the shows Pete attended in January 1980 was a Clash gig in Brighton, where he performed 'Louie Louie' with the group during the encore. "It was one of the best concerts I've ever seen," Pete told *Trouser Press*. "It was fucking

---

[7] In 1985, a clean-cut, sober Townshend wore a gold lamé jacket for his *Face The Face* performance in the *White City* film.

[8] Townshend estimated that he saw "about a hundred" bands in 1981 alone.

incredible. They asked me to go onstage and play, which was a bit embarrassing because I'd only had *London Calling* about a week, and I wasn't too sure of many of the chords, so I tuned the guitar to one and just pretended. It was really exciting."

At the beginning of 1980, The Who signed a new multi-album record deal with Warner Brothers, reputedly worth around $12 million. The deal gave Warner Brothers the rights to the band's US and Canadian releases, while Polydor retained the band's marketing throughout the rest of the world. "Apparently Mo Ostin, chairman of the board of Warners, was a big reason the group signed with that label," *Rolling Stone* reported in March, citing Townshend's friendship with the man. A few months earlier, Pete had signed a solo deal with Atlantic subsidiary Atco ("my favourite record label," he declared in 2005) through which he was committed to recording three solo albums over the next six years.

Townshend had bitten off more than he could chew. "I'd made a whole series of insane decisions: signing a new Who deal for five albums, within two months of signing a solo deal for three albums," he told Q in 1996. "In five years, I had to produce eight albums. Write all the songs, tour, do the PR, record . . . there was no way I could have done it. There was that, and I had started a very ambitious publishing company, I decided to start a floating studio . . . started to build a house. That was just fucking mad."

CHAPTER TWELVE

1980–1981

"It was a waste of time. Heroin is an utter, complete waste of time."
                                                    – Pete Townshend, 1985

*"From my point of view, I like to be like a reed. You get blown
backwards and forwards by the ebbs and flows of what is happening in the
world. But you don't break – and I have never broken and I will never
break."*
                                                    – Pete Townshend, 1982

IN early 1979, Pete had begun work on a solo album starting with two
songs which were leftovers from the *Who Are You* period: 'Keep On
Working' and 'Empty Glass'. The latter originally had a working title of
'Choirboy' during the *Who Are You* sessions in April 1978. "Pete might've
called it 'Empty Glass' 'cause he was singing 'Empty Glass'," Jon Astley
recalls, "but on the tape box, it's called 'Choirboy' . . . I didn't know what
to call it [at the time of the recording], maybe because of this little falsetto
Pete singing, I called it 'Choirboy', I don't know."

The rest of the tracks that ended up on what became *Empty Glass* were
composed over the following year and recorded in demo form at Pete's
24-track recording studio. In a break with tradition, Townshend resisted
giving his best material to The Who.

"The only distinction I made," he told the *NME* in April 1980, "was
that if I was really going to do a solo album deal properly . . . the only way
I could do it would be to take the best of any material that I had at any particular time, rather than knock together solo projects of any sort based on
material that The Who had rejected. So my album – though I was able to
take a lot more risks with the material than The Who would – could have
been a Who album if we'd happened to be recording at that time . . . I just
decided to write – to write straight from the hip and offer everything to

the project that's going on at the time, not earmark stuff. I think that what's quite interesting is the way that *I* do a song as distinct from the way The Who would do it, and I don't want to deny myself all The Who-type material because y'know, that's what I am."

Astley recalls complimenting his brother-in-law about the quality of the songs during the recording sessions. "He said, 'Yeah, they're the ones that Roger rejected!' And you think to yourself, in the case of 'Rough Boys', 'Roger rejected 'Rough Boys' as a Who song?' It's madness!"

Since *Who Came First* consisted of a collection of pre-existing demos and songs from the Meher Baba albums, and *Rough Mix*, a collaboration with Ronnie Lane, *Empty Glass* was the first bona fide Pete Townshend solo album. Musicians playing on it included bassist Tony Butler and drummer Mark Brzezicki, from the band On The Air (who also featured Simon Townshend on guitar) who went on to achieve substantial success as the rhythm section of Big Country in the early Eighties.

Recording took place at Wessex studios, north London (with additional work done at Eel Pie and AIR studios), overseen by the production-engineering team of Chris Thomas and Bill Price. A highly regarded producer, Thomas had started his studio career in 1967 working for George Martin's AIR company and had recently produced The Sex Pistols and The Pretenders.

"Most of the material is pretty uptempo," Townshend informed Kurt Loder in 1980. "I did have a couple of ballads I was thinking I might include, but I didn't – mainly at the behest of Chris Thomas. He figured the album should be pretty ballsy, and that's the way it's come out."

Thomas was also credited with transforming Townshend's voice. "I always had quite a nice voice, but I never owned it until 1980, when I did *Empty Glass*, with Chris Thomas," Pete recalled to *Rolling Stone*'s Jenny Eliscu in 2000. "He said, 'Why don't you just sing?' And I said, 'Because I sound like Andy Williams.' And he said, 'So?' And I sound like Andy Williams – I've got a beautiful voice."

Pete recalled in 1996 that the opening track 'Rough Boys' was "made up on the studio floor. Entirely . . . I just made it up as I went along, and Kenney Jones played along. I had a synthesiser guitar which was running into . . . two early primitive guitar synthesisers . . . each of which went to a huge Hiwatt stack in the middle of Wessex studio, so I stood there on my own with Kenney bashing away on the drums, and produced this huge noise, which sounded like about 30 guitars . . . And what you hear is me going nuts in the middle of the studio."

The horns at the end of the song proved difficult for Raphael Rudd to arrange. "The reason it's so complicated at the end harmonically is because I was just playing anything that came under my fingers," Pete recalled. "It took [Raphael] a long time to analyse some of those chords at the end. Anything that didn't work, we snipped out with a pair of scissors."

Originally titled 'Tough Boys', the song was "a rant about the British punks [like Sid Vicious] I had come across in recent years who wore outfits I had come to know in New York as the apparel of 'rough' gays," Townshend wrote in the *Scoop 3* liner notes in 2001.[1]

'Rough Boys' was followed by 'I Am An Animal', "a song about the evolution of the individual in a spiritual way," Townshend explained, "about all the different roles we go through in one lifetime." Like 'Rough Boys', 'And I Moved' could be construed as having a gay theme, thanks to the lines, *And his hands felt like ice exciting, as he laid me back just like an empty dress.*

"I don't really know what that's about," Townshend told *Trouser Press*. "Originally I wrote it as a song about a voyeur, but it went through some permutations. A lot of people feel that it's about me and my father or me and Meher Baba or me and a relationship with a woman, but I listened to it last night because I was checking the pressings, and I thought it was a bit like an admission of homosexual tendencies."

"Of course, a literal reading of a songwriter as complex as Townshend can be deceptive," a retrospective review of the album in *Rolling Stone* pointed out, "as in 'Rough Boys' and 'And I Moved' . . . taken by some as confessions of homosexual lust."

"A lot of gays and a lot of bisexuals wrote to me congratulating me on this so-called coming out," Townshend revealed. "I think in both cases the images are very angry, aren't they? In 'Rough Boys', the line 'Come over here, I want to bite and kiss you' is about 'I can scare you! I can frighten you! I can hurt all you macho individuals simply by coming up and pretending to be gay!' And that's what I really meant in that song, I *think*."

The fact that the central figure in 'And I Moved' is a male who is seemingly seducing the singer is better explained when considering the following: "I think it's probably best not to try to explain it," Townshend said. "Originally I wrote it when Bette Midler's manager had written to me and said she was doing an album, she liked what I wrote and asked if I could

---

[1] This probably explains Daltrey's reluctance to record the song.

send her a song. He said, 'Make it a bit dirty, because that's the kind of thing she likes.' So I sent it to her [along with an electro-pop song entitled 'You're So Clever'] and heard nothing for a couple of months; then I heard from him and he said, 'I couldn't really give it to her because it's smutty.' I said, 'What? You asked for something dirty' and he said, 'It isn't dirty, it's smutty.'"

The vagueness of the song's lyrics reflected a change in Townshend's stance on his public image.

"All of a sudden I've initiated this process of not caring about looking a bit of an idiot, saying the wrong thing or being told that you're wet," he told *Trouser Press*. "There's nothing more annoying than someone who is so full of their own semi-consciousness that they can't be themselves in front of you . . . it makes you realise that you're not free. Anything that inhibits freedom is damaging in the end.

"It's not just society, but in rock. People in rock imagine that they're so incredibly fucking liberated and anarchistic. But they're not. They're so incredibly closed up and macho. In many ways rock is more reactionary than the rest of society, because the business side of it is so super-corporate, the money flow of it so controlled, and the forefront of it is so commando-trained, so macho, so concerned with uniforms and hardness."

The most commercial track on *Empty Glass* was 'Let My Love Open The Door', "one of those songs where you end up shooting to write something really deep and meaningful," Townshend said in 1996, "and what you end up coming up with is something that appears to be froth. This was a song about love, but this is actually about divine love. It's supposed to be about the power of God's love, that when you're in diffi-culty, whether it's major or minor, God's love is always there for you. But I suppose, because I used the royal 'we' – I sang with God's voice – it became a song about, you know, 'Hey, girl, I'll give you a good time, if you're feeling blue, come over to my place, and we'll catch a movie,' very much a soap opera version of what it was all about . . ." Eventually released as a single, the song reached a very satisfactory number nine in the American charts.

Townshend attacked journalists on 'Jools And Jim' – the title a pun on Francois Truffaut's innovative film *Jules et Jim* – which was inspired by the *NME* writers Julie Burchill and Tony Parsons.

"I wrote the song after someone from the *Guardian* wrote an article about them to promote their book [*The Boy Looked At Johnny*], and he got very animated about how they didn't give a shit about Sid Vicious going down," Pete told *Trouser Press* in 1980. "Then [Parsons] brought up Keith as well and said, 'Fuck Keith Moon, we're better off without him. Decadent cunt driving Rolls-Royces into swimming pools; if that's what rock'n'roll's about, who needs it?' To a certain extent I agreed with a bit of it, but I feel that it was a bit of opportunist cock . . . I just wrote the song as a reaction. I changed the title from 'Jools And Tone' to 'Jools And Jim' because it's not directly about them, it's about taking a stance and believing what you read. It's just another 'Don't believe what you read' song. I think it's one of the best songs on the album. The energy's great and I really like the singing on it."

'Keep On Working' was Townshend's attempt at writing like Ray Davies. "Ray's always been a big influence on me," he told *Musician* in 1982. "I've never been able to write in the same way, though I've often tried. In fact, I'm terrible at it. I think 'Keep On Working' tries to be a Kinks song but it just doesn't work."

'Cat's In The Cupboard', featuring a galloping beat and Hope-Evans' Larry Adler-like harmonica work, could have easily been adapted into a Who song. 'A Little Is Enough', which remained a staple of Townshend's solo live shows, was "a really great favourite of mine," he said in 1996. "Around the time when I was making this record, I was having my first difficulties in my marriage and feeling that I'd allowed my career to take far too much priority in my life. My wife had warned me I was taking on too much, and I just wasn't really listening to her, and one day I came back from the studio or a gig or maybe even from a party, weeping, crying – 'This is all too hard, I'm depressed, I can't do it, I can't handle show business, nobody loves me, they're not giving me enough money, they're giving me too much money, I'm too big, I'm too small,' whatever it was . . .

"Anyway, I went to Adi Irani, who was Meher Baba's secretary for a long time, and he was doing a lecture tour over here, and he said, 'You look a bit sad.' So I said, 'Well, I'm going through my first real hiccup in my marriage,' and he said, 'Oh, what's it about?' And I said, 'My wife doesn't love me anymore.' And he said, 'Well, she's there, isn't she?' And I said, 'Yeah,' and he said, 'Then she must love you a little bit,' and I said, 'Yeah, yeah, she probably loves me a little bit.' And he said, 'Well, when you're talking about love, which is in itself by nature infinite, then a little is enough.' And it solved my immediate problem, but also seemed to me to be a very, very wise thought, and a very romantic thought, too, you know, if you only have a moment of love in your life, it's enough, because it never evades you and it always returns."

"['A Little Is Enough'] was purely personal; instinct and purely transparent," Pete told Greil Marcus. "It's very emotional, but it's also very straightforward and clear. Just the fact that you can't fucking have the world. If you're lucky enough to get a tiny piece of it, then – fine. I suppose I wrote the song about a mixture of things. I wrote it a little bit about God's love. But mainly about the feeling that I had for my wife – and the fact that I don't see enough of her and that when we are together there are lots of times when things aren't good, because of the period of adjustment you require after a long tour; stuff like that. She would always want a deeper, more sustained relationship than I would – but in the end I suppose we're lucky that we do love one another at all. Because love, by its very nature, is an infinite emotion – just to experience it once in a lifetime is enough. Because a lot of people don't – don't ever experience it."

'Empty Glass' provides Townshend's condensed rock'n'roll adaptation of the Book of Ecclesiastes. "The spark-off for the song was when I read Ecclesiastes again, and it was so powerful," Pete told *Trouser Press*. "You got King Solomon talking about how after he's fucked everybody and had everything and gone through everything, the only piece of advice he's got is that life is useless. But it also contains some great inspirational poetry: 'There is a time', and all that. It really reminded me of a lot of Persian Sufi poetry- that it's only in desperation that you become spiritually open . . ."

The power chording of 'Gonna Get Ya' rounded out the album. "That song's nonsense," Townshend said in 1980. "It's just a word game. I don't think it means anything."

"*Empty Glass* is a direct jump from Persian Sufi poetry," Townshend told Greil Marcus in explaining the album's title. "Hafiz – he was a poet in the 14th century – used to talk about God's love being wine, and that we yearn to be intoxicated, and that the heart is like an empty cup. You hold up the heart, and hope that God's grace will fill your cup with his wine. You stand in the tavern, a useless soul waiting for the barman to give you a drink – the barman being God. It's also Meher Baba talking about the fact that the heart is like a glass, and that God can't fill it up with his love – if it's already filled with love for yourself."

"Spirituality to me is about the asking, not the answers," he elaborated to *Trouser Press*. "I still find it a very romantic proposition, that you hold up an empty glass and say, 'Right. If you're there, fill it.' The glass is empty because you have emptied it. You were in it originally. That's why it's only when you're at your lowest ebb, when you believe yourself to be nothing, when you believe yourself to be worthless, when you're in a state of futility, that you produce an empty glass. Normally, you occupy the glass. By emptying or vacating the glass, you give God a chance to enter it. You get yourself out of the way . . . you ask for help.

"I can't back this up, but I think that when I've sincerely prayed, I've gotten an answer of some sort. Not in the ways I'd ever imagined I'd get an answer, but I've gotten one. If you go on challenging life, saying, 'Why won't life do something for me? Why am I the one who's always losing?' then all you're doing is perpetuating life as is, the idea that life revolves around you as the centre of the universe, which is not true. It's not realistic and it's not practical. You're just another fucking cog in the wheel and you're nothing. You only mean something and you only become something when you believe yourself to be nothing. That's why I put that little footnote on the cover [*Desire for nothing except desirelessness, hope for nothing except to rise above all hopes, want nothing and you will have everything*], which was only a repeat of something Meher Baba said: 'If you want nothing, then you've got everything.' "

Empty Glass was a tight, well-produced album, full of quirky but commercial songs which were loaded with impressionistic writing. Pete credited much of the album's vitality to the British punk movement.[2]

"I had invented punk a thousand times in my head," he said in 1980, "and when it finally happened it really inspired me. It came just as rock was getting so rigid and formatted and it was a reaction to boredom . . . I hold rock above most forms of art because it is one of the few forms of communication where there are people who are idealistic in the medium. And there is a very high percentage of people who listen who are looking for idealism and are disappointed when they get empty crap. I aspire to music that has brains, balls and heart."

Released in April 1980 in the UK and a month later in the US, the album was an immediate critical success. "*Empty Glass* contains the least stiff-necked music that Pete Townshend has made in ages," Dave Marsh wrote in *Rolling Stone*, adding that it "may be an album without much innocence . . . but that's only because Pete Townshend is past the point where he can fake acceptance. You can hear it in his vocals, which are the most – and probably the only – assured ones he's ever done."

---

[2] Pete dedicated *Empty Glass* to Karen, while 'Rough Boys' was for his daughters Emma and Aminta, and The Sex Pistols.

The *NME*'s Paul Morley, one of a new breed of iconcoclastic journalists, came to praise not bury the album. "Townshend has to be respected for his convincing, almost radiant response to the past few years. The frankness and determination of this LP cannot be undermined. This is quite a recovery. We're so fond of knocking those elder statesmen . . . who mess it up and make fools of us and themselves. Townshend should first of all be acknowledged for producing something that isn't pathetic, self-congratulatory, feeding on his own myth, and then congratulated . . . for making songs that have real relevance. It shouldn't be a big deal, but it is."

Guitar magazine's retrospective look at the record seven years later described, "a frightfully revealing and appealing album. While *Glass* may not contain the usual dose of Townshend's manic, mashing guitar, it is surely the guitarist's most personal pop statement, and a rich and diverse musical document."

"If I disagree with the fact that [*Empty Glass*] is the best work I've done in a long time, I would be fooling you," Townshend said in 1982. With hindsight, he admitted that the album further paved the way for his solo career. "I think the only thing that really went wrong was that I realised, as soon as *Empty Glass* was finished, 'Hey, this is it. I'm not able to achieve with the [Who] what I've achieved here.'"

As 1979 had drawn to a close, *Lifehouse* was once again back on the drawing board and another script was written by Michael Hirst, a script-writer Townshend had met during *The Kids Are Alright* filming at Shepperton Studios in 1978.

"Michael helped me to trawl all my short stories into shape," Pete told Matt Kent in 1999. "I'd sent him a bunch of short stories and he had been an editor. He sent them back to me with annotations and stuff and encouraged me to write, but we also had a load of meetings on the story of *Lifehouse*."

Hirst's script eventually made it through to director Nicolas Roeg. "Roeg is loosely interested, I don't know if it's the kind of thing that he would want to do," Townshend told *NME* in 1980, "but I really love the films he's directed, he's English, and his new film *Bad Timing* just smashed me."

Roeg, a British director whose impressive resumé included *Performance*, *Don't Look Now*, and *The Man Who Fell To Earth*, liked Hirst's *Lifehouse* script, but Townshend thought "it was a bit weird." Pete submitted his own recently rewritten script to Roeg, who thought "that it was too sci-fi and not well-written enough," Townshend told Kent. Though married with children, Roeg was living in LA with 23-year-old actress Theresa Russell who had appeared in *Bad Timing*.[3] Townshend wanted to visit Roeg to discuss the script he'd written, setting in motion a chain of events that only exacerbated Pete's midlife crisis. He developed an unrequited obsession for Russell whom he described as "the most spectacular creature on the face of the planet."

"I was going over to LA [in February 1980] to do some demos," Townshend explained to Kent, "so I was going to talk to [Roeg] about the script I had written and how Michael Hirst might be able to bridge the gap . . . I could sense that he wasn't all that mad about it but Jeremy Thomas [Roeg's producer], too, felt that this was a huge project . . . I rang one day, knowing that Nic had just left LA to come back to London for a funeral of a friend . . . and his girlfriend came to the phone. I said, 'Can I speak to Nic?' and she said, 'Oh, Pete he's just left for London,' and I knew that so I said, 'Oh fuck, I was just coming over and was hoping to see him. Never mind, maybe I'll give him a ring when I'm there,' but my intention was to see her. So, I'd fly over there and get into this whole obsession about realising that I had to move very, very quickly, that Nic Roeg and she were obviously living together, he was obviously living there and not in London, they weren't working on a project, what was going on, were they in a relationship, were they not?

"I rang up a couple of friends and asked advice . . . I hadn't even met her yet! I decided that in order to find out what was going on it would be OK to take her out, not one-to-one as I couldn't reveal what was going on, and so I got [some friends] to come with me and her to go and see [Pink Floyd's] *The Wall* [concert at the LA Sports Arena].

"We went and got very pissed and it was the first time in my life I'd ever taken cocaine and she took a bit . . . I completely, totally . . . without any real encouragement from her at all, apart from the fact that she was herself and she was great to be with . . . totally fell in love with her . . . partly I must say fuelled by the fact that it was the first time I'd taken cocaine. What then happens is I jump in a car, it's Valentine's Day, and I go and buy her some tequila and loads of flowers and she wouldn't let me in, wouldn't let me see her and I completely fell apart. I had the most spectacular emotional crash and came back and immediately became a serial drug addict. I was really in a terrible state . . . up to that point I had a lot of drink

---

[3] The pair eventually married in 1982.

problems and a lot of emotional stuff; Cincinnati, Keith dying . . . I was drinking, drinking, drinking but this was the thing that really started to push me over the edge."

When Pete returned to London, he had to deal with Roeg's wrath. "Nic, of course, was fucking furious with me," Townshend recalled, confirming that his indiscretion spelt the premature end of the production. "Jeremy Thomas is a big, powerful producer, he was behind it. Mike Hirst is a great writer, has written some fantastic films since. We would have done it," Pete lamented. *Lifehouse* once again disappeared from view, not to resurface for more than a decade.

Townshend channelled his experience into a new song, 'Theresa' which he demoed on February 16 – just two days after his Valentine's Day rebuke – at the Warner Brothers recording studio in North Hollywood. "When I came to do the vocal on this," Townshend wrote in the *Scoop 3* liner notes, "I was really out of my mind with frustration and grief because she didn't reciprocate. But as you can hear, I was obviously enjoying myself."

He eventually changed the title of the song to 'Athena', "Because I didn't want to blow the whistle on myself," Pete said, "I didn't want to do anything which, at that time, would hurt her, would hurt Nic any more than I already had." He also perhaps did it to keep Karen from finding out about his indescretions, although they were by then estranged. "I'd been through a period of being fairly promiscuous, which was unusual for me because I'd always been very loyal to my wife, but when I'd hit an emotional rock bottom after Keith's death I'd started to get quite promiscuous and nobody had ever turned me down. So, when I was finally turned down it hit me hard."

"It is so wonderful to feel in love like that," Townshend said in 1999. "I felt like I was made of dissolving concrete. The song that I wrote about it, that's all the feelings I was feeling at the time [one line from the song certainly summed up the letdown: *I felt like one of those flattened ants you find on a crazy path*]. I felt like I'd been trodden on. I felt fractured, my emotions were huge. I hadn't felt that kind of feeling for a long time and so I felt bad but I felt alive. It started a whole train for me of looking for that kind of experience, to try to bring myself alive again through pain."[4]

Having managed to gain something from the experience, Pete played

---

[4] A story which obviously drew from the Theresa Russell incident, *Champagne On The Terraces*, surfaced in *Horse's Neck,* Townshend's 1985 book of short stories.

the demos he'd recorded in LA to his bandmates. "I walked into a Who session – didn't even go home to say hello to my little girls – ran through the stuff, and there were all these whispers: 'This is OK, but it isn't great,'" Townshend told John Harris in 1996. "And Kenney Jones, who was new in the band, his first response was: 'You used all the best material for your solo albums.' And my inner reaction was, 'Who the fuck are you? You're only in this fucking band 'cos I wanted you in it.' Roger had never wanted him in in the first place.

"Anyway, I just kind of medicated myself. I turned round to Bobby Pridden and said, 'Could you go out and buy me some coke?' and he said, 'You don't use coke.' I said, 'Listen, I do now, go and buy me some.' Anyway, he went out and bought me some terrible coke, laced with speed . . ."

"I started drinking about a bottle and a half of cognac a day," he told *Omni* in late 1982. "And to cut through the drunken stupor I was in I got into this deadly alcohol cocaine oscillation."[5]

"I adjusted to what was happening in the world," Townshend said in *The Courage To Change*, "people weren't drinking quite as much as they used to – certainly not as much as I was. They were using cocaine in the music business – at the dentist, the hairdresser, the lawyer's office, the record company, the recording studio, on the bus, on the taxi. They were using coke everywhere, and I quickly got into this routine, too. Having plenty of money, I was able to supply myself and also about 50 other people who followed me around London . . . it was a cycle. It was a way of getting out of something, of getting away from the band. It was a way of getting away from rock'n'roll. The only way I could face the work was by destroying myself. I didn't have the guts to stand up and say, 'This is a bunch of shit. I've got to go.'"

In the midst of Townshend's worsening personal state, The Who went back on the road. After a short run through five European cities in late March, the band began the first leg of a North American tour with 18 dates stretching from mid-April through the first week of May. Despite rumours of the band adding an extra guitarist, Pete had decided to keep things as they were. "I think we'll keep the horn section for this tour," he

---

[5] "I went to lunch with the guy who was my driver through that period," Pete told John Harris in 1996, "and I said to him, 'I've really got to apologise to you, for all that, drinking two bottles of brandy a day.' He said, 'No. It was five . . .' He said, 'Pete, I once saw you drop a bottle of brandy, and you got down and licked it up.'"

told Kurt Loder in April. "It really does add extra colour. But apart from that, we're sticking with the same line-up – Rabbit on keyboards, and that's it."

An interesting snapshot of The Who at this stage was provided when *Rolling Stone*'s Greil Marcus took in the first of the band's three shows at Oakland's Alameda County Coliseum on April 18: "If the show was not quite The Who's Greatest Hits, it was the History of The Who . . . Technically, the show was superb: shot through with fun and movement . . . Townshend's crouched leaps were thrilling – spectacular but not gaudy, aggressive but not cruel. No one in The Who ever seemed bored by the material. The band changed the show over the next two nights. They cut it down, stretched it out, shuffled the songs, varied the encores – and, according to one fan who saw all three concerts, Townshend never played the same solo twice . . . he appeared onstage in an impressive navy blue jacket: he looked like a world-beater. When, after a few numbers, he took it off, revealing a Clash T-shirt with sleeves rolled up, his pants suddenly seemed baggy – and he struck me as just another rock & roll anomaly. Just another Buddy Holly: the kid you laugh at, if you bother to do that, the kid who one day comes out of his shell and changes your life."

It was after one of the Oakland shows that the infamous 'bloody hand' *Rolling Stone* photo of a cleanshaven Townshend[6] was taken by Annie Leibovitz. "By the time we got to start taking pictures, the blood was badly congealed," Pete recalled in 2004. "Annie got me to swing my arm afresh to generate more blood. Then she actually found some fake blood and added a little to create the runny effect. But I have to say, my hand was a fucking mess before she started to embellish it . . . I loved how that photo turned out . . ."

Despite the fact that almost all of the venues sold out as the tour wound on through the central United States and Canada, Townshend rapidly lost his enthusiasm. "I don't think I'd go and watch The Who even if I lived in America," he declared. "I mean, I'd sit and wait until The Clash came: I'd go see them. And hope I'd get one of their good nights!"

---

[6] "I shaved it off about a month ago, mainly for medical reasons," Pete told the *NME*'s Charles Shaar Murray in April 1980. "My face started moulting, so I shaved it off and my kids started screaming and my wife started screaming. I've had a beard since 1970, so my youngest kid has never see me without one except for when I played Widow Twankey in the pantomime. At that time the Kenny Everett false chin was not available, otherwise I would have worn one. The director said I had to shave. Nobody knew who the fuck I was."

Pete, 1976. "I did a lot of stuff with the Who and a lot of extramural stuff, too... I think already by '76, I was running out of ideas as to how to get the Who to move to the next level, if there was one." (PENNIE SMITH)

The Who backstage at the Saville Theatre, London, with Jimi Hendrix, January 29, 1967. (J. BARRY PEAKE/REX FEATURES)

Pete attacking his amp, at Granby Halls,
Leicester, March 13, 1967 (PICTORIALPRESS.COM)

From the photo session for *The Who Sell Out*
album cover, October 1967.

(DAVID MONTGOMERY©)

Pete pictured outside Battersea Power Station, 1967.
(CHRIS MORPHET/REDFERNS)

Pete backstage at the Saville Theatre, with twin neck
Gibson, October 22, 1967. **(CHRIS MORPHET/REDFERNS)**

Pete on his wedding day with wife Karen Astley,
May 20, 1968. **(HULTON ARCHIVE/GETTY IMAGES)**

Pulling a face, 1968. Richard Barnes:
"Pete had lost all his sneering unpleasantness
and the 'I'm A Big Shot Pop Star' ego trip had
disappeared. He was relaxed, interesting and
for the first time in years, very, very happy." **(LFI)**

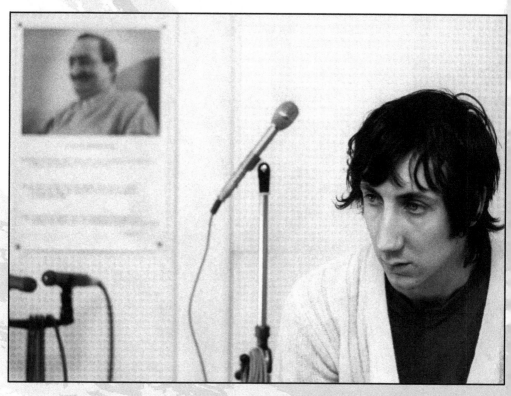

Pete pictured in his Twickenham studio, 1969. Meher Baba's picture is pinned to the wall. (CHRIS MORPHET/REDFERNS)

In the studio, 1970. (CHRIS MORPHET/REDFERNS)

On stage at the Isle Of Wight Festival,
August 30, 1969. (PETE SANDERS/REX FEATURES)

The Who photographed in the grounds of
Keith's Chertsey house, on the occasion of the
party to launch *Who's Next*, July 14, 1971.
(CHRIS WALTER/WIREIMAGE.COM)

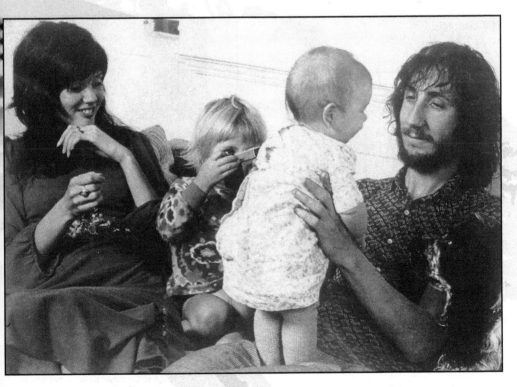

Pete at home with wife Karen and daughters Emma and Aminta, 1972.
(TONY MCCRATH/GUARDIAN NEWS & MEDIA LTD 1975)

Pete on stage with Ron Wood and Eric Clapton
at the Rainbow Theatre, London, January 13, 1973.
(BARRY PLUMMER)

Pete with his dad Cliff making sound
recordings at Goring-On-Thames, 1973.
(CHRIS MORPHET/REDFERNS)

Pete, with Ronnie Lane, in a shot promoting their *Rough Mix*
collaboration, 1977. **(MICHAEL OCHS ARCHIVES/STRINGER/GETTY IMAGES)**

On stage at Shepperton for what was to
be Keith Moon's last gig, May 25, 1978.
(ROSS HALFIN/IDOLS)

Pete and Keith at opening of the exhibition
'Who's Who?' at the ICA, London. August 1978.
(GRAHAM WILTSHIRE/REX FEATURES)

On location in Brighton during the filming of
Quadrophenia, 1978. **(URBANIMAGE.TV/ADRIAN BOOT)**

Pete on stage with Keith Moon's replacement, ex-Small Faces / Faces drummer Kenney Jones, 1979.
(RICHARD YOUNG/REX FEATURES)

With Paul McCartney backstage at Kampuchea benefit, Hammersmith Odeon, December 1979.
(ANDRE CSILLAG/REX FEATURES)

With Mick Jones of The Clash, Brighton, January 1980. **(KATE SIMON/DAVEBROLAN.COM)**

His contempt towards his fans and the touring machine had become obvious. "We don't give a shit whether the audience has a problem or not. All we know is that for us, to go on a stage, get instant communication . . . have an instant connection with the audience, go backstage afterward into a dressing room full of the most beautiful women you can ever hope to lay your eyes on, never have anybody say anything nasty to you, everybody's friendly, everybody's wonderful, people don't throw us out of hotels anymore – I mean life revolves quite nicely – you know what I'm saying? I'm getting paid a lot of money for the privilege. The first 10 years in The Who were fucking awful; miserable, violent, unhappy times. It's nice to now sit back and enjoy it."

Following the tour, Pete spent two weeks at AIR studios assembling the demos he'd recorded earlier in the year for the next Who album, eventually titled *Face Dances*.[7] Although he told *Rolling Stone*'s Kurt Loder that he had found working on *Empty Glass,* "very, very exhausting," he added, "I didn't have any difficulty at all coming up with what I think is some exciting, new-sounding material for The Who quite quickly."

Some of Pete's demos, such as 'You Better You Bet', demonstrated that Townshend was still revelling in the British punk movement – his vocals have a clear John Lydon sneer.[8] "I think I've changed my style slightly through working on my solo album," he told Loder. "Because I was singing every day, my voice improved a hell of a lot, and that affects a lot of the melodies I'm writing and also the kind of diction I can get across."

The argument was later made that some of Pete's demos were of better quality than the finished product.

"Sometimes I feel that I get a little too precious about a song," Townshend told Charles Shaar Murray, "and I feel that I don't really want to hear the band play it because I like the way it is on the demo. But I'm always pleasantly surprised. Some of the material that we've been

---

[7] A last minute replacement for the unimaginative original title *The Who*, *Face Dances* originated from a phrase Townshend coined when he saw a friend in front of a mirror with a match between her teeth, moving the match and her eyes to a beat. The song 'Face Dances Part Two' on *All The Best Cowboys Have Chinese Eyes* references this incident. "I said to her, 'Face Dances' and she just laughed," Pete said in 1981. It wasn't until later that he remembered the 'face dancers' in Frank Herbert's *Dune* trilogy. "That must have stuck in my head because I really loved the first [book]," he recalled.

[8] Townshend enjoyed Lydon's company during this period. In the *Scoop* liner notes, he recalled that the demo of 'Cache Cache' was recorded "between drinking bouts with John Lydon and his brother Jimmy one night."

recording with The Who I've sung with a half-English accent – as is the current trend – and I never thought Roger would be able to do it, but he just lunged right in and did it and it sounds much more natural than singing in his normal Bob Seger accent. He was pleasantly surprised and I was pleasantly surprised . . . The first band that made me feel that it wasn't being deliberately done but that they were just singing was The Sex Pistols. I really got into their albums and played 'em all the time, so when I was ready to do demos it felt quite natural just to do it myself . . ."

Recording sessions for *Face Dances* began in June. With a new recording contract and personnel, The Who elected to use a new producer, Bill Szymczyk, who chose Odyssey studios over the band's familiar choice of Ramport. Szymczyk, whose resumé included production credits on the Eagles' *Hotel California* and *The Long Run*, recalled in the 1982 book *The Record Producers* that the former was one of Townshend's favourite albums. "Really, that's what got me the job with them, that album. Your reputation goes before you, and its like, 'You hear the way that sounds? Do that to me.'"

The sparse guitar and liberal use of keyboards (a theme repeated throughout) on album opener 'You Better You Bet' led some to wonder if Townshend was veering away from his signature guitar work. "I always get very worried about the guitar because I tend to come out with the same three or four chords again and again and again," he said in an interview used on the February 1981 promotional album *Filling In The Gaps*. "I don't even sometimes know that I'm doing it. So I still look to keyboards, particularly to synthesisers and stuff like that as a way of breaking my own preconceptions, breaking my own habit patterns. 'You Better You Bet' was a very spontaneous lyric and a fairly spontaneous, sort of peppy song. I think it's a pop song, really, just a pop song."

His comments were spot on because when released as a single in February 1981, the song reached number nine in the UK and 18 in the US – The Who's biggest chart success since a reissue of 'Substitute' in 1976. In 2006, Townshend remarked that 'You Better You Bet' was "a surprise hit single for us . . . we even ended up back on *Top Of The Pops*."

'Don't Let Go The Coat' was inspired by a Meher Baba expression "hold fast to the hem of my robe". "I wrote this one in London," Townshend recalled in 1982. "I was thinking about all the things you cling onto, and that the most important thing for me at that particular time was to cling to some semblance of a spiritual equipoise. The verses of the song talk about 'things might change', and 'things might explode', but just as long as you hang onto that thread, that apron string of a real affection and love for the people around you, and for whatever else you're into, God, whatever it is . . . mum and dad!"

'Cache Cache' was "a weird kind of song which I wrote to celebrate a wonderful two days I spent living as a tramp in Switzerland," Townshend said referring to an episode which took place during The Who's European tour at the end of March 1980. "I decided I was going to give up the music business forever, and I got my wallet and passport, and a bottle of brandy, and went off in a town called Berne. Berne is famous for its big brown bears and these cages up in the hills. I spent about 16 hours walking around, sleeping under trees and all that, and I was thinking, 'I don't know if I want to be a tramp now,' but I was drunk enough to decide it would be worthwhile just going and visiting the bears. I don't know whether or not I really wanted to get torn to pieces or not, but I think I was in that frame of mind when I really just did not give a damn.

"I went up to this bear pit and I went down this bit where all the apple cores are and climbed up the rocks on the other side. I was always thinking 'If I could get in, I wonder why they couldn't get out?' I went into this big sort of cage at the back and walked inside. It really stank but luckily the bears aren't there in the middle of winter. Really, it's just a song about sometimes you can go and say, 'Right! I'm going to do something really amazing and stupid and devastating,' and then you end up looking like a complete idiot."

He recalled the writing of the demo in his *Scoop* liner notes:

> "I had written this about a very screwed up time in Europe, a time that from my point of view still seems strange; The Who too long on the road, me totally schizophrenic and everyone simply reacting by saying that I was schizophrenic. The song is a jibe at them, the band, the managers, the hangers-on, asking them if they know what it's like. It's a bitter piece, but powerful. Roger saw immediately what it was about when I tried to get him to do it on Face Dances and made me sing it myself. By the time I came to do The Who version I had forgiven everybody, or realised that they hadn't really been guilty of anything in the first place. When I sang this demo I meant it."

(Daltrey did end up singing The Who's version).

Not surprisingly, given Townshend's mood during the writing of both albums, *Face Dances* could be classed as being thematically close to *The Who By Numbers*: 'Did You Steal My Money' is almost the next logical step from 'How Many Friends'.

"The true story behind this doesn't make anyone look good – especially me," Pete said of 'Did You Steal My Money' in 2001. "It is not the time to tell it." When asked about the song's meaning today, he told the author, "It's private. But those involved know who they are, and we are friends again, and probably always were – it was only money after all. Quite a lot of money. But only money."

'Daily Records' contains a similar tone of introspection and self-pity as 'However Much I Booze':

> *I just don't quite know how to wear my hair no more*
> *No sooner cut it than they cut it even more*
> *Got to admit that I created private worlds*
> *Cold sex and booze don't impress my little girls*

"I think it was basically about the music drug," Pete recalled in February 1981. "That's all, just the fact that music does become like a drug and I can't get enough of it. It's not a testament to spending endless hours in smoky recording studios, it's about the business of making records, the business of using . . . it's about what I said, music being like a drug to me, to a great extent. When I say music, I suppose I mean songwriting."

Lines like *You still support me now, you love me anyhow, and I am still under your influence* and *I'm still amazed at your omnipotence* could be construed as a nod to Meher Baba despite the life Townshend was living when he wrote them.

'Another Tricky Day', which, along with Entwistle's two contributions, 'The Quiet One' and 'You' was sonically the closest the album got to the classic, guitar-oriented Who sound, touched on the same theme of despair:

> *Another tricky day*
> *Another gently nagging pain*
> *What the papers say*
> *Just seems to bring down heavier rain*
> *The world seems in a spiral*
> *Life seems such a worthless title*

'How Can You Do It Alone?' was inspired by Townshend's late night encounter with a flasher, which the lyrics recount in literal detail.

"I was actually going up Holland Park Road and I wanted a cigarette . . ." Pete recalled in 1982. "It was about two in the morning, and this guy came out of the station and I asked him for a light and he looked very afraid and he stepped back and I said, 'Listen, all I want is a light from your cigarette,' and he said, 'Oh, all right.' He opened his coat up and got a lighter out and before he'd known what he'd done, he was completely naked underneath . . . he was a flasher! He'd obviously just come off the tube doing a bit of flashing. He saw that I saw that he was naked and that I knew what he was up to. I looked into his eyes and he looked into mine, and the *shame* on his face!

"I felt like saying to him, 'Listen, don't be ashamed. I don't give a damn.' Then I was walking up the street and I thought I should have asked him, 'How do you do it all on your own? How do you live that solitary . . . how do you get your kicks?' Because that's more alone than masturbation. So I started to explore that idea and that turned into the song. How can you do anything on your own ultimately?"

"I quite liked The Who's rendering of this song," Townshend wrote in his liner notes to *Scoop 3*, which included the song's demo. "Roger sang it really well. But it is probably one of those songs that needed my acidic tone to work without awkwardness. Whichever version is your favourite [and you may hate both of them] it's good to be able to compare."

Aside from the songs appearing on the album, The Who also recorded 'I Like Nightmares' (sung by Townshend), 'It's In You', and 'Somebody Saved Me', a different version of which would appear on Pete's next solo album. Among the rejected demos was 'Zelda', an unusual song featuring synthesised strings, which Pete named after his niece, and 'Dirty Water', featuring Jones on drums, which ended up on *Scoop*. "I sang the vocal lying flat on my back on the studio floor," Townshend wrote. "The Who didn't record this song as it was too ordinary."

During an autumn break in recording, due to Szymczyk's injury in a car accident, shortly after which he was committed to mixing a live Eagles album, Townshend recorded a batch of demos, but was taken aback by the band's reaction. "I went and wrote four songs while everybody else was resting," he later recalled. "When I played them nobody said anything, not a dicky bird. Eventually Rabbit said, 'I like such and such a song, that has some good bits in it.' He was trying to be positive because he was aware of this big pregnant silence. I just picked up the tape and walked out. I thought, 'I'm not breaking my back for these cunts.' "

One of the demos (included on *Scoop*) was called 'Popular'. "The band reaction was lukewarm, we were close to ending the [*Face Dances*] album and were all unsure of what was happening," Townshend commented in

1983. "I later removed the 'Popular' chorus, replaced it with 'It's Hard' and managed to sell another song!"

Recording on *Face Dances* was wrapped up in late 1980, with the mixing done at Szymczyk's Bayshore Recording Studios in Coconut Grove, Florida. Townshend visited Bayshore to assist in the process, but he and the other band members weren't particularly pleased with the result, when it appeared in early March '81. "If we'd been there to mix it, it might have been a bit better," Entwistle lamented, "but I don't think it was actually on the tape anyway."

Townshend explained that his feelings for the album were "kind of mixed . . . I think the chemistry was wrong, and it wasn't just Bill Szymczyk.[9] I don't think we were really quite working together. Roger says that you could feel on *Face Dances* that the band wasn't a band."

Daltrey's frustration was largely aimed at Kenney Jones. When looking back on the album in 1994, Roger declared, "I love all the songs on *Face Dances*. Imagine if they had been played with a great drummer . . . listen to the drums on that album and you tell me if they're any fucking good."

Townshend, at the time, still stood loyally by his choice. "Kenney Jones has been a tremendous blood transfusion," he told *Oui* magazine's David Rothman in 1980. "Not just as a player – 'cause he's different from Keith, very much a fundamental backbone drummer – but he's a much more positive individual. Keith was a very positive musician, a very positive performer, but a very negative animal. He needed you for his act, on and off the stage. Kenney fits in very well as a person with the other guys in the band."

While taking more than his share of the blame for the album's shortcomings, Szymczyk commented in *The Record Producers*, "I have to tell you one thing, the songs that Pete Townshend wrote are just amazing, and when I can stand back from it and listen to it as a whole, the album is brilliant, and as a writer, Pete has grown by leaps and bounds. I think that Kenney Jones has been a great addition to the band, and I really love the record, but it was such a big deal to me that I can't be certain that I'm being completely objective about it."

Being the first post-Moon studio Who album, *Face Dances* fell victim to

---

[9] *Mojo* reported that "Szymcyk demanded that at least three replica recordings be made of each individual track, doing away with any spontaneity." Townshend defended Szymczyk's work in the *Scoop* liner notes. "Much has been said about *Face Dances*, especially by the band, some of it to the irritation of Bill Sz. He is a great producer."

extremely high expectations. Unfortunately, the album failed to justify the hype.

"It was ineffective; it didn't work," Townshend admitted. "I think the songs weren't right for the band. I can probably get more introspective and examine myself more on [solo] records than anybody else I know and get away with it. I can get all curled up in myself and people don't mind too much. Can't do that with The Who."

"As an album, *Face Dances* neither triumphs nor fails," *Rolling Stone* reported. "Instead, it makes you wonder if The Who, without social – i.e. internal – crises, have any reason for being." Ira Robbins, a staunch Who defender and editor of *Trouser Press*, was similarly unimpressed: "In context with The Who's enormous and illustrious body of work, *Face Dances* is a pleasant and rather meaningless album that proves, not The Who's continuing genius, but rather their ability to churn out 'product', watered down from their days of glory."

Despite a general thumbs down, *Face Dances* charted well, reaching number two in the UK, and four in the US – perhaps due to the inclusion of a hit single in 'You Better You Bet'.

The Who returned to the US in mid-June, commencing their summer tour in San Diego. After the show, Townshend punched a wall backstage in what he later told an interviewer was a moment of "sheer exuberance" and broke a finger on his right hand, requiring a cast and bandage for the rest of the tour. Again there was an overreliance on familiar past glories such as 'Substitute', 'I Can't Explain', 'Pinball Wizard', 'My Generation', and 'Won't Get Fooled Again'. Other less popular album tracks in the set included 'Drowned' and 'The Real Me' from *Quadrophenia*, and 'Music Must Change', 'Who Are You' and 'Sister Disco' from *Who Are You*. An early preview of material from *Face Dances* was played in the form of 'Another Tricky Day' and 'How Can You Do It Alone'.

The band performed seven sold out shows in LA prior to winding through the south for two weeks, playing to packed houses. However, Townshend's substance abuse caught up with him as the tour continued.

"Occasionally he would play brilliantly . . ." Barnes recalled in *Maximum R&B*. "More often, however, Pete would be so 'out of it' onstage that he would start to wander off on his own, jamming away at the end of numbers that the other three had thought had finished. Many of these guitar solos would catch Roger out and he would be left in the middle of the stage marking time and wondering what was happening. To a certain extent, I suspected that Pete would do this simply to wind Roger up, but many nights he just selfishly played away totally ignoring the other three . . .

"Pete was also taking a great deal of amphetamines to get him through the tour. However, it would mean that he would talk his head off after a show backstage. He was always the last to leave. One night he spoke for hours to some fans, who couldn't believe their luck at getting backstage and having Pete talk to them. Eventually, even they were exhausted by him and left. After talking about everything to everybody, there wasn't anybody remaining as it was about three in the morning. There was only our bodyguard, a driver and myself left. But Pete ended up talking for another hour to the cleaners as they seemed prepared to listen."

"I became involved in a much higher level of promiscuity than ever before," Townshend told *Penthouse* in 1983. "It was not through any increase in appetite. I was just so socially demented all the time that I didn't realise what I was doing. I was very gullible. When I was on the road, I would often wake up in the morning with a roomful of girls whom I'd never seen before, simply because I had been so drunk the night before that I didn't throw them out or politely ask them to leave or whatever it is that you do."

After the last show of the tour on July 16 at Toronto's CNE Stadium, the band attended an all-night party after which, thoroughly exhausted, they flew to New York to board Concorde for the trip back to England. Barnes described the eventful flight home in *Maximum R&B*:

"There was a particularly attractive blonde stewardess on board and every time she passed, Pete would make a determined but drunken lunge from his window seat and try to grab her. Every so often, he would stand up and attempt speeches, often attacking his fellow passengers. ''Ere we all are sitting 'ere travelling faster than a bullet in this supersonic rocket that I paid for with my fucking taxes . . .' and would quickly collapse. Then he took a liking to my meal and would scoop up a handful of lobster, chew it and start spitting it out at everybody nearby . . . The pretty blonde stewardess was removed to work behind a curtain up the front of the plane and the passengers nearby were all moved away. The stewards, however, were all smiles and didn't seem to notice, even when I almost had him in a headlock. The head steward came up and asked if the pilot could have his autograph. Pete started to write it in his wobbly hand and then with a flourish circled the autograph. He went on circling it for about five minutes, so that it looked like a large spiral had been

drawn on the page. The steward returned and was delighted, no doubt impressed at what an elaborate autograph Pete had.

"After leaving the Toronto party a kid in the street had presented him with a packet of cocaine. Pete threw the lot at his nose and it went all over him. Fellow passengers on Concorde probably thought that he had talcum powder all over his face and hair, not realising that it was really $100 worth of cocaine . . . Roger and I were concerned about Pete returning to his family covered in spilt wine, brandy, cocaine and bits of food. Roger found a clean T-shirt in his bag, which I took for Pete to change into. Unfortunately, Pete tossed it out of the car window after we left the airport."

Back in England, Townshend returned to a solitary life. "I lived away from my family for quite a long time," he said in 1982. "We have a house in the country, and I was living there, mainly . . . I spent a lot of time in the country working on a book of short stories and other times just knocking about with some of the London club scene people. I enjoy a lot of that life, in a way."

Pete recorded 'Driftin' Blues', which surfaced on *Another Scoop*, in the kitchen of the house.

"I can remember doing it," Pete told *Guitar Player* in 1989. "I had been living away from my wife for about nine months, had had a string of unsatisfactory relationships with young women, and was feeling like shit because I wasn't able to accept their love, either because I wasn't completely cut off from my wife or just because I wasn't man enough to do it. I was drinking a lot, I'd gone back to using cocaine, which I despised in other people, and I wasn't in very good spirits. I just started to play that song, and suddenly I just felt happy with myself. You know, I felt I had a friend in me. And I suddenly realised what the blues was.

"I was living alone at the time," he wrote in the *Scoop 3* liner notes. "I spent a lot of time at my big kitchen table, looking at the River Thames flowing by outside my windows. I used to knock out little songs like this, or short stories that I later published in *Horse's Neck*."

'A Death In The Day Of', a short story portraying a suicidal figure included in *Horse's Neck*, inevitably invites parallels to what one imagines to be an accurate depiction of Townshend's life during this period.[10]

---

[10] A reference to "the kids of Toxteth and Brixton", respective areas of Liverpool and London where riots broke out in the spring and summer of 1981, appears to date it to the winter of that year.

"I wake up about four or five in the afternoon; at this time of the year I rise in darkness. At better times I might awake with a lover, hopefully the one I really care about. The trouble is that the good times are inextricably tangled with the bad. If I am on the wagon I become reclusive and antisocial. I tear out the phone or, if forced to answer, pretend that I'm too ill to move. So if there is a lover, she will have slept with a drunk.

My days in London are not much use to anyone, but fun. I buy clothes, pop in to see friends and endure disturbing business appointments. Everyone is in the same boat: interest rates are running well over 22 per cent, I can't really catch up until they fall. In the evening I used to go and see a lot of bands, but at the moment I prefer a quiet dinner with a friend, and then a nightclub.

I have an office which I rarely visit. My secretary is ready to quit. She's seen too much of my self-obliterative nature. My wife, living separately (lucky thing), signs the bills. I have a studio, but most of the time other people use it. I suppose I get pleasure from that. Just now I can't work. Getting up so late, I have a short day. I live in a paradox: I feel comfortable with this unhappiness. I am content with misery.

Living by the river, I can row and I do this frequently. I have a sun bed. I sit under it and listen to Radio 4. In the summer the garden is wonderful. I grow vegetables and prune fruit trees.

I try to write every day. Solitude is vital . . . I read about six books at once so I can adjust my reading to my mood. If I'm feeling delicate, I might read P.G. Wodehouse or H.E. Bates. If I feel strong, I'll tackle biographies . . . I read fairly heavy stuff . . .

In spurts I answer fan mail and business letters, play snooker, strum my guitar into a cassette machine, pray for forgiveness and think about what a total mess I've made of a life that had everything, and everyone, going for it."

The character's desperation becomes increasingly evident:

And so, once more, to bed . . . the cask of grief that cracks as I lie back always brings tears . . .

What's the date? Does it matter? Nothing significant about today. What would I write if I were keeping a diary? 'Didn't want to live anymore', or 'I've always wanted to try it, just to see what it was like', or 'This showed you, didn't it, you load of bastards?' or 'Please water the plants'.

I imagine slashing my stomach and watching my guts emerge; I envisage a mirror image as I draw a rusty razor blade slowly across my throat from ear to ear. Then, simply swallowing a few tablets doesn't seem quite so bad.

Townshend maintains that the story's autobiographical nature has been overstated by some observers, telling the author, "My life, most of the time, was divided between the band, and my family. There was a very short period indeed when the pressure of my career and family became too much for me, between 1978 and 1981. During this time I occasionally parted with my wife for quite long periods and lived in our house in the country. My daughters sometimes came to stay with me, and we took vacations as a family. But my work load was colossal. 'A Death In The Day Of' could describe one of my days in the country, it could even be based on some diary pages. But it is a preposterous romanticism of my reality around that time.

"The truth about this time will only emerge when I properly engage it in my own memoirs. At that time I will have to trawl through my diaries, and speak to those with whom I came into contact, and try to put together an accurate account of what happened to me. It was only in the last few months of 1981 that I believe I really became delusional, although I had had many short periods of delusion from 1978 onwards because of my extremely heavy drinking."

If any further evidence were needed that Townshend's problems had reached a critical stage, The Who's extensive British tour in early 1981 removed all doubt. "Like every arsehole writer I felt that drinking was helping me to work or at least helping with some of the pressure I was going through . . .," he told Chris Salewicz in 1982. "I was drinking myself into oblivion in order not to face up to the fact that there were certain things I couldn't do and certain things I just didn't want to do. I wasn't running away from life but from particular issues."

While the previous year's US tour had been aimed at large arenas and stadiums, The Who chose to play in smaller theatres for the 26-date British tour which spanned seven weeks, beginning with a January 25 date at Leicester's Granby Halls. With *Face Dances* about to be released, 'You Better You Bet', 'Don't Let Go The Coat', 'The Quiet One', along with an occasional rendition of 'Did You Steal My Money?' were inserted into the setlist. Although Townshend managed to turn in an at least capable performance most nights, as with the American shows, his insobriety resulted in unexpected solos and diversions that caught the rest of the band offguard.

By now, Townshend's utter disdain at what The Who had become was beyond all doubt. "If touring is just getting up every night to play old favourites that I'd written out of my system years ago," he said at the time, "then I don't want to do it."

This disenchantment was notoriously demonstrated at two high-profile, fundraising shows The Who played on February 3 and 4 at London's Rainbow Theatre.[11] At both concerts, Townshend made an embarrassing display of himself, drinking a large quantity of brandy onstage. "I was so completely out of my brain that I actually humiliated the band in public . . . I kept stopping songs and making speeches to the audience," Townshend told *Penthouse* two years later. "I kept playing long, drawn-out guitar solos of distorted, bad notes. I'd alter the act, making up songs as I went along. And I knew it was London, and I knew that everybody's friends and family were there, and I deliberately picked that day to fuck up the show. I just ceased to care. I threw my dignity away."

Townshend's antics at the second night led Daltrey to throw his mike stand at the guitarist and storm offstage, followed by Jones and Entwistle. "Basically I decided to go out and not play," Pete told Chris Salewicz in 1982. "I was just going to talk until somebody stopped me from talking by knocking me out."

The inevitably heated confrontation in the dressing room brought things to a head as Townshend recalled, "Far from kicking my head in, Roger was worried I was killing myself. Roger's always said over the last year or so when I was going through a lot of shit, 'Listen, stop the band if it'll keep you alive. You're the important one to me.' I think what I was doing at the Rainbow was testing that."

"The English tour last year was just too much to take," Townshend said the following year. "We weren't playing well enough. And a lot of that was because I was pretty peculiar most of the time. I think we all were, though. And Roger was really having serious doubts about whether or not we should go on."

He further described his fragile state in August 1982 to the *NME*'s Paul Du Noyer: "Towards the end of [the UK tour], my mind started to turn

---

[11] The first show was a benefit for the Chiswick Family Rescue while the second aided Meg Patterson's financially beleaguered Pharmakon Clinic in Sussex. Patterson's memoirs state that both Townshend and Eric Clapton held separate benefit shows at the Rainbow during this period, raising £20,000. Unfortunately, the funds arrived too late to save the facility which closed in January 1981. Patterson then moved to California to continue her research.

inside out in a way, and I had almost decided to blow the London gigs. There was so much animosity around the band . . . anyway, after that I did cancel a European tour. I just said to everyone I wasn't ready to do it. I didn't really know what was going on in my head, but I could see trouble coming. And I started to work on my own record."

The final date on the English tour took place at the Poole Arts Centre, Sussex on March 16. Rumours circulated throughout the media that The Who's breakup was imminent and conventional wisdom had it that this was to be their last show. "Pete and Roger were both in great moods, laughing onstage," Barnes described in 1982. "It was a tremendous show and the audience, which numbered only 2,000 [due to the venue's small size] were wildly enthusiastic . . . Later at the stage door, a large crowd of fans waited, many in floods of tears, to thank the band and implore them not to break up."

The only remnant of the cancelled European tour took place in late March as The Who appeared in a live TV and radio simulcast from Essen, Germany for *Rockpalast*. Appearing on the bill were The Grateful Dead and after The Who's set, a chemically enhanced Townshend joined the Dead onstage for one of their trademark marathon jam sessions, which ended shortly before dawn.

Meanwhile, work on Townshend's solo album was at a near standstill. Producer Chris Thomas was also growing increasingly concerned at Townshend's cocaine use and the effect it was having on his voice, and attempts at recording were, according to Barnes, "going very slowly. Progress could usually be made only on Mondays and Tuesdays after a weekend of rest. By Wednesday, [Pete] was already exhausted from his destructive nocturnal lifestyle. Chris Thomas remembers one day talking to Pete at the mixing desk, only to realise that Pete had been sitting at the controls fast asleep. Pete got stranger and stranger, dropped his friends, had gone in for a succession of unflattering haircuts, taken to wearing makeup . . . and was 'generally weird'."

On April 7, Kit Lambert died, aged 45, from an irreparable brain haemorrhage which he'd sustained from falling down the stairs at his mother's house. The fact that he'd been beaten up in a nightclub earlier that evening was a major contributing factor. The news reached Pete, "right in the middle of a period when I was in New York," Townshend said in 1984. "There had been no contact for a long time, but I still adored him," although he later admitted to Andrew Motion that, "I didn't feel very much at the time."

While he missed Lambert's funeral, Townshend arranged a memorial service on May 11 (what would have been Lambert's 46th birthday) at St Paul's Church, in Covent Garden. "[Pete] organised about 100 members of the London Symphony Orchestra to perform," Motion wrote in *The Lamberts*, "they played 'some of *Tommy*, music by Constant, and Kit's favourite piece of Purcell, *The Gordian Knot Untied*' – and gave one of the two addresses."

After the service, a contingent of mourners, including Townshend and Chris Stamp, "had a bash in a studio in Covent Garden," Pete told Motion. "We went from this beautiful elevated atmosphere, to this seedy place with cheap wine and beer and all the low lives together snorting coke in some back alley. Chris was saying, 'It's what Kit would have wanted,' but I wasn't sure. Something around that time happened to me, and I turned away from the light and faced the darkness. I felt I had to experience a shadow of the suffering and isolation that Kit had had. When he died I felt I'd lost the last sense of everything coming into my life; I felt from now on I was never, never going to get topped up again. On one hand it made me want to kill myself, on the other it made everything come together. It was so beautiful."

CHAPTER THIRTEEN

1981–1982

*"It's very, very difficult to live in the present. If you can live in the
present, it's a divine quality. It leads to selflessness, it leads to happiness,
it leads to a smiling face. It might lead to what a lot of people feel is kind
of almost like hippie-esque, dopey consciousness. I don't aspire to that, I
aspire to living in the present, accepting what I am and where I am and
what's happening to me and trying to make the best of it. That is what I
was fighting, I think, for such a long time, was actually what I was. I've
always said that happiness is not something which anybody has a right to
at all, and if you get 10 per cent of it a day, you should be delighted."*

– Pete Townshend, 1985

O N May 30, Townshend participated in an all-day concert (billed
as 'Rock Against Unemployment') at Brockwell Park, Brixton,
arranged by the Trades Union Congress as part of the People's March For
Jobs campaign. Pete's band, featuring Mark Brzezicki, Tony Butler, and
Peter Hope-Evans, performed 'A Little Is Enough' (two versions since
Townshend apparently wasn't happy with the first), 'Cat's In The Cup-
board', 'Big Boss Man', 'Substitute', 'Corrina Corrina', 'Body Language',
'Join Together', and 'Let My Love Open The Door'. Pete openly quaffed
Remy Martin straight from the bottle throughout the show.

A much-needed wake-up call arrived soon after when Townshend discovered that his Eel Pie business group was in severe financial trouble.
"What happened to arrest me was that the money ran out," he told Dennis
Wholey in *The Courage to Change*. "If there was an act of God in this
whole thing, which I call a miracle, it was that." Desiring a new mixing
desk during work on his next solo album, Pete discovered that he not only
had no money for the £130,000 desk, but that he was also in debt to
several banks, owing a total of over £500,000.

"I went to the bank and said, 'Listen, I've got to get this record finished.'" Townshend recalled. "They said, 'No, you can't have any more money.' The fact that Pete had kept the same bank account since the beginning of art school didn't assist his plight. "I said, 'Come on . . . all I have to do is deliver the record and they'll give me two million dollars. So if we can just finish the record . . .' No, we're not going to give you any more money."

The Eel Pie companies had virtually run themselves into the ground, and the bank was seeking some security. "The National Westminster Bank wanted my bollocks," Townshend recalled, "despite the fact that I'd put every personal penny I had into the company to keep it afloat they wanted more. They wanted my house, they wanted my recording contract, my record label. I was caught in an incredible cleft stick; I'd not wanted to blow the money I had on mansions or Rolls-Royces or homes in LA, because I thought it was much better to create jobs or put the money into something which helps other people create, and to accept that this was part of my responsibility. But then I was unable to follow it through, either because I was so fucked up, or distracted, or simply not here because I was on the road with The Who. Also the people I'd appointed to do the work thought there was an endless supply of money . . . people were spending my money faster than I could earn it."

The royalties and profit Townshend received from tours and record sales were simply unable to surmount Eel Pie's losses. "I was selling records. I sold a lot of copies of *Empty Glass*, and The Who's first album for Warner Brothers, *Face Dances*. I had money coming in, of course, because a songwriter is buffered. The record was selling in 1979 and I'd be getting money in 1984. I certainly didn't need to steal an old lady's handbag to get my bottle of Remy or my drugs. But then my book publishing company went to the wolves, and it took every penny I had with it – about a million dollars. I had not supervised the company and it had no separate bank of its own. It was badly managed, overstaffed, over-invested, and contracts were too generous to authors; on the other hand, we did some good stuff and I'm very proud of it. But the company collapsed."

Simply going on the road wouldn't raise enough money, even if Townshend made it through another tour intact which, given his condition, wasn't guaranteed. "When I realised that I couldn't earn a million dollars after tax in a year," he told *Penthouse*, "I started to go round and round in circles, getting very upset at the idea of having to sack people."

The situation did at least have one positive outcome as Pete recalled, "I had to go back to Karen and say, 'Can we raise money on the house? Can you sign this piece of paper, which allows the bank to do this and that? Can we sell our country home? Can we at least borrow against our country home?' And she said, 'Before I sign this piece of paper, maybe we could talk about us.'"

"I was getting used to living away from my family," Townshend told Paul Du Noyer in 1982. "It was a mistake, which both my wife and I realise now, but it was something we were trying out. But it didn't protect the kids from my lunacy which I was going through, and it didn't help my old lady, and it didn't help me."

Although Townshend with hindsight points to his dire financial state as the turning point, his two-year spiral into depression and drug addiction continued unabated. His alcoholism had reached the point where he drank a glass of brandy each morning, "because it was the only thing that would make me feel normal," he told Dennis Wholey. "Wouldn't make me high, wouldn't make me low, just make me feel normal. It would stop my feeling sick."

In a 2001 entry on Townshend's website he wrote, "By 1981 my quite restrained cocaine use had nonetheless allowed the quantum increase in my intake of brandy to around three bottles a day. I drank it neat; I loved it so much I used to sometimes sleep with a Remy Martin bottle in my arms like a pet cat. Predictably, I started to become ill."

"Pete would often take Concorde to New York only to spend most of his time sleeping in some hotel suite," Barnes wrote in *Maximum R&B*. "He got very friendly with Bowie,[1] and once passed out in the cloakroom of Mick Jagger's Manhattan apartment after a night's drinking with Mick and Charlie [Watts]."

Townshend bumped into a familiar face during one New York visit – his brother-in-law who was experiencing his own marital problems at the time. "I saw Pete while I was out partying in New York one night," Jon Astley recalls, "and we both kind of went – double take, you know. 'What the fuck are we doing?' We were both abusing ourselves."

On one of Townshend's transatlantic Concorde flights, there was engine trouble. "I understand it wasn't a near-death incident at all," Pete recalled in early 2000, "but it certainly felt like that to Elton John. When

---

[1] "We went out on two occasions," Townshend told Stuart Grundy and John Tobler in 1983. "I like him because he's very intelligent, but he's also very relaxed and easy company, not the glamorous distant figure some of his fans imagine him to be. He took me to this Japanese restaurant and I went into shock when he ordered the food in Japanese!"

we got down on the ground, I said to him, 'It must have been horrible for you – some woman up in your cabin was screaming her head off.' He said, 'That was me, darling!'"

In early September, Townshend went out drinking in London at the Club For Heroes, at 1 Baker Street, with near-disastrous results. "It was the first time I'd spent any time with Paul Weller and his girlfriend, and they were being so nice to me," Pete told *Q* magazine in 1996. "Anyway, [Thin Lizzy bassist/leader] Phil Lynott said, 'I can give you something to perk you up.' I held out my arm, had the injection, and the next thing I know was that I was being carted away."

Several accounts name Lynott as the guilty party, but in 2000, Pete said, "I don't know that it was Phil Lynott. I think Phil and I went down to do some coke, but there were five or six other people there." Townshend told the author that "someone injected me with a speedball [a mixture of cocaine and heroin] when I was extremely drunk. I had told them I was a seasoned user for some insane reason."

A bouncer carried Pete's unconscious body out of the club and deposited him on the back seat of his car while Townshend's driver, Paul Bonnick tore through the traffic to reach the nearest hospital.

"When they carried me into the hospital, I was dark blue," Townshend said. "The nurse said my heart had stopped beating. They gave me a massive cortisone injection, and it didn't work. They gave me another one under the chest, and they were about to give me an electric shock, and I came round. I think I owe my life to my driver, Paul. He said, 'We've got to get Pete to a hospital.'"

The comparisons with Keith Moon's descent were now eerily apparent. Townshend stopped work on his solo album in October.

"I gave up," he told Dennis Wholey. "I went to Chris Thomas and said, 'Stop the record. I'm going to take three months off.' It was crazy, but I was tired. I had worked very hard and done a lot of writing and I wasn't very healthy. There was a doctor looking after me and I was doing a lot of exercise, so I was alive by the skin of my teeth. I was in reasonably good shape, but I was drinking a hell of a lot and not eating very well, staying out late and fucking people around. I felt the best thing to do was stop and regroup. I went to New York and spent a week there. I came back. I got in with a guy who was deeply into free-basing cocaine, and I started to dabble in that, still drinking very heavily all the time.

"Then I went to work with Elton John in November 1981 [playing on 'Ball And Chain' off Elton's *Jump Up* album]. I went to Paris. I took my mother and father and a girl I was seeing at the time and a few friends. I would go to the studio at nine o'clock in the morning, run through a tune with the guys in the band, and Elton would come about midday. We'd work until nine. Then I'd go out to a club, come back to the hotel, and spend some time with this unbelievable woman. God only knows what she was doing there. About 5 a.m. I would get the energy from some- where to get out of bed and go and say hello to the minibar. I would drink the soft drinks, the tomato juice, the Perrier, that horrible French lemon juice, then go through the brandy, the wine, and think, 'Fuck it, the grain, let's have some of the grain.' In the end there would be nothing in the fridge. It would be about 7 or 8 a.m. and I had drunk everything. So I would ring up and get some breakfast. The next day I would do the same thing. I don't think I have ever, ever, ever been quite that bad, and yet I didn't feel any remorse about what I was doing. I didn't know that what I was doing was particularly exceptional."[2]

Coincidentally, Betty Townshend had recently been treated for alco- holism. "She was actually the person who made me think about starting to treat myself as an alcoholic . . . She decided she'd had enough, and she stopped. And I knew, this time, that she'd stopped for life. They said it probably would be a good idea if she didn't go home straight away, so she came to live with me. And two things happened: first, I was really inspired by her, and I wanted to show solidarity by stopping myself, once and for all. But also, a lot of my excuses were taken away. There's absolutely no question of it being genetic, anyway; I couldn't really say, 'Oh, it's because everybody in my family is a drunk, that's why I'm a drunk.'"

"I approached my doctor just after Halloween in 1981 asking for help with my drinking," Townshend told the author. "I had just done a recording session with Elton John in Paris and I was starting to get full-blown delirium-tremens [DTs]. My doctor referred me to a lovely fellow who treated me with hypnotherapy, I am a good subject and it worked. I stopped drinking. However he also prescribed fabulous Ativan that I quickly became stuck on, but which soon stopped working. At one point that winter I switched to heroin, which seemed to me to replicate Ativan [now a restricted drug I believe]."

"Now these Ativans were really the business," Pete told *Penthouse*.

---

[2] Richard Barnes wrote in *Maximum R&B* that Townshend ended his stint in Paris "by throwing up his champagne into the ice bucket in the restaurant of the exclusive Hotel Georges."

"They made me feel incredibly good. I felt as if I could cope with everything."

"I just took anything I could lay my hands on," he said in 1982. "I hated the sensation of not being drunk."

"Someone would be freebasing, and you'd see them puff in a bit of burning junk through a straw," Townshend told Chris Salewicz. "And that's it! A lot of people don't realise you are going to get addicted to heroin instantly by smoking it. If you snort it you don't get addicted instantly, but if you smoke it you do. It's not as dramatic as sitting at a party and drawing out a hypodermic and banging it in your arm, but it's the same thing. What was incredible to me was to watch the pushers sweetly come in and say, 'I've got some nice stuff here, but it's not good enough for snorting, it's really for smoking.' And that was it. At least 50 people I know got addicted in the space of six months last year."

"I went to New York, I needed something . . . I just replaced the booze with drug abuse," Townshend said in 1984. "I was still very, very fucked up. I came back and went to my doctor and said, 'I've got a serious problem with drugs. I'm getting more into drugs. I'm not drinking, but I've got to do something about the other drugs' . . . I was using the whole prescription [of Ativan] at once. Then I would get another supply from a dealer. I wasn't drinking, but I was still using coke, free-basing it. I was smoking heroin, too, quite a lot of it, which I was buying privately and doing completely in secret. Nobody knew except me. I would take two or three Ativan tablets when the heroin wore off, plus sleeping pills. I remember going to see my parents around Christmas time, and my Dad said to me, 'You say you're not drinking?' I said, 'No, no, no. I haven't had a drink for a month now.' He said, 'You're on something and it's a damn sight worse, in my opinion.' And he got up and walked out. He was the only person who seemed to know that something was fatally wrong."

The rest of Pete's family had no idea what was going on. "We were all blissfully unaware," Simon Townshend confirms. "Because Pete came over very rarely, maybe Christmas, couple of times a year . . . when he'd actually given up was when everyone found out. Realistically, if he was using drugs, he was probably having periods where he was off it, trying to get clean, 'cause that's how it works, it's a sort of cycle and I think perhaps those were the times he would come over, during those good periods."

"At the end of 1981, I started to get into real difficulties and I missed my family a lot," Pete recalled in 1984. "I suddenly realised that I couldn't live without my wife, and she was falling right out of love with me. I couldn't handle that."

The holiday season brought a contrite, dejected Townshend back to his family, privately pleading for help. "I went back to Karen and my kids," Pete recalled in a 1985 radio interview, "and I said, 'I don't think I should really stay. I'll go and stay at the country place and I'll come back again tomorrow.' And she said, 'No, stay,' and I said, 'Well listen, the point is that I'm using smack at the moment and I don't think I should be around the house,' and she said, 'No, you stay anyway.' I think that was the thing that really triggered it for me, the fact that I thought I was a worthless piece of crap, not worthy to be in the house that I'd bought, with the family that I'd brought into the world and sustained and fed, and all that stuff, and yet they, particularly my wife, didn't feel that way. I think it was that gesture that meant such a lot to me and I immediately determined that, in fact, in the rest of the sentence I said, 'OK, I'm addicted now, but I mean to get off as soon as the New Year comes.'"

Pete was floored by his wife's compassion. "It's a golden opportunity to demonstrate unconditional love for somebody," he said three years later. "You're faced with somebody who feels such a low sense of their own value that they've turned to drugs, they've destroyed themselves and they stand before you and you say, 'Well, still, come home every night, we don't care if you're a junkie, come and stay with us. Steal the silver if you want to. It's you we care about.' Now how many opportunities do you get to demonstrate that kind of unconditional love? I always urge people that I come across to do what Karen did for me."

By early 1982, Meg Patterson had been active in the field of drug and alcohol rehabilitation for more than a decade with her Neuro-Electric Therapy (N.E.T.), or 'Black Box' treatment, claiming a 98 per cent detoxification success rate. Having settled with her husband George in Corona del Mar, just south of Los Angeles, she was continuing her research in the hope of obtaining US Food and Drug Administration approval, when Townshend approached her asking for help. According to her memoirs, she dispatched her clinician son, Lorne, to accompany Pete during his flight to the US, although Townshend told the author that "my guitar tech Alan Rogan travelled with me and looked after me half the time, Lorne Patterson looked after me the other half of the time."

Townshend also revealed that he took a massive dose of heroin to get through the flight to California. The Pattersons brought an N.E.T.

stimulator with them when they drove to the airport, anticipating Pete to be in steep withdrawal. "I could see from his agitated appearance that he was desperately ill and craving as he came out of the customs area, so I hooked him up to the machine right away," Meg Patterson wrote in 1994. "I was horrified to discover that he was also hooked on Ativan, a tranquiliser which could well cause convulsions when it was stopped. But it was late at night and not possible to change arrangements. We had two hours' drive to the flat and before we reached there he had demonstrably calmed down."

During his detox and rehabilitation, Townshend stayed – under constant supervision – in a small rented flat near the Pattersons' residence. Pete spoke in great detail about his experiences in an interview with *Omni* magazine editor Kathleen McAuliffe, which was published in *Penthouse* in August 1983.

"The first frequencies they gave me were low ones for heroin," he told McAuliffe. "I think it was kept on that setting for about eight hours . . . I just got this sense of a natural energy flowing into my body. It was as if all sorts of dormant feelings were being rekindled. The inner joy of recovery, and becoming independent from drugs, it produced this tremendous feeling of rejuvenation. By the second day, in fact, I knew I was on the home stretch."

On the second day of his treatment, Pete was reminded of the severity of drug withdrawal when the nine-volt battery in the electrical stimulator went dead.

"We were totally unaware of this until it became clear that I was going into steep withdrawals," he recalled. "I got the full belt of the symptoms back – the panic, the nose-running and fantastic cramps, particularly in my arms and legs. When they got the machine working again, I got only some of the symptoms – and they were less severe. I got a runny nose and I did have muscle cramps. I had a certain amount of difficulty sleeping, but it wasn't too bad, really. I felt fairly warm. But most important of all, I got back the ability to act."

Townshend wore the 'black box' throughout the first seven days, and then wore it only during the day for the last three days, being able to obtain restful sleep unaided by this point.

"On the third day I started to look and feel human again," he told McAuliffe. "I started to read newspapers and to write about the way I felt. I remember writing things like, 'I want to go out for a walk. I don't believe it.' I could really feel my passion for life returning. Another thing was that I'd had traces of returning sexuality . . . for about a month, maybe two months, before being treated I'd felt no sexual feelings whatsoever, so the treatment definitely had a rekindling effect . . .

"But then on the fourth day, I woke up with this aggressive, angry attitude toward life. No, arrogant is perhaps a better word. I believed that I could take on the world. Later on, though – on the fifth day, I believe – I started to get depressed. Meg would then turn the machine up to a high frequency for an hour or so to stimulate the cocaine-type receptors in the brain. And if it was left on too long at this setting, I would start babbling away and everything in the room would start to go *wooooooo*. The intensification of colour and sound, often in a very pretty way, was just like acid. But there was no confusion of sense channels – that didn't happen. I really felt up until the next day, when I woke up nauseous and achy. A lot of the withdrawal symptoms had actually returned in their own shape."

After 10 days of N.E.T. the detoxification was complete. Townshend's mood stabilised and the black box was removed, resulting in "very, very minor withdrawals". He entered the rehabilitation phase of his treatment, undergoing three weeks of psychotherapy with Dr Patterson, focusing on emotional and spiritual redevelopment.

"When you first start to recover you feel superhuman," Pete told McAuliffe. "You get swept away by the euphoria of the natural high and the feeling of being able to handle any crisis . . . The feeling of *I'm going to get this lot behind me*. But this is where I think Meg is so clever. It seems she understood that, and in the month I stayed with her she helped me to sublimate that and balance it – in other words, not to overreact, and thus swing the pendulum too far in the other direction. She constantly stressed the spiritual rebuilding I had to do, which I'm still dealing with: the importance of getting closer to my children again, and if it was possible – and at the time it didn't look like too hot a situation – to re-establish my relationship with my wife."

By the third week, Townshend's appearance had remarkably improved. "People who had seen me taking brisk walks would come up to me on the street and say, 'That's California for you. When you first arrived you looked like a corpse. We gave you half an hour to live. And now look at you. All you needed was a few days in California."

"Pete made a remarkable recovery considering how far gone he had been, both in London and when he arrived in Los Angeles," Patterson recalled in *Dr Meg*. "Again, it was not enough simply to detoxify from his drugs of addiction, for his return to drugs had been caused by a variety of problems which had to be sorted out to effect a real cure. Some of these were begun while he was in Los Angeles, such as the agreement of his wife to help him by trying to make their broken marriage work again, and the sorting out of his complex business affairs."

On the last day of his rehab programme, Townshend and a friend were walking along Laguna Beach, just south of Corona Del Mar where he was staying, when they came upon a medical bottle which had washed ashore.

"I said, 'That bottle is full of cocaine,'" Townshend recalled in a 1989 radio interview. "I said, 'I just know that the devil is here now.'"

The pair examined the bottle and Pete's friend tasted it. Sure enough, it was cocaine, probably thrown from an inbound boat whose crew had been startled by an approaching customs craft.

"I said, 'Give it back to me,'" Townshend continued, "and I just threw it into the sea, and he went, 'NOOOOOOOO Pete!'"

Townshend considered 'Laguna, Valentine's Day, 1982' the "most optimistic" story in *Horse's Neck*, explaining that it served "to kind of explain what I was going through."

> "*I sit in a small armchair upholstered in an understated flower pattern and contemplate the view. Before me stretches a vast, shining beach covered with dry sand. There is no wind. In the distance I can see the edge of an ocean that stretches away to a horizon that seems unusually high and straight . . .*
>
> "*In the distance I can see two tiny figures on horses by the water's edge . . . The riders in the distance are much closer now, and I can see that they have a mount for me on a rein. It is a white horse . . .*[3]

The character penetrates the horse as a metaphor for the banishing of his demons and thus becomes one with what is often a symbol of purity and beauty throughout the book.

> *. . . When my orgasm comes, it is without sensation. I am no longer an animal . . . At last I can ride. I am in perfect control. I urge the horse into a gallop and the wind cools my face. I am riding towards the water's edge.*"[4]

After 30 days with Meg Patterson in California, in mid-February, Townshend began weekly psychotherapy in Britain in a continuation of

---

[3] Delia DeLeon wrote that "Baba was known as the 'White Horse' or 'Kali' Avatar by His Hindu followers."

[4] "Somebody said to me when they finished reading *Horse's Neck*, 'You know, people are going to think you really fucked the horse!'" Pete revealed in 1989.

his rehabilitation.[5] He compared emerging from rehab to "like walking out of darkness. And this feeling that what I'd thought of as darkness was actually just standing in a door and *facing* darkness," he told the *Sunday Times'* Mick Brown in 1985. "We're in that doorway all our lives, and what life is about is deciding which way you face.

"I'd become the personification of my own worst fears, and I really wanted to be beaten for it. But I was staggered to find that people did not want to beat me or piss on me; neither, it seemed, did they want to ignore me. What came from the media, in fact, was a tremendous compassion and a desire that I get myself together. That wasn't what I expected at all, and it helped me to realise that I wasn't in the hole I thought I was."

On returning from America, Townshend moved back in with his family and set about rebuilding his marriage.

"Karen said I could stay in the family house in the basement," Pete told Dennis Wholey in 1984. "I stayed there for a couple of weeks and eventually we got close enough together to be able to rebuild the family atmosphere very quickly. It was hard for Karen but the kids were able to erase the problems completely. I just hope that, over a period of years, it hasn't left them with any scars. But, certainly, as far as my being there, they made me know it was great 'to have you back, Dad.' They made a big fuss over me and made it clear that they really enjoyed having me around. The terrible, terrible nightmare turned back into normality."

Pete obviously deeply regretted his actions over the last two years which had taken a toll on his family. "I just wish the consequences hadn't been so fucking hard for the third parties involved," he told *Musician* in 1989. "There are advantages and disadvantages to the life I've led. The kids have financial security but there was a time when they suffered a certain amount of fear and deprivation as a direct result of my behaviour. We try to talk about it regularly. Awful, awful thing to contemplate. You don't want to hurt anyone in your life but when you do . . . At least my old lady knew I was in a rock'n'roll band when we got married. She knew I was an arsehole. It's not like that with kids. They're born and they're subjected to all this shit."

Along with regaining the love of his children, Pete and Karen managed

---

[5] Townshend revealed to the author that the Patterson family did not charge him for his treatment because he had been their patron. Meg Patterson died on July 25, 2002 after suffering a stroke. For further information on Dr Patterson's life and NET, visit www.drmeg.net.

to rekindle their relationship. "Really, apart from a few ups and downs, we never suffered any major problems until the last couple of years," Townshend commented that April, "and we both feel that one of the problems was that I did overcommit when I took on a solo career. It was a great strain. And living in the same house and everything, we literally became estranged – we were like strangers. And it was only when I actually became so ill that I couldn't work that we had the time to sit down and talk. And then we stopped being strangers and we became friends and lovers again, and life is back to the way it was. Our marriage was made in heaven, there's no question about it. But you've got to work at marriage, and it's a different kind of work from what you do normally, and it's got a different end product. I'm sure this stuff is familiar as hell to everybody else, but it's all new to me.

"Anyway, once I stopped taking everything – not just drinking, but doing *anything* at all – and started to be careful about my diet and got into a routine of regular exercise, the transformation was instant. Now I feel superhuman. Also, I had managed, with a lot of assistance from my wife, to re-establish myself in the family, and that's great for me. I mean, it's something I desperately missed."

Another facet of Townshend's personal life which needed reaffirming was his spiritual beliefs.

"It's very hard to talk about," he told *Musician* in September 1982, "because . . . it's very easy to look like you have some kind of phony humility. But Meher Baba's teachings on the subject were expressly clear, and my conviction for Meher Baba as the pinnacle and focus of spiritual wisdom in the West is paramount in my life. His statement is that whatever you do, however small or big you feel yourself to be, you're always a channel and a servant of God. Even if you're a *rat*, you've got the hotline to God. Even rats are servants of God whether they know it or not . . . I'm *embarrassed* to be in God's presence – not afraid. Once I would've been ashamed, but not now."

His personal life thus realigned, Townshend next faced the daunting task of getting his finances back in order. "What had gotten me into so much trouble to begin with was my refusal to face up to various problems," he told *Penthouse*. "So one of the first things I did after getting back was deal with the bank. I gave them my record contract and said, 'Listen, hold on to that. Don't charge me any interest. I'll get on with delivering the record and you just take the lot. I'll pay you over three or four years.' I also sold a lot of assets. I closed my bookshop and sound equipment company. I sacked a few people. I raised the rates at my recording studios. I cut down on personal spending. I sold my Ferrari and my boat.

"I also managed to convince the guys in the band that I would stay alive if they allowed me to work with them again. After the Rainbow fiasco, I had difficulty proving to Roger in particular that I was going to enjoy working with The Who, and that it was important to me that the band end properly, rather than end because of my fucking mental demise. I love the group. What I couldn't stand was the tension of not knowing when it was going to end. I just had to know when it would finish. I couldn't stand the indecision. So we agreed to wind everything down between 18 months and two years from that time . . . I have to be very careful about my tendency to overwork. I really know how much I'm capable of now."

Because he had put so much hard work and money into it, the hardest blow to Townshend was scaling down the Meher Baba Oceanic Centre. In a 2001 essay posted on Townshend's website, he wrote that Oceanic ". . . had in any case slowed down to a crawl while I descended into self-obsession. Several of my employees there had gone through problems of their own, and some time in 1982, I impolitely sacked everyone. I then shut down the living quarters and confined the Meher Baba Association to a single room in the building. They moved within a year to new premises they still occupy in Shepherd's Bush in London."

Townshend's overdue solo album was taking longer than expected due to a substantial amount of material being rewritten after the initial tracks had been laid down the previous year. "Originally, I did a series of experiments, basically just rhythm tracks with poetry over the top," he told *Rolling Stone*'s Kurt Loder in 1982. "When I took the first tracks to New York and played them for the record company, you would have paid money to have seen their faces! They said, 'Leave it to the avant-garde.' Bowie was with me at the time and he said I should just go ahead and do it, what do the record companies know, anyway. But I came back and rewrote half the album. 'Cos there's little point in sitting and writing material, and getting obsessed with whatever you choose to get obsessed with, and then have nobody to listen."

Ironically, due to problems obtaining studio time at either of his own recording venues, Pete resorted to using other locations to put his demos on tape. In addition to using the small studio in his new home (located just a short walk east from his former dwelling on Twickenham's Embankment) he recorded several demos on a 120-foot long Dutch canal barge on the Thames.

In February, sessions resumed on what became *All The Best Cowboys Have Chinese Eyes*, at Eel Pie with work being completed by April in the familiar surroundings of AIR and Wessex studios. The production and engineering services of Chris Thomas and Bill Price were retained, as were drummers Mark Brzezicki and Simon Phillips, bassist Tony Butler, and harmonica player Peter Hope-Evans. Chris Stainton, who'd played piano on several *Quadrophenia* tracks, assumed keyboard duties, along with Townshend's sister-in-law, Virginia Astley. Jody Linscott contributed percussion while Ann O'Dell arranged the brass on 'The Sea Refuses No River'.

"At that particular time I decided I wanted a band of women," Townshend told Paul Du Noyer, "and that was basically because I was fed up with men. I really was. I was fed up with male sensibilities. I was fed up with fighting for everything I wanted, sometimes physically fighting. I was fed up with the macho music press . . . and I was under the misapprehension that maybe if I surrounded myself with female players that a lot of that would recede."

Chinese Eyes focused on the principles Townshend considered to be of the utmost importance in his life. "When I started *Empty Glass* . . . I was hoping that I was going to pursue two careers at once, not realising that they're irrevocably knotted together. I hadn't quite realised how much what I did as an individual would affect The Who, and vice versa. The new album was a big difference, in the approach to it and with the ruthlessness with which I had to deal with The Who, with everything around me, in order to get it made. It's actually a recognition of . . . a commitment to a set of principles which I've debated over the last 10 years: the importance of a family, the importance of my role with my peers and the band, the importance of my freedom of self-expression, and lastly but not at all least, the importance of becoming actively immersed again, for only the second time in my life (and the last time was when I was 17) in politics. I really do feel that I can't sit and watch any longer."

Townshend's political activism, which had been rekindled after the Rock Against Racism concert, was aimed at the current apathy he saw.

"I get worried about people, who right now more than ever, believe they are impotent, that they are powerless, that the circumstances of hierarchical control, of apparent control of our planet, are irrevocably destined to fail," he told *Musician*. "I think that is a mistake, because if the individual feels he can't change anything, then what is the point of being alive? You can be a *rat* and still change the world."

When *Spin*'s Kristine McKenna asked Townshend to define sin, he replied, "Waiting for things to get better. Saying 'Look to the future, things will get better.' That's as much a sin as saying things will be awful in the future because the future doesn't count. What counts is now, and this moment does shape the future. If you look out at the city you live in and see that it's full of garbage you should whistle a happy tune like a character in a Disney cartoon and start collecting the garbage. To sit at your window and say that someday someone will come and clear up all the garbage is bullshit. And a sin."

This attitude was reflected in his opinion of contemporary Britain in the early Eighties. "I suppose what's lacking is the depth," he told *Musician* in 1982, "and the commitment to the depth you put in. You know, if you put in too much, people become almost embarrassed! I don't know how it is over in the States, but over here if you try to get in a conversation about arms build-up or nuclear weapons, people turn away and order another pint of Guinness, and they want to talk about bloody Arsenal! They're gonna be dead tomorrow if they don't start thinking about it . . . but they're *embarrassed*; 'It's annoying – oh, don't talk about *that*! We're impotent, we're neutered.' Now *that* is what's happened to rock'n'roll. People have actually started to say, 'What's the point of trying to make a really great record, when we know that just a well-constructed, well-produced piece of crap is gonna sell six million copies, and everybody's gonna think we're great.' And to be brutal for a second, I think one of the dangers of middle age in rock'n'roll is that it's very easy to take the easy way out. You have to be very angry, in a sense, to stay honest."

Townshend felt it was part of an artist's responsibility, "always to challenge, but first he must gain the public's ear and heart by making an attractive offering," he told *Spin* in 1986. "Entertaining first, challenging and inviting debate later . . . I want to please people, then possibly slip them something that I feel I've been able to make some kind of acute judgment about."

Chinese Eyes concerns Townshend's recent personal upheavals more than any form of political activism. The album's opener, 'Stop Hurting People', delivered in an almost theatrical spoken voice, was, as Pete explained in 1982, a plea to be reunited with his wife. "I wrote it last summer. I suddenly broke down and scribbled it out on a piece of paper, and didn't realise until later quite to what an extent it was a prayer." The song was a strident declaration of the power of love (*Love conquers poses, love smashes stances, love crushes angles into black*) and a statement of determination. (*A love born once must soon be born again.*)

Like 'Empty Glass' from Townshend's previous album, 'The Sea Refuses No River' was inspired by Eastern literature, specifically the poetry enjoyed by Meher Baba. "His interest in this poetry led me to go and look at it," Townshend said in 1996. "I was very struck by the use of wine as an analogy for God's love, and therefore by association that the tavern is the heart. The tavern is the place where you receive God's wine, and what you have to do is you have to hold up an empty cup – which is where I got the title of my first album – in order to receive. Anyway, this song is about all of the different qualities of love, and I remember once Meher Baba freely interpreting a poem about the fact that if God's love is wine, then human love is like water, and lust is like the stuff that runs into the sewer, but that in the end it all combines in this huge ocean which is the infinite presence of God, and therefore it's all subsumed and mixed and one. And that's what the song is about."

A 1932 Baba quote reflects a similar sentiment:

Baba is like the sun . . . anyone whose heart is pure can receive the rays. Make the heart pure by thinking of the Master, and then loving Him.

Baba is like the sea, which receives weak or strong, diseased or healthy, dotard, sinner or saint.

Baba is like an Infinite Ocean, and in order to realise Him the ego must be annihilated altogether.

The brief but striking 'Prelude', co-written with Pete's old friend Andy Newman, "is a simple prayer for change in a world that from my viewpoint had gone crazily wrong," Townshend said.

'Face Dances Part Two', "is the anthem of the soul in solitary confinement . . ." Townshend explained. "It's like feeling in jail and the face that I sing about is my own, I wrote the words while I was looking in a mirror. The cause of the loneliness is partly obvious. I've become incredibly confused over the years with The Who. I think anybody that's read interviews I've done over the years and seen the work of the band knows the kind of confusion and perhaps it's a kind of self-inflicted torment. I know a lot of people reckon I couldn't live without it. A lot of the values I'd held to be important in the early part of the band's career and in the early Seventies – spiritually and morally and creatively – got let down somehow, compromised. I think because I wanted an easier, happier life, I've always found it difficult to say no and I think that applies also to 'no' when somebody asks you for a favour and also 'no' when somebody is trying to [enter] into your life in some way."

'Exquisitely Bored', sung in a distinctly Mark Knopfler-style vocal, features the lines *exquisitely bored in California/we take our troubles to the crest* and *walking in Laguna* which reference Townshend's recent rehab stint.

The album's most avant-garde track was 'Communication'. "I deliberately take the word 'communication' and break it up into bits," Townshend said in 1982. "I mean I literally hurl the letters of the word at the listener. And then I show a literal example of how not to communicate, which is with flowery, meaningless prose. You know, 'briolette tears drip from frozen masks, the back of the whale cracks through the ice floe,' blahblahblahblahblah – who needs it?

"Just as years ago, when I used to smash guitars because I just couldn't play them the way I wanted to . . . now I smash words."

In 'Stardom In Acton', Pete contemplated the sweet smell of success as a youngster in west London. "It's incredible to think that music began so simply for me when I was a kid in Acton and I had no idea how much it would challenge me when I got older. And how much the simple thing I call rock'n'roll could give and how much it could take – try to take." 'Uniforms (Corp d'Esprit)' was "obviously double-edged," Townshend told *Musician*, pointing out how the song acknowledges that uniforms can lead to unity in some cases, but a herd mentality in others. "It also recognises the fact that there are behavioural uniforms as well."

'North Country Girl' derived from Bob Dylan's 'Girl From The North Country' (originally appearing on *The Freewheelin' Bob Dylan*) which, in turn was 'borrowed' in part from British folk musician Martin Carthy's interpretation of the traditional 'Scarborough Fair'.

'Somebody Saved Me', a leftover from the *Face Dances* sessions, struck many as Townshend's eulogy to Kit Lambert, or perhaps even a more veiled reference to Meher Baba:

> *I lived hippie jokes getting stoned insane*
> *Till the rain looked just like snow*
> *But there was a soul in whom I could depend*
> *He worked himself crazy while I laid in bed*
> *I never leaned on a person like I leaned right then*
> *And when I finally woke up clean*
> *My friend was dead – stone dead*

Townshend explained to *Musician* that the album's final track, 'Slit Skirts' was (along with 'The Sea Refuses No River') a demonstration of Bruce Springsteen's writing form and that the song was a conscious attempt "to break that form down, to smash at it."

" 'Slit Skirts' was written at the absolute depths for me," Townshend admitted in 1985. "I was just barely alive when I wrote that . . . and I think you can feel that when you hear it."

" 'Slit Skirts' is about getting to that place in middle age where you really feel that life is never going to be the same," Townshend explained in 1996. "You're never going to fall in love again, it's never going to be quite like it was – and it's a song about getting drunk, about being maudlin and sentimental, and looking back, and, as always, the irony of the intention was lost on most people. I got very, very upset when people said, 'This sounds like a song that Pete Townshend wrote when he was getting drunk,' and I'd very carefully stayed sober in order to write it, so that I could get drunk to listen to it. It evokes that feeling that sometimes I have at my age, which is that one minute I'm sitting there looking at some old crap on the TV thinking, 'If I was just 10 years younger, I'd probably be in a night club right now,' and suddenly you get to the end of the song, and you go from that reflective pseudo-tragic piano motif to the 'Slit skirts, slit skirts, we're rocking out now – more champagne!' The futility of it, the bathos of it, and it's not unlike how I was living when I was working on the record."

Due to the solemn nature of much of the material, *Chinese Eyes* struck many as particularly downbeat. "Unfortunately, a lot of unhappiness comes through," Townshend told *Rolling Stone*, "but there's also a great feeling that I seem determined to win, somehow. You can feel it in a lot of the songs, there's a determination to overcome. And I managed to do it."

"This is the first record I've ever made during which I felt that there was no hope whatsoever to try to repair my lost love for my wife and family or to repair the damage I felt I'd unwittingly laid on my friends and my relationship with the other guys in the band, The Who. And the songs, as a result, each a reflection of an aspect of what it's like to feel alone, I think, and yet still be yearning for lost emotions and power."

Like *Quadrophenia*, the album was rife with metaphors concerning water, particularly the River Thames. "It always reminds me of a soul irrevocably plodding on towards God," Pete said in 1982. "It's full of food for fish and it provides London with most of its water and yet it's also treated like a rubbish dump . . . people chuck their cars in and their beer cans, their used contraceptives and everything else. And many rivers still get used as sewers and yet they all get to the sea in the end. And so the analogy with the human soul always appeals to me, the fact that it doesn't matter how clean or dirty you are, you get there in the end. It reminds me constantly, the river, of immortality and of my goal and in a strange way – however I feel – it reminds me of my permanence."

Townshend told *Musician* that the album was designed to awaken the listener into accepting their own personal responsibility. "This is something that I tried very, very hard to get across: not to point a finger and say *they're* the evil ones. It's *us*. We're the ones who are guilty – as a group, and as a race, for allowing things to get out of hand.

"I do believe that everybody on the planet, whether they like it or not, is a spiritual aspirant, and that the most valuable demonstration of how he deals with his or her problems can be seen in how he handles the commitments he makes to the most important human beings in his life, whether it's his wife, his offspring, his workmates or whatever. And that includes how the individual deals with his own contradiction and problems . . . his conscience. That's the place to start."

The curious title inevitably drew queries regarding its significance, something which the liner notes did little to explain:

> They were being attacked from all sides, everything seemed hopeless. There seemed to be no language in which they could communicate to their adversaries, to beseech them for mercy. At a crucial moment a natural leader emerged. His horse was dry and cool when all others were frothing and bleeding, his leather clothes dusty and worn. His face was keen and firm, lightly lined and weather beaten. The most remarkable thing about him was his eyes; half shut against the wind blown dust and the noise of guns.

The title was an allusion to "the fact that you can't hide what you're really like", Townshend told Loder. "I just had this image of the average American hero – somebody like a Clint Eastwood or a John Wayne. Somebody with eyes like slits, who was basically capable of anything – you know, any kind of murderous act or whatever to get what was required – to get, let's say, his people to safety. And yet, to those people he's saving, he's a great hero, a knight in shining armour – forget the fact that he cut off 50 people's heads to get them home safely.

"Then I thought about the Russians and the Chinese and the Arab communities and the South Americans; you've got these different ethnic groups, and each has this central image of every other political or national faction as being, in some way, the evil ones. And I've taken this a little bit further – because I spent so much of my time in society, high society, last year – to comment on stardom and power and drug use and decadence, and how there's a strange parallel, in a way, between the misuse of power and responsibility by people who are heroes. If you're really a good person, you can't hide by acting bad, and if you're a bad person, you can't hide it by acting good. Also – more to the point, really – that there's no outward, identifiable evil, you know? People spend most of their time looking for evil and identifying evil outside themselves. But the potential for evil is inside you."

All The Best Cowboys Have Chinese Eyes was finally released in May. Atco, who were expecting a repeat of the success and acclaim that greeted *Empty Glass*, were unreceptive to the album's experimental and introspective nature and when *Chinese Eyes* reached only number 26 in the *Billboard* Top 40, the relationship between artist and record company cooled.

"I enjoyed working on *Chinese Eyes*," Townshend said in 2005. "I feel it was an honest album, and more courageous creatively. With this record though my relationship with Atco changed, I felt they disliked the record, and from there onwards we operated at arm's length."

The reviews were a mixed bag. Kurt Loder (in *Rolling Stone*) commented that "this sort of sophomoric spew disfigures most of the album's 11 tracks, which is a shame" in reference to lines such as *Love crushes angles into black* and *For that's what true beauty is – time's gift to perfect humility* (from 'Stop Hurting People'), and *Just like the stub of that long cigarette full of hash / I'm the first to get booked* (from 'Stardom In Acton').

"Because in some ways, *Chinese Eyes* is Townshend's most accomplished and admirable solo LP . . . Rock'n'roll has less need of gratuitous high-culture flourishes than perhaps any other artistic form – a lesson one might have thought we'd all learned back in the bad old art-rock days. Townshend is a gifted rocker, and that should be enough. That he apparently yearns for some higher form of quasi-literary respectability is sad, not simply because he's so unsuited for it, but because his particular form of pop genius is direct observation."

Dave Marsh was kinder in *The Record*. "What's certain is that Townshend is now making a kind of music that doesn't have much to do with The Who. It still rocks, but it's more devoted to studio intricacy than interplay among band members. It's also certain that this music is a hell of a lot more interesting, even in its use of the same structures and elements, than the tired stuff with which The Who have toyed lately. If you are looking for an explanation of the catastrophe The Who (on record) has become, it's not in any waning of Townshend's abilities."

Marsh's perceptive comments were to prove prophetic when Pete directed his attentions to The Who. Following his return from California, he found that the other band members had been rehearsing without him, with Daltrey and Andy Fairweather-Low assuming guitar duties.[6] Tim Gorman (from the Glyn Johns produced band Lazy Racer) was enlisted in a limited role to augment the band's sound as John Bundrick was absent, drying out from alcoholism. Kenney Jones was also on the wagon, keen to be seen in a more favourable light by Daltrey. In June, The Who began work at Turn-Up Down studios, located at Johns' home in Surrey.

Townshend was armed with "just two songs when I went down to the studio," as he told *The Record* in December 1982. "The band was working, they were active, they were writing . . . If I had said right then and there, 'Listen chaps, I don't feel like making the record,' they looked as if they would have gone on and done something without me. And they weren't making any demonstrations to me, either. They were just doing it because they wanted to do it. It was really strange. I thought, 'I'd really like to play with those guys.'"

"I don't see The Who going on for very much longer," Townshend announced to *Rolling Stone*. "I think that with this next album, and with the next protracted period of work we do, we're really gonna throw ourselves into it 100 per cent. And then we're gonna stop. I'm pretty sure of that. It's not because we want to, but because we've come to the point where we don't really want to go through all these periods when the public and our fans and the record company and even we don't know what the fuck's gonna happen next. The tension is just too much. And this period when we work on the band, I'm gonna really think about very little else.

"I'm worried about it, because I've become accustomed to doing lots of other things. And I like the richness of what I do in other areas. That's become almost as important to me as being in a band. And I think when you get to that point, you have to think very seriously about what it is you're doing it for. Because it's always been too important for us to do just because we enjoy one another's company. And I think basically one of the

---

[6] Fairweather-Low, who had contributed backing vocals on *Who Are You*, received a rhythm guitar credit on one track, 'It's Your Turn' (on *It's Hard*).

reasons we're working together at the moment is that we enjoy one another's company. It's as simple as that."

"I don't see any reason why we shouldn't do a certain amount of work," Pete further stated just prior to the recording sessions. "But after that, I really think we've had enough. At least for now, we seem to have to know that we're making one last big effort. We have to feel that there is an *end* to it; otherwise, I don't think we could really go in the right mind."

Townshend's assertion that he was going to focus all of his efforts on what was hinted as the last Who album, combined with the fact that Johns was back on board as producer, created high expectations. Rather than approaching the band with a collection of demos, Townshend asked for the others' input.

"I sat round with everybody and I asked them, 'What do you want to fucking sing about? Tell me, and I'll write the songs,'" he told Paul Du Noyer. "It's a piece of piss! I've been writing songs for 20 years. D'you wanna sing about race riots? D'you wanna sing about the nuclear bomb? D'you wanna sing about soya bean diets? Tell me!

"Well, after establishing, quite quickly, that there was very little common ground, we did find that we all cared very deeply about the planet, the people on it, about the threat to our children from nuclear war, of the increasing instability of our own country's politics. There's the fact that we've actually infiltrated the establishment, in a way that younger bands haven't been able to do. It's taken us a long time to do, but now we can see that even the establishment is impotent, it's not just us, and we're really in a danger zone, and not to cry *panic*; panic! But it was something we need to express. Consequently, a lot of material we're doing at the moment is quite anguished."

The result of this band meeting seemed to provide a sense of purpose that was missing from *Face Dances*. "It really did unify us a lot," said Townshend. "It made us feel like human beings, part of society, living on a planet, not as isolated superstars who were worried about advancing middle age, money problems, whether they could buy another radiator cap for their Rolls-Royces."

Pete further whetted appetites for a killer Who record in an interview with *Musician* in September 1982, when he asserted that the album in progress was "probably the most dangerous one The Who have ever made" and "The new Who songs are violently aggressive, the most aggressive stuff we've ever come up with," and "from our point of view it's a tremendous record." He referred to 'I've Known No War' as "the key song on the next album. We just started with the word 'war' and went from there. It's possibly one of the best Who tracks we've ever done, I believe. It's a very archetypal, very Sixties issue, but it's also bloody great."

During the recording of 'It's Your Turn', 'Dangerous', and 'One At A Time', all Entwistle compositions, Townshend's hearing concerns surfaced again. "The only time I [hurt my ears] recently was on a couple of John's songs, because it was what he wanted," Pete told *Musician* in 1982, "and I came out of those two sessions with my ears ringing for a week. And I thought, 'Well, there's another db lost, you know.' I'm just very anxious to preserve my hearing."

It's Hard opened with 'Athena', the song Townshend had written following his embarrassing episode with Theresa Russell in 1980. 'Cooks County' was inspired by a documentary Pete had seen about Cook County hospital in Chicago, a free hospital which was in dire financial straits and had applied for government grants to stay open.

"The grants were refused so the hospital was going to close," Pete said. "It was in a ghetto and it was mainly black people and it was mainly drug abuse and everything else, ghetto-influenced problems, which this hospital dealt with. Of course a lot of these people, you get blasted by a shotgun in a Chicago street and you get picked up by an ambulance, you get taken to hospital and unless you've got a Medicare card or insurance or something you get shoved straight out again. I just felt so moved by this that I just felt in a sense that I had to scribble out a few lines about it and that's how it came out. I just went in with the poem I'd written 'people are suffering . . .' and we turned it into this particular track."

'One Life's Enough', written for Karen and perhaps the most un-Who like track ever to appear on a Who record, was symptomatic of the album's undistinguished nature. 'Why Did I Fall For That?' and 'A Man Is A Man' were redolent of the type of American radio-tailored AOR that Johns had aimed for on the *Who Are You* album. The former was written to address the apathetic attitude of society during the cold war. "We've just sat back under the nuclear umbrella and lived our lives, taken our drugs, listened to our blues," Townshend said. "I don't want to sound like fucking Pravda or anything, but we have been a pretty impotent, unthinking [generation]."

The undoubted highlight of a lacklustre collection was 'Eminence Front', a Townshend-sung observation on the hollowness of Western materialism, which would not have sounded out of place on *Chinese Eyes*.

The final song, 'Cry If You Want', a Daltrey favourite, featured the only example of the promised aggression Townshend talked about, in the form of a frenzied series of slashing power chords as the song faded out.

The album sleeve depicted the band members – Townshend sporting an unflattering, New Romantics-style haircut – standing in front of a child playing a 'Space Duel' arcade game, perhaps an updated reference to *Tommy*. "I had very little to do with the cover and the title," Townshend said, commenting on what was obviously a sore subject. "One of the problems with the band is that we very, very rarely agree on policy. So where we should have had a terrific album cover, we have a rather spineless cover because nobody works hard enough for it. Nobody fights."

It's Hard was released in September, climbing to number eight in the US and 11 in the UK – the first Who album since *The Who Sell Out* not to reach the Top 10 in the British album charts. It received a puzzlingly glowing review from *Rolling Stone*'s Parke Puterbaugh, who called it The Who's "most vital and coherent album since *Who's Next*," and "a strong affirmation of this band's ability to reach millions with powerful rock'n' roll and trenchant, galvanising politics." Puterbaugh went on to praise the pompous 'I've Known No War' as "a song that could become an anthem to our generation much the way 'Won't Get Fooled Again' did a decade ago," and compared 'Cry If You Want' to 'I Can See For Miles'.

Sounds' Gary Bushell was less enthusiastic: "The music on *It's Hard* is worse than the record's cheapo cover. Most of it sounds like the watered-down bits of other Who LPs. It's sort of like a footballer who's got old and fat and out of condition but keeps on kicking a ball about."

"*It's Hard* should never have been released," Daltrey later declared. "I had huge rows with Pete . . . when the album was finished and I heard it, I said, 'Pete, this is just a complete piece of shit and it should never come out!' It came out because as usual we were being manipulated at that time by other things. The record company wanted a record out and they wanted us to do a tour. What I said to Pete was, 'If we'd tried to get any of these songs on to *Face Dances*, or any of the albums that we've done since our first fucking album, we would not allow these songs to be on an album! Why are we releasing them? Why? Let's just say that was an experience to pull the band back together. Now let's go and make an album.' He said, 'Too late. It's good enough.'"

"*It's Hard* was a mistake," Townshend admitted to *Mojo* in 2004. "I was fresh out of rehab and went straight into the band who were already recording without me. They didn't understand the depth of my problem."

CHAPTER FOURTEEN

1982–1985

"I see a society, or a race which I feel lucky to be a part of, and lucky to be a little bit unique, and in my own arena of activity, obviously, especially unique, and I really enjoy that. But at the same time, I don't want to face up to the inevitable fact that if life is as I see it, as I'd like it to be, then I am no better than anybody else. And that occasionally throws me into a bit of a turmoil and that's where I'm at odds to a great extent. I don't quite know how to deal with it all the time. Sometimes I've got it in control, and sometimes it gets out of control."

– Pete Townshend, 1982

"I've just made a decision to take on a few things. I won't put my stability or my family at risk, but I have to do something with some risk attached. So far, I've turned away from all big chances and all big risks. I think there is a point where the individual who is involved in the rehabilitation process has to start to run . . . One has to test the water."

– Pete Townshend, 1984

BY 1982, Simon Townshend had been writing and performing as a singer and guitarist for at least eight years, forming several bands along the way. Pete generously gave his younger brother some recording time at Eel Pie, where Simon laid down demos of several songs he'd recently written.

"He came in and said, 'This song's great. What is this?'" Simon recalls. "It was one of the songs I'd written called 'So Real' and when he heard about five or six songs, he said that he had some time, and would I like to do an album?[1] Of course I jumped at the chance because at the time I

---

[1] Following the *It's Hard* sessions, Townshend was scheduled to produce an album for The Pretenders, but these plans were cancelled when 25-year-old guitarist James Honeyman-Scott died of a drug overdose in June 1982.

couldn't get a record deal. I had no manager that was really actively working for me, but I was being very creative."

The sessions for the album, entitled *Sweet Sound*, took nearly three months. "It dragged on a bit," Simon admits, "it was too long for Pete, I think, in terms of working on somebody else's record, but he was very committed to it." Pete also wasn't averse to offering constructive criticism to his younger sibling. "He said, 'Why don't you go away and work on that,' or 'that's not as good as other stuff'."

Pete offered to help promote the album, accompanying Simon on a promotional trip to America that autumn. In the press release with the album, Simon was quoted, "Pete's a great producer. He has a special relationship with the engineer, Bill Price, and that really helped the sound. I got to know Pete for the first time during the recording of this record. He's so much older that I never knew him well growing up. In the studio we could really get close for the first time."

The Simon Townshend Band included Mark Brzezicki on drums, while Chris Stainton played keyboards on the album. Released by Polydor in 1983, "*Sweet Sound* was close to being a hit record, at the time," Simon recalls. "But you know, those things, if they're meant to be, they happen, and what I got out of it was a great deal of satisfaction to have made that album. And to work with Pete, 'cause that was great, as well."

On July 21, Pete made a solo live appearance – his first since the Rock Against Unemployment show at Brockwell Park 14 months earlier – at London's Dominion Theatre, marking the first Prince's Trust Gala Benefit. Dressed in a rather gauche grey, side buttoning suit, Townshend performed 'Let My Love Open The Door' and 'Amoreuse', and sat at the piano for 'Slit Skirts' in addition to playing with the house band, which featured Robert Plant, Kate Bush, Gary Brooker, Phil Collins, Ultravox's Midge Ure and Japan bassist, Mick Karn. Other guests performing that evening included Jethro Tull and Madness.

Townshend followed this busy period with a short holiday in Cornwall during which he indulged his lifelong passion of sailing, finding time to record three demos, 'Cat Snatch', 'Ask Yourself', and 'Baroque Ippanese', during the break.

What became known as The Who's 'Farewell Tour' began to take shape. When asked by *Rolling Stone* if anything would be missing from his life if the band broke up, Townshend quipped, "Yeah, I would say about a million dollars a year . . .

"I think that, far from there being something missing, the very fact of not being involved in it any more would allow us to take a different stance on what we've done – to enjoy it, to luxuriate in it, to celebrate it, to cherish it and to draw the best from it. Rather than always see the past as something that threatens our future – which is something that seems to be an irreversible feature of the band today. I don't know: I think The Who will break – not break up, but stop working – before the Stones do."

"The Who have stopped and regrouped several times in their career, at one point for two whole years," Townshend told *Musician,* "and those times were vitally important for the band. So what we're talking about at the moment is a year of exploitation, but under our own control, of live performances of [*It's Hard*]. And then we're gonna stop. What happens then is an open book."

Inevitably, his ongoing hearing problems were an important factor. "One reason I don't like playing that kind of heavy-metal guitar any more is because it hurts my ears. It's the frequencies at which my ears are irreversibly damaged . . . they're very, very sensitive. Say you damage your ears at two kilohertz; any loud noise at that frequency produces pain, which is the ear's warning system not to screw around at that frequency. So I'm in a kind of Catch-22 situation, 'cause what I've done best for 20 years has damaged that part of my hearing."

Plans were made for a US tour over the autumn and winter, followed by an extensive tour of Britain and European venues in early 1983. Australia and Japan were pencilled in for spring, and, according to an optimistic report from *Rolling Stone*'s Kurt Loder in November 1982, "Bill Curbishley, the group's enterprising manager, is already talking about the possibility of playing a quick cluster of dates sometime in 1984 and perhaps fulfilling The Who's long-standing plan to play eastern Europe – maybe even doing *Tommy* at Moscow's opera house."

"I'm never gonna drink again," a newly sober Townshend told Loder. "In a way, I'm quite looking forward to [the tour] as a test. I'm happy to have sorted out my family problems once and for all. I always felt and hoped that it was possible. I didn't want to be a rock casualty in any sense, because I've always felt that one more rock casualty is just another headline for a couple of weeks, and then everybody gets really . . . not only bored, but everybody feels *betrayed*. Because although rock casualties make good copy in the *NME Book Of The Dead*, they don't make good copy in the lives of rock fans, who have a slightly higher emotional involvement in the musical form than it's just being, you know, like a circus, full of

351

Berlinesque, decadent arseholes who don't know how to spend their money, etc.

"I didn't want to end up just another rock statistic," he later remarked. "My kids were still quite young. Up to that point, apart from smashing up a few guitars, there was nothing I'd done which they had to be publicly ashamed of, and suddenly there were lots of things, my alcoholism, people dying at concerts. I'd become a real rock'n'roll seedy figure. I didn't really want to go on in that direction. So I actually agreed to do that last tour really to close the book."

The tour began on September 10 – a week after the release of *It's Hard* and over 17 months since the last Who live performance – with a two-night warm-up at Birmingham's National Exhibition Centre. Tim Gorman performed keyboard duties on the UK and US dates.

In his review of the Saturday night show, *The Times'* Richard Williams wrote: "This elderly group delivered 24 songs in two hours with polish, panache and evident enjoyment. Only once or twice was there a suggestion that Pete Townshend, whose devilment is born out of an honest self-dissatisfaction, might wish to send the group hurtling off the rails. In general the performance was as compact and unsurprising as their early shows were erratic and electrifying.

"The highlights of any show by The Who, therefore are likely to be provided by the old songs. This time they included 'Substitute', 'I Can't Explain' and the under-regarded 'Naked Eye' which has some of his most moving lines. More recent material such as the inflated 'Sister Disco' and the rowdy new 'Cry If You Want' sounds tame by comparison. Townshend probably knows this; Roger Daltrey the singer who has acted as his mouthpiece for almost two decades probably does not.

"Nonetheless it was impossible neither to feel a tug when the house lights went up during the inevitable medley from *Tommy*, nor to be warmed by the triptych of encores which included 'Shakin' All Over', 'Twist And Shout' (with a raging vocal treatment by John Entwistle) and 'Summertime Blues'. The latter, an Eddie Cochran song whose words and music played a vital role in shaping Townshend's compositional style, was a particularly appropriate choice; outside there was an autumnal nip in the west Midlands air."

Following the Birmingham shows, The Who began the first leg of the US and Canadian trek on September 22 with two nights at the Capital Centre in Largo, Maryland.

"There are moments in the show when the desire, drive and urgency of

The Who combine into something truly resonant," wrote *The Record*'s Jonathan Gross when reviewing the opening night. "But for the most part, the boys use this indoor date as a warm-up, having had only a Birmingham, England date coming in . . . They close with the exultant strains of 'Won't Get Fooled Again', with Townshend offering some of his most graceful leaps of the night. Still, no big deal this one, and The Who pack it up after one encore, which includes the set's most enjoyable tune, 'Twist And Shout' . . . for a brief moment, it appears Townshend is going to smash his guitar for this next-to-last D.C. area audience. Alas, he pauses at the top of his backswing and slices instead through a convenient microphone stand. Maybe later for a Fender splinter bomb. Control, Townshend says, is the operative word this year."

The outdoor shows in the States featured an elaborate stage set-up, with 'WHO' spelled out in forty-foot high letters, while the stage itself, situated under the bar of the 'H', featured a 110,000-watt PA system. Some 11 tractor-trailers were needed to transport the band's equipment from show to show, while a Boeing 707 was chartered – at around $5,000 per hour – to transport the band and its entourage. Kurt Loder outlined the tour's financial details in *Rolling Stone*:

> "When 90 people are eating and sleeping off a band's profits, some sort of compensation becomes essential . . . The Who have signed a lucrative sponsorship deal with Schlitz beer. In return for appearing in two 30-second Schlitz commercials,[2] allowing their music to be used in other Schlitz ads and permitting the Schlitz name to be used on concert tickets, The Who will receive a pot of money [described by a Schlitz spokesman as a seven-figure amount and "the biggest corporate-sponsored rock music entertainment ever undertaken"]. Then, there is merchandising – the sale of tour T-shirts and jerseys [$10 to $18 apiece this year], tour programmes [$5 each] and, in an innovative move, an authorised biography called The Who: Maximum R&B, a four-colour trade paperback that is being sold for $14 a copy. Every little bit helps."

Dave Marsh, who was writing his own Who biography, *Before I Get Old* at the time, penned an article in *The Record* entitled 'The Who Sell Out' which criticised the band for accepting sponsorship. Pete fired off a

---

[2] The footage used in the Schlitz commercials was filmed "at a rehearsal, backstage and at their first concert," according to Stroh VP of Brand Management Hunter Hastings. "You won't see Pete Townshend singing the Schlitz jingle."

venomous response printed in the subsequent issue, dated December 1982:

> *"An inference that The Who are now motivated only by greed indicates that this ace rock parasite, now working on a book about The Who, is taking leave of his senses . . . I refused to do a tour of such gruelling length (10 weeks) without a private plane. The sponsor's fee nearly pays for this plane and makes for better shows without raising ticket prices. We are doing this tour for our fans, for rock'n'roll and hopefully to make some sense out of 20 years of confusing history in which none of us became millionaires, despite much written to the contrary.*
>
> *"We are not ashamed to be paid well for what we do, nor for what we have done in the past. I think rock music carries people like Marsh on its back. Until he and others like him realise that until they take a chance, like Cameron Crowe did with* Fast Times At Ridgemont High, *and do something of worth outside of rock'n'roll criticism, they have to face up to that charge . . . A few Schlitz flyers in the arena won't sublimate our passion."*

Townshend was now favouring Schecter Telecaster-copy guitars, which he'd begun using back in 1979. "We used to use Gibson Les Pauls," his guitar tech, Alan Rogan told *Guitar World* in 1983. "One day I spotted a Schecter Telecaster-type guitar and I took it down to the shows we were doing in '79 at Madison Square Garden and [Pete] used it immediately, then we had backups and spares made of that."

The tour continued through the east coast and Midwest, playing to over 91,000 at JFK Stadium, Philadelphia and 85,000 at Buffalo's Rich Stadium. Further massive crowds gathered at the Silverdome in Pontiac, Michigan (75,000), and CNE Stadium, Toronto (68,000).

Kurt Loder caught up with the tour one week in for a *Rolling Stone* report. "Townshend has already caught a cold, which may explain the two sweaters he's wearing, if not the faded pink handkerchief that's knotted around his wrist. A copy of *Nostromo*, the Joseph Conrad novel, lies on a table near the sofa where he's sitting, and a stack of portable recording equipment – an adjunct to on-the-road songwriting – stands against a far wall.[3] One year after nearly cashing in his chips, Townshend

---

[3] Townshend reviewed *Nostromo* for the *Mail On Sunday* newspaper in September 1983. His Portastudio recording equipment, which accompanied him throughout the tour, was used to record several demos, including 'Holly Like Ivy' and 'Prelude #556', both of which appear on *Another Scoop*.

looks a little ragged, but he's obviously sober and straight. His only remaining vice is a penchant for miniature Indian cigarettes, which he smokes steadily. 'I do miss a drink before going onstage,' he admits, raking a hand through his dishevelled hair. 'Even just a small brandy would always stop me from feeling nervous. But once I get on the stage now, I'm OK. I don't miss it,' he says, waving the bad old days away. 'I don't miss any of it . . . I think there's a certain amount of relief about the fact that it's the last tour.'

"There's a tremendous amount of sadness, though, as well, because I know it's not what everybody wants . . . I think John is probably . . . *more* than sad. He's not at all vocal, and that makes it very difficult, because he's actually sittin' and tryin' to work out how he feels half the time. But I think I know him well enough to know that he will probably mourn The Who more than anybody in the world. He's losing a vehicle for his talent and *passion* that he knows he'll never be able to find anywhere else."

On October 12 and 13, The Who played two nights at New York's Shea Stadium – the site of two Beatles' concerts in 1965 and 1966 – supported by The Clash. All 72,000 seats for the first show sold out in under two hours, making it the fastest selling concert in the history of ticket agency Ticketron (the second show sold out the following day).

An increasingly apathetic Townshend wasn't impressed as he told Matt Kent in 1999, "When I was going to Shea Stadium and Robin Denslow was talking to me saying, 'There's a 100,000 people here, you've sold out two dates, you've got the record for selling it out, how do you feel?' and I said, 'I'm bored.' 'Oh, so you're washed up and arrogant and finished?' 'No, I'm not. This bores me!'"

His boredom was reflected in the shows on the tour. While sell-out ticket sales demonstrated the audiences' enthusiasm and fans' loyalty, the by rote quality of the performances was brought into question early on. When inevitably compared to past Who concerts, the 1982 model of The Who looked and sounded bland for a band whose reputation was built upon spontaneity and musical dynamism. Loder was surprisingly complimentary toward these uninspired live showings. "Buoyed by what they conceive as a spring toward some sort of final curtain," he wrote, "the [Who] have been *burning* through their two-hour-plus sets, lashing out the songs from their new album, *It's Hard*, with all the fire of their great, anthemic hits. So far, it seems like a great way to go out – on top, as Roger says."

★　　★　　★

The tour continued westward – a show attended by 44,312 at Sun Devil Stadium in Arizona ending the first leg on Halloween night. The second leg began a month later in Orlando, Florida, before 65,000. A show in Dallas on December 4 marked the only occasion on the tour that Townshend smashed his guitar, frustrated at the cold wind that caused his guitar to continually go out of tune and reportedly, still smarting from a mid-set argument he'd had with Daltrey.

Towards the end of the tour, "after many hints," according to Barnes, "Pete stunned everyone by announcing he was finally and definitely leaving the group." The ongoing plans for further tours of Britain, Australia and Japan were consequently scrapped. On December 16, the Farewell Tour reached its final stop, a two-night stand at Maple Leaf Gardens in Toronto, the second and final night being featured on North American television as a pay-per-view event. While it wasn't originally planned as the site for the last concert, Maple Leaf Gardens was an appropriate venue for several reasons – it was historically significant being where Moon officially played his final Who show in 1976, with a sizeable crowd capacity (14,300), plus it was easily accessible for a satellite feed, and, being in Canada, enjoyed a favourable exchange rate.

While the crowds were appropriately enthusiastic, the shows – the first of which was taped as a safeguard in case of technical problems the following night – were described by *Rolling Stone* as near duplicates of each other: "The band didn't seem concerned about spontaneity: the song blocking and between-tune patter were virtually the same on both nights. Unpredictability, a quality with which The Who established their reputation in the Sixties, was apparently not a priority anymore. But, as the kids who roamed up Yonge Street after the last concert shouted, 'Who cares?'"

Variety offered the following assessment of the December 17 show: "There was little in The Who's pay-per-view concert to distinguish it from performances seen on the stadium tour of North America just concluded. The two-hour-plus performance . . . capped one of the most commercially successful – and commercially exploited – rock tours in history, and was in fact being billed as the veteran UK band's final appearance on this continent. But aside from a montage of vintage photos of the group, the 20th Century Fox Telecommunications-distributed event stuck to the playbook of the tour. And like the tour concerts, the show lacked the sense of anything special being contributed by the band.

"The close-up view of the group afforded by the 11-camera production, however, communicated this more clearly than the stadium shows did. One had only to look at guitarist Pete Townshend's bored expressions to understand that the emotional punch was lacking. The "very special finale" promised by 20th Century Fox, which hinted that Townshend and company would reprise their trademark destruction of instruments from years past, did not occur. Instead, a very scaled-down version of the fireworks display which ended the stadium shows was reprised."

The purported 2.5 million homes which were projected to order the special were similarly unimpressed as less than half tuned in. While the Farewell Tour had grossed at least $40 million, The Who had gone out on a whimper with the worst live performances they'd ever performed.

"The band became *just* a power chord," Townshend told the *Washington Post*'s Richard Harrington in 1989, "and you can't imagine how *boring* an album can be when every song starts off . . . [*imitates windmill and power chord*] it sends you to sleep. Somehow in the live context, it's acceptable because of the fact that not everybody receives it at the same time. In a way, it's as if you're rallying a whole group of people, some of whom may not have emotionally arrived yet and you make sure they hear one of the rallying calls and they go out ready to fight.

"But *what* are they fighting for? That's the thing that's so extraordinary. We forgot that The Who had already won the battle, that we are a generation that had already taken over society. There's no need to infiltrate the establishment because we've actually inherited the establishment by virtue of growing old. In a sense, we could have just waited quietly in the wings."

Upon completion of the Farewell Tour, engineer Cy Langston compiled a three-album set of live material spanning The Who's career which drew rave reviews from those who heard it. "Unfortunately," Barnes recalled in *Maximum R&B*, "in their wisdom, MCA Records insisted only tapes from the Farewell Tour be used. The band couldn't believe this but gave in. As a result, *Who's Last*, their farewell album, is thought by the band to be one of their worst."[4]

The album reached number 48 in Britain and 81 in the US. "To put it bluntly, The Who never sounded worse – more impotent and eviscerated – than on this dismal double album . . ." Kurt Loder opined in his *Rolling Stone* review, "several of the 16 songs here are available in far superior

---

[4] In late 1984, the author wrote a fan letter to Pete. "Glad you liked *Who's Last*," he mentioned in his January, 1985 reply, with an asterisk: "I didn't."

live versions on such albums as *Live At Leeds* and the soundtracks of *Woodstock* and *The Kids Are Alright,* and even the most casual comparison with those previous LPs exposes *Who's Last* as the disgraceful cash-in that it is . . . I can't think of another band as committed and allegedly idealistic as The Who that has ended its career on so sour and sickening a note."

Despite the cancellation of further tours, the decision was made to record one more Who studio album before the band finally called it quits. In January 1983, Townshend started work at his Eel Pie studios in Twickenham and Soho, writing songs based around the notion that "each of us is a soul in siege," he explained in 1987, continuing an idea he'd first addressed on *Chinese Eyes.* He wrote and recorded several experimental demos for the project, including 'Prelude, The Right To Write', in addition to 'Ask Yourself', 'Cat Snatch' and the various pieces he'd recorded on his Portastudio during the Farewell Tour.

In searching for an appropriate sound for *Siege,* Pete came up with what he called a 'Myriad Speaker System'. "I organised a synthesiser whose 16 unison 'string' voices were reproduced through 16 separate small speakers on mike stands at about head height, distributed around the recording studio in formal string section grouping," he wrote in 1987. "As soon as I played a note I knew I'd hit on something. The synthetic string sound was rich and spacious . . . It's a wonderful system, but is complex and takes many hours to set up."

However the *Siege* project was abruptly dropped in March, when Townshend decided that the material was unsuitable for The Who. After several weeks of deliberation, he informed the rest of the band that he was no longer able to write appropriate material for them, and that he was leaving The Who. Since this wasn't the first time a break up had been threatened, his announcement was taken with a pinch of salt.

Meanwhile, a 26-song collection of Pete's demo recordings entitled *Scoop* was released that same month. "I'd like to put together an album package of old demo material that I've done which has never been commercially released," Townshend had said in a radio interview five years earlier. "Every time The Who have made a record I've made a little demo and I thought that'd be quite an interesting thing to put together. An anthology of the old material, you know."

Scoop consisted of demo versions of The Who songs 'So Sad About Us', 'Squeeze Box', 'Circles', 'Melancholia', 'Bargain', 'Magic Bus', 'Cache

Cache', 'Behind Blue Eyes', and 'Love Reign O'er Me' alongside out-takes and experimentations from various periods in Townshend and The Who's history. *Rolling Stone*'s four-star review said, "This album is an open invitation into the root experience of songwriting, a rare glimpse of those secret explosions when words first collide with music."

"A chronicle of Pete's love affair with the recording process . . ." wrote *People Weekly*, "the collection is unpretentious and meant, apparently, to recapture some of the innocence that has been lost in making popular music under constraints of commercialism and band compromise. This is the rock'n'roll equivalent of a writer publishing his notebooks, and because Townshend is as talented as he is, it's a fascinating project."

Scoop was followed by two further collections of Townshend's demo material, *Another Scoop* in 1987, and *Scoop 3* in 2001. Despite complimentary reviews and healthy sales, the first two collections did not prove profitable.

"Although the first *Scoop* sold more than Mick Jagger's last solo album, I've still got a kind of minus figure on my budget," Townshend said in 1989. "They're expensive to produce because they're quite lavish, the packaging, the double albums, and they're sold at budget prices. Neither I nor the record company are making any money out of it, but you know Atlantic have been great to allow me the space to do it, they really have. I think Doug Morris, who's the president, loves me, most of all because I gave him his first hit in a sense with the *Empty Glass* album . . .

"So the company has given me that space and it's something that I love greatly. It's one thing that has made me feel that Atlantic is a wee bit more than just a front line record company . . . understanding that modern rock musicians, although they tend to be honest enough to put their commercial interests first, in a lot of cases, the music is very much an abstract and that it needs attending to on an abstract level. So I hope that there will be some more stuff, 'cause I produce music all the time, and I write all the time. I write constantly . . . I've got barrels of stuff."

"I never felt I had a cache of great unreleased music," Pete said in a Sirius radio interview in 2006. "If I'd ever had great music, I'd have put it out. What I felt I did have, was music that I really loved working on, and it might not fit anybody's idea of what was commercial, but I enjoyed the process of recording it. I love recording, I love the studio, I love the technology. For me, it's my link to music and I love music . . . In a way, when I go to something like [the *Scoop* albums], what I'm trying to do is to demonstrate the way I think music works in my life."

On July 7, Pete took a significant step away from the music world when a press conference was held to announce his new position as an acquisitions editor for the esteemed London book publishers Faber & Faber. Faber had an important literary tradition above most other British publishing houses, having published T.S. Eliot, William Golding and Lawrence Durrell as well as other important poets and playwrights. Townshend had initially contacted the company the previous year to see if they would be interested in purchasing his financially beleaguered Eel Pie publishing company.

"Faber was interested in modifying its culturally rarified image and reaching a younger, wider audience," wrote the *Sunday Times*' Mick Brown in 1985. "It did not want Eel Pie but it did want Townshend, both for his ideas and, says Faber chairman Matthew Evans, as a way of attracting writers who would otherwise have regarded Faber as a 'cultural no go area'.

"Townshend's arrival was widely held to be a gimmick . . . even *The Times* was moved to note with some irony, that Townshend arrived for his first day at the office wearing a suit. This tradition has not continued. It is possible that Townshend is the only associate editor in the company to arrive at editorial meetings in a chauffeur-driven limousine with a two-day growth of beard, wearing cowboy boots and smoking fragrantly scented Indian *biddhis*. 'Pete has brought a breath of the street to the place,' says his fellow editor, Robert McCrum. And, suit notwithstanding, Faber has brought a breath of traditional propriety to Townshend. Twice a week he appears at the offices, attending editorial conferences armed with his share of ideas; at home he reads manuscripts assiduously, a dictionary and thesaurus by his side. It is, he notes without irony, 'the best job I've ever had.'"

Pete explained his new position to Hugh Foley. "I'm an editor. Sometimes I actually physically edit books, you know, I go through text and edit, and talk to the authors about . . . structural changes, and with some writers I do a good job and with other writers I do a bad job. I do books about music. I try to do high quality photo books if we can do them. It's a natural thing for me to do, I find working with words quite easy.

"When I left The Who I knew I had music, but I was also very keen to have a different life, to work in a different team, to get some different influences. I wanted to regularise my life a little bit and meet new people. My work at Faber did that: I got involved with people from the theatre, with people involved with medicine, with poets and writers, and with people from the merchandising/production side of publishing. It's a new life really, because people have come to embrace me without having any strong feelings about rock'n'roll at all."

"Pete has brought us an independent voice and a list of contacts which have been invaluable," Faber chairman Matthew Evans told Brown. "He is an extremely smart, bright guy, who fits in with a group of people who also see themselves as smart and bright. Any reservations anybody had about him joining the company have gone, I think."

While at Faber, Pete acted as commissioning editor on a variety of projects that varied from popular music (including Eric Burdon's auto-biography, *I Used To Be An Animal But I'm All Right Now*, *Like Punk Never Happened* – Dave Rimmer's study of early Eighties pop, *Expensive Habits* – Simon Garfield's dissection of shady dealings in the music business, and *Crosstown Traffic*, Charles Shaar Murray's award-winning Jimi Hendrix biography) to a volume of Prince Charles' collected speeches.[5]

As a result of his position with Faber and Faber, Townshend became professionally involved with radical playwright Steven Berkoff,[6] and developed a friendship with Sir William Golding, the Nobel prize-winning author of *Lord Of The Flies*. In 1989, Townshend read a newspaper interview with Golding in which the author expressed his loathing for popular music. When Pete began writing a riposte, he realised that Golding identified with Townshend the editor, not the musician. Another acquaintance Pete made as a result of his position at Faber was British Poet Laureate, Ted Hughes – an association that would lead to an artistic collaboration six years later.

When Warner Brothers terminated The Who's recording contract in December 1983, Townshend released a written public statement regarding his status with the band which left little room for any misinterpretation:

"I will not be making any more records with The Who and I will not perform live again, anywhere in the world, with The Who.

In the first three months of this year, I wrote songs for the next contracted

[5] In a January 2000 interview with Q, Townshend named Brian Eno and Russell Mills' *More Dark Than Shark* as the best book he published at Faber & Faber, commenting, "Russell Mills did illustrations of some of Eno's notebooks, which are hilarious."
[6] Matthew Scurfield, who appeared with Townshend in Richard Stanley's 1968 film *Lone Ranger*, performed roles in four Berkoff stage productions from 1976–1980.

Who album, and I realised after only a short time that they weren't suitable for The Who. In March I informed the other members of the band and our manager that I was in difficulties. Several ideas were thrown around but none helped me.

Therefore in May, I met with the band again and to tell them that I had decided to quit, leaving The Who ball in their court. I did nothing more until September when I felt that, out of courtesy, I should explain my problem to the chairman of Warner Bros USA, Mo Ostin. He was sympathetic and made several suggestions, none of which helped me.

On December 7 we received Warner Brothers' notice of termination of contract. I feel sad that I cannot honour our commitment to Warners – and that many of our fans, both old and new, will be upset after being exposed to rumours that we were recording all this year. The fact is we didn't even book studio time.

My solo deal with Atco will continue, and I hope to record an album next year. I wish Roger, John and Kenney the best of luck with their future work and thank them for their patience.

The announcement, contained within the news pages of the Christmas editions of various music-related magazines passed almost without comment. As Chris Charlesworth pointed out in his Townshend biography published the following year, "In 1970 the news would have called for banner headlines – 'PETE QUITS WHO SHOCK!' – and a sensational front-page story. Now it no longer mattered; if Pete Townshend no longer cared about The Who, neither did the rest of the world."

Townshend viewed his decision as a personal choice – he stated that the others could continue if they wished, surely realising that without him, it was The Who only in name. Upon the band's inevitable disintegration, their contract with Warner Brothers had to be addressed.

"What stunned me was that I was going to have to pay back money that had been paid indirectly, for the use of the name to the Keith Moon estate, and directly, to Kenney," Townshend later said. "We'd just had an instalment of something like $1,750,000 and Warner Brothers wanted it back."[7]

Once payment was delivered, Pete felt a great weight had been lifted. "I feel greatly liberated," he said in 1985. "At the beginning of The Who's career we had the world before us, and a tremendous amount of creative –

---

[7] Townshend picked up Moon and Jones' shares as the latter reportedly couldn't afford the amount.

and every kind – of freedom. When we became an enormously successful group, I think we ended up – *I* ended up – feeling very caged. When I finally did face the future and had the courage to leave the band, I felt like I'd been released and I still feel very much that way. I feel I can control my own destiny and I still find that a great novelty."

His former bandmates were left considering their next move. "I would get regular visits from Roger saying, 'I want to do this, I want to do that,'" Townshend told *The Observer*'s Simon Garfield in 2006, "and I would say, 'Listen, it's over. Fuck off.' Well, I wouldn't say fuck off, but 'I'm not your man.' Watching him pretending to be who he was . . . it was all just pathetic. I had very little sympathy for him. I thought he should really go back and be a builder . . . Looking back now, it does seem very cold of me to have brought down such a heavy door. John Entwistle was very resentful as well. What happened with John was that he'd got used to living high, and his money supply was cut off."

The turn of 1984 marked the beginning of Pete's third year in a continuing programme of weekly psychotherapy. "Of course the problems are still there, but therapy helps to draw back the veils that we use to obscure them from ourselves," Townshend told *Spin* in 1986. "Therapy, particularly the old-fashioned kind of analysis, takes a very long time and half the time you don't know what it is you're going to find. I remember missing four weeks of sessions once because I was working on something, so I decided to write down what I might have said to my therapist. I started writing this story about something that happened to me as a child and began to grow very frightened because I knew I was approaching something that was very painful. I finally came to a point which was like a curtain and I knew I shouldn't go any further. By the time I realised how perverse my ideas about beauty had become I was ready to handle it. You must be prepared to accept what you learn about yourself."

The period which had elapsed since his return from Meg Patterson's detox treatment provided Pete with enough perspective to persuade him that the wisdom gained from his experiences might help others. He recounted his substance abuse to author Dennis Wholey, who was compiling *The Courage To Change*, a book of "Personal Conversations About Alcoholism," which featured the stories of Gary Crosby, Grace Slick and Jerry Falwell, among others.

Townshend also became vocal with regards to Britain's poor drug rehabilitation facilities. "It's not a problem you can separate from other problems," he told a meeting of Young Conservatives in 1984. "In this society oblivion is one of the only ways you can find balance because everything seems so frantic, so dangerous. With a right-wing [Conservative] government everything also seems so uncaring. People tend to become absorbed in their own emotional physical feelings. Most people go to the pub and get wrecked and that's what I did until my liver more or less gave out. I needed these moments of oblivion and when that stopped working I needed to find something else."

Pete specifically focused on drug rehabilitation, as he felt that efforts to prevent hard drug abusers from using in the first place were largely ineffective.

"I don't think there's much you can do to combat the use of heroin," he said in a 1985 radio interview. "What I'm most active in doing is raising money to provide beds in clinics to help people that have become victims of drug abuse. When somebody's about to embark on a course of oblivion, it's like somebody's about to throw themselves off the top of a tower block – you say, 'Listen, you shouldn't do that 'cause it's gonna hurt you,' it doesn't work too well, because their whole object is to hurt themselves. So what you have to do is you have to be ready at the bottom of the tower block, so that if they survive, and they want to get well, then you can help them.

"In Britain, the facilities are very, very, very lean indeed . . . although we have a national health service, a free medical system, it does nothing particularly for class A drug addicts – cocaine abusers, heroin abusers . . . we're making a lot of progress . . . The British government embarked on an anti-heroin campaign with advertising, and I was co-opted by them as a kind of figurehead, and then the various other people co-opted me into their own campaigns, but my main work is raising money to try and open a large clinic."

The clinic Townshend referred to was a drug treatment facility he and Meg Patterson had intended to open in London. The plan eventually had to be abandoned when, under duress, Patterson signed an agreement with a rabbi ("a decision that I was to regret deeply for the next several years," she wrote in her memoirs) who endeavoured to financially gain from Patterson's N.E.T. practice by misleading her friends, colleagues and patients by claiming to be her 'worldwide representative'. When Townshend refused to cooperate with the rabbi, he was mailed a letter from the man's lawyer threatening a lawsuit. It took three years of legal wrangling for Patterson to rid herself of the rabbi, by which time he had inflicted a substantial amount of damage to her work.

"Meg and George were blinded by the 'rabbi of Bethlehem'," Townshend told the author. "I was not. Yes, he turned out to be a con-man. However Meg never received the credit or funding she deserved and I don't think George helped. He always had such enormous global, spiritual and evangelical visions that he hoped to base on Meg's soon-to-land success (or his own success as an author). I really loved George, his son Lorne is an angel in many ways, but I think it was hard for all of them to see Meg denied proper recognition for her 'Black Box' detoxification system. It worked for me. I think it worked for a number of other famous people who then simply paid their bills and left her behind . . ."

Further examples of Townshend's anti-drug activism during this period took place in the form of a benefit concert in April 1984 with Siouxsie & The Banshees and an article he penned a few days later for Britain's *Mail On Sunday* urging better care for the nation's growing number of addicts. Pete became chairman of Double-O Charities, taking a more active role in raising funds for the causes he'd recently championed. Other examples of his involvement with the cause during this time included personally selling fund-raising anti-heroin T-shirts at a series of UK Bruce Springsteen concerts, and financing a trip for troubled former Clash drummer Topper Headon to undergo Neuro-Electric Therapy.

Most significantly, Townshend collated a series of short stories he had written between 1979 and 1984 with a view to publishing them. "It started when I kept a detailed journal of my dreams for a few months," Townshend recalled, "and I discovered that I don't have the sort of dreams most people have. I turned several of the images into stories and then I went on and did a series of erotic stories as well. My wife was shocked when she discovered them. She said she didn't know I had it in me."

The resulting book, *Horse's Neck* was partly motivated by a sense that, as an editor, Townshend needed to gain some credibility in the literary world.

"I thought it's wrong of me to be editing people's work and telling them what's wrong and everything else and they're sitting there, thinking, 'Can this guy write? And if he does write, do I respect the way he works as a writer?'" Pete told Hugh Foley in 1989, "so I put the book together and people can see me, warts and all. They can see me really trying . . . there are great moments in the book, there are also quite kind of sophomoric moments in the book, so you can see that's as good as I can do, and if you can do better, you deserve a deal."

Writing prose as opposed to songs proved a completely new experience for the musician. "It was different because I felt unfettered by the need to fit my thoughts into the context of a rock'n'roll song," Pete told *Spin* in 1986. "Except for two stories where I was going for what's known as a shaggy dog ending, 'Fish Shop' and 'The Plate', I didn't feel the need to entertain. Most of the book was written with the feeling that I was just laying it out there, and if you didn't like it, tough, because the things I was trying to share were very painfully observed by me and there was no way to sugarcoat them."

The book contained 13 short stories, tackling subjects such as childhood, stardom and spirituality. A recollection of one dream, entitled 'Horses', provided some startling imagery:

> *Confronting the white horse I put out my hand and brushed hard down the flank as if to smooth away the mark of a girth strap. As I did so, the skin fell away, and the dry white bones of the rib cage appeared. Beneath the ribs, living within the body of the horse, moved a massive snake. Its skin shone green and blue. It was bloated and overfed; full of the heart, the liver, and the intestines of my perfect horse, my symbol of purity. It moved within the body of the horse in a circle.*

A similar striking equine image had appeared in 'Athena' (from *It's Hard*): *Consumed, there was a beautiful white horse I saw on a dream stage/ He had a snake the size of a sewer pipe living in his rib cage.*

'Fish Shop', based on the television script Townshend wrote back in 1978, ostensibly provided an evocative glimpse of his early career:

> *Performing with his band on the stage was my friend Pete, a narrow man with eyes like the eyes a child sees when he stands on his head and looks into a mirror. He was swinging his guitar like a battle-axe, slicing a microphone stand in two and sending the tragic instrument hurtling across the stage, its cable curling . . . The band began the song and Pete sang venomously. The words celebrated men being real men; real men didn't need to display their toughness but needed to be able to know compassion and self-sacrifice . . . Pete says that night was important to him. The event seemed to be symbolic: the moment when he finally decided to break away from the little town and the people that he had grown up with.*

Over the years since its publication, Townshend has had to repeatedly point out that the majority of *Horse's Neck* is fictional. "It wasn't as autobiographical as a lot of people took it to be," he said in 1989. "I was upset that the word *autobiographical* even appeared on the jacket of the paper-back, 'cause it's not autobiographical at all."

"[*Fish Shop*] was the most real story that I had in that book," Townshend told *Guitar Player*'s Matt Resnicoff. "Most of the stuff was complete fiction. I was trying to write a Bukowski kind of thing, actually taking people through a really quite nightmarish thing and then out the other side, and little bits of autobiographical things slipped in. You know, you only have one life and only one set of influences. And, if something slips in which anybody can recognise as being real, they immediately think the rest of it must be real."

Regardless, certain stories – most notably 'A Death In The Day Of' and 'Champagne On The Terraces' – bear an uncanny similarity to events in Townshend's life at the time they were written, while 'Thirteen' evoked his childhood when Pete's parents were entertainers at Britain's seaside resorts:

> The beach at Filey was a Northumbrian miracle; sandy hollows exposed wind-eroded wombs to a sometimes raging sea. At certain moments you could believe that no one had ever run his fingers through the golden dust, or that no cigarette had ever been discarded. The exploring hand of an inquisitive child would belie that fancy. Even at the water's edge the flotsam of civilization floated gently home. Between the waves the heads of seals would bob, their whiskered noses inspecting the shore. Nearby, a more complete invasion threatened: holiday camps and railways, ice-cream parlours and penny arcades at Whitley Bay. Yet in the hollow of a sand dune, a child could well be on a desert island.

Another true-to-life scenario was 'Pancho And The Baron' which appeared to reflect Townshend's state of mind in 1981 as he pondered the early demises of Keith Moon ('Pancho') and Kit Lambert ('the Baron'):

> When I first heard that Pancho had died all I could think of was that I had survived. I had outlasted him. In a sense, I had won . . . Three years later, in my seedy hotel room in New York, I sat with Able and we talked about the old days. I kept saying over and over again: 'I survived.' I was about two weeks into a desperate recording session in a small studio there. As a professional drunk I was a great success with the New York musical elite, and I had been entertaining people night after night in my room, at restaurants and nightclubs . . .

'The Baron's dead. He died yesterday. Fell down some stairs. Got beaten up apparently.'
'Shit.'
I got up and looked over Central Park.
'I've survived.' That was all I could think of to say before I went to the studio and finished work on another song. 'First Pancho, now the Baron.'

When the author attempted to ascertain whether Townshend was pre-pared to concede that some of the book's stories were based on fact, Pete replied, "I think it's a stretch to try to find accurate correlation in any of the stories. I took such liberties with the truth that if I made connections it would be insulting and hurtful to some of the characters I developed, and make me look half-insane. For a biographer . . . there is an obvious desire to find the links between the creative output and the input, but there will be so much you might like to interpolate that is faulty, and so much that might be real that I probably simply will never see [or admit to]. *Horse's Neck* was a real attempt to write short fiction, a tricky form but one I felt I might rise to because of my skills as a lyricist.

"Where I chose to write in the setting of rock'n'roll, or touring, or dark and dingy nightclubs, I wrote about what I knew, and had observed, but changed names, and invented new characters. Later, my editor Robert McCrum warned me that wherever the setting was familiar, the reader would set out to try to place me inside the story, and that I might as well make the stories appear to be autobiographical. This does make the stories more plausible perhaps and easier for a reader to get into without too much concentration. But it also makes me look as though I led a life more like some of the lunatics that surrounded me, than the life I in fact lived. This state of affairs is confused by the fact that there are of course occa-sional true autobiographical references. But those that are unembellished are few."

Overall, *Horse's Neck* was acknowledged as a worthwhile departure when published in May 1985. "For Townshend, the book was partly a valediction for a passing era, partly a cathartic exercise to unravel the conundrum of self and public image," Mick Brown wrote in his *Sunday Times* review. "It is measure of the disparity between the two, he says, that he was deluged by letters from Who fans who had read the book, 'all saying they had no idea just how unhappy I had been'."

"*Horse's Neck* has established Townshend as a legitimate literary voice," proclaimed the *Wall Street Journal*. *Time* magazine's reviewer took Pete's predilection for pretentiousness to task, but was ultimately complimentary:

> "Townshend can be lyric and affecting, but too often he is portentous: *'Almost as soon as the window had misted up, a great blast of steam wafted into the street. Pete felt like the witness to some awesome nuclear test of devastating power . . . We were the frayed rubber band inside the enormous balsa-wood airplane of rock'n'roll.'*"

"Readers looking for the continuity and facts of Townshend's life will be disappointed. Yet there is enough evidence of innovative talent in these pages to indicate that if the author would write acoustical rather than amplified prose, he might have another promising career."

"The audience I had in mind was people who had enjoyed my songwriting, and those are the people who bought the book," Townshend told *Spin* in 1986. "Considering the price of the book in hardback, I'm amazed at how many people did buy it. I'm sure there were a few new readers, but I wasn't looking for a new audience. If I wanted a new audience, I'd use a nom de plume – and then I'm sure I'd sell zero copies. In England it was given a mixed reception, and I was pleased with that because I thought the book was mixed. Parts of it were good and parts of it were flat and confused. I re-read it once after it was published and some bits of it embarrassed me. The reviews in America did surprise me. It's been quite encouraging, because I imagined that rock critics and literary critics alike might resent the fact that a guy who makes enough dough selling records was trying to infiltrate new territory."

In 1984 Townshend started an occasional working relationship with Pink Floyd guitarist, David Gilmour. The previous year, Eel Pie Studios had been used by the band when recording their last studio album, *The Final Cut*. "[Townshend] stopped me in the corridor to say how much he had enjoyed my first solo album [released in 1978]," Gilmour told author Nicholas Shaffner in 1991. "I thought that was very nice of him – and also he said that if I ever needed any help with anything, to give him a ring."

With Pink Floyd on ice, Gilmour began work on his second solo album, *About Face*. "I was getting a little stuck for words, as is my wont . . ." Gilmour told Shaffner, "so I called [Pete] and said, 'Fancy writing a couple of lyrics?' He said, 'Sure, love to, send down the tape.' He sent back the first run of lyrics the next day; he'd been up all night working on it. That was 'Love On The Air'."

"I've always found it very difficult to collaborate and I haven't yet collaborated on a song," Townshend said in 1999. "Songs that look like collaborations, like the Dave Gilmour songs that I wrote, were either me writing the music or finding lyrics to music that was already done."

Pete also contributed 'All Lovers Are Deranged' to *About Face*,[8] but 'White City Fighting' was left off to be used by Townshend for his next project. "[Gilmour] didn't feel he could include it on *About Face* because, he said to me 'I don't know what goes on in the White City' – he came from Hampshire or somewhere," Townshend revealed the following year.

In addition to giving studio time to his brother Simon, Pink Floyd and Mick Jagger during this period,[9] Pete also continued to allow lesser known artists to record at Eel Pie, sometimes at no charge.

"I've been in and out of various levels of this type of work, either running co-ops with people or working directly with one or other new band, or doing special deals for young bands, new bands, sometimes new *old* bands," Townshend explained in a 1989 radio interview. "A studio is a studio . . . when you have a bad week, and there's nobody there who wants to come in and use the studio or if, like me, you don't even really run a commercial studio but you run a studio which is designed expressly to suit a particular artist on a project, if there's no music being made it starts to die . . . it's an interesting equation, you know, a place like this building right now if there's no music happening for, say, two weeks, and then an artist comes in, it will often take about two weeks to get it trucking again. You know, the people that work in a place like this, the engineers, the maintenance people, the administrative people, they all live for the day when the studio is full of music, full of action. Without the music, they have no purpose, certainly the building itself has no purpose . . .

"These are very, very functional places. So, to bring new music in, par-ticularly young players, not only familiarises them with the process, but it also plants seeds. When I've given free time to people, they've often come back at later dates and bought time just like everybody else. To that extent, it's obviously a commercial thing to do, but . . . selfishly the reason that I

---

[8] A demo song with the same title and lyrics as 'All Lovers Are Deranged' but with differ-ent music was recorded by Townshend in January 1983 at his Soho studio. "Another lyric based on a true story," he explained in the liner notes to *Scoop 3* in 2001. "Two people attempt to conduct a love affair over the telephone, from different sides of an ocean. Not to be recommended."

[9] Jagger recorded some of his first solo album *She's The Boss* at Eel Pie Studios. Pete was among the session guests.

do it has got nothing to do with money. It's to do with the fact that I come in contact with people that are breaking into the music industry. I come in contact with their problems, their difficulties . . . I see that side of the record companies that only the new artist sees . . . the last band we had in was Cleveland Watkiss' band . . . They got a five album deal from Polydor on an album that we did for them for nothing. The first album they're putting out is those tapes, so we're very proud of that. Also, by the by, we get our studio charges. So what would have been a dull period for us has actually turned into cash, it's turned into energy and we had three or four weeks of sessions in there where . . . not just me, but everybody that worked there, got some real feedback."

The subject for Townshend's next project, a progression on his *Siege* idea, evolved into a study of the emasculation of the postwar male.

"Throughout history, men have satisfied the drive to create and control by leading, writing, and governing," Townshend told *Spin* in 1986. "Men gained power through traditionally rewarded acts of heroism, self-sacrifice, and at the most mundane level – and to this day the thing we find hardest to let go of – by doing a hard day's work and bringing home the money. There are so many men who are unable to do that now, and it's backlashing against society in a monumental way. I work with a refuge for battered women in England, and working there has led me to conclude that domestic violence is often the last resort of men who are lost and emasculated. The popular solution is to separate men from wives and children because society refuses to tolerate violence in the home. Yet for millions of years violence has been the way we've run our countries and protected our causes."

The struggle of the male to maintain his place (Townshend specifically had the British male in mind, as the problem hadn't "crystallised" to such an extent in America) had moulded a generation of "desolation and decadence". The footsteps of those heroic soldiers who had assembled the vast British Empire, and those who had bravely and victoriously fought in two World Wars were impossible to fill, especially in an environment where the notion of conventional warfare had faded during the Cold War and its threat of nuclear annihilation. It had become increasingly more difficult to prove one's manhood through traditional acts of heroism, or even simply through providing for one's family, given the high rate of unemployment at the time. The typical man had no direction, and no avenue to demonstrate his validity.

"In a strongly feminist climate of the Eighties, men were increasingly being made conscious that without wars to fight they must struggle ever harder for some kind of male validity – and had to learn to face that their inbred machismo and violence were unacceptable and abhorrent."

"It's unfortunate that sexuality is a component in the nature of freedom," Pete wrote in early 2002, pointing out that with the advent of feminism, women were in a stronger and more favourable position than men by the fact that they retained their primal abilities to give birth and raise children.

"With the advance of feminism in western society . . . women can shape the future," Townshend told *Spin's* Kristine McKenna. "I don't object to feminism, but I think men should have a version of it for themselves." While the modern woman had gained considerable ground, many men – particularly those within the New Romantics movement – had deliberately changed their appearance, dressing and styling their hair effeminately and wearing make-up, something which Townshend had flirted with a few years earlier. "In some way I experienced triggered identification with those young men who wanted to defy macho conventions of the post-military epoch," he wrote.

Townshend's weekly psychotherapy sessions had unlocked some disturbing skeletons from his childhood. "Through therapy I had come to realise that I had been quite seriously emotionally abused as a child," he wrote in an early 2002 posting on his website, saying that the abuse had occurred while staying at his grandmother's house when he was a child. "Like many other celebrities . . . I turned to creative work and finally incomprehensible self-destruction as a means to draw attention to my subconscious difficulty."

With hindsight, this 'subconscious difficulty' was evident in Townshend's writing, from 'I Can't Explain' and 'I'm A Boy' via *Tommy* and *Quadrophenia* – both stories of young, desperate men suffering various degrees of mental and physical abuse – up to his most recent work, which was originally to be titled *The Tragedy Of The Boy*.

The setting for this urban story of male identity crisis presented itself during Townshend's regular drive from Twickenham to his office at Faber & Faber in London. "I used to drive home back through a familiar territory, the White City estate, which lies just next to Shepherd's Bush, which is where The Who's career really began," he said in a 1985 radio interview with Dan Neer. "I used to cut back through it, and I was looking for a place which would act as a symbol setting for a story which I had in mind about life in post-war Britain and suddenly I realised that this place contained all these street names which were connected with the British Empire: Australia Road, Canada Way, and New Zealand Road and South Africa Road and then I thought – 'White City – it's such a wonderful name, and it's a promise of a vision.'"

In 1908, the White City area became the site of the world-famous Franco-British Trade Exhibition, featuring exotic buildings which represented countries from all across the British Empire, and a spectacular arch which served as the main entrance. The dazzling white plasterwork of the buildings, which were erected especially for the exhibition, inspired the area's name. The White City stadium, the world's largest at the time with a reported capacity of 150,000, was erected for the 1908 Olympiad. In 1936, Hammersmith Council bought the majority of the exhibition grounds to build apartment buildings. The streets were named after exhibits, such as Commonwealth Avenue, Australia Road, India Way, Canada Way, South Africa Road and White City Road. By 1984, the area had badly deteriorated, a shadow of its glorious past, and the stadium was demolished the following year.

The White City estate provided Townshend with a suitable "metaphor for neighbourhood" through which he could explore his thoughts on male emasculation and his memories of child abuse. His musings led him to the conclusion that a film would be necessary in order to fully articulate his ideas. "Many of the songs needed images, many of the images needed poetry," he later wrote. Pete's original idea for a story, which "was simply going to be 24 hours in the life of somebody who spends a day literally wandering through that area . . ." as he described in 1985, became an examination of the behaviour and relationships of the central character Jim, an embattled, frustrated male struggling to express himself. "The story is a follow on from *Quadrophenia*," Pete said in 1985. "Jim might be Jimmy from *Quadrophenia* 20 years on."

Like its predecessors, *White City* was full of autobiographical elements. In the film, for example, Jim states that as a child, he was sent off to live with his grandmother and that his mother was often involved in affairs with other men. This inclusion of autobiographical information proved cathartic, as Townshend wrote in 2002: "Writing *White City* was – for me in therapy – a way of facing some of the anger I felt towards the adults in my childhood, who had done their best, but failed to be perfect parents [if there can be such a thing]."

A film script was duly written, the original synopsis of which Townshend later outlined as:

A violent young man ends up in a wheelchair after a drunken car crash. He descends into anger and self-pity, after driving away his wife with acts of violence. She takes up a job in a women's refuge on the multi-racial White City estate on which they live.

The young man has a friend who takes him to various local pub gigs. At one of these gigs he attempts to perform, wearing a daft transvestite's outfit and a lot of make-up. He starts well, but booze gets the better of him. He has a terrible row with his mother who runs the pub.

In the middle of the row he suddenly remembers some childhood trauma involving his mother, and rushes to consult his estranged wife who is training some young swimmers at the local swimming baths. She is planning a special event to raise funds for the Refuge.

At the pool the young man comes across a rock star – myself [10] – who had gone out with his wife before they were married. I have offered to perform at the fund-raiser. My obsession at the time is with South Africa and the curse of apartheid. At every chance I get, I engage people [possibly bore them?] with the issues there, attempting to alert people – who really don't need to be reminded – to the fact that racism is everywhere.

During the rehearsals I find myself attracted to my old girlfriend and there seems to be a chance we might reunite.

The young man, believing himself to be on the brink of redemption with his wife, is infuriated by me and storms out of the baths.

Later that night, while I am onstage performing, he arrives, dressed absurdly, somehow managing to walk, and to my chagrin convinces his wife to go back to him.

I sulkily leave town, back on the road, hopeful I can find love and help Mandela to rescue Soweto.

Pete showed his completed script to Bill Curbishley, who reacted favourably and encouraged him to write songs based around the story. During the summer, Pete concentrated on writing songs and refining the story,

---

[10] Townshend revealed in a 2005 interview posted on his website that "the original story was less about me as a rock star than a group of people I'd met in connection with the work of Erin Pizzey who founded the first Women's Refuge [from male domestic violence] in London, and who The Who had started their charity Double-O to help. As the script changes evolved, I became more the subject of the movie rather than simply the writer-composer . . ."

which he referred to as a 'musical teleplay'.[11] On the recommendation of a friend at Faber & Faber, producer Walter Donahue, he contacted Australian film producer Richard Lowenstein. Townshend had been impressed by Lowenstein's award-winning feature *Strikebound*, and invited him to London to collaborate on the script and shoot the film.

"I badly needed help from Lowenstein," Pete recalled in a January 2002 web entry. "In the UK in 1984 no one knew whether I was a distinguished publisher, a reformed junkie, a writer of short stories or a rock star. I was trying to do too many things at once, possibly in a confused battle for some meaning in my post-Who life."

Armed with a script and extensive "location reconnaissance video movies of the White City estate" which he'd filmed with a pre-production team assembled by Donahue, Townshend felt primed to deliver a groundbreaking feature-length film.

"It would be wrong to say Lowenstein and I hit it off. He seemed slightly sceptical of me. He later referred to my script as 'pretentious'. My script had been intended as a jumping off point for our collaboration on a finished version, but the more we spoke, the more I realised that Lowenstein found my ideas confused. Looking back today, I can see why . . ."

A 'confused' assessment of a Townshend script was now something to be expected. "Indeed, [*White City*] was – on the surface – a confused tangle of ideas and images," Pete wrote, "but from my point of view, no more complex than those gathered for my first few songs written for The Who. Songs like 'I'm A Boy' or 'Join My Gang', and the background stories for projects like *Tommy* or *Quadrophenia* all tapped into similar veins."

"[Lowenstein and I] stripped away quite a lot, we stripped away a lot of the music which we felt was superfluous and the whole thing did evolve," Townshend said in 1985. "In small steps, I'd do a bit of recording and then we'd together do a bit of writing for the screenplay. We were inching forward step by step . . ."

---

[11] While working on the demos for *White City*, Townshend also continued to work on *Siege*. In early 1987, he purchased a large Synclavier synthesiser. "One of the first things I did on my new Synclavier at this time was to conduct a series of exercises round the *Siege* canon I composed on sheet music . . ." Pete wrote in his *Scoop 3* liner notes. "I had hoped to complete a symphonic piece based on the canon, but really such a task was – and still is – out of my scope. But I produced a large number of simple variations." A handful of these variations were included on *Scoop 3*.

Pete, however, still wanted to maintain the integrity of the teleplay, with its interspersed songs and poetry. "I hoped to demonstrate to him [Lowenstein] that the song lyrics, and possibly some poetry sequences in the soundtrack, would both deepen and clarify the confused plotting and give it substance and edge," he wrote in 2001. However, time was against him. Lowenstein had already been in Britain for two weeks and the budget was in place. In the interest of getting the film underway, and trusting that Lowenstein was the man for the job, Townshend agreed to relinquish control. "At Donahue's suggestion, and with my complete blessing, Lowenstein finally retired to a posh hotel and completed his own shooting script without any further involvement from me."

Meanwhile, recording for the *White City* album began at Eel Pie studios in Twickenham and Soho, and AIR studios in London, with a familiar cast of Simon Phillips, Mark Brzezicki, Tony Butler, Peter Hope-Evans, Rabbit Bundrick and producer Chris Thomas on board. Other guest musicians included Dave Gilmour, bassists Chucho Merchan, Pino Palladino, Phil Chen and Steve Barnacle, the five-man brass section Kick Horns, and ex-Blondie drummer Clem Burke. The band was dubbed Deep End, referring to the film's concert stage, located at the deep end of the White City Pool. An interesting addition on backing vocals was Pete's 16-year-old daughter, Emma.

Recording and mixing of the album concluded in early October, although some work remained unfinished due to Pete's commitment to the accompanying film. "My daily involvement in the film as an actor meant that several pieces of music intended to be in the soundtrack weren't even completed in the recording studio prior to filming. Two quite important songs, 'After The Fire' and 'All Shall Be Well', emerged from the *White City* songwriting demo sessions but were never completed at the time. The first I gave later to Roger Daltrey to use on one of his solo albums, the second I adapted as a pivotal closing celebration in my next project *The Iron Man*."[12]

Shooting on the film got underway with Lowenstein at the helm. Pete appeared, rather self-consciously, alongside the other principal actors, Andrew Wilde ('Jim') and Frances Barber ('Alice'). "It was the first time I ever had to sit with an actress and pretend to have feelings for her,"

---

[12] Other unfinished songs included 'Life To Life', which was later used as the title song on the *Playing For Keeps* soundtrack, and 'Night School', a version of which appears as an extra on the *White City* video.

Townshend wrote in early 2002. "I just felt and looked shy." In one scene, Pete and Jim told stories, reminiscing. "I found that much easier to negotiate," Townshend recalled. "The rest of my 'acting' was confined to wandering around the White City estate in a Metropolis-label overcoat."

Pete's relationship with Lowenstein improved once filming was under way. "He incorporated into his own script many of the stronger conventional elements of my own, and honed together a solid story," Townshend said. Unfortunately, the end product failed to live up to expectation.

"With more money and more screen time – [*White City*] would have made an impressive and moving major feature film with substantial music sequences," Townshend wrote in January 2002. "With a bigger budget I believe Lowenstein would have made a film for me that provided a British complement to *Purple Rain*. As it was, we shot on 35mm rather than the first proposed Super 16 and ran out of money and movie stock with about 20 minutes of film for music video still to shoot."

The record company investors had insisted that three usable music videos should be incorporated within the story, which act as a distraction from what would otherwise have been a far more conventional and satisfying full-length feature.

"I still think the songs from *White City* work better if you imagine the young hero is disabled, and drunk," Pete wrote in the *Scoop 3* liner notes in 2001. Instead, the film became "an anachronism – too short for cinema release, too long for music video TV, and too insubstantial for my more intelligent and incisive fans."

"I remember working on *White City* with great pleasure . . . Lowenstein was really wonderful to work with once filming started and we have remained friends."

Two decades on, Townshend said that he would "very much like to novelise" his *White City* story. "It touches on so many areas of the kind of world in which I grew up that it seems a shame to have it fail to properly flower."

CHAPTER FIFTEEN

1985–1989

"Commercially, leaving The Who was the dumbest thing I've ever done in my life but artistically, it was undeniably the most logical thing for me to do. It was the most important thing I've ever done for me – to allow me to have a new beginning, to actually grow."

– Pete Townshend, 1987

THE *White City* album was released in November 1985 – its official tag being *White City: A Novel.* "Well, I thought, if I could get away with Rock Opera . . ." Pete told Dan Neer, "[that's] a bit of a gag, you know, to address the fact that I'd been working as a book publisher lately and that if I was gonna make a record and a video, that I should call it a novel."

The album's opener, 'Give Blood', addressed the film's central issue of emasculation, as Townshend attempted to explain: "The idea behind the thing was to both honour the old values, the idea that somebody would be prepared to fight for something that they believed in, but to face the fact that that won't work any more, you know, and that we have to find a new way of giving blood, of proving that we are capable of self-sacrifice. It seems to me that the way that we are confronted with now is just to make some kind of sacrifice for the people that we live alongside, you know, we can't really hope to gain heroism through acts of valour abroad any more, it just doesn't seem to work that way . . . I think really that the idea was also that 'keep blood between brothers' – you can still shed blood, but do it wrist to wrist."

In contrast to the lyrics, the song's musical structure was arrived at in a relatively simple manner. "'Give Blood' was one of the tracks I didn't even play on," Pete said in 1996. "I brought in Simon Phillips, Pino Palladino and Dave Gilmour simply because I wanted to see my three favourite musicians of the time playing on something and, in fact, I didn't have a song for them to work on, and sat down very quickly and rifled through a box of stuff, and said to Dave, 'Do one of those kind of ricky – ticky – ricky – ticky things, and I'll shout 'Give Blood!' in the microphone every five minutes and let's see what happens.' And that's what happened. Then I constructed the song around what they did."

Gilmour recalled to Nicholas Schaffner that he arrived at the studio thinking he would be recording the guitar track for 'White City Fighting'. "Simon Phillips was there for something that I wasn't needed on, so Pete found something else for both of us to do . . . That I was on 'Give Blood' as well was an accident."

The relationship of 'Brilliant Blues' to the *White City* theme seems to lie in its depiction of the British male's resilience in the face of adversity. Townshend said in a 1985 radio interview that the song was "dedicated to a Liverpudlian performer called Pete Wylie [singer with early Eighties group, Wah!] I particularly like Liverpudlian performers, 'cause when they get big in England, they stay in Liverpool – they don't leave, and I kind of admire that – sticking to your ground . . . I just had this idea that in a way the whole statement that the Liverpudlian performers were making by staying in Liverpool, it was a renouncing, this true blue British way . . . We have two colours in Britain – we have blue for the right and red for the left, and so it was quite simply just to say the brilliant blue doesn't flow in Merseyside, you know, the Mersey is a grey, neglected river with a run-down port and a lot of problems in the area. But when you go to Liverpool they've still got that incredible Merseyside spirit."

'Face The Face' drew comparisons to the T.S. Eliot poem *The Love Song Of J. Alfred Prufrock*, which contains the line, *We must prepare a face to meet the faces that we meet*, but it was only after he'd written the song that Townshend discovered the poem.

"In that line what he's talking about is . . . it's a kind of contrast to Dylan Thomas' line, that thing of fighting death: *Rage against the dying of the light*. He's talking about preparing a certain dignity, to meet your destiny, that's really what this song is about. It's both about preparing to meet whatever's gonna hit you, but also seeking it out – seeking out, certainly not death, but seeking your destiny."

" 'Face The Face' was done on a new keyboard . . ." Townshend said in 1996, "and I was very keen to get something very, very fast and upbeat knocked out, and I knocked out a few sections that I couldn't play all together. I could play bits of it, but try and do it all together and it confounded me, so I did a bunch of building blocks and said to Rabbit, 'I want 40 of them' – this is a Mozart technique – 'five of those, six of these, seven of those,' and he wrote it all out and played it to a drum loop . . . and that became the beginning of the track. This was very much a new age type of recording, and that's why it sounds pretty modern, I think. Simon Phillips overdubbed the drums, we later overdubbed the brass, we over-dubbed backing vocals, we overdubbed everything. It was all overdubbed onto Rabbit's synthesiser playing." When released as a single in late 1985, 'Face The Face' peaked at number 26 in the US charts.

The inspiration for 'Hiding Out' addressed a more physical aspect of Townshend's 'soul in siege' notion, as he told Dan Neer: "If you look at a place like Tokyo, where there's an enormous population, the space in which people live gets smaller, but there's always the fact that you can look out of a window and see the stars. In fact, to somebody who's in jail, just a tiny, tiny, tiny, tiny window so that you can see the sky is all you need to keep you sane. And that's really what the song is about."

'Secondhand Love' was Jim's statement to Alice that he wanted her to himself, while 'Crashing By Design', with its line *Another man without a woman, too many rages have cost you this time* was an assessment of Jim's life.

'I Am Secure' was Townshend's observation of the White City area, but was also perhaps a statement about his view of life from the elevated platform of rock stardom:

> *My room looks out to the wide open spaces*
> *My heart is touched by awakening faces*
> *I see the panic of people in motion*
> *I can stand here and look out on an ocean*

The song also mentioned apartheid, which provided yet another metaphor for the soul in siege. "I've always been very interested in the poignancy of the situation in South Africa," Townshend told Neer, "where black and white are not even allowed to make love. I wanted to use it in a poetic way, to look at the way that people in modern urban areas are kept apart by the conditions in which they live."

Apartheid also provided an ironic example of the decline of the British Empire and its idealistic vision, all of which were represented in the White City estate. "The nationalistic images of Empire sparked by the historical street and building names jarred against the main political issue of the day, which was the dismantling of apartheid in South Africa," Pete explained in 2002. "Through my friendship with David Astor [once the owner-editor of *The Observer* newspaper in the UK] I had – with Peter Gabriel and others – become involved in fund-raising for the ANC via less radical black South African organisations based in the UK. I was also supportive of the sanctions imposed against South Africa which I knew Nelson Mandela endorsed."

'White City Fighting' became the album's central track, having been turned down the previous year by Gilmour. "I was extremely pleased about that," he told Nicholas Shaffner, "because I'm probably the only person who's ever written a song on a Pete Townshend album apart from Pete."

The music to the album's final song, 'Come To Mama', began life as 'Commonwealth Boys', an experimental demo recorded in late 1984 which, according to Townshend, "didn't fit the story".[1]

White City was well-received by critics, described by *Rolling Stone*'s Rob Tannenbaum as "a clear, organic parable of hope triumphing over despair, making this Townshend's best work since *Empty Glass*."

Despite Pete's reservations, the film also received polite reviews. The images of Jim's life are, in fact, so harsh that Townshend's songs come as a tangible relief from the unrelenting horror of the rest of Lowenstein's hour-long nightmare. The movie has disarmingly surreal elements, such as a prepubescent girls' synchronised swim team. Pete's decision to include the scene was partially due to the fact that the sport had recently been added to the 1984 Olympic Games, held in Los Angeles, as he told Neer: "I was very amused with the way America presented the Olympics, to see that synchronised swimming was included and I thought that if Esther Williams has finally made it to the Olympics then maybe in 20 years' time there'd be *cardboard guitar* Olympics or *breakdance* Olympics. I was so struck with it and I found that there were a lot of young kids who'd felt the same way, and in Britain particularly little girls, my daughters were mad keen on it, they used to have all these funny nose clips and I just wanted to bring it into the film because I thought it was so beautiful and so wonderful."

To promote the album and film, Deep End played live three times, twice at south London's Brixton Academy on November 1 and 2, in a drug rehab benefit aiding Double-O Charities. Townshend described Deep End onstage as "me running through solo stuff and jazz stuff and blues stuff and dancing around like a lunatic." The set list included the *White City* songs, 'Secondhand Love', 'Give Blood', 'Hiding Out' and 'Face The Face', in addition to covers of Screaming Jay Hawkins' 'I Put A Spell On You', James Brown's 'Night Train' and Robert Parker's

---

[1] 'Commonwealth Boys' was later included on *Scoop 3*.

'Barefootin'', along with such Who/Townshend classics as 'Behind Blue Eyes', 'Won't Get Fooled Again', 'The Sea Refuses No River' and 'A Little Is Enough'. In addition, Dave Gilmour sang his own 'Blue Light' and 'Love On The Air'.

"[Pete] asked me if I would do the shows with him because he wanted to move away from being the guitar hero," Gilmour told Nicholas Shaffner in 1991. "He refused point blank to play electric guitar, and people said, 'Oh, come on, at least 'Won't Get Fooled Again' – strap on a guitar and do it.' But he refused, he wanted the whole project to be not 'Pete Townshend, guitar hero' but 'Pete Townshend, singer, writer, bandleader.' It was great." (An album, *Deep End Live*, was released from the concerts).

Pete participated in another fundraiser just prior to Christmas at the Dominion Theatre, London. The "Snow Ball Revue", featuring musicians, comedians and TV personalities, was staged to raise monies for the Chiswick Family Rescue Centre, of which Karen Townshend now served as chairwoman. Townshend's band, featuring Rabbit Bundrick, Simon Phillips, Billy Nicholls and the Kick Horns, played a five-song set including 'Pinball Wizard' and 'Slit Skirts'.

In January 1986, Deep End played once more at the Midem festival in Cannes and a month later, Gilmour again joined Townshend for a benefit show at the Royal Albert Hall, organised by bassist Chucho Merchan for the victims of the Columbian volcano disaster.[2] Also on the bill were The Communards, Annie Lennox, and Chrissie Hynde. Emma Townshend joined her father onstage to perform 'Eyesight To The Blind', 'Hiding Out', 'I'm One', and a cover of The Beat's 'Save It For Later'. It would be Pete's last solo date until July 1993.

"The Deep End, as I called them, played a show or two," Townshend told Hugh Foley in 1989, "and straight afterwards they all said, 'God, this is the best band that we've ever been in, we must go out on the road!' and I said, 'It can go out on the road – but not with me.'"

While Townshend was in the middle of the *White City* sessions, Boomtown Rats' singer Bob Geldof (with the able assistance of esteemed promoters Harvey Goldsmith in the UK and Bill Graham in the US) was busily coordinating Live Aid, a live music event to be staged in both

---

[2] The volcano, Nevada del Ruiz, melted glaciers and triggered a massive flood of water and debris which killed over 25,000 people in November 1985.

London and Philadelphia, with simultaneous broadcast worldwide to raise funds for victims of Ethiopia's horrific famine. The majority of the world's top artists – over 60 in total – agreed to participate, including Paul McCartney, Mick Jagger, Bob Dylan, Eric Clapton, David Bowie, Elton John and a reunited Led Zeppelin with Phil Collins sitting in on drums. Townshend had already pledged to perform but this wasn't enough for the persuasive Geldof who was insistent that The Who perform. After being called off several times due to bickering among various members – Geldof later likened it to "getting one man's four ex-wives together" – The Who only finally agreed to play because of the anticipated harsh media and public reaction if they turned down such a worthy cause.

The Who's set at Wembley Stadium on July 13, 1985, in front of a reported 1.5 billion television viewers worldwide, consisted of 'My Generation', 'Pinball Wizard', 'Love Reign O'er Me' and 'Won't Get Fooled Again'. Their underwhelming performance was marred by several technical problems, the most glaring of which was a satellite transmission breakdown which resulted in a large chunk of the band's performance being lost. When the coverage resumed, the television audience saw Townshend attempting a trademark sweep of his right leg over his mike stand which resulted in him falling flat on his back. Without his regular bass tech, Entwistle experienced last-minute problems with his main instrument just prior to taking the stage. "I ran for the backup bass but couldn't tune it because there were no transformers backstage," he told *Guitar Player* in 1989. "At that point we were introduced, and I barely managed to get back onstage in time to start 'My Generation'. If you listen closely to the video, you can hear me tuning the D string as we go. I just about got it in tune in time for the bass solo."

At the London concert's conclusion, Townshend and McCartney hoisted Geldof onto their shoulders. "I nearly died of embarrassment," Geldof later recalled. "It was terrible. These people were pop greats . . . I am still embarrassed but intensely proud that I was carried on Paul McCartney's and Pete Townshend's shoulders."

Townshend had originally intended to showcase a new song, 'After The Fire' during The Who's set at Live Aid. The song ended up being recorded by Daltrey for inclusion on his latest solo album, *Under A Raging Moon*.

"I actually wrote it for the Live Aid concert," Pete told Dan Neer. "I thought it would be really good to have a new song which we could do, but we really didn't have time to do it. I wrote it two or three days before, and then I met Roger in a club, told him I'd written it and that it was ready and he had three days of recording left and managed to squeeze it in. I'm absolutely delighted with the way he's done it . . .

"I got the idea from thinking about things that people were saying about the aid that was going over to Africa, you know, the fact that this will help put the fire out, but it will still smoulder in the future, and it just seemed to me that the line also fitted pretty much the kind of thing that's happened in the past with The Who, you know – the fire might be out, but it's still smouldering."

The band's Live Aid appearance brought the inevitable questions regarding the possibility of further Who shows. "I think The Who is almost certainly over with as a recording act," Pete told Neer. "I don't want to be a big tease here, but we didn't think that we'd ever get together and do the Live Aid concert so I suppose if an opportunity like that came up again we'd certainly consider it. But what I'm looking forward to is the possibility of working in new ways with the other members of the band, in a way which would bring me the same kind of enjoyment that I get from functioning as somebody that, say, could write songs for Roger, or to work with John or Kenney on musical things in the future. I do want to get away from The Who years. The Who went round in a great big circle and it was a *great* circle, but in the end it stopped working, for me anyway. I certainly wouldn't pursue that."

In mid-1986, Townshend returned to the recording studio. "I was recording a follow-up album to *White City*," he wrote in 2001. "Chris Thomas was producing for an album that was intended to support a series of story videos that I was planning that would have come out very much like that wonderful movie *Strictly Ballroom* had I the talent of its director Baz Luhrmann.[3] However, my father died [in June] during the sessions and I had to let the idea go. There were a number of tracks recorded at this time, 'All Shall Be Well' and 'Lonely Words' are worthy of a mention. There is even another song from these sessions with the same title which has a tango beat. The subtitle of this song was 'Real World' and I used the idea later in a different form as a song for *Iron Man*."[4]

The second instalment of the *Scoop* series was released in March 1987. As a continuation of its predecessor, *Another Scoop,* dedicated to Cliff

---

[3] Australian director Baz Luhrmann's *Strictly Ballroom* was released in 1992. Luhrmann was also behind the 2001 movie hit *Moulin Rouge*.
[4] *Real World (Can You Really Dance?)* ultimately surfaced as an instrumental.

Townshend, represented a wide range of Pete's demo recordings, from one of the earliest, 'Call Me Lightning', through Who hits such as 'Substitute', 'Pinball Wizard', and 'You Better You Bet' up to his recent *Siege* work, represented by 'Cat Snatch', 'Prelude: The Right To Write', and 'Ask Yourself'.

"The greatest strength of *Another Scoop*," wrote *Rolling Stone*'s David Fricke, "is its revealing portrait of the artist in his private song lab, testing and editing his creative impulses before broadcasting them to the world at large. *I want my voice to cut over mountains*, Townshend declares in a 1984 gem called 'The Shout'. *And I want my soul to gush up like fountains to where you reside*. He needn't worry – these recordings have a resonance that will carry far beyond his studio walls."

On February 8, 1988, The Who regrouped (the apt term "persuaded to perform" was used by the *Washington Post*) for their first show since Live Aid, an appearance at the Royal Albert Hall for the British Phonographic Industry (BPI) Awards, the British equivalent of the Grammies. In addition to performing, the band was to receive a Lifetime Achievement award for "long-standing services to the music industry."

The Who's disastrous appearance at Live Aid came back to haunt them, as Townshend explained to the *Washington Post*'s Richard Harrington the following year:

> "*As I was about to leave for the Albert Hall, my 17-year-old daughter Aminta was taken to the hospital with pneumonia; she'd been in bed with bronchitis for a while and just as I was about to leave, the ambulance was coming. And it was a real test of the show-must-go-on dictum. And all these things flashed through my mind: Maybe the reason she's got a weak chest in the first place is psychosomatic . . . Is she the way she is because I put so many other children before her? But I went to the hall and did the gig. And I thought, damn you, Townshend – given the gun, you will still kill. I just can't get it out of my blood.*"

With a family crisis hanging over him, Townshend's frame of mind could not have been improved by The Who's brief but ragged performance being faded out during 'Who Are You' due to the show overrunning its allotted schedule. Because one of the previous acts had been given extra time, the transmission was halted to make way for the BBC's nine o'clock news report, resulting in a huge backstage row. The BPI event also marked Kenney Jones' last appearance with The Who.

With the follow-up to *White City* put on ice, Townshend considered his next move. "The first thing I did to try to give myself some roots in the publishing world was to write a book," he said in 1989. "The next thing I thought was I should try to forge some musical links to my publishing life, that I should do something which is actually embedded in the literary world. I was very determined to achieve something that attended to both sides of my career."

Pete decided to write a musical based on an existing literary work, with specific designs regarding the songs.

"I've got this bee in my bonnet about the fact that the term *musical* has moved into the Eighties, but the music has been the only thing that hasn't moved into the Eighties," he told Hugh Foley in 1989. "Everything about modern musicals is new, except the music . . . I went to see a bunch of musicals over the last four or five years, a lot of which I liked for various reasons, particularly *Les Miserables* . . . but the music was junk – not just junk, but old-fashioned junk, it just didn't belong . . . you can understand the mechanic behind it but it doesn't move you. So I wanted music that was a wee bit more up to date. Even my music isn't new – I'd like to see somebody like Thomas Dolby working on a musical, too, but maybe if I do it, he'll do it."

"I just felt that I had the experience of working with conceptual pieces; I've done it since the beginning of The Who," Townshend told *Musician* in 1989, "and I thought, I should really attend to this again. I'm not just a songwriter; I'm a storyteller. And my experience has been acutely a rock'n'roll one and very, very reflective."

In searching for an appropriate subject, Townshend said, "I looked for a fairy tale. I think that the term fairy tale is something that you can only apply to those universal stories that work at every level – they work for children, adolescents, and older people alike. In *The Iron Man*, I think I've found it."

Pete had first read *The Iron Man* – a 1968 children's story written by British Poet Laureate Ted Hughes – back in 1976 when he started Eel Pie Publishing. While most of the company's books concerned pop culture, some such as *Hepzibah* by Peter Dickinson [published in 1978] were aimed at the children's market. "We were hoping to produce better books for children," Townshend explained, "books in which illustrations were vital and yet in which the prose had a kind of poetic weight, and was not con-descending to kids. *The Iron Man* was our model."

In 1986, through the Faber & Faber connection, Hughes met Townshend, who explained his plans to create a musical based on the story. "I asked him if the rights were available," Townshend later recalled, "and I told him what I was contemplating, turning it into a musical, and obviously as a rock musician, a rock musical – I hate that term. I found that he was very open-minded and certainly not at all concerned about the idea of his story being adapted and perhaps distorted by being swallowed up in the world of rock'n'roll. He was quite keen to see what would happen."

The Iron Man was a great metal giant who emerges from the sea and terrifies a rural English farming community because of his intimidating stature and a habit of eating anything made of metal – notably cars, tractors and fences. The townsfolk trap the giant in a huge pit and bury it but a year later, the giant manages to dig himself out and once again terrorises the town. A small boy named Hogarth suggests that the giant be taken to a local scrap metal yard, where he would have all the 'food' he wanted. All was well until a massive dragon from outer space lands on Earth, covering the whole of Australia. It eats all manner of living things – trees, people, and animals. A massive war is waged in vain against the Space Dragon, who gives the world's population a week to deliver its first meal, threatening to devour entire cities if it isn't satisfied.

Hogarth pleads with the Iron Man to do something to stop the Space Dragon. The metal giant takes action by challenging the much larger creature to a "test of strength". If the dragon declines to accept, it would be labelled a "miserable cowardly reptile, not fit to bother with." The Iron Man lies on a massive grid of iron girders and submits to a fire which turns him red-hot. He tells the Space Dragon that if it can't withstand the same degree of heat from the sun, then it would have to be his slave. The battle lasts three excruciating rounds until the Space Dragon could withstand no more. "The fires of the sun are too terrible for me," it said. "I submit . . . I'll do anything you like."

Upon discovering that his foe is a "star spirit" whose function is to make "the music that space makes to itself", the Iron Man tells the Space Dragon to take up residence inside the moon and sing for Earth. "It's a long time since anybody here on Earth heard the music of the spheres. It might do us all good." This the Space Dragon does, and the population of the Earth is deeply affected by the beautiful music that emanates from the moon. "The singing got inside everybody and made them as peaceful as starry space and blissfully above all their earlier little squabbles," Hughes wrote. "The strange, soft, eerie space music began to alter all the people of the world. They stopped making weapons. The countries began to think how they could live pleasantly alongside each other."

Pete discovered in the book a great deal that could be related to the contemporary world ("It is about fear and deprivation of children and the ignorance we display towards both history and nature. You can read many different morals into the tale") and was particularly struck by the tale's symbolism.

"There was so much more to it than there appeared to be on the surface," he said in 1989. "I was deeply struck by the story. It fitted my life at the time, it fitted my childhood, and to some extent I hope that it fits my future. It's a very, very simple story in structure, and yet such a powerful story."

In a July 1989 interview with the *Washington Post*, Townshend outlined perhaps the most important connection he made with the work.

"What is at the centre of *Iron Man* is a little boy who is isolated and afraid. It's the *Tommy* story, it's the *Quadrophenia* story, it's my story, which is why I was attracted to it in the first place. What I found when I got deep into it, it's also about that little boy taking power, taking control of his own life and doing it with such a vengeance that he actually over-comes fear by taking control of the very things that are threatening him. And in a sense, I think that's what I've done in my life and what I intend to continue doing."

"I identify very much with Hogarth myself," he elaborated to *Musician* in 1989. "I have to remind myself sometimes that I'm a big, strong man. We're all big people with nothing to be afraid of. We're the masters of this planet and nothing should frighten us except our own actions and their consequences, our carelessness, the possibility that we are our own undoing."

Armed with a story and a head full of ideas, Pete retreated to his home in Cornwall where he spent an intensive two weeks writing lyrics and music.

"In the two weeks I spent on the actual lyrics," Townshend told Dan Neer in 1989, "I surrounded myself with books about robotics and space machinery and dragons and myths and legends and the Beowulf stuff, and all kinds of stuff that I felt was relevant to what I was doing, and just immersed myself . . ."

In addition to around 20 songs, he also wrote a dramatic scenario, a libretto, an overture and recitatives for the project. "I tried to construct a complete musical work which I could put into the Library of Congress and then anybody who wanted could do it," Townshend told *Rolling Stone* in 1989. "It seems mad to spend two and a half years making a record which is in and out of the American shops in three months, so I just thought maybe I could write something which had a chance of having a long life. And I thought maybe I could make it have a longer life by giving it more depth, allowing it to touch a wider audience, allowing it to live in different ways and by not being so central and fundamental to it as an artist myself."

Recording sessions for *The Iron Man* began in early November 1986. Townshend decided to handle the production himself because "I wanted complete control over the voicings of all the chords, so that nobody would ever play a note that I didn't want, and the structures would be very, very pure . . . my first hope was that I would be able to pick up a guitar or sit at a piano with a bunch of vocalists, and the thing would hang together. And it does; you can strip away everything."

Pete's fragile hearing was a major factor as to why the songs mainly used acoustic guitar. "I haven't written a song on this record on electric guitar; I just can't do it anymore. I was working mainly with acoustic . . . I also listened very, very quietly . . ."

"It's been a great help to me that I haven't actually done any songs with heavy guitar . . ." he told Hugh Foley in 1989. "It's actually produced a different kind of dynamics and a different kind of record, which is actually suited to this project, but if I do want to do a very heavy song, I have trouble, because if I sit with a guitar amplifier and thrash away with it, if I want to hear what I'm doing, I have to wear headphones, and even if I don't have the headphones too loud, the very sound of the guitar the way that I play it, which is the sound that's obviously caused the damage in the past, aggravates my current problem, and it sets up dead parts in my hearing spectrum, and also very, very loud ringing to the extent that now I have permanent ringing in my ears – this has developed in the last three years – to such a level that it amounts to something akin to shell shock. You have to constantly tell yourself that it's not happening, whereas what is actually happening is that I can right now hear the most unbelievable row in my head.

"If I expose myself to loud electric guitar, particularly my own loud electric guitar, my hearing suffers and I have to take about two or three weeks away from any loud noises. So it's very difficult for me to work at music. I've taken two years to make a record for myself which should have taken about a year. A lot of that has been that I've had to give myself long rests."

Townshend considered using other guitarists for the album. When *Guitar Player*'s Matt Resnicoff mentioned that the track 'Over The Top' was similar to Larry Carlton's 'Blues Bird' (from the album *Sleepwalk*), Pete replied, "Yeah, I've got that album – probably something else that's gotten into the back of my brain. At one point I actually thought about inviting him onto the record, because I was afraid that I wouldn't be able to play lead guitar. I also thought of Pat Martino, who I desperately want to work with sometime . . ."

Eventually the electric guitar parts on *The Iron Man* were added at the last minute by Townshend himself. "None of the solos were worked out," he told Resnicoff. "They were all just off the top of my head, and they were all done in two days, because I didn't think the album was going to have any lead guitar on it."

Townshend had recently visited George Harrison's Friar Park home in Henley during the time that Harrison was working on the Traveling Wilburys' first album. Roy Orbison and Mark Knopfler happened to be there at the same time.

"They were playing the tracks in George's studio," Pete recalled, "and Mark Knopfler kept coming up to me and saying, 'Strumming, man, that's what everything's about: strumming, great strumming!' . . . I went back and took the first song, 'I Won't Run Anymore', and I thought, 'I'm going to try two guitars on this, strumming.' I tried it, and my assistant producer, Jules Bowen, said, 'It really picks it up; it sounds lighter.' So I went through and put strumming guitars on everything, and then it begged an *electric* guitar. I realised I was going to have to do lead guitars."

Once the tracks were completed, Townshend began to visualise who would play each role in the story. "It was great fun, not so much actually casting it, but thinking about casting it," Pete said in 1989. "I suddenly thought, well I've got this list of characters, the Iron Man, some woodland creatures, namely a fox, a badger, an owl, a frog, the boy, Hogarth, the Space Dragon, the children, and the girl who lived inside the Space Dragon . . . This is my interpretation of the story."

Roger Daltrey played Hogarth's father while an Australian singer named Deborah Conway portrayed the vixen (representing Hogarth's conscience). A former model and singer for the Australian band Do Re Mi, Conway was originally chosen to play Hogarth. "I went to see her play," Townshend told Dan Neer in 1989, "and she was wearing a slinky red dress and she had her hair flying around, and she's just about one of the sexiest presences I've ever seen on the stage. I thought, this is not gonna work. I went up to her afterwards, and I said, 'Listen, would you mind playing something a little more foxy?' And she said she wouldn't, and what would I suggest, and I said, 'Well, how about a fox?' I've now bowed to the sexist implications of that and allowed her to be a vixen."

After much deliberation, Pete decided to play Hogarth himself. "I tried all kinds of stuff with children's voices and girls' voices, and in the end I figured, no, there has to be a centrepiece for the story," he later recalled. The woodland creatures' parts were covered by backing singers Chyna, Nicola Emmanuel, Billy Nicholls, Simon Townshend, and Cleveland Watkiss.

Townshend's initial choice for the role of the Iron Man was Lou Reed; in fact, Pete wrote the song 'Man Machines' for Reed's voice. Reed initially agreed; however, he later had to withdraw when it became clear that the project wouldn't be completed on time, creating a conflict with the recording of Reed's own album, *Songs For Drella*.

"I was kind of sorry not to have him," Townshend told Neer, "because at that time I was going to use John Lee Hooker for another role, the father, or a farmer, or something. I then just wondered what the hell I was going to do . . . I had this fixed idea that Lou Reed was the kind of robotic man that I required, and how was I going to replace him, and I thought, hold on a minute, you're missing the point here. It's not about the person, casting like that is a bit obvious, it's a bit kind of naïve . . . It's the kind of casting that means that when you do *Tommy* on Broadway you have to have Roger Daltrey and nobody else, like Lou Reed just symbolised something, but wasn't necessarily that person. In fact, when I heard his album [*New York*, released in 1989] I realised that what Lou was doing in life was actually taking that preconceived image that we have of him and screwing it up and throwing it away, showing us that he's grown as a man, and as a family man in particular. And I suddenly thought well maybe if Lou can't do it maybe John Lee Hooker can do it."

Townshend felt he had made the right choice. "I wanted a primordial voice," he wrote in a 1997 letter to Charles Shaar Murray, author of the 2000 Hooker biography *Boogie Man*. "The voice from R&B that I remember first being disturbed by was Howlin' Wolf, but John Lee Hooker's voice is less that of a macho monster, more of a dark, frail masculine soul. He evokes something whale-like in a way, a spirit that is thrashing powerfully beneath the surface, but in grave danger from the world and his own restrained anger and vengefulness. Ted Hughes' Iron Giant in the story has no history; we must project it onto the story for ourselves. Hughes invites us to ponder with him: 'Where had he come from, nobody knows.' The first time I heard the blues by John Lee Hooker that's how I felt – where does this come from? It was so familiar to me, so resonant, and yet so obviously not of my experience or society."

Hoping to persuade the blues master, Townshend sent Hooker a demo tape. "When Pete Townshend asked me to do it I laughed at him," Hooker told Murray in 2000. "'Iron Man? Gargling gasoline? What do you mean by this? That ain't me. That ain't the blues.' But he just said to me, 'If anyone can do it, you can.'"

Since Hooker liked the songs, he agreed to voice the part. "'The Iron Man' had been one of Hooker's nicknames back in Detroit," Murray wrote in *Boogie Man*. "The honorific bestowed on him by his friends to acknowledge his powers of stamina and endurance during those long years of working in steel mills by day and playing in bars by night. Now he was The Iron Man once more: not just to his friends, but to the world."

"It was a great, great, great thrill for me to work with John Lee Hooker," Townshend confessed to Resnicoff in 1989. "You know, just to hear him saying my name on the [studio intercom] talkback. I mean, he was the first blues performer I really adored."

Hooker's vocals were recorded in New York. "It was completely natural," Pete said of the session. "It was tricky to get used to the fact that his young blonde girlfriend was younger and prettier than any I had known, but despite his crisp suit, elegant hat and sharp demeanour, there was humility. He couldn't read music or text, and learned each line parrot-fashion. He said it wasn't blues, but he could feel it nonetheless. It was an affirmation for me to sense that he felt at home with what I was doing because I know how deeply everything I do is rooted in his own work."

"This was a very rough day in the studio," recalled Hooker's manager Mike Kappus in *Boogie Man*. "The words and phrases were completely out of John Lee's vocabulary and even with on-the-spot coaching, Pete ended up just having John speak most of the words, later using a synclavier to make them sound sung."

'Over The Top' described the Iron Man's reassembly and mindset after he fell over the cliff, while 'I Eat Heavy Metal' was a humorous dissection of his diet. "[Hooker's] got a wonderful sense of humour, and it really conveyed itself through the work," Pete said in 1989. "Certainly it was great fun working with him . . ."[5] 'I Eat Heavy Metal' also provided Townshend with a subliminal double meaning: "One thing I do know is

---

[5] Hooker was also slated to sing 'Man Machines', but he "couldn't manage to do this particular song," Townshend wrote in 2001.

what music is made of, where *Live At Leeds* came from, and where heavy metal began."

For the role of the Space Dragon, Townshend aptly cast the notoriously truculent jazz singer Nina Simone. "She was great," he told Hugh Foley. "What was interesting was I'd done a demo vocal for her, on 'Fast Food', which is the song she sings on this album. I felt like running in to her when she first sang it and saying, 'Listen, you don't have to copy my demo vocal, you do it your way,' until I suddenly realised that, of course, it was the contrary that was true. It was me that had been copying her for 25 years."

The album began with 'I Won't Run Any More', where Hogarth faces his fears. "When he sees the shining lights of the iron man on the top of the hill, the first thing that comes into his mind is, I can't run from this anymore," Townshend told Neer. "I can't run away. The story is about nightmares, in a sense, it's about fear, and what happens in children. And what happens in the story is that you see how we finally get to grips with encountering that."

'Man Machines', which Pete demoed back in 1985, was sung by Simon Townshend. Concerns were apparently raised that Simon's voice was too similar to his elder sibling's, but Simon remembers a different parallel being drawn when he sang the lead vocal on an unused take of 'Dig'. "The record company thought I sounded too much like Roger, that was the ironic thing. That's strange. I sang it quite nicely [but] I think that actually Roger's vocal was better."[6]

An unlikely Who studio reunion took place on 'Dig' and 'Fire'. "I wanted to work with Roger, but I was not keen on working with The Who again and just sounding like the band of '82," Pete told the *Washington Post* in July 1989. "This was a potential area in my solo work for The Who to come together without that programmed quality, without that need to kill, that need to complete the mission, however you feel about it emotionally . . ."

The Who acted as "my guests on this record," Townshend told Neer. "I really wanted Roger on the record. 'Dig' had a synthesiser bass on it. Once Roger was on there, something seemed to be missing and I figured it was really live bass, and I asked John if he minded doing it, and he agreed to do it. We were in the studio together, we worked together on it . . .

[6] The version of 'Dig' featuring Simon Townshend's vocal was released as a bonus track on the remastered *Iron Man* in 2006.

well, it wasn't quite the old magic, but there was certainly a chemistry there."

The Arthur Brown hit 'Fire', originally produced by Pete, represented the Iron Man's challenge to the Dragon. It also provided "a gift to AOR programmers who won't know what the hell else to do with the record," *Rolling Stone* reported in August 1989.

"When I first put the collection together, there seemed to be a hole in the fire scene," Townshend told *Musician* the previous month. "I said to my manager that the trouble with fire songs is that it's all been said. As recently as Bruce Springsteen, 'You can't find a flame without a spark.' You go back in history and the fire cliches make you want to vomit. I said the best song is just '*Fire, fire, fire, fire/ You're going to burn*. And Bill [Curbishley] said what a great idea. I said, 'No, I didn't mean the actual song.' But I sat down and thought that it wouldn't hurt. I used 'Eyesight To The Blind' by Sonny Boy Williamson on *Tommy*. Then I got a letter from Arthur in Texas. He's running a small commune there and I thought let's go for it. He wrote asking if I could help get him some money through publishing. I wrote back and said I've got a better idea. We'll put 'Fire' on the album and pray for a hit."

"'A Friend Is A Friend' is the centrepiece song from *The Iron Man*," Pete said in 1996. "There's a point in the story where the Iron Man has been trapped in a pit that's been dug for him by the hero of the story, this little boy called Hogarth, and as they're throwing earth onto his face, his eyes meet the little boy's, and the little boy realises that there had been a friendship developing between him and this iron giant, and he's worried that he's betrayed it. So it's just a song about the nature of childhood friendship, and what happens when you say to somebody when you're a little kid, 'I'm going to be your best friend for ever and ever and ever,' whether that is actually true, or can be true. And if it turns out not to be true, how does it make you feel?"

The song is "actually trying to get across the warmth and the mystery of friendship and what it is, the realisation of it," Townshend told Neer. "The words are very clear in the context of the story, but I felt that there's something about friendship that is that it's just a recurring pattern. It's not like love; it doesn't have the pain of love . . . you can actually become friends with somebody who you never know their name, who you meet every day on the train on the way to work. And that that experience, once that has happened, you have a contract . . . it's about how Hogarth has just suddenly realised that the Iron Man and he are in the same place and time, and are both facing the same kind of destiny and that a contract has been written. Hogarth has actually found his first real friend, you know."

'All Shall Be Well', a leftover from the mid-1986 recording sessions with Chris Thomas, represents the love story Pete included in his interpretation of *The Iron Man*. "I think I just felt that you couldn't have a musical without a love story . . . I also felt that there was a woman somewhere in the story and I just had to find her . . . I found her in two guises in the Space Dragon, I found her both as a mother, and also as a lover, and I don't mean that in a Freudian sense . . . but rather the idea that the first woman that any child, male or female, falls in love with is their mother. And you fall in love with your mother when she's, in most cases, certainly, in a kind of prime. After a great act of creation, a great act of self sacrifice to bring you into the world . . . the kind of thing that a mother says, with no guarantees, she's powerless to deliver what she's promising, but she knows she has to say it: 'Hush little baby don't you cry, everything's going to be all right,' and you trust that.

"This tearing that Hogarth goes through in this song, he is dealing with burgeoning lust, he's dealing with wanting to tear himself away from his mother, he's dealing with the idea of making new commitments of taking on new challenges, and all under the banner of a world which is in a sense pretending that nothing can go wrong. Or what I wanted the song to do was to make people think well, if this is so, if all shall be well, this is the way we get through life, we say, have a nice day, isn't everything nice, the sun is shining, how are we gonna solve the problems, how are we gonna grow, how are we gonna move forward. And of course what it comes down to is our primal urges, what finally gets Hogarth moving, despite the fact that everybody's telling him now that you've got the Iron Man in the scrap yard, everything's fine, life will be great, is that he wants to fall in love, he wants to find a partner, he wants to create, his animal urges take over, and he's actually quite a dangerous little character at this point."

Admittedly "an arch show tune", as Townshend described it, 'Was There Life' became the only one of "about four or five" that were written for the project to make it onto the album. "The music took me ages to write, and it was tortured and painful, and when I finally got it right, I thought this is the one I'm going to include, and I just know there's a lot of Who fans and in particular Pete Townshend fans are going to hate it, and I thought, 'I don't give a shit.' If you want the rest of the stuff, you listen to this at least once."

'Fast Food' was the Space Dragon's 'I Eat Heavy Metal' – a humorous song which described her desires. "It was fun writing the words for this," Townshend said. "Man actually is the junk food. He is the fast food."

'A Fool Says' reflected Hogarth's contemplation of the approaching Space Dragon. At first glance, the Dragon appeared to be a sparkling star from which emanated beautiful music. As it moved closer, its ugliness became apparent, and the façade of beautiful music became the screams of countless children. Hogarth's love for the approaching object was in vain, and his love could do little to conquer the Dragon, nor to satisfy her demands.

"It's not a denial of the value of love, it's just imagining that love can really conquer everything," Townshend explained. "It can't – love is an energy, but it's not an act until you turn it into an act. You have to *do* something – you have to be motivated by love to do something. He feels cheated; he feels that he has to do something."

'New Life/Reprise' rounded off the album. "I try to musically create the fact that the dragon is subordinated and the horrible screaming that she produces turns back to beautiful music and she flies off back into the sky," Townshend told Neer. "And then the cast gathers for a song called 'New Life', which is really about the fact that now is an opportunity to go ahead and do something new, create a better place. This is a song that I really did write very much with musical theatre in mind, kind of a show closing song."

The Iron Man was released in Britain and the US in June 1989 to mixed reviews. "This is a Pete Townshend solo album in the most liberal sense of the term," said *Rolling Stone*. "[Townshend] appears as part of a sizable cast of vocalists, singing on just about half of the album. There is also a noticeable shortage of ripping guitar . . . But if *The Iron Man* is short on rock'n' roll wham, its spiritual tensions are still cut from familiar Townshendian cloth . . . some guitar hooks and vocal flourishes, like the choruses in 'Over The Top' and 'Dig', sound like missed opportunities, the kind of grabbers that Townshend would have pumped up to anthemic proportions 15 years ago. It is also jarring to hear a Townshend record so bereft of ironic sting, power-chord rage and torturous self-examination. In remaining true to the innocence and wide-eyed wonder in Hughes's story [yes, dragons can fly and we can all live happily ever after], Townshend has erred on the side of compassion."

"The sentiment, however, becomes the middle-aged Townshend. The optimism and hope in songs like 'I Won't Run Anymore', 'Dig' and 'All

Shall Be Well' are refreshingly free of the confessional angst that nearly deep-sixed *White City* and *All The Best Cowboys Have Chinese Eyes . . . The Iron Man* is not lightweight art pop, nor is it the great Townshend record we've all been waiting for since *Empty Glass*. It is Pete Townshend's *My Generation* for the next generation."

People Weekly's David Hiltbrand was less kind. "Boy, will you be disappointed by this turgid fare. 'A Friend Is A Friend' and 'Was There Life' are nearly passable melodies, but only by comparison with the rest of the album. Measured against the body of Townshend's work, these efforts are third-rate. The rest of the songs, whether sung by Townshend or by such guest vocalists as John Lee Hooker or Nina Simone, are stunted and curiously devoid of charm."

Among the more positive reviews, the *Oakland Tribune* called the album "Townshend's tightest and most accessible work in years," while the *Atlanta Journal* described it as, "a musical and lyrical tour de force." "*The Iron Man* resounds with some of [Townshend's] most adventurous playing in almost seven years," *Guitar Player* reported in September. "It's also a perfectly executed pop album."

Townshend was eager to explore the visual potential of the work. At the end of 1989, he engaged in talks with London's National Theatre about the possibility of staging *The Iron Man*, while entertaining the idea of an animated film. "I'm keen to do it," Pete told *Musician* in July. "I want to see it tested in the theatre, get it into workshop as soon as possible. And if it develops, get it funded and out there."

That same month Townshend told the *Detroit Free Press* that he was "starting to look forward to the idea of getting it finished off. I'm going to try very hard to get it onto the stage, even for a limited season. I think it would actually make a greatly entertaining story."

Townshend revealed to Hugh Foley that he'd "written a whole musical, you know, with an overture, bits of recitative, and a narrative and stuff, and maybe about another eight or 10 songs which aren't on this first record – I don't think they're the kind of songs which people would miss on an album, they're songs which would only really work on a theatre stage." This caused some observers to ponder why *The Iron Man* wasn't expanded into a double to accommodate the extra songs and a more palatable plot.

"For financial reasons," Pete explained to *Musician*. "I got a nice deal from Atlantic in the States and Virgin worldwide, but I had to contract all the different singers on the record and I spent two years in the studio. It cost me a lot of money. I couldn't afford a double album because neither company was willing to pay me a double-album rate. They would have put it out, but I wasn't willing to risk my own money. It would have taken another six months and another $200,000. John Lee Hooker would have sung five or six songs as opposed to two, and there would have been an enormous amount of detail work. I was working with six singers at once, all of whom were getting £600 a day. The money was just disappearing."

Despite Pete's evident enthusiasm, it would be some years before a staged and animated version of *The Iron Man* came to fruition. Interestingly, around late 1988, he almost became involved with another feature animation project involving the character of Sinbad, thanks to old friend Richard Stanley.

"I suppose the basic theme would be that all the children of the world would come together, tacky as that sounds," Stanley recalls. "It was kind of Sinbad as a catalyst for children wanting to change everything." Most of the animation was to be drawn in Iran, "because at that time there were several very, very interesting key animators who would bring a whole new look to the film, and also they had fantastic studios with artists who were not expensive, because frame-by-frame, hand-drawn animation was really, really expensive at that time."

Stanley and project leader Michael Frank travelled to Tehran to discuss the project further. When the conversation turned to the film's music, Stanley suggested Pete, "because of the Baba sort of themes, and [Pete] was very interested. We talked about it quite a lot." Unfortunately, the project was soon derailed when in February 1989, Ayatollah Khomeini, Iran's spiritual leader, issued a fatwa against British author Salman Rushdie, claiming that Rushdie's book *The Satanic Verses* was blasphemous against Islam. As a result, Townshend declined to become involved. "Pete thought that as a member of PEN,[7] he couldn't support it," Stanley recalls. "I think it was a fairly minor thing, some meetings and some phone calls, it didn't get much beyond that . . ."

Towards the end of 1988, after several promoters had made overtures to Bill Curbishley, Townshend found himself contemplating a 25th anniversary Who tour but had been racked by doubts. Were they too old to tour? Did anyone care anymore? The Who had marked the occasion earlier that year by posing for photographs (with Kenney Jones) outside the Marquee

---

[7] PEN is a worldwide association of writers which promotes freedom of expression.

on Wardour Street, but as Townshend erroneously claimed the following year, "*nobody* ran the photos."

"I'd spent an immense amount of time thinking about the negative aspects: the trouble that I might have with my hearing, the fact that The Who are a spent force creatively and so couldn't ever go into the studio and produce a decent record. And we're too old, and this group kills people, and music does not belong in stadiums."

However the financial incentives were difficult to overlook. "To be 100 per cent honest, the first thing that made me think about touring was the money," Townshend told *Musician* in 1989. "The commercial force behind such a venture is fantastic. I started to think what it would mean to have so much money that I would never have to make records at all. But around Christmas I decided I couldn't face doing it in spite of the fabulous sums of money involved. I said, 'No, I want out.' I thought what I'd be doing this year was put out my solo album, do a week of interviews, make the videos and go sailing."

On January 18, Pete was in New York for a Rock'n'Roll Hall of Fame dinner at the Waldorf Astoria, delivering a speech inducting The Rolling Stones, which *Rolling Stone* described as "biting".

By the end of the evening, he was starting to reconsider his decision. "I saw The Soul Stirrers onstage, and this 86-year-old guy was onstage talking about music, and I realised that this undeniable American art form of rock'n'roll had given me a reason for being, a focus, a destiny, a past, a present and a future."

In addition, Soul Stirrer R.H. Harris' speech had a profound effect as Townshend explained to Dan Neer, "I experienced something there that was very, very important and that was the perspective and the context that I live in and that I'd grown in, and that was a black American heritage . . . I felt a kind of a spiritual buzz from it . . . [Harris] said, 'We've waited a long time for this award, and it's come from you white folk and you rock'n'roll people . . . but rock'n'roll comes from R & B and R & B comes from gospel music with a swing, and gospel music with a swing comes from the Soul Stirrers.' I looked around me and there's Paul Simon, nodding, 'This is true, this is true,' and Bruce Springsteen, 'Yes, yes of course, this is very true,' and I thought, 'I'd never even heard of them,' you know and I thought, 'I'm in the presence of the people who created rock'n'roll . . .'

"And I just thought, faced with all this unbelievable history which was kind of descending on me . . . that I shouldn't be obdurate about this. If they want to honour The Who, if they want to bring The Who back through the Hall of Fame, so be it . . . If fans out there are willing to pay us to go and attempt to do something, then who are we to argue? And I know I'm going to have trouble with the stadium thing, I know I'm going to have trouble with journalists telling me that I'm a hypocrite, I know I'm going to feel a bit of a hypocrite, I know it's going to be very difficult for me to work with my hearing problems, I know there are going to be a lot of problems, but I also know that I am still at heart and always will be, a marine. I know that once you give me my gun, I will just go out there and I will kill, and so maybe right now I shouldn't intellectualise this whole thing too much. I should just get down, grab my guitar and go out there and do what I've been trained to do, and hope that it all works out."

"I just felt that this is the music I was partially responsible for bringing back to America when The Who came over in the Sixties with a catalogue of R&B songs," Townshend told *Rolling Stone*. "And I suddenly thought, 'This is shit. They want us to come back and tour, and this is their music. It's not my fucking music.' And I suddenly felt that I'd been obstructive, obdurate and obstinate. All the *obs*. And I thought that I should get my shit together."

The trip back to London removed any further doubts from his mind. Having intended on flying club-class, he decided to switch to economy when his flight was delayed by fog. Trying to find a way to cope with his unfamiliar and uncomfortable surroundings, Townshend decided to pass the time by figuring out how much he'd saved by downgrading his ticket. It turned out to be about $165 an hour. "By the time we landed," he told *Rolling Stone*, "I suddenly realised that the whole nub of the thing, the other thing about coming back to America and touring, was that America was gonna insist on sending me home very, very rich. And that's a good feeling."

Pete arrived home and told his wife, "Listen, I've procrastinated a lot about two things: one is whether or not to do this tour, and the other is whether or not we should adopt children. And you know, I think I'm gonna do both. Let's get some kids, and let's do this tour." A couple of weeks later, the tour was being booked and Karen Townshend was pregnant.

CHAPTER SIXTEEN

1989–1993

"What has bothered me is the echoes of people like Bob Dylan, Tom Petty and Neil Young talking about the evil of nostalgia and sentimentality in rock. Part of me kind of agrees, but I don't really know why. I've been trying to find out in my own mind why nostalgia or sentimentality of any kind is such a bad thing. Certainly there was a lot of it on The Who tour."

– Pete Townshend, 1990

"I was very worried that if Broadway failed, it would halt Tommy as a property for probably another 10, 15 years. And that would have been a shame, because my instincts told me this is the right time. One of the things that was very disturbing is that I knew that if it was successful, it would change my life. I was excited that if the show did well, it could feed my future creative life, but I was also frightened that maybe I should be retiring, you know? Maybe I should be just taking the money I already have and slowing down, getting out of show business."

– Pete Townshend, 1993

IN early spring, The Who started rehearsals for their reunion tour at Bray Studios, outside London. Anyone who stumbled upon the band within the vast, aeroplane hanger-type space could have been forgiven for not recognising The Who. A total of 12 outside musicians were being used, which prompted many observers to question the use of the name.

"What you're hearing today is not The Who," Townshend clarified to Matt Resnicoff during rehearsals. "It's a sophisticated bunch of session musicians who, because of the way they've been picked and the way they've evolved in their relationship to me through my work as a writer, feel very deeply about what they're doing. But nonetheless, they're session musicians, who, when this is finished, will go back to Mick Jagger or whoever it is they were with. The Who, if you like, is John Entwistle,

Roger Daltrey, and Pete Townshend, three kids who met at school when they were 14, and we're still here."

Conspicuously absent was Kenney Jones, whose working relationship with Daltrey was still strained. Jones' original ally in The Who also clearly despaired of the drummer.

"Kenney [has] given me an extremely hard time lately," Townshend told *Musician* in July. "Firstly about our not going on the road for so long. And he said I denied him the opportunity to make a good Who album. When I broke the deal with Warner Brothers, he felt we were just revving up to make a great album. And he became mesmerised by The Who in a worse way than anyone I've come across. I said to him that I wanted to work with Roger and I think there will be difficulties, but it's not my battle. You've got to sort yourself out with Roger. Got to convince him you can do the job. Nothing seemed to get done. One day Kenney's wife, or girlfriend, or whatever she was, rang me up and she said, 'Listen, he's not going to wait while you fuck around anymore. He's going to get this band together with Paul Rodgers' [The Law] and he went ahead and did it . . ."

In explaining his choice of Simon Phillips as Jones' replacement, Townshend gave further insight into the formation of the new band. "What we can do with Simon is probably a lot more ambitious than anything we could do with Kenney. Kenney isn't here. I chose the new drummer. You could go down the rest of the band and I think you'll find that I chose most of them. In fact, I chose the whole fucking lot of them. There's no conflict. This is my band. The only potential conflict is based on how John and Roger feel about working in that environment and calling it The Who. Maybe they would prefer going out as a four-piece and I had a stack and we thrash away like we did in the Sixties. I don't know what's on their minds. They're not entirely honest with me all the time. They treat me like a lunatic sometimes."

The large collection of musicians Townshend assembled was chiefly intended to create a "powerful sound without too much volume," thus keeping any discomfort stemming from his hearing troubles to a minimum. "My reasons for wanting a larger band are technical, really," he explained. "With a larger number of musicians you can keep the stage sound level a lot lower."

Without the ability to reduce the onstage volume, Pete would have regarded the proposition of the usual Who-style tour too hazardous as he confirmed in a radio interview in May, "Contemplating going back on the road with The Who for all the reasons that are involved in it, for the celebration, for getting together to celebrate 25 years of our history, our part in rock, to raise money for charities that we believe very strongly in, to honour the audience that want to come and see us play, and to take home their money, if we want to do any of those things, we've got to find a way of doing it, in my case, without actually making my hearing worse . . ."[1]

In addition to Townshend, Entwistle and Daltrey (or 'TED' as Entwistle now called them), the touring band consisted of Phillips, a five-piece brass section (The Kick Horns), three backing vocalists (Chyna, Billy Nicholls, and Cleveland Watkiss), percussionist Jody Linscott, keyboard player Rabbit Bundrick (who was readmitted) and an auxiliary guitarist, Steve Bolton.

The relatively unknown Bolton, described by *Rolling Stone* as, "a tall Scotsman with a mountain of hair and a rockabilly wardrobe," played "merely competent, chorused-out, whammied-up Eighties style service to a library of classic crunch," according to *Guitar Player*.

"I felt the best thing to do was to make the line-up of the band as anonymous and capable as possible," Townshend told *Guitar Player* which helps to explain why Bolton was chosen over Joe Walsh, who offered backup if Bolton didn't work out. "Walsh's and The Who's managers decided they might as well draw up a contract just in case," the magazine reported.[2]

While the rather bloated line-up had very little in common with the original Who, Townshend acknowledged that a glimmer of the old magic still remained. "The three of us, when we work together, have part of the magic that the early band had," he told *Rolling Stone*. "I think, in a sense, Keith's death had a kind of compounding reduction in that magic, and Roger, John and I add up to about 50 per cent of the old Who. But it's there . . . In a sense, the name refers to the audience's feeling about what the band means to them. And that's got very little to do with what the band actually does these days, which is *nothing*. The band has done nothing in years. There *is* no band. It's wrong, really, to call it The Who, because it isn't The Who. It's a bunch of session musicians brought together to play

---

[1] At the press conference announcing the tour, Townshend had problems hearing many of the questions asked by reporters – Daltrey repeated them for him.
[2] In the end, Walsh went out on the road with another of his Sixties' pals, Ringo Starr, as part of the All-Starr Band.

Who material. It's kind of authenticated because of our presence, but that's all, really.

"It's very difficult, when you've changed your mind, to explain why you've changed it. But this is an anniversary year for the band, and I desperately wanted to do something. I wanna see The Who's catalogue out there, I wanna see people buying the early records."

Another worry of Pete's prior to the tour was his physical conditioning. He hadn't exposed his body to any lengthy travelling and performing in seven years, and, at the age of 44, he wanted to ensure that his system could handle it. "Before this tour, I had to lose 20 pounds," he told the *San Diego Union* in August. "I had to have a heart scan, and I actually had to change my diet. When I come offstage I need a two-hour cool-down period, and I have to sleep 10 hours a night."

While the presence of a large group of musicians eased the damage on Townshend's fragile hearing, further steps were necessary during rehearsals in order to minimise his tinnitus. A Plexiglas enclosure was constructed in which Pete could see the band while playing guitar, but which shielded him from any extraneous noise, particularly the high-pitched squeals of feedback often emanating from the amps or microphones.

While the booth was primarily intended for use during rehearsals, Townshend planned to take it on the road as a precaution. "On the stage itself," he told *Rolling Stone*, "I'm really hoping that I'm going to be able to just stand out there and work . . . If I get a bad feedback shriek, it disables me for between five and 15 minutes, so I would then just have to go into the booth. Roger doesn't really want me in this booth at all. He wants me to wear earplugs, but I haven't yet found any that I've felt comfortable with . . ."

As the rehearsals continued, Townshend gradually discovered that if he kept the volume on his side of the stage to 98 decibels ("about the level of a loud, fairly squawky hi-fi"), he could leave the sound booth without any discomfort.

Townshend also made it clear in several pre-tour interviews that his trademark windmilling was a thing of the past.

"I've got to be careful because I knock my fingernails off and because when you connect [with the strings], you hurt yourself very, very badly," he told the *Washington Post*. On previous Who tours, he explained to *Guitar Player*, "as soon as we'd hit 'Baba O'Riley', I'd go *Djaaang*, swing, swing, all my fingernails would just get broken off across, and from then on I would be in absolute agony for the rest of the tour. I wouldn't be able to sleep; you know, at night my hand would be throbbing. I'm not allowed to use any kind of opiates at all, so I can't use strong pain-killers, and aspirins don't do anything. And the other thing is, when you swing your arm and you've got a cut finger, blood pours out of it at a great rate, and it goes all over your strings. So one of the other things I decided to do on this tour was be a little bit more careful with my *hands*."

"There are two ways to windmill," Pete told *Rolling Stone*. "There's the way I windmill, and there's the way that every other arsehole windmills. When I windmill", he explained emphatically, "I . . . break . . . off . . . the . . . ends . . . of . . . my . . . fingers. Flesh flies off. Blood runs under my fingernails. When I windmill, I fucking *windmill*, right? And I can't do that to myself. I really can't. I don't care enough about the audience, and I don't care enough about the music anymore. I care more about the state of my fingernails."

While the windmill was, at least for the time being, not an option, Townshend's equally distinctive onstage leaps remained in consideration for the upcoming tour. "I haven't really tried to do that lately," he told the *Washington Post*, "but I'm too young and fit to injure myself doing something as easy as that . . . I'm going to be careful, but I'm still going to kill people."[3]

Primarily, while it was Townshend's hearing difficulties that led to the unusual move of an extra guitarist, an underlying desire to function as a rhythm player also influenced his decision. "I can't hear the high notes, or the top octave of the piano at all," he told the *Washington Post* in July. "The second guitarist is there because I want somebody to play the solos, but also because I want to play rhythm. That's what I'm looking forward to on this tour because I play *great* rhythm guitar – I'm up there with Don Everly, or whichever one it was."

The acoustic guitar is "something which I feel is a very, very powerful instrument," Townshend told Hugh Foley. "'Pinball Wizard', for example, is a front line, famous, loved classic Who track, and it's actually a song that, on the record, is an acoustic track. It's not an electric guitar song at all . . .

---

[3] This recurring theme to "kill people" summed up Townshend's feelings about performing live with The Who after a long hiatus. "At times like this I just see it like a Marine: I'm just going to go out there and kill people. I don't really know whether I'm going to come back in one piece or not, and I can't really afford to contemplate that. I know that my gun is going to be my best friend and that's it . . . I'm not sure I'm going to be able to sustain 12 weeks of touring and a three and a half hour show without literally getting varicose veins or something. I don't know. There are no guarantees."

the actual rhythm of the song, that's what gives it its powerhouse thing, and it's an acoustic played in that slightly kind of Spanish-y way that I play. I really feel I'm a definitive rhythm player on acoustic and electric. I've had people that I regard as the top players in the world tell me that – I'm increasingly told that by young guitarists who by the time they're *six* can play faster than Jimi Hendrix ever dreamed of, and I'm proud of that, and I enjoy that and I also think it's a fundamental part of Who music. It's not to say that when The Who go out on the road I won't play some electric, but I don't think I'll ever play the way I used to play."

Townshend was won back to the electric guitar after buying a Casio MIDI guitar with a locking-nut tremolo system. "I started to play around and thought, 'So that's how they do all this unbelievable string bending; it's this thing that you can wiggle all over the place . . .'" Townshend told *Guitarist* the following year. "I always used to take the arm off. So I pulled off some solos I was proud of and it kind of brought me back to the electric guitar. I was studying pull-offs and all that stuff and deliberately trying to keep away from the Townshend clichés . . ."

Further changes were reflected in the tour's set list, which included a wide variety of songs, including cover versions of other people's material, such as Jimi Hendrix's 'Hey Joe', James Brown's 'Night Train', Bo Diddley's 'I'm A Man' and Creedence Clearwater Revival's 'Born On The Bayou'.

"I'm sounding a bit like a cracked record on the subject," Townshend told *Rolling Stone*, "but I just feel that the audience needs a little bit of perspective. I want people who listen to Prince to know *why* he is there. I want The Who to lead irrevocably to Cream and to Jimi Hendrix. I want people to understand the fucking *context*. 'Cause, you know, if you're just presented with Prince out of context, he's not so much a genius as a weirdo."

"Prince is such a kind of quantum genius that the guy doesn't even really know what he's doing half the time," Pete further explained to Hugh Foley. "He means something if you know the music of The Who, if you know the music of Jimi Hendrix, if you know the music of Little Richard . . . It's only then that you can perceive the scale of his genius. If you don't know that music, then he's just another jerk from Minneapolis who wears funny trousers . . . You have to know the context. It's too easy to belittle some of the fairy-tale superstars of this age like Prince, like Madonna, like Michael Jackson, if you take them out of context it's very easy. The reason why they are so enormously popular is because they understand their context. And so that's something that is happening very much at the moment and which I like to feel that not only have I begun to contribute to a bit in my own work but that The Who will do when they go out on the road, it's something that we're trying to look at in a slightly different way, I'm not saying we're gonna play old blues songs all night . . . but we're gonna try and evoke the atmosphere we grew up in. So we're going to do four hours of Everly Brothers songs!"

In addition to the covers, among the more than 70 songs rehearsed for The Kids Are Alright tour were obscurer Who tracks such as 'Mary Anne With The Shaky Hand' and 'Tattoo', alongside the band's recent studio tracks, 'Dig' and 'Fire' as featured on *The Iron Man*. Also included in the repertoire were solo Townshend songs such as 'Give Blood' and 'Let My Love Open The Door' because, as Pete told *Rolling Stone*, "I'm anxious that the traditional Who set doesn't sound or look or feel like a traditional Who set."

Wishing to avoid adhering to what he described to the *Detroit Free Press* as the "heavy electric guitar music" of The Who's more popular work, Townshend wanted to spotlight some of their more subtle side. "All we're really doing, I think, is letting them hear a little bit more than they hear on the radio or that they heard in the old concerts. We only made 10 studio albums, so it shouldn't be that difficult to keep up with us."

Pete's mention of the same staple Who tracks being played on contemporary radio was an important reason for the introduction of more obscure material into the repertoire. "What I *don't* want to do with The Who, and I think it would be fatal if we did it, is feed radio and reinforce what radio has done to music," he said in 1989. "Radio is unbelievably important, but it has become too much of a slave to ratings and demographics, and we tend to become too much of a slave to that response. You go out and play a song like 'Behind Blue Eyes', 'Won't Get Fooled Again', 'Pinball Wizard', any of the tracks that get a lot of FM airplay and the crowd immediately responds."

Despite all his intentions, Pete ended up deferring to Daltrey and Entwistle on the song selection. "I don't think any of us are happy with the set," Entwistle remarked. "We have got different ideas about the music, different ideas about how The Who should sound and what The Who should play, and we'll never, ever agree on that." The end result of these divergent views meant that the shows on the tour often lasted for over three hours.

The 43-date, 27-city 25th Anniversary Kids Are Alright tour kicked off at Glens Falls, New York on June 21, in front of what the *Detroit Free Press* described as an "astonishingly enthusiastic" crowd of 5,000, prior to two sold-out dates at Toronto's CNE Stadium on June 23 and 24. Most of the shows on the tour began with a 40-minute version of *Tommy*, omitting songs such as 'Eyesight To The Blind', 'Sally Simpson' and 'Sensation'.

In fact, a chief reason for the tour's existence was two charity performances of *Tommy*: the rest of the tour dates providing the financial wherewithal to pull off the two free fundraisers.

"The economics of it started to beg the question: how much is it going to cost us to get a band together to play Radio City Music Hall?" Pete said. "How much does it cost to get The Who Machine in action? When I looked at the budget, I went into shock. A lot of things have changed in seven years, and not just the music."

The first full *Tommy* performance by The Who in 19 years occurred at New York's Radio City Music Hall on June 27.[4] After the opera was played in its entirety, a selection of Who classics followed, including 'I Can't Explain', 'Baba O'Riley', 'Love Reign O'er Me' and 'Won't Get Fooled Again'. Together the *Tommy* performances raised $6 million for the Nordoff-Robbins Music Therapy programme for autistic and abused children and the non-profit Rock'n'Roll Hall of Fame, while other children's charities also benefited from shows on the tour.

"I feel that The Who is one of the very few fund-raising outfits of our power and potential with a social conscience, willing to address certain domestic issues," Townshend told the *Washington Post*. "Since rock'n'roll grows from the streets and sewers – we're not talking in clichés – it also blossoms from the fertiliser of blood and death, deprivation and starvation and, in a lot of cases, domestic melodrama – the angst of youth, the pain, the loneliness and the isolation. It *thrives* on that and therefore it's got a strong linking of hands with Narcotics Anonymous and Alcoholics Anonymous and all these other street causes.

"I didn't want to say 'no more' because what if somebody comes to us with a heavy cause and says for every dollar you raise, a life can be saved? What's our response? 'No, we won't do it because artistically it's not satisfying anymore?'

A series of sold out dates were played at massive East Coast venues,

---

[4] On the same day as the *Tommy* performance, Townshend appeared on *The David Letterman Show* performing 'A Friend Is A Friend', with Billy Nicholls and Chyna on backing vocals.

including four nights at Giants Stadium in East Rutherford, New Jersey, and two at Washington DC's RFK Stadium. 'Irish' Jack Lyons flew to America and saw the shows at Giants Stadium and RFK Stadium, travelling on the band's Learjet between cities. "[Pete] was amazed that I would go to all the trouble of flying to New York to see The Who," Lyons recalls. "I told him it had always been a personal dream of mine to see The Who in America."

As the tour wound through the Northeast and Midwest, Pete's attitude toward touring, shaky at first, began to change. "I'm a late convert, I guess," he told the *Detroit Free Press*' Gary Graff on July 18 at Buffalo's massive Rich Stadium. "Every now and again I have a slight misgiving about what we're doing, but then I have to remind myself of the size of the misgivings I had before I came out. Without seeing the audiences, I could remain a sceptic. But there's something about how the crowds are responding that's rebuilding a lot of the faith I had in the music I've loved all my life, that it can keep people together and bring pleasure . . . It *is* stimulating. I'm not suffering from the kind of musical boredom that I used to have on the road with The Who.

"I think we've succeeded. What happens onstage is that every now and again you think, 'Ah yes, this is The Who,' and at other times you think, 'Oh yes, this is people gathering together to celebrate The Who.' That's good enough, really; it would be cruel for outsiders to say that because we can't do the whole book, we can't do any of it."

"Whatever has happened since the band hit the road is very good, and my view has changed," Pete told the *San Diego Union*'s George Varga a month later, by which point he had markedly increased his use of electric guitar onstage. "I now like to think that I made the right decision. Never has a man come under so much fucking pressure to put a band of old warhorses back together again, and it's not because I wanted it; it's the *last* thing I wanted. It's what the audience wants. It's not up to me to define when it finishes. It's up to the audience to say, 'No, this is wrong. You now are too old.' But rock has to have the courage to define itself. That's the thing, and it's not up to the performers. I've tried to do it; I tried to do it in 'My Generation' and I've tried to do it since. I tried to say in 1982, 'OK, The Who is finished. It's ended.'

"[The Who] have to define our limits. I'm surprised at what we've been able to do this time . . . the Stones [who were about to embark upon their first major tour in seven years] are never going to stop, and if The Who lives another 25 years, I'm sure we'll be tempted to get up there and party down. And that might be the day somebody has a heart attack onstage. I have to be honest. It's quite possible that I've had a heart attack on this tour! So, it's whether or not it repels you, that's what's important. It's about entertainment, and you can't be entertained by people who are repellent because of their age. We can go onstage with 16 layers of make-up, and I'm sure on the video [screens that flanked the stage] we look two, three, maybe five or 10 years younger than we really are. The people we are really confronted with are the people in the front row who can see the lines, can see the thinning hair and see the make-up. Now if you can make them happy, and if you can mainly convince yourself, I suppose, that you're happy with it, then you can go on. But I think it's still a real problem. There has to be an end to it; rock isn't like blues or jazz."

On August 16, the tour, which was being disparagingly referred to in some quarters as 'the Las Vegas tour' or 'The Who On Ice', reached the Tacoma Dome in Washington. Despite having sworn off executing his more physically demanding moves, Pete's trademark windmill action was such a powerful and effective gesture, he couldn't resist giving people what they wanted on occasion. "It was like . . . like Hitler arriving!" Townshend said of the crowd's reaction, "and all I'm doing is swinging my bloody arm."

During 'Won't Get Fooled Again', the final song prior to the encore, as Pete windmilled, his hand collided with the tremolo arm, which was jutting backwards rather than hanging down in its customary position. "Suddenly I just felt my arm stop," he told *Guitarist* in June 1990. "I thought I'd just banged my hand but I looked and it was actually still in there . . . sort of hanging. I thought, 'Shit! That's gone in quite a way,' then I realised it had gone right through the hand!" The tremolo had pierced his right hand between the fourth and fifth finger. "Well, I picked up the guitar and held it from the tremolo so that everybody could see what had happened," Pete told *Q*'s David Cavanagh in 2000. "Then I pulled it out and blood started to pump out. And then it fucking hurt. I ran offstage and ended up having oxygen, so I don't remember much after that."

Unable to move his fingers and in "quite severe shock", Townshend was rushed to hospital, leaving the band to perform an encore consisting of 'Twist And Shout' and 'Hey Joe' without him. "It just so happened that in Tacoma there's this brilliant microsurgeon who irrigated [the hand] with a saline solution for an hour and a half," Pete recalled in 2000. After series of dexterity tests was performed, it was discovered that no nerves or tendons had been damaged. The tremolo arm had pierced the webbing between Pete's fingers and nothing more.

"That night I was sufficiently coward enough to pray," he told *Guitarist*. "I didn't care about rock'n'roll, or the guitar, or performing, or having money, or being thought of as an important this or an unimportant that or a has-been this or a has-been that. But never to be able to hold a pencil again or, as I said to the doctor, have a good wank . . . It was just so shocking to realise that for the sake of a catchphrase I'd put myself in a position where I might have disabled myself for life. I so desperately want what I do *not* to be circus and it *is* circus. So much of it is tightrope walking and so little of it has to do with what I write, what I play and the quality of it.

"What I was actually doing when I speared myself on my whammy bar was a kind of humorous impersonation of what a silly fuck I was when I used to do that before . . ." Townshend told *Guitar*'s H.P. Newquist in August 1996. "My heart wasn't even in it. Maybe that's why I speared myself."

Following two dates in Vancouver and a stop at San Diego's Jack Murphy Stadium, on August 24, The Who played a second complete rendition of *Tommy*, this time at Los Angeles' 5,800-seat Universal Amphitheater. The televised, pay-per-view performance, which was later released on video, was an all-star affair, featuring Elton John as the Pinball Wizard, Billy Idol (Cousin Kevin), Phil Collins (Uncle Ernie), Patti LaBelle (the Acid Queen), and Steve Winwood (the Hawker).

Another date in LA followed two nights later at the more sizable Memorial Coliseum in front of 65,000 fans while the two Oakland shows on August 29 and 30 brought in another 100,000 fans.

Two September dates in Texas marked the end of the tour's American leg. The shows in Houston and Dallas, which were sponsored by Miller Lite beer and raised $1 million for the Texas Special Olympics, also featured the only opening acts of the entire tour, locals Stevie Ray and Jimmie Vaughan and their respective bands, Double Trouble and The Fabulous Thunderbirds. According to Townshend, the use of corporate sponsorship was simply a means to funnel more funds to worthwhile charities, as he told the *Washington Post*.

"It seems that charity in the music business has come to consist of the same half a dozen people – me and Peter Gabriel and Sting and Phil Collins and a few others – calling each other on the phone and saying, 'You owe me a favour.' And I've had enough of that bullshit. This way we're taking money from these corporations and making sure it goes somewhere where it can help."

Nearly a month after the conclusion of the North American tour, The Who embarked on the English leg faced with the prospect of having to scrap the last few concerts due to the imminent arrival of Pete and Karen's baby. (However, Joseph Townshend delayed his arrival until 21 November.) The tour commenced with four early October dates at the Birmingham NEC followed by almost a fortnight's break. A four-night stand at Wembley Arena starting October 23 was memorable when, towards the end of the penultimate show on the 26th, Daltrey's hoarse voice gave out and he stormed offstage in apparent disgust at himself, not to return. Townshend, who was obviously not pleased at this turn of events, was forced to sing 'Won't Get Fooled Again' at the end of which he smashed his Stratocaster against the front monitors but the guitar refused to break.

Townshend contemptuously described his own actions as "pathetic" during a BBC TV chat show appearance he and Eric Clapton made the night after the final Wembley concert. (The pair treated host Sue Lawley to a rendition of Muddy Waters' 'Standin' Around Cryin'', while a video clip of Townshend and his band performing 'I Won't Run Anymore' closed the programme).

The Kids Are Alright 1989 trek closed with two further charity performances of *Tommy* on October 31 and November 2 at the Royal Albert Hall. In just over four months, the tour had raked in over $30 million, not including the sponsorship the band received from Miller Beer (reported to be in the seven figure range). Some inevitably questioned if the band really needed the money, to which Townshend responded, "The sad answer is, 'Yes, we do.' It would be pointless to pretend that we don't . . . It would also be pointless to pretend that John Entwistle is making the kind of money he used to make in the heyday of The Who. So, money was an important factor. The reality of the money was one of the first things that made us consider whether or not our party was a possibility. But what's been nice is the money *has* led us to the party, and the party has turned out be a good party, [and] an expensive one, in that it's making lots of money, unless that seems like an upside-down statement."

"What was very important to me about that tour – which in hindsight, I greatly regret doing – what's hard about it was that I fucking *enjoyed* it," Townshend told Q's John Harris in 1996. "I think I regret it because finally, as it got closer and closer, I realised that I was doing the job I love to do the most *purely* for the money. And some of the celebration of our 25th anniversary got lost, because I very quickly realised that other people had another agenda. Their motives were not to celebrate the past 25 years but to look forward to the next 25. This was the re-birth of The Who – for Roger, for John, for a lot of the fans, for the record company, the promoters, everybody. It was, 'Oh great, we've got one of the few super-groups back that can fill up fucking Pontiac Stadium.'

"The Who got back together and what people were hoping was, through this Townshend will get a taste for it again and we'll be back with the one band who can consistently fill 86,000-seater stadiums. We never ever fucking failed to do it. With a shit record out, with a *dead drummer*, we could still do it. That's the dream that John and Roger have had to let go. But I'm grateful that we did it and I'm grateful that we made the money that we made."[5]

1990 saw a limited amount of Who activity, with the band's induction into the Rock'n'Roll Hall of Fame taking place on 17 January at New York's Waldorf Astoria. Pete, Roger and John attended with Keith Moon's daughter Mandy also present.

In March, *Join Together*, a boxed set featuring live recordings from the 1989 tour was released. It reached number 24 in the UK, and a lowly 180 in the States. "I don't really know what the significance of this album is," Pete told *Rolling Stone*. "I don't think it's a groundbreaking live album like *Live At Leeds* was. I don't know whether it will mean anything in Who history."

He was spot on. "*Join Together* is the inevitable live-album curtain call designed to squeeze the last dollar out of The Who's 25th anniversary tour . . ." read the two-and-a-half star review in *Rolling Stone*. "*Join Together* is not the work of a seminal rock quartet. Instead, it's a meticu-lously rendered performance of the rock opera *Tommy* plus selections from The Who songbook played by a 15-piece group that just so happens to include three of the band's original members. Call it The Who Revue, featuring the durable voice of Roger Daltrey, the dour throb of bassist John Entwistle and the deaf-defying antics of Pete Townshend . . .

On purely musical grounds, *Join Together* cannot be faulted: the

---

[5] A large percentage of the money Townshend made went to charity. In 2006, Q maga-zine asked him, "What was the most money you spent? And what did you spend it on?" He answered: "I gave away more than £4 million to charity in 1990."

recorded sound is exquisite. It's a highly professional rock'n'roll record of a kind that was inconceivable when a far angrier Who defined itself by bashing its rebellious way through *My Generation* all those years ago. It's also thoroughly redundant and as predictable as the answer that Pete Townshend himself would no doubt give if asked to name The Who's best concert album: *Live At Leeds.*"

Around this time, Townshend was asked to produce Liverpool group, The La's, whose memorable pop song, 'There She Goes' eventually became a UK Top 20 hit. The story had it that their eccentric leader and songwriter, Lee Mavers knocked on Townshend's door, asking, "Can Pete come out to play?" Townshend, who deferred working with the band, supposedly after he and Mavers fell out over which recording equipment was to be used, recommended them to Bob Pridden, reportedly warning him, "If I was you I wouldn't touch 'em. Do you remember what I was like when I was 22?" (Pridden wasn't used for their album though he did go on to produce bassist John Power's post-La's band, Cast.)

In late 1990, Townshend found himself in the news following some comments he'd made in an interview with Timothy White for White's book, *Rock Lives*. The two spoke about the homosexual innuendo in 'Rough Boys', of which Pete said, "What, in a sense, 'Rough Boys' was about was almost a coming-out, an acknowledgment of the fact that I'd had a gay life, and that I understood what gay sex was about: it was not about faggery at all. It was about violence in a lot of senses. It leans very heavily into the kind of violence that men carry in them. If men have a violence which cannot be shared with women, then it can't be shared with them sexually. And so there's only one place for that violence and that's with other men.

"One of the things that stunned me when *Empty Glass* came out was that I realised I'd found a female audience, just by being honest. Not necessarily by saying, 'I am gay, I am gay, I am gay.' But just by being honest about that fact that I understand how gay people feel, and I identify. And I know how it feels to be a woman. I know how it feels to be a woman because I *am* a woman. And I won't be classified as just a man."

The ensuing reports of Townshend's 'coming out' and his supposed admission of bisexuality naturally drew plenty of media attention, and the fact that he didn't immediately refute the charges provided enough evidence of guilt for many observers. Pete offered a Wildean response to the furore: "Scandal is fabulous. No artist ever suffers from it. The people who suffer are the artist's family and friends. When Reuters put out on the wire that I was a transsexual, cross-dressing sheep fucker, I was laughing until I saw my cleaning lady's face. It was a weird day."

Townshend further commented on the incident in a 1994 interview with *Playboy*: "['Rough Boys'] is ironic because the song is actually taunting both the homosexuals in America – who were, at the time, dressing themselves up as Nazi generals – and the punks in Britain dressing the same way. I thought it was great that these tough punks were dressing as homosexuals without realising it. I did an interview about it, saying 'Rough Boys' was about being gay, and in the interview I also talked about my "gay life", which – I meant – was actually about the friends I've had who are gay. So the interviewer kind of dotted the T's and crossed the I's and assumed that this was a coming out, which it wasn't at all. But I became an object of ridicule when it was picked up in England. It was a big scandal, which is silly. If I were bisexual, it would be no big deal in the music industry. If I ran down a list of the men who have tried to get me into bed, I could bring down quite a few big names in the music business. And no, I won't do it . . .

"I don't want to deny bisexuality as if I were being accused of child molestation or murder, as if it were some crime or something to be ashamed of, because that would be cruel to people who are gay. But I was bitter and angry at the way the truth had been distorted and decided never to do any interviews again. Not because I had been manipulated but because I didn't trust myself to be precise about what I was saying."

In a February 2001 letter to *Mojo*, Townshend attempted to address the issue of his sexuality (an earlier issue of the magazine printed a reader's letter criticising Pete's flippant references to homosexuality in an interview).

"If it is un-PC to even mention whether someone is gay or not, then I am guilty," he wrote. "But to give some background to the qualification: I did live with Kit Lambert for six months in 1964 after leaving art college and he was open about his sexuality with me, and – unlike the wonder-fully vulnerable Robert Stigwood – never attempted to seduce me. I sometimes met Kit's rent boys the morning after, and we swapped little purple pills. I genuinely liked the gays I knew. They seemed to have a conviction about their entire identity that – at the time – I lacked . . .

"The Who had always had a huge male audience who, on the outside, might be entirely populated by lager louts. Keith Moon with his blondes and his press stunts may have seemed to be a lad. Roger was obviously a lad. But what was I? In a couple of early auditions the other guys were urged to 'chuck out the gangly one with the big nose'. Before I called my beautiful art school friend Karen Astley, I was a Kings Road swan, unsure whether to be gay or not. It was not about fashion, it was about the fact that all the men I admired seemed to be gay, bisexual or just not give a shit. I still don't give a shit. Weren't the Sixties great!"

In a 2002 interview with *Rolling Stone*, Chris Heath pointedly asked Townshend if he considered himself bisexual.

"No, I don't. I know that I've got – and this has got nothing to do with anything I've actually done, or not done – a very, very feminine side. I think my creative side is very feminine. And I went so far as to say in that interview [with Timothy White] that I often feel like a woman; I can see what a woman feels – the whole act of submission sexually. But, in a sense, what I was talking about was the act of submission sexually in a male-female relationship, that you can swap roles. But that's very common and corny now, in a sense, to even bring it up. And I suppose what I'm doing is taking all of the feminine attributes and regarding them as being passive, gentle, submissive or whatever. But in the sense that my creative side is archly feminine, it is 'I want the baby and I want it now!' It's biological. It's absolute. It's the feminine side that says to you [raises voice], 'If I need to take heroin, I'll fucking take heroin – who are you to even raise an eyebrow? If I need to give birth, I shall do it!' But it's got nothing to do with my sexuality."

Further speculation as to Townshend's sexual orientation was caused in 2002 when former music business journalist, A&R man and manager Danny Fields revealed that Pete was a boyfriend of his in the late Sixties in the book *In Their Own Write: Adventures In The Music Press*. Of more concern to Townshend was the fact that he knew nothing about it until the subject was broached by Heath. A flabbergasted Townshend acknowledged that he and Fields were friends, but he firmly denied it went further than that.

"I just don't know what he is fucking talking about. I have no idea . . . I haven't spoken to him since this has come out. I'll just look him in the eye and say, 'What the fuck are you talking about? Please tell me' . . . If Danny fucked me, Danny drugged me first. So if you want to fucking print that, then print it. Because that's the truth. It fucking hurts, that he so fucking carelessly said this in the papers. He should have fucking told me what he did to me first."

When Heath asked if he'd had many physical encounters with men over the years, Pete laughed and said, "No, I haven't", adding "I'm from the Sixties. You know, we tried everything, but . . ." He later acknowledged to *Rolling Stone* in an email that he distinctly remembered "experimenting, consciously", on only two occasions and that the encounter with Fields, if it happened at all, must have been a case where he "experimented unconsciously". (Fields later acknowledged that his comments had been misinterpreted in the book).

Townshend attributed the few sexual encounters he'd had with men to being in a state of severe inebriation and having impaired judgement. "I think what it had to do with – and to be honest, I can't remember much about any of it – was to do with the fact that I was actually completely smashed out of my head," he told Heath. "I'm not interested in men. I don't think I ever really have been."

July 1991 saw a Who reunion of sorts, as the band contributed a track to the Elton John/Bernie Taupin tribute album, *Two Rooms*, which was released in October. The Who covered 'Saturday Night's Alright (For Fighting)', but didn't record the song as a band – in fact, Townshend's guitar and vocal work was recorded second only to Jon Astley's programmed drums and keyboards (Entwistle and Daltrey added their parts about a week later).

In an interview with The Who fanzine *Generations*, Astley recalled Townshend's performance during the session at Eel Pie: "All in one afternoon we had to do two acoustic guitar passes, a couple of electric guitar passes – one of which was fantastic. It's a funny thing about Pete in the studio; he'll go through the motions and then suddenly he'll get interested and then everyone's just rooted to their seats . . . it doesn't last long but it's brilliant, he's really going for it and his hand is moving as fast as his brain. He doesn't know what he's going to play next, it's all off the top of his head and then he'll lose interest again. So unless you catch it . . . I mean, it was a brilliant pass."

Townshend later expressed his disdain for the recording. "I saw Pete about a month later and said, 'What do you think?'" Astley recalls. "He said, 'Well, I hate it . . . it's just a Who pastiche.' I said, 'Well, what else was I supposed to do? It's got to sound like The Who, and therefore it's a pastiche,' and he went, 'Yeah, but it should have been something new.' I think it was all tongue-in-cheek and a good bit of fun, but Pete must have seen it, although he didn't convey this to anyone, as a possibility for trying something new out, a new direction. He'd had to have been much more hands-on if that's what he really wanted."

In September, Pete sailed his 60-foot yacht off the coast of Cornwall to vacation in the Scilly Isles, a tiny cluster of islands about 30 miles west of

Land's End. The Townshend family stayed in a cottage on Tresco, a small island which contains the ruins of a 10th century abbey and fortifications known as Oliver Cromwell's Tower and King Charles' Tower. Cars are not permitted on the island since it has no proper roads, so Pete's inland transportation consisted of a rented bicycle.[6] It was on Friday, September 13 that he fell off his bike and severely broke his right wrist and forearm. "I was on a bike, completely exhilarated, going down this hill, and I hit a pothole and went over the handlebars," Townshend told *Playboy* in 1994. His wrist "shattered into a dozen fragments", as he described it. Pete was promptly flown by helicopter to Truro City Hospital for emergency treatment, which involved the insertion of metal pins and plates into the damaged limb and a cast from fingertips to elbow.

"I really smashed my wrist up," Pete said in 1993. "I think if they had invented a nylon wrist joint I would be using it, because my wrist is very, very bad. But for a long time I thought I wouldn't play the guitar again, I didn't think I'd be able to type. One doctor I spoke to said that I might have difficulty even writing . . ."

The possibility that his life as a musician was over proved devastating to Townshend. For years, his right hand had taken a great deal of punishing, and not all of it as a result of his guitar playing. During an argument at his parents' house, he'd smashed a window and rubbed his hand in the glass fragments, he'd punched a wall backstage during a tour, breaking a finger and only recently, he'd severely tested his luck by impaling his right hand on his guitar's whammy bar. The considerable damage to his right wrist seemed to spell the end of his guitar – and piano – playing.

In November, the PACE Theatrical Group approached Townshend about the possibility of taking *Tommy* to the stage. The group, which operated theatres and subscription series in over 20 American cities, had taken shows such as *Evita*, *The Secret Garden* and *Fiddler On The Roof* on the road. The last time Pete had seen a stage production of *Tommy* was in 1978, at the Queen's Theatre in Hornchurch, Essex. He was impressed enough to help the production transfer to London's West End the following year.

"In the past 15 years," Pete told the *New York Post*'s Lisa Robinson in

---

[6] On the subject of cycling Townshend was later named to the honorary board of 'Trips For Kids', a non-profit organisation based in California which provided disadvantaged children the opportunity to embark on mountain bike outings.

1993, "I've blocked every single production [of *Tommy*] – I've been very adamant – until the public were ready, and until Roger Daltrey was ready for a *Tommy* that didn't have him involved in it. Until I could sit down and say to Roger that I wanted to do it my way, but [that] it would be very different. Now Roger and I see very much eye-to-eye; we've had a lot of conversations and we're nicer to each other than we've been in the past."

"If I did anything smart with *Tommy* it was to register a grand right with the Library of Congress in 1969 and sit on it," he declared. However, this time the PACE group caught Townshend at an interesting juncture in his life. In addition, his recent interest in stage work, which had led to *The Iron Man*, piqued his interest. He made an agreement with the PACE group, in partnership with a group of theatrical producers known as Dodger Productions, one of whom was Des McAnuff, director of California's La Jolla Playhouse (and also a guitarist) who ended up producing the work. McAnuff, who won a Tony award in 1985 for the musical *Big River*, already had specific plans for staging *Tommy*.

"I wasn't interested in doing another unofficial version of *Tommy*, which is what the other stage versions that I'd heard about seemed to have been," McAnuff commented in the 1993 tie-in book *The Who's Tommy*, he co-authored with Townshend. "I also knew that we'd have to work hard to adapt *Tommy* to the stage; it wasn't going to be a natural leap, because we were dealing with a song cycle. And in order to maintain the integrity of the piece, I wanted to be able to work with Pete. Of course, I didn't really expect him to say yes, but I immediately began to prepare. I listened to the original album, and the only decision I made firmly at that point was that I wanted to maintain real respect for the original recording. I wouldn't want to update it or make it sound like a Nineties version.

"I wanted to capture the sound and spirit of the original and treat it as a classical piece of rock'n'roll, rather than doing what Ken Russell ended up doing with the film, which was to let people bring their own sound to a song – so that Elton John makes 'Pinball Wizard' sound like a Bernie Taupin/Elton John song, and Tina Turner makes 'Acid Queen' into a Tina Turner song. That's the only decision I made before meeting Pete."

McAnuff also wanted a more realistic *Tommy* than Russell's cinematic version. "We were not interested in exploring *Tommy* as a fantasy," he wrote in *American Theatre* in 1993. "We believed that the 'Amazing Journey' described in the lyric was best achieved by grounding the members of Tommy's family, the Walkers, on some kind of recognisable landscape . . . Ken Russell had, in his 1974 motion picture, already given

419

us the fantasy extravaganza [which lives on as a prime example of that particular genre of film-making from the Seventies] and we were more interested in exploring *Tommy* as a dramatic theatre piece."

Townshend and McAnuff first met in November 1991 at a London hotel with four other representatives from Dodger Productions and PACE. "He and I managed to have this little private conversation in the middle of the larger meeting, while God knows what was being talked about at the other end of the table," McAnuff recalled, "But we got about 15 minutes in and agreed to meet again alone."

The pair hit it off immediately. "From the moment I met Des in London, I felt he was absolutely right," Townshend recalled in 1993. "What struck me was that he understood the rock'n'roll ethic that underlays *Tommy*. He never let go of it. He's always held on to the fact that the original songs are all a very important part of the spiritual quality of the piece."

The day after their first meeting, Townshend had a recording session but his injured wrist certainly precluded him from playing any instruments which gave McAnuff some time to reflect.

"The breathing space turned out to be great for me," he recalled. "I was staying at the Portobello Hotel, and I had 36 hours before our next meeting. Pete and I had had just enough of a conversation for me to get a sense of what he was concerned about. He wasn't sure whether the musical danced, and that came up strongly in that first meeting. I thought it did, and I felt that the instrumental sections would be very useful as storytelling . . . With these ideas in my head, I spent 36 hours listening to all of the recordings of *Tommy*. I truly basked in the original and also all the cover versions . . . I steeped myself in it, took some notes and came up with a kind of outline to start our conversations about song order and what the bare bones of the story might be."

"Every designer on *Tommy* listened to the original album over and over," McAnuff wrote in *American Theatre*. "They paid great attention to the music," confirming that the original album "eventually became the bible for everyone on this project."

Townshend and McAnuff's first proper meeting the following day became a creative brainstorming session. "That meeting was about five hours long," McAnuff recalled in 1993. "We just talked and talked and talked and talked about the outline. Pete had a lot of comments, and we switched some things around, and we talked philosophically about the piece. I think quite quickly in that five hours we also made the biggest decisions – the decision about having more than one Tommy, the critical decision to keep Tommy a local hero for as long as possible, to keep that rise to power very brief; and the decision to create a story about a west London family and to ground it in some way – not to make it a fantasy or go in the direction that I think it's gone in other versions."

The decision to have more than one Tommy character was an unusual move. "Considering his total isolation in most of the story, how were we to find an emotional throughline for the character of Tommy?" McAnuff explained to the *Washington Post*'s Lisa Leff in 1994. "The basic conflict in the story, we agreed, was between Tommy and Tommy. This gave birth to the idea of the multiple Tommys [i.e. Tommy at four, Tommy at 10 and the adult Tommy – our narrator]. It was the interaction between these characters that created the magical layer which led to many of the most exotic visual elements in the production."

McAnuff explained the play's timeline to *American Theatre*: "Pete and I agreed that what we were dealing with was, in essence, a postwar story set against the background of historical events that led up to the 1960s, so the blitzkrieg of 1940 and the rock'n'roll British invasion of 1963 became the bookends for our timeline."

With that much mapped out, McAnuff flew back to La Jolla to begin work on the project. "By Christmas we'd really made most of our decisions," McAnuff wrote. "We'd pitched the song order back and forth by fax . . . What we did was tell each other the story, more or less. We would walk through each act, scene by scene, and I would describe some of the visual work that I thought we could do, and Pete would talk about philosophy and then we would discuss themes and characters."

Townshend made several trips to New York and La Jolla in late 1991 and early 1992 as *Tommy* rolled slowly towards its projected summer debut. While in New York, he stayed in a top-floor suite at the Royalton Hotel.

"It had this kind of Bauhaus theme," McAnuff told the *LA Times* in 2007. "The chairs were all three-legged chairs, so we'd be getting into these intense discussions about Tommy, and every two hours, one of us would go arse-over-teakettle back over the chair. He'd be waving his arms and doing a windmill and go flat on his back, and I'd do the same thing. It took a month to get these chairs changed because of some contractual rule with the architect that they couldn't change anything without approval. Because he was Pete Townshend, he made such a ruckus. It kept everything in perspective."

A key piece of *Tommy* which needed attention was the ending. "I have learned there is a vital difference between the simple rock song and the conventional music theatre play – that it's necessary to bring a story to a conclusion, something you never have to do in rock'n'roll," Townshend wrote in *The Who's Tommy*.

"When I originally created *Tommy*, I did it with the understanding that people of the time were exploring the limits of their imaginations," Pete told the *San Jose Mercury News* in July 1994. "They were in pursuit of spiritual awakening. When they sat down to listen to *Tommy* with a joint in hand or whatever, they were saying to themselves – and probably to me – 'We want to go somewhere.' And I specifically left parts of the story open to allow them to reflect and review. But with this version of *Tommy* I approached it from the point of view of the dramatist. Onstage, you have to tie things up in a sense. And I did tie it up at the end. But I didn't add anything that wasn't there to begin with."

Townshend was referring to the 'Listening To You' finale during which Tommy reunites with his family, embracing each of them, including Cousin Kevin and Uncle Ernie. Many observers were critical of this 'happy ever after' ending.

"We've had people come away thinking it's a Nancy Reagan 'family values' message," Townshend told the *New York Daily News* in July 1993. "We'd like to make it clear that it's not." Indeed, he informed the *LA Daily News* in 1994 that Tommy's return to the family fold could be for other more sinister reasons, suggesting that it may have initially occurred for Tommy "to wreak vengeance. Tommy's embrace of Uncle Ernie is immensely cruel . . . You think, 'What's he up to? He's obviously about to embark on retribution'. But he snaps out of it. He ends up accepting who he is, what he is, what he's been through. And [he accepts] the people around him."

Other lyrical adjustments to the original work drew additional criticism with the removal of many religious and mystical references. For example, the *tall stranger* with the *silver sparked glittering gown whose golden beard flows nearly down to the ground* in 'Amazing Journey' was replaced with a description of Tommy himself. The 'kids' rather than the 'disciples' lead Tommy in 'Pinball Wizard', while *Freedom tastes of reality*, a key line in 'I'm Free', became *Freedom tastes of normality*. Also, in 'The Acid Queen' sequence, Tommy's father whisks him away before she has a chance to begin her peculiar brand of therapy.

"It was clear I couldn't compete with the acid trip someone had when they first listened to the album," McAnuff told the *Washington Post*'s Lisa Leff in December, 1994. "All I could do was carry out Pete's vision and my own vision of the piece. There was really no other choice. I knew we would take some lumps from people who had a very strong personal relationship with *Tommy*. But as it turns out there has been far less of that than I ever would have expected."

To facilitate the parental decision making which must have taken place between 'Tommy, Can You Hear Me?' and 'Smash The Mirror', Townshend wrote a new song, 'I Believe My Own Eyes'.

The song was "a conventional music-theatre number in many respects," he wrote in 1993. "This is because it performs a conventional function. It has a job to do. It has to suggest the passing of time and patience and must strengthen the audience's feeling that the parents are exhausted but still young enough at heart to hope for their relationship. It also must keep the audience's focus on the mirror, about to be smashed by the mother. And it has to attend to the idea that when there are no answers we have to look inside. There was one other, less specific, part of the brief – and that was that we wanted a ballad, something like 'Behind Blue Eyes' from The Who. I trawled all these elements together and came up with the song. By doing so, I surprised myself and everyone else. It is not as popular a song in the show as I had hoped, but it is vital and it works. It is the one piece of new writing I have done for the show that makes me feel I can really write music drama in the future."

It wasn't until Townshend revisited *Tommy* that he began to realise the story's strong autobiographical nature.

"What actually happened was I'd fallen off a bike, smashed my wrist up, thought I couldn't play any more so thought I'd better write a book, an autobiography," Townshend told *Uncut*'s Simon Goddard in 2004. "But then I thought, I can't write a book until I know what happened to me as a little kid. So I went back to my mum and I said, 'Listen, I can remember being young on the beach, I can remember being in the tour bus with you and dad, I can remember having a lovely childhood and then I can remember going to live with my grandmother and I've got two blank years. I want to know what happened.'

"She fussed and kept avoiding it and I said, 'No, Mum, I want to know what happened.' I made her sit down and she kept changing the subject. I kept banging the table going: 'Tell. Me. What. Happened!' And in the end she told me the story. She didn't look good when she told me. I was a very, very clear-cut post-war victim of two people who were married in the war too young, had problems because of the war, so I went to stay with my grandmother, who happened to be off her fucking head. It was a horrible story."

Although Townshend wrote in 2002 that he remembered "no specific sexual abuse," he told *Q*'s John Harris in 1996 that "I think it's quite possible that when I was with my grandmother, she had a boyfriend who came into my bedroom. I don't know quite what happened, but I've got that far in my mind. I've tried to bring it out through therapy and I've failed. She used to make me call all her boyfriends – and there were several – 'Uncle'. I think that's where it [Uncle Ernie] came from."

"I didn't know that my mother and father had split up. I didn't know that my mother had a lover who was prepared to marry her and be my father. I didn't know that my father had said to her, 'You can fucking go to Aden with this new bloke, but you can't take Peter, I'm keeping him.' Where did I get the idea for a woman living with a lover, having a child, the father going off, disappearing, shooting the lover, and on we go to have a dysfunctional family? That's the story of my life, but I certainly wasn't conscious of it."[7]

"We recognised in our excavation of the rock opera that the story was at least to some extent autobiographical – not that Pete was personally traumatised to the point of becoming deaf, dumb and blind, but rather that he was writing an autobiography, perhaps unconsciously, for a generation," McAnuff told the *Washington Post* in December 1994. "*Tommy*'s physical and metaphysical journey is largely a metaphor and this, we came to understand, helps explain the *Tommy* phenomenon – the fact that the character became an icon, even a mascot, for a whole generation. It may explain why he lives on with such vitality today."

"Even though Roger Daltrey played Tommy," McAnuff told the *LA Times* in 2007, "there was no question that the principal creator of *Tommy* is Pete Townshend, so he was projecting himself on that little child, and that had to do with his experience growing up after the war. I always saw it as a World War II story, that rock'n'roll had essentially been born out of the turmoil of World War II. I felt that was what *Tommy* was about. The journey Tommy goes through is the journey Pete went on in terms of coming out of complete obscurity to sudden superstardom."

"This is going to sound incredibly impetuous, but the fact is, I set off on

---

[7] Another autobiographical feature was the Walker family's address: 22 Heathfield Gardens. Townshend's childhood home was 22 Whitehall Gardens in Acton.

two pathways [in my life]" Townshend told the *LA Daily News*. "One was the ideological pathway of rock'n'roll. We were going to change the world. We didn't. The second was a spiritual pathway. I thought I was going to grow spiritually by following an Indian master and meditating and being a good boy. And I didn't. If I'm going to grow, do anything of any good, it's all still to be done."

Townshend compared the end of the show, when Tommy embraces his family and then turns to face the world, to his own experience. Having completed one journey, he's ready to begin the next. "That's the sobering message of *Tommy*," Townshend pointed out, "but it's also very real: every day is a new day. Every day we have the chance to start over."

Once he and McAnuff had refined this new Nineties version of *Tommy* with, in the latter's words, "a fair bit of detail", the La Jolla Playhouse workshop was brought in. As well as a retinue of 24 actors, the show featured nine rear-projection screens to aid in visual presentation (this number increased to 18 when the show transferred to New York), a nearly full-size aeroplane out of which actors 'parachuted', a huge pinball machine (one of nine custom-built machines used in the show), dozens of television monitors which showed footage filmed live from the stage, and eight tons of scenery. On average, costume changes took place every three minutes, as cast members donned one of over 1,000 costumes made for the show, one of which was a $3,000 white leather jacket.

Curiously, on the musical side, Townshend's involvement with the stage adaptation was not as extensive as one might have expected. He was not involved in choosing the seven-piece band (two guitarists, bass, French horn, drums, two keyboards), nor did he meet them until two weeks prior to the show's premiere on July 9, 1992 in the Playhouse's 492-seat Mandell Weiss Theater. The opening served as a benefit for the London-based Nordoff-Robbins Music Therapy Foundation. Entwistle and Daltrey joined Townshend in attending the occasion, which received rave reviews.

"The show here is one continuous aural and visual orgy," proclaimed the *LA Times*, "a movable feast of sound and colour, flying props, swirling doors, projections and flashing video for the very senses Tommy was so long denied . . . a roiling, high-tech piece of theatrical wizardry for the Nineties." *Rolling Stone* called the show ". . . an ingenious and visually smashing telling of the familiar tale of a deaf, dumb and blind boy who is taken for the new messiah . . . musical director Joseph Church has assembled a fine seven-piece band, with drummer Luther Rix even contributing some powerful Keith Moon-like bashing from the orchestra pit." The *San Jose Mercury News* stated, ". . . the next big British rock musical to hit Broadway may come from a California theatre."

"I wasn't surprised, when I first saw it, as much as I was relieved," Townshend told the *San Jose Mercury News* in July 1994. "I thought, finally someone has done what they said they would do. I had worked with a number of people in the past . . . but Des made good on his promises."

Nine months after its debut in La Jolla, *The Who's Tommy* opened on Broadway at the St James Theater on 22 April, 1993.[8] In 2007, Townshend indicated to the *San Diego Union-Tribune*'s George Varga that he didn't appreciate the fact that the stage show was named in this way. "I have to admit that back in 1993, with *Tommy* on Broadway, I had absolutely no intention of working with The Who again . . . From an authorial point of view *Tommy* is my story, no one else's."

A review in the notoriously hard-to-please *New York Times* appeared in the following morning's edition.

"*Tommy*, the stunning new stage adaptation of the 1969 rock opera is at long last the authentic rock musical that has eluded Broadway for two generations . . ." critic Frank Rich wrote. "This show is not merely an entertainment juggernaut, riding at full tilt on the visual and musical highs of its legendary pinball iconography and irresistible tunes, but also a surprisingly moving resuscitation of the disturbing passions that made *Tommy* an emblem of its era. In the apocalyptic year of 1969, *Tommy* was the unwitting background music for the revelation of the My Lai massacre, the Chicago Seven trial, the Charles Manson murders. Those cataclysmic associations still reverberate within the piece, there to be tapped for The Who's generation, even as the show at the St James is so theatrically fresh and emotionally raw that the newcomers to *Tommy* will think it was born yesterday . . .

"Instead of merely performing the songs, or exploiting them as general riffs of dance and psychedelia, the evening's creators, who also include the choreographer Wayne Cilento and some extraordinary multimedia artists led by the brilliant set designer John Arnone, use the singing actors to flesh out the drama of *Tommy*. Better still, they excavate the fable's meaning until finally the opera's revised conclusion spreads catharsis like wildfire through the cheering house . . .

---

[8] That same month, Pete recorded a cover of 'Substitute' with The Ramones for the band's *Acid Eaters* album.

"As played by Michael Cerveris with the sleek white outfit, dark shades and narcissistic attitude of a rock star, the grown-up Tommy is nearly every modern child's revenge fantasy come true: the untouchable icon who gets the uncritical adulation from roaring crowds that his despised parents never gave him at home . . .

"The isolated young Tommy's totemic, recurring cry of yearning – '*See me, feel me, touch me, heal me*' – flows repeatedly between inner child and grown man, giving piercing voice to the eternal childhood psychic aches of loneliness and lovelessness. It is this primal theme, expressed with devastating simplicity in Mr Townshend's score and lyrics, that has made *Tommy* timeless . . . Yet it is the evil of the authority figures the hero must overcome – a distant father, a dismissive mother, a sexually abusive Uncle Ernie and various fascistic thugs – that also makes *Tommy* a poster-simple political statement reflecting the stark rage of the Vietnam era . . .

"Dominating the stage instead of being usurped by the hardware, the performers can shine as well . . . When the time comes for the entire company to sing the soaring final incantation – "Listening to you I get the music. Gazing at you I get the heat" – *Tommy* has done what rock'n'roll can do but almost never does in the theatre: reawaken the audience's adolescent feelings of rebellion and allow them open-throated release . . . Far from being another of Broadway's excursions into nostalgia, *Tommy* is the first musical in years to feel completely alive in its own moment. No wonder that for two hours it makes the world seem young."

While it was well received in most quarters, *Tommy* had its detractors. "The classic rock anthems are still there in orchestrations by Steve Margoshes that respect the original voicings and are played by a gutsy pit band," *Newsweek*'s Jack Kroll wrote, "but the mystery and ambiguity, the poetic richness of the original has been flattened out . . . The scenes of little Tommy are the strongest in the show – poignant evocations of an autistic child. But McAnuff has been seduced by Broadway's high-tech rollers into an eclectic style that echoes *Dreamgirls* (tall towers), *Chess* (video screens), *Miss Saigon* (flying airplanes), *Les Misérables* (the people). The audience cheers the special effects, climaxed when Tommy hops onto a flying pinball machine, which explodes in a fireball. But there's almost as much cheering when sodden old Uncle Ernie chug-a-lugs a beer and emits a burp like a sonic boom.

"This *Tommy* has energy, and some witty choreography, but no sensuality or soul. Michael Cerveris as the grown-up Tommy epitomises the cast, attractive but without real charisma. The new *Tommy* spurns charisma.

'The point is not for you to be more like me,' he tells his followers. 'The point is I'm finally more like you.' Townshend, the old guitar-buster, has created a new category. Wonk rock."

Time was similarly unimpressed: "There's not much emotional depth or adolescent rebellion left in the granddaddy of rock operas."

Thanks to word of mouth, Townshend and the work's reputation, alongside a welter of positive press coverage, *Tommy* was a smash hit on Broadway.[9] Attendance was such that Townshend told the *New York Daily News* he'd recoup his investment only six months after opening. The musical went on to make a reported $150 million, and in 2002, *The Sun* reported that Townshend's take was £45,000 per week during this period. In June 1993, the *Tommy* Broadway show received five Tony Awards, including one for Townshend, for Best Original Score, and one for McAnuff, for Best Musical Director.

"You know, the Tony is the first artistic award I've ever had," Townshend later remarked. "I've only ever had performance-related awards before, you know, special services to the music industry, that type of thing. I've never won a Grammy or anything for my creative work. At this time in my life, it's like getting a knighthood."

After the awards presentation at the Gershwin Theater, the *Tommy* crew headed to the theatre district for a party which lasted well into the following morning, and where Townshend and Michael Cerveris performed 'Pinball Wizard'.

With the Broadway success of *Tommy*, Townshend's attraction to the Big Apple grew. "When I come to New York now, I have a family," he told *Rolling Stone*'s Anthony DeCurtis in late 1993. "I can go to my little yellow theatre, and there are people there that love me. I have investors lining up to invest in any crazy idea I come up with. So, I'm pulled to New York – and pulled out of a rather unsatisfactory life at home, where for 25 years I've been married to somebody who doesn't like show business very much. It's quite a good thing that my wife doesn't like show business, but it does make it difficult. I've got a young son, and I don't like to be away from him, but I feel dragged into the excitement and vigour of New York."

With his home life under renewed strain, the amount of attention and recognition he received as a result of his theatrical recognition was

---

[9] According to a 1994 edition of the *Chicago Tribune*, one of the few regrets Pete had about the Broadway *Tommy* was that his father didn't live to see it.

overwhelming. "The thing I had to worry about [prior to the Broadway opening of *Tommy*] is not that the show was going to flop but that it would be too much of a success. It could destroy me."

His words were to be somewhat prophetic. "Commercially the success of *Tommy* changed my life, and not entirely for the better," he admitted to the *San Diego Union-Tribune* in 2007. "It took me some time to get used to making so much money without having to stand on a stage myself; I went a bit crazy."

CHAPTER SEVENTEEN

1993–1996

"I've been pitching to work in theatre for a long time. I started to show an interest in it in 1970. I was hoping to do a theatre-film project back then with The Who called Lifehouse. *When The Who finished I was keen to move into theatre just because of the fact that it was another showbiz area which didn't require me to drag my body around the world like a hunk of meat, which I was rapidly turning into, with holes in various bits and blood pouring out of various parts of my hand most of the time."*

– Pete Townshend, 1993

"I don't like *The Who. Do I have to like them? My feelings about the band are much deeper than that, incredibly ambivalent. I feel like the proud housewife who cooks a lovely dinner, takes it in to this wonderful man she married . . . who's sitting and watching TV with his shirt hanging out, belching and drinking beer. And she thinks, 'I* love *him, but I don't* like *him.'"*

– Pete Townshend, 1994

AS *Tommy* began its initial run at the La Jolla Playhouse, Townshend returned his attention to the group of songs he'd begun work on in 1990, which had been readied for release just prior to his bicycle accident.

"Rather than put out an album I wouldn't be able to play live, or even feel inclined to talk about much, I held it back," Pete explained in 1993.

In its first incarnation, Townshend described *Psychoderelict* as "a conventional solo album, which – I had been warned by my manager and record label – had to be a 'real' rock record."

However, due to the severity of his wrist injury, Townshend reassessed the project. "I was kind of coming at it as though it was the last thing that I was ever going to do," he told Dia Stein.

"I had been obsessed with an idea: that in this highly computerised age the truth is being lost in our easy access to facts," he wrote in the *Psychoderelict* press notes. "I saw some moral issues too; is the nature of truth actually changing? Each song I'd written addressed this in a different way. It was a good notion. They were good songs. But the real idea didn't come across."

Pondering how best to translate his ideas more effectively, Townshend recalled the work of one of his favourite authors, Joseph Conrad whose *Heart Of Darkness* was performed as a radio play by Orson Welles in the Thirties. The recent transformation of *Tommy* from a series of songs into a successful stage work was enough to convince Townshend that he could successfully mix dialogue and music. After briefly considering using Conrad's *Nostromo* in a radio play format intermingled with the songs he'd written, Pete decided instead to use a story which he'd been working on since 1989 called *Ray High And The Glass Household*.[1]

With his new record label, Atlantic subsidiary East West[2] offering "greater creative scope", Townshend recalled. "I came back to this album and thought, 'Fuck it. What I'll actually do is say what this thing is about. I'll use a play or drama to describe what I'm trying to get across. The music can act as highlights.'

"*Psychoderelict* feels like a part of a big continuum, now that *Tommy* is doing so well. I felt that I could be specific, that I could skip the vague, metaphysical language of music and say what I wanted to communicate, write it out, make it really punchy, and make it work."

Previously, Townshend had generally been less direct, often hoping that the finished song as a whole would get the meaning across.

"I was obeying the old set of rules which is that you don't fuck with people when they're listening to music. You don't play them a piece of music and slip them a subversive idea that happens to be your idea of the month. I do that in interviews. I take an interview as a chance to say, 'Let's talk about Bosnia or Amnesty International.' Interviews are a good place to explore these things because journalists are well-read, they're activists, they're smart, and they know what you're talking about. They can get

---

[1] In 2001 Townshend described *Ray High And The Glass Household* as "a novel", and that "part of this book was complete enough to send a first draft to my editor . . ." The name Ray High was concocted as an amalgam of Ray Davies and Nick Lowe – two rock contemporaries Townshend admired.

[2] In the midst of working on *Psychoderelict*, Townshend was "sacked by EMI which had been bought by UK label Virgin to get hold of The Rolling Stones and a few others."

your crazy rock star ideas in order and ask the right questions if you're going off on the wrong tangent."

Townshend brought in his old art school flatmate Richard Barnes as a soundboard for his ideas. "I wrote scripts and I'd throw them at [Barnes] and he'd blue pencil them and tell me this was happening, that was happening, and we honed it down to [a] finely edited form. So the story definitely came afterwards, but I think the story was always there, because I'd written the songs around a theme, the theme was, what is the difference between facts and truth – in society, in the press, in music business, in my life, and in rock'n'roll."

The convoluted plot of *Psychoderelict* concerned Ray High, a washed-up rock star whose best years were supposedly behind him. Having suffered a nervous breakdown, High has become a recluse, cutting himself off from most of society.

"What *Psychoderelict* is about," Townshend told Matt Kent in 1999, "is a man . . . I suppose men in particular do this, some women, but mainly men . . . men who decide to opt out, men who run away, men who go and live on desert islands, men who leave their jobs, men who decide to become Richmond Green drinkers, men who just turn their back on everything around them."

High's self-imposed exile allows him contact with very few people bar his manager, a reporter, and a fan who manages to "penetrate his existence," as Townshend put it. At the fan's urging, High reworks an abandoned project from his past entitled *Gridlife*.

Townshend wrote in 1999: "Ray is cajoled by Rastus [his manager], manipulated by Ruth Streeting [the reporter] and intoxicated by Rosalind [the fan, for whom he writes a hit song] and manages to get [*Gridlife*] onstage. It is a tremendous success, but he remains a little jaded, and yet nostalgic. I tried to deliver a double irony: Ray prefers to look back to a time when he was still able to look ahead. The play closes as he begins to forget his recent success, pores over new letters and pictures from new fans, and resentfully bemoans his great, lost hippy days of the Seventies.

"It was deceit and scandal that had delivered High's most recent success, which rendered the experience bittersweet. He preferred to dream about the futuristic visions which had occupied his time while writing *Gridlife* some 20 years earlier. At the end of the play, High yearns for those days, wondering 'Whatever happened to all that lovely hippie shit?'"

The obvious parallels between *Gridlife* and *Lifehouse* were the result of Pete's recent push to finally turn the latter into a reality. "After 20 years, I became obsessed with telling the story behind my failure to complete what was a genuinely good idea for the first genuine rock musical film," Townshend later wrote in the *Richmond Review*. "The obsession to do this was greater than the desire to complete the original film itself, and led to *Psychoderelict* . . ."[3]

The project provided Pete with an opportunity to revisit some of the *Lifehouse* instrumental demos he'd recorded more than two decades earlier.

"On the album, the songs associated with *Gridlife* are prefixed 'Meher Baba' and originated on eight-track demos first recorded in 1970/71 for *Lifehouse*," he explained in 1993. An unused, extended interlude from the demo for 'Who Are You' – written during another surge of *Lifehouse* activity – surfaced on *Psychoderelict* as 'Meher Baba M4 (Signal Box)'.

The majority of the album's songs were recorded in demo form in late 1990 and early 1991 at The Cube, Townshend's home studio. Recording sessions then took place on *Grand Cru,* the Dutch barge Pete had converted into a recording studio, which was moored on the Thames behind Eel Pie studios.[4]

"I used my usual group of musicians," Pete told Dia Stein. "I like to have the same people that I used on *Chinese Eyes*. Jody Linscott on percussion, Peter Hope-Evans on harmonica, John Bundrick – Rabbit – on keyboards, and if I can get them, Mark Brzezicki or Simon Phillips on drums, Pino Palladino or somebody like him on bass, and nowadays I like to have a guitar player around.[5] We kicked off with that group of people and they played along with the things that either I was doing in the studio, or that were on tape, and then I started to finish the tracks off. I suppose I play really about 80 per cent of the music on it. 'Cause some of the stuff on it I dumped."

"The engineer and Pete weren't getting on at all," Jon Astley recalls of the *Psychoderelict* sessions. "For some reason, Pete had decided not to use a

---

[3] In keeping with the Townshend tradition, *Psychoderelict* was originally substantially more complicated. The radio play, according to the *New York Daily News*, "incorporated even more big-issue ideas in its original form, since it started with 12 major characters before being whittled down to the current three." Incidentally, one of the characters deleted during creative workshops was played by Broadway *Tommy* lead Michael Cerveris.

[4] "It had once carried live eels (which I thought was amusing because my company is called 'Eel Pie')," Townshend wrote in the *Scoop 3* liner notes in 2001.

[5] Credited with playing bass on *Psychoderelict* were Paul "Tubbs" Williams and Jaz Lochrie. Guitarists, in addition to Townshend, were Adam Seymour (of The Pretenders), Phil Palmer, and Gavin Lewis. Simon Rogers and Ian Broudie of The Lightning Seeds, were credited with programming on 'Meher Baba M4 (Signal Box)'.

producer. I think Pete needs a producer in the studio, even if it's someone like Glyn [Johns] who'd say, 'Yeah, that's good, but let's try it this way,' or 'Do we really need that?' With Pete producing, it was very long-winded . . ."

Astley, who was in demand as a drum programmer during this period, was brought in for the rhythm programming. "They got a drummer in [Brzezicki] who replaced me on three or four songs but actually you'd be amazed what's real and what isn't on that record."

Townshend examined several areas within *Psychoderelict*: the roles of people — especially males — in post-war society (a theme previously explored in *Siege* and *White City*) and the effects of the media on the general public.

"Through a series of unfortunate accidents and predicaments, I ended up doing things in a better order than I had planned," Townshend told Matt Resnicoff in 1993. "I wanted to write songs about the nature of truth, how it's changing in the modern world, how computers — data banks and computer preservation of newsprint in particular — are elevating fact to a level of truth. Facts, as I say on the record, don't always lead to the truth. They should, but they don't always. I think that journalism, particularly criticism, is the foundation of the support system for the musician like me. It doesn't always feel entirely just, because what you work in as a musician is a big picture. It's very difficult to communicate that you desperately need to say something that is very difficult to say, and that is why you've chosen music to start with."

"These new songs are for you if you still believe in truth, or you still believe you can find truth if you try hard enough," Townshend wrote in the album's press kit. "Whether you read newspapers or listen to the radio, you probably think that what you *suspect* is what is really going on is — in fact — close to the real truth. I know I do. We need to be told."

Townshend elaborated on this theme in 1996. "One of the things that happens today is that, because of the incredible effectiveness and the huge appetite of the media for sensational stories, a tiny incident that might happen 80 miles away becomes as significant to me as though it happened in my own neighbourhood, and this song is about that, and we allow it to make us afraid when we're walking down the street. We should only be afraid if we've got experience of something. If some old lady's been banged on the head in your street, then be afraid, but if she hasn't then don't be afraid until it happens. Don't go looking for it."

In an amusing anecdote, Townshend used the media scandal of his supposed bisexuality as an example: "On this album, I've tried to make clear that you always try to win over the people who hate you. The more people hate you, the more you want them. You don't learn from adverse criticism or scandal alone. The press actually hand the story on, then the reaction happens. In the bar in La Jolla, after the opening party for *Tommy*, two girls attached themselves to me. One of them was really game. I'm old and wrinkly and she was young and beautiful. I thought about it briefly, then decided to go to bed. As I said goodnight, one turned to the other and said, 'See, I told you he was a fucking faggot.' It's not about the story. It's about how the public respond."

Townshend's decision to convey these weighty ideas coincided with his renewed, if ultimately short-lived, belief in the power of rock'n'roll music.

"What we're going through on the planet today, with over-population, global warming and so on; the ageing process; the feeling of the loss of a dream, rock'n'roll can deal with all of that," Pete told the *New York Daily News*. "Unfortunately, it usually doesn't. It's rare when a Bob Dylan grabs an issue and holds our feet to the fire to feel it. What bothers me today is that rock'n'roll has become so *conservative*, so resistant to change. That's something else I'd like to figure out: 'Why has rock'n'roll straitjacketed itself?'"

'English Boy', the opening track on *Psychoderelict*, was the focus for virtually the entire album.

"It's about the emergence of the modern punk; those post-war years in the late Fifties and the early Sixties in England where they stopped conscripting people into the army. They said: 'Listen there's gonna be no more war. We've solved that problem. We don't need you anymore.' And I think there are a lot of kids running around England trying to find something to do . . . And the song is really about that . . . the fact that those boys, those men, those people are kind of made redundant, in a sense, by peace . . . and now being held up, in some way, responsible for many of the things that are wrong with modern society."

Pete elaborated on this idea in his *Guitar Player* interview with Resnicoff: "'English Boy' is a story about young men being undervalued and made to blame. What was so awful for me, and it's painful to talk about because I didn't handle it very well, was that my great years in America were so fucking shaky for many men my age because they could have been and they did get drafted. It was *Apocalypse Now*, *Heart Of Darkness*, it was dead people in rivers of mud in the middle of jungles.

Mothers, fathers, and families were wondering what the fuck they were doing there. It was Vietnam, and I was trying to pretend that it wasn't happening. I wasn't going to get drafted. I wanted to be a pop star. I felt that politics and pop didn't mix. I had no idea that the music we were playing was so vital to their very survival. Although it's called 'English Boy', it could just as easily be called 'American Boy'. It's about the guys who died in that war . . .

" 'English Boy' is about the idea that you're good enough to go and die in a fucking war for your country, but if there happens to be no war then fucking behave. Cut your hair. Wear a grey suit. Do your job. Clean the lavatories. Count the money. Sell the stocks. Fix the car. Keep your fucking mouth shut. That's the establishment picture that young kids grow up with. That's wrong. That's not who we are. If I'm a member of the establishment now, that's not what I want my kids to think of me. I want them to feel free, to be themselves, to be fucking wild, and to make mistakes."

Obviously self-aware of his penchant for cerebral concepts, Townshend had thought of writing a song like 'Let's Get Pretentious' for some time, "cause I just like the idea that I had my moment of courageous pretentiousness, jumping in with *Tommy*," he told Stein. "It felt very pretentious at the time to be writing something that was a song cycle, let alone something that later became known as a rock opera. So I've never had a problem with people that call me pretentious . . . I don't regard it as an insult! But in the context of the piece, the song is actually about what Ray feels is the setting for his manager and the journalist's lifestyle. He feels that it's frippery, it's fluff, it's puff, to use the modern expression."

Townshend described 'Outlive The Dinosaur' as "one of the smartest songs I've ever written. My hero, a drunken rock-star is living alone in his glass mansion. He takes on all the issues of ecology with a sense of duty and responsibility to our dying planet. And yet he cannot move, cannot reach the outside world, cannot even write a cheque. The word dinosaur was of course first used to describe ageing rock stars with vicious irony, and I use it here with vicious irony redoubled."

'Now And Then' was "just a song that I wrote for somebody that I care about and addressed the original idea of the whole album which is really whether or not when you actually feel, or say, that you're in love with somebody that you actually know what you mean. It was the first principle for trying to find out . . . when we think we're speaking the truth, whether it's possible for us to ever know that we're speaking the truth. And then, if that's true in relationships, then is it possible that when we accuse the totalitarian media of sometimes bending the truth – which obviously, in this particular story I do to some extent – are we actually being hypocrites? That was the first song that set up this idea for the record that, in a way . . . when you see somebody, . . . you look in their eyes there's something goes between you and you both recognise that and you both might feel very, very different things. But if one of you decides that it's – let's say love – what that actually can set up is a very kind of fatal circle."

'I Am Afraid', inspired by and written and recorded in demo form within a few months of Pete's son's birth, referred to the "future phobia" experienced by Ray in the story.

'Predictable' was "about somebody saying, 'What I like about you is that I know what's going to happen,'" Townshend told Stein. "'I *know* what's going to happen. I *know* I'm not going to have an orgasm . . . I know how it's going to feel. I know how it's going to go today. That is what makes it exciting is I'm certain it's going to go a certain way and that often it doesn't . . .'"

'Flame', the hit song in the story written by Ray High and performed by Rosalind, was co-written by Simon Townshend.

"Around that time, there was a band called Huge Big Thing," Simon recalls, "that was Mark Brzezicki on drums, Jaz Lochrie on bass, a couple of other guys, really good musicians, and me singing. We did a tour in the States, we did loads of gigs around and we were trying to break, and 'Flame' was one of our songs. I wrote the lyrics to it, and we recorded it for *Psychoderelict* and I think then Pete had a girl sing a vocal on it which gave it more meaning in his production."

Apparently Pete tried to record the song at Simon's home recording studio at Woodgrange Avenue, but according to Simon, "it didn't work out. We had a big argument that day, and ended up at Eel Pie to record it."

'Fake It' concerned fulfilling an audience's expectations, no matter what the cost. The memory of hitting rock bottom in 1974 at Madison Square Garden was obviously still at the back of Townshend's mind. "It goes back in my career to somebody saying, 'Jump, jump, jump, jump . . . smash a guitar' and me saying, 'But this is crap,' and them saying, 'But we don't care, do it anyway.'"

The lyrics to 'Fake It' and 'Don't Try to Make Me Real' were written simultaneously. "What they were supposed to be was a conversation between a man and woman, and the way that men and women traditionally seem to fall into stereotypes of requirement in relationships," Pete told Stein. "The man says often, 'Don't try and put me in a pocket. If I say I love you, it doesn't mean I love you. It was something I just said at the time.' And in 'Fake It', a woman's saying, 'I don't care if you really love me. Bring me flowers, touch me, hold me, because it's now that matters to me. You're passing through my life from one end to the other. Grab me as you're passing – I don't care if it's not true. You tell me anyway.' In the play, 'Fake It' becomes about information, about law, about justice, about orgasm rather than just about 'Say you love me, and that'll get me through the day.'"

Like 'Flame', 'Fake It' was credited to several composers, namely Jon Astley, Pete Townshend, Billy Nicholls and Jon Lind.

"Pete had this song he'd been asking Billy to try and sort out, 'cause he was struggling with the verses on it," Astley recalls. "He had this chorus – *fake it, fake it* – it was actually in half time . . . Billy was writing with a Los Angeles songwriter called Jon Lind at the time, and they go back a long way. They sat down again and tried to do some stuff, and Billy came round [to Astley's home studio in Twickenham] and played what he'd been doing, and I had computers and programming machines and Fairlights and stuff, and I said, 'What about this idea for a rhythm for the verses, and get away from this half time thing, and actually make it [imitates the song's rhythm].' And they all went, 'Oh, that's good.' John Lind had gone home by this point, he wasn't involved any more.

"So we suggested it to Pete who said, 'Fine, great,' and then he insisted that Billy and I had a writing credit on it. John Lind heard about this and insisted on a meeting, so we sat down at this meeting and I just thought, 'Christ, I'm not going to get involved in this,' because American songwriters tend to believe that if they're in a room at the time anything is done whether it is used or not, they're part of the song! So Pete kind of went, 'Oh, all right, fine, if that's what you want, fair enough.' So we ended up with four co-writing credits on that song which really Billy and I put together."

The final song was a reprise of 'English Boy' which featured a heavier emphasis on guitar. "I did about 15 solos," Townshend told Resnicoff. "My original idea was that there should be hundreds of guitar solos, but the guy who did the remix, Jeremy Allom, just took one. I'm happy with it . . . My idea was to have a guitar wall of noise." He described the solo as a homage to Carlos Santana. "We were at Woodstock together. We've been together with John McLaughlin, who Carlos works with all the time and who sold me my first Fender amp and a couple of guitars when he worked in a guitar store. I just wanted to evoke that feeling."

Several of the songs recorded in demo form didn't make it onto the finished article, mostly as a result of his decision to release *Psychoderelict* as a single, rather than double, CD. Among these was a guitar piece entitled 'Wistful', which was intended as "an incidental underscore for some dialogue," according to Townshend, and 'Squirm Squirm', which was reinstated into *Psychoderelict* during creative workshops in New York in 1999, when the story was being considered for a Broadway run à la *Tommy*.

"At last, a song with a happy inspiration," Townshend wrote in his liner notes for *Scoop 3*. "One day I was holding my newborn son Joseph and singing him to sleep. It came into my mind that seen from high above we humans must look just like insects, or worms. As he wriggled in my arms I sang to him about the messages we all believe we get sometimes from above. At the time I was gathering material for *Psychoderelict* . . . The song seemed to contain and reflect both the peace and safety of this child in my arms, and the chaos and danger that surrounded us out there in the crazy world."

'Uneasy Street' eventually surfaced on the 1996 Townshend compilation, *Coolwalkingsmoothtalkingstraightsmokingfirestoking*.

"There's a very difficult area on *Psychoderelict*, which is unexplored, which is the notion that if 'English Boy' is about the exaggeration of evil in society, that there is also real evil in the world and it's important not to forget this. There is real evil at work. It tends to express itself through the individual, who indeed, if charismatic, can inspire masses of people. But 'Uneasy Street' was supposed to be about that moment when the hero of the story, Ray High, suddenly realises that his sexual passion, his desire to be seduced by a glamorous woman that he meets – and the reason the song's not in is that I wrote her out of the play in the end – is bowing to something in himself which is incredibly self-destructive . . . heavy stuff but a nice little ditty!"

When released in July 1993, *Psychoderelict* sold poorly; indeed, it soon became Townshend's worst selling solo album, selling only about 200,000 copies.

"I abandoned my recording contract after *Psychoderelict*," Pete told *The Times'* David Sinclair in 1998. "I'd always told myself that when I sold less than 200,000 I'd stop. I had imagined myself triumphantly arriving at the Edinburgh Festival with it, so it was a bit of a blow."

"It's a tricky thing to get on the radio, and some of the critics have dismissed it," Townshend told the *Orange County Register* in August, explaining that *Psychoderelict* was perhaps somewhat difficult, given the format. "Some of it works, some of it doesn't." He also conjectured that "If *Tommy* were released today, it would probably fail. It's not quite fair to say people are lazy. Their listening habits have changed."

Most reviewers appreciated the music, but found the dialogue a distraction. "Townshend is now in the midst of his fourth decade as a bona fide rock star", wrote *Guitar Player*'s Chris Gill, "so it's no wonder that his latest work for Atlantic, *Psychoderelict*, deals with the artistry and business of rock'n'roll . . . The record breaks rules and challenges listeners, but Townshend hopes his audience will approach it with an open mind. Dialogue links the songs together, but because it often interrupts the music, it may annoy listeners who simply want to boogie to the tunes. However, those who tolerate the dialogue will discover Townshend's strongest musical work since *Empty Glass*."

Time's Janice Simpson and *People Weekly*'s Ron Givens also subscribed to the opinion that the format got in the way of the songs: "This melodrama, overstuffed with who-knew-what-when twists and weighed down by lyrical significance, intrudes upon the songs in the form of dramatised soundbites," wrote Givens. "Nevertheless, these tunes glow with vitality. The riffs come at you with just the right amount of Who-like snap, Townshend's voice crackles with gusto, and he combines tenderness with sweet pop on 'Now And Then' and 'I Am Afraid'. Townshend may have thought the play's the thing with *Psychoderelict*, but he was wrong. Rock'n'roll is."

Perhaps in answer to the critical consensus, a 'music only' version of the album was released in an attempt to make the songs more accessible. "[*Psychoderelict*'s] complexity meant that it has been largely ignored by radio," Townshend remarked. "Even some fans can't cut through the wrappings to get to the music on the disc."

Early in the evolution of *Psychoderelict* Townshend realised that touring might better communicate the work to the audience. "I feel it's essential to promote this record," he told the *New York Daily News* in July. "The record is very difficult for radio."

"Impetuously and perhaps pompously, I wanted to do something a bit different with the rock format," he told the *Orange County Register*. "I was worried that these great songs would get ignored altogether if I didn't do something drastic to attract attention to the record . . .”

Despite the fact that Townshend estimated touring would cost him approximately $500,000, the decision was made to take the show on the road. “When I finished *Psychoderelict*, I was *shocked* to find I wanted to perform it live,” he told the *New York Daily News*. “My son was born and I took a year off to be with him, and I assumed writing and producing would be enough from then on. But in some way, on some level, it wasn’t. I needed what I got from being onstage.”

“I’m extremely ambivalent about performing, period,” Pete told the *Los Angeles Times*. “I know when I perform and when I hear music, I love it and I’m energised by it, but I have a great difficulty committing . . . I became a drunk for three months, and in that three months I made about four or five serious commitments which I wouldn’t have made sober . . .”

However, he added, “I feel good about [touring]. I think I was a brave guy, and I think I can do the job. I’m certainly confident that I can do the job sober. I’m not trying to make a case for alcoholics going and getting drunk in order to make important life decisions.”

The numerous compliments which Townshend received for his guitar playing on *Psychoderelict* were welcomed, given the serious injury he’d had to overcome. “A lot of the guitar playing was post-accident . . .” he said in 1993. “I’m actually becoming a guitar player,” he said, as if he wasn’t much of one before. “I love the guitar now, and I never used to. I used to hate it.”

The 1993 *Psychoderelict* tour was not a lavish affair – 14 dates in mostly smallish venues in eight North American cities[6] – but it meant a lot to Townshend.

“As a solo artist, I’ve only done two, three shows in my life,” he told Stein. “Really, I’ve hardly done anything. As a solo performer I don’t exist, really, so I’ve got no career. So this is a big moment for me. If I actually do this, this will be the first solo tour that I’ve ever done. I’m not wildly anxious to get back up on the stage, because I’m not wildly keen to be a performer. I don’t feel comfortable as a performer, particularly. I’m much happier as a writer or a band member. It’s ironic for me that after years in The Who, being frustrated because I couldn’t express what I felt I needed to express because the band was such a big force and had such a big personality, and I had to write for *it*, that I left, got my moment of personal

---

[6] “Playing smaller places, the scope of expression is so much broader,” Townshend told the *Orange County Register*. “You can converse with the audience.”

freedom, said my piece, and then missed the fact that whenever I go on a stage now, I'm in the front . . . it's hard work, to have to write it and to have to carry the show as well.

"This isn't quite like that. This, I would be one of the people in the show, I would have my little rests. I think it would be quite good for me. And I think that I feel comfortable that I could do this where I don't necessarily feel that I could do a tour of just me solo, you know, like a two hour show with me jumping about all over the place. You know, I don't find performing hard. What Roger does as a performer is so much bigger and harder than what I do. He takes on the whole audience. He makes a pact with them when he walks on – 'I am going to hold your attention for two hours and I'm going to give you every ounce of adrenaline and blood and guts in my body.' I go out there and say, 'Hi guys.' What you get is what you see is what you get, you know, and if you like it, fine, and if you don't, then fuck off. I'm a working musician. That's how I see myself. I really do . . . I was in a band. And it's the writing that's made me a bit of an icon as a performer."

The first live rendition of *Psychoderelict* took place on July 2 at the Mayfair Hotel in London, a press-preview in much the same vein as that which unveiled *Tommy* at Ronnie Scott's back in 1969. Pete, performing solo for the first time since February 1986, played acoustic guitar unaccompanied, but with three actors, John Labanowski (Ray High), Linal Haft (Rastus Knight, High's manager) and Jan Ravens (reporter Ruth Streeting) performing their parts of the story. A Q&A session followed the performance.

Townshend's first fully fledged solo tour began with a July 10 date at Toronto's Massey Hall, with the musicians trooping on to the stage playing 'Cobwebs And Strange' on toy instruments. Richard Barnes, who came along on the tour, wrote that Pete said this "was to get rid of their egos." The band consisted of regulars Simon Phillips, Pino Palladino, Rabbit Bundrick, Peter Hope-Evans and Billy Nicholls (who was joined by backing singer Katie Kissoon). Guitar duties alongside Townshend (who played the majority of the set on a Fender Telecaster) were provided by Eric Clapton band regulars, Andy Fairweather-Low and Phil Palmer.

As with the album Jon Astley was asked to programme the drums during the tour in place of a conventional drummer. "Pete said, 'Why don't you come out on tour and do it?'" Astley recalls. "So I said, 'OK,' and got in touch with Bill Curbishley. Bill said [*adopts gruff voice*], 'How much are you going to cost?' I said, 'It's not me so much, Bill, I've got cases of gear to cart around!' 'I'll have to talk to Pete about this.' I probably asked for too much money."

Another addition to Townshend's band who ultimately didn't make it was Roger Daltrey. "When *Psychoderelict* came out Roger called me and said, 'You know, this would've made a great Who record.'" Pete told Howie Edelson in 2006. "And I said, 'Well, yeah, you're always going to say that. It's my record and you know if we'd have been doing it with The Who you probably wouldn't have liked it.' And he said, 'No, this is a part that I could play. If you're ever going to do it as a theatre piece, think of me.' So when I took it out on the road, I did call him but he'd just taken another job. But we would've gone out together with *Psychoderelict*."

Rolling Stone was impressed with the two shows at New York's Beacon Theater on July 12 and 13, as the review of the first night revealed:

> *"Dressed in a natty, humidity-be-damned black suit, Townshend kicked off the American leg of his first full-fledged tour as a solo artist by playing nearly three hours without taking a break; and neither his energy nor his charm wilted a jot during that time . . . The actors were on hand to enact the witty spoken portions of the libretto, and behind the stage hung a giant screen on which psychedelic patterns and symbolic images were projected to further embellish the plot and themes . . .*
>
> *"In addition to Psychoderelict's 'English Boy', with its effervescent chorus and jazzy bridges, the evening's most invigorating moments included a buoyant rendering of 'Let My Love Open The Door' and a radiant 'Pinball Wizard', on which Townshend – who played both acoustic and electric guitar throughout the set – strummed with dazzling dexterity and coaxed sounds from his instrument that were at once clamorous and pretty. Most importantly, Townshend seemed to be having a grand time – poking fun at his serious-songwriter image ['A Quick One While He's Away' was introduced as a song of "deep, deep social significance"], careering across the stage, jumping around and doing windmills against his guitar as if threatening to remind youngsters like Kurt Cobain that trashing one's axe after a night's performance is hardly a new trick. Pete Townshend himself is no more a new trick than Ray High, of course; but with his muse and his sense of humour in good health – to say nothing of his cardiovascular system – High's creator appears in little danger of becoming media fodder any time soon."*

At one point during the Beacon gigs, Townshend grew angry at the crowd's incessant shouted song requests, saying, "I play what the fuck I like. You don't think I've worked for 30 years to get to this place to have you fucks tell me what to play."

The gig at Chicago's Arie Crown Theater on July 17 assumed significance but for all the wrong reasons. "I decided to have a bottle of vodka before going on the stage," Townshend told *USA Today's* Edna Gunderson. "I made a terrible mess of it." Barnes recalled that "Pete played a lot of the show flat on his back."

"I hadn't had a drink for 11 years, then I decided I was rich enough, so I deserved one, and I began allowing myself an occasional beer," Townshend told David Hinckley of the *New York Daily News* in July, 1999. "Then, for some reason, before a show in Chicago I drank a bottle of vodka. I don't remember a thing, except I'm sure the show was a fucking mess."

While short-lived, Townshend's relapse was certainly a full-blown affair. "I had *Tommy* on Broadway and it went to my head," he told *The Sun's* Dominic Mohan in 2002. "I thought, 'Even if I have got a bit of a problem with alcohol, it doesn't matter,' but of course it did. It doesn't matter how much money I had, I still ended up coming out of a club, seeing a builder's skip and thinking, 'Oh, what a lovely place to spend the night.' My head went completely. I used to do that all the time. My limo driver would be waiting for me to wake up. There were probably people walking past saying, 'Isn't that the bloke from The Who asleep in that skip?'"

A scheduled 12-day break followed Chicago with the first of two shows at LA's Wiltern Theater on July 29. John Entwistle took the stage for the encore, playing bass on 'Magic Bus', 'Let's See Action', and 'Won't Get Fooled Again'. Before the second show the following night, Townshend and company all stood on one foot, "to show that we're all completely sober."

"The cranky, overly analytical, musical-genius side [of Pete Townshend] was put aside Thursday night," wrote Mark Brown in the *Orange County Register*. "The cheery guy who loves to play smart songs and flail away at his guitar in every way imaginable was there instead. Better than on most Who tours, rawer and more stripped-down than in his 1986 'Deep End' big-band concerts, this rare Townshend solo tour is everything his fans could possibly hope for.

"*Psychoderelict* stands tall among Townshend's work, whether with The Who or without. Grinning like a madman and chasing harmonica player Peter Hope-Evans all over the stage while ripping out guitar leads, Townshend was more than full-on for most songs."

After the show, a clearly torn Townshend told Fred Shuster of the *LA Daily News* that he was "far more interested in holding my family together and bringing up decent kids with principles than in being a rock star. As long as I can hang onto that, I think I'm a worthy member of society. The job that I do as an artist depends on my survival as a person that can tell the difference between decent behaviour and otherwise."

Shuster was not impressed with *Psychoderelict* live, calling it "pretentious, dull, stale, silly, amateurish and thoroughly boring". The *Oakland Tribune*'s Dave Becker was similarly unenthusiastic after witnessing the August 2 show at the Community Center in Berkeley, California. "While the ageing-rock-star angle, obviously has more than a few parallels to the life of the 48-year-old Townshend, the self-absorption *of Psychoderelict* isn't nearly as annoying as the fact that it's simply a weak, dumb story. Especially coming from the man who set the standard for mixing rock and drama with *Tommy,* the piece is piffle . . . Townshend himself seemed to recognise the limitations of his new work, murmuring before the performance began that 'It's not meant to be the greatest thing since rock'n'roll' and pleading with the audience to 'roll with it'."

During the second concert at Berkeley, Michael Cerveris guested on 'Pinball Wizard' and as he had done the previous evening, Townshend performed 'My Generation' solo as part of the encore. The *San Jose Mercury News* described the rendition as "stunning", gushing "it was one of his *Scoop* albums come to life, a stark onstage 'demo' – a one-of-a-kind performance from a one-of-a-kind rock titan."

At the show was self-confessed Who fanatic, Pearl Jam singer Eddie Vedder. "I recognised him in the audience, but he looked bemused, a little lost," Pete told *Spin* in 2001. "[Afterward] I spent an hour with him. It could have been ironic, the play I was performing – about old, worn-out stars trying to pass on their 'wisdom' to younger performers."

"Eddie was in great distress," Townshend told *USA Today* in October 1999. "He was worried that he had become a huge celebrity and couldn't sit in audiences unmolested to watch his favourite artists anymore."

"I was in a terrible space," said Vedder. "I enjoyed the show incredibly, but I was ready to fall apart mentally. We just kind of stared at each other for the first two minutes. Pete really helped me with a couple things. I had a friend in a bad situation that I didn't understand. In 45 minutes, Pete dispensed information I couldn't have gotten anywhere else. I just appreciate his wisdom and experience."

At the time, "[Vedder] was interested in developing *Quadrophenia* as some kind of stage vehicle," Pete said in 2000. "We became friends because he listens to me when I speak. I just love that! I also admire the way he lives his life. He values friendship and love, and gives those around him space."

The next night was a benefit show for the La Jolla Playhouse, at San Diego's 2,200-seat Copley Symphony Hall, which raised approximately $100,000.

"Townshend was by turns inspired and indulgent, provocative and pretentious . . ." wrote the *San Diego Union-Tribune*'s George Varga. "[*Psychoderelict*'s] muddled dramatic staging by three London actors underscored the continuing problems in marrying theatre and rock live onstage . . ." Cerveris again joined Townshend onstage, providing vocals that Vargas described as "too slick" on a 12-minute *Tommy* medley consisting of 'Captain Walker'/'It's A Boy', 'Christmas', 'Sensation', 'Pinball Wizard', and 'See Me, Feel Me'.

Pete and band returned to the East Coast for a show at New York's Brooklyn Academy on 7 August, which was recorded for pay-per-view broadcast and released on video as *Pete Townshend Live* (and later on DVD as *psychoderelictliveinnewyork*).

"The music from *Psychoderelict* is far superior to the story line . . ." reported the *Boston Globe*, echoing what was a familiar sentiment by this point. "The three actors who play these roles drift around the stage in a kind of script-induced fog. Townshend's reach exceeds his grasp – he even uses the actors to comment on everything from hippie dreams to technological overkill – but the music redeems the whole enterprise . . . Townshend rages through new rock songs and ballads that represent some of his best material since his prime with The Who. Although you'll scratch your head at the *Psychoderelict* story line, you'll still be in awe of his music."

Technical problems occurred during the early part of *Psychoderelict* at the August 9 show at Great Woods Amphitheater in Mansfield, Massachussetts. After dispensing with both the behind-the-stage projections and onstage actors, Townshend stormed off into the wings, leaving the band wondering what was going to happen next. Some of the older Who fans in the crowd knew that they might be in for a treat, as Pete had demonstrated many times in the past that his most passionate shows often occurred when his anger boiled to the surface.

Dean Johnson of the *Boston Herald* recalled the ensuing fireworks: "An infuriated Townshend returned for an unscheduled 'Magic Bus' that lasted 10 minutes and featured four grinding, sprawling guitar breaks from

Townshend. He leaped on amps, scampered Groucho-like around the stage and unleashed his windmill guitar riffs . . . the rest of the night was so intriguing because no one was sure what was next, including Townshend . . . Good rock is all about attitude, and Townshend's spit-and-vinegar show proved he still has it by the truckload. But he was clearly embarrassed. The crowd was cheated out of seeing his new rock opera. A better show resulted, but that provided him little solace."

Two days after a stop in Philadelphia, the final date of the *Psychoderelict* tour took place on August 12 at one of Pete's favourite venues: Jones Beach Theater, New York.

"The Jones Beach show is the one that I remember as the most successful amalgam of a rock concert and a theatrical piece," Townshend told *Cleveland Live*'s Ira Robbins in 1996. "It was a little bit circus-ish in a way, a little bit bawdy . . . By the time we got to the end, the actors were rather parodying themselves and having fun with the thing.[7] But the audience was familiar with it, they were comfortable with it, they knew what was going to happen, they knew that there were going to be people acting, they'd heard from their friends or whatever. By the end of the tour, people knew what was going to happen, and it worked."

At home after the conclusion of the *Psychoderelict* tour, Townshend found himself at a personal crossroads, as he told *Rolling Stone* in December. "Going on the road with my album, deciding that it would be my last album – I don't know if it will be or not – and deciding that I would do some shows was partly to see whether I could still do it. But I also felt I had to prove to myself that having a show on Broadway didn't mean that I wasn't still a rock star. All those things are about turmoil really. The beginning of the year, I was very happy. I was meeting wonderful new people, making regular trips to New York. But toward May, June, I started to get uneasy, and I'm still in that place. I'm still not sure how I'm going to do the things I want to do without traveling an enormous amount – which is again something my wife and I find difficult. So there's a kind of feeling of dread which runs through me, my oldest daughter, my younger daughter and all my friends, including my wife, feel that we're heading for difficult times, because of the career I want, which is a

---

[7] During the scene where Ray High is 'swimming' – actually John Labanowski walking around the stage in swimming trunks waving his arms in a swimming motion – Townshend knelt on the stage breathing through a snorkel while observing Ray's dialogue with Rastus.

show-business career, and show business is destructive. It's both disturbing and incredibly exciting."

While Townshend had originally intended staging his version of *The Iron Man* back in 1988, it wasn't until November 26 that the work was performed in front of an audience – at the Young Vic Theatre, the site of the experimental *Lifehouse* shows more than two decades earlier.

"It was a marvellous, small production with a lot of promise and a great cast," Townshend recalled in 2005, "but I found the work impossible to advance after such a busy couple of years mounting three different theatrical productions of *Tommy*, releasing *Psychoderelict* and touring it. I was shattered."

His drinking didn't help either. "I remember one of the worst states I saw Pete in was when I went round to the house one morning to ask Karen something," recalls Jon Astley, "and he looked grey, dreadful."

Townshend asked his brother-in-law if he'd like to accompany him to the Young Vic. "He got into my car and he stank of booze," Astley recalls, "and he burst into tears about his life. The whole thing . . . he was in a desperate way about his marriage and Karen . . . I mean, Pete didn't really talk to me about his marriage – that was the only time, actually. He was more excited about going to watch his performance, I think. During the interval we went across the road and had a glass of white wine, and he was quite happy to drink away his problems, you know."

Pete's marriage ultimately didn't survive this latest rift and he separated from Karen not long after. In 2000, when *Rolling Stone*'s Jenny Eliscu asked him what he considered to be the best and worst aspects of being Pete Townshend, he responded, "It's all pretty good. The worst thing is having a failed marriage. I regret that. Although we've been separated for a long time, I think this is the year we've finally properly given up on it."

As 1994 approached, rumours circulated of a Who reunion to mark the 30th anniversary of their formation. Daltrey and Entwistle had periodically attempted coercing Townshend into resurrecting the band but were consistently met with strong resistance. When asked about the prospect of a reunion the previous year during an interview with the *New York Post*, Townshend replied, "[Roger] and I are cooking up something really fucking bizarre, but it's much too soon to talk about it. It'll be one of the wildest things we've ever done, something you can do only when you're really old and really rich."

Whatever scheme he was referring to, it dissipated quickly. By mid-1994, Townshend was bluntly quashing any notion of a Who reunion. "I thought briefly about doing it," he told the *Detroit News and Free Press*. "There's never been a tour planned, to my knowledge. There was lots of supposition about it, but nobody ever ran a list of dates or a budget by me. Ultimately it's not something I really want to do. It's an absolute no – forever."

"I think there are days when he doesn't like The Who; he's definitely in his Who denial period now," Daltrey said at the time. "I don't even talk to Pete about The Who anymore. If he changes his mind, he knows my number."

The closest thing to a Who reunion that year came on February 23 and 24 when, just before his 50th birthday, Daltrey performed a selection of Who songs at New York's Carnegie Hall accompanied by a 65-piece orchestra from Juilliard, with guests including Sinead O'Connor, Eddie Vedder, Linda Perry, Alice Cooper, Lou Reed, The Chieftains, and The Spin Doctors. Daltrey's band featured Pino Palladino, Simon Phillips, Phil Palmer, Billy Nicholls, Cleveland Watkiss, Rabbit Bundrick, Jody Linscott, and Jon Carin. *Daltrey Sings Townshend*, a sold-out affair and pay-per-view telecast, was initially to include Entwistle and Townshend onstage with Daltrey, but Townshend decided nearer the date that he wasn't comfortable with the idea, citing the fact that he didn't enjoy playing onstage in front of an orchestra and that he was unwilling to perform a 'Greatest Hits' show. Richard Barnes revealed that "after a 'robust' phone call from Roger [Pete] was talked round but he stipulated that the three members of The Who didn't appear together."

Pete was initially "comfortable" with *Daltrey Sings Townshend*, as he told *Cleveland Live* in 1996. "Where I started to feel uncomfortable with it was when Roger's manager started to suggest that I might change horses as well, and move away from what I was doing in my life and turn Roger's tribute to Pete Townshend into the new Who. I'm not suggesting that that was [the manager's] motive, but like a lot of Who fans, his dream was to find some way to get The Who back together. That is still probably Roger's self-confessed dream. That was a real problem for me, because what I felt at the time was that I couldn't see a creative route to that state of affairs. I couldn't see us going into a studio and coming up with songs that were a credit to each of us as human beings."

Rolling Stone described Daltrey as "livid" when told of Pete's proposed set list during rehearsals: "Shaking his full head of curly blond tresses in disbelief, Daltrey complains about Townshend to orchestra conductor

Michael Kamen: 'What do you mean he's decided to perform 'The Shout'? [from *Another Scoop*], I don't even know that song, I just think that to do something that obscure at that point in the show is suicide.' Kamen tries to appease Daltrey, but the well-tanned singer isn't having any of it. 'He changes his mind every day,' Daltrey says with a stomp. 'You just don't do that to friends, do you? He's mad, isn't he? The man's obscene.'"

Ultimately, Townshend performed 'And I Moved' – not exactly a crowd-pleasing Who classic, although better known than 'The Shout' – and 'Who Are You'. Neither Daltrey nor Entwistle were onstage for either song although the three did appear together, along with the rest of the artistes, for the 'Join Together' finale.

"[Townshend] appeared onstage dressed as an English gentleman, with a charcoal suit, wire-rimmed glasses and a white shirt buttoned to the top," the *New York Times* reported. "Yet as soon as he started strumming his acoustic guitar, the music had a new immediacy."

"The dour-looking Townshend appeared none too pleased to be onstage," wrote the *San Diego Union-Tribune*'s George Varga, "and his interaction with Daltrey was almost non-existent."

Among the other guests, Lou Reed performed 'Now And Then' from *Psychoderelict*, while Linda Perry sang what *Rolling Stone* called a "wicked" version of 'The Acid Queen' (although Varga called her singing "wretched" and "off-key"). In a spirited performance, Eddie Vedder contributed 'Sheraton Gibson', 'My Generation', 'The Kids Are Alright', and an impromptu rendition of 'Squeeze Box' in response to an audience member's shouted request for the song. Vedder, who once told an interviewer that Townshend's influence on him was such that he should be sending him father's day cards, resorted to Who-like methods of preparation for the show when he (and Jim Rose of Jim Rose Circus notoriety) trashed a backstage dressing room. Townshend, who wasn't present during the destruction, commented, "No one thought it was particularly well executed. But after all, he's a fucking surfer!"

Daltrey took the *Daltrey Sings Townshend* show on the road, bringing Entwistle along on selected dates. Ringo Starr's son Zak Starkey played drums, while Simon Townshend filled in on guitar. "He looks so much like Pete it's uncanny," Daltrey told *Music Connection*'s John Lappen in August, obviously realising that what he'd put together was a surrogate Who. "I could have used The Who name on this tour; I have Pete's blessing. However I won't do that because it's not The Who."

Daltrey continued to long for a genuine reunion but it wasn't to be. "I'd love to see the band get back together. I still feel we have better work to do. But I'm just taking it a day at a time. Pete isn't interested in doing it right now. But tomorrow, who knows? I hear rumours that he might appear at some of the shows on this tour, which pleases me very much."

"Around the time of his tour, [Roger] was out there doing his thing and I was going through probably one of the worst chapters of my life, having just messed up in London with *Iron Man*," Townshend told *Cleveland Live* in 1996. "Although it was a success in its way, I was emotionally fucked up by it. I couldn't work out what had gone on. I knew that *Tommy* was hugely successful and I knew that *Iron Man* had somehow failed and it didn't have to do with the disparity in their budgets, it was something else . . . I went away to review my life and think about what I was going to do next. Meanwhile, Roger's tour was rolling and I was somehow expected to be a happy-go-lucky part of it all. I couldn't do it. I couldn't do any more than I did, which was to run on the stage and give him a birthday hug, sing a couple of songs and then go home. I was not a well boy, I don't think."

With his marriage on the rocks, Pete had stopped drinking and was attending Alcoholics Anonymous meetings by this point.

"There was one day when I just said, 'That's enough,'" he told Dominic Mohan in 2002. "I didn't go to a clinic, I just stopped. What I'd managed 11 years before I thought I could manage again. It was messing up my life. But I've certainly had help over the years. I've had counsellors. I had a therapist for three years, I don't know if that really helped or not. I just know I'm all right now. I don't think about alcohol but I know I wasted a lot of money on it."

Despite this positive change in Townshend's life, he appeared, at least to be distancing himself from those close to him. "Pete, at that point, cut himself off from everybody," Jon Astley observes. "All his friends, family – he's never been the same with me, and probably with most other people that he knew really well, since he joined AA."

With Daltrey's hopes seemingly lost on an indifferent Townshend, the two men obviously still weren't seeing eye-to-eye after all these years.

"No question, it's a strange relationship," Roger admitted. "People outside the band just see it as Pete and me fighting. But they don't understand that the fighting between us was the spark for our creativity. What is any artist without opposition? We've never really been chums, but there is a deep love there. If he were ever in trouble, I'd be the first one by his side. We don't need to see or speak to one another. We do fight a lot, we do disagree on a hell of a lot. But what we do have in common outweighs all of that."

The pair were eventually persuaded to open a dialogue. "Our counsellors kept telling us that we had to sit and talk, and it was frightening," Townshend told *Cleveland Live* in 1996. "In the end, we got the courage, and we sat down and we talked to one another about it. And it was hard, but we resolved it."

In May, an official boxed set entitled *Thirty Years Of Maximum R&B*, assembled by long-time Who associates Chris Charlesworth and Jon Astley, hit the stores. Charlesworth, who had rekindled an interest in The Who after witnessing one of the band's shows at Wembley Arena in 1989, was disillusioned at the lack of a representative box-set on The Who when many lesser acts had already been enshrined in this way

He was moved enough to pen a letter to Townshend, dated February 24, 1993, to point this out and to offer his services as compiler and coordinator for such a project. "[Pete] rang me up the next day, and said that I should put a Who box together," Charlesworth told *Mojo*. Unbeknownst to many, Polydor were actually working on a similar project but this tended to put too much emphasis on the post-Keith Moon period with a distinct lack of unreleased material that would interest the hardcore fan. Charlesworth, Astley, graphic designer Richard Evans and Polygram's George McManus returned to the archives for a proper attempt to document The Who's career.

Unfortunately all The Who's radio sessions recorded for the BBC couldn't be included, and the early Shel Talmy-produced material could not be properly remixed because of a long-running legal dispute with Talmy. Regardless, reaction to the boxed set was ecstatic. *Q* magazine even labelled it "the best boxed set ever released."

Townshend wrote a sarcastic, occasionally scathing foreword to the set's liner notes entitled 'Who Cares' in which he gave vent to his feelings for the project and on the history of The Who in general. While he acknowledged that Charlesworth and Astley had done "an OK job", he felt that "being dragged through your life like this is strange." He signed off with a venomous jab at his critics: "So to my detractors, to detractors of The Who, to critics of Moon and his diabolical certain-death style of rock'n'-roll nihilism, I say 'Fuck you.' And not for the first time. I'm still briefly alive. Be kind, be real, or get out of my face. Pete."

"I said to Pete, 'Isn't that a bit negative?'" Charlesworth told *Mojo* in 2004, "and he said, 'Well, that's the way I feel.'"

Townshend was "delighted" with the 79-song collection, according to a July article in the *Detroit News and Free Press*, "and feels it shows the many facets of the band – not just the heavy, arena rock outfit it became during the Seventies." The success of the venture led to talk of producing an expanded version of the originally abbreviated *Live At Leeds*.

"I've got a huge warehouse full of reels of tapes and movie film," Pete said. "Anybody who's interested enough to come in and wade through it and find stuff to put out can do so. That interests me more than the idea of trying to find new product."

Pete attended daughter Aminta's college graduation in October (older sister Emma was studying at Cambridge University during this period), prior to flying to Los Angeles for the premiere of the touring *Tommy* stage show at the Universal Amphitheater. The *Chicago Tribune*'s Jessica Siegel caught up with him backstage, noting that "he was kinda deaf, so I had to talk loud during the interview," and "he still chews at his fingernails, which are bitten to the quick. Occasionally, he smokes." Siegel also noted that Townshend carried a "little red book" in the pocket of his denim jacket: a "guide to local Alcoholics Anonymous meetings in Los Angeles . . ." Pete met the cast backstage between acts, and signed autographs. "After writing 'You were O.K.' on one cast member's playbill," Siegel reported, "Townshend pauses just long enough for dramatic effect before adding 'until you joined the show'."

Having celebrated his 50th birthday the previous month, in June 1995, many internet users were stunned by a bizarre news story which hit the worldwide web: "I was very saddened to hear of the death of Pete Townshend, formerly of The Who. His *Tommy* will be missed by millions." Before obits could be prepared, a statement emerged qualifying that it was actually Group Captain Peter Townsend, who had an ill-fated romance with Princess Margaret in the early Fifties, who had passed on. "I think you're confusing Peter Townsend, who died but wasn't very famous for almost marrying someone royal, with Pete Townshend, who hasn't died [as far as I know] and was very famous for being in The Who!"

In September, a very much alive Townshend played solo at a benefit show, also featuring Annie Lennox, organised by Paul Simon at Madison Square Garden's Paramount Theatre, for the Children's Health Fund.

"Agreeing to appear, I picked up a guitar and I realised that since the middle of 1992, I had probably spent more time at home playing piano than guitar (I was recovering from a serious wrist accident and keyboard practise was more useful physiotherapy)," Townshend wrote in the liner notes to

Scoop 3. "So it seemed to me that I should play piano in public for the first time. On this occasion the Wynton Marsalis orchestra, some of the best jazz musicians on the planet, were in attendance. I was nervous. But I did well." Pete's set included 'Save It For Later', 'Slit Skirts', 'Cut My Hair', 'Love Reign O'er Me', 'I Am An Animal', and 'Drowned'. Paul Simon and band joined him onstage for 'The Kids Are Alright', while Townshend returned the favour by assisting Simon on 'You Can Call Me Al'.

In November, a preview run of *Tommy* opened at the Shaftesbury Theatre, London, with Paul Keating playing the lead with Eighties pop star Kim Wilde taking the part of the mother. In February 1996, a private party for the cast and crew was staged at the Orange, a bar in West Kensington, where Pete played 'Pinball Wizard', with Keating guesting on vocals. Despite the fact that it topped two Andrew Lloyd Webber shows to take an Olivier award for 'Most Outstanding Musical Production', the West End production closed within a year of its opening on March 5. As *The Times'* Helen Johnstone put it, "After rave reviews fell on deaf ears, it became clear that the story of the deaf, dumb and blind boy who becomes a rock messiah was not catching on this side of the Atlantic."

It was around this period that Townshend was lined up to appear in a film, based on an art project that his friend Richard Stanley and artist Alvar Gullichsen had devised over the previous four or five years for Finnish television. (Stanley had moved to Finland in the Seventies, becoming a respected music producer and film-maker). The outlandish plot involved a fictional corporation named Bonk Business, Inc., and its role in a massive, mysterious electromagnetic phenomenon which wipes out all electronics built with processors – cars, computers, aircraft, etc. Pete's role was that of journalist Jack McHine who sets out to uncover the cause of the phenomenon, which turns out to be a malfunctioning radioactive waste-disposal contraption called the Cosmic Sucker.

However time constraints meant that he had to back out of the project and Townshend's character in the hour-long film, released in 1997 as *The Cosmic Sucker*, was taken by Matthew Scurfield, who had appeared alongside him in Stanley's 1968 short, *Lone Ranger*.

"The character was written with Pete in mind from the beginning," Stanley confirms. "He read the script, and he liked it and so forth, but once again, he sort of cancelled quite late, before the production . . . I think that it would have been really interesting to use him in the movie, simply because he is quite a media person. But anyway, it wasn't meant to be."

CHAPTER EIGHTEEN

1996–1999

"Roger speaks a lot about the magic that happens when the three of us get together to play. I have to say I've yet to experience that! I'm trying hard not to be cynical. It doesn't feel that magical to me, but I am enjoying performing for the first time in a long time. I must give myself some credit: I've worked very hard learning to do that. The Supper Club dates that I did recently were all part of a programme to try and get myself to ease back into being in the public eye and accepting the fact that my audience – my fans, The Who's audience and Who fans – are people that I utterly depend on, and I should accept that with some good grace and enjoy it . . ."

– Pete Townshend, 1996

"I've never apologised for restoring and reshaping things I've already done. Partly, that's because there's a quality of energy in my early work that's really difficult to emulate. It's not because I can't do it, I think I can do it sometimes, it's because I don't want to do it. I suppose the work that I did when I was young stands on its own two feet, and I don't want to go down the same road again. I've never been afraid of going and looking at that stuff and trying to make it better. I feel like, in a way, what I'm doing is honouring my job as a writer and making up for the fact that, in many respects, a lot of The Who's music was underrated and undervalued."

– Pete Townshend, 1996

IN late April 1996, Townshend travelled to America for a five-date tour set up to promote *Coolwalkingsmoothtalkingstraightsmokingfirestoking*, a 'best of' compilation.[1] He reportedly let the record company choose the

---

[1] During the visit Townshend met with the designers of a *Tommy* CD-ROM, to be released in June. The CD-ROM featured interviews with the three surviving original members of The Who, Ken Russell, Des McAnuff, and soundtrack producer George Martin. It also featured some original Townshend demos. "I wasn't involved in the authorship of the CD-ROM at all," Pete told *Addicted to Noise*'s Mark Brown in April. "I was a producer and obviously a participant."

album's title and content, as he told *CNN*, "I told them, 'You look, you take what you think is cool, because as far as I'm concerned, it's all genius,' or, if I get up on the other side of the bed, 'Don't do it, it's all rubbish.'"

The shows, containing a mixture of solo material along with a handful of Who songs, were well-received, notable for their intimacy and back to basics feel. Accompanied only by ex-Pink Floyd sideman Jon Carin on keyboards, Townshend seemed in good spirits and at ease onstage. After making a brief appearance at LA's Universal Amphitheatre on April 28, Pete performed two shows at the LA House of Blues the next day, one at 9 p.m. and another at midnight. Eddie Vedder sat through both sets, and "mouthed most of the words", according to one reviewer. Also in attendance were *Cheers* cast members George Wendt and Woody Harrelson, along with actor John Cusack and former Yes bass player, Chris Squire.

On April 30, Pete performed at one of the original venues that broke The Who in America, the Fillmore in San Francisco. "For his screaming crowd, the show was a two-hour high," reported the *Daily Californian*. "When Townshend sang the line, 'I wish I was home this time' from 'Sheraton Gibson' a fan quickly quipped, 'You are home, Pete!' The musician's gentle smile cemented the love affair between him and his audience . . .

"Rarely can a rock musician manage to captivate his public without actually playing music but Townshend's friendly chit-chat about the most improbable subjects [his masturbation habit, spirituality and paganism, Rod Stewart's sexiness] made the interludes between songs so entertaining that fans kept asking the rock legend to keep on talking. The range of Townshend's well-informed interests was best illustrated by a seamless segue between a discussion about Cybill Shepherd's recent *TV Guide* interview and a song based on a saying of Julian of Norwich, a medieval English saint."[2]

While the *Oakland Tribune*'s William Friar reported that the Fillmore show was mostly an acoustic affair, it was clearly the occasions Pete picked up his Telecaster that he appreciated most: "When Townshend wanted to play, he *played*. Lightning-fast riffs. Thundering power chords. Spidery finger-picking. It didn't matter that he never pulled out his

---

[2] Townshend was referring to 'All Shall Be Well'. Julian of Norwich said, "I learned that it is more worship to God to know all-things in general, than to take pleasure in any special thing. And if I should do wisely according to this teaching, I should not only be glad for nothing in special, but I should not be greatly distressed for no manner of thing: for *ALL shall be well*. For the fullness of joy is to behold God in all . . ."

trademark windmill strum, and no one really expected him to break a guitar, a rock-concert tradition he started and tired of before many of today's modern rock rebels were even born. However, that didn't stop Tuesday night's audience from begging him to do it. 'If I smashed this up, then I'd go to hell,' Townshend said, cradling his American-made vintage electric guitar."

Townshend was not above any imperfections in his performances as the *Daily Californian* remarked upon: "Near the end of 'Rough Boys' as Townshend was about to bring the song to a triumphant climax . . . he stopped and calmly re-tuned one of the strings. He then launched back into the closing chords, but it was a disaster, cracking up both him and his keyboardist. Similarly, during a rollicking encore of 'Magic Bus', Townshend stopped playing mid-song to take off his shoes, while his keyboardist tried to cover for him. Townshend then proceeded to talk about the incident – again, while he was still ostensibly playing the song."

Following the San Francisco show, Townshend travelled to New York for two shows at the 1,000-seat Supper Club in the theatre district on May 3 and 4. The set lists remained essentially the same for both the West and East Coast performances and the amount of *Quadrophenia* selections included might have provided a clue to the more discerning that Pete was toying with the possibility of giving the album more exposure – an idea which would soon prove a reality.

On June 29, a reunited Who (in all but name) performed the entire album at the Prince's Trust "Masters Of Music" Benefit Concert staged in London's Hyde Park. Having experienced a renewed enthusiasm for playing onstage, Townshend had originally agreed to perform solo but his plans were dramatically altered when it became apparent that the show was on a much larger scale than any of the concerts he'd performed recently.

"I learned that the expected audience was 150,000 people and essentially I thought, 'What the hell am I going to do? Stand up there with a guitar?' What I did with Paul Simon [at the Paramount in New York] was play a bit of piano, play a bit of guitar and it was a very intimate occasion. I realised I really couldn't do that and thought about what I could do as an alternative."

Townshend put it more bluntly in an interview with the *Los Angeles Times* in May 2000: "The promoter, Harvey Goldsmith, told me half a million people were coming and I said, 'I'm scared, I don't think I can do it.'"

Pete had been entertaining the idea of "rescuing" *Quadrophenia* for over two years, even considering a stage show à la *Tommy* and *The Iron Man*.[3] The prospect arose after *Tommy*'s Broadway success, when Townshend began to evaluate his back catalogue for further stage possibilities.

"I have lots of ideas for plays and musicals that I want to pursue," he told the *San Jose Mercury News* in July 1994, "and the way this version of *Tommy* has worked out, it makes me think there's hope for some of the pieces I wrote for The Who that nearly worked but didn't – things like 'Rael', 'A Quick One (While He's Away)' and *Quadrophenia*. Maybe I should try them again."[4]

His interest in reviving *Quadrophenia* was further stimulated to a degree by the *Daltrey Sings Townshend* concert. "I remember when I did Carnegie Hall with Roger in 1994, and hearing 'Dr. Jimmy' and thinking how wonderful it sounded, but chiefly how wonderfully he sang it and how explosive it was."

Another reminder of the album's power and durability came with the arrival in March of Townshend's advance copy of the remastered CD, released in July.

"I put it on, and 'I Am The Sea' comes up, and it was just spectacular. Something happened in the original mixing process which destroyed the record . . . Fuck knows what I did. It was some sort of phase problem. *Quadrophenia* now sounds very much like it sounded in the studio, as I remember it."

"I got a beautiful e-mail from Pete when he heard [the reissued] *Quadrophenia* . . .," says Jon Astley, who supervised the remix. "He just said something like, 'Fantastic, I just couldn't believe it. You brought *Quadrophenia* to life, saved it.'"

"I really want to see *Quadrophenia* turn into a theatrical property of some sort," Townshend said. "It's a much more cohesive, dramatic work, really, than anything I've ever done. The problem with it is it's an inside view. It's an internal story. So it's quite difficult to realise without quite a lot of suspension of disbelief on the audience's part. What I'd really like to see happen is to see it as a touring production that would feature major rock star celebrities like Roger, like a number of other people who may be slightly disenfranchised by their bands breaking up earlier than they would

[3] During a *Rolling Stone* interview in late 1993 Townshend remarked, "If it [*Quadrophenia*] had female voices, I think it would have *West Side Story*-type potential."
[4] Another idea of Townshend's during this period was "an idea for a musical based on five pages of playwright Arthur Miller's autobiography [*Timebends*, published in 1987]," according to the *Los Angeles Times* in August 1993.

like. Certainly it's a piece that would work well in the Hard Rock Hotel in Las Vegas, in Atlantic City installations, and in sheds on the road, with a band. It would be Who music and Pete Townshend's story. And it might turn out to be a really strong vehicle for Roger. But we'll have to see about that."

"I never really thought about [staging *Quadrophenia*] seriously until about a year ago," Pete said in 1996, "when Bill Curbishley came to me with a proposal to do a European tour of a rough treatment that I'd done, which was very, very expensive. It was a very ambitious project, a bit like [U2's] Zoo TV, with two bands. I was very excited. Then I told him that I wouldn't appear in it, and he said he didn't think it would sell out, and therefore the funding wasn't available in advance.

"And then Des McAnuff came to see me in February or March of this year with a proposal to do a celebration for 50 years of the Vespa motorscooter from the Piaggio company in Rome in August.[5] That's when I started to think about it seriously. I started to think about the fact that a company like Piaggio might be able to put up the money required to do a fairly simple but elegant staging. And then the Prince's Trust thing came up."

It was now obvious to Townshend that staging a version of *Quadrophenia* at Hyde Park was an attractive alternative to performing solo. "We're getting *Quadrophenia* done because we went straight to [the sponsors] Mastercard, cut out all the people in between, got $400,000 and put the thing up. It's a strange place to be to realise that all I have to do is stroll into a room with a few old guys and say, 'I fancy doing *Quadrophenia* as a dramatic work,' and they say, 'Hey, we'll give you money.' That may sound cynical, but the fact is I can do it, and I trust myself to do it well."

Drawing from his recent experience with stage work, Pete examined potential methods to "advance the story" of *Quadrophenia*, since it suffered a similar problem to *Lifehouse*, though to a lesser degree.

"What happened with *Quadrophenia* is it's a very elegant piece of work that to an extent is confused by its grandiosity," Townshend told *Addicted To Noise*'s Mark Brown in April, "but it's a very, very simple story. A young man has a bad day, basically, and that's really all there is. It's a series of events . . . He just realised that all he has in his life is himself and some

---

[5] The Piaggio anniversary show, which was slated for August in Rome, didn't take place due to scheduling problems.

spiritual future. Very much like *Tommy* in a way, the end of it. What's happened to me in my life is I've had kids come up to me like Eddie Vedder and say, 'I used to listen to *Quadrophenia* because it was my childhood. I could see my childhood in it.'"

Realising that The Who's British audience were not as deeply committed to the band and its back catalogue as their American counterparts, Townshend decided to employ a "visible link" to the 1979 movie, bringing in lead character Phil Daniels as on-stage narrator, assisted by film projected on to a behind-the-stage screen. This gave the story context and continuity, and advanced some of the less stage-friendly nuances of the plot. With an eye to strengthening the dramatic aspect of *Quadrophenia*, additional cast members were brought in, including Seventies UK glam pop star Gary Glitter as the Godfather, and actor/comedian Adrian Edmondson as the Ace Face.

The 16-piece band, featuring three backing singers (including Billy Nicholls) and a five-piece brass section, soon came together. "Obviously my first choice for a main voice was Roger," Pete said in early 1996. "I asked Roger if he'd appear, and Roger said, 'You must get John to play.' Roger had done a tour last year with John on the bass and Zak Starkey on drums. So they became the nucleus of the band around the time of the announcement, so it kind of amounts, in a sense, to a Who reunion. Though that's not how it's going to look because I'm not going to play guitar, I don't think. I'm going to be in it, performing some songs. It's exciting. But that's where it stands."

Starkey had strong Who connections, and would prove to have a better chemistry with Townshend and Entwistle than Kenney Jones or Simon Phillips.

"We're really pleased to have him in the band," Pete said in early 1996. "He's just stunning. He's very easy to play with. Mind you, I'm very spoiled with drummers. I don't fuck around anymore . . . Simon Phillips is a different kind of drummer, but he's very easy to play with, he's very much a listening drummer. But what Zak has is a lot of karmic Keith Moon about him, which is wonderful. It's easy to make too much of that – he really is his own drummer. He has his own style. But he's very intelligent. What he did was adapt his own style as an imitator of Keith Moon – he does a garage band imitation of Keith Moon which is probably unbeatable – but he's modified that, moderated it, in a very intelligent and musical way so that he won't be directly compared. He won't evoke uncomfortable memories for the audience. I've known him for a long time. Keith used to be a kind of musical godfather to him. He gave him his first drum kit, which I think is rather strange. Ringo may have actually given him his first drum kit, but I think Keith gave him the first drum kit that he really wanted. It had nude women on it."

Guitar duties were split among Simon Townshend and former Procol Harum/session player Geoff Whitehorn. Pete enjoyed working with his brother again. "I'm glad he's comfortable doing this, because it's a chance to spend time together, which we tend only to do when we're working. We see each other at Christmas and birthdays and other occasions, but we both shut ourselves out in our respective studios and write, write, write, write. He's been doing it since he was eight, so he's been doing it nearly as long as I have."

The main reason Pete delegated the majority of guitar work was the poor condition of his hearing. "I won't be playing guitar . . . I can't play guitar the way I used to," he said in early 1996. "I'd fucking kill myself. I'd make myself deafer than I am already . . . I'm fucking deaf. I'm damaged."

"It's amazing that in the debate about whether or not Pete should tour with The Who that the question of hearing is never thought about, and yet it's the first thing that comes to my mind," Townshend told *People online* in 1996. "It makes me angry. When I'm in the back of my car, I can't hear a word my wife and six-year-old son are saying in the front. On aeroplanes I can only hear children or people with high squeaky voices if they're looking right at me. I lip-read. I don't have hearing aids in my ears, but it wouldn't hurt for me to wear one, and I eventually will when I can no longer get through the day."

The concert also starred Alanis Morissette, Eric Clapton, and Bob Dylan with Ron Wood, and raised approximately $1 million for the Prince's Trust. Daltrey had to wear an eye patch after being hit in the eye by a Gary Glitter-wielded microphone stand during the previous day's rehearsal. The Prince's Trust show turned out to be one of the largest single-day events ever staged in Britain with an audience of around 150,000 who braved the unseasonably cold weather.

"[*Quadrophenia* in Hyde Park] was a reckless move and in a lot of ways it didn't come off," Townshend told *The Times*' David Sinclair in 1998. "We played to 200,000 people, half of whom had come to see Alanis Morissette. I spoke to a lot of young people about it afterwards and they said they didn't really know what was going on. It was all a bit confused."

While the show might not have been an unqualified success in Townshend's estimation, it did demonstrate the potential of *Quadrophenia* as a stage piece.[6] "At the moment I'm considering the idea of bringing it to Giants Stadium or something like that," Pete said at the time. "But I don't want to tour the world because it's actually a workshop. It might be crap." Six nights at Madison Square Garden were booked for mid-July and to Townshend's relief, all were sell-outs. The only cast change was the substitution of Billy Idol in place of Edmondson.

"What makes *Quadrophenia* resonate today, so long after its inception, is its powerful, universal theme and its killer songs, many of them simultaneously bombastic and introspective," wrote the *Boston Globe*'s Jim Sullivan in his review of the opening night. "Inner angst meets arena rock; power chords mesh with quasi-operatic singing; sentimentality runs headlong into stridency . . .

"There is still no bona fide Who reunion – these six shows are the extent of it and Townshend doesn't even like to call it The Who. Still, Daltrey must be in heaven. The 14,000-strong Garden audience [a quarter of the house seats weren't sold due to staging] went bonkers over *Quadrophenia* – and got an unexpected encore treat with 'Behind Blue Eyes', 'Won't Get Fooled Again' and 'Magic Bus'."

Variety's Kevin Zimmerman was similarly impressed with the opening show: "Townshend stuck with acoustic guitar and was notable mainly while exhibiting his famed wrists of rubber on a solo 'Drowned' and trading vocals with Daltrey on a fiery 'Helpless Dancer'. Entwistle characteristically stayed well in the back, delivering a thumping bass solo during a roof-raising take on '5:15' . . . Apparently a tune-up for the inevitable Broadway production, *Quadrophenia* nevertheless retains much of its nimble, muscular brilliance. More to the point, perhaps, is the fact that there's clearly life yet in this particular brand of rockers."

Encouraged by the response, a full US tour was arranged to commence in October. "With Zak Starkey on drums and my brother Simon on guitar, we've managed to spin some karma into the piece which makes it feel very comfortable for me," Townshend told *Cleveland Live*'s Ira Robbins. "When the three of us [Townshend, Entwistle, Daltrey] stand

---

[6] The night after the Hyde Park concert, at midnight, Townshend played a four song, 30-minute set at a private party at Thunder Drive nightclub which included 'Pinball Wizard' featuring West End *Tommy* lead Paul Keating, and 'My Generation' with Joe Walsh on guitar.

together with a piece like this you can get more of a sense of it having genuine authority . . . The three of us are 'from the neighbourhood', it just somehow feels right . . ."

"I've enjoyed the concerts so far. I'm not sure how I'm going to feel about being on a long, drawn-out tour again, but I'm sure I'll be OK. I absolutely loved the New York show. We'll probably do a few more shows with it in London and Europe, and after that I really don't know. I'm already getting interest from theatrical producers in developing it as a simple sit-down theatrical production with a band onstage, like *Rent*, that kind of thing. I've had a couple of offers already, which I'm thinking about. What I think *Quadrophenia* lends itself to, and what I might be able to pull off where others have failed in the long term is to create a rock'n'roll event of great integrity and authenticity which can sit down somewhere in an installation . . . This is what interests me for the future, not so much music theatre in the old tradition, but an aspect of music theatre that allows technology to play an important part without being subject to the vagaries of Broadway."

Following the New York shows, several changes were made to the line-up and visual presentation including the removal of Whitehorn, with Townshend playing more electric guitar. "My brother Simon is still playing most of the work," Townshend told Robbins, "but I decided I would actually get myself a rig like the one I used in '89, which certainly didn't hurt my ears, and play a few solos, basically because I felt that Geoff Whitehorn was getting a bad rap. I thought he played beautifully and elegantly, and people seemed to think in some way that he shouldn't have been there. So I just thought that I would bow to public opinion and play a bit of electric."

It was also felt that the onstage narration and film presentation were confusing. To correct this, Daniels was dropped. As Pete said, "We're in the process of tidying that up a bit. We're shooting a lot of film, another half-a-million dollars worth of movie."

The North American tour began with four dates in the Pacific Northwest, with Townshend appearing unannounced for an early evening set at Neil Young's Bridge School Benefit on October 19 at the Shoreline Amphitheatre, Mountain View, California, before playing with The Who in San Jose. Also appearing over the two nights was an impressive artist line-up of David Bowie, Patti Smith, The Cowboy Junkies, Pearl Jam and Young himself.

Townshend's half-hour set consisted of 'The Kids Are Alright', 'I'm A

Boy', and 'A Legal Matter' (which he introduced as songs he "wrote when I was young about being young"), 'Let My Love Open The Door', 'Drowned', and 'Behind Blue Eyes'. At one point, he joked with the audience, "Muddy Waters once said, 'My guitar is my thing!' If my guitar was my thing, then I used to bounce my thing all over the stage!'"

The *San Diego Union-Tribune*'s Dennis Hunt wasn't impressed with the LA *Quadrophenia* show on October 22, citing the "muddled story line", Gary Glitter ("second-rate"), Billy Idol ("feeble-voiced") and Daltrey's "totally shot" voice, which "kept cracking in the wrong places and he was having trouble sustaining notes . . . Townshend was the best performer of the lot, but couldn't carry the show by himself."

The tour wound on through Las Vegas and Denver prior to stopping in Chicago for two shows (October 31 and November 1) at the United Center. *Rolling Stone*'s Steve Knopper reviewed the second night.

"What's this? A flash of inspiration? From The Who? The 32-year-old band's short *Quadrophenia* tour, like its 1989 reunion hype extravaganza, is three old rockers and 12 of the best touring musicians money can buy. But unlike 1989 – and certainly unlike the listless 1982 'farewell' tour – singer Roger Daltrey, guitarist Pete Townshend and bassist John Entwistle decided to make *Quadrophenia* count.

"As unlikely as it may sound, their best hire was Zak Starkey on drums. He mimicked the late Keith Moon perfectly, wearing all white and recreating the chaotic explosions that hold *Quadrophenia* together. His presence alone energised the surviving trio. The other good choice was *Quadrophenia* . . . it holds up after two decades infinitely better than the impossible-to-kill *Tommy*, The Who's first rock opera . . . *Quadrophenia*, a tale of mods battling rockers in Sixties England, was about rock nostalgia when it came out in 1973. So it works better than, say, singing, 'Hope I die before I get old' . . ."

The first half of November saw the tour move through Michigan and Ohio, and on to the East Coast – Pennsylvania, New York, Maryland, Massachusetts, finishing with an additional show, in East Rutherford, New Jersey. Two weeks later, the band played two shows on December 6 and 7 at Earls Court and Manchester's Nynex Arena on 11 December, with Sixties singer and all-round hellraiser P.J. Proby assuming the role of the Godfather in place of Glitter.

During the four-month break that followed the UK dates, Townshend resumed work at his home studio, 'The Cube'.

"What I'm writing today is very different from anything that I've ever written before," he told Robbins. "I don't know that my audience would feel comfortable with it. I started to demonstrate some of that – I suppose it's the style in which I've been playing for almost the last 10 years – in my recent solo concerts. As I grew in confidence I also grew in pragmatic sense of self-preservation, where I would have been quite happy to sit and bang away at the piano all night, or play John Fahey ragtime all night. That's what I do.

"I also do a lot of extended compositions – I wouldn't call them jazz, but they're very modal, they're very simplistic. It's a style of composition I've been developing to support dramatic language. I've never been interested at all in film composition, so everything I've been doing is about training myself for another life as somebody who could write for the stage. While I've been trying to learn to play the piano a little bit better, trying to learn to score a bit more elegantly, trying to learn to deal with other players without being quite so dictatorial, show business is changing under me. Las Vegas is a good example. The whole world of theme parks is an area where specially commissioned music from somebody like me is welcomed. So I don't quite know where I'm gonna go.

"The piece I'm working on at the moment is quite a modest piece called 'Stella'; out of that grew another piece called 'Trilby's Piano',[7] which was a thing about something that happened to me when I was a kid with an aunt of mine – a very positive experience for me. I've started to look at the more positive experiences I've had in my life, and I find it very difficult to compose for that stuff because I've spent most of my time drawing on my negative experiences, or what I would call my growth experiences."

The majority, if not all, of the pieces Townshend recorded during this period were written and recorded on piano, specifically a "six-foot Yamaha Conservatory Grand piano that was equipped with a MIDI send", as he wrote for *Scoop 3*. An example of the work was 'Wired To The Moon' and its successor, 'Wired To The Moon (Part 2)'. The former was offered in free mp3 download form on Townshend's website, while the latter surfaced on *Scoop 3*, for which he explained the song's subject matter: "I have experienced a number of strange attacks in recent years that I call 'dream attacks'. I fall into a state in which I remember dozens of

---

[7] 'Trilby's Piano' later surfaced as part of the 'Wire & Glass' mini-opera on The Who's *Endless Wire* album.

recent dreams. In fact they start to rerun like several movies, but all at once."

Also during the tour break, Townshend celebrated the eight Olivier award nominations *Tommy* garnered by throwing an invitation-only party in early February at London's LA 2 club. The 500 guests including John Entwistle and the Daltrey family (Roger was absent in LA) were treated to a two-hour-plus set with Townshend and band Zak Starkey, John Bundrick, Jody Linscott, Billy Nicholls, Jon Carin and Pino Palladino, performing selections from his solo work, in addition to familiar Who standards such as 'Pinball Wizard' and 'Won't Get Fooled Again'.

It was also during this period that Pete bought his current home, 'The Wick', on Richmond Hill. The historic mansion (which was reported as being bought for prices ranging from £3 to £8 million, with the higher end being the more oft-reported amount) was previously owned by esteemed British actor Sir John Mills, and in the early Seventies by Faces and Rolling Stones guitarist, Ron Wood. Richmond Hill is especially noted for its spectacular views of the Thames, and the Wick's semi-circular rear wall and large glass conservatory afforded the occupants breathtaking views from several vantage points. Townshend also owned property near the Helford River in Cornwall, a popular yacht racing venue, and Chapel House, a former residence of poet Alfred Lord Tennyson, on Twickenham's Montpelier Row.[8]

When Townshend first viewed the Wick, he noticed that the full-scale studio he had helped install in the basement at Wood's request had been converted into a gym by the current resident, but without changing the room's interior dimensions. After moving in, he prised up a floorboard and found the original wiring for the studio was still intact. Having retained one of its old recording desks, he painstakingly had the studio reinstalled.

In April, The Who commenced a month-long tour of Europe, winding through nine countries prior to the final show at Wembley Arena on 18 May. The following day, Townshend recorded *Prelude 970519* on his birthday. "This piano 'prelude' was intended to evoke serenity, calm, and ultimately – in a very short space of time – readiness to sleep," he wrote in

---

[8] Around 1990 while living on Montpelier Row, Townshend visited old friend Tony Palmer's house in Notting Hill Gate, with an eye toward purchasing it. "He came to look at it. Partly because I had a big sound studio in the basement," Palmer recalls. "He had a sort of sound studio out in Twickenham, but I think that there had been an awful lot of complaints, and he was looking around for another one."

his *Scoop 3* notes. "So it is intentionally soporific and light. Occasionally, for a month at most, I would try to record at least one piece every day as part of what I called my 'Daily Project'. This idea was inspired by my reading of *The Artist's Way*,[9] and the course work I did on the 12-week programme of creative stimulation the authors recommend. If I didn't record any music, I might instead try to write a short essay or poem of some kind."

On June 14, Townshend performed a solo benefit show at the Chicago House of Blues for Maryville Academy, a local children's charity. Having drunkenly messed up his appearance at the city's Arie Crown Theatre on the 1993 *Psychoderelict* tour, he was keen to make amends.

"Early in his three-hour-plus set, Townshend paused to present the Reverend John Smyth, executive director of Maryville, a cheque for more than $200,000" reported the *Arlington Heights Daily Herald*. "Townshend's relegation to mammoth arenas showed, as he took his time getting comfortable with the more communal environment. He fumbled with his lyric book, flubbed words and chords on the keyboard and admitted his jetlag. Jon Carin helped as a one-man Who, gracing Townshend's guitar with drum rhythms, vocals and keyboards. But Townshend's aloof humour and, in particular, choice of songs he hasn't played live in years or ever, gave the marathon evening more of a campfire feel . . ."

Having invited Townshend to a Chicago Bulls game the night before the show, Eddie Vedder volunteered to join him onstage at the House of Blues. The pair had no rehearsal prior to singing duet on 'Heart To Hang Onto' (which Townshend dedicated to Ronnie Lane, who had succumbed to multiple sclerosis, aged 51, on June 4, in Trinidad, Colorado), 'Magic Bus', and 'Tattoo'.[10]

"It's a good thing I listened to those records hundreds of times in my youth," Vedder told *USA Today*. "I've known these songs since I was 17 and they still resonate."

In late summer, The Who opened the second leg of the US *Quadrophenia*

---

[9] *The Artist's Way*, written by Julia Cameron, was published in 1992. The book inspired Townshend to write a letter to his younger self. "I think in my letter to young Pete I told myself that I shouldn't worry," he told *Salon.com*'s David Marchese in 2006. "There would be no nuclear holocaust. The planet would not become so polluted that we would all have to live in suits like they do in *Dune*. I think young Pete told this old fart to mind my own business. I think he was right."

[10] The performances of 'Magic Bus' and 'Heart To Hang On To' from this show later made it on to 1999's *Pete Townshend Live* CD.

tour – with Ben Waters taking over the role of the Ace Face – at St Louis' Riverport Amphitheatre on July 19. The *Chicago Tribune*'s Rick Reger filed a lukewarm report on the performance at Tinley Park's World Music Theater the following night, opining that it "mingled moments of decrepitude with passages of inspired playing . . . when the band dispensed with the excess keyboards, percussion and brass and simplified songs down to bass, drum and guitar, as they did on 'I'm One' and 'Is It In My Head?', they mustered that blend of pathos and searing anger that's always defined The Who's sound."

Brian McCollum of the *Detroit Free Press* concurred when reviewing the show at the Pine Knob Music Theatre five nights later: "With a five-piece horn section, two synthesisers and auxiliary percussion, most every song Friday became an awkward anthem. If The Who – and other grown-up rock acts – would recognise the overload, where washes of superfluous sound dilute the essential backbeat, such shows would stand even taller."

The tour ended in Florida with an August 16 date in West Palm Beach. Back in London, Townshend was working on several projects. The August 18 edition of *Publishers Weekly* reported that he had signed a "world rights deal" with the publisher Little, Brown to publish his autobiography. The memoir, the contract of which was worth reportedly "in the seven-figure range" was due out in late 1999.

The deal had been in preparation for at least a year. "It's not so much about money as about how much the book would cost to produce if I were to decide to fill it with black-and-white pictures of my dear old dad or something," Townshend said in 1996. "I'll probably start early next year and it'll take me two years. The term autobiography is a bit mischievous; what I'm really doing is writing about my life and my music. About life and music in general. It's going to be an artist's view of the last 50 years and what's been going on with music in that time. I don't pretend to be an arch academic musicologist, but my journey is a unique one, and does give me a very special and acute view of where popular music came from and what it means.

"I hope this book will elucidate a lot of that stuff simply by me telling my story without any frills. Just talking about my grandparents and my parents and the music that they listened to, and what they did when they were young, and my life and how I grew up and what I did when I was young and the people that I met and then suddenly 'Hey ho, here we are'. I'm looking forward to it. I've been gathering materials for it, most of which has been a bit of a waste of time, but it's all good memory-jogging stuff."

1999 came and went, with no sign of the finished book. "I've written about 250,000 words and I've taken a break for a while," he told *Q's* David Cavanaugh in 2000. "I've done the difficult part, which was my childhood, and I'm up to the art school years . . ." Townshend further explained the publishing delay in an online chat hosted by American book chain Barnes & Noble: "I'm afraid I put it down. My publishers were wonderfully supportive, and I found writing about my childhood very natural. But when I reached The Who years, I started to panic. There is, you see, so much documentary evidence that suggests that the way I remember things is wrong! I need to do more research, speak to friends, find out whether I can really write down what I remember without being dishonest or careless over the truth. I will pick it up again very soon."

Also in 1997, an animated version of *The Iron Man* went into production. Des McAnuff declared his faith in the work's ability to translate to the big screen, and the rights to the story were eventually acquired by Warner Brothers. Animation writer and director Brad Bird, whose work included *The Simpsons*, *King Of The Hill*, and *The Critic* was hired, and the $30 million feature was released in 1999 as *The Iron Giant*. Townshend was named executive director, McAnuff producer.[11]

"I love animation, but I wanted the film to be a musical," Townshend said. "That didn't happen, but I'm still immensely proud of what has become perhaps the last true cell-animation film to be made on a big budget. We shall see."

Ted Hughes was sent a copy of Bird's script during the making of the film. "I want to tell you how much I like what Brad Bird has done," Hughes wrote in a letter to the film-makers. "He's made something all of a piece, with terrific sinister gathering momentum and the ending came to me as a glorious piece of amazement. He's made a terrific dramatic situation out of the way he's developed *The Iron Giant*. I can't stop thinking about it . . ."[12]

Another ongoing project that Townshend was determined to see realised after nearly 30 years was *Lifehouse*. "In staging *Tommy, Psychoderelict*

---

[11] "[Brad Bird] was dead set on avoiding a Disney-style musical [which I happen to like] with songs, etc.," Townshend revealed in an online chat in 2000. "So although we did not argue over this – he is a great film-maker – I stood down."
[12] Ted Hughes died in October, 1998 at the age of 68 following an 18-month battle with cancer, just 13 days after being awarded the Order of Merit by the Queen.

and *The Iron Man* in 1993, I learned some of the dramatic writing and stagecraft skills I need to go forward," Pete had written in his essay accompanying the 1995 CD reissue of *Who's Next*. "*Lifehouse* will probably emerge as a kind of musical or newfangled opera rather than as a film. But I assure you it will make sense to you, just as in my mind it always has. Critics will probably call it naïve. I hope so. I wrote it when I was a child."

He started to think of the arrangements of the original songs in more grandiose terms and brought in outside musicians to help, one of them being Rachel Fuller. "He hired me as an arranger and orchestrator when he was working on *Lifehouse*," Fuller told the *Chicago Sun-Times*' Jeff Elbel in 2006. "I did some orchestrations on 'Behind Blue Eyes', and themes based on *The Iron Man*. I also orchestrated some Scarlatti harpsichord sonatas for *Lifehouse*."

The two struck up a friendship which, over the ensuing year, blossomed into a romantic relationship. "It's the first time since I've been separated that I've been out with an English woman," Townshend told *Rolling Stone* in 2000. "I've mainly gone out with American women."

On September 14, Pete gave a speech and unveiled a blue plaque in honour of Jimi Hendrix at 25 Brook Street, Mayfair, next door to where 18th century composer Handel had once lived. "There's been a lot of talk about whether a rock performer deserves to be on the building next door to George Frederick Handel, and I think he does," said Townshend to the gathered crowd of around 2000. "[Jimi] was so special, so extraordinary; he's up there for me with Miles Davis and Charlie Parker as somebody who was a virtuoso, an innovator. He was different, extraordinary and new."

Apart from this rare public appearance, Pete continued to compose and record demos; one of the first such recordings was '971104 Arpeggio Piano'. "This piece was recorded to DAT tape at my home in London on November 4, 1997," he wrote in his *Scoop 3* notes. "When I first moved into the house in London in which I now live I chose the tiniest room [an ante-room off the main living room] and set up a keyboard on which to practise and compose . . . I used the keyboard every day for about a year, recording to DAT tape or cassette."

Another example, 'Variations On Dirty Jobs', was recorded a few nights later. "I fully orchestrated it earlier this year," Townshend wrote in 2001. "Although the chords are similar to 'The Dirty Jobs' from *Quadrophenia* it is an entirely original composition. It is intended to demonstrate the kind of tonal effect I could achieve should I develop a full orchestral version of *Quadrophenia.*"

1998 saw the release of Emma Townshend's *Winterland*. In its three-star review, *Rolling Stone* said the album "carries enough promise to make Townshend an artist worth watching." Her father called the album "pretty great", adding, "I can't tell you how strange it is. Her voice is so beautiful." Due to its low-key reception, *Winterland* remains Emma's only recording to date.

On May 19, Pete's 53rd birthday, his father-in-law, Ted Astley, passed away aged 76. A few weeks later, on 8 June, Townshend delivered an address towards the end of a 90-minute memorial service at St Martins-in-the-Fields, London, for Linda McCartney, who died in April from breast cancer. In his speech, he paid tribute to the durability of the McCartney marriage, saying "They achieved it by staying together," although some of the 700 mourners present took umbrage at his more candid remarks.

"I've lived in a bit of a fantasy, I think," Townshend told *Rolling Stone* in 2000, when discussing his own marriage. "I always wanted there to be a kind of Paul Newman and Joanne Woodward story but they're one of the great exceptions. I did hold Paul McCartney in high esteem because of the way that he conducted his relationship. I have those kind of old-fashioned family values."

In August, Pete slotted in a series of solo shows around an appearance at Max Yasgur's farm in Bethel, New York, the original site of Woodstock. Prior to the gig, Townshend made an appearance on David Letterman's late night television show on August 13, followed by a warm-up performance the next day in Boston.

"The Harborlights show was everything a fan could hope for," reported the *Boston Phoenix*. "With a five-piece band in tow, Townshend remained onstage for two hours plus; he pulled favourite Who hits and solo rarities from his catalogue; he was loose and chatty between songs; he did a few tunes [including the folk standard 'North Country Girl'] that he's never played live before, and he drastically rearranged nearly everything . . .

"As much as you wanted to cheer Townshend for the irreverence with his own oldies, the new arrangements missed as often as they hit. Although the stripped-down band didn't include a drummer, it did have keyboardist Jon Carin, who saddled nearly everything with overloud, monochromatic drum-machine parts; percussionist Jody Linscott had to make do with slapping cymbals and shaking maracas. More's the pity, because Townshend was in the mood to jam, playing more electric guitar than he had on the last two Who tours . . . Almost electrifying, but you just can't get funky without a drummer.

"The surprise Woodstock homages were a pair of Canned Heat covers, 'On The Road Again' and 'Going Up The Country' – both beautifully done, with Townshend's falsetto echoing the late Al Wilson's. He and back-up singer Tracey Langran [a member of the *Tommy* Broadway cast] duetted on 'The Acid Queen' . . . But as the night went on there was more dead air onstage, culminating with a glitch-ridden version of 'Won't Get Fooled Again' during which Townshend threw down two guitars, stopped the band twice, and finally left the stage."

The following day, Townshend headlined in front of an audience of 26,000 at 'A Day In The Garden', the Woodstock 29th anniversary event which took place on the site of the original festival. Other performers appearing included Ziggy Marley, Ten Years After, Melanie, Stevie Nicks, Don Henley, and Lou Reed.[13]

"There were 30 food vendors and 400 portable toilets, in marked contrast to the absence of both at the first fest," reported *USA Today*'s Jim Bessman. "There was a phone bank and a mobile cash machine and a play area for kids, a field hospital and four satellite first-aid stations – and a sturdy chain-link fence to keep '69-style gatecrashers from sharing space with those who'd shelled out up to $69 to get in . . ."

Pete's set opened with 'On The Road Again', and incorporated a blues segment featuring guitarist Taj Mahal. He dedicated 'Behind Blue Eyes' to late Yippie leader Abbie Hoffman, whom he had infamously thrown off the stage at the original event, and closed the day with a grand finale of 'See Me, Feel Me', featuring a local 26-piece gospel choir. The following evening, Townshend returned to the Chicago House of Blues for his second annual Maryville Academy fundraiser, which generated over $300,000.

Rolling Stone's Blair Fischer reported: "An orchestra stand was in place to help Townshend remember the lyrics he penned, a drum machine provided the backbeat for the grungy 'Anyway Anyhow Anywhere' and 'Save It For Later', and horns and harmonica accompanied pop jigs like

---

[13] The Who were invited to play at a 30th anniversary 'Woodstock 99' festival. "We were earnestly invited to appear," Townshend told *USA Today*'s Edna Gunderson. "And I half considered getting The Who together for it, but only half. I feel that I hadn't ever been honest about how important Woodstock had been to me and to The Who."

'Let My Love Open The Door' and 'A Little Is Enough'. Blonde song-stress Tracey Langran joined Townshend on acoustic guitar for much of the night and lent silky pipes to the ballad 'A Friend Is A Friend' and the cheery 'Sensation' . . .

"Long before Townshend lost his hearing, most of his hair and his bandmate, Keith Moon, Townshend was a juggernaut onstage. He ripped into his strings until his fingers bled and he had no compunction about puncturing amplifiers or splintering his guitar on a nightly basis. That, of course, was a long time ago. Preparing to play Canned Heat's 'Going Up The Country', his guitar strap broke and his guitar fell to the ground. Some laughed, but Townshend didn't. Rather, he slowly, calmly picked it off the floor and said, 'Just dropping them doesn't do anything.' Meet the new boss. Almost the same as the old boss."

Upon his return to England, Townshend lent his services to another cause, this time the striking (and subsequently fired) Liverpool dock workers. The invitation-only October 16 Rock The Dock show took place at London's Sound Republic Club, with Pete supported by Oasis guitarist/songwriter Noel Gallagher, and Ocean Colour Scene. At the end of Townshend's seven song set, Gallagher and Ocean Colour Scene guitarist Steve Cradock joined him on 'Magic Bus'.

The following month, Townshend performed a series of UK solo performances, billed as 'Pete Townshend And Friends' (Jon Carin, Peter Hope-Evans, Chucho Merchan and Tracey Langran) – the first at London's Shepherd's Bush Empire on November 9.

"I have to start from the bottom again,' Pete told *The Times*' David Sinclair a few days prior to the show. "I've got to convince people that it's worth coming to see me play and worth looking at my body of work. I'm still passionate about pop and feel that by doing a show that takes snapshots from throughout my story you get a sense of what it means and what it adds up to."

The set list was similar to his recent US shows, with Townshend and Langran duetting on 'Sensation', 'The Acid Queen' and 'A Friend Is A Friend' but the most noteworthy addition (and not entirely for the right reasons) was a New Zealand-born rapper named Hame who delivered a freestyle rap during 'Baby Don't You Do It', 'Who Are You', and 'Magic Bus'.[14]

---

[14] The following year, Hame's vocal was recorded for a track entitled 'Vivaldi', included on *The Lifehouse Chronicles*.

The following night, the band played in Truro, Cornwall. The band walked on to 'Cobwebs And Strange', Pete started playing 'Sheraton Gibson' but stopped, due to him ripping a fingernail off the previous night, while the show ended with a traditional ditty, 'The Lobster Song', sung by the Kneehigh Theatre Company, for which the gig was a fundraiser. An early January 1999 gig in front of 80 people at the Oxford Museum of Modern Art marked the final night of an exhibition of Gustav Metzger's work.

On July 28, Townshend performed a 15-song show at the Supper Club (advertised as a 'listening party') to promote the release of *Pete Townshend Live*, recorded during the 1997 and 1998 shows at the Chicago House of Blues, with proceeds from both show and album going to Maryville Academy.

After the opening 'Won't Get Fooled Again', Pete set aside his red Fender Stratocaster in favour of a Gibson J-200 for the next two songs, 'Behind Blue Eyes' and 'Drowned'. Bruce Simon of launch.com opined that the reason for the songbook Townshend used was due to the diversity of the set. "It seemed as if he was deciding what songs to play on the fly, using the options in the book for reference." Pete sat at a grand piano for renditions of 'Slit Skirts', 'Let My Love Open the Door', and an off-the-wall version of the Screamin' Jay Hawkins number 'I Put A Spell On You' which, according to the *New York Post*'s Dan Aquilante, "was so eccentric it took a few seconds to decipher that he was playing the usually recognisable song."

Townshend then introduced guest Eddie Vedder, with whom he'd taped performances of 'Magic Bus' and 'Heart To Hang Onto' at the Ed Sullivan Theatre with David Letterman's band earlier that day for broadcast on Letterman's show. The pair duetted on 'Heart To Hang Onto' and then both strapped on acoustic guitars for 'Let's See Action', prior to Pete switching to his Stratocaster for Pearl Jam's 'Better Man'. Don Williams' 'Till The Rivers All Run Dry' and 'Sheraton Gibson' followed, the latter featuring Vedder on lead vocals, with Townshend playing acoustic and singing harmony. Following 'Magic Bus', the pair left the stage. After a short break, Townshend came out alone, picked up his acoustic guitar and played part of 'I'm One', changing the lyrics to "I'm a loser, just like Eddie."

"It was the kind of rock event that fans of either man would have given anything to see," Aquilante wrote, "yet in spite of that, for some bizarre reason, those present – especially in the balcony – loudly squawked at each other throughout the performance. If the show had been a stinker, maybe their lack of respect and courtesy might have been justified. But the concert was terrific. Had the rudesters in the balcony listened more and talked less, Townshend might have stayed longer than an hour."

The crowd chatter continued the following night when Townshend and Vedder performed a slightly shorter show at the House of Blues. "The last couple of days, spending time with Pete has taught me new things about music and new things as a human," Vedder anounced from the stage. "One of those things is to say what you feel. And I feel like you people talking between songs are driving me nuts."

After returning from the States, Townshend was busy as ever with various projects. In addition to continuing writing his memoirs, reports had surfaced that *Psychoderelict* was being readied for the a stage. The *New York Daily News* reported that Townshend was to begin work on a script with director Ethan Silverman and had visited the Guthrie Theater in Minneapolis and met with artistic director Joseph Dowling to discuss the possibility of staging *Psychoderelict* there.

"I went to several theatres on that trip," Townshend told the *Minneapolis Star-Tribune*'s Jon Bream in December 2006, "including the Ordway, and the one run by Garrison Keillor and one more experimental one in a huge empty shell of a building."

In October 1999, *USA Today* reported "producer John Scher says confidently that *Psychoderelict* will appear next year on Broadway," and "there have been various workshops over the past five years; one is planned for this spring."

Ultimately, the work wasn't staged. "*Psychoderelict* will never happen," Townshend told the author. "I did a workshop in New York a few years ago with my friend Ethan Silverman directing and with the actor Peter Gallagher in the lead role. It was a great workshop – but at the last minute I felt I could not proceed."

Ultimately, the project that was to consume the majority of his time and effort was the resurrection of *Lifehouse*, the first official mention of which emerged in the February 7, 1999 edition of the *Sunday Times*. Nicholas Hellen reported that Townshend had been commissioned by the BBC "to create a musical from unperformed fragments that he first devised at the height of The Who's success. His concept embraces computer technology, science fiction and eastern mysticism in a visionary future cityscape."

A radio play, already in rehearsal, was set to debut December 6 on BBC Radio 3 and talks were reputedly under way with Daltrey and Entwistle to stage it.

"The story of *Lifehouse* was, in a nutshell, of a family, under considerable stress," Townshend explained in 1999, "who had been affected by the changes in the world, the changes in the way that people communicated and about the tribalisation of society, the splitting up of society, which replaces the class system, very much an English story."

For the site of the concert at the original story's end, he chose "somewhere like the Millennium Dome, to celebrate the millennium. This millennium tag has been added on just because of where we are but it fits very well with the notion that we're at the dawn of a new age and this group of people get together to throw a concert."

The play's characters espouse "New Age millennial notions . . . these may appear to be rather cosmic ideas, but I implicitly believe in them."

The BBC's interest in *Lifehouse* lay in the project's relevance to the significant changes technology introduced as the millennium approached – most notably the advent of the internet. This entirely new method of communication, which changed the face of global business, had far-reaching social implications, bearing an uncanny resemblance to the 'grid' Townshend had imagined.

"It's extraordinary when you think about what Townshend was writing in 1971," said Kate Rowland, the BBC's head of radio drama, who Pete enlisted to assist him in dramatising the production. "It was like he was projecting ahead. He didn't use the words 'net' or 'web'. He called it 'grid'. But he was hitting the nail almost right on the head."

When Rowland's comments were disseminated through the media, Townshend copped a certain amount of derision for what many mistook as his taking credit for predicting the internet.

"*Lifehouse* was never meant to be about 'prediction' . . ." he wrote in the *Richmond Review*. "I've had a certain amount of sarcasm directed at me. That's OK.

"The feeling that you get when you read that early script, which is very naïve and very cobbled together, is that I was trying to describe a world that is maybe in the future without understanding what it would be like. I didn't think I would wake up in the year 1999 and it would be like this . . . I wasn't pretending to be a seer and I don't like the fact that recently I've been portrayed in that way, that wasn't my notion . . ."

Along with Rowland, Townshend enlisted the help of seasoned radio playwright Jeff Young to adapt the story.[15] Pete's decision to solicit outside help was partly based on his recent theatrical experiences. "I just felt that what I had learnt in projects since I'd done *Lifehouse* – the stage version of *Quadrophenia*, the *Tommy* film, the *Iron Man*, *Psychoderelict* – I'd learnt that I am not a dramatist yet . . ." he told Matt Kent in 1999. "I can sit and write a fairly good story, but I don't think that necessarily entitles me to write all the music and whatever. What I wanted to do here was simply to get together a truly great team, who could honour the work I have done in the past, and that other people have done in the past, on this project."

Lifehouse underwent a significant overhaul for the radio dramatisation. Since the idea was now almost 30 years old, Pete and his consultants – who shaped the story during a series of meetings at the Wick – decided to change the perspective from a vision of the future to a contemporary story.

"In this playscript – the definitive version of *Lifehouse* – Jeff Young, Kate Rowland and I decided not to try to further predict any problem with the current march of technology and ignore common phobias about it," Townshend wrote in the *Richmond Review*. "After all, in the current climate, to describe the future is to describe tomorrow, possibly even some daft science fiction writer's yesterday. Here we speak not of 'grids', or the virtual reality 'experience suits' of my 1971 story, but of 'tele', 'hackers', 'pirates' and of course 'websites'."

When updating the story from its fictional, post-apocalyptic setting, Townshend realised that the play's backdrop was much closer to his original idea than perhaps he'd first imagined.

"I've started to realise that I have lived in a post apocalyptic period," he told Kent in 1999. "My life began with a huge atomic bomb, which killed loads of Japanese people and ended a bloody, terrible world war and there's been nothing like it since. It's totally transmogrified the world, transformed it and distorted it. We look out and see green fields and think everything's fine but it is actually an apocalyptic world we live in, the rules have changed."

Townshend also began to see that his life's work as an artist was a reaction to the post-war climate in which he was immersed as a child in bomb-damaged London, a theme he reiterated in a 2006 *Rolling Stone* interview: "I was born on the very last month of the fucking war, and out

---

[15] The collaboration began by Townshend giving Young a batch of old *Lifehouse* scripts in 1998. "Pete felt a sense of loss about never finishing *Lifehouse* and, more generally, about the failures of the Sixties generation," Young told *Mojo* in 2004.

I come into the world looking for laughter and fun and what happens is I land in this peculiar planet called England, and it was weird. My entire function is about trying to deal with expiating my childhood difficulty that came from the denial of previous generations."

"There was a lot of pride in what we'd done [in World War II], but for us younger ones trying to see what had happened there was a lot of denial," Townshend told the New Jersey *Courier-Post* in 2006. "So I suppose my entire work is dedicated to trying to overcome that denial, to break out and help our fans – and me too – to face what happened and how we should go forward . . . In any case without the 'Great Silence' of the post-war years, rock music as we know it today would never have been born. We'd still be dancing to saxophones and living in romance."

"There has been no great bomb since that last one dropped on Japan, but there has been a steady erosion of what is natural," Townshend wrote in the *Richmond Review*. "As my art school mentor Gustav Metzger says, nature has been replaced by 'environment'. We no longer know the true values of natural life and art. We are slowly destroying ourselves in an 'autodestructive' society."

When analysing the *Lifehouse* characters, the creative team soon realised that "my phantom presence in the story was more forcefully felt than I had intended," Townshend said in 1999. The three arrived at a way to articulate Townshend's viewpoint by incorporating two voices heard by the main character, Ray. The two additional characters reflected his conflicting thoughts – Rayboy, Ray's "childlike voice of around nine or 10 years old, imagining the future, delighting in the certainty that we would all one day blow ourselves to bits," in Townshend's words, and the Caretaker, "an imaginary friend from that childhood, a kind of Uncle-In-Overalls who replaces the emotionally distant, war-ravaged father who can only recommend to the kid that he sits and quietly watches the newly acquired miracle of a tiny, grey-screened telly."

Rayboy, whose character was created after Young studied tape recordings of Townshend recalling his childhood, reflected the older Ray's lost aspirations. While it could be argued that many of the young Pete's dreams came true, Pete pointed out that, "Ray and Rayboy are still very much of me. Perhaps they are also of my audience and childhood friends: all those who sometimes turned to me and said that I had a knack of putting into words what they could party-dance away, but found hard to otherwise express. It turned out that what I was best at putting into words for them was the frustration that they could not put anything into words."

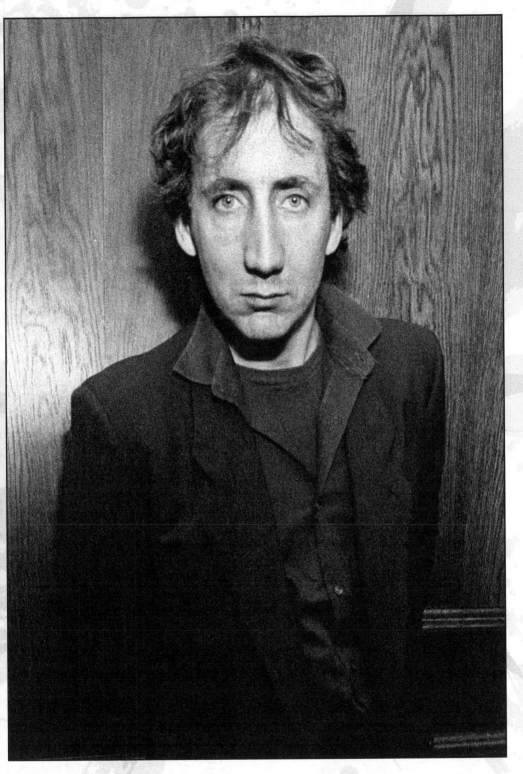

Pete, 1981. "Something around that time happened to me, and I turned away from the light and faced the darkness… When [Kit Lambert] died I felt I'd lost the last sense of everything coming into my life… on one hand it made me want to kill myself, on the other it made everything come together. It was so beautiful." (URBANIMAGE.TV/ADRIAN BOOT)

The post-Keith Who: Kenney Jones,
John Entwistle, Pete and Roger Daltrey, March 1981.
(URBANIMAGE.TV/ADRIAN BOOT)

Pete attacks Mick Jagger, 1981. **(LFI)**

Pete with Roger on stage during the Who's 'farewell' tour of 1982. **(ROBIN ANDERSON/REX FEATURES)**

With Bob Geldof and Paul McCartney at the climax of the
Wembley Live Aid concert, July 13, 1985. **(STEVE RAPPORT/RETNA)**

With daughter Aminta, 1985.
(RICHARD YOUNG/REX FEATURES)

And with elder daughter Emma at the *Hope And Glory* film premiere, London. September 4, 1987.
(RICHARD YOUNG/REX FEATURES)

The Who in 1989, the year when the original trio reformed with 11 additional musicians to perform *Tommy* in the US and UK. **(MICHAEL PUTLAND/RETNA)**

"The Who got back together and… we never ever fucking failed to do it [fill stadiums]. With a shit record out, with a *dead drummer*, we could still do it." Pete on stage at the Birmingham NEC during the 'Las Vegas' tour, October 1989. **(REX FEATURES)**

With poet laureate Ted Hughes, 1993. **(NILS JORGENSEN/REX FEATURES)**

Pete on stage in California during 1993's
PsychoDerelict tour. (TIM MOSENFELDER/GETTY IMAGES)

Pete with director Des McAnuff at the
premiere of the stage version of *Tommy*, July 1994.
(TAMMIE ARROYO/CONTRIBUTOR/GETTY IMAGES)

The Who in 2002 with Zak Starkey, son of Ringo Starr,
who became their drummer of choice from
1996 onwards. (PETER SIMPSON/REX FEATURES)

On stage with Noel Gallagher, 1998.
(RICHARD YOUNG/REX FEATURES)

Pete and Roger embrace on stage at the Hollywood Bowl, following John's
death the previous week, July 1, 2002. (JEFFREY MAYER/WIREIMAGE.COM)

Pete in the back of a police car following his arrest for allegedly
downloading child pornography, January 13, 2003. (SEAN DEMPSEY/PA ARCHIVE/PA PHOTOS)

The Who arrive in Sydney in 2004, for their first tour of Australia since 1968. **(LFI)**

Pete with long term girlfriend Rachel Fuller at the launch of her *Cigarettes And Housework* album at the Opium Club, London, July 28, 2005. **(LFI)**

With Roger at the *Tommy & Quadrophenia Live in Concert* DVD launch, New York, October 7, 2005. "We two old buggers have one of the great banners of rock history to wave, and we are determined to wave it, partly in memory of our two buddies who flew the coop. Roger and I have each other, and that means more today than it did when we first crossed angry paths as kids in Acton in 1960, 46 years ago." **(LFI)**

Still windmilling in 2007. (LFI)

"The play that is going to go on the radio is a final realisation, the last stop café of the story, the story that I've always carried in my head and that ran through the original and tied all the songs together . . ." Townshend told Kent in 1999. "What we have for the radio play is something that is about as close to the telling of that story as I want to get."

The basic plot remained essentially unchanged from its original form but with several additional twists. "In the story, what we have now is a family, they live up north – they have run away from the media age – they're supposed to be farmers, which is all very true to the original pattern that I'd placed behind the songwriting. Their daughter grows up in Scotland . . . she's a good kid, but she runs away and they don't really know why. The father is distraught and takes it very, very badly and the mother doesn't quite know why this is happening and doesn't understand what his reaction is about . . . she's worried that he may have driven her away somehow, she's quite down on him because she's not sure he's made a commitment to their new life.

"He worked in media, television and advertising and run away from it but seems obsessed by it. He's constantly logging on, constantly watching TV, and constantly throwing things at the TV! He gets up one day, gets a bit drunk, jumps in his old van and heads for London to try and find his daughter and he discovers that what's going on in London is a bit of a revolution. That a bunch of young people, renegades, people on the streets have decided to defy the media, who have control of all music, all art, all thinking, all news, all political views, on the basis that the only way 'we' can keep you safe is if we nanny you. Whereas in fact it's all about control. The young renegades decide to voice their defiance of the controlling media by arranging a huge concert but this is complicated by the fact that the media is supported to a degree by the government."

"There's some sense in the story that the authorities are, in some ways, in league with the media . . ." Townshend said in 1999. "In other words, if I could put faces to the figures, imagine Tony Blair gets a phone call from Rupert Murdoch, who says, 'Listen, Tony, I hear that these bunch of kids are going to go on air with this *Lifehouse* thing. I have the rights to that, I own all the media in the UK you mustn't allow this to happen.' 'Well, I'm very sorry Rupert but I don't think there's much I can do . . .' 'Well fuck that, you stop them, or I will . . .' kind of thing.

"What happens is that the bunch of kids get together and it turns out to be a big smash. The philosophy of the *Lifehouse* is very much like the philosophy in the original story; it's a metaphor for what was happening in the earliest, I think healthiest, part of rock'n'roll, which was when the music reflected the audience. I've taken that metaphor and embellished it a little. What happens at the end of the concert . . . I don't want to give the ending away but it doesn't end quite as you'd imagine."

The root of the story lay in the power of communion, as Townshend wrote in the *Richmond Review*, as the end of the decade – and the century – approached. "*Lifehouse* is essentially about the necessity for human beings to congregate regularly in order to share their emotions, and their responses to the spiritual challenges of art, great and small . . . In this play, as a writer of fiction, and the bearer of post-apocalyptic wounds and generational shame, I suggest that the party might not end quite as they hope. Less seriously, I predict most of us will merely get drunk and laugh a lot, just like any other December 31.

"What's missing today for me is the kind of congregation that went on when I was younger. What *Lifehouse* means, what the metaphor means, is that what works today is what worked in the past, which is that as many people as are able to gather and readdress their personal position and their future will do so. If they do so in a selfless, happy, positive manner, in other words to have a laugh as much as anything else, what comes out of that should be positive."

"As everything gets bigger, technology makes the world smaller," Townshend told the *New York Daily News* in 1999. "At some point, there will be an explosion – pollution, political, whatever – and we will re-learn that the only way we can survive is congregationally. We can't do it alone."

With today's widespread use of the internet, the social implications of people favouring interaction through a computer rather than personal contact could be realistically contemplated. "People understand virtual reality, the internet and being linked to each other through a grid," Townshend told the *New York Post*'s Dan Aquilante. "We can now start to reflect on the spiritual consequences of living our lives as 100 per cent couch potatoes. The conclusion hasn't been decided. Will people stop reaching out? Will they stop congregating?"

The music featured in the radio play was, rather surprisingly, limited to Townshend's *Lifehouse* original demos and some orchestrations, reflecting his confidence in the ability of the revamped script to carry itself. Pete's decision to exclude Who versions of the songs was made on a more practical level, "so I didn't have to wrestle with the record label over the rights to my own songs," as he told the *New York Daily News*.

"What is probably important to say now is that when you hear this play on the radio, the music will not change your understanding of the story," he wrote in the *Richmond Review*. "That was never my intention. Much of the music featured in the play is used by Kate Rowland in an almost incidental way, but I hope in a manner that could not be improved upon. She is especially good at using music in drama . . . In *Lifehouse*, music itself is a fundamental and rudimentary principle, almost a functional character. To a musician like me, music is what is 'inside us all'. It represents experience, emotion and spiritual potential. I have invested my leading characters with this belief."

The radio play aired in early December to unenthusiastic reviews as exemplified by *The Guardian*'s Anne Karpf: "Dispiritingly, *Lifehouse* sounded almost exactly the way you'd expect a play by a rock star in his fifties to sound. Both Mary and Ray are rebelling against a grey future, but so many fine artists have depicted grey futures that this one needed to be a lot greyer to have any impact . . . The only memorable tunes were ones he wrote earlier, specifically for 1971's *Who's Next* album. Neither the echoey, multi-track production nor the first half's slightly fractured narrative managed to give it a modern feel. Townshend may be a rich and once creative musician, but someone should have had a word in his ear."

Despite its muted reception, the completion of the radio play gave its creator a mixture of satisfaction and relief.

"For 29 years I have been entangled in this thing called *Lifehouse*," Townshend wrote in the *Richmond Review*. "I blamed the frustration it caused me on its innate simplicity and my innate verbosity; one cancelled out the other. The story contained ideas that were once regarded as overly ambitious. I felt like a jungle explorer who had stumbled upon an Inca temple of solid gold and become impeded by roots and vines in a knot of undergrowth, only yards from civilisation. One day I would emerge crying aloud that I'd discovered something marvellous, but would be patted on the head and indulged in my triumphant ranting. The playscript is the result of this awkward, though not particularly heroic, journey. I have come to the end of a creative adventure in which I struggled as much to overcome my own impatience as obstacles in my path."

After losing sight of his ambition to make a *Lifehouse* film in 1971, Pete was eager to revisit the notion. "I have dozens of ideas," he told the *New York Post* in 1999. "In fact I'm about to break a long-held rule and going to start making my own films." He also mentioned the "strong possibility" of some live work, similar to the *Lifehouse* concert referred to in the play.

"I imagine a celebratory gathering at which a large number of individuals hear modest compositions or songs created specifically for them," he wrote in the *Richmond Review*. "In a finale, all those pieces could be combined, perhaps with creative and engaging images of each subject. I believe the result would have enormous impact and significance. I recently wrote a proposal to a friend of mine who owns a computer company that is going to sponsor events of this kind. But this is perhaps just my composer's megalomaniacal dream. Such visions must be realised rather than described. That much I have learned on my *Lifehouse* journey, which ends here. Thus I move quickly onto the reality."

CHAPTER NINETEEN

1999–2001

"Most people out there are just so fucking stupid on this subject. They say to me, 'Why don't you just write songs? You're good at that. You're no good at plays.' Some people feel, for example, that some of my song collections are encumbered by literary pretensions. I've been in a fucking rock'n'roll band all my life! People just don't understand what I actually need, and the demands that are implicit on my thinking processes to produce material which has depth . . . We have to engage life, and for me, stories help me to engage it from a different angle. What I've realised in my journey through life is that what's really important is the human story. It's not what goes on around us but how we respond to it."

– Pete Townshend, 1996

"Outside The Who I am working on a number of projects, which may or may not come to fruition. They all require money of course, so I am glad I earned some this summer. I have a music publishing company, a recording studio, a sailboat, a domestic life. I also run a really good charity which usually keeps a low profile, but does a lot of valuable work with addicts, alcoholics and both the victims and 'recovering' perpetrators of sexual abuse. But I myself am always a Grade One addict-accident waiting to reoccur. Certainly what I do onstage always surprises me. It doesn't feel like me sometimes. I have to measure my lust for life very, very carefully and I take impartial advice wherever I can on how to live a relatively normal life (I have a counsellor rather than a therapist today). Like most people in the entertainment industry I'm a nut."

– Pete Townshend, 2002

AS *Lifehouse* approached a state of finality for Townshend, in October 1999, reports surfaced that The Who would reunite for a series of concerts.

"I had originally intended to present *Lifehouse* in concert form, at the

Royal Albert Hall, during the millennium celebrations," he told Matt Kent in 1999. "It wasn't just going to be me playing the *Lifehouse* music but a whole day of music that inspired *Lifehouse*, including Terry Riley and some orchestral work . . . I invited Roger and John to come in at the end and play some of the songs from the original album. What then happened was that it exploded very, very quickly, as everything does when you talk about anything to do with The Who, it just got incredibly out of hand. Robert Rosenberg [of The Who's management company Trinifold] rang Gateway Computers, who had used one of my songs in a campaign, asked for $20 million for sponsorship, or whatever the figure was, and got it arranged in return for a 25-date Who tour and all of a sudden the whole thing was totally out of whack."

Back in May 1998, Daltrey had emphatically expressed his profound disappointment at Townshend's neglect of The Who, and his feeling that he and Entwistle had been pushed aside while Townshend enjoyed the considerable fruits of being The Who's chief composer and publisher. "I wasn't particularly sympathetic," he told Phil Sutcliffe in May 2000. "Roger and John were, after all, residing in mansions about 40 times the size of my house."

However, Daltrey's heartfelt and plain-speaking words had an effect.

"It was pretty scary," Townshend told *Rolling Stone*'s Chris Heath in June 2002. "He felt that I had fucked him over. He also went on to say a whole load of other things, which were to do with unspoken contracts from childhood: that we were a band, we were lads from the street, he was going to go into the gutter. We looked at each other in the eyes, we swore to be together for the rest of our lives . . . Halfway through the conversation, this stuff that he was saying was making me cry – it was so brutal, it was so nasty and it was so aggressive. And elements of it were true, but lots of it wasn't.

"So in the end I stopped him. I said, 'Roger, listen, this is hurting too much, you're just going to have to stop. And all I can tell you is to go away, and I swear to you I will think about it.' And so he left, and then he called me back about two hours later and he said, 'I've been thinking about this, and I went too far – and I'm really sorry.' He said, 'I just want you to know, I don't care what you do, I don't care if we ever go out again. I'm your friend, I love you, and all I care about is that you're going to be OK.' And I said, 'What I feel proud of is that at our age you feel you can come and do it. It's nice that you can be fucking honest.' Because years ago I would have had to read this in a newspaper."

"I felt I had been offered unconditional love," Townshend wrote in a web diary entry from August 2000. "The truth, his truth. Within a month I had decided that there was unfinished business for Roger, Pete and John. I knew it would cost me very dearly, and it has. But I was not being heroic or patronising. I was doing what had to be done, out of love, in response to love . . . I decided that rather than appear to be patronisingly returning to The Who to prop up Roger and John's declining egos or sagging bank balances, I would turn everything on its head. Roger had asked me to help him and John. I asked them instead to help me."

Townshend asked Daltrey and Entwistle to perform with him at the annual Chicago House of Blues benefit, "to placate my own uneasy soul," he wrote. "They both agreed without a moment's hesitation. At the time they agreed there was nothing in it for them but hard work. There were no guaranteed spin-offs, no deals, no tours, no reviews, no assured fan support. Not a single journalist feels that this mechanism is worth a serious or uncynical mention. Maybe nobody knows the background yet. It was a selfless and unconditional response from Roger and John to a pre-established plan of mine. I realised these two guys would do almost anything I asked, and ask for little or nothing in return, apart from my company."

Zak Starkey and Rabbit Bundrick were added to the line-up to bring The Who back to a five-piece as opposed to the substantially bloated versions of previous years. The band were subsequently asked to headline *iBash*, a show on October 29 in Las Vegas celebrating the opening of the streaming video website Pixelon.com, to be broadcast live on the internet. They were reputedly offered $2 million plus an undetermined amount of stock in Pixelon.com to do the show. Two benefit appearances at Neil Young's Bridge School Benefit were added on October 30 and 31, since the *iBash* concert revenue would offset their expenses.

The heavily touted return of The Who took place as scheduled at the MGM Grand Garden on the Vegas strip, headlining a bill which also featured Kiss, The Dixie Chicks, Sugar Ray and Brian Setzer. While the show was well-received, the heavily publicised live web broadcast was a damp squib – much of the concert was unavailable for internet viewing due to technical problems, perhaps an omen of Pixelon's impending demise.[1]

---

[1] In April 2000, Pixelon.com's founder, 'Michael Fenne', was discovered to be David Stanley, a bail-skipping felon who was on Virginia's most wanted list for several years for embezzlement and stock fraud. The company, which had amassed $35 million in investment capital but blew $16.2 million on *iBash*, soon dissolved amid an onslaught of lawsuits. A DVD of The Who's concert, *The Vegas Job*, was released in November 2006.

However, The Who seemed to thoroughly enjoy proceedings, playing for well over an hour when they were scheduled for just a 45 minute slot.

"The singer's microphone did a lasso twirl and the guitarist's arm windmill-whirled, all before the end of the first song," wrote the *Las Vegas Review Journal*'s Mike Weatherford. "The Who were back, all right . . . Townshend was plugged in and wailing away, reminding the sold-out crowd he's a phenomenal guitarist as well as a songwriter. He supplied both the power chords and intricate melodies on big-finish tunes such as 'Pinball Wizard' and 'Listening To You' without the help of a rhythm guitarist.

"Townshend has resisted doing a hits tour for years now, perhaps fearing The Who would come off like a washed-up oldies revue. But after a playful night onstage Friday, he hopefully will look at recent shows by The Rolling Stones – long-time rivals for the 'World's Best Rock Band' title – to see what can happen when veteran rockers get back to work on a regular schedule. With any luck, Friday's show will not be seen as a last hurrah preserved as a digital museum piece, but as a new beginning."

Indeed, *iBash* signalled a new beginning for The Who. The Bridge School Benefit shows a couple of nights later at San Francisco's Shoreline Amphitheater were all-acoustic (Entwistle played an acoustic bass). The Who climaxed a day of performances including Brian Wilson, Pearl Jam, Tom Waits and Green Day. The school's students, all of whom suffer from severe speech or physical impairments, sat on a raised platform behind the stage.

"This most electric of rock bands played unplugged, as is the custom at the Bridge benefit," wrote the *San Francisco Chronicle*'s Joel Selvin. "Pete Townshend even pulled up a chair to play his clattering solo on 'Who Are You'. They may look like old bankers, but The Who's members played like juvenile delinquents. It was utterly magnificent – a towering close to an epic concert."

Despite the fact that they were priced at $300 a seat, the 1,300 tickets for the show at the Chicago House of Blues on November 12 sold out within minutes. (A second night was added due to the demand, with a similar rapid sell-out ensuing.) Prior to the first concert, a silent auction included among the lots a 12-string guitar Townshend had used in the writing of *Tommy*. While some reviewers bemoaned the predictability of the set list, the first show included rarities such as 'A Legal Matter' (during which Townshend forgot the words despite the aid of a Teleprompter), 'Tattoo' and in a nod back to their roots as The Detours playing C&W at Douglas

House, a Johnny Cash medley of 'I Walk The Line' and 'Ring Of Fire'. 'Magic Bus' turned into a ragged jam which ultimately fell apart ("shit" was Townshend's onstage opinion) while support act C Average (featuring Eddie Vedder) retook the stage to help out on 'Let's See Action'. The band presented a cheque for $1,000,000 to the Reverend John Smyth, Maryville's executive director.

"We had just finished the [second] show and someone sent a message backstage saying that they would pay $100,000 to the charity if we would play 'Eminence Front'," Daltrey told *The Guardian*'s Bill Borrows. "Pete said, 'We're not going on again,' and I said, 'We fuckin' are!'"

In November, Townshend continued his embrace of technology when he opened his official website, www.petetownshend.com. The website offered MP3 downloads of unreleased music,[2] streaming video entries, a chat room, a news section, details of various projects, a complete concert guide with an updated Who section and a regularly updated internet diary from Townshend himself. These snippets of thoughts and observations provided a glimpse into Townshend's mind in much the same way that his 'Pete Townshend Page' columns in *Melody Maker* did almost 30 years before.

"I spend no time on it at all really," he said in June 2001. "I'm an artist. You've seen my guts already, you just don't know it. The diaries are nothing more than what I've always done in interviews. I'm not interested in secrets or facts, just truth."

Townshend invited Matt Kent, who ran the semi-official fan club *Naked Eye* and had co-organised two UK Who conventions in 1995 and 1998, to run his website, which received over two million hits during its first six months of operation.

The website gave Townshend and Who fans an unprecedented amount of information, reflecting Pete's eagerness to disseminate information.

"I love the internet because it's a place to share," he told the *New York Post*'s Dan Aquilante in July 2000. "On my website, I share my process with those who are interested. I am an art school boy, and sharing process is part of how I work. I do love talking about what I do. In concert, some find it irritating as hell. All they want is for me to stop talking

---

[2] "I give some stuff away, like I've always done on loss-making tours, the radio and in home taping, and I sell some stuff," Townshend told *The Hollywood Reporter* in June 2001. "The one feeds the other."

and pick up the guitar and play. That's why the internet is so good for me. I can talk."

Townshend's cyberspace outlet for his ideas provided an unexpected boost. "It has sharpened my sense of myself as an artist . . ." he told the *Hollywood Reporter*'s Chris Marlowe in 2001. "I am far more willing to attend to my old established and readily recognised methods. This has allowed me to do Who touring in the old manner without feeling I am letting my artistic vision fester."

Buoyed by the success – and enjoyment – of recent performances, The Who wrapped up the millennium with two hastily arranged shows on December 22 and 23 at the 2,000-seat Shepherd's Bush Empire.[3]

"The whirlwind opening salvo of 'I Can't Explain', 'Substitute', 'Anyway Anyhow Anywhere' and 'Pinball Wizard' set the tone for a show that was an uninhibited celebration of the group's glory days . . ." *The Times* reported. " 'My ears have gone', Daltrey complained towards the end. 'You don't need to hear anything these days,' Townshend replied, sounding and indeed looking a bit like Spike Milligan. 'There's nothing worth listening to these days. It was different when I was a lad.' Minutes later, the ageing rocker smashed his guitar to pieces in one well-practiced but still surprisingly ferocious movement, before leading the group into an encore of 'My Generation', a lyric which has now taken on a somewhat different complexion to when it was written. The dads are all right."

In addition to the disposal of superfluous musicians onstage, a major reason for The Who's rejuvenation was the addition of Starkey on drums.

"We always had an orchestra to hide behind – we never really felt like The Who back then," Entwistle said in April 2000. "It's much more like the old Who – we're actually playing together." Daltrey added, "The band hasn't been this raw since Keith died. Kenney Jones, although he's a great drummer, was never the right drummer for The Who. With Zak on the drums now, we can get back a lot of fire that has been missing for so long in the band. His style is very similar to Keith's . . . if you close your eyes, it's so similar musically, it's uncanny. It's eerie . . ."

A few months after the introduction of Townshend's website, a commercial website, www.eelpie.com was set up which sold recordings and

---

[3] "We always did Christmas [shows] because then we didn't have to buy gifts," Townshend joked to *The Times*. "We'd say, 'We're far too busy – we have to learn our lines.' "

various merchandise, such as copies of the new *Lifehouse* script (autographed versions were available), books and posters. Since Pete had parted with Atlantic following the poor sales of *Psychoderelict*, Eel Pie served as his new label.

"This site is for everything I do," he said at the time. "I will only get back to record labels if I really must." The venture soon proved "hugely lucrative for me," Townshend told the *Hollywood Reporter*'s Chris Marlowe in 2001, justifying his statement by adding that the website's "dollar gross ran into seven digits in the first year of trading."

One of the first items sold via the site was a four-CD boxed set entitled *Avatar*, released in February 2000; each of the three privately produced Meher Baba albums (*Happy Birthday*, *With Love*, and *I Am*) were reproduced, along with a CD-ROM movie entitled *Parvardigar*.

"The three British Meher Baba group albums were never meant to be commercial releases, and neither is *Avatar*," Townshend told *In Music We Trust*'s Alex Steininger in 2000. "There are only 2001 copies, so if you have one, you're lucky. There may be a reprint. But it's doubtful."

The release of *Avatar* was Pete's first public acknowledgement of his continuing devotion to Meher Baba since his involvement in Raphael Rudd's 1996 album *Awakenings*. "I still read Meher Baba and I still believe he is an authentic spiritual master," he told *Q*'s David Cavanagh in January 2000.[4] "Currently my connection with him is that I look after and fund archival film work."

Townshend further addressed his devotion with *Meher Baba – The Silent Master: My Own Silence*, an essay posted on his website in July 2001 which was interspersed with images of Baba, and some of Townshend's personal photos from the pilgrimages he made to India in 1972 and 1976. Pete indicated that, given his battle with alcohol and drug abuse, he felt unsuitable as a public spokesman for Baba, and would be uncomfortable in such a role.

"Today I avoid making public pronouncements about his status as a spiritual master. He claimed to be the Avatar but so do other self-appointed masters in India and elsewhere. I have my own conviction, and I enjoy a very intimate and special relationship with him that – because he passed away in 1969 [two years after I started to follow him, and before I had a chance to meet him] – is entirely spiritual in nature. I enjoy his sense

---

[4] "Townshend still prays and meditates every day," *Rolling Stone*'s Chris Heath reported in 2001.

of humour if that doesn't sound too daft. I often feel that I can see mischievous signs of his presence in my daily life, coincidences or delightful moments.

"But I feel Meher Baba too in the darker side of life we all face today. My own journey required that I learn some true humility, and also not to take myself so seriously. My drinking and drug crash would have meant little had I been content to be just a rock star, it might even have helped my career. But, as someone who had vaunted so often the spiritual power of music and audience congregation, I fell further when I crashed. I am thus – I hope – more tempered and less melodramatic about spiritual matters. I hope too that I am in a better position now to speak about what it is that really makes me continue to follow Meher Baba.

"It is quite simply that I have come to love him unconditionally. That might seem dangerous, but I am asked to give no money; I am asked to make no public statements on behalf of those who carry out the work of carrying his message to the world. I am asked for nothing, except sometimes my presence in India to say goodbye to the remaining older disciples who fondly remember my musical visits in 1972 and 1976. I remember my friends in India fondly too, and I miss them. I hope it is true humility and not lost pride that prevents me from running back like some kind of Prodigal celebrity. I concentrate my efforts on the MEFA film archive project,[5] and in finding Meher Baba in the rhythm of my daily life."

The same month that *Avatar* appeared, an ambitious six-CD boxed set entitled *Lifehouse Chronicles* was also made available exclusively via the eelpie.com site. The package contained all the music inspired by the *Lifehouse* story over the past 30 years, including an extensive collection of related demos and orchestral recordings as well as the entire BBC radio play. Assembling the project took "about a year," according to Townshend.

"For me, one of the things that I want the *Chronicles* to do is to chronicle my own 'experience'," he told Kent in 1999. "I was listening to a lot of avant-writing at the time, such as Tim Souster and Stockhausen, and I was trying to find out what these people were trying to do with music . . . [*Lifehouse* is] a living project and as a result, what I needed to do in order to put it to bed, was to chronicle it up to the present day. It's always been an idea that has stimulated me. When I've gone back to *Tommy*, to *Quadrophenia*, they are stories that are finished; you can only change the

---

[5] MEFA, or Meher Baba European Film Archive, works to collect and maintain an archive of Baba related films. For more information, visit www.meherbabafilm.com.

shade of them. With *Lifehouse* it was always alive and living, particularly in the area of music creativity and music as a reflection of the human spirit."

A single CD containing a selection from the set, entitled *Lifehouse Elements,* was released to music stores. "I did it to reach the audience who do not want the bigger more comprehensive package [and thus pay more money], and of course those who do not yet use the Internet," Townshend explained in 2000. In keeping with the grandiose ideas connected to the original project, he planned to release a limited edition of 2001 boxed sets entitled *The Lifehouse Method,* containing the same music as *Lifehouse Chronicles,* but each also containing an individual code and a ticket to a proposed *Lifehouse* concert, "either with or without The Who, which would embrace some of the hopes of the original concert parts of the story, which was quite simple."

"I still have this crazy urge to make the fiction real," Pete wrote in the *Richmond Review.* "Sadly, this particular package will not be cheap. It contains four hours of music and is lavishly packaged. It also contains that guaranteed concert ticket and my promise that the buyer will be treated there like a V.I.P."

Perhaps too widely ambitious, neither the *Lifehouse* concert as Townshend envisioned it nor *The Lifehouse Method* reached fruition. Instead, following a fortnight of rehearsals, two shows featuring the music from *Lifehouse* were staged at London's Sadler's Wells Theatre (a venue of which Kit Lambert would have been proud) on February 25 and 26, 2000. Along with the 28-piece London Chamber Orchestra, the musicians featured Rabbit Bundrick, Chucho Merchan, Phil Palmer, Peter Hope-Evans, Jody Linscott, Billy Nicholls, Chyna, and Cleveland Watkiss. Pete had asked Roger Daltrey to provide lead vocals but he was away touring in Australia with the British Rock Symphony (featuring Simon Townshend) at the time.

Each show, comprising two-and-a-half hours of music, was opened by Piano Circus playing the Terry Riley composition *In C.* The song order on the first night (adjusted slightly for the following evening) was 'One Note (Prologue)', 'Purcell One Note (Quick movement)', 'Baba O'Riley' (orchestral), 'Teenage Wasteland', 'Time Is Passing', 'Love Ain't For Keeping', 'Going Mobile', 'Greyhound Girl', 'Tragedy', 'Mary', 'I Don't Even Know Myself', 'Bargain', 'Pure And Easy', 'Let's See Action' followed by an intermission. The second half consisted of 'Hinterland Rag' (orchestral), 'Baba O'Riley', 'Behind Blue Eyes', 'Sister Disco', 'Getting In Tune', 'Relay', 'Who Are You', 'Join Together', 'Won't Get

Fooled Again', 'Tragedy Explained', 'Song Is Over', and 'Can You Help The One You Really Love?'[6]

Rolling Stone's Jenny Eliscu witnessed the second night. "Even when Townshend and his band flubbed their parts – starting a couple songs over from the beginning – the audience's support was unrelenting . . . From where I was sitting on Saturday, I could see the back of John Entwistle's noggin, and he seemed to be digging it, too . . . Townshend offered a brilliant set, full of emotion and resounding proof that the man can still play the fuck out of his guitar. He played only acoustic guitar, having said at a small Q&A session a couple days earlier that if he got his mitts on an electric, he would become too absorbed in his instrument to keep control over the proceedings.

"Aside from a couple of orchestral numbers – each beautiful, but largely a distraction from the rock'n'roll main event . . . Townshend introduced ['Bargain'] by explaining – in the kind of relaxed manner that characterised most of his between-song chatter – that in the course of revisiting his *Lifehouse* demos, he had found that while some songs would benefit from further musical elaboration, others were impossible to better. So, for *Bargain*, he had the tape of his guitar part from a 30-year-old demo piped through the speakers, and the band played along with it . . ."

The Times' Nigel Williamson wrote, "Townshend had given warning that the sound might be 'clunky', and at one point he apologetically announced that 'some of these numbers could have done with a little more rehearsal.' There were rough edges but, as he had claimed, there was also a passion that was undeniable . . . but many were disappointed that he stuck to acoustic guitar, denying us those famous electrified pyrotechnics . . . It was a flawed but fascinating exercise."

If The Who's late 1999 benefit appearances did little to swell Daltrey and Entwistle's coffers, the resurgence of Who activity in the summer and autumn of 2000 helped to remedy this. Introduced by David Letterman band leader Paul Shaffer as "the most exciting band in rock'n'roll," Townshend, Entwistle and Daltrey held a press conference from the stage of New York's Supper Club on April 10 to announce a 25-date US summer tour, in addition to promoting the release of a 20 track live album,

[6] Townshend described the idea behind this new song as: "If you had found *your* Lifehouse [a place you felt your journey might end in joy and fulfillment], would you be able to persuade your parents to join you?"

entitled *The Blues To The Bush*, selected from the 1999 Chicago House of Blues and Shepherd's Bush Empire shows. The album's internet-only distribution via musicmaker.com also meant that fans could customise their own disc by dictating the song order, or select only a few songs for a reduced price.

One of the more interesting subjects at the press call concerned rumoured new Who material. "The plan is to go into my studio, because it's comfortable and it's in the house and there's plenty of room in the house to hide from each other," Entwistle joked. "We're just going to go in and try it. I think, hopefully, we can find some common ground on recordings that we've done of these shows. Some of the improvisations may give us inspiration for new songs. A lot of my songs come from what I'm playing onstage, and Pete gets inspired by stuff he sees us work up."

Daltrey revealed that he had also written three songs "which lyrically I think are really good." He added that he'd played demos of the songs to Townshend, and hoped that he and Entwistle would aid in fleshing out the material. "I don't want us to get back to the situation we used to have with Pete in the latter days," Daltrey said, "where he would come up with such a perfect demo that you'd end up just trying to copy it. I want them to be organic from the band."

He insisted that new Townshend compositions for The Who would be relevant. "There's a courage and an honesty about [Pete's songs]. And I know they were written really about problems of adolescence and just a little bit beyond that, most of them, but they equally apply to problems of middle age and onwards too. I think there are other problems of middle age and onwards, but it's frustrated me that Pete has never managed to put pen to paper or pen to guitar and write more about them. It always frustrated me that Pete could do it so well about adolescence and about the young boy growing up, but he can't write about the middle-aged man figuring out his life with all the problems he faces. I mean, what's the fucking difference?"

The three hoped to write during breaks on the tour, and perhaps produce an album for 2001. "It's a hope, not a promise," Townshend said. "We're in our mid-fifties, so if we don't do it now . . ."

The tour was organised into three legs, each about two weeks in length, beginning in late June and ending in early October ("not an arduous one at all," Pete commented), to facilitate Townshend spending more time with his son. In a cost-cutting measure, Jimmy Page and The Black Crowes played consecutive nights on the itinerary. This led to the inevitable question as to whether there would be any onstage jamming. "Short answer: no, I think," Townshend told *Launch.com*'s Gary Graff. "I'm really looking forward to them being days off. You know, I'm definitely going to go and watch. I'm kind of more of a fan of Black Crowes than I am of Jimmy Page, but that's because I grew up with Jimmy Page."

"We're picking up where we left off in '81, the last year we were a creative force," Townshend told *Newsday*'s Letta Tayler. "All the stuff that's happened in between has been distraction, really, and procrastination. This is a real 'Well, let's grab it and see what's really there.' And what we know is there is the joy of one another's company . . . that blood-brother stuff is very important."

In May, Townshend arranged an online auction on his Eel Pie site to raise funds for Oxfam's emergency services in helping those affected by floods in Mozambique and a combination of drought and food shortages in Ethiopia. "It will be an opportunity for you collectors of memorabilia, precious guitars and other interesting things to contribute to a very good cause," he wrote. "I have gathered together a number of items I regard as precious. I will miss them when they're gone, and I sincerely hope they mean as much [or more] to you as they have to me while I've been custodian."

Among the list of items made available for the auction were a selection of gold and platinum awards, the trombone used during the *Psychoderelict* tour, letters from Paul McCartney, Keith Richards, Arthur Miller, and Eric Clapton, the white jacket worn for 1998's A Day In The Garden, one of Pete's bicycles, and two sets of author's proofs for *Horse's Neck*.

Other more important items on the auction block included a "classical Spanish guitar circa 1971" on which he composed 'Behind Blue Eyes' "and a number of other important songs. My daughter Minta used it to learn on, and I got it back from her about three years ago. It is a very good guitar which I bought in LA from West LA Music." In addition, a Gibson SG Pete Townshend edition, was offered. "This guitar is the very first of the numbered line to be built in this limited edition series. My son Joseph has the prototype." A Rickenbacker Pete Townshend Model 335 was also offered. "This is the very first of a numbered line to be built in this limited edition series. I have used this guitar around the house. The prototype of this series needed some work, which I did myself, and sent the resulting guitar as a gift to Paul Weller." Another Rickenbacker guitar in less playable condition and up for grabs was one that Townshend smashed, arranged and had mounted.

The centrepiece, though, was a 1957 Fender Stratocaster which was given to Pete as a gift by Eric Clapton in thanks for Townshend arranging Clapton's 1973 Rainbow show. However, four days into the auction a message appeared on the webpage: "The Fender Stratocaster has been withdrawn. It has been purchased for an unspecified, but astronomical, price by a syndicate of buyers. David Bowie, Mick Jagger and Pete Townshend have bought the guitar and given it to Tony Blair, the British Prime Minister. Tony Blair is a guitarist himself, and the three rock stars are hoping for knighthoods and think this gift might help." As a result of the auction, Townshend's Double-O Charities donated a reported £300,000 to Oxfam for the relief effort.

On June 6, The Who played a charity gig in New York for the Robin Hood Foundation, an organisation dedicated to ending poverty in New York City. Comedian Robin Williams MC'd the fundraising event, individual tickets to which cost $2,000, tables upwards of $20,000. Simon Phillips filled in for the unavailable Zak Starkey with minimal rehearsal taking place in the days leading up to the show.

Pete flew back to the States in good spirits a few days prior to the North American tour opening at Chicago's New World Music Theater, on June 25. "I'm feeling pretty good, and I am really looking forward to this first leg of the tour," he wrote in his web diary, which was regularly updated during the trek. "The rehearsals went well, Zak and Rabbit both playing brilliantly as ever. John with a very cool new bass rig, Roger in a really upbeat mood, talking through a new song he's been working on. I'm carrying a full demo studio rig on the road in case Roger or I get to write anything. I am also carrying a large MiniDV editing rig so I can produce some video diaries. I'm hoping to carry a camera onto the stage at some shows, it should be amusing . . ."

"It was really noisy last night, the band and the crowd," Townshend wrote in his diary the following day. "I came off the stage with my head screaming, and as with the recent indoor shows we've done, it is as much from the noise of the hall as the sound onstage. My amps were set at number '3' . . . not like the old days . . . For a first show it wasn't bad, a little bit out of control maybe, but I had fun."

Despite the improved condition of his hearing,[7] Townshend's ears took a beating as a result of this opening show, as he wrote a few days later: "My

---

[7] "I've had some treatment for it," Pete told Q's David Cavanaugh in January, 2000. "I found a homeopathic practitioner who has really helped reduce it tremendously."

ears were screaming, my head throbbing [with high blood pressure], my limbs aching and the appreciative sound of the audience somehow lost down the short corridor to my dressing room . . . I always feel bad about subjecting my body [mainly my ears, of course] to such an assault as it gets onstage with The Who . . . looking at myself on video after the show, my heart breaks a little for two reasons.

"One, because I do love what I do so much and I am grateful to be doing it. But two, because it is so sad that this music I helped to refine seems to demand so much human food – like the Space-Bat-Angel-Dragon in Ted Hughes' *Iron Man* story, it seems insatiable. While I seem unable to come up with great new songs, I suppose it is enough to feed the Dragon more little pieces of the tips of my fingers, or the edge of my hearing . . . sounds melodramatic, doesn't it? But that's how it feels, you know."

Following a show at Detroit's Palace of Auburn Hills two days later, Pete made note of reviewers focusing on his renewed energy.

"Reviews speak of some new spark in me. You know there is no new spark. The old spark has always been there, I've chosen not to ignite it. Solo shows of late have helped me refine a good electric guitar sound I can use at medium level and still get off, and the fact that no one is putting me under pressure to be creative for The Who [as a songwriter] helps me a lot. I am still a very active composer, but writing songs for a deeply established rock band [that many musicians I admire don't even like] isn't coming easy to me . . . If it happens, it happens. If it doesn't, well enjoy the 'new' spark."

"When Pete Townshend confessed his sniffling nose had nothing to do with cocaine use, you believed him," wrote the *Washington Times'* Christian Toto of The Who show at the Nissan Pavilion on July 5. "Mr Townshend, who emerged from the shadows in hip shades and a dark trench coat, quickly cocked his arm for his patented windmill moves. Stiff-legged and chrome-domed, the guitarist propped up the evening with his keening background vocals and precise strumming . . . A few numbers wilted under the strain of elongated jams. As much as Mr Townshend's handiwork should be admired, his guitar solos took precious time that could have been used to squeeze in some lesser-known gems. The guitarist seemed to be enjoying himself too much to care about neglected classics . . ."

"There is still quite a lot of creative space to be found with this band and material," Pete noted on July 6. "Rabbit and Zak can be especially inspiring and surprising. But the front line is surprising, too, sometimes. Roger has been singing powerfully, but also with a lot of new deep feeling. John is visibly cheering up as the prospect recedes of going to jail for tax evasion . . .

"And me? Well I still can't believe myself to be honest. About eight years ago I had a bad wrist accident that I thought would end my decent playing forever. I thought I was consigned to a computer to write and play music. But I practised hard, and did 18 months of physio to retrieve still-restricted movement, but that practise opened up a lot of skills to me that I'd never tapped before. I'm enjoying taking off in solos and actually having to land carefully in case I crash-land . . ."

The final show of the first leg at Jones Beach show on July 9 served to reaffirm at least one original Who fan's faith in the band.

"The show was simply incredible . . ." wrote *Rolling Stone*'s Anthony DeCurtis. "The fire and force of their performance echoed the great Who shows I had attended in the Sixties and Seventies, shows that are among the best I have ever seen . . . But The Who meant something very different to me this time around. When I was young, The Who perfectly caught my anger and my gruelling sense of physical discomfort. While the Stones and Beatles always seemed Olympian, remote and somehow perfect, The Who [like The Kinks] seemed very much like me – nervous (that stuttering), vulnerable and really pissed off . . . Watching Townshend stand onstage in the middle of a great rock'n'roll show and calmly, even gently, explain to a fan who wanted him to smash his guitar that 'I'm 55' was inspiring. That about an hour later he smashed the guitar to bits – because he felt like it, not because the audience expected it – made the gesture even more powerful . . ."

The Daily Telegraph's Neil McCormick was similarly impressed. "Dressed like a distinguished pallbearer at a state funeral, but throwing shapes like a hyperactive punk on speed, [Townshend] attacks his poor Stratocaster guitar as if it might be forced to yield up the secrets of the universe, thrashing out power chords with his windmilling right arm, bending notes hopelessly out of tune with a whammy bar, squeezing the last drops of feedback from his amplifier before [apparently incensed by the guitar's failure to surrender its mysteries] he lifts the Strat above his head and brings it down on the stage with a force that cracks the neck and sends a shockwave through the stadium.

"The crowd roar and Daltrey grins with astonishment as Townshend enacts a ritual of autodestruction long absent from his repertoire, smashing that guitar again and again until there is nothing left but some broken bits of wood and a scrawl of electric noise. Then he spits on it and stalks offstage. OK . . . I know Townshend has got through an awful lot of guitars in his time and perhaps this really was nothing more than a moment of high theatre, an act of showmanship certain to delight an audience keen to rekindle the fires of their collective youth . . . but I'm not sure. If this outburst of musical violence retains the power to astonish, it may be because [now more than ever] it is a genuine expression of Townshend's tormented relationship with his band, his audience, his muse and, ultimately, himself."

In July, as The Who began their summer break, Gibson announced at a trade show that they were issuing a limited edition of 250 Pete Townshend SG guitars. A replica of the instrument Townshend used during The Who's *Live At Leeds* era. A special set of 10 prototypical models were available on his website, each complete with a photo of Pete posing with that particular guitar, and a CD containing a snippet of him playing it.[8]

In addition to spending time with his children and attending Bill Curbishley's wedding, Pete spent some of his break sailing in Cornwall. "Yesterday was my first race aboard 'Deejay' the J24 I part-own with my friend Tim," Pete wrote in his August 3 web diary. "We were first in a fleet of 12 . . . Sadly, we won't get a cup to add to my collection of about 20 [none of which I can pretend I had anything to do with, I was performing in the USA!] because the committee were 'protested' for restarting the race too early after a false start . . ."

Touring resumed on August 14 as the second leg kicked off at the Hollywood Bowl – The Who's first appearance at the venue since 1967.[9] Pete's daughter, Emma, joined him in time for the next show at LA's Verizon Ampitheater. That day, Pete and Emma took a helicopter ride to Irvine. "Flew over the new Getty museum," Pete wrote in his web diary, "with a running commentary from my daughter Emma on what is inside, and the beauty of the gardens."

"I got bored yesterday," he wrote the day after. "About halfway through 'Magic Bus', I suddenly felt like I'd been doing this for too long. I

---

[8] The guitars were £10,000 each – part of the proceeds going to Double-O charities. To date, one remains unsold.

[9] In 1933, Meher Baba had planned to appear at the venue and speak for the first time in eight years. "He told us we would be with Him forever, and we would get God-Realisation, when He broke His silence in the Hollywood Bowl," Delia DeLeon wrote in 1990. However, this plan changed – Baba ultimately kept his silence for another 36 years.

snapped out of it, I have to laugh at it all. I never expected this to be challenging. It is the ease with which we can knock this stuff out that leaves me aching for musical challenge. All I have to do to raise a cheer is swing my arm. It ain't art. But don't try it at home when you're holding a pick unless you want to lose your fingernails."

San Francisco Chronicle veteran writer Joel Selvin witnessed the August 21 show: "The sun may long ago have set on the British Empire, but not all its glories have faded. Returning to action with the swashbuckling verve of musicians half their age, the three surviving members of the storied British rock band nearly destroyed a capacity crowd at Shoreline Amphitheatre on Monday with what bandleader Pete Townshend called 'Who brutalism'. Comeback tours by ageing rockers tend to be wobbly affairs, with the musicians propped up by additional players, light shows, set design, anything to distract the audience from the band's lack of vitality . . .

"Who concerts for the past couple of decades have been largely lacklustre, hollow shells of the towering emotional sieges that people who were there 30 or more years ago remember as if they were last month. As with last year's acoustic preview of the full reunion at the annual Bridge concert, the musicians onstage at Shoreline played for keeps. That, of course, was the real trademark of The Who. Townshend's guitar was an instrument he used to wage war. The entire range of human drama – hope, anguish, anger, rapture – was there for all to see. It was never merely a performance. It was life and death. Such urgency is hard to keep up, but Monday's concert was more than a reminder."

Townshend attempted to explain the motivation behind such an incendiary performance. "When I went onstage I expected a feeling of God's presence," he wrote. "The two shows I'd done there before had been for Neil Young's Bridge School charity and there is no question that on those occasions a very powerful and benign spiritual presence warmed the event. At The Who show this month . . . there was not a trace of any benign and unconditional spiritual energy. Not that I could feel. It surprised me. I thought it was a de facto element of any Bay Area event. I was not angry, I was suddenly exposed and determined. So what I had to do was work, just to survive."

The second leg finished with an August 27 date in Dallas, and Houston two nights later. "I am just about as bored as it's possible for a spoiled brat like me to be," Townshend wrote in Dallas. "I sleep for as many hours as possible so I don't have to pretend I like being awake in the latest hotel room. I bury myself in the absorbing brilliance of a Jeffery Deaver novel and refuse to emerge until the next performance. I do not play golf or go sailing, for if I did I would not have enough energy or desperation left to play a decent show. I do not visit the local sites or go to art galleries. I do not accept invitations to dinner or 'home-cooked' meals. If the most glamorous woman in the world presented herself to me for sex and romance I would be unable to demonstrate even the slightest enthusiasm . . ."

"Good show tonight," he wrote in his web diary after the Houston concert. "Very hot and sweaty, just how I like it . . . I'm home tomorrow to see my son, partner, friends and Flash my dog. I'll be happy to put my feet up somewhere other than a hotel room – but life has not been hard. In Dallas the late meal I had yesterday (Swordfish) was just superb, one of those TRULY GREAT MEALS. Not sure how they do it in hotels with 400 rooms. I've lived well, and the reviews have been generous for a band that hasn't recorded a great new song for 20 years."

The Who returned in late September for the third and final leg of their North American tour, the first show taking place at the outdoor MARS Music Amphitheatre near West Palm Beach, Florida. A calamity occurred during the third show at Phillips Arena, Atlanta on September 28. "I banged [my wrist] on my guitar," Townshend wrote, "and not entirely by accident I'm afraid to say . . . I can hardly type. I have re-damaged it where I broke it in 1991 . . . I think there may well be some lumpy shows ahead for me."

He continued his diary report two days later: "Found a good ortho surgeon who with his physiotherapist X-rayed, heated, cooled, steroided, anti-inflammatoried my wrist and told me he really loved *Quadrophenia*. My hand was in good hands . . . Both the good surgeon and the physio are coming to see me tomorrow and I'm sure I will be fine for the show in Cleveland. The prognosis is that I can jump around and swing my arm as much as I like, what I have to watch is the flamenco! It's exacerbating the deeper arthritis I built up since the accident. I wish I could show you my X-ray. My wrist looks bionic. One of the old 1991 screws appears to have split the bone. But it's all healed pretty solid."

His wrist appeared to have soothed in time for the final stop of the US tour, three shows at Madison Square Garden in early October. The Wall-flowers (featuring Bob Dylan's son, Jakob, whom Townshend described as "a very smart and balanced guy") replaced The Black Crowes at short notice when Jimmy Page was sidelined with a back injury.

"I'm looking forward to going home," Pete wrote in his web diary on October 7. "This has been just about the most pleasant, easiest and incident free tour I've ever done. I've had fun sometimes onstage, and always offstage . . . the shows have always been fulfilling for me. I've enjoyed playing my long self-indulgent solos, not just because I'm self-indulgent – it's just rare to be playing with such incredible musicians as Zak, Rabbit and John, I get going and I don't want to stop."

After a three-week break, The Who played UK dates, the first on October 30 at Birmingham NEC. On top of the band having to fly through terrible weather to get to the venue, "they were not helped by the uncannily quiet crowd," David Cheal of the *Daily Telegraph* appraised in his review. "This show was hard to fault, except perhaps for some rather aimless extemporisation during 'The Kids Are Alright'. They were tight, controlled, focused. If only the audience had done their bit and made some noise, this show would have been elevated to another level." The band returned to Birmingham a week and a half later, this time to a more enthusiastic crowd.

The second concert took place in Manchester on November 2. "Definitely *the* show of the whole tour so far," webmaster Matt Kent commented in his online news posting. "The look on Pete Townshend's face for the first few minutes of Thursday night's triumphant gig in Manchester is really quite disturbing – in a way that it wasn't when he was 25," wrote *The Observer*'s Sam Taylor. "It's the façade of serene respectability that makes Townshend's clenched jaw and frenzied windmilling arm seem more than an old rock star's stage tricks. You can practically see the demons seeping smokily from his fingertips."

The poor weather followed the band to Sheffield prior to arriving home in London for four sold out London dates – the first at Docklands Arena on November 13, followed by Wembley Arena on November 15 and 16 (supported by Townshend's old friend Joe Strummer with his band, The Mescaleros) which officially completed The Who's UK tour. The final date was nearly cancelled due to Pete's worsening chest cold, which dictated that he had to drop his usual acoustic solo spot. An additional concert at the Royal Albert Hall on November 27 was a fund raiser for the Teenage Cancer Trust, a charity for which Daltrey was the patron and which The Who continue to support. "It looks like the Albert Hall will raise twice as much for the Teenage Cancer Society as anticipated, and ending this current phase of Who work with a charity show is appropriate and logical. It is how we began again after all."

The band had reportedly donated £250,000 from their US tour earnings to the Teenage Cancer Trust, and presented the charity with an additional £1,000,000 at the time of the Royal Albert Hall show, the proceeds of which were slated for facilities and services for cancer-stricken teens. Special guests at the event included comedian Phill Jupitus, Kelly Jones (from The Stereophonics), Bryan Adams, Eddie Vedder, Paul Weller, and Noel Gallagher. Weller brought the sheet music for 'Sunrise' (from *The Who Sell Out*) to the rehearsal as a potential song for he and Townshend to duet on during the show.

"It was much too complicated for me though," Weller wrote in *Mojo* in 2004, "so he saved the day by suggesting we do 'So Sad About Us' instead. I managed that one, but just being able to share a stage with The Who was something else."

The sold-out show wound up lasting three and a half hours. As well as the Weller/Townshend duet, the guest appearances consisted of 'I'm One', 'Let's See Action' and 'Getting In Tune' with Vedder, 'Behind Blue Eyes' with Adams, 'Won't Get Fooled Again' with Gallagher, and 'Substitute' with Jones. The show closed with a medley of 'My Generation/ 'See Me Feel Me'/ 'Listening To You', with Vedder, Adams, and teenagers representing the Teenage Cancer Trust.

The Royal Albert Hall benefit marked the end of all Who activity for the foreseeable future. A European tour had been considered, but Townshend opted out.

"I really do need to catch up on some vitally important solo projects and personal work," he wrote in his web-diary on November 15. "But I hope we tour in Europe before we pretend to die, perhaps in early 2002? We left the matter until today to decide, and I have decided I can't go on – not right now. I need rest, but I also need to recharge . . . Roger, John and I intend to go on seeing each other as often as we can to continue to explore what we might do next as a creative band. The Who brand has never been stronger.

"So the future's been seen, and it is not the void it once was, neither does it need to be ever again – not while I'm pretending to be alive. So take heart. There will be a pause. Maybe even a long pause. There will probably be no new Who studio album in 2001, it doesn't quite seem possible. But there may well be new Who songs – though today I have no idea quite where they will come from. What there will not be is an end.

"I have profited from this tour in more ways than I can explain. There has been money of course. And there are cynics who will say that's the only reason we got together. It doesn't matter. What matters is that it was – all in all – wonderful . . . My legs hurt, my teeth hurt, my ears hurt, my fingers hurt, my brain hurts and my whole psyche burns from all the stuff – good and bad and in between . . . But my heart feels good. It feels like one of those extraordinary days that Keith Moon didn't die. They were always good days."

In January 2001, Townshend and his son Joseph logged on to the Napster website, where music could be downloaded free of charge. While amazed "how quickly one can gather together good quality tracks," Pete ultimately judged the site as exploitative which forced him "into reliance on what only I can do – that is, to perform live, and to constantly produce new work."

While unimpressed with Napster as a money-making venture, Townshend expressed his faith in broadband as the future of entertainment. ". . . once the cost comes down, there will be no stopping the artists of this world," he told the *Hollywood Reporter*. "Freed from promoters, managers, agents, fixers, middlemen, press, and even accountants, they will perform like buskers whenever they have the need. It's true piracy."

Townshend had foreseen music downloads in a lecture he gave at the Royal College of Art back in 1986. "I think I first told a dark short story about a man who gassed hitch-hikers in the back of his black limousine, then sexually abused them when they were unconscious," he wrote in a January web diary entry. "The point of that was that the web brings us sharply up against our own narrow and lonely fantasies. It gives us the illusion of control. But although we can make our target passive in the back of our 'limousine', it is only a perverse few who want sex with unconscious partners. Listening to music on the web forces us to face our possible lack of social contact with others, and leads us to action. Music on the web should lead people to concerts, congregations, travel, real sex and the ownership of some copyrighted music."

Having donated a pioneering Atari MIDI sequencer to their music department, regardless of his good intentions, the audience wasn't impressed with Townshend's lecture and "walked out".

Having spent the previous month sifting through the mountain of demos he'd accumulated since *Psychoderelict* in 1993, in the New Year, Townshend reported that he had approximately 1,400 pieces of music logged, "of which 400 might be potentially good", and only 40 of which were actual songs.

"[*Scoop 3*] is still a little in the air," Townshend told *In Music We Trust* in 2000. "The producer [Helen 'Spike' Wilkins, the producer of the first two

Scoop collections] has had some personal problems and we slowed the whole business down to give her some space. So the next *Scoop* is as yet unfashioned. It will represent the closest thing to a new studio album for me. It will certainly contain brand new music as well as old demos and live material."

"I had a good Christmas and New Year, but I've been finding it rather strange doing creative work again in a home studio," he wrote in a January 5 diary entry. "I keep wanting to work deep into the night, and feel irritated with anyone who, or any event or commitment that threatens to prevent me working whenever the whim takes me. I am really enjoying it though. My studio is powerful and simple. And I now have a dedicated DV editing suite [which is just a computer on a table!] so I feel very professional."

In an update a month later, Pete stated that he'd now readied 12 pieces of music for *Scoop 3*, and had spent the "first six weeks of the year going through piano pieces written between 1995 and 1999 . . . They are pseudo-classical-cum-jazz pieces. No words." After taking a short break at the end of February, Townshend returned on March 8 with another web entry. "I have now completed about 14 'free' piano pieces and I'm moving on to another period of writing. I have come up with a few lyrics that seem quite cool, but I am going to begin the next batch of recording with a few new acoustic guitar pieces."

The guitar pieces Townshend was referring to were recorded on one of his Collings acoustic guitars which he'd recently purchased during a trip to New York. He recorded a piece of music while 'playing-in' one of the guitars a few days prior to Christmas. 'Collings' was posted as an audio and video download on Townshend's website and also included on *Scoop 3*.

"Helen included it here and I am glad because I am especially proud of it . . ." Townshend wrote in the album's liner notes. "I used a tuning here that is quite new to me. Reading recently about Bert Jansch, one of the guitar heroes of my youth, I saw reference to 'DADGAD'; a tuning that allows unskilled folk players to knock out a three chord trick using a single finger . . . A very useful tuning I find."

"For those of you looking forward to conventional songs I'm sure some stuff will surface soon," he wrote in a January 2001 web update. "However, I will be less likely to put demos of 'proper' songs up as mp3s, at least until I've shared them with Roger and John, just in case they will work as Who songs. So what goes up will tend to be Who rejects."

Released in October, *Scoop 3* continued the series' tradition by presenting familiar Who/Townshend songs in demo form, along with experimental tracks and several items which were omitted from their relevant projects' final form.

"It may mean that those legions of diehard fans looking for a collection overflowing with unheard songs, starkly revelatory early demos, and covers – like on the first two *Scoop* releases – may be a little disappointed, because there simply aren't as many . . ." wrote music.com's Stephen Erlewine in his review. "But they are here, in the form of previously unheard songs like 'Commonwealth Boys' and 'I Like It The Way It Is' as well as early versions of 'Rough Boys', 'However Much I Booze' and – most remarkably – 'Eminence Front' and 'Athena', in slower renditions that reveal the heart of the songs . . .

"It does wind up sounding like a musical diary, and if that isn't enough to satisfy listeners who have eagerly awaited a third *Scoop* for over a decade, they're simply ungrateful, since few musicians would have the guts or the inclination [or the material, for that matter] to release something as raggedly lovely and personal as this."

In February 2001, The Who were invited to perform at the 43rd Annual Grammy Awards in Los Angeles as well as receiving a Lifetime Achievement Award but declined since Pete was busy in the studio. Following up on his promise to get together with Daltrey to work on possible Who material, Townshend posted a March web entry stating, "Roger and I are not working together yet. He has played me three really good songs, but I don't feel they quite fit the current Who brief." He added that he had written some songs of his own, "but I am certain they will not work for The Who without a major change in our musical direction." Two months later, he told the *Daily Telegraph*, "I have my usual clutch of daft ideas. Probably the daftest is to try to write some grand new project that might suit The Who. We shall see."

Townshend's interest focused on a stage version of *Quadrophenia*. Much to his delight and anticipation, Trevor Nunn, the director of London's National Theatre had given his blessing to the development of a script and new score for a theatrical musical version of the work, with playwright Joe Penhall enlisted.

"Joe produced a very striking and original dramatic treatment for the major part of the story," Townshend wrote. "With a few clever strokes he solved many of the structural and dramatic problems of staging this work. Then he and I had a couple of creative meetings to establish how to get the most out of the music without overloading any future production with over ambitious production values. As I played some of the songs to Joe on acoustic guitar and keyboard – demonstrating how well some of the pieces work when played in a simple way – he hit on the phrase '*The Cappucino Kid* version' of *Quadrophenia*. We decided it was important to try all the songs and music from the piece, however complex they may sound on The Who's album, to test a very simple band line-up. We decided on acoustic guitar, acoustic piano and percussion [not drums].

"I was certain the music would be wonderful played in this way, but only if we could test it with musicians who would play my music really accurately. This meant using musicians of the calibre of those who toured the piece with The Who for their multi-media stage presentations in the USA and Europe from 1996 to 1998. I decided to ask John Bundrick to play keyboards, and my brother Simon to play guitar."

A four-day workshop was held in late April at the Bush Theatre (formerly the New Carlton Irish Club, where The High Numbers had auditioned for Andrew Oldham in 1964) to work through the new version of the play. In addition to Rabbit and Simon, percussionist John O'Hara, the Bristol Old Vic's music director, was brought in. Musical director Billy Nicholls enlisted two vocalists – Richard Oliver and Suzi Webb. Webb had toured with The Who on the 1996–97 *Quadrophenia* tour as a backing vocalist. The proceedings were recorded by Oceanic technical manager Lincoln Fong.

"That was fun," Simon recalls. "It was good, interesting, we were doing very different arrangements, very different sort of approaches to the songs. All the songs were stripped to a different slant – that was the whole idea. I think it worked as well."

"The workshop went very well . . ." Pete confirmed on eelpie.com. "Everything sounded terrific played by Rabbit, Simon and John O'Hara (who mainly banged away at bongos and congas). The singers worked hard, aided by Simon on certain character vocals, and we knew with absolute certainty that Joe's *Capuccino Kid* version was going to work."

Townshend and Penhall went their separate ways after the workshop. Townshend was committed to a benefit performance at the La Jolla Playhouse and working on the completion of *Scoop 3*, while Penhall readied his play *Blue/Orange* for London's West End. When the pair met up again to review Penhall's newly completed script, Townshend's enthusiasm hadn't waned.

"It is excellent," he wrote on his website. "I am really excited now that we have a solid theatrical foundation for *Quadrophenia*. The completed script was duly submitted to Nunn. "Trevor Nunn knows Joe's work and is a great ally. I have invited him to consider this project. But as we stand today, the paper feels right at last, the music has always been great – but now it works in a truly theatrical framework – and all we need now is a starting gun."

All activity surrounding the project went quiet until more than three years after the initial Bush Theatre workshop. "There is exciting news in the wind about *Quadrophenia* and its theatrical life," Townshend wrote in a November 2004 web entry. "The development during 2002 with Trevor Nunn for the National Theatre hiccupped, but various provincial British theatres have shown very serious interest in mounting a production. There is also an investigation of its theatrical potential by a major American producer."

Townshend's jubilation was somewhat premature as it would be another two years before *Quadrophenia* reached the British stage – albeit on a much less ambitious scale.

On a warm May afternoon, Pete attended the 46th annual Ivor Novello Awards ceremony at Grosvenor House on London's Park Lane to receive a Lifetime Achievement award.[10] Others up for recognition included David Gray, Stevie Wonder, The Clash, and Iron Maiden. It wasn't until some three hours into the ceremony that Townshend was called up to the stage.

"Despite enthusiastic applause," wrote the *Daily Telegraph*'s Neil McCormick, "I think it is fair to say the rock legend was not particularly overwhelmed. Casually attired in short-sleeved shirt and jeans, Townshend announced to the designer-clad assembly: 'I did all this crap so I could have my own swimming pool. And I'm not in it!' He suggested that if they speeded proceedings up a bit, he might still catch a few precious rays of sunshine . . . Townshend was joking, of course, but there was a tangible edge to his remarks. As soon as the last speech was made and the lights in the ballroom went up, Townshend could be spotted pulling on his denim jacket, brushing off the attentions of well-wishers as he made a beeline for the exit."

"The problem is they seem to have forgotten they gave me a very similar award at the 'end' of my career 20 years ago," Townshend added,

---

[10] The Ivors are known as the top internationally recognised honours for British songwriters.

referring to a 1981 award for Outstanding Services to British Music. "As for Lifetime Achievement – I'm far from dead."

On June 22 and 23, Townshend performed two solo benefit shows for the financially troubled La Jolla Playhouse. Ticket prices for both sold-out performances at the tiny 550-seat, San Diego theatre ranged from $100 to $1,000, raising over $360,000, with fans flying in from as far away as Japan and Australia to witness him perform in such an intimate setting.

"I'm going to be really quiet . . ." Pete told the crowd on the first night, pausing to add: "to start with." During his 100-minute set, alternating between guitar and piano, Townshend paid tribute to recently deceased blues legend John Lee Hooker by performing a spare, Mose Allison-styled rendition of the Cab Calloway hit, 'St James Infirmary'.

Following a quiet summer (Townshend had announced plans to "take the entire summer off to go sailing"), on October 10, The Who were stirred back into action by the Concert for New York, a star-studded benefit concert at Madison Square Garden organised by Paul McCartney for the victims of the September 11 terrorist attacks on the World Trade Center and the Pentagon. Due to the sensitive nature of the proceedings, the content of the set list was carefully considered.

"There was a lot of talk about 'Should we play the heavy stuff or not?' and I just said, 'We should just do what we do, we shouldn't rationalise this too much,'" Townshend told *Rolling Stone*'s Chris Heath in June 2002. "I went into Eric [Clapton]'s dressing room and into Billy Joel's dressing room, watching the monitors. James Taylor was on, singing 'Fire And Rain', and everybody was crying . . . I think if we had known what the atmosphere was going to be like in advance, we would have played a different kind of show. When I came off, I thought, 'I went out there with a fucking sneer on my face and I machine-gunned the audience! What the fuck?' But it was OK."

In front of a mostly uniformed crowd of police, firefighters and other emergency workers – and a TV audience of several million – The Who stole the show with a 20-minute set consisting of 'Who Are You', 'Baba O'Riley', 'Behind Blue Eyes', and 'Won't Get Fooled Again'. "Although the majority of performers erred on the side of reverential sentimentality, The Who turned in an emotional yet powerful and electric performance," Matt Kent wrote in a special Who edition of *Mojo*. Daltrey and Townshend returned at the end of the show to join an all-star singalong on 'Let It Be' and McCartney's new song, 'Freedom'.

While in New York, Pete was also slated to record a guitar track for

David Bowie's album, *Heathen*.[11] The last time the two had collaborated was 21 years earlier when Townshend played on 'Because You're Young', a track from Bowie's album *Scary Monsters (And Super Creeps)*. His playing on 'Slow Burn' was "the most eccentric and aggressive guitar I've heard Pete play, quite unlike anything else he's done recently," Bowie told Bruce Simon in 2002. The following month in London, Pete was again in the studio, contributing guitar work on three tracks for Mick Jagger's fourth solo album *Goddess In The Doorway*.

Townshend had originally planned to spend much of 2002 writing a novel, entitled *The Boy Who Heard Music*, which he expected to finish by June. He would then have "the rest of the year to go sailing or do whatever I want," he told *Rolling Stone*'s Chris Heath. However, as 2001 came to a close, plans were under way for The Who to be fully reactivated. Townshend had originally agreed only to perform some shows in New York, "to keep [Roger] amused," in his words. "Our manager was on the phone the next day to say, 'This is arrogance, to think that you can go back to America now and just play a couple of shows.' I said, 'OK, just book what you need to book.' Soon, a North American tour was on the cards by which time, Townshend found himself uncharacteristically in a positive mood at the prospect of a Who tour.[12]

"This is something that I'm really quite inclined to do at the moment . . ." he told Heath. "It is something I am doing for Roger and John and for other people in The Who's camp. It's not just a favour, it's also, in a sense, a thank-you, an acknowledgment of solidarity and friendship. It sounds patronising to say that [Roger's] grateful, but I think, in a way, I'm grateful, too, for pushing 60 and being in a band where you can get together with a couple of old mates and rely on some kind of weird cosmic energy to inhabit you and inhabit the audience. And it's pretty bloody reliable. And you can use it for all kinds of things. You can use it for charity events, you can use it to buy yourself a boat if you want to, you can use it to simply go out and enjoy playing music. What you can't use it for is creative work. Unfortunately.

"So the next bit of The Who's jigsaw puzzle has been the bit where Roger has been fighting hardest, which is to get The Who back into the

---

[11] *The Guardian*'s Dave Simpson reported in June 2002 that "Townshend eventually had to mail his contributions by post, after arriving at the studio with "bloodied knuckles" from, implausibly, doing windmills while practising."
[12] Pete later revealed that his partner Rachel Fuller was instrumental in encouraging him to resume touring and playing live.

studio and doing new, fresh creative work. What's been an uphill struggle has been for me to get Roger to accept that it's going to be incredibly fucking hard, and it'll probably be terrible. And he's willing to spend a couple of years producing something which is absolutely terrible. I can't afford to do that."

CHAPTER TWENTY

2002–2005

"In the past 30 years I have amassed a huge amount of research about the issue of child abuse and the way damage has recently been spreading via the internet. I was concerned for a number of years in anticipation of awful problems the 'miracle' of the internet might pose when it finally reached the billions of homes it touches today. I also still have a buzzing head full of opinions, anger, frustration and energy I want to bring to bear on the authorities and treatment charities who I once thought needed my ideas. But today, without my help, fantastic work is being done by good people who are fighting hard to combat both the spread of sewage on the internet and the terrible psychological effect that it could have on the minds of the children of the future."

— Pete Townshend, 2003

IN early January 2002, in a web posting entitled "Oh dear, I have to get off my arse", Townshend announced that The Who would be playing three warm-up shows prior to two previously announced charity concerts in early February at the Royal Albert Hall. "A US tour in three legs is also emerging in sketch form from the desk of Who manager Bill Curbishley – probably starting in LA in June and ending in the Northeast in August. It could all change though . . ." In its final form, the scheduled North American tour was a 26-date affair, and was expected to draw $1 million per night.

The UK warm-ups took place on January 27 and 28 at the 2,000-seat Portsmouth Guildhall, followed a few days later with a concert at the 1,400-seat Watford Coliseum. The Royal Albert Hall shows for the Teenage Cancer Trust, organised by Roger Daltrey and Harvey Goldsmith, took place on February 7 and 8 as part of a five-night run of benefits for the charity.

A number of songs from *Tommy* were reinstated into the set, as well as some old covers, including 'Summertime Blues', 'Baby Don't You Do It' and 'Young Man Blues'. "The actual reality of it is when you start to play something that you haven't played for a long time and in some cases 20 years," Pete told *The Sun* the day after the first TCT show, "it takes you back in a very, very real way to when you were younger, when you were, in my case, sadder and more frightened and more arrogant and when Keith Moon, our drummer, was alive. Yesterday we started to play a song called 'Young Man Blues' and I got into it and my hand was completely covered in blood. I was playing the way that I used to play – I used to knock a couple of fingernails off within about five minutes. There's an adrenalin rush – you don't feel anything."

The first night found Townshend curiously disengaged from proceedings. *The Guardian*'s John Aizlewood offered the following report:

> "*'God, this is boring,' sighs Pete Townshend, before embarking upon a version of '5:15' that ends in a 10-minute, instrumental free-for-all of such dreariness that The Who's leader is not the only one to feel downhearted. Townshend's mean-spirited capriciousness is all part of The Who's volatile marriage, but, like a boorish uncle at a family christening, he can't help but overdo it . . . Daltrey, all oafish charm and hairless chest, does an impassioned charity awareness speech before the encore. Townshend returns to the stage muttering, 'I don't know what he said, but it's all lies. Who gives a shit?' The toes of the Royal Albert Hall's crowd collectively curl.*"

Pete later attributed much of his contrary behaviour that evening to pretending to be intoxicated onstage. While this might not provide a convincing reason for him aborting a solo acoustic version of 'Drowned' after forgetting the words, it could certainly explain his falling off the stage during 'Young Man Blues' on the second night. "I enjoy the fact that if I pretend to be drunk for 15 minutes, the crowd go wild," he explained to Chris Heath. "And, you know, I'm a recovering alcoholic and it's a good laugh to pretend to be drunk. But to be celebrated for it, there's a kind of weird irony of it where, in actual fact, one of the only reasons I can be up there at the moment is because I'm healthy."

As a result of Townshend's fall, a female fan Melissa Hurley was slightly injured. "I actually had to meet with a girl who I hurt," he told Heath. "I fell on her with my guitar, and she could have sued me or sued the band or the hall or something, but she didn't – because she's right in the front row, she's obviously a hard-nosed fan. My guitar fell on her neck and damaged her collarbone. And I didn't hear about it until quite recently, and she wrote a letter saying, 'I can't believe that you haven't sent a letter saying sorry.' And I was – I didn't fucking know about it. And she came and we talked about it. And I was, 'What was I doing? Oh, that's right, I was pretending to be drunk!'"

A week of rehearsals for the 2002 US summer tour taking place at Oceanic studios in mid-June were filmed for use by tour sponsor JBL. The band tried out several seldom-heard songs during the rehearsals, including 'I Can See For Miles', 'Eminence Front', 'Sea And Sand', 'Another Tricky Day', 'Music Must Change' and Entwistle's 'Trick Of The Light'. Several observers wondered why the hard-living bassist was seated throughout the run-throughs but concluded he was saving his strength for the tour. Two weeks later, just before noon on June 27, the day prior to The Who's first scheduled show at The Joint in Las Vegas, Entwistle was found dead in his sixth floor room at the Hard Rock Hotel & Casino.

Already taking medication for a heart condition, Entwistle had "a significant amount of cocaine" in his system at the time of death, according to Ron Flud, the Clark County coroner, and this combination brought on not an overdose, but a fatal heart attack. As a state of shock set in, the question of continuing the tour hung over the band's heads. Daltrey, who Townshend described as "really ragged with worry", deferred to Townshend as to the decision.

"I had to push down a lot of emotion . . ." Pete told *Mojo* in 2004. "It took me all night to decide." "I would have loved to cancel [the tour]" he told the *Vancouver Sun*. "I was so appalled that I just wanted to go home. I had been worried about John's health for a long time, but he had kept his heart trouble secret."

"I decided in favour of the road crew and the fans who had travelled to the USA from Europe rather than John's family and friends who might feel we were being insensitive to carry on. I was concerned that the unknown circumstances of John's death might preclude those people being paid by the insurers of the tour, and I certainly didn't have the $20 million it would have taken to cover damages. In the end I think I made the right decision. John's family received compensation for the use of The Who brand name, as did the estate of Keith Moon."

Townshend chose to contact old friend Pino Palladino, who'd worked with Townshend on *White City* and had been in the *Psychoderelict* tour band.[1]

---

[1] Among the dozens of artists on Palladino's session resumé were Roger Daltrey, Jeff Beck, Eric Clapton, Peter Gabriel, David Gilmour, Elton John, Phil Collins, Tina Turner, Melissa Etheridge, Don Henley, Celine Dion, Rod Stewart, Paul Young, Tears For Fears, Gary Numan, Joan Armatrading, Chaka Khan, B.B. King, and Luciano Pavarotti.

About to leave Philadelphia having just wrapped up recording sessions with hip-hop artist Common, Palladino was notified of Entwistle's death by his wife. Shocked at the news, he was even more surprised when on June 28, he received a call from Bill Curbishley, asking if he could fill in as bassist on the tour. Despite the awkward and potentially uncomfortable transition that awaited him, he agreed and flew to Los Angeles that evening.

"When I got to the hotel in LA that night, Pete met me and said, 'We don't expect you to copy John's parts or playing entirely; it wouldn't be right, anyway,'" Palladino told *Bass Player* in 2004. "'We just want you to play as loud as you can bear. This is a loud band and the bass plays a key role, so you'll have to fill that space.'"

The decision to continue was alternately praised or damned among Who fans and the media. "For my part I am not attempting to deliberately establish any sense of memorial or tribute to John," Pete wrote in a web update shortly after his decision was made public. "Unlike others I entirely respect [including many of John's friends and family] I don't feel I know for certain that John would have wanted us to go on. I simply believe we have a duty to go on, to ourselves, ticket buyers, staff, promoters, big and little people. I also have a duty to myself and my dependent family and friends. I also want to help guide Roger and the rest of the band at this time, all of whom have been shaken by John's death . . . My immediate mission is to complete this tour in good heart, and to remember John in my quiet and private times. It is easy for me to smile when I remember John. I loved him unconditionally."

The dates set for Vegas on June 28 and Irvine's Verizon Amphitheater on the 29th were cancelled to be rescheduled. "I knew some Who tunes, but not a whole lot, honestly, especially from the bass perspective," Palladino told *Bass Player*'s Chris Jisi in March 2004. The first night in LA was spent making notes while listening to Who CDs. "It was pretty scary listening to John's amazing playing. We had two short rehearsals [over June 29 and 30] to learn about 25 songs. By the second one I realised I had to play a lot more notes than I was used to playing to fill up the spaces between Pete's guitar and Zak Starkey's drums. Pete or Roger would say, 'When we get to this section, step out a bit more.'"

On July 1, Palladino had his baptism of fire in front of a sold-out crowd of 18,000 at the Hollywood Bowl. As footage of the pre-tour rehearsals with Entwistle played on giant video screens on either side of the stage, the band walked on to a standing ovation before a single note was played.

Pete and Roger, dressed in black, hugged each other prior to launching into 'I Can't Explain', 'Substitute', and 'Anyway Anyhow Anywhere', after which Daltrey told the crowd, "Tonight we play for John Entwistle. He's the true spirit of rock'n'roll, and he lives on in all the music we play." Introducing 'Bargain', Townshend announced, "For fans that have followed us for many years, this is gonna be very difficult. We understand. We're not pretending that nothing's happened."

Palladino played the first few songs "off to the side, often in shadow," as *Billboard* reported. While Palladino appeared subdued, it was undoubtedly out of respect to Entwistle. "There were times during songs when I'd suddenly realise I'm occupying one of the immortal bass chairs in music," he told *Bass Player*, "or I'd look over and see Pete flailing away and Roger swinging his mike and I'd be like, 'What in the hell? I'm playing with The Who!'"

At the end of the show, Townshend and Daltrey embraced and waved farewell to a giant screen beside the stage on which images of Entwistle – ranging from his youth to his latter days – were projected.

Two nights later the band played to a sold-out crowd at Mountain View's Shoreline Amphitheater, the site of Neil Young's Bridge School benefit shows. "Rock'n'roll was never meant to be easy," Daltrey told the crowd, "Nor was life. You just get on with it."

Following a July 6 gig at Washington's the Gorge during which Townshend smashed his guitar at the show's conclusion, the band headed home for Entwistle's funeral. The July 10 service took place at St Edward's Church near John's home at Stow-on-the-Wold, Gloucestershire. The entrance to the church was surrounded by floral tributes including one reading "RIP Ox", referring to the bassist's nickname. In the hearse were tributes shaped like a champagne bottle and a guitar. Among the hundreds of mourners was Entwistle's family, girlfriend and first wife, Alison. Outside after the service, which was broadcast on loudspeakers to the crowd of well-wishers and fans gathered outside, Daltrey and guitarist Townshend hugged as they left for the private cremation.

As the tour continued on July 26 in Mansfield, Massachusetts, opinion continued to be divided as to whether the decision for The Who to carry on was appropriate. "Pete Townshend and Roger Daltrey could be accused of callous indifference and barely disguised greed in cancelling a mere two shows before resuming the lucrative trek," the *Chicago Sun-Times'* Jim DeRogatis wrote after seeing the August 24 show in Illinois. "So much for a mate who'd been with them for four decades. But while one can't entirely discount those motives, after seeing the show, it seems they felt they still had something to prove.

"The argument that continuing the tour is a 'tribute' to Entwistle is nonsense – his role was acknowledged only by a brief video montage that preceded the encore; his replacement, Pino Palladino, was barely audible in the mix, and Townshend actually made two rather snarky remarks about the bass giant, noting that he was now floating somewhere above Las Vegas spending even more money [Entwistle was deep in debt when he died] and the other that his voice was shot, so the band had already recruited Pete's brother Simon to sing backing vocals before they had to replace the Ox on bass as well."

The matter was brought into stark focus on September 14 when The Who returned to the Hard Rock Hotel in Las Vegas, for a makeup date. The intimate setting at the Joint dictated ticket prices of $350 and up, but nevertheless the 1,600-seat venue was packed. The atmosphere was sombre as the band took the stage wearing black with the exception of Townshend's blue jeans, but they launched into their set with typical abandon, "thundering from the start," according to the *Las Vegas Sun*. Uncharacteristically silent between songs, Townshend paid tribute to Entwistle with some improvised lines during 'The Kids Are Alright': "*I met this guy. He had a horn. It became a bass. He gave me his hand. I joined his band . . . We used to share that red wine. It wasn't worth a dime. We'll have to share it some other time. See ya, John.*"

At the following night's show in Irvine, according to the *Orange County Register*, Townshend launched into a "typically delightful tirade about the Hard Rock in Las Vegas, the hotel at which Entwistle died. He mixed in a few four-letter words as he went off about the joint's huge pictures of 'my dead friends', naming Jimi Hendrix and Janis Joplin in particular."

The second rescheduled show at Irvine took place the following night. On September 23, The Who played a fifth benefit show in less than four years for Maryville Academy at the Chicago House of Blues. Individual tickets went for $400 while balcony boxes cost as much as $25,000. Pearl Jam opened the show, including a rendition of 'Leaving Here', which The Who had recorded back in 1965, in their set. "It takes a lot of guts to come onstage when you know a guy named Pete Townshend is gonna come out later and wipe it with you," Eddie Vedder remarked.

Prior to playing 'The Kids Are Alright', Townshend dedicated the song to Maryville director Reverend John Smyth, and spoke of the problems the academy had encountered recently with incidents of fights, attacks on staff members and suicide attempts. "When I was a teenager, I never, ever realised that one day we would be able to use our music to help kids," Townshend announced from the stage. "There has been some controversy regarding the way Maryville does business, and I can tell you, I never do anything like this without first going through the books and going through the underwear drawer. This one is kosher!"

"It's taken such a long time to come back to this city," Townshend told the 13,000 crowd at Toronto's Air Canada Centre on September 28. "Tonight, in true tradition, this is the last show we're doing on this tour."

Two weeks later, Townshend wrote a web diary entry entitled 'Ah Ha! You thought I was sulking':

> *[Roger] is upbeat and energetic about the future, but as ever – worried that he may be unable for various reasons to sing my songs for very much longer . . . Because of the power of the shows, and their financial success in a slightly depressed marketplace, there are those who conclude that I will naturally continue to perform with Roger under The Who banner. There are those, who perhaps think they know me better [as a grouch, a spoiler, a self-obsessed creative, an insecure and pretentious self-styled artist, etc.], who conclude that now it is all over.*
>
> *The truth is rather less sparked with drama . . . Many people think of me as a rock performer first and foremost. A guitar smasher. An arm swinger. An innovator of very loud chord work. But primarily, after art school, I turned my attention entirely to writing rock songs for The Who. Without that creative work I would not have stayed in the band. There have been times I've hated it. When I began to find that songwriting work impossible to do well, I felt there was no point in carrying on with all the other stuff that related to my rock 'image'; it was all real, but very heavy to carry . . .*
>
> *I still don't think I can write new songs for this thing we all call The Who. Good news? Roger and I met under Bill Curbishley's watchful eye in Boston for a short meeting before we all came home to catch up on our domestic lives. Bill said that The Who are attracting audiences in the US out of all proportion with our visible and measurable status in the record and entertainment industry; if we tour once a year for another four or five years we will make money and make a lot of people very happy. I suggested Roger and I meet as often as possible when we get home, and attempt to write some music together . . .*
>
> *My old friend Tom Wright, who some fans will know as the guy who left*

his collection of great R&B recordings for me to plunder when he went back to the US in 1963, feels Roger and I need to make a 'last' album. One that is real, passionate, earthy, and innovative – but also accessible . . . Anyway, Roger and I haven't managed a meeting yet. But we will do something I'm sure . . .

I'm a nut. But please trust me. I'm going to attempt to get out of my own way, and stay out of my own way. That will be hard for me. It's not exactly a spiritual discipline, but for someone like me who has no regular confining daily schedule of work and responsibility outside the time I spend with my young son, it's hard to remain focused on remaining unfocused.

Townshend could only focus on one thing in the New Year of 2003, though he would have preferred it not to have been the case. On January 11, right-leaning London newspaper the *Daily Mail* ran a report that an unidentified rock star was one of over 7,000 British citizens suspected of viewing child pornography on the internet. The list of suspects, provided by the FBI, was compiled from data that traced a quarter of a million suspected paedophiles worldwide through their credit card information, obtained from a targeted website known as *Landslide*. The British component of this worldwide hunt was known as Operation Ore.[2]

Rumours quickly circulated that the celebrity in question was Pete Townshend and tipped-off reporters descended on the Wick. "I was having a cup of tea, looking out at the river, when I got this phone call, and someone says, 'Have you seen the *Daily Mail?*'" he told the *Observer*'s Sean O'Hagan in December. "I said, 'No, I don't take it,' and they said, 'Well this is what it says.' They read me the front page down the phone, and then they said, 'It sounds like you, Pete,' and I said, 'Yeah, it sounds like me.'"

Townshend "went into deep panic and anxiety. I had sensed, or I knew that there was a developing witch hunt in progress, and I thought, 'Oh my God, this is going to be hung on me.'" When he looked out of his front window, he saw that his house "was surrounded not just by scores of reporters but a ring of satellite vans. I was just spinning. It was a bit like being shot. I didn't really quite know what to do. When I recognised

---

[2] Operation Ore later came under fire when the police's central claim that everyone who visited *Landslide* entered by clicking on a button which said "Click Here (for) Child Porn" was found to be untrue. According to *The Times*, Steve Barker, "a solicitor who acts for one Operation Ore suspect in a High Court appeal, said that in many prosecutions police were unable to disprove defendants had simply accessed legal adult porn rather than paedophile material. In other cases, child porn might have been accessed accidentally by those looking for adult porn."

myself in the *Mail* piece, I called my lawyer and he called the police. I very nearly went to the local police station. I was half-way there with my girl-friend, then I said, 'Maybe I shouldn't do this.'"

"If I had a gun, I would have shot myself," Pete told the *Observer*'s Sean O'Hagan in a stunning revelation that December. "And if I had shot myself, it would have been fucking awful because it would have confirmed what everybody thought."[3] Townshend later said that he'd perhaps over dramatised when he made this statement. "It was pulled out as a headline and I don't think it's true," he told *Mojo* in 2006, but qualifying, "I think it's the first time I've felt that kind of fear and panic."

In the afternoon, Townshend appeared on the front porch, in a white dressing robe, to speak to the assembled media, acknowledging that he was the rock star in question and that he'd been in touch with Scotland Yard. He also read a prepared press statement:

> *I am not a paedophile. I have never entered chat rooms on the internet to converse with children. I have, to the contrary, been shocked, angry and vocal [especially on my website] about the explosion of advertised paedophilic images on the internet.*
>
> *I have been writing my childhood autobiography for the past seven years. I believe I was sexually abused between the age of five and six-and-a-half when in the care of my maternal grandmother who was mentally ill at the time. I cannot remember clearly what happened, but my creative work tends to throw up nasty shadows – particularly in* Tommy.
>
> *Some of the things I have seen on the internet have informed my book which I hope will be published later this year, and which will make clear to the public that if I have any compulsions in this area, they are to face what is happening to young children in the world today and to try to deal openly with my anger and vengeance towards the mentally ill people who find paedophilic pornography attractive.*
>
> *I predicted many years ago that what has become the internet would be used to subvert, pervert and destroy the lives of decent people. I have felt for a long time that it is part of my duty, knowing what I know, to act as a vigilante to help support organisations like the Internet Watch Foundation,*

---

[3] In a 1996 interview with *Q*'s John Harris, when discussing the emotional depths of his early Eighties drug addiction, Townshend explained that the act of suicide was pointless to Baba followers. "What you have to remember intellectually is that it's a completely futile act. You have to remember that deep down, my rationality was telling me, 'There's no point killing yourself, 'cos you'll be reborn 15 seconds later with exactly the same set of problems.' I believe that."

the NSPCC [National Society for the Prevention of Cruelty to Children] and Scotland Yard to build up a powerful and well-informed voice to speak loudly about the millions of dollars being made by American banks and credit card companies for the pornography industry. That industry deliberately blurs what is legal and what is illegal, and different countries have different laws and moral values about this. I do not. I do not want child pornography to be available on the internet anywhere at any time.

On one occasion I used a credit card to enter a site advertising child porn. I did this purely to see what was there. I spoke informally to a friend who was a lawyer and reported what I'd seen . . . I hope you will be able to see that I am sincerely disturbed by the sexual abuse of children, and I am very active trying to help individuals who have suffered, and to prevent further abuse.

Outspokenly honest, Townshend only added fuel to the flames by stating, "I have always been into pornography and I have used it all my life, but I am not a paedophile. I was worried this might happen and I think this could be the most damaging thing to my career. I think I'm fucked."

While stories circulated worldwide which portrayed Townshend as a paedophile, many friends and celebrities, while still digesting the few available facts related to the case, jumped to his defence including Bob Geldof, Bono, David Bowie, Jerry Hall, and Pete's estranged wife Karen Astley. "Pete is no paedophile," veteran showbiz journalist and neighbour Chris Hutchins, told the media. "There's no question about that. Pete absolutely lives by his honesty. He's in a programme of recovery where to tell a lie could lead him back to a drink or drug problem. If Pete says that it was for his book, then that's true." Old friend Tony Palmer sent him a letter of support ("I think I said, 'Tell the police to bugger off,'" Palmer recalls).

Others like Elton John were supportive if more measured in their response. "I'm very shocked and I hope it's not as bad as it sounds. I'm a friend of Pete's. I love Pete and my thoughts are with him."

"My gut instinct is that he is not a paedophile," Roger Daltrey said, "and I know him better than most. Pete has perhaps been a little naïve the way he's gone about it, but I believe his intentions are good."

Townshend's assertion of being "shocked, angry and vocal" at child pornography was corroborated by the lengthy essay 'A *Different* Bomb', which he'd posted on his website back in early 2002 and copies of the six-page document were presented to the media attached to his written statement. The essay, written after 'Jenny', an AA friend of Pete's and a victim of childhood abuse at the hands of her father, committed suicide, outlined Townshend's thoughts on the scourge of child abuse and its consequences, his own childhood abuse, and characterised the climate in the media, government and law enforcement towards child abuse as a "witch hunt" – a prescient observation, given the events of the following year.

"In my work fund-raising in the field of drug and alcohol rehabilitation I have come across hundreds of individuals from the UK and Europe whose problems have been triggered by childhood abuse," Townshend wrote. "Not always, but often, the abuse is sexual. Sometimes it is quite minor, but even in those cases – for some reason – spectacularly damaging . . . In some cases, what is so distressing is how little it takes. For me, a few minor incidents seem to have created a dark side to my nature which thankfully emerges only in creative work like *Tommy*."

Pete's disgust at the child-porn industry was made plain in 'A *Different Bomb*', which detailed the events leading to his direct involvement in the efforts to eradicate it.

"Ethan Silverman, a film director friend, had made an extremely moving documentary about an American couple who adopted a Russian boy. As a charity fundraiser [and, I suppose, philanthropist to boot] I wanted to support the work of such orphanages and decided to see if I could – via the internet – find legitimate contacts to help. [I had tried many other methods and failed]. The various words I used included 'Russia' and 'orphanages'. I used no words that could usually be taken to be sexual or lascivious, except – perhaps ill-advisedly – the word 'boys'.

"Within about 10 minutes of entering my search words I was confronted with a 'free' image of a male infant of about two years old being buggered by an unseen man. The blazer on the page claimed that sex with children is 'not illegal in Russia'. This was not smut. It was a depiction of a real rape. The victim, if the infant boy survived and my experience was anything to go by, would probably one day take his own life. The awful reality hit me of the self-propelling, self-spawning mechanism of the internet. I reached for the phone, I intended to call the police and take them through the process I had stumbled upon – and bring the pornographers involved to book.

"Then I thought twice about it. With someone on trial who had once been connected with me – however loosely[4] – I spoke off-the-record to a

---

[4] "In 1997 a man who had briefly worked for me was arrested in the UK for downloading paedophilic pornography," Townshend wrote in the same essay; a reference to Gary Glitter, who appeared with The Who during their 1996 *Quadrophenia* tour. Glitter was arrested and convicted in 1997 and 1999 for possession of child pornography.

lawyer instead. He advised me to do nothing. He advised me that I most certainly should not download the image as 'evidence'. So I did as he advised. Nothing."

Shocked at the ease with which he could stumble upon such a disturbing image, Townshend began "attempting to prepare some kind of document with respect to all this for wider publication . . . The pathway to 'free' paedophilic imagery is – as it were – laid out like a free line of cocaine at a decadent cocktail party: only the strong willed or terminally uncurious can resist. Those vigilantes who research these pathways open themselves up to internet 'snoops'. Many are willing to take the risk. They believe the pathways themselves must be closed. They must be totally and completely eradicated from the internet. If that is not possible they must be openly policed by active and obstructive vigilantes – not just 'snooped' by government agencies and police."

It was his own vigilante attitude that landed Townshend in hot water in early 2003. "The internet provides a very short route indeed to some of the most evil and shocking images of rape and abuse," he concluded in his essay. "The subconscious mind is deeply damaged and indelibly scarred by the sight of such images. I can assure everyone reading this that if they go off in pursuit of images of paedophilic rape they will find them. I urge them not to try. I pray too that they don't happen upon such images as did I, by accident. If they do they may like me become so enraged and disturbed that their dreams are forever haunted."

In October 2002, Pete posted 'A *Different* Bomb – Revisited', in which he outlined his plans to talk to "someone at a large children's charity here in the UK about creating some safe User Group forum for the rehabilitation of those who, addicted to internet porn, begin to be enticed into unacceptable stuff. I know that 'Just Say No' never worked with heroin, I didn't expect it to. But internet pornography depends on addiction for its massive profits.

"['A *Different* Bomb'] was first posted early this year. At one point recently I decided to take it down at last, but I just heard that another young woman who Double-O had put into treatment for depression and anxiety related to sexual abuse at the age of eight, had started drinking again. Sometimes this all feels so bloody futile. But I am determined to do my bit. I made a lot of money out of that poor little sap in *Tommy*. Now I understand how easily he could be recreated as a real child in our present society. I feel driven to try to change things."

Meanwhile, two days after his implication in Operation Ore was made public, Townshend granted an interview to Dominic Mohan of *The Sun*, another conservative British daily tabloid.

"I am not making any excuses. I am angry about child porn on the internet, and deeply wounded at the inference that I might be a paedophile. I have looked at child porn sites maybe three or four times in all, the front pages and previews. But I have only entered once using a credit card and I have never downloaded. With hindsight it was very foolish but I felt so angered about what was going on it blurred my judgement. I have never purchased any forms of child pornography or wished to own any. I saw the first, awful photo by accident. It repelled me and shocked me to my very core. I was not breaking the law at the time. This was in the winter of 1996/1997.[5] It was then illegal to download, which I did not do, not to search and view. I did not think using a credit card was illegal either at the time. As a public figure I would never have given details had I known I would be breaking UK law. I need to regain the trust of police and authorities involved in protecting children to continue to use my energies and determination to help what they do.

"If my therapy revealed anything, it indicated that I might regard myself as the victim of paedophiles. I was stupid to try to deal with my anger about child porn on the internet alone . . .[6] It is important that the police are able to convince themselves that – if I did anything illegal – I did it purely for research. I am not a paedophile. I agree with what the police are doing. I did not expect to be targeted in their swoops. Foolish of me but not arrogant. I sincerely believed that the police would know my history as someone who works tirelessly to help the abused, and that since 1978, I have run a charity which has contributed millions to organisations working to prevent violence and abuse."

While Townshend's actions in taking it upon himself to investigate child porn, especially going as far as to use a credit card on an illicit site, were, in the words of UK Internet Watch Foundation vice chairman Mark Stephens, "incredibly foolhardy, naïve and misguided," most were of the belief that Townshend's defence was credible.

It was a fact that Townshend had been in touch with Scotland Yard the

---

[5] In December 2003, Townshend told the *Observer* that he saw the first image, by accident, in early 1999. He claimed that the incident in which he used his credit card took place in May that year.
[6] "God, the arrogance of me!" Townshend told the *Observer*'s Simon Garfield in 2006. "I looked at myself and I thought, 'Fucking hell, Pete, what did you think was going to happen?' . . . The conceit of me! I was thinking, 'I'm going to be the one to stop this . . .'"

previous October (former Detective Chief Inspector Jackie Malton asserted her willingness to verify that this communication took place) in an effort to spearhead a website providing information on the dangers of child pornography, possibly with the involvement of the NSPCC. Further verification of his defence was belatedly provided in March, when the Internet Watch Foundation confirmed that he had reported a list of child-porn web sites to their office although unfortunately this was too little, too late as an IWF spokesman initially stated that there had been no such contact.

Townshend told Mohan that he would commit himself to campaigning against the evil of child pornography, even at the expense of his career. "I want to live my life, enjoy my family and continue with my work. But if all I can do from now on is fight the sexual abuse of children, and to help those who become victims, well that wouldn't be too bad a way of living the rest of my life . . . At heart I think the internet is a wonderful thing. But it is allowing child porn to be circulated freely around the world, crossing borders, allowing laws to be ignored, and there are real children behind the images, children like I was."

On January 13, after meeting with his attorney, John Cohen, Townshend arrived home at 2.30 in the afternoon, using the private drive at the rear of his house. Cohen briefed the gathered media a few minutes later, informing them that by mutual agreement his client was scheduled to meet with the police at 3 p.m. As scheduled, four plain-clothes detectives armed with two search warrants entered the house, followed 15 minutes later by a dozen more officers, one of whom carried a crate containing plastic evidence bags. Pete was interviewed while his home and business addresses were scoured for potential evidence. "There will be a thorough and detailed search of the premises," a Scotland Yard spokeswoman told the BBC. "It will take as long as necessary."

Four hours later, the police left, loading several personal computers and laptops along with diaries, videos and computer disks into a van. At 7.30 p.m., a wearied and unshaven Townshend was driven away from his house in the back of a car, accompanied by police detectives and taken into custody at Twickenham police station. "He has been arrested under the Protection of Children Act of 1978," a Scotland Yard spokesman said, "on suspicion of possessing indecent images of children, suspicion of making indecent images of children and on suspicion of incitement to distribute indecent images of children." After nearly an hour and a half of questioning, he was released on bail shortly after midnight.

"Mr Townshend has been interviewed this evening by the police," Cohen told waiting press. "He has not been charged with anything and he has been bailed till a future date when he may be required to come back and answer some more questions."

Naturally, regardless of assertions of his innocence, the British gutter press in particular damned Townshend before he had a chance to defend himself. Daltrey fumed about the media's ravenous appetite for the story, telling journalist John Crook, "The list that Pete's name appeared on also had the names of a dozen judges, 30-odd policemen, three MP's – we don't know who the hell they were, because everyone focused on Pete, because his name sold papers . . . There were people in authority, people other than just the police, who should have known better but who were inflaming the press with sweeping, untrue statements that Pete had actually downloaded this stuff. These people were telling what, well, let's kindly call 'variations on the truth'. What Pete told was the whole truth, from day one, namely that he never downloaded even one image to his computer. That stuff, the pornography, makes him physically sick, he hates it so much."

Meanwhile, the support of Pete's friends and fans continued to flow in. A fan website – petetownshendisinnocent.com – surfaced, featuring relevant news articles and information, alongside media contact information to balance what many considered was one-sided coverage of the story. The site even contained a link where supporters could purchase "Pete Townshend Is Innocent!" T-shirts.

The Townshend family weathered the storm in different ways. "We are, and remain, a loving Christian family, and will continue to stand by Pete," his 79-year-old mother, Betty, told the press. "I'm unaware he suffered abuse. If what he says is true, he's carried it privately." His brothers, however, refused to play the media game. "Neither of us spoke out," Simon recalls. "Paul and I saw no need to sensationalise it in any way. They came to our door and they'd camp outside, sometimes. But we wouldn't speak to those people because they were coming here to talk about something that we were not willing to even contemplate. Because we know Pete so well and we know that it was all a complete misunderstanding . . . I know what Pete's prying mind is like. And if he's writing a book, then he's going to research it, and *that* is Pete, if you know him, that's the bottom line. Nothing would stop him."

Jon Astley was also the object of media prying. "We had newspapers knocking on our door, but we did actually invite the reporters in and we said, 'Listen, we've never had any problem with Pete and we've got two young children . . . he's not Uncle Ernie. He is Pete, the very dear uncle who wouldn't dream of doing anything like what is being suggested or whatever, and we trust him, implicitly. That's it. End of story.' "

"That whole period was horrible," Simon recalls. "I mean, it's hard to explain, just little things . . . You got the feeling that people were talking about it around you, behind your back, but then it might be something that you're imagining, you know what I mean? You don't know where the line is. But certainly I'd be with some people and they would be talking to me like they didn't realise that Pete was related to me, and they're talking about the latest news. It's *gutting*, you know, that people believed it. That's what really hurts, is that people out there still to this day probably believe that of Pete, and that is *heartbreaking*. It's heartbreaking because it's just so far from what he is as a person, if you knew him."

With his personal computers impounded, Townshend found himself at a loose end until receiving an offer to create a 5.1 surround sound remix of *Tommy*. "I did it because I got arrested last year and I had nothing else to do," he told *Uncut*'s Simon Goddard in 2004. "That's the only reason. I knew that I'd have to wait two or three months, because the police took 12 computers from my house. I knew that it takes them about a gigabyte a week to look through so I just thought, 'This is gonna take fucking forever. I knew I couldn't work. I thought, 'Fuck, what can I do?' So that's why I did it, but I also felt I should go back to the emotional source."

Jon Astley points out that there were more practical reasons involved. "There was pressure from the record company, 'cause there was some kind of anniversary for *Tommy* and they wanted to do a special issue. Everyone at Universal was talking about 5.1 sound and Universal was getting paid by Sony to give money to musicians to remix their records in 5.1."

In April, Townshend played the original *Tommy* studio session tapes at Oceanic in preparation for the remix. "I put the tapes up and kind of went into shock," he told Goddard. "It's not what I remembered . . . What actually happened with this remix thing is that I rediscovered it. I rediscovered it in its original flawed, incomplete, innocent, naïve, wonderfully gauche form. It's a part of The Who's story and I'm so glad I did it. If I'd done a biography and written about The Who years without having done this remix, I'd have told a very different story. It's not perfect, nothing is, and it was never meant to be perfect. It's probably always going to be the most important thing that I've written."

"[Pete] got the tapes out and he was blown away," Astley confirms. "When he was mixing it he called me down to listen early on, to see what I felt. He doesn't trust his own hearing . . . He called me over and he said, 'I want to mix this really dry, I've never been happy with the mixes,' and I said, 'Why, what happened?' and he said, 'Well, I wasn't there,' because they were touring so much – even if it was just to Scotland and Manchester. They were playing practically every other night when they were on the road, and they were late finishing the record, so they were out on tour and it was mixed in their absence. And that's what really grated with Pete. When he heard it, he kind of went, 'Oh, OK,' but he wasn't ever really that happy."

Astley recalls Pete being obviously preoccupied with more pressing matters during the *Tommy* remix. "He had to go off to do counselling and stuff and he had to report to the police every so often, I think . . . [Astley's wife] Judy and I saw a lot of Pete during that time and we both gave him a lot of support."

Once *Tommy* was completed, *Quadrophenia* was also in line for a 5.1 remix. Astley and Andy Macpherson started by working on 'Love, Reign O'er Me' and 'The Real Me' on Pete's barge studio. "They were both fantastic," Astley says, "but Pete didn't like them. I don't know why – he didn't really explain. He just said, 'No, I don't like this, I don't like the way it's going.' I think we probably were taking too long."

After an excruciating wait of nearly four months, Townshend was summoned to Kingston police station on May 7 for the hearing of his case. He was informed that he would face no charges, but would receive a caution which meant his name would be placed on the Sex Offenders Register for five years and that any further improprieties would almost certainly result in charges being filed against him. Being on the register also resulted in him being required to check in with the police annually and upon any change of address. After submitting to fingerprinting, a DNA sample and a photograph, he was released.

Scotland Yard confirmed that they had found no downloaded images of child abuse on any of the computers that were confiscated and analysed.

"As I made clear at the outset, I accessed the site because of my concerns at the shocking material readily available on the internet to children as well as adults . . ." Townshend wrote in a web update. "The police have unconditionally accepted that these were my motives in looking at this site and that there was no other nefarious purpose, and as a result they have decided not to charge me. I accept that I was wrong to access this site and that by doing so, I broke the law, and I have accepted the caution that the police have given me."

The less-than sensational news that Townshend was exonerated predictably made few column inches.

"He was telling the truth, all the way, and the whole thing is appalling to me, the way he has been branded this dreadful thing, which he is not . . ." said Daltrey, who described the whole ordeal as "the worst thing I have ever had to deal with in my life." "I have never known anyone in my life who has helped [victims of paedophilia] more than Pete Townshend. You should see some of the letters he has gotten from [people he has helped], and I am talking about hundreds of people, and he also does just incredible work in prisons.[7] Most people don't even know about that, because Pete doesn't have a publicist following him around calling attention to all he does to help people. He says, 'No, these people have to be protected,' bless him, so imagine how I feel, knowing all this about him, and watching these second-rate journalists feeling they can kick him around all they like . . .

"I wouldn't lie for him. Child pornography is so completely abhorrent to me, that no way would I defend him if I had even a shred of doubt, but I tell you, no one has done more for these people than Pete Townshend. He did what he said he did exactly for the reasons that he said he did it, and he was found not fucking guilty . . . I have to wonder what's going on here . . . There is a civil liberties issue here, a big one. We can't have the police making judgements on people with no crime. It's not good for democracy, and it's not good for the police, either. This could be done to you tomorrow, or to me, in the same way . . . It's disgusting."

A few weeks after the resolution of his case, Townshend sent an email to *Rolling Stone*'s Jenny Eliscu outlining his plans.

"I intend to work my way back to normality. As a result of all this shit, I've decided to greatly formalise the structure of my charity [Double-O] and the way I work with 'survivors' – so that in future my work is more well-known to everyone. I've kept my profile low in this area out of

---

[7] "I do a lot of work at Feltham Young Offenders' Institution [about five miles from Townshend's home] working much more ground-level again," Pete told the *Radio Times* in 2006.

modesty I suppose, and it has worked against me. I am going to complete my autobiography, *Pete Townshend (Who He?)* I put it down and did not plan to finish it until much later. But now I am going to push ahead until it is done. People need to read about my entire life to get a real picture of who I am. I hope to finish it by the end of the year. So it may come out next year sometime. I am also going to get up and play just as soon as I can.

"Finally, I'm going out onto the street to meet people, to smile and shake hands with everyone who has been supportive of me in my home town but also to give those people who are "undecided" a chance to look me in the eye and make their own decision. Going on TV won't help me. I'm too wounded, too crazy, too happy and grateful, too resentful and too busy."

"There was a huge anger there, and I think a lot of it came out when I performed," Townshend told the *Daily Telegraph*'s Neil McCormick in 2006, referring to his own memories of childhood abuse. "But having technically committed a crime in the process of research, I remember suddenly feeling, 'I really do have to stop this. I have to stop being angry.'"

According to McCormick, Townshend "wrote a symbolic letter of forgiveness to the deceased relative he held most responsible for his childhood traumas . . ." – presumably his maternal grandmother. "I suppose for a while I thought that maybe I would re-channel the anger back into my performing work, but the trouble is I wasn't angry any more. It says something for forgiveness and it does make for a happier Pete, I suppose. Not that it's incredibly useful."

A July 8 report in the *Daily Mail* stated that Townshend was a "changed man" who had, by necessity, become a recluse due to hate mail and other threats he'd received as a result of the recent investigation. Townshend refuted these claims in a web diary entry posted on July 10 – 'Silence Day' for Baba followers.

"Silence is what I would like for a while – but it seems impossible. I don't want to pick a fight with any British newspaper, but some of them are starting to make things up. This year has been a tough one for me, but contrary to what one British tabloid wrote yesterday, I am not depressed, my neighbours are not abusing me – far from it, they go out of their way to show me warmth and understanding – and I have not received death threats. I have a driver who acts as a kind of bodyguard and I have a night security man – but I always have. No change there. I walk freely in my town, I eat in local restaurants and everyone is very good to me.[8] I take what happened to me very seriously indeed, and I hate the idea that anyone might believe my intentions were criminal, but I do believe great good has come out of it all.

"One message I want to send. I know I am not above the law, but the law on the access off indecent images on the internet was changed in this country *after* I did my research. While doing research I knew the law. I was not breaking it. I'm not stating this to make an excuse. But surely anyone can see if that is a fact, and it is, why would I be ashamed of the subsequent due process of law acting against me? But I am deeply sorry for the trouble and pain I've caused: even the investigating officer [in Texas] who first found my name on a porn site database was a Who fan and was saddened.

"But I am not sad. I am out of the war against child porn, but the war continues and that is what matters. I'm happy, strong, sober, humbled and for the rest of the day I'll try to stay silent."

Pete was deeply touched by the outpouring, telling the author that his vocal supporters "helped save me from penury and ostracism. Even a slight shadow of such an accusation would have made it impossible for me to live a normal life. Those who came to my support so unconditionally made me aware that there was some magic at work to counteract the mischief that sparks sometimes between celebrity and the press."

Daltrey continued to be vocal in his defence of his colleague, for which Townshend was profoundly grateful. "He said all the stuff that I couldn't say, because my lawyers told me to keep my mouth shut," Townshend told *Mojo*'s Pat Gilbert in 2006. "He went to Howard Stern and threatened to nut him. He was such a fucking hero for me. I know that he was worried about his future, there was a bit of self-preservation there too. But he went further than he needed to go. That was a real act of friendship."

Because of this unexpected show of strength from someone he often viewed as a professional adversary, Townshend reviewed his partnership with Daltrey. In mid-November, Pete announced in a web update that he and Roger had completed recording a new Who song, 'Real Good Looking Boy'.

---

[8] Jon Astley recalls a point when Townshend employed a bodyguard "because he was getting abuse if he was driving and someone recognised him – people were shouting and screaming stuff and so he had to get a bodyguard and he just started being driven more and he'd hide and put a hat on."

"We did it in fairly raw form, but it brought together the band from last year's tour [apart from Pino who is out with Simon & Garfunkel – Greg Lake[9] filled in beautifully. Smashing fellow.] Zak, Rabbit and my brother Simon played brilliantly and Roger and I were bloody useless. But what do you expect of two such creaky old tossers? I am back in my own studio again preparing songs and visual material for some kind of future project, which I hope will provide a pathway of some kind for Roger and me in the future. Whatever happens, Roger and I are facing our 'new' Everly Brothers format with excitement and trepidation. I sense great chaotic madness ahead . . ."

'Real Good Looking Boy' was "a song I wrote quite a few years ago about two young men who worry about their looks," Pete wrote in a February 2004 web diary entry. "One of them, based on me – hopes and believes he might look like his best friend who is a conventionally handsome fellow. [He is disavowed of this notion by his mother.] The second, based on Roger – hopes and believes he will one day turn out to be like the young Elvis. [He, more happily, sees part of his dream come true.] They both find love in later life."

Pete also announced in mid-November that he and Daltrey would play at the Royal Albert Hall in March. "We will perform something quite surprising I think," he commented. It was rumoured that this something would be *Tommy* in its entirety but according to Townshend, that idea was never in the running.

Late February saw Pete in New York City for twin purposes. "Firstly, Eel Pie Publishing artist Rachel Fuller has a showcase for Universal Records," Townshend wrote in a web entry. "Secondly, I want to play two new Who tracks to Doug Morris, the CEO of Universal. The Who are now handled by Geffen which is based in LA and – though owned by Universal – has different staff. But Doug signed me to my first real solo deal at Atlantic in 1978 . . . He also signed Rachel in 2002. I want him to be the first person in Universal to hear the new Who music . . ."

Alongside 'Real Good Looking Boy', the other new Who track since 1982's *It's Hard* was 'Old Red Wine', a song Townshend wrote in New York about John Entwistle. "He loved expensive claret, and often drank it past its prime. There is an irony there somehow: John never seemed to realise how perfectly *mature* he had really become as a rock musician. He

---

[9] Lake was singer and bassist for King Crimson in the late Sixties prior to becoming singer and guitarist for Emerson, Lake & Palmer.

didn't need the trappings he thought essential, and that – in my opinion – led directly to his premature death."

"I had to try to rescue [the situation] because Roger had committed publicly to the idea that we were going to make a record, and he felt he'd look like a complete idiot if we didn't make any new music," Townshend told *Rolling Stone* in 2006. "So we did 'Real Good Looking Boy' and 'Old Red Wine' for [the 2004 Who compilation] *Then And Now*.

Interestingly, both tracks carried a Simon Townshend production credit. For years, he had been recording music at his home studio in a front bedroom at the Townshend family home on Woodgrange Avenue, and was growing weary of the studio's limitations. "I'd done some things with Pete in there before and I think he had sussed that the problem was this small area, so he used to let me go down to Eel Pie and record drum tracks, and then come back to my home studio and do overdubbing, which worked perfectly, 'cause if you've got good backing tracks, you can do anything."

Soon, Simon found himself producing *Invisible*, the debut EP of Rachel Fuller's friend, Mikey Cuthbert at Eel Pie. Pete was sufficiently impressed to ask his younger brother to produce The Who songs at Oceanic once some of the backing tracks had been recorded.

"[Pete] came to a sort of point where he was too close to it to be able to be critical any more," Simon recalled, explaining that Pete felt "I was somebody who could be perhaps a little less close to it."

"Pete gave me so much respect and freedom to do what I wanted. He was sort of executive producer in some ways, he'd pop in and out here and there, check things out and if he didn't like something, he would say. He's like that with all producers, really. It worked well for me, because I really was able to enjoy the experience of working with people like Zak . . . We did an advert, as well, for Hewlett Packard, for 'Baba O'Riley' where we used outtakes." Simon was later awarded a gold record for his work on 'Real Good Looking Boy'. "I was very proud of that."

As a warm-up to their March 29 appearance at the Royal Albert Hall for the Teenage Cancer Trust, The Who played three nights at the Forum, a 2,000 capacity venue in London's Kentish Town, their first shows in the UK since Entwistle's death. In addition to Townshend and Daltrey, The Who line-up now consisted of Pino Palladino, Rabbit Bundrick, Simon Townshend and Zak Starkey. "As they started with a lean, powerful version of 'Who Are You' they sounded like a band that has rediscovered its sense of purpose," reported *The Times*' David Sinclair.

Backstage at the Albert Hall was original Detours drummer, Doug Sandom, who was a frequent attendee of Who gigs in London. Sandom hadn't communicated with Townshend for decades. "I mainly used to go and see John in his dressing room and have a chat. I'd never get hold of Peter, 'cause he was a bit aloof, he always had lots to do . . ." Just prior to the show, Doug received a message that Pete wanted to see him. "He invited me into his dressing room, and that was great." The pair buried their past differences. "We had a nice chat, a little hug, and we're all mates again now," Sandom says.

As at the Forum shows, Townshend spoke about the harrowing experience he'd endured the previous year. "Visibly moved onstage, Townshend admitted that he had been 'nervous' about stepping out in public again before thanking the packed-out crowd and his bandmates for their support," reported the *NME*.

A little over a week later, he was back onstage at the Royal Albert Hall for a Ronnie Lane tribute show which served as a fundraiser for both Lane's family and multiple sclerosis research. *Billboard*'s Paul Sexton called the show "a thoroughly merited testimonial for an artist who's rarely received his due." Other guests included Ronnie Wood, Kenney Jones, Paul Weller, (ex-Clash guitarist) Mick Jones and former Sex Pistol, Glen Matlock. Townshend played 'Evolution' and 'Heart To Hang Onto', the latter of which Sexton wrote, "was moving both for his affectionate introduction and its signal that Townshend's artistic mercury is rising again."

If Pete's artistic mercury was rising, his penchant for outspoken comments during interviews made other's blood boil when some tactless remarks regarding departed bandmate John Entwistle were published in the aptly named *Uncut* in April.

"I think John was in the wrong band," Townshend remarked to Simon Goddard. "John wanted to be in, I dunno, Whitesnake. Really. But he loved me and he loved my writing and he loved playing the music but I think he wanted there to be lines of coke in the dressing room and groupies on the end of his knob all the time. And when he was left to his own devices, that's what he did and that's how he died."

Shortly after, Townshend received a letter from Entwistle's mother who took exception to his remarks, compelling him to pen an apology via his website:

I think I am still very angry about John's death, and some of that came out. I feel very sad to have upset Queenie and have apologised to her as best I can . . . Let me just say that I do not think of John in the way it appears I might through that particular comment in the Uncut *interview. Morally speaking, he was certainly never worse than I was; I suppose I got beaten in a different way, and – thankfully – my personal crash in rock'n'roll came early enough that I was able to save my health. I remember John only as a great genius of the bass guitar . . . I also genuinely loved him, he was a supporter and proper friend of mine from the age of 13. We first met even earlier than that. He was funny, generous and caring. We shared a great passion for dogs.*

John, typically in very few words, thanked me lovingly recently for allowing him his dignity back by touring with The Who – the one place he really truly shone. I think in 1982 John was as relieved as I was that The Who were going to stop. He very much enjoyed working with his own band, and was always the most sociable and accessible member of The Who, he loved to mix with people and talk. However, recently all of us who worked with him, but who were unfortunately not close to him day by day were worried about his health. He was truly a very quiet and secretive man and none of us were entirely sure what was going on. It has emerged since his death that several people very close to John fought hard to help him – as I felt I did by touring with him.

We are all still deeply shocked by our loss, and I think I can speak for many of us when I say that we are angry too. But it is an aimless and probably quite futile anger. For a while I was even angry with the Las Vegas hotel chain in which he died! I had to apologise to them too.

I am sorry this stuff keeps rearing its ugly head. Jimi Hendrix, Peter Meaden, Kit Lambert, Keith Moon, the Cincinnati 11, John Entwistle. I suppose we have to accept that everyone has to die in the end, but in every one of the cases above I have at some point said things in pain that I have later regretted.

John was a celebrity. He is still celebrated, and in and around The Who, as long as Roger and I continue to work under The Who name, he will be honoured.

Sorry Queenie.

Pete

On May 19 – Pete's 59th birthday – The Who played a short unannounced set at Carnegie Hall in New York at the end of a CBS presentation of highlights from its upcoming season for TV business insiders. The band played 'Baba O'Riley', 'Who Are You' and 'Won't Get Fooled Again' – the three songs used as themes for the *CSI* television series. "Townshend and Daltrey barrelled through the songs – Pete windmilling on the guitar, Roger unleashing his trademark screams – as if they were in front of any other audience, say, one composed of people with souls," wrote *Time*'s James Poniewozik. "That, I guess, is what great entertainers do, in popular music or popular TV: they forget, for a while, about the compromises and cynical dealing that keep their business afloat, and occasionally manage to create something wonderful and transcendent."

Townshend put a more positive spin on circumstances in his web diary: "In a very real way the use of Who music in this manner keeps it alive, and brings it to a new audience in an era when our music would otherwise never be heard on the radio or TV . . ." The following day The Who played a full set at Boston's Tweeter Center ("It was a little rusty," Pete commented, "but what a welcome we received.") while May 22 marked The Who's return to Madison Square Garden. "This was just the best thing that's happened to me in two years," Townshend wrote the following day. "So many beautiful, friendly faces, and at a show that sold out in just 20 minutes. Roger connected with the crowd just as he had on the last dates in 2002. I was just happy to be up there, grateful to be alive, and lucky to have such a great team around me."

After a month's rest and relaxation, The Who embarked on a nine-date tour which saw them perform in the UK prior to playing their first ever dates in Japan and their first shows in Australia since 1968. After shows in Birmingham and Cardiff, on June 12, the band followed the Manic Street Preachers on the second day of the 2004 Isle Of Wight Festival. Obviously enjoying themselves throughout the set, Daltrey and Townshend found time to poke fun at Paul McCartney and reminisced about the last time they played the festival back in 1970. Townshend joked that some of the younger ones present were conceived there.

Less than two weeks later, The Who arrived in Japan to play a couple of shows as part of the Rock Odyssey Festival. Other performers on the bill were Aerosmith, The Red Hot Chili Peppers, Paul Weller and Lenny Kravitz. The festival stopped in Tokyo on July 24 (where Townshend smashed his guitar) and Osaka the following day. The band then travelled to Australia for the first time since their problematic jaunt 36 years earlier, the first two dates taking place at the Sydney Entertainment Centre. The band then performed in Melbourne prior to heading to Hawaii for the first time since the Herman's Hermits tour in '67 with two early August dates, one each in Honolulu and Maui. The worldwide trek ended with a pair of gigs in California – the first at the Shoreline Amphitheater, followed by the Hollywood Bowl.

The conclusion of this latest tour begged the usual question about a new Who album, which had been talked about since the 2000 tour, but nothing had emerged. Townshend attributed part of the problem to the band being active on the road. "I think we didn't make enough albums because our energy came from playing live," he told *Mojo* in early 2004. "We reflected the energy from our audience. So what we did was often rushed, especially the writing. That is happening again. I should be writing songs today. Instead I'm playing charity gigs and going to Japan and Australia. I'm doing what I want. I'm not complaining, but people – Roger! – should not expect a miracle this year. If we are on the road, even for a month, it breaks my stride as a writer and takes me a very long time to settle."

In a November 10 web entry, Townshend mentioned a possible collection of new material. "*Who2* will not be a concept album. That is, in itself, a concept for me. Roger and I meet in mid-December to play what we have written. If we move ahead from there, we may have a CD ready to release in the spring. My working title for the project – *Who2* – is only partly tongue-in-cheek. If the recording works out we will tour with the usual band in the first half of 2005."

"The new Who album has been delayed, not cancelled," Pete wrote in a further update on March 21, 2005. "The release date I had hoped for in the late spring or very early summer was whipped from under my nose after three years of writing. Shows we hoped to do in the early summer seemed to fizzle, and we lost our drummer to Oasis until January 2006.[10] All alternatives proposed, and which I have desperately considered, do not fit in with my current commitments. I am committed to record the music for my new story *The Boy Who Heard Music*. I am also completing my autobiography later this year. Sadly, this forces a postponement of the planned Who activity this year for some indeterminate time.

"I had lots of plans, but no hard schedule. And that is what has created this predicament. It's probably my fault, because I work very slowly in the studio, and either no one believed I was actually recording, or they got tired of waiting. I should say that Roger has done what he calls sketch vocals on several tracks I produced, and the results are very exciting. But I

---

[10] With future Who plans uncertain and not being on a retainer, Zak Starkey accepted an offer to fill in on a world tour with Oasis after the departure of their drummer, Alan White.

feel I can't tour any more with The Who without a new record. So until that record is actually in my hands, I must hold my breath and live in hope."

Townshend later revealed to the *Boston Herald* in December, 2006 that he and Daltrey had discussed the possibility of replacing Starkey, "but decided to wait. It turned out to be a long wait. However, as I didn't have a complete album of songs ready, I didn't panic. By March, however, things had deteriorated somewhat between Roger and myself, only with respect to communication. It was a rather bleak period, and in the end we agreed to cancel the plans on the table."

Townshend described that bleakness to *Goldmine*'s Ken Sharp the following year. "2005, Roger and I had almost lost hope of doing any more Who work outside of charity shows. We pledged always to be friends, and to love each other and try to support each other, and possibly to try some musical things together if the opportunity ever came up."

On June 13, Townshend and Daltrey played at New York's Gotham Hall for Samsung's 'Four Seasons Of Hope', an annual children's charity fundraiser. "It was a grand and generous gathering of good-hearted, and slightly sceptical business people, some of whom had shelled out $30,000 for a table to be served [but not consume] a beautiful, rare tornado steak and listen to two 60-year-old men who call themselves 'The Who'," Pete wrote in a June 22 diary entry. "Roger sang my last published song 'Real Good Looking Boy' entirely unaccompanied by me, or Jon Carin who was along for the ride with us on keyboards and memory stick. When Roger plays guitar for his own voice the dynamic is gentler, more intimate, more delicate. It's hard to reconcile that this is the same straining voice that has struggled to be heard over the loudest band in rock for 40 years. It was a rare treat, like the Tornado, but better received."

While rehearsing in London for the performance, Townshend received a request from Bob Geldof for The Who to perform at Live 8, a worldwide "day of action" on July 2 designed to draw attention to poverty in Africa, and scheduled to take place at the beginning of the Gleneagles G8 Summit, a policymaking gathering of the leaders of the world's richest nations. Two decades on from Live Aid, this new series of concerts (which took place in the UK, France, Germany, Italy, the US, Canada, Japan, South Africa and Russia) had similar superstar drawing power. After some discussion with Daltrey, it was agreed that The Who would perform.

"It may have escaped everyone's attention that in photographs of the 1985 Live Aid concert I am the only man present with a sensible, classic, short haircut," Townshend joked in a web entry. "I also look very handsome indeed, especially as photographed by David Bailey and displayed in the Gents at the Caprice. I point this out because, musically on that occasion, we were trounced by Queen, who were in the middle of a tour. This time, no doubt, we'll be trounced by U2 who are in the middle of stadium rock's answer to the ANC revolution. What are we in the middle of? We are in the middle of 'resting'. Again. I have a feeling my haircut will again prevail. I wonder suddenly, is this truly something I should be bragging about?

"It will be the only big show we do this year, or at least the only one we do until someone asks us to do another one. Our career is so *ailing*. We badly need to have our career *revived*. I write this at 2.30 in the morning. Fretting so much about my *ailing* career I can hardly sleep. I have worries. I'm sure I do."

The British Live 8 concert attracted 200,000 fans to Hyde Park. Other artistes appearing in London included Paul McCartney, Elton John, R.E.M., Stereophonics, Annie Lennox, Snoop Dogg, Madonna, Coldplay, U2, and a highly touted Pink Floyd reunion. With Palladino and Starkey unavailable, Paul Weller's band was tapped for drummer Steve White and bassist Damon Minchella to play along with Rabbit and Simon. The Who only played two songs, but the *Daily Telegraph*'s Neil McCormick was impressed.

"Still angry after all these years. [The Who] tore it up with a snarling 'Who Are You' directed at the G8 leaders, and an epic 'Won't Get Fooled Again'. Pete Townshend remains the most radical, art-school guitarist in rock, with power chords that really convey power."

Sales of the *Then & Now* collection skyrocketed after Live 8, which was watched by nearly 10 million British TV viewers. "Our sales went up 832 per cent over the weekend – that's because we sold one record on Saturday and 832 since," Townshend quipped to the press. The Who, among some of the other performers, agreed to pledge the extra profits to charity.

CHAPTER TWENTY-ONE

2005–2006

"Rock'n'roll is getting old. If it embraces the issues of ageing, it will age. Or would you say it is becoming universal now, free of limitation and constraint? Against all the odds I put up in my own jaundiced middle-age, rock is not dead. Neither is it right. Or wrong. Or a new religion. Or an answer. Or even a question. It's a process. An island. Walk on, walk off. . . ."

— Pete Townshend, 2006

"I wanted what we did after our last album to connect back to Who Are You *or* Quadrophenia, *not to the post-Keith Moon years, and I knew deep down it was not about who played drums, or how they played them. I knew I had to find a mindset that was almost Zen-like, I had to allow the music to flow. God, this sounds so pretentious. In truth, I just waited. I had no idea I would wait 24 years."*

— Pete Townshend, 2006

WITH the fresh triumph of Live 8 behind him, Townshend continued to keep busy at home and in the studio. His autobiography, *Pete Townshend (Who He?)*, was reported to be just over half-finished at this point, with a planned completion date of late 2005/early 2006. Two other key projects were also under way that autumn, namely Pete's recently written play, *The Boy Who Heard Music*, and the long-mooted Who album still labouring under the working title of *Who2*.

Townshend had readied a demo-DVD for submission to Daltrey, which contained "the music tracks of songs I've recorded so far, demos for songs in progress, some videos of me pitching various songs, and printed lyrics and photographs," he wrote in the June 22 instalment of his web diary. "I hope that viewing this DVD will help him to feel that all is not lost by my delaying the work we started last September when we set out to produce a

539

new Who album. It will get finished, as long as we stay healthy." The pair met in August to further discuss The Who's future, and agreed to revisit the situation in February 2006, after Zak's Oasis commitments had ended.

On September 24, Townshend began serialising his fictional story, *The Boy Who Heard Music* in an online chapter-a-week blog format on his website. He had originally intended to present it as a web-based live radio play, but he "couldn't quite crack that," as he told *Pitchfork's* Rob Mitchum in October 2006. Inspired by Rachel Fuller, who began her own blog a month before, Townshend chose an online format over a printed publication because he felt that "if I published it, it would make it too important, and it wasn't as important to me as the music that it has produced," he told Fuller in a Sirius satellite radio interview in October 2006.[1]

Like *Psychoderelict*, *The Boy Who Heard Music* was derived from the unpublished *Ray High & The Glass Household*; in fact, Townshend described the story as "a sequel to *Psychoderelict* if you like."

"Since [1993] I have been struggling to come up with a new dramatic music piece," Pete told newhousenews.com's Kevin O'Hare in September 2006. "I have been drawn in a number of different directions. I always come back to the same themes over and over again: the problems of young people growing up in post-war British society, and the echoes of denial and rebellion that generates. In 1996 I started work on my autobiography and very quickly realised that I still had a great music story to tell, based on what had not been touched on in *Psychoderelict*. So I went back to my novel of *The Glass Household* and found three kids from different religions who form a band and go and watch an older band blow themselves to pieces – that band looking quite a bit like The Who . . . The Glass Household is the name of the young band who decide to try to revive some lost visions and ambitions of their ageing and decadent rock hero Ray High."

"The new story is, like the first mini-opera ['A Quick One'], *Tommy*, and *Quadrophenia*, set in a neighbourhood where young people look for answers and their parents seem unable to help," Townshend told *Pitchfork's* Rob Mitchum in October 2006. "So they look to art, to music, to spirituality, to congregation, and finally to the endless wire for solutions."

---

[1] Interestingly, Dave Marsh reported in the December 2006 issue of *Mojo* that two publishers rejected *The Boy Who Heard Music*, quoting Townshend: "They said that they felt that it was over complex and . . . anyway, they didn't get it."

"The wire is the internet, but also all the lines of communication that envelope the globe," he explained.

Also in common with *Psychoderelict*, *The Boy Who Heard Music* was rife with themes explored in *Lifehouse*. In November 2004, Townshend wrote that his new story was "a continuation of the *Lifehouse* chronicles, and features the *Lifehouse Method* [music generated from data gathered from various individuals]. I hope to develop this as an animation feature with music in the second half of 2005. I would also like to see a concert version. With everything *Lifehouse*-related I know I must dream on."

Townshend described the plot for *The Boy Who Heard Music* in concise fashion to the *Desert Sun*'s Bruce Fessier in November 2006. "A retired rock star meditates. From the heights of his stratospheric point of view he sees three children from his old neighbourhood exalt and revive his early, flawed but most ambitious work. He watches them rise. He joins them in their attempt to realise the most important part of his vision: the unification of a global audience, in a single moment. He then watches them fall."

However, as with most Townshend-penned storylines (especially those connected to *Lifehouse*), many website readers were left perplexed by certain details. "The story is not chronological, so it can be a confusing and even irritating read," Pete admitted to *Goldmine*'s Ken Sharp.

"Those that wish to go deeper and try to sort it out can do so . . ." Townshend told *PopMatters*' Justin Cober-Lake in November 2006. "I only write these stories to inspire music, once that is done I feel satisfied."

"I use concepts mainly to keep myself interested or inspired," he elaborated to the *Salt Lake Tribune*. "Narratives can be inspiring, but also limiting if they are too complex or deeply plotted. Maybe that's why the plots of some classical operas are so clunky. I've always felt great music allows you to enter into it, and make it your own. Too much narrative can prevent that happening. I was very careful in *Quadrophenia* to keep the 'story' thin, as I did with *Tommy*. Interesting that it is this 'weakness' of plot that critics sometimes feel is the result of some laziness or inability on my part. It's deliberate . . . What the music and the idea touch on is what matters: the proposition that something metaphysical happens when thousands of people gather to hear great music."

As with much of Townshend's work, *The Boy Who Heard Music* is rife with autobiographical connections. However, as with *Horse's Neck*, it's often difficult to differentiate between the non-fictional elements and those which may have been embellished or otherwise altered. "[*The Boy Who*

Heard Music] is a misleading title because it suggests the story is auto-biographical," Townshend confirmed in July 2005. "It is rather a divergent spur from my life in music: a story about an imaginary concert, not a boy, and so is closer to my script for *Lifehouse* . . . than my own life story. I was once a boy. So it might be partly about me."

Indeed, Pete used a couple of strong childhood memories in his story, both of which served to develop the character of Gabriel. "There was for me as a boy a series of revelations . . ." he told the *Desert Sun*'s Bruce Fessier in November 2006. "I dramatise them a little in the story. What happened was that I began to hear imagined music when playing my aunt's delightfully out-of-tune piano. I was about eight years old." He was referring to his aunt Trilby, who in the story is Gabriel's aunt. "The part of Gabriel's story that is closely based on my own is when Trilby applauds his naive piano playing while he is hearing his own sounds in his head," Townshend told the author.

The second childhood memory involved an incident on the River Thames, when Pete was in the Sea Scouts at around 11 years old – an experience he also tapped for *Quadrophenia*, as he related in a 1983 interview with *Penthouse*:

> "We went out for a ride in a boat with an old, rusty outboard motor on the back. As we bobbed along in the water, the engine made these funny noises . . . By the time we had gone up the river and back again, I had to be carried off. I was in a trance of ecstasy. When they turned the outboard motor off, I broke down – I actually physically broke down. At some point in the journey I had gone off into a trance. I began hearing the most incredible sounds – angelic choirs and celestial voices. What I heard was unbelievably beautiful. I've never heard music in my imagination like it since. But I've always realised the potential for sounds to ignite my imagination like that. To this day, I'm a bit scared to let a sound take me that far."

In *The Boy Who Heard Music*, Gabriel's trance-like state ends with a horrific case of sexual abuse at the hands of two Sea Scout leaders. Bearing in mind that he dramatised the two childhood incidents only "a little" for the story, whether Pete actually endured a similar experience is open to conjecture, but he did tell *Rolling Stone* that *The Boy Who Heard Music* was "underpinned by rage and passion about events of abuse in my childhood that had been re-triggered as I wrote about them in my autobiography, and my mother's recent return to active alcoholism."

In addition, Townshend also sought inspiration from those around him.

"Rachel influenced the story of *The Boy Who Heard Music* in ways that sadly cannot be elaborated without giving away her secrets," Pete cryptically remarked. Fuller seemed to identify in particular with the character of Leila, a young Muslim girl who lost her mother at a young age.[2] "When I first shared *The Boy Who Heard Music* with Rachel she immediately wrote several songs for the musical play I hope the piece may one day become," Townshend said in 2006. A segment of the lyrics to Fuller's song 'I Can Fly' (which was later included on her EP *Shine*) are used to develop Leila's character.

Although *The Boy Who Heard Music* evolved naturally over the 15 years from the period *Ray High And The Glass Household* was written to the time that the blog appeared in 2005, some aspects of the story – notably the terrorist attack which one might assume was influenced by 9/11 and the London transport bombings on July 7, 2005 – were apparently there all along.

"For a moment I believed I had foreseen the attack," Townshend told the author. "In all my early treatments of *TBWHM* the concert in Central Park was interrupted by terrorist bombs, however in my story this is something that happens almost entirely in the delusional mind of Gabriel."

However, his 2003 arrest dictated that certain changes were made to the original story. "I had to clean up quite a bit of the story out of respect to those who had supported me," Townshend told the author, "my own childhood had exposed me to many instances of sexual abuse, my own and my friends. I had to soften all that as I had revived it in my novella. I don't think it hurt to soften it. This stuff may be better touched on in a single sentence rather than elaborated. Survivors of abuse have a tendency to spew out their stories in the hope they will not be rejected as damaged goods or whingers – but sadly, they are often rejected. Thank God, I am an exception."

The *BWHM* blog, posted over a period of 25 weeks from September 2005 to February 2006, also offered another advantage in that it provided Townshend with a conduit for direct audience feedback. "I developed the novella as I went along with feedback from about 800 readers who commented," he told the *Vancouver Sun*. "It gave me a real feeling of being a part of a new creative community, and that my fans are often a lot smarter than I am. It was humbling and extremely valuable for me as a writer."

---

[2] According to a 2006 blog entry on her website, Fuller lost her mother "very suddenly six years ago."

"The blog I did when I serialised *The Boy Who Heard Music* was meant for me, and everyone who came on to post messages really helped me tremendously to realise that the novella was in many ways a very flawed piece of work," Townshend told the *Omaha Reader*. "Nonetheless I could see that what it contained was precious to the readers. Without that blog serialisation I don't think there would be 'Wire & Glass'. Without 'Wire & Glass' there would probably not be a new Who CD. Without the CD there would be no world tour."

The Who's reactivation in 2006 removed the focus from any further *TBWHM*-related plans Townshend may have had at the time. However he revealed several proposed ideas. "I would like to see a 'Talking Book' with incidental music and a few songs perhaps," he said in October 2005, while the blog was still ongoing. "There is also a version of the story that I am preparing for a Las Vegas producer, I have no idea whether it will happen."

"*The Boy Who Heard Music* would include quite a few songs from *Psychoderelict* if it was ever produced as a play or film," Townshend said in 2005. "Such a story would also include music from The Who's *Lifehouse* experiments, and hopefully new writing. I suppose since 1993 I have been waiting for the emotional strength to complete this piece."

"I did have [plans for developing *TBWHM*], but I have almost abandoned them all now that the new Who album is about to come out," Pete told *PopMatters* in November 2006. "I still have a yen to see each song from the mini-opera inspire unique, individual animation films, but this is something someone else will have to drive." In January 2007, he told *Metro France* that he hoped "the music (and additional music) will be used to make an animation film."[3]

In *The Boy Who Heard Music*, Ray High observes Gabriel communicating with his Glass Household bandmate Josh via an imaginary 'Vox-Box'. Townshend had an actual 'Vox-Box': a web cam set up in his Oceanic studio which could deliver live, streaming footage. "I had arranged it so I could relate the story of *The Boy Who Heard Music* as a narrator," he explained in a November 2006 web posting. "I never got round to using it, so suggested to Rachel she might find some use for it."

---

[3] In mid-July 2007, a workshop of *The Boy Who Heard Music*, adapted and directed by Ethan Silverman (who was involved in the *Psychoderelict* workshop in 1999), took place over two nights at Vassar College in New York. Curiously, the play included no songs from *Psychoderelict*.

Fuller did just that, devising a show which initially served to promote her 2005 debut album *Cigarettes And Housework*. "I had a blog site which was getting quite a lot of hits so I started doing In The Attic [named after Fuller's home studio] with Mikey Cuthbert, an old friend of mine," Fuller told Pierre Perone of the *Independent* in February 2007. The setting was informal ("somewhere between Jools Holland and *Wayne's World*" as she described it to Perone) with a couple of chairs and a microphone set up in front of a piano.

"It was really silly. Music was the serious part of it. I would sing and play piano and Mikey would sing and play guitar and we would do stuff together. And then we would just be silly and I would do fashion tips. Because people could blog and watch the show in real time, they would ask questions and we would answer them."

During the first webcast on September 21, 2005, "Pete kind of popped his head around the door, and then he played 'Heart To Hang Onto'," she recalled.

"He thought it was amazing and became a regular on the show, which became a bit of a joke," Fuller told the *Daily Record* in July 2006. "Sometimes he'd make the tea and sometimes he'd fix the lighting. He would always come and play something, whether it was a song nobody had heard before or one he was working on for The Who album or an old classic."

Despite the fact that the audience was tiny, Townshend found In The Attic an exciting and liberating format, reminding him of past acoustic sessions he had with musical friends like Ronnie Lane or John Sebastian. "What happened was I realised I could feel the audience in a way I wouldn't have done if it had just been recorded," he told the *Independent*. "We had an upper limit on our bandwidth, believe it or not, 50 people, so it was a tiny audience and yet an incredible power. The following week, there they all were. It was one of those things where you see something creative evolving, quite intriguing."[4]

Guests were invited in, including Simon Townshend – who quickly became a regular – and even Pete's son, Joseph dropped by and contributed a guitar instrumental. "We did a thing called Basement Jam at the Bedford in London in November, and that Christmas we decided to do a

---

[4] Townshend's old friend Chris Morphet was brought in at one point to lend a hand as cameraman. "I did one of the very early editions of In The Attic," Morphet recalls. "I filmed some of it with the people at Eel Pie."

Christmas special," Fuller told the *Independent*. "Our mate Jerry Hall came down and did a song, Mikey and I did a fake nativity play. We also went into the big studio here, it was the first thing we'd done here with a live audience."

In The Attic also offered Pete and Simon Townshend an opportunity to informally work together. "I love Rachel for getting that going," says Simon, "'cause every week in the winter time when there's no work on, just regular shitty old life, I'd be going backwards and forwards from the studio, just to do that, and it's something to look forward to when you're actually creative and we talk about new and old ideas, or whatever. And it really did just bring us together, and being able to just be together with Pete, so when I get those chances I cherish them."

After the broadcast went off the air, the two would "sit around and play and chat for hours," Simon says, adding that he'd often use the opportunity to quiz his older sibling. "Obviously, I tend to sort of ask Pete stuff about chords and tunings and stuff, 'cause he's got some very interesting stuff that he's got in songs that . . . it's hard to work out chord charts for them without knowing the secret, if you like." When asked if he and Pete have ever entertained the notion of a musical collaboration outside The Who, Simon revealed, "We talked about it . . . we'll see. It'd be great to do – I'd love to."

In early January, as *TBWHM* blog neared its conclusion and In The Attic was gaining popularity, the prospect of new music from The Who was becoming a reality. "Sometime around the middle of January . . . I had about 12 tracks that I would have been happy to release – if I'd been working on a solo album," Townshend wrote in a March 18 web diary entry. "But more than half the songs were intense, slow tempo and very mature in tone."

Townshend had written 'Black Widow's Eyes' and 'In The Ether' back in 2002, "when John Entwistle was alive, and he always had lots of songs ready," Pete told *Metro France* in 2007. "At that time Roger was promising to write songs as well, so I concentrated on trying to produce songs that were arch, dark and extreme – leaving the lighter stuff to John and Roger."

"I had 'In The Ether', I had 'Black Widow's Eyes', I had 'Mike Post Theme', I had a song called 'Cinderella', that's about a friend of mine that was abused as a child," Townshend told Dave Marsh. "I had a song called 'He Said, She Said', which is an account of listening to a man talk about his partner, and then an account of the girl, the woman, talking about her partner . . . I wrote a song called 'There's No Doubt' about a conversation I had with Bill Curbishley. I asked, 'How's the marriage?' He said, 'It's great.' I said, 'Is she the one?' Is she the one for the rest of your life?' And he said, 'There's no doubt, there's no doubt.' I had this idea that it's very nice, this idea that there's no doubt, that there is no doubt, and turned that into a song. So I had enough music to make a record, but it didn't feel to me like it was truly about anything."

Townshend had floated the idea of *TBWHM* past Roger Daltrey "a few times in 2004 and 2005, but he never showed very much interest," Pete told *Metro France*. "In any case I wasn't sure it would make a good basis for a Who album. I had already written some lyrics and made some demos for the play as it stood in early 2005. I had the rough lyrics for 'Fragments' and a demo for 'In The Ether'."

"I played it ['In The Ether'] to Roger," Pete told the *Observer*'s Simon Garfield, "and about a month passed. In the end, I got on the phone and said, 'So, what did you think?'" He said, 'It's a bit music theatre. Maybe if you didn't have piano but just had guitar . . .' 'Yeah, and maybe if it was three guitars and was rock'n'roll and sounded like 'Young Man Blues' it would be OK," an exasperated Townshend responded, hanging up the receiver. "I was really, really hurt," he admitted to Garfield.

Adding to Townshend's resigned attitude at the time was the news that his mother had broken her hip, but her response to this setback soon served to motivate him. "She's had an alcohol problem all her life, and she suddenly started to drink around Christmas time," Pete told the *Philadelphia Inquirer*'s Dan DeLuca in September 2006. "We all thought she would wither away, and maybe go nuts and die. But she didn't. She rallied. She got herself together, healed up, and continued to cause lots of trouble. I kind of dusted myself down and thought: 'Well, if she can fucking do it, I can do it.'"

As well as In The Attic ("I learned a lot on the show," Pete told the *Independent*. "It definitely bumped up my writing. It had kind of slowed down. But suddenly I felt that I didn't have to write the fucking song of my life every time I started to knock songs out"), the final source of motivation came from Pete's friend and business manager Nick Goderson, who suggested exploring the possibility of creating a mini-opera based on *TBWHM*.

"This was what I needed," Pete wrote in a March 18, 2006 diary entry. "With the story fresh in my mind, and with hundreds of useful comments from those who had responded as I had published the chapters one by one, I was able to quickly scratch out a lyrical synopsis of *The Boy Who Heard Music*. This comprised seven or eight short lyric-poems. I took into account none of the depth, background or complexity of the story. In a way, I deliberately skipped over what I had explored and elaborated in my novella, and just grabbed at whatever came into my mind as I sat with pen and paper. I had the benefit of my notes from the *Lifehouse* script and lyric guides from as far back as 1971, one of which – 'Sound Round' – I used to start the collection. I also used some of the lyrics I had written especially for the novella. Quickly I found I had enough coherent lyrics to comprise a short song-cycle or 'mini-opera'."

By the end of February Pete had "completed 10 songs, two of which were full length and quite complex, the rest shorter, punchier or simple and ballad-like," to add to the batch of songs he'd written over the last few years. "Once I had those lyrics, I called Roger and told him we were back in business."

Still smarting from Daltrey's response to 'In The Ether', Townshend was rather pessimistic when presenting some of the new demos. "I'm chucking tracks at him over and over and over again," Townshend told Marsh. "Towards the end I thought, 'OK, I've got as much as I can do, now I'm gonna send him the real tricky ones.' 'Tea & Theatre' – he's gonna hate this. 'Unholy Trinity'. 'Man In A Purple Dress' and '2000 Years'. He might like '2000 Years' 'cos it's a bit of hoedown. But is he still in that place? Fuckin' went apeshit for them!"

On February 28, work began at Oceanic studios with Pino Palladino, Simon Townshend and John Bundrick in their usual roles, with Peter Huntington, from Rachel Fuller's backing band, on drums, due to Zak Starkey being on tour with Oasis. Billy Nicholls was on hand to help with backing vocals, while Daltrey later added his lead vocals. In addition to playing guitar and an assortment of other instruments, Townshend acted as producer. (Jon Astley points out that he, too, "worked on the mini-opera, but that was it. Pete and I had a falling out at that point.")

The 10-song mini-opera, initially entitled *The Glass Household* but which later became known as *Wire & Glass*, kicked off with the uptempo 'Sound Round'. "A young man [the young Ray High] is driving a large camper bus with extreme air-con around an estuary close to a large power station," Townshend wrote in the *Endless Wire* press notes, evoking memories of him driving 'Maxine the Motor Home' to Osea Island back in the summer of 1970. The song served to set the scene as High looks to the sky, where "he sees the future – nothing ecological or apocalyptic, more a vision of a society strangled by wire and communications."

'Pick Up The Peace' followed, with a glimpse of an elderly High 'in the ether' – meditating in his cell. He "sees three teenagers from his neighbourhood getting together as kids do, playing, flirting, talking, and forming a band. Then he has an intuition that they are going to become stars. They are Gabriel, Josh and Leila. [They call their band The Glass Household]. In striking contrast he sees scenes from his own childhood in the same neighbourhood, bombed buildings and old soldiers."

While the origins of both 'Sound Round' and 'Pick Up The Peace' can be traced back to *Lifehouse*, the remainder of the mini-opera was "entirely new, if anything I do can ever be described as entirely new," Townshend told Kevin O'Hare in September 2006. 'Unholy Trinity' highlights the markedly different backgrounds and religions of The Glass Household members. "Gabriel is from a showbiz family of lapsed Christians," Townshend wrote in the press notes. "Josh is from a fairly devout Jewish family [they observe Sabbath] who have suffered a tragedy, the loss of their father in an incident in Israel. Leila, from a Muslim family who have also suffered a loss: that of her beautiful and charismatic mother who died when she was very young. They each share fantasies, and afflictions, gifts and ideas, and become deeply committed friends. Like urchin-angels they share their secrets: Gabriel hears music; Josh voices; Leila can fly."

'Trilby's Piano' was easily the most un-Who like piece in *Wire & Glass* (and in the finished *Endless Wire* album). "Josh's widowed mother vests all her hopes in her brother Hymie becoming a great man. He falls in love with Trilby, Gabriel's goofy blonde Aunt. Trilby is the one who has nurtured Gabriel's great musical talent, unnoticed by his preoccupied mother. The kids decide to put on a musical play at Leila's father's studio featuring this song, and it finally breaks Josh's mother's resistance to the love match. The song is sung by Gabriel."

Townshend orchestrated the strings in 'Trilby's Piano' under the watchful eye of Rachel Fuller. "She has skills I do not have, and may never have, and I have skills she needs to learn," Pete said in an interview posted on his website. "But one thing I was able to do for the first time on this Who record was to confidently orchestrate a string section for ['Trilby's Piano'] and fix the players and record it without any adaptive work from an outsider. Rachel checked my work, added some dynamics here and there, and supervised the musicians on my session. Without her help I would have lost control."

The first of two longer pieces was 'Endless Wire'. "At some point in their rehearsals for the play, the three teenagers unearth documents that turn out to have belonged to Ray High, Leila's father's old studio partner. The documents refer to a crazy scheme to use the global wire network Ray saw as a young man to spread unifying music to everyone. [This matches my own vision for the *Lifehouse Method*, a computer-driven website through which people can commission their unique musical portrait.] They pore over the plans and realise that his scheme might be something they can make happen." Townshend later dedicated the song to Vint Cerf, "the internet guru who invented the TCP/IP protocol that underpins the experience we know as the internet."[5]

'We Got A Hit' describes the success of The Glass Household ("The hit referred to in the lyric is 'Fragments'," Townshend explained),[6] followed by 'They Made My Dream Come True'. "Still in his cell, Ray High can observe the kids' rise to fame while meditating. He foresees a tragedy, someone at the band's biggest ever, and last, concert will die. He rues the fact that the rock industry seems unable to change. What is never clear is whether the concert he foresees ever takes place in reality, or actually remains a dream forever."

The song featured the line: *People died where I performed*. "In this part of the story the ageing narrator who is singing refers to two tragedies," Townshend told *Newhouse News*. "One is an incident a little like the Stones' Altamont or The Who's Cincinnati, where audience members die. The other incident is the possible death of a member of the young band, maybe murdered by one of his bandmates, it isn't entirely clear. The dream he sings about is that they bring computerised tailor-made music to the internet, something I myself will be doing shortly through my *Lifehouse Method* website."

The second of the longer pieces was 'Mirror Door'. "The three pursue their own dream to perform an extraordinary elaboration of their children's play in Central Park in New York that is webcast to the entire world for charity, and during which they demonstrate Ray's idea to 'turn everyone into music'." Where there was once a small puppet theatre stage, there is now a massive one; where there was once a small stairway to the

---

[5] "If you have the ivory tower view that the internet is good only if everything on it is good you are mistaken," Cerf told the BBC in 2004. "The internet is a reflection of our society and that mirror is going to be reflecting what we see. If we do not like what we see in that mirror the problem is not to fix the mirror, we have to fix society."

[6] Not a part of the mini-opera, 'Fragments' became the opening song on *Endless Wire*.

back of the stage, there is now a stairway hoisted by blimps that seems to reach into the heavens. The band play, it becomes clear that there are terrorists on the streets trying to distract from the celebration, but the show goes on. At the top of the stairway appear gathered a series of legendary singers from popular music, all dead. A shot rings out and the tragedy is established. Josh, a paranoid schizophrenic, has stopped taking his medication and grabbed a pistol from someone and shot Gabriel. We cannot help our own. He ascends the stairway to join the dead. Even now, it is not clear whether this particular series of events actually takes place."[7]

"The mirror door came out of a kind of a rant I had with myself," Townshend told *Rolling Stone*'s Jenny Eliscu. "When I was young, I used to talk about the fact that The Who were like a mirror, and then I realised that wasn't quite right. What we were was very transparent. The true great artists, the Dylan's, make you believe you're looking into a mirror, and then, 'Bang!' You're changed. So 'Mirror Door' is how I would describe the artistic process. You walk up to something you believe is going to tell you something about yourself and then it tricks you and you change. The mirror is actually a doorway. You're changed and you can never go back."

The plaintive 'Tea & Theatre' rounded out the mini-opera. "Years later Josh and Leila – now old – take tea together. Coincidentally Josh's protective sanatorium cell is next to Ray's and they have just – together – revived once again the children's play, this time with the inmates of the sanatorium. They reflect on their career and lives together. The inference here is that perhaps, just maybe, Ray [the narrator] has confused the play he just saw in the sanatorium with the one they all hoped to see happen one day in New York, in the sky, and up into the universe."

While 'Tea & Theatre' ostensibly describes two fictional musicians reminiscing, the parallel with Townshend and Daltrey was easy to draw. The song's inclusion as the final number in The Who's set list during the upcoming tour gave credence to the notion that the song was autobiographical. "I don't know what Pete wrote ['Tea & Theatre'] about, but I think the audience thinks it's about us," Daltrey said in an October 2006 radio interview.

"I do regard myself as a survivor, but this is not a song about me," Pete told the *Minneapolis Star-Tribune* in December 2006. "I wrote it about two

---

7 While writing 'Mirror Door', Townshend accidentally named Doris Day among a list of dead stars. "I was absolutely convinced she was dead," he told the *Observer*'s Simon Garfield. "But I went to the internet and there she was – a fucking happening website!"

old folk in that retirement home Roger and I refuse to attend. Roger makes this song his own and I wouldn't want to challenge that. It is great that it speaks for us as older performers, but my survival is something I feel grateful for, not incredulous. I am hugely supported by so many people around me. This isn't because I am rich or talented. It is because I am loved. I cherish that support above everything else today. For years I think I knew how to love unconditionally, but not how to receive and accept unconditional love. I suppose I was – like most people – suspicious of the motives of those who claimed to love me. Now I know I can depend on that support. Life is too short to waste time doing measurements."

With recording sessions running up against pre-tour rehearsals, Townshend decided to prepare a condensed version of the mini-opera, prior to going on tour. "I wanted the incomplete mini-opera released so that The Who would at least have some music released before we started our European tour," Townshend told *Pitchfork*'s Rob Mitchum in October. "I didn't want to tour unless I had new music," he reiterated to the *Philadelphia Inquirer* in 2006. "I couldn't really see the point of taking the old circus around the world, I just felt there was a kind of pointlessness to it." Released on July 10 as a maxi CD and 12-inch single which Townshend insisted should be issued complete and unedited, the condensed *Wire & Glass* mini-opera consisted of: 'Sound Round', 'Pick Up The Peace', 'Endless Wire', 'We Got A Hit', 'They Made My Dreams Come True', and 'Mirror Door'.

"The Who's first proper record in 24 years is nothing so humdrum as a single," reported the *Times*' Paddy Jansen. "*Wire & Glass* is a suite of six thematically linked songs with a radio-unfriendly running time of 11 minutes, 26 seconds . . . The Who were one of the few highlights of Live 8 and remain a potent force as a live act, belting out classics such as 'Won't Get Fooled Again'. But will anyone be interested in their first album since the lacklustre *It's Hard* in 1982 when it comes out in October? On the evidence of *Wire & Glass*, the answer is yes . . ."

"[*Wire & Glass* is] all faintly preposterous. But there's something great about it too; something noble in Townshend's belligerent insistence that there's nothing the novel, say, can achieve that rock music can't. At 61, he seems to have been revitalised as a creative force by his relationship with the singer-songwriter Rachel Fuller . . . you miss the rococo rumble of Entwistle, who died in 2002. And while Townshend's playing is incendiary, 62-year-old Roger Daltrey's voice has inevitably lost some of its range and power. Beggars can't be choosers, though, and whatever the limitations of *Wire & Glass*, it's still way better than anyone had a right to expect."

In an ambitious and financially costly move, Townshend encouraged Fuller to host live, on-location webcasts along the way during The Who's summer 2006 European tour. He bought an Airstream trailer – similar to Ronnie Lane's old mobile studio – for this purpose, interspersing the live action with clips of The Who onstage. These innovative webcasts were available for a nominal fee, proceeds from which went to Double-O Charities. Plans were also afoot to offer full-length live webcasts of all the concerts on the upcoming US tour. In addition, Townshend organised a lottery (funds from which would go toward building a music-based school in hurricane-ravaged New Orleans) to auction off the remains of the Fender Stratocaster he smashed in Tokyo in 2004 – announcing it as the last guitar he would ever demolish in concert. He signed the reconstituted guitar, had it mounted to a small table, and planned to take it on tour, asking In The Attic guests to sign the display. Unfortunately, his good intentions were ultimately derailed due to lottery laws in the US.

The Who also continued their practice of making official CDs of each live performance available in their Encore series, but this year adding an accompanying professionally shot DVD. Again, proceeds from these recordings, which were available at themusic.com went to Double-O Charities.[8]

"Really the significance of the world tour really ties to the significance of us having new material for the first time – enough for an album," Townshend told BBC Radio 2's Johnnie Walker in July. "You know, for many years we've dodged the whole issue, not only of what was going to happen to the future of the band, which just lived up in the astral space, really. The brand name existed, back catalogue and lots of new fans because of the fact that so many of the modern crop of guitar bands would refer to The Who and our music got played a lot in movies and in commercials and stuff like that, but the band didn't really exist, it didn't record.

"But for the first time, we've got new material, got 15 to 20 tracks to choose an album from. I really felt, we've got new music, let's get out there and do it properly, so let's do the real thing. Let's do a big tour, let's

---

[8] Before the 2006/2007 World Tour, it was reported that sales of live CDs/DVDs from the band's tours in 2002 and 2004 had raised approximately £1 million for Double-O Charities.

play all the territories we haven't played in the past, and let's play at the ones we haven't played for a long time, let's play our favourites too."

As the tour preparation intensified in late spring 2006, the Eel Pie camp was shaken by the sudden resignation of Matt Kent. Townshend described this news as a "shock. This tour is the most web-intensive we have ever embarked on, and Matt's role was central to the provision of the portals we need to make it work," he wrote in his June 1 diary. "Luckily everyone has rallied around me to help drive this forward, especially the people at StreamingTank who are providing the bandwidth."

Bearing in mind Townshend's treatment of his work associates often left a lot to be desired, Kent's surprise departure was apparently far from amicable.[9] According to Jon Astley, who worked closely with him on the reissue of Townshend's solo catalogue that year, "Matt just said, 'I've had enough abuse.' Most of the time, Pete's a dream to work with and some days he's the worst person in the world to work with. That's the problem with Pete. He can be the nicest person – and he is, very often, the nicest person in the world, and you love him to death. And for no reason at all, he can be a complete arsehole, and make you feel completely wretched. And it gets worse. As he gets older, it actually gets worse."

In June, Townshend came under fire in the tabloid press for posting a piece on his blog which contained a description of a sex act between two teenagers. He removed the story, a novella posted in instalments entitled *The Comedian*, advising readers, "I'm afraid I have had to end this blog. I'm so sorry for those of you who were beginning to enjoy it, but it has upset certain people, and I sincerely do not wish to offend anyone." Pete commented that "the point of *The Comedian* was to develop a series of angles on the drift we are making towards an extreme form of political correctness, and the fact that the internet seems to be making it worse, not better."

A June 3 web diary entry described some of the stresses he was dealing with at the time. "My partner Rachel and I are both having to struggle through complex business problems and personal stuff too – friends who are falling by the wayside that we cannot help [because we are busy], really tricky staff problems and a building sense of awe, frustration and excitement as the tour approaches. I don't usually get so wound up about performing, but this is the first time for 24 years that I've produced a record

---

[9] Matt Kent declined an interview request for this book.

just prior to the tour and I'm reminded how chaotic it can make the whole business feel. So many events all coming together at almost the same moment."

Townshend enjoyed working with Fuller, who he has cited as a positive influence in both his life and career, telling the author: "When Rachel and I began our relationship I immediately began coaching her into the mysterious and disruptive ways of show business. We agreed to support each other's creative needs whenever possible, and to try to work out our respective calendars so that was possible. Recently Rachel and I have worked more and more as one – and although I am still the bigger earner, her talent and her show business acumen will probably overtake me one day.

"She is great fun to be around. She is like me and can be a little obsessive about her pet projects, but we talk everything through. She has been a good and pragmatic advisor to me and helped me to avoid making the current evolution of The Who an insoluble problem or show business an 'enemy'. We work together, and so far it has been very positive. I do enjoy her company, and I love working with her. She is tough and focused now, and determined to make her own way and prove her own talent, but also committed to make sure we do nothing to create unnecessary separations between us."

"Townshend is still not divorced [complex property issues], but he is contemplating the matter again now that [his] third child is 16," wrote the *Observer*'s Simon Garfield in September 2006. "He says that Rachel Fuller would like him to be divorced, and when I ask whether he plans to have children with her [she is considerably younger than him], he says they haven't talked about it. He adds: 'And as we don't have sex at all, it's not a problem.'"

Early June saw The Who rehearsing at the familiar location of Bray Film Studios, although Townshend was somewhat frazzled from the added workload due to both Kent's resignation and Eel Pie managing director Nick Goderson's ongoing battle with cancer. "I've had to learn to help look after my own financial direction while he's away," Townshend wrote. "I'm not very good at it. We were all hoping he'd be back before the tour – he especially – but it is not to be. He needs more time to recover. He is getting well slowly."

Despite these impediments, the rehearsals, "all went very well . . ." Pete wrote. "We are knocking the old Who show from the 2004 tour into shape for our first outing which is at Knebworth for Teenage Cancer. This is next week. Then we go back into rehearsal to learn the mini-opera [that Zak hasn't even heard yet] and maybe a few 'rarities' to spice up the summer shows."

On June 7, The Who played their first show since Live 8 in the grounds of Knebworth House, north of London. Hedgestock, as the event was known, was a hedge fund industry gathering, attracting an estimated 4,000 fund managers and investors who paid upwards of £500 each for this networking opportunity. Stock market types are not renowned for their rock'n'roll credentials, so it was no surprise that The Who's set was met with a subdued reception.

"Have you lot been drinking all day?" *The Times*' Penny Wark reported Daltrey asking the politely clapping crowd, opining that she'd seen more passion at her local supermarket on a Friday night. "Everyone still has their mobile phone on and even Daltrey's belting lyrics don't stop them taking calls. Eventually Townshend loses it. 'Turn yer mobiles off!' he yells. There is no noticeable response."

Despite the lukewarm reception, the fundraiser was a resounding success with a reported $3.4 million being raised for the Teenage Cancer Trust.

"We've got The Who machine back up and running, and the band sounds good," Pete wrote in a web posting three days after Hedgestock. "We are developing a special six screen video system to provide an alternative and a complement to our lighting rig . . ."

The week after saw The Who back in rehearsals, focusing on the mini-opera. "We are playing it," Townshend wrote in a June 13 diary entry. "It sounds great. It's new, and that feels strange, we haven't played anything new for such a long time, but it's also familiar – I remember playing new songs to audiences who were really unsure they wanted to hear them. This selection is 11 minutes long, we will blast through it, and if the crowd get distracted they can buy our fabulous merchandising."[10]

In addition to such hardy perennials as 'I Can't Explain', 'Anyway Anyhow Anywhere', 'Behind Blue Eyes', 'Who Are You', 'Won't Get Fooled Again', and 'My Generation' (which now segued into 'Cry If You Want' from 1982's *It's Hard*), the band rehearsed several less frequently played songs, including 'Pure And Easy', 'I Don't Even Know Myself',

---

[10] For the stage, *Wire & Glass* typically consisted of six songs – 'Sound Round', 'Pick Up The Peace', 'Endless Wire', 'We Got A Hit', 'They Made My Dreams Come True' and 'Mirror Door'. On a handful of occasions, 'Unholy Trinity' was added.

'Getting In Tune', 'The Seeker', 'Bargain', 'Relay', 'Naked Eye', 'Another Tricky Day', 'I'm A Boy', 'Tattoo' and 'Let's See Action' alongside even more obscure tunes from The Who's back catalogue such as 'A Quick One (While He's Away)', 'Here For More', and 'Blue, Red And Grey' (performed solo by Pete on ukulele).

Townshend wrote that he hoped to introduce the songs "one by one on the American tour later this year . . . Working with Rachel on In The Attic has made me quite a bit braver about tackling unusual songs, and I'm hoping that on occasion – where a 'rarity' may not work on the big Who stage, I might be able to play it live on In The Attic.[11] I may be able to persuade Roger to join us sometimes. So there should be some interesting times ahead."

The Who's European tour – with opening act Casbah Club, Simon Townshend's latest venture, featuring Mark Brzezicki, rhythm guitarist Bruce Watson (from Big Country) and bassist Bruce Foxton (ex-Stiff Little Fingers, The Jam) – began on June 17 when, some 36 years on from their now-legendary performance, The Who returned to the 2,000-capacity Leeds University refectory venue. Townshend and Daltrey unveiled a blue Civic Trust plaque commemorating the refectory as a "legendary concert venue" and The Who's live recording there, while Sir Peter Blake devised a special artwork, *Live At Leeds 2* for the occasion.

The next night the band played in Brighton, returning to Leeds a week later to headline their first festival date of the summer, the two-day O2 Wireless Festival, in the grounds of Harewood House. The Who headed a line-up which featured Massive Attack, The Zutons and The Flaming Lips in front of a 40,000 crowd. "We're only really here to see The Who!" Flaming Lips' frontman and über Who fan, Wayne Coyne announced from the stage. Prior to the show, Townshend squeezed into the airstream trailer and accompanied The Flaming Lips on a piano-based 'I Can't Explain', and sat in with 'E' from The Eels for 'Substitute'. Pete also previewed 'God Speaks Of Marty Robbins' (from *Endless Wire*).

The Who returned to Bristol for the first time in 35 years on June 28, performing in front of 20,000 at Ashton Gate Stadium. After a cool reception at the O2 festival, The Who dropped *Wire & Glass* for the festival shows and concentrated on familiar material. 'Let's See Action', 'Love,

---

[11] During The Who's European tour, Townshend played lesser-known songs such as 'Too Much Of Anything', 'Greyhound Girl', 'Cut My Hair', 'Acid Queen', 'Sensation', 'Time Is Passing', and 'A Quick One' during his pre-show In The Attic appearances.

Reign O'er Me', 'Bargain' and new song 'Mike Post Theme' were the only interesting inclusions in a mostly 'greatest hits' set list.

After a June 30 gig at Belgium's Werchter Festival, on July 2, a year on from Live 8, The Who returned to Hyde Park for the Hyde Park Calling festival, which attracted around 60,000 fans. Co-headlining a 20-band bill alongside Roger Waters (whose set included a complete performance of Pink Floyd's *Dark Side Of The Moon*), The Who delivered an impressive performance that eclipsed those who came before them.

The touring schedule continued the following day with a show at the Beaulieu Motor Museum, then a stop in Liverpool for two shows on July 5 and 6 – The Who's first appearance in the city for over three decades, which took place under canvas in the 'Big Top Arena', prompting Daltrey to make the onstage remark: "The historical importance of Liverpool and fuck me, you're still stuck in a tent!"

Following a wind-and-rain-soaked performance at the Oxegen Festival in Dublin on July 8 (headlining a 50-act bill which featured the likes of The Arctic Monkeys and James Brown), The Who headlined the T In The Park Festival in Kinross, Scotland. "We're The Who – what's left of us," Townshend told the crowd, which totalled an estimated 120,000 over the weekend – the year's biggest UK festival – featuring The Red Hot Chili Peppers, Paul Weller, Arctic Monkeys, and The Strokes, among others.

"In the hippie days, stuff like Woodstock and Monterey and the Isle of Wight were terrible," Townshend told the *Daily Record*. "I hated them. I felt the whole philosophy of the hippie era was hypocritical. I much prefer it now. T in the Park is just wonderful." He had previously played the festival the year before as part of Rachel Fuller's band. "We had such a great time that I said, 'If [The Who] ever get an album together, this would be the festival we would want to do."

The European tour continued through July, with 10 more dates in Germany, Switzerland, Monte Carlo, France, Austria, and Spain.

"The rewards [of touring] are huge," Townshend said in September. "In Madrid, we had never played in Spain, a crowd of 10,000 young men applauded every tiny guitar line I played. I got better and better with their encouragement until I was playing like Jimi Hendrix, in fact several local newspaper reviews made that claim, not me. That's some place to go to. I don't want to leave my friends, my home, my neighbourhood, my kids and my dogs behind me – but for this kind of moment in the life of someone who is after all just another musician most of the time, the price is worth paying."

As the European leg reached its conclusion, a frustrated Townshend announced via his web diary that the live webcasts of Who shows on the tour would cease.

"Webcasting The Who, whether live or pay for view, and donating profits [not proceeds] to various causes, was entirely my idea. I was unable to share my plan properly with Roger prior to the tour because we were having such trouble meeting our recording deadlines. My feeling, still, is that webcasting allows us new ways to get our new music across that our traditional live show does not. I have yet to convince Roger of this. Sadly, I announced my grand plans, and put them in action, before Roger really had a chance to digest what I was doing.

"Roger is my partner in The Who. He is not my partner in anything else. We love each other but we are not regular social buddies like Bono and Edge, we do not discuss or share ideas, and we have no unified joint vision or strategy for The Who or for creative projects in general . . .

"I had hoped that Roger would fall more actively behind me, and we could secure a solid sponsorship deal that would make everything flow smoothly, and repay some of my initial investment. Roger has been recorded in the media several times saying that I benefit from publishing income while The Who are not touring, and that allows me greater personal, creative and financial freedom. This is true. But with no promise of any investment from inside or outside The Who I need to stand back now and review my commitment."

Townshend went so far as to set up an email address for Who fans to write and try to convince Daltrey of the virtues of webcasting. "Of the 250 mb of emails, only two were negative," Pete told *Billboard*. "Roger and I were not at war," Townshend told Kevin O'Hare in September, in response to several overblown stories which had appeared in the media, "but I did act to webcast The Who in Europe quite independently, and when it came to the future US tour, and Roger committing to investment at the same level as I was willing, he demurred . . . This is something we remain divided over."

"I think the internet is just an advertising device of very dubious returns," Daltrey told the *New York Times* the following month. "Also, I haven't got the luxury of throwing the kind of money at it that he can . . . I haven't got the publishing, I'm just the singer. So I have to look at it much more hard-nosed as a business and ask if I can put a million dollars into it, and the answer is no."

Although the notion of live webcasts from the upcoming American tour was no longer an option, The Who's music soon reached audiences through another medium: radio. In September, a 'Who Channel' was introduced on Sirius satellite radio, featuring 24 hour programming dedicated to The Who, including broadcasts of shows from the tour and backstage interviews.

"This is the last day I spend with my son, my family, our five dogs, in my garden, enjoying the end of the English summer, the blue dragonflies over the mill-pond, the sound of the coots," Townshend floridly wrote in a September 3 diary entry entitled 'A Letter To America'. "Tomorrow I begin my journey to come and play to you . . . We've recorded a few great new tracks of [Rachel's] at home together, and she's been working out how best to arrange her time on tour to promote her EP *Shine* and keep up her work on In The Attic . . .

"This entry is a kind of goodbye – for now – to this pleasant English life I lead when I am not being a rock musician. It is hello to hotels, media inquisitions, being shouted at in the street, and the security and safety of being sequestered at Who shows, ready to play, ready to fly, ready to try to forget who I was, who I am, and who I might one day soon become, and occupy the 'zone' for a few moments – and perhaps play as well as I did in Madrid. I'm not going to pretend I'm looking forward to being away from home, but neither am I going to pretend I'm not looking forward to the tour. These are the last few hours I have to enjoy the almost absolute silence of the countryside, and the ability to instantly meditate as one can when sitting on a bench in a wood, or a field, or on a hill, with no body and no building in sight."

After conducting closed pre-tour rehearsals with The Who in Bridgeport, Connecticut on September 9 and 10, Pete joined Rachel Fuller the following night for the first in a series of performances scheduled at Barnes & Noble bookstore, promoting her EP, *Shine*. His appearance at these in-store performances was not pre-publicised, but soon became anticipated by diehard Who fans. Townshend joined Fuller on the song they wrote together, 'Just Breathe'. "Pete and I wrote that in New York together on his birthday about three years ago," Fuller told the *Chicago Sun-Times*. "We were trying to decide what to do, and he just picked up his guitar. He does that a lot; he can actually have a conversation while he's playing, and he always has an acoustic knocking around. I said, 'Ooh, ooh, I like that!' And that's how it happened. In the end, we just sat down and wrote a few songs together."

On September 12, the first leg of The Who's 2006–7 world tour got underway in Philadelphia's sold-out Wachovia Center. Townshend based himself in New York for the early dates, flying out to each show and then back the same evening. With the upcoming *Endless Wire* album incomplete, he was still mixing the album while on the road.

"In New York the mixing desk was squeezed into a tiny room at a mid-priced mid-town hotel where our In The Attic crew were staying," Pete wrote in an October diary posting. "I had to mix two extra tracks there for the forthcoming Who CD that were intended for radio, but which both the American and European record companies wanted to add as 'bonus' tracks. These were extended versions of two of the shortest mini-opera tracks 'Endless Wire' [which now has a middle part and a repeat verse at the end] and 'We Got A Hit' [which has a new middle and a completely new verse at the end].

"I was thinking I might have time to record some more demos, and do some creative work on a possible theatrical incarnation of *The Boy Who Heard Music*, but I simply haven't had the time."

As became typical during the tour, Townshend appeared humble and almost contrite when introducing the *Endless Wire* material, telling the crowd at Philadelphia, "Thank you for putting up with it. We're very proud of the new music." Roger added, "You are so loud. It's really hard playing music for the first time. You were very gracious."

Townshend seemed overly obsessed with the band's performance during their September 13 show at Jones Beach. "The sourpuss guitarist unhappily and unnecessarily pouted his way through the two-and-a-half hour gig with sarcastic between-song patter that attacked his bandmate Roger Daltrey, the fans, and even his own new music," reported Dan Aquilante in a *New York Post* article titled 'Baba O'Nasty'. After a seemingly flawless rendition of 'Baba O'Riley' that concluded with Daltrey blowing a mean blues harp, Townshend judged the rendition worthy of a 'Jewish wedding'. Whatever that meant, it drew a burning glare from Daltrey, and the tension in the air made drummer Zak Starkey go rigid behind his drum kit.

"Later, Townshend diluted his acid with just a hint of humour, calling Daltrey 'a rock'n'roll casualty' just before the band launched into 'Real Good Looking Boy' . . .

Then there was the introduction to 'Who Are You' in which Townshend mused about what it means to be a rock star and, in the final breaths before launching the tune, spat unexpectedly at the crowd, 'Who the fuck are you?' . . .

"Behind wraparound shades and slightly slurred elocution, the real problem with Townshend was the weight of the giant chip on the shoulder that made him defensive and timid about the new songs from the band's upcoming *Endless Wire* album . . . As for the quality of those new tunes, Townshend shouldn't have had a concern. They were pretty good, and given a tour's worth of live performance, the gems will certainly emerge from the set."

On September 14, after a performance of 'Man In A Purple Dress' was taped for David Letterman's show, the first Attic Jam on the US tour took place in New York City's tiny Joe's Pub with a capacity of approximately 160. Irish musician Foy Vance was first up, playing three songs, followed by Martha Wainwright. Townshend, Fuller and Wainwright joined Vance onstage for his final song, 'Indescriminate Act Of Kindness', and later Townshend and Fuller joined Wainwright for the second of her two songs, 'Factory'. A solo Townshend then performed 'Greyhound Girl', 'Endless Wire', 'Lets See Action', 'Blue Red And Grey' (on ukulele), finishing with 'In The Ether' accompanied by Fuller on piano. Following Fuller's own set (which included Townshend accompanying her on 'Just Breathe'), the ensemble returned to the stage for a communal 'I'm One' and 'Shine', the theme for In The Attic.

Following shows in Ottawa (their first since 1969) and Boston, The Who played Madison Square Garden over two nights on September 18 and 19. "Roger told me not to say anything tonight," Townshend told the crowd in reference to his comments onstage at Jones Beach a few nights earlier.

"When the band played what's emerged thus far from Mr Townshend's latest opus, *Wire & Glass* its exuberance brought to mind the excitement of hearing new Townshend compositions three and four decades ago," reported the *Wall Street Journal*'s Jim Fusilli. "Mr Daltrey and Mr Townshend performed two songs from the album by themselves, including the night's finale, 'Tea & Theatre', which finds the *Wire & Glass* characters looking back on their lives and careers. While the parallel to the men's long, occasionally troubled relationship was obvious, the duo shunned the easy play for sentimentality. They ripped into the song, then left the stage."

On September 23, The Who played the outdoor Virgin Festival at Baltimore's Pimlico Race Course in front of 40,000 on a bill with more than 20 bands including The Red Hot Chili Peppers, The Flaming Lips, The Killers and The Raconteurs.

"Never mind the group's advanced age vis-à-vis the rest of the V-fest field," reported the *Washington Post*, "The Who sounded more vital than any of the bands that played before them, tearing through their rich catalogue with abandon. Daltrey's voice was frayed and parched after so many years of braying onstage, but it added new texture to the old standards. And the windmilling Townshend can still summon wicked riffs with the best of them. No wonder so many of the festival's other performers watched the set from stage left, mouths agape."

Two-thirds of the way through The Who's set at Chicago's sold-out United Center two nights later, Daltrey left the stage, leaving Townshend to sing lead vocals on the 'My Generation'/ 'Cry If You Want' medley.

"It was up to Pete Townshend to carry the load," wrote the *Chicago Tribune*'s Greg Kot. "He overcompensated, and uncaged one of the finest performances I've seen at a Who concert in decades. 'My Generation' became not a nostalgia anthem that looked back to 1965, but something that spoke to who Townshend and his audience are now. The 61-year-old elder statesman turned the now infamous line, *Hope I die before I get old* into a howl of dissent. *I can't die . . . We can't die . . . There are too many of us!*"

"Townshend's guitar strafed Zak Starkey's drumbeat with shuddering sustains and staccato runs, then landed one final, crashing windmill chord. *This . . . is . . . my . . . generation, baby!* he exulted. It was Townshend tipping his mighty axe to Dylan Thomas: 'My Generation' transformed into 'Do Not Go Gentle Into That Good Night' and its exhortation to *rage, rage against the dying of the light.*"

Daltrey returned to the stage for the encore. "It was just an allergic reaction . . ." he explained in a radio interview on the Sirius Who channel. "Someone was smoking a joint in the audience, and I got a whiff of it."

Two days after playing in front of a disappointingly low turnout of just over 6,000 fans in Des Moines – The Who's first show there in 30 years – the second Attic Jam on this leg of the tour took place on September 28 at a substantially larger venue than Joe's Pub, the Chicago House of Blues, in front of an audience of about 600. In addition to joining in on a song with guest Willy Mason, Pete performed 'Greyhound Girl', 'Blue Red And Grey', 'In The Ether' (with Rachel on piano), 'Endless Wire', and 'Let's See Action'. Townshend later joined Fuller for a rendition of 'Just Breathe', prior to returning to the stage near the end of the show to jam with Rose Hill Drive on their song 'Raise Your Hands', and the more familiar 'Young Man Blues'. The broadcast closed with the usual ensemble performance of 'I'm One'.

The following night The Who performed in Detroit, prior to heading to Canada for a gig in Ontario the next night prior to a two-day break. Townshend was using Chicago as his between-show base and he detailed aspects of his road life in a October 3 diary entry.

"I travel pretty heavy myself. I carry a lot of books,[12] a small recording system based around an Apple computer, a keyboard, four guitars and a ukulele, tools [including soldering gear], a whole bunch of identical black trousers and jackets, black and white stretchy T-shirts, and a few shirts for stage shows, a computer printer, loads of cables for various things, a small MiniDV camera system with a very wide angle lens so I can use it in cars and on planes, a kettle, a toaster, tea bags, biscuits, bread, Marmite, marmalade, cups [that most hotel maids eventually steal from me for some reason], little digital cameras, a spare mobile phone, and a couple of iPods I never listen to . . . It is on such occasions, like today in Chicago, that I understand how much I like to have this stuff around me. It makes me feel I am at home.

"At every show I have a luxury bus out in the yard or down in the basement instead of a dressing room, so that after afternoon soundchecks I can cook my own basic food, drink English tea, read, watch DVDs and even take a short nap. After shows I can shower on it, but the best thing is being able to leave a lot of my stage gear on it for the duration of the tour leg . . ."

On October 3, the tour picked up where it left off in Canada, starting in Winnipeg before heading west to sold-out Calgary on the 5th. "[Townshend] recounted The Who's Calgary shows of the late Sixties when the stage was set up on a Corral floor covered in cow dung," reported the *Calgary Herald*. "When we first came to Edmonton, it was the first time we had ever met mods outside of London," Pete told the 12,500-strong crowd from the stage of Edmonton's Rexall Place the following night.

Townshend was beset with technical troubles at the Edmonton show, having to switch guitars mid-song during 'Won't Get Fooled Again', and

---

[12] An avid reader, Townshend listed some of the books he brought along during the US tour in a 2006 interview with the *Des Moines Register*'s Kyle Munson: "*The Name Of The Rose* by Umberto Eco. *JapanAmerica* by Rolan Kelts (early copy), a number of crime novels." In January 2007, Pete noted in a web entry that he'd recently completed *Against The Day* by Thomas Pynchon. "It has been reviewed as a very thick book, it has over 1,000 pages. Yet as soon as I began to read I knew I was happily hooked for the entire journey . . ."

delaying the start of 'Behind Blue Eyes' due to another glitch. He also received an electric shock on the mouth from his microphone, knocking him backwards into his amps. Despite these setbacks, the 61-year-old still delivered, causing many reviewers to remark on his onstage vitality. When asked how he maintained his good physical condition, Pete told the New Jersey *Courier-Post's*, "It's more about what I don't do. I don't drink. I don't smoke. I don't have a lot of sex. I don't take risks. I eat carefully [with enjoyment]. I sleep quite long hours. I try to stay calm whatever I'm faced with. I work a lot to help other people face their troubles, that keeps my mind off my own."

The first leg of the tour finished on the West Coast, playing Vancouver, Portland and Seattle where, again, Townshend faced technical problems. "Things got off to a sketchy start as Townshend wandered offstage midway through 'I Can't Explain' in search of a functional axe," reported the *Tacoma News Tribune*. "'They don't make guitars like they used to,' Daltrey declared, stalling as a roadie got everything properly plugged in after the opener."

Two weeks after the Seattle show, Townshend was set to play live with Daltrey via satellite on Howard Stern's radio show on Sirius satellite radio. However, prior to going on the air, Townshend walked out of the studio after hearing Stern and co-host Robin Quivers in characteristic form, discussing his 2003 arrest and the long-standing rumours of his bisexuality. Later that day, he posted a message on his website which simply said, "Howard – Let's Have Lunch."

"I would not agree with reports that I stormed out of the interview with Howard Stern; I would say that I walked away before the show when I heard Robin saying they were going to ask me about my sexual history," Townshend told the *San Jose Mercury-News*. "I am not angry with Howard or his team, and they have a perfect right to discuss my sexual past whenever they choose; I am a public person. I decided not to join what was threatening to be a light-hearted inquisition of sexual subjects that cause widely felt discomfort when not seriously addressed."

On October 29, The Who played their last British show of 2006 when they closed the annual BBC Electric Proms in London with an impressive performance at the newly refurbished Roundhouse, in Chalk Farm. "Last time I played here [in 1970] it was dirty," Townshend told the crowd. "Now it's clean and I'm dirty."

CHAPTER TWENTY-TWO

2006–2007

"I now find myself thinking and sometimes even singing, 'I hope I die before I get old.' This time I am not being ironic. I am 61. I hope I die before I get old. I hope I die while I still feel this alive, this young, this healthy, this happy, and this fulfilled. But that may not happen. I may get creaky, cranky, and get cancer, and die in some hospice with a massive resentment against everyone I leave behind. That's being old, for some people, and probably none of us who don't die accidentally can escape being exposed to it. But I am not old yet . . ."

– Pete Townshend, 2006

ON October 30, 2006, to a certain amount of anticipation and trepidation, *Endless Wire* was finally released.[1] The album kicked off with the 'Baba O'Riley'-esque introduction to 'Fragments', "based on the continuation of the *Method* music way of creating individual pieces of music dictated by parameters and information from individuals, which I first explored in the *Lifehouse* project in the early Seventies," Townshend sought to explain in a song-by-song commentary on music.aol.com.

'Fragments', based on initial experiments Townshend conducted with Lawrence Ball, a composer and mathematician who devised a programme called 'Harmonic Mathematics' back in 1983, was credited to 'Townshend/ Ball'. (An instrumental version, entitled 'Fragments Of Fragments', was included in *Wire & Glass*. Ball's software was also used to create the album's sleeve.)

Townshend was inspired to write three of the album's songs after watching Mel Gibson's controversial movie *The Passion Of The Christ*. "When I saw the film, what I think I felt was pain and I think it was my pain," Pete told the *Daily Telegraph*'s Neil McCormick in December. "It

---

[1] Pete told the *Des Moines Register* in 2006 that he "would not have released the new Who album as a solo album, I wouldn't have had the nerve. It is far too epic."

was the unbelievable fucking humiliation that I'd been through when I was arrested." Townshend said in the *Endless Wire* press release that 'Man In A Purple Dress' was "not so much a rail against the principles of justice through the ages, but a challenge to the vanity of the men who need to put on some kind of ridiculous outfit in order to pass sentence on one of their peers. It is the idea that men need dress up in order to represent God that appals me. If I wanted to be as insane as to attempt to represent God I'd just go ahead and do it, I wouldn't dress up like a drag-queen."

Pete told *Billboard* that 'Man In A Purple Dress' and 'Tea & Theatre' represented something of a breakthrough for The Who. "Back in the days of *Who By Numbers*, I did a song on ukulele, 'Blue Red And Grey', but even then, we didn't feel comfortable leaving it unadulterated, so John added some beautiful brass-band brass to it. This is clean. If Roger sings and I play acoustic guitar, what we actually have is a band, a brand and acoustic music. It focuses the attention where it should really be, which is on the song."

Another *Passion Of The Christ*-inspired tune was 'Two Thousand Years'. "This one is about the fact that Judas may not have been acting to betray Christ at all, but precisely following his instructions," Townshend wrote in the press release. "He waits 2,000 years for us to consider this a possibility. We wait 2,000 years for the New Christ. We need a lot of patience."

"The larger theme in the background [of 'Mike Post Theme'] is the statement that we are no longer strong enough or young enough to love. In a very real way, movies, novels and TV series do help us to express selfless emotions as we once did when we were in love. Men cry quietly watching TV and movies, women maybe a little more openly, but when we do that we are reconnecting with our innocent and free-flowing feelings. If only we could still do that with the principal lover in our lives."[2]

And not only the "principal lover", but our fellow man in general: "['Mike Post Theme'] is about our inability to find the strength and resources to love other human beings who are different to us," Townshend told *PopMatters*.

"TV series, and their theme tunes, do two impossible things," he told

---

[2] Mike Post is a popular TV theme writer who has penned the themes for dozens of US television programmes, including *The Rockford Files*, *NYPD Blue*, *Hill Street Blues*, and *The A-Team*.

the *San Jose Mercury News*. "They defy time and ageing by allowing us to live forever vicariously in the characters we watch, but they remind us that time is passing, show by show, week by week.

"When I first came to the US in 1967, *I Love Lucy* was always on TV somewhere. When I saw her pretty face, I was reminded how much older she must have become, how much younger I was [then] than she. Today the same shows remind me I have overtaken her TV persona. There is a valuable poignancy there that is not sentimental in any way, and yet reaches to the heart of human vulnerability. Mike Post's theme from *Hill Street Blues* reminds me that once I associated the sound with a cop who couldn't deal with his drink problem. Now I hear it and I remember a brother, for pretty soon I was facing the same problem."

Townshend described 'Black Widow's Eyes' (the only track on *Endless Wire* featuring Zak Starkey drumming) as "a love song. We sometimes fall in love when we do not want to, and when we do not expect to. Suddenly. Foolishly. This song is about the man holding a child in the Beslan massacre who described the female terrorist who blew herself up, killing the child he held, as 'having the most penetrating and beautiful eyes'."

'In The Ether' (which Pete cited as his favourite song on the album) concerned Ray High's meditation. "This song reinforces how lonely it is to be 'spiritual'," Townshend wrote in his press notes. "If the intention of the spiritual aspirant is to 'become one with the infinite', and yet life is almost the universally finite antidote to the infinite, isn't he likely to get very lonely?"

He also described the song as expressing "how it feels to be getting older and feeling lost – as lost as one felt when young and yet feeling at last that pain may have a purpose." His raspy vocal – described by several critics as "Tom Waits-style" – drew a fair amount of criticism. "I'm 60 years old pretending to be 80," Townshend explained to the *San Jose Mercury News*. "My voice is an instrument I can't always control. I love Tom Waits, but listen to him, he sounds like gravel being hauled through an oil can. I just sound a teensy bit gruff. Tom is the man. There is really no such thing as Tom Waits 'style' singing."

The simple, acoustic 'God Speaks Of Marty Robbins' started life on Townshend's *Scoop 3* album as an instrumental entitled simply 'Marty Robbins'. In his press notes, Pete described the song as "very simple . . . God is asleep, before creation – before the Big Bang – and gets the whim to wake, and decides it could be worth going through it all in order to be able to hear some music, and most of all, one of his best creations, Marty Robbins."

"God is not in awe of Marty; he imagines him," Townshend explained to *Goldmine*'s Ken Sharp. "Marty is no more or less important than any other singer God has imagined. I just like him, and always have, and love the sound of his name."

Another beautifully sparse acoustic track was 'You Stand By Me'. "I wrote this a few minutes before appearing on my partner Rachel Fuller's In The Attic Live webcast show from my studio in London," Townshend wrote. "I had nothing new to play and decided to write a song. This just came out. It is for her, and for Roger, for believing in me, and standing by me when I have been completely out of order. It could be for many of my family, friends and fans who have done the same. I have often been a very tricky man to live with."

'It's Not Enough', the track selected as a single, was credited to Townshend/Fuller, featuring Rachel on keyboards, with her drummer, bassist and guitarist who played acoustic while Pete played electric.

"One day I suggested to Rachel that if she wanted to write a radio hit she should try my fail-safe technique: find a rolling, rhythmic electronic loop that might be fun to listen to while driving your car or jogging, add an overlay of several very simple repetitive chords [as heavy as possible] and an earnest lyric. She did this with a tune she called 'Magic Flute'. For a while she tried to complete it, but I saw her heart wasn't in it. As I'd let her appropriate my jazz-style guitar chords for 'Just Breathe' I asked if I could appropriate her backing track for The Who album. I changed the words, imposed an extremely aggressive guitar part and some big backing vocals and 'It's Not Enough' was the result."

Townshend described the inspiration behind the song in the album's press release: "Watching *Mepris*, the Sixties film by Jean Luc Godard starring Brigitte Bardot, I found myself wondering why it is that we choose people to partner who we feel aren't quite right. Bardot asks her lover, 'Do you adore my legs?' He nods. 'My breasts?' He nods. 'My arms?' He nods. She goes over her entire body. He nods every time. When she's finished she gets up and tells him, 'It's not enough.'"

Among several other Townshend compositions up for inclusion on *Endless Wire* but ultimately left off were 'Ambition', 'Uncertain Girl' and 'How Can I Help You, Sir?' 'Uncertain Girl' was at least partially recorded, while in December 2005, Pete posted a film on his site which chronicled the making of the demo for 'How Can I Help You, Sir?' which he described as being "about a sick person's refusal to allow anyone to help them, a lonely person refusing to allow anyone to get close . . ."[3]

The *Endless Wire* liner notes stated that the album was "recorded discontinuously at Pete Townshend's home studio and at Eel Pie Oceanic Studios, Twickenham between autumn 2002 and summer 2006," unwittingly revealing Townshend's difficulties in writing what he felt was appropriate material for The Who.

"The album is recorded in a simple way," he told newhousenews.com. "I made it in my home studio that is arranged around an old vintage mixing desk and an old-fashioned 8-track tape machine. We went on to add certain things in a big studio, but all the tracks have a simple audio backbone, nothing too fancy, nothing too self-indulgent."

Townshend told *Artist Direct* that Daltrey had "wanted to record a conventional record in the studio with a band. I wanted more control, wanted the record to be as much as possible about just Roger and myself . . ." Because of this approach, Pete played a variety of instruments, including drums on 'Mike Post Theme', violin and viola on 'Two Thousand Years', and programmed drums, mandolin, and banjo on other tracks, in addition to his usual guitar work.

Despite the fact that the band weren't recorded as an ensemble (Daltrey added his vocals separately in the studio at the end), Townshend attempted to capture the 'classic' Who sound and mixed the album while on tour in Europe. "I think the album that this one most closely echoes is one I made with Ronnie Lane in 1976 called *Rough Mix* – but sonically it stands as a Who record somewhere between *Who By Numbers* and *Who Are You*," he told *Rolling Stone*.

"The way I shape chords or work with keyboard patterns gives a certain stamp of The Who sound," he described to the *Daily Telegraph*'s Neil McCormick in December. "But when Roger adds his vocal and turns it into a bravura performance, that's when it becomes something else."

"I wanted Roger to love this new record," Townshend told the *Long Beach Press-Telegram* in February 2007. "I wanted him to love it more than fans. That is very different from in the past when I was glad if he liked what I did, but I didn't mind if he didn't like it. I have been the creative guide for The Who, but now it is just Roger and me, I feel we need to be more balanced."

---

[3] All three songs were performed by Townshend on In The Attic ('Ambition' and 'Uncertain Girl' in 2006 and 'How Can I Help You, Sir?' in 2005).

Somewhat to his relief, Daltrey appeared delighted with the finished product. "It always felt that if [1982's *It's Hard*] had really been the end, it wouldn't have been right," Roger told the *New York Times'* Alan Light. "With this new album, now there can be an ending. I don't want it to be, but it can be, and I'm at peace with that." Townshend told *Associated Press* that he feels "it's a good record. It feels like a record I may have made way back, back in 1968 or 1970."

Endless Wire debuted at number seven on the *Billboard* chart and went on to sell 88,000 copies in its first week of release. The album received a positive critical reception although some writers were perhaps overawed by what the album represented rather than how it sounded. *Mojo's* Pat Gilbert called it, "Fantastic – arguably the best Who album since 1973's *Quadrophenia*" while *Rolling Stone's* David Fricke opined that *Endless Wire* was "brazen in its way and right for its day as *The Who Sell Out* and *Tommy* were in theirs. Daltrey's voice is deeper and darker now, even in total roar – you can hear the extent to which he has punished it in long service to Townshend's songs. And it must be said: bassist John Entwistle, who died in 2002, is sorely missed here. His stoic baritone and ghoulish lyric wit were reliable black humour relief on Who albums, especially when Townshend was at his most conceptual and argumentative. But this is the only Who left, and at times on *Endless Wire*, Townshend wields it like an avenging sword . . ."

Of the more objective reviews, a common complaint was that the album sounded unfinished, based on Townshend's decision not to consistently use The Who touring band, especially Zak Starkey, and that the mini-opera felt only half-formed, with its components not presented as fully formed songs.

"It's a fascinating but messy work which embraces and comments on much of what has made Pete and The Who great," said the *Daily Mirror*, "though it does sometimes labour under an inevitably portentous Pete concept. Exactly what that concept amounts to is as clear here as it was in 1971's abandoned, internet foreseeing *Lifehouse* project. That is to say there are lots of interesting details but not even Pete could explain it all. The concept does, however, serve as a launch pad for memorable music."

However reviewers tended to agree that the mini-opera was the strongest part of the album. "Taken on its own, *Wire & Glass* does stand as the greatest Who music since *Who Are You*," wrote allmusic.com, "so it's a bit hard not to wish that the entire album had its thematic cohesion, muscular melody, and sense of purpose, but if it meant losing the quite wonderful highlights of the first half, it may not have been worth it because they're not only strong songs, they give this record its ragged heart."

Townshend flew back to the US on October 31, a few days prior to the resumption of The Who's tour. Rabbit Bundrick was unable to join the band for this second American leg, as he was caring for his wife Sue, critically ill with cancer. Filling in on keyboards was Bundrick's roadie, Brian Kehew.

"Rabbit cannot leave her at such a time so we are going to continue the tour without him, but we will not replace him," Townshend wrote in an October 31 web entry in which he asked for "prayers and positive thoughts please for Sue, Rabbit and Sue's family and friends."[4]

On November 3, Townshend and Fuller made an in-store appearance at a Los Angeles-area branch of Barnes & Noble, where Rachel performed four songs. The following evening, The Who played the first of two consecutive nights at the Hollywood Bowl.

"On this tour leg's opening night, guitarist Townshend and the other four instrumentalists didn't mount the most powerful and dynamic playing ever delivered under The Who banner," reported the *Los Angeles Times'* Richard Cromelin. "The mix of new Who and classic Who might have been inevitably uneasy, and the band could have followed the Rolling Stones' example and minimised the momentum-interruptions of new songs. But there are demands other than crowd-pleasing in the artist's heart, and it's good to see Townshend heed them."

Another Attic Jam took place in Los Angeles on November 7 at the small Hotel Café. Along with regulars Fuller, Cuthbert and Simon Townshend, guests included actress Minnie Driver, E from Eels, and a rather nervous Smashing Pumpkins frontman, Billy Corgan. Pete played along with nearly all of the guest musicians – including a rendition of Thunderclap Newman's 'Something In The Air' with Billy Corgan and run-throughs of 'Let My Love Open The Door' and 'The Kids Are Alright' with E – in addition to performing his own set, which consisted of 'Greyhound Girl', 'Endless Wire', 'Blue, Red And Grey', 'God Speaks Of Marty Robbins', 'Let's See Action', and 'In The Ether' with Fuller on piano.

[4] Sue Bundrick passed away on April 9, 2007.

The Who tour continued the following night at San Jose's HP Pavilion. Joel Selvin was present for the *San Francisco Chronicle*. "Although they sprinkled Who concert staples through the show, the programme concentrated on material from the new album that kept the audience in their seats. The songs from *Endless Wire* were so listless and obscure they made something like 'You Better You Bet' sound like a classic. Since when was 'Eminence Front' a towering peak in The Who repertoire? . . . The band played the six-song 'mini-rock opera' included on the new album . . . the songs just zipped by, inconsequential, harmless and obscure.

"Some of the other songs from *Endless Wire* – the pseudo-folkie 'A Man In A Purple Dress' or 'Black Widow's Eyes' – have some heft, but they are instant trivialities in The Who's distinguished catalogue . . . With The Who, Townshend is mired in music he made as a youth in the spirit of collaboration with three very disparate accomplices. The combination made some great rock music – as great as it gets. But now as a tribal elder, he appears caught between his desires to forge ahead and his debt to the past. He refuses to be simply an oldies act, reliving past glories, but his latest work is remote from the body of great work he created in those magic years with The Who."

By the time of The Who's performance on December 5 at Toronto's Air Canada Center, Daltrey's voice was feeling the strain. "As you can probably hear, I've got a bit of a cold tonight," he told the crowd. His illness meant that Townshend had to pick up the slack. "Guitarist Pete Townshend ably stepped forward to become the magnetic force that held the show together," Aaron Brophy of chartattack.com reported. "For a near senior citizen, Townshend was a ball of fury. Stooped over his guitar, he pounded out power chord after power chord before launching into trademark windmill spasms.

"His tones were vicious, snarling things, the sort of violent noises more closely associated with gutter punk than cinematic rock operas. It was a display of virulent guitar power that left his increasingly complacent peer group in the dust. Indeed, with Keith Richards reduced to foolish blubbering, Eric Clapton churning out increasingly tepid blues-pop and Neil Young ever oscillating between country, rock and misadventure, Townshend's dynamic bursts are now just about as close as any students of classic rock will ever get to reliving the primordial power of Seventies rock'n'roll."

Daltrey's illness continued from this point forward, but he fought throughout to deliver onstage. "Whatever I've got, you'll get," he told the crowd in Grand Rapids, Michigan on December 5. Following a show in Omaha two nights later, Roger was unable to finish the show in St Paul, Minnesota on December 8. "After clutching his chest throughout 'Won't Get Fooled Again', the obviously uncomfortable singer declared, "I'm going to make this night up to you. We'll come back,'" reported the *Minneapolis-St Paul Tribune*. "Well, he didn't even come back for the encore, leaving Townshend to sing three songs, including 'My Generation'." The customary *Tommy* medley was dropped.

As Daltrey took a much-needed break over the weekend, on December 9, another Attic Jam took place at Martyrs', a tiny Chicago club with a capacity crowd of 200. Guests for the evening's performance included singer/songwriters Alexi Murdoch and Joe Purdy, along with the usual regulars. In addition to accompanying Murdoch and Purdy on their own songs, Townshend duetted with Purdy on The Everly Brothers' 'Bye, Bye Love' and later performed 'Sunrise', 'In The Ether' (both with Fuller), 'Drowned', and 'God Speaks Of Marty Robbins'.

The second leg of The Who's 2006 US tour came to a close on December 11 in Columbus, Ohio. Daltrey's voice had improved since the previous show in Minneapolis, but his throat was clearly still suffering from the effects of his cold. "I have really bad bronchitis," Daltrey croaked. "But it was either we cancel the show or we play. But it doesn't fucking matter. It's rock'n'roll, right?"

According to Columbus' *The Other Paper*, at the show's close, when Daltrey had sung the last words of 'Tea & Theatre', "Pete turned to him and shouted loudly and joyfully, 'You fucking did it!' Then he gave the much smaller Daltrey a loving parental pat on the head as they walked off stage."

On January 21, 2007, Townshend performed alongside the likes of Steve Winwood, Paul Weller, and Joe Walsh as part of Dear Mr Fantasy, a charity concert at the Roundhouse celebrating the life of Traffic's Jim Capaldi, who had died of cancer two years earlier. Funds raised from the event went to Capaldi's pet charity, the Jubilee Action Street Children Appeal. As he had done at his 1974 solo appearance at the same venue, Townshend played Traffic's 'No Face, No Name, No Number' (off the band's debut 1967 *Mr. Fantasy* album) solo on acoustic guitar.

Two days after the concert, Townshend met with Daltrey and The Who's management to formulate plans for the next couple of years. "We all feel that 2009 – as the 40th anniversary of *Tommy* – will be one to celebrate; we may not be around for the 50th," Townshend wrote in a diary entry the following day. "This coming year already looks chock full, at least until the summer. We will soon announce European shows that begin in May, and will end in the festival season in July. It looks almost certain we will visit Japan, Australia and Hawaii in winter 2007. We also discussed the launch of a dedicated new Who website planned later this year. There is no schedule set for a new album, but I will probably drift into it using the same process as last time and start work at home."

That evening, Daltrey and Townshend attended the *South Bank Show* Awards, where they received an award for 'Outstanding Achievement'. "I sat next to the artists Gilbert and George, and that was a treat," Pete wrote. "We three agreed we looked like gathered bankers or vicars rather than the groundbreaking radicals we were and still are." The *Independent* quoted George as telling Pete, "Oh, you really were a handsome thing, weren't you? But look at you now, you look like a vicar or a bank manager." To which Townshend replied, 'Fuck off, so do you. We all do.'"

On February 8, at a press conference at the Hospital, a basement club in London's Covent Garden, Daltrey and Townshend announced The Who's 28-date, 14-country 2007 European tour, set to begin on May 8 in Lisbon, Portugal, and ending on July 9 in Helsinki, Finland. The pair played four songs – 'Won't Get Fooled Again', 'Behind Blue Eyes', 'Mike Post Theme', and 'Tea & Theatre' – with Townshend on acoustic, before answering questions from the media.

On February 12, Townshend and Fuller held a special Attic Jam at the Pigalle Club in Piccadilly Circus, London, to mark the release of *Attic Jam*, an iTunes-only compilation of 19 songs recorded during appearances by guests including The Raconteurs, The Zutons and The Flaming Lips.

"If somebody came and asked me to give permission for something I'd strummed away in the back of a caravan with people laughing and the microphone moving around, I just wouldn't do it," Townshend told the *Independent*. "These are big name bands, but she [Rachel] got all of them . . .

"We carried a satellite, we had sliding bandwidth. Most of the time it was about 5,000 or 6,000 but at Hyde Park it went up to 50,000. Going into that little caravan with a band like The Kooks and starting to chat was interesting. All the performers came and played live without any pretentiousness. It was the generosity of spirit that I found so extraordinary, and also the lack of that sense of being so up your own arse that you have to control everything. It might have been to do with the internet, or the festival season, but people felt they could play music, allow themselves to go into an informal environment. They didn't have a manager or a PR person looking over their shoulder."

"The sound isn't great and Fuller has an annoying habit of squawking, 'Aw, that was brilly-unt!' after every song, but there are some worthwhile tracks," wrote the *Guardian*'s Chris Salmon. "They include The Zutons' duet with Townshend on a breezy camp-fire version of The Who's 'Mary Anne With The Shaky Hand', Editors' menacing stripped-down version of 'All Sparks' and The Fratellis' sprightly 'Got Ma Nuts From A Hippie'. The album's flaw, though, is that while songs such as the distinctly under-rehearsed Who covers from The Flaming Lips ['Baba O'Riley'] and The Raconteurs ['The Seeker'] probably made for entertaining viewing, they simply don't stand up to a proper release." At the album's release party, Townshend performed 'Drowned' and 'The Acid Queen'.

Just before departing for America, on February 14, Townshend managed to squeeze in a trip to Wales to see the first official workshop theatre production of *Quadrophenia*. After Trevor Nunn's development of the idea stalled, Tom Critchley and Jeff Young, who had worked on the 1999 *Lifehouse* radio play, decided to take matters into their own hands. "When Jeff and I were working at Bristol Old Vic in 1993 we said, 'Wouldn't it be great to stage *Quadrophenia* together?'" Critchley told the *Western Mail*'s Karen Price in February 2007. "That was long before I'd even met Townshend . . . Pete was given the choice of a large-scale production or a more intimate production . . . he chose the latter option."

Like the stage version of *Tommy*, Critchley and Young's *Quadrophenia* featured no dialogue, being based on the original album rather than Franc Roddam's 1979 film. "Pete Townshend's frustration with the film was that the music was used as a background," Critchley told the *Western Mail*. "We are using the music and songs as our primary language. I believe this is some of the best narrative rock music ever written. Many of the current musicals seem to assemble songs around a flimsy story. We have one of the best pieces of rock music which needs no words."

Young and Critchley's interpretation, performed by a 12-member cast of students from the Royal Welsh College of Music and Drama, premiered at the Sherman Theatre, Cardiff, on 9 February. The play's eight-day run was intended as a test, with the hope of staging it in London's West End if reaction was sufficiently enthusiastic.

Preoccupied with the imminent Who tour, Townshend missed the premiere, and almost missed witnessing the show at all. "In the middle of packing, I suddenly realised at about 3 p.m. that if I didn't get in my car and drive, I would miss seeing the [play]," Pete wrote in his online blog. "On an impulse I set off west down the M4 motorway and three hours later was watching the show . . .

"The Cardiff show was a conventional production in two acts, and that made me very happy – I'm keen that whatever happens with *Quadrophenia* in its theatrical incarnation doesn't preclude it from being seen in older theatres. It featured a young, energetic company, and a terrific band with horns and strings. John O'Hara [who was involved with the Bush Hall presentation] was the music director and orchestrator, and he was very faithful to the nuances that make this piece my favourite. The choreography, set design and lighting were all excellent. There were some wonderful moments in the play, but I have high hopes we will move on to another production level soon, so I won't give too much away. What is important to say is that everyone threw so much passion, talent, energy and wonderment into their work that I felt humbled."

The following week, on February 19, Townshend attended Rachel Fuller's appearance at the Lincoln Triangle Barnes & Noble store. He was only peripherally involved in this event, as Fuller performed with Barnes & Noble CEO Steve Riggio's 18-year-old daughter Melissa, an aspiring poet and musician who had Downs Syndrome. She had recently been featured in a *National Geographic Kids* magazine article which caught Fuller's attention. Using Melissa's poetry, she and Fuller co-wrote and recorded two songs ('The Ring' and 'Love Is A Potion'), produced by Townshend. "[Melissa has] a lovely voice," he told the *New York Times*. "As a producer, I can't see any reason why with a bit of time, she couldn't make an album utterly of her own right." The event was emceed by Bob McGrath, an original character on the children's programme *Sesame Street*.

The following night, Townshend returned to New York City's Joe's Pub for his and Fuller's third Attic Jam at the venue. Guests included co-host, comedian Jimmy Fallon and musicians Amos Lee, Rachel Yamagata, Dinosaur Jr's J. Mascis, and most impressively, Lou Reed. "Amos Lee and Rachel Yamagata both began their sets alone, clearly floored to be on the same bill as Townshend – who joined them both on acoustic guitar for the conclusion of their brief sets," reported *Rolling Stone*'s Andy Greene.

"It was during J. Mascis's set, however, that the show shot into the stratosphere. Mascis, dressed in purple T-shirt, a black tracksuit jacket and an enormous pair of glasses, played a set of Dinosaur Jr tunes, before bringing Townshend out for the closer. "I'm a little surprised J. wanted to play this one," Pete said,[5] before singing the opening of 'See Me, Feel Me', which caused the entire audience – including a rather stoic Matt Dillon who had been stashed away in a corner booth – to go absolutely ballistic."

Townshend then launched into his own solo acoustic set which consisted of 'The Acid Queen', 'The Real Me', 'Drowned' and 'Won't Get Fooled Again'.

"If all this wasn't enough," wrote Greene, "as the clock approached midnight Lou Reed came onstage . . ."

Reed played electric guitar while Townshend played acoustic in their first-ever performance together. "It was great to see how it caught fire," Townshend told the *New York Post*. "It was magical for both of us."

The two sat side-by-side and launched into 'I'm Waiting For The Man', followed by 'White Light/White Heat', a choice Reed said was inspired by seeing Jack White play it recently. "Yeah, well, I'm better than Jack!" Townshend shot back. They closed their all-too-brief set with 'Pale Blue Eyes' (from the Velvet Underground's 1969 eponymous third album).

"Every previous In The Attic show has ended with a jam featuring all the guests," Greene concluded, "but apparently realising nothing could top the Townshend/Reed duets the show simply ended as a stunned crowd emptied onto the street."

The Who resumed touring – with Bundrick back on keyboards – on February 23 in Reno, Nevada. When snow-bound opening act Rose Hill Drive couldn't make the next show two nights later in Fresno, Simon Townshend played a solo acoustic set as an impromptu warm-up. Three more dates followed – Long Beach, Phoenix (in a disappointingly half-full US Airways Arena)[6] and San Diego before another Attic Jam took place on March 3 at the Hotel Café in Los Angeles.

Tenacious D (featuring comic actor Jack Black) opened the show with

---

[5] "[Mascis is] quite shy," Townshend told the *New York Post*. "At soundcheck I asked him, 'How do you want to do this?' He said he just wanted to do 'the end of Woodstock.' I said to him, 'I'm not entirely sure about this.'"

[6] Townshend dedicated 'Man In A Purple Dress' to Britney Spears, who had been in the press for bizarre behaviour, including shaving her head, and had entered rehab. After the crowd's laughter subsided, Pete explained that he wasn't joking, saying, "Let's not be too quick to judge is what I mean."

an over-the-top *Tommy* medley prior to Joe Purdy's set, which featured his father on mandolin. Pete also joined Purdy for a rendition of 'Let My Love Open The Door'. After Fuller's set (which featured Townshend providing acoustic guitar accompaniment on her rendition of Eels' 'It's A Motherfucker'), Pete joined Alexi Murdoch onstage for Murdoch's single 'Orange Sky'. Ben Harper followed, joined by Townshend and Fuller for his 'Diamonds On The Inside'. Townshend finished the evening with a Harper duet on 'I'm One', followed by 'The Acid Queen', 'The Real Me', 'Drowned', and 'Won't Get Fooled Again'.

The Who tour continued two nights later in Chicago, making up for the strain that Daltrey's vocals had been under when visiting the Windy City the previous September. However, the same problem returned to haunt him in Tampa, Florida, on March 13. "The group took the stage at 8.40 p.m., following an opening set by Rose Hill Drive," reported the *Tampa Tribune*. "Townshend slashed out the familiar three-chord riff opening 'I Can't Explain', but Daltrey walked offstage before singing a note. Townshend waved the song to a halt. 'Roger has bronchitis,' Townshend told the crowd. He and the other musicians left the stage for a few moments before Townshend returned with the bad news. 'I've just been with Roger and he can barely speak,' Townshend said. 'We're going to have to cancel.'"

The following day, to a standing ovation, Pete delivered the keynote address during the first day of the 21st annual South By Southwest (SXSW) Music and Media Conference in Austin, Texas, the recording industry's largest annual gathering. His speech, delivered to a packed Hilton Grand Ballroom, focused on the power of the internet.

"Music is about congregation, gathering and sharing. The gathering that the internet offers is meditation. You lose yourself when you're listening to good music." He also encouraged the practice of live webcasting as opposed to the common practice of delayed feeds. "What do we do with [live music broadcasts on] the internet? We delay them! You can have it later, when it fits into your work day. Fuck it – I want it live!"

Pete also used his speech to discuss his *Method* project, the beginning of the realisation of a dream he'd conjured more than 30 years earlier. Thanks to Lawrence Ball's software, users would soon be able to log on to a website, enter some personal information, and listen to a piece of music uniquely designed for them. A flyer stated, "*The Method* offers subscribers the opportunity to create their own unique musical composition by 'sitting' for the *Method* software composer, just as you would sit for a painter making your portrait." Pete told the audience that further details on the *Method* – which had already undergone testing using a small number of 'sitters' – would be revealed at a forthcoming press conference in London.

Later that day, Townshend appeared onstage at the Austin Music Awards, during a set by Ian McLagan and the Bump Band, guesting on The Small Faces' 'Whatcha Gonna Do About It' and Ronnie Lane's 'Kuschty Rye'. The following day marked a special SXSW edition of Attic Jam, which took place at Austin's La Zona Rosa. With British performer Mika running late, Townshend opened the show with 'Drowned', prior to giving way to Rachel Fuller, Willy Mason, Alexi Murdoch, Mika, Martha Wainwright, and Joe Purdy.

"Each performer played a song before Townshend and Fuller would join them onstage," reported *Earvolution*'s David Schultz. "Without exception, each musician had a look on their face that expressed their amazement that they were not only onstage with the legendary guitarist but that Townshend was accompanying them on their material.

"Purdy opted for one of Townshend's songs and their acoustic duet of 'Let My Love Open The Door' transformed the song from a cocky demand to a yearning plea. Ever the comic, Townshend kept the mood light, good-naturedly letting the various singer-songwriters shine while letting his star provide the glow . . .

"Accompanied by Fuller, Townshend sang 'In The Ether', the weakest effort off of The Who's recent *Endless Wire* before picking up the guitar and closing the show with what he believed to be the first ever public performance of 'I Can't Reach You' from *The Who Sell Out*. Given the wealth of material at his disposal, the performance of an obscure track from 40 years ago felt a tad anticlimactic."

On the third day of the festival, dressed in a dark suit and dark glasses, Townshend dropped in unannounced during The Fratellis' afternoon performance. Later that same day, Townshend and Fuller appeared in a performance at the Lone Star Lounge, broadcast live by Direct TV. Fuller performed several songs with guitarist Jolyon Dixon (who played on *Endless Wire*) prior to introducing Martha Wainwright and Townshend. Fuller, Townshend and Wainwright together played 'Factory', a Wainwright composition while Townshend and Fuller performed 'In The Mix' and 'Sunrise' together.

Meanwhile, as a result of Daltrey's bedridden battle with bronchitis, The Who's dates scheduled for Mexico City and San Antonio scheduled for March 17 and 20 respectively, were cancelled. Because the band were scheduled to play at the Royal Albert Hall at the end of the month, and with the make-up Tampa show having been rescheduled to March 25, it was not possible to reschedule the two cancelled dates.

Daltrey was sufficiently recovered for the tour to resume on March 22 in Little Rock, Arkansas, the band's first ever show in the city.

"Windy, rainy but nobody cares," Townshend wrote in a diary entry during a day off in Miami. "The rescheduled Tampa show is tomorrow, and I intend to throw sparks. Roger seems back closer to his usual self. There has been talk of an extension of the current tour in the USA through August. Under the present uncertain circumstances I have decided it might be better to abandon this plan, and get the European shows behind us first. I'm sorry to have raised the hopes of some fans in Vegas and the Northeast, but all good things must come to an end. The US tour is now two shows away from the end. Sad, but I'm looking forward to a proper rest in April without the stress of worrying about Roger's uncertain health."

Plans to take the tour to new Who territories like Mexico, South America, Russia and, possibly, China were put on hold. The day after the final show of the US tour, at the Seminole Hard Rock hotel and casino in Hollywood, Florida, The Who flew back to London to play the Royal Albert Hall on March 31 as part of the venue's annual week-long benefit for the Teenage Cancer Trust.[7]

Townshend wrote on his blog the day after the show that despite his jet-lag, "at the moment of truth the adrenalin of walking onto the stage last night kicked in and I careered off in a rock trance. I really have no idea what the show was like. I was too zapped for a soundcheck and it all felt very loud. The band seemed pretty great to me and Roger sang well after his recent troubles. We both desperately need a rest and we are about to get one."

On April 25 – more than 36 years after his press conference announcing *Lifehouse* at the Young Vic – Townshend held a press conference at Eel Pie Oceanic to officially unveil his long-held dream, the *Lifehouse Method*. Pete said that he wanted the launch of the internet-based *Method*, which would open to subscribers on May 1, to "in essence, close the book on the great lost project of *Lifehouse*, as a Who legendary non-event."

---

[7] Pete dropped in on frequent *Attic Jam* guest Joe Purdy's performance at the Bar Academy in Islington the night before The Who's Royal Albert Hall performance.

"Today it is possible to do what in 1971 I could only dream about," Townshend told *Pitchfork*'s Rob Mitchum in October 2006. "I have a website prepared, you visit it, enter some data, and get tailor-made music back. Your music, and that of everyone who visits the site, will blend together."

Townshend pointed out that the 1999 *Lifehouse* radio play was the final realisation of only one facet of his vision. "The *Method* is of course what I always called 'Barrel Two' of The Who's *Lifehouse* project – the bit we were supposed to actually make happen in reality. 'Barrel One' was what was finalised in the radio play – the fiction," Townshend told the author.

The breakthrough which led to the fruition of Pete's *Lifehouse Method* took place around 2004 when he began working with Lawrence Ball. "Lawrence listened to my brief, changed very little from the *Lifehouse* story of 1971, in which people logged onto a virtual internet Grid were each given their own tailor-made piece of music, and adapted a programme he calls 'Harmonic Maths' to deliver me what I wanted," Townshend told *PopMatters* in 2006.[8]

Visitors to the *Lifehouse Method* website could simply upload a sample of their voice, a sound, a rhythm, and an image, all of which should reflect the user in some way.

"Sitting online you are invited to share some sounds and visual material," Ball wrote in the liner notes of the double-CD collection entitled *Method Music – Imaginary Sitters, Imaginary Galaxies,* released on iTunes on April 23 and dedicated to Terry Riley. "This personal interface acts as a fine tuning that creates a very specific character and composition of music . . . When we become more aware, we see how our music fits together with that of others. 'Two Sitters' can be played together in parallel, either synchronising their beginnings, or the beginnings of any two segments. Pete's idea in his novella *The Boy Who Heard Music* is that we all have our own music, and at some great future event we might see how our music fits together with everybody else's . . ."

"This is a step in doing something which is a true, authentic, elegant artist process, based on the incredible [software] system," Townshend said at the press conference. "I love what this produces and my vision for it now is that I think, yes, we could have a gathering in some future time where we could share our music together." As of late summer 2007,

---

[8] Playing a key role in the adaptation of Ball's programme was software developer Dave Snowdon, who designed and engineered the *Method* web user interface.

several thousand 'sitters' had enrolled for a musical portrait on the *Method* website.[9]

Pete elaborated on his vision of a future *Method* 'concert' in an interview with BBC radio's Johnny Walker in July, 2006:

> *"My idea there is that maybe 1,000 people will produce really good interesting pieces of music, and the software has been constructed in such a way so that all the pieces of music fit together. We think — maybe we have this big gathering, invite all these people, we play a bit of the music, we chat to them, we talk to them, we congregate, in the flesh, and then we play all the music. And we'll see what it sounds like. My notion is that it'll probably sound a bit like the sea, but it could also sound like London on a bad day when you can't get a taxi in the rain, I don't know."*

Today, Pete Townshend splits his time between his homes in London and the south of France, prompting him to learn the native tongue as he told *France Metro* in early 2007, "I already speak a little German, but French is the language I wish I'd taken at school."

As a result of extra care over the last few years, Townshend has noticed an improvement in his hearing condition. "My upper-frequency hearing is actually returning, and that's become a great relief. I think one of the things about tinnitus and hearing damage is that you psychologically close yourself off. You don't fight for hearing. The reverse happens: You kind of say, 'No, no, please, no more loud noises. Stop. Stop!' . . . yesterday my alarm in my car went off, and I lifted up the bonnet to switch it off, and I couldn't get *near* it. I thought, 'If I get close to this fucking alarm, I'm going to blow my brain out.'"

He continues to work on his autobiography, entitled *Pete Townshend: (Who He?)*. Writing chronologically, as of autumn 2006, he had reached the end of the Sixties.

"When I have clear periods I sit and write and very much enjoy it. I can't do it in and around other work though. So it keeps getting delayed while I do all the other stuff . . . the complete uncondensed and unexpurgated book will probably now be published conventionally in 2010," Townshend told the author.

---

[9] "The website is still operating with a small beta group of testers, and the results are encouraging," Townshend told the *San Jose Mercury News*. "Some of my own sittings have produced music that amazes me. Not sure I like it. I fancy myself as a piece by Henry Purcell. I sound more like a rather sad Terry Riley. Still, pretty impressive for a piece of software."

As of early 2007, he had no publishing deal, "and no plans to pursue one." In February, Townshend's website was shut down, while a blog page – petetownshendwhohe.blogspot.com was opened where he periodically posted short extracts from his incomplete memoirs. However, by August, all the entries had been removed.

In addition to continuing work on his autobiography, Townshend has been tempted by the idea of another solo album.

"A lot of the songs [from *Endless Wire*] either I excluded from presenting to Roger or Roger passed on once he'd heard them, [because] they don't actually make a particularly powerful record," he told *Billboard*'s Jonathan Cohen in October 2006, "but wow, they would make an extremely interesting record. So I might actually look at the possibility of putting out a solo record. But again, the only reason I would do that is if I felt I could support it."

"I have enjoyed making solo records, especially working with Chris Thomas and Bill Price on the first three," he said in 2005. "I don't think I'll ever work that way again. I can't imagine how I would promote a solo record in the present millennium and who would want to buy it. I think my creative work is spread out now over a number of different arenas, and I have to face the fact that simply making a record has never quite felt enough to me – however good the finished product."

When asked if there are any plans afoot for a fourth *Scoop*, Townshend told the author, "Nothing planned. *Scoop*s I could knock out by the dozen, but I have no desire to trawl through all those thousands of tapes again – at least for a while longer."

His ongoing obsession to make *Lifehouse* a functioning reality continues to occupy his imagination: "I will never tire of exploring the notions behind *Lifehouse*, of audience congregation synthesising magic from music and how much more powerful that might be one day if we can 'congregate' using the web."

If anything positive resulted from the deaths of Keith Moon and John Entwistle it was – for Townshend and Daltrey – a deeper appreciation of their empathy for one another.

"After John died, I was left with one very clear relationship and that was with Roger, which was probably the least important to me in the band," Pete candidly admitted to the *New York Times*' Alan Light. "We had a lot of discussion that our friendship meant more to us than anything else."

"I don't care when people say we're not getting on – it's not fucking important," Daltrey told the *Observer*'s Simon Garfield. "All that matters is what exists onstage and in our music. In that music is our relationship, is our love. I have such a deep love and respect for him, and that goes through all of it. He forgives all my foibles, and I forgive all his, and underneath all that I love him dearly."

"Roger and I have found a way to work together now and we will not let it go," Pete told *France Metro* in early 2007, adding that he has "some ideas for a new record."

"While we can we will always perform together now in some shape or form," Townshend told newhousenews.com. "This is not an end, it really is a beginning for us. We two old buggers have one of the great banners of rock history to wave, and we are determined to wave it, partly in memory of our two buddies who flew the coop. Roger and I have each other, and that means more today than it did when we first crossed angry paths as kids in Acton in 1960, 46 years ago."

Acknowledgements

The 'amazing journey' behind this book began back in 1997 when I decided to gather information about Pete Townshend as a hobby – partly to fulfil an urge to write, and partly to learn more about my favourite artist. The project grew as the years passed, and in February 2005, I began a chapter-a-week posting of my 'book' online, at www.townshendbio.com. Several months and 20 chapters later, I had received a great deal of encouragement to publish what I'd written, from both Townshend fans and friends alike.

Accordingly, at the end of 2005, I published the first self-published version of this book as *Amazing Journey* via Lulu Press, an on-demand publisher. The following year, I met Pete Townshend in London, sold the book at a Who convention in Shepherd's Bush, and appeared at the Lulu Press booth at the Book Expo America in Washington, D.C. By this time, the book – which became a Lulu Press bestseller – had garnered a warm reception from hardcore Townshend fans, and had won positive praise from several publications, including *Mojo* magazine.

By late 2006, I'd landed an interview with Pete Townshend and by early 2007, I'd visited London again, had conducted several interviews, and was closing in on a conventional book deal.

At every turn in this adventure, I have encountered a host of friendly, warm, encouraging people. Without them, this project would not have been possible. I would therefore like to thank the following people for their assistance, support, encouragement, and advice:

Bonnie Bartman at Hawley-Cooke, Ross Butler, Sheree Bykofsky and Brian Rubin, Brian Cady, Rick Chapman, Chris Charlesworth, Martin and Christine Cook, Ron Dovey and the team who organised the 2006 Who Convention, Yvonne Elliman, Jason Gilder, Ross Halfin, Kay Hamada, Sarah Hardin, Stella Hernandez at the Meher Spiritual Center, Nicola Joss at Eel Pie, Matt Kent, Bob Kowalski at Stir Music, Martin Lewis, 'Irish' Jack Lyons, Lorne and George Patterson, Carrie Pratt at www.longliverock.org, Mark Richardson, Dave Rimmer, Johnny Rogan, Ken Small, Amy Smith,

Scott Smith at www.thewho.net, David Spain and the staff at Lulu.com, Eddie Vedder, Rich 'WhiteFang' Weiner, and Lianna Wingfield.

I would also like to thank everyone who viewed the original edition of this biography on my website, www.townshendbio.com, and those who took the time to read and review *Amazing Journey*. Your support and feedback was greatly appreciated.

As well as a special thanks to Pete Townshend, much appreciation is due to the following interviewees, some of whom welcomed me into their homes, all of whom graciously and patiently answered this novice writer's many questions: Peter Amott, Jon Astley, Chris Charlesworth, Sheila Krynski, 'Irish' Jack Lyons, Chris Morphet, John Otway, Tony Palmer, Alan Pittaway, Doug Sandom, Richard Stanley, Simon Townshend, and Dana Wiffen.

Finally, a project of this scope could not have been completed without the support and understanding of my family – my wife Melissa, and my children Alex, Nick and Sam. Without their selfless love and determination to help me see this project through to its completion, I would surely have failed. This book is therefore dedicated to them.

Mark Wilkerson

References

In addition to the following references, information in this book is drawn from interviews conducted by the author, liner notes, promotional interviews, press kits, transcripts and recordings of radio and television interviews, and postings on Pete Townshend's web site, www.petetownshend.com, which was active from November 1999 to February 2007. The majority of the articles listed below were obtained from library archives.

The following websites are also indispensable sources of information for fans of The Who and Pete Townshend:

Fan sites:
www.thewho.info
www.thewho.net
www.thewho.org
www.thewhothismonth.com
www.quadrophenia.net

Official sites:
www.eelpie.com
www.longliverock.org
www.intheattic.tv
www.lifehouse-method.com

Books

Atkins, John, *The Who On Record*, London, McFarland & Company, 2000.
Baba, Meher, *Discourses*, Myrtle Beach, SC., Sheriar Press, 2000.
Baba, Meher, *The Everything And The Nothing*, Myrtle Beach, SC., Sheriar Press, 2000.
Barnes, Richard, *Mods!* London, Plexus Publishing, 1991.
Barnes, Richard, *The Who: Maximum R & B*, New York, Plexus, 1996.
Black, Johnny, *Eyewitness The Who*, London, Carlton, 2001.
Charlesworth, Chris, *The Complete Guide To The Music Of The Who*, London, Omnibus Press, 1995.
Charlesworth, Chris, *Pete Townshend: A Career Biography*, London, Proteus, 1984.

Charlesworth, Chris, *The Who: The Illustrated Biography*, New York, Omnibus Press, 1982.

Clark, Steve, *The Who In Their Own Words*, New York, Delilah/Putnam, 1979.

DeLeon, Delia, *The Ocean Of Love*, Myrtle Beach, SC, Sheriar Press, 1991.

Fletcher, Tony, *Moon: The Life And Death Of A Rock Legend*, New York, Avon, 1999.

Goldrich, Henry, and Goldrich Schoenfeld, Holly, *The Wall Of Fame: New York City's Legendary Manny's Music*, Milwaukee, WI., Hal Leonard, 2007.

Guiliano, Geoffrey, *Behind Blue Eyes*, New York, Penguin Putnam, 1997.

Grundy, Stuart and Tobler, John, *The Guitar Greats*, London, BBC, 1983.

Grundy, Stuart and Tobler, John, *The Record Producers*, London, BBC, 1982.

Marsh, Dave, *Before I Get Old: The Story of The Who*, New York, St Martin's Press, 1983.

McMichael, Joe, and Lyons, Jack, *The Who Concert File*, London, Omnibus Press, 1997 (revised in 2004).

McKnight, Connor and Silver, Caroline, *The Who: Through The Eyes Of Pete Townshend*, New York, Scholastic Books, 1974.

Motion, Andrew, *The Lamberts: George, Constant And Kit*, London, Hogarth Press, 1987.

Murray, Charles Shaar, *Boogie Man*, New York, St Martin's Press, 2000.

Neill, Andrew, *A Fortnight Of Furore*, Muttley Press, 1998.

Neill, Andy, and Kent, Matt, *Anyway Anyhow Anywhere: The Complete Chronicle Of The Who 1958–1978*, New York, Barnes and Noble Books, 2002 (revised in 2005).

Oldham, Andrew Loog, *2Stoned*, London, Vintage, 2003.

Palmer, Tony, *Born Under A Bad Sign*, London, William Kimber, 1970.

Patterson, Meg, *Getting Off The Hook: Addictions Can Be Cured By N.E.T.*, Wheaton IL., Harold Shaw, 1983.

Patterson, Meg, *Dr. Meg*, Milton Keynes, Nelson Word, 1994.

Purdom, C. B., *The God-Man*, Crescent Beach, SC, Sheriar Press, 1969.

Shaffner, Nicholas, *Saucerful Of Secrets: The Pink Floyd Odyssey*, New York, Dell, 1991.

Smith, Larry David, *Pete Townshend: The Minstrel's Dilemma*, Connecticut, Praeger, 1999.

Swenson, John, *Headliners – The Who*, New York, Ace Books, 1979.

Townshend, Pete, with Young, Jeff, *Lifehouse*, London, Simon & Schuster, 1999.

Townshend, Pete, *The Who's Tommy*, New York, Pantheon Books, 1993.

Townshend, Pete, *Horse's Neck*, New York, Harper & Row, 1985.

Townshend, Pete, and Barnes, Richard, *The Story Of Tommy*, London, Eel Pie Publishing, 1977.

Tremlett, George, *The Who*, London, Futura, 1975.

Wholey, Dennis, *The Courage To Change*, New York, Warner, 1984.

Wolter, Stephen and Kimber, Karen, *The Who In Print*, Jefferson, NC., McFarland and Co., 1992.

Magazine/Internet articles

(unsigned), "Coming your way – Tamla Motown." *Melody Maker*, 6 June 1964.
(unsigned), "The Who." *Melody Maker*, 9 January 1965.
(unsigned), "Who – And Why." *Melody Maker*, 20 March 1965.
(unsigned), "The Who." *Melody Maker*, 5 June 1965.
(unsigned), "The Who Use Force To Get Sound They Want!", *NME*, 18 June 1965.
(unsigned), "Who Make Drastic Policy Changes." *Melody Maker*, 17 July 1965.
(unsigned), "The Beat Elite." *Melody Maker*, 25 September 1965.
(unsigned), "Who Split Mystery." *Melody Maker*, 20 November 1965.
(unsigned), "Who Hates Who?" *Melody Maker*, 11 December 1965.
(unsigned), "Who In Record Rumpus." *Melody Maker*, 12 March 1966.
(unsigned), "Who's Record Row Still Rages." *Melody Maker*, 19 March 1966.
(unsigned), "Who Record Injunction Is Lifted." *Melody Maker*, 26 March 1966.
(unsigned), "At Last! Entwistle's Silence Is Broken." *Melody Maker*, 16 April 1966.
(unsigned), "Who Cause Thousands Of Pounds Of Damage At Festival." *Melody Maker*, 6 August 1966.
(unsigned), "*I'm A Boy*." *NME*, 27 August 1966.
(unsigned), "Smash – Up TV Show For Who." *Melody Maker*, 1 October 1966.
(unsigned), "Schhh . . . You Know Who." *Melody Maker*, 8 October 1966.
(unsigned), "Who – Finally Reaching The Sounds They All Search For." *Melody Maker*, 19 November 1966.
(unsigned), "Who In New Single Delay." *Melody Maker*, 10 December 1966.
(unsigned), "*Pictures of Lily*." *Melody Maker*, 22 April 1967.
(unsigned), "Who Move Into A Class Of Their Own." *Melody Maker*, 29 April 1967.
(unsigned), "Really Smashing." *Guitar Player*, October 1967.
(unsigned), "The Who Sell Out – And How!" *Melody Maker*, 16 December 1967.
(unsigned), "Tour Extended." *Melody Maker*, 4 May 1968.
(unsigned), "Traffic Warden Takes Magic From Who's Bus!" *NME*, 19 October 1968.
(unsigned), "Scene", *The Village Voice*, 22 January 1970.
(unsigned), "Five Days That Rocked Britain." *Melody Maker*, 5 September 1970.
(unsigned), "Who's Future In The World of Science Fantasy! At Last Pete Tells All! *Disc and Music Echo*, 24 October 1970.
(unsigned), "Quadrophonic Beach Boys." *Melody Maker*, 7 November 1970.
(unsigned), "Pete's Plan for the "New" Who," *Record Mirror*, January 1971.
(unsigned), "It's About Time For Townshend," *Rolling Stone*, 5 August 1971.
(unsigned), "Pete Townshend at 26. Just an Old Fashioned Guy," *NME*, 21 August 1971.

(unsigned), "Pete Townshend Won't Get Fooled Again," *Crawdaddy*, 28 August 1971.

(unsigned), "Time For The Who To Put Their Balls On The Rails," *Time Out*, 27 August–21 September 1971.

(unsigned), "Beaty, Big and Bouncy Who." *Melody Maker*, 13 November 1971.

(unsigned), "Pete Townshend," *NME*, 1 April 1972.

(unsigned), "Townshend Delay." *Melody Maker*, 23 September 1972.

(unsigned), "*Who Came First* (review)." *Rolling Stone*, December 1972.

(unsigned), "*Tommy* Repeat For Rainbow." *Melody Maker*, 27 October 1973.

(unsigned), "Who's Quad Christmas!" *Melody Maker*, 10 November 1973.

(unsigned), "Dr. Who Signed." *Melody Maker*, 8 December 1973.

(unsigned), "Random Notes." *Rolling Stone*, 20 December 1973.

(unsigned), "Who La La!" *Melody Maker*, 16 February 1974.

(unsigned), "Chatting With Pete Townshend," *Zig Zag*, July 1974.

(unsigned), "Let's Stay Together." *NME*, 18 October 1975.

(unsigned), "*Rough Mix* (review)." *Rolling Stone*, 6 October 1977.

(unsigned), "Who Said That!" *NME* 12 August 1978.

(unsigned), "Townshend," *Penthouse*, December 1974.

(unsigned), "Peter Townshend Sees Videodisk As Wave Of Rock Music's Future; Who Plans Video-Angled Albums." *Variety*, 9 May 1979.

(unsigned), "Polygram's 100% Bankrolling Of The Who's Pix Paves Way For Major Move Into Production." *Variety*, 9 May 1979.

(unsigned), "The Who Set To Show Cannes The What & How Of Ballyhoo." *Variety*, 9 May 1979.

(unsigned), "The Who Survives From 1960s As Disk-Concert-Pix Industry; 'Tommy' Take Tops $60-Mil." *Variety*, 9 May 1979.

(unsigned), "Who Aiming At 'Fever,' 'Grease' Pix-LP Parlay." *Variety*, 9 May 1979.

(unsigned), "Who's Roger Daltrey Scores As Film Thesp, Sparks New Project." *Variety*, 9 May 1979.

(unsigned), "Deaths at Who Date Seen Spurring Tighter Security at Concerts." *Variety*, 5 December 1979.

(unsigned), "Blame For Crush That Killed Who Fans Laid To Four Major Factors; Cincy Mayor Moves On New Rules." *Variety*, 12 December 1979.

(unsigned), "Who Cincy Concert Results In $27-Mil. Negligence Action." *Variety*, 19 December 1979.

(unsigned), "The Who sign with Warner Brothers" *Rolling Stone*, 6 March 1980.

(unsigned), "Simon Napier-Bell Producing 'Fictionalized' Kit Lambert Life." *Variety*, 17 June 1981.

(unsigned), "Punitive Damages Nixed In Case Of Concert Tragedy." *Variety*, 15 December 1982.

(unsigned), "The Who – The Final Concert (review)." *Variety*, 22 December 1982.

(unsigned), "*Scoop* (review)." *People Weekly*, 4 April 1983.

(unsigned), "Townshend Splits The Who." *Melody Maker*, 24 December 1983.

(unsigned), "*Horse's Neck* (review)." *Time*, 30 September 1985.

(unsigned), "*Empty Glass* (review)." *Rolling Stone*, 16 November 1989.

(unsigned), "Poet Ted Hughes Dies." www.bbc.co.uk, 29 October 1998.

(unsigned), "Townshend Eyes Great White Way." www.wallofsound.com, 25 March 1999.

(unsigned), "Who-Ray!" www.nme.com, 28 November 2000.

(unsigned), "The Who's Entwistle Dies On Eve Of Tour." www.cnn.com, 27 June 2002.

(unsigned), "Fans Touched By Who gig." www.bbc.co.uk, 2 July 2002.

(unsigned), "Who Launch Tour After Death Of Bassist." *Associated press release*, 2 July 2002.

(unsigned), "The Who Play On, Four Days After Bassist's Death." *Reuters press release*, 2 July 2002.

(unsigned), "Final Farewell To Entwistle." www.bbc.co.uk, 10 July 2002.

(unsigned), "Cocaine Killed The Who star." www.bbc.co.uk, 26 July 2002.

(unsigned), "Trips For Kids Names Honorary Board." www.bikemag.com, 4 November 2002.

(unsigned), "Townshend 'Wrong' Over Child Porn." www.bbc.co.uk, 12 January 2003.

(unsigned), "Police Arrest Who Star In Child Porn Inquiry." www.cnn.com, 13 January 2003.

(unsigned), "Police Arrest Townshend." www.bbc.co.uk, 13 January 2003.

(unsigned), "Who Star Released On Bail." www.cnn.com, 14 January 2003.

(unsigned), "Who Star Townshend Bailed." www.bbc.co.uk, 14 January 2003.

(unsigned), "Who Star Freed After Porn Arrest." www.cnn.com, 14 January 2003.

(unsigned), "Townshend Victim Of 'Witch-hunt'." www.cnn.com, 11 February 2003.

(unsigned), "Townshend Affirmed." *Rolling Stone*, 6 March 2003.

(unsigned), "Who Star Cautioned Over Child Porn." www.cnn.com, 7 May 2003.

(unsigned), "Caution For Who Star Townshend." www.bbc.co.uk, 7 May 2003.

(multiple authors), "The Who: The Inside Story." *Mojo*, March 2004.

(unsigned), "The Who Live Raise $3.4m For Charity." www.therockradio.com, 13 June 2006.

(unsigned), "The Who Close The Proms." *NME*, 30 October 2006.

(unsigned), "Pete Townshend." *Q*, November 2006.

(unsigned), "Billy Corgan Plays Low-key Show With Pete Townshend." www.nme.com, 8 November 2006.

(unsigned), "New Solo Pete Townshend Collection Out Now." www.therockradio.com, 31 January 2007.

(unsigned), "Pete Townshend Delivers SXSW Keynote." www.nme.com, 15 March 2007.

Altham, Keith, "Who Admit They're Feuding." *NME*, 10 December 1965.

Altham, Keith, "Who Are Going Around In 'Circles'." *NME*, 18 March 1966.

Altham, Keith, and Smith, Alan, "Mightiest Ever!" *NME*, 6 May 1966.

Altham, Keith, "Lily Isn't Pornographic, Say Who." *NME*, 20 May 1967.

Altham, Keith, "California Screaming." *NME*, 24 June 1967.

Altham, Keith, "Who All Ready To Hit You With New Ideas." *NME*, 28 October 1967.

Altham, Keith, "Pete Townshend Keeps The Who Live." *NME*, 16 November 1968.

Altham, Keith, "The Rock'n'Roll Circus." *NME*, 21 December 1968.

Aquilante, Dan, "Townshend Tells All On Lost Who Album." www.nypost.com, 2 July 2000.

Arrington, Carl, "Pete Townshend: Who's He?" *Creem*, November 1980.

Atlas, Jacoba, "Caught In The Act: Who In LA." *Melody Maker*, 25 December 1971.

Bailey, Andrew, "Roger Daltrey: A Who Sings His Heart Out In The Country." *Rolling Stone*, 26 April 1973.

Benton, Michael, "Who's Next Monster." *Melody Maker*, 23 December 1972.

Bierbaum, Tom, "Hope The Who Date Will Hype Pay-View Status." *Variety*, 15 December 1982.

Bohn, Chris, "You Better You Bet." *NME*, 28 February 1981.

Brandle, Lars, "Townshend's 'Method' Finally Ready For Unveiling." www.billboard.com, 25 April 2007.

Brooks, Michael, "Peter Townshend." *Guitar Player*, May/June 1972.

Brophy, Aaron, "Townshend Bails Daltrey Out At Who Gig." www.chartattack.com, 5 December 2006.

Brown, Mick, "Who's Still Angry? Roger Daltrey is." *Rolling Stone*, 2 June 1977.

Browne, David, "*Tommy* (review)." *Entertainment Weekly*, 7 May 1993.

Burman, John, "*The Kids Are Alright*." www.hollywoodreporter.com, 24 September 2003.

Burr, Ty, "Rock Opera Wizard." *Entertainment Weekly*, 25 June 1993.

Bushell, Gary, "*It's Hard*." *Sounds*, Sept. 1982.

Carr, Roy, "*Join Together*." *NME*, 17 June 1972.

Carr, Roy, "Pete Townshend: *Who Came First*." *NME*, 7 October 1972.

Carr, Roy, "Pete Townshend." *NME*, 24 May 1975.

Carr, Roy, "That Was Then." *NME*, 4 October 1975.

Cavanagh, David, "Pete Townshend." *Q*, January 2000.

Charlesworth, Chris, "I See A Mad Moon Rising!" *Melody Maker*, 7 November 1970.

Charlesworth, Chris, "Whole Lotta Who Gear." *Melody Maker*, 7 November 1970.

Charlesworth, Chris, "Where To Now, Who?" *Melody Maker*, 17 July 1971.

Charlesworth, Chris, "Caught In The Act: The Who." *Melody Maker*, 23 October 1971.

Charlesworth, Chris, "Rock Comes In From The Cold – At The Rainbow." *Melody Maker*, 13 November 1971.

Charlesworth, Chris, "*Meaty, Beaty, Big And Bouncy*." *Melody Maker*, 4 December 1971.

Charlesworth, Chris, "Thumbs Down In Rome . . ." *Melody Maker*, 23 September 1972.

Charlesworth, Chris, "Personal Opinion." *Melody Maker*, 23 December 1972.

Charlesworth, Chris, "Giving It All Away." *Melody Maker*, 7 April 1973.

Charlesworth, Chris, "A Piece Of Cake." *Melody Maker*, 8 December 1973.

Charlesworth, Chris, "March Of The Mod." *Melody Maker*, 18 May 1974.

Cheal, David, "A Whiff Of The Old Magic." www.telegraph.co.uk, 1 November 2000.

Clarke, Steve, "Silver Screen: *The Kids Are Alright*." *NME*, 30 June 1979.

Cober-Lake, Justin, "Our Story Is A Perennial One: An Interview With Pete Townshend." www.popmatters.com, 10 November 2006.

Cocks, Jay, "A New Triumph For The Who." *Time*, 1 October 1979.

Cocks, Jay, "Rock's Outer Limits." *Time*, 17 December 1979.

Cohen, Jonathan, "Pete Townshend and Eddie in Secret NYC Club Show." www.spin.com, 29 July 1997.

Cohen, Jonathan, "The Who launches Tour After Entwistle's Death." www.billboard.com, 2 July 2002.

Cohen, Jonathan, "Who Needs Webcasting? Not Us, Daltrey Says." www.billboard.com, 27 July, 2006.

Cohen, Jonathan, "Townshend Mulling Solo Set, Hopes To Jam With Vedder." www.billboard.com, 10 October 2006.

Cohen, Jonathan, "Townshend Townshend Reveals The 'Method' To His Madness At SXSW." www.billboard.com, 14 March 2007.

Coleman, Ray, "Who's Next." *Melody Maker*, 21 August 1971.

Collins, Abbie, "Isle of Wight Festival 2004 Review Day 2." www.bbc.co.uk. 21 June 2004.

Collins, Michael, "Pete Townshend: Busy Days." *Rolling Stone*, 20 June 1974.

Connelly, Christopher, "1982: Who Won, Who Lost; Winner: The Who." *Rolling Stone*, 17 February 1983.

Coon, Caroline, "Squeeze Box." *Melody Maker*, 17 January 1976.

Cooney, Patrick, "The Modfather." www.telegraph.co.uk, 10 January 1998.

Cott, Jonathan, "A Talk With Pete Townshend." *Rolling Stone*, 14 May 1970.

Crook, John, "Daltrey Blasts Press, Politicos for Townshend's Ordeal." www.zap2it.com, 30 September 2003.

Dawbarn, Bob, "Dogs." *Melody Maker*, 15 June 1968.

DeCurtis, Anthony, "Opera Man: The *Rolling Stone* Interview With Pete Townshend." *Rolling Stone*, 23 December 1993.

DeCurtis, Anthony, "Opinion." *Rolling Stone*, 24 June 1993.

DeCurtis, Anthony, "Getting Old With The Who." www.rollingstone.com, 20 July 2000.

Denselow, Robin, "Townshend Prays, Writes New Opera." *Rolling Stone*, 26 October 1972.

Di Perna, Alan, "*Tommy*." *Guitar World*, June 1999.

Di Perna, Alan, "Machine Gun." *Guitar World Acoustic*, No. 38, Summer 2000.

Di Perna, Alan, "Smoke Stack Lightning." *Guitar World*, September 2002.

Doherty, Harry, "The Who / The Stranglers / AC/DC / Nils Lofgren: Wembley Stadium, London." *Melody Maker*, 25 August 1979.

Du Noyer, Paul, "Interview: Pete Townshend." *The Record*, August 1982.

Du Noyer, Paul, "*It's Hard.*" *NME*, 4 September 1982.

Elder, Bruce, "The Danger Behind The Daltrey Mask." *Melody Maker*, 16 August 1980.

Eliscu, Jenny, "Pete Townshend Opens the *Lifehouse* Door." www.rollingstone.com, February 28, 2000.

Eliscu, Jenny, "People of the Year: Pete Townshend." *Rolling Stone*, December 14–21, 2000.

Eliscu, Jenny, "Pete Townshend Says Who Reunion A Cure For Loneliness." *Rolling Stone*, June 16, 2000.

Eliscu, Jenny, "Pete Townshend Speaks Out." www.rollingstone.com, May 20, 2003.

Eliscu, Jenny, "Dr Who." *Rolling Stone*, October 22, 2006.

Epstein, Dan, "Feel Me: Pete Townshend And Raphael Rudd – *The Oceanic Concerts* (review)." *Guitar World Acoustic*, no. 48, 2001.

Erlewine, Stephen Thomas, "*Endless Wire* (review)." www.allmusic.com, 2006.

Evans, Allen, "My Generation." *NME*, 17 December 1965.

Evans, Paul, "*Psychoderelict* (review)." *Rolling Stone*, 19 August 1993.

Fantoni, Barry, "Various Artists: *Tommy.*" *Melody Maker*, 9 December 1972.

Fletcher, Tony, "Red, White And Who." *Revolver*, Fall 2000.

Flippo, Chet, "Entwistle: Not So Silent After All." *Rolling Stone*, 5 December 1974.

Flippo, Chet, "Rock & Roll Tragedy." *Rolling Stone*, 24 January 1980.

Fricke, David, "*Scoop* (review)." *Rolling Stone*, 14 April 1983.

Fricke, David, "*Another Scoop* (review)." *Rolling Stone* #498, 1987.

Fricke, David, "Pete Townshend." *Rolling Stone*, 5 November–10 December 1987.

Fricke, David, "*The Iron Man* (review)." *Rolling Stone*, 10 August 1989.

Fricke, David, "Then & Wow." *Rolling Stone*, 29 April 2004.

Fricke, David, "*Endless Wire* (review)." www.rollingstone.com, 27 October 2006.

Fu, Lily, "Recording Academy Names Lifetime Achievement And Trustees Award Recipients." www.grammy.com, 9 January 2001.

Gambaccini, Paul, "Quadromania: The Who Fuss, Fight And Hit The Road." *Rolling Stone*, 4 December 1975.

Gambaccini, Paul, "British rockers Unite In Concerts For Kampuchea." *Rolling Stone*, 21 February 1980.

Garbarini, Vic, "Pete Townshend: Behind Chinese Eyes." *Musician*, August/September 1982.

Gardner, Elysa, "Pete Townshend (performance review)." *Rolling Stone*, 2 September 1993.

Geelsin, Ned, "*White City* (review)." *People Weekly*, 16 December 1985.

Gilbert, Pat, "Bigger Than Mod." *Mojo*, September 2000.

Gill, Chris, "Psychodrama: Pete Townshend Stages His Return." *Guitar Player*, September 1993.

Givens, Ron, "*Psychoderelict* (review)." *People Weekly*, 5 July 1993.

Glasner, Joanna, "Perilous Fall Of Pixelon." www.wired.com, 16 May 2000

Goddard, Simon, "See Me, Feel Me." *Uncut*, April 2004.

Goldman, Albert, "Gap-bridging Triumph Of Rock: The Who At The Met." *Life*, June 1970.

Goldman, Vivien, "*Don't Let Go The Coat*." *NME*, 9 May 1981.

Graff, Gary, "Not F-F-Fade Away." *Guitar One*, September 2000.

Graff, Gary, "Older, Wiser Townshend Focuses On 'Unfinished Business'." www.yahoo.com, 16 June 2000.

Graff, Gary, "Pete Townshend Says No Jamming With Page & Crowes." www.launch.com, 13 June 2000.

Graff, Gary, and Simon, Bruce, "The Who Rehearse? Only A Little, Says Pete Townshend. www.launch.com, 1 June 2000.

Graff, Gary, "The Who – The Blues To The Bush." www.wallofsound.com, 10 May 2000.

Graff, Gary, "Townshend's *Lifehouse* Triumph." www.launch.com, 28 February 2000.

Green, Richard, "Who Try To Ward Off Trouble." *NME*, 22 March 1969.

Green, Richard, "Who's Sick Opera." *NME*, 24 May 1969.

Green, Richard, "200,000 Roar Approval." *NME*, 6 September 1969.

Green, Richard, "Who 'Leeds' The Pack." *NME*, 16 May 1970.

Green, Richard, "Woodstock: Best film Ever Made About Pop." *NME*, 23 May 1970.

Greene, Andy, "The Rock Was Opera At Pete Townshend's Star-Studded NYC Show." www.rollingstone.com, 21 February 2007.

Gross, Jonathan, "The Who: A Last Stand." *The Record*, December 1982.

Halfin, Ross, "Mods & Sods." *Guitar World*, September 2002.

Harris, John, "Did Loads Of Drugs, Made Loads Of Money, Smashed Loads Of Guitars." *Q*, June 1996.

Heath, Chris, "The *Rolling Stone* Interview." *Rolling Stone*, 8 August 2002.

Heath, Chris, "Townshend Fights Back." *Rolling Stone*, 20 February 2003.

Henke, James, "Who To Rake In Millions On Tour." *Rolling Stone*, 14 October 1982.

Henry III, William A., "*Tommy* (review)." *Time*, 3 May 1993.

Hewitt, Paulo, "The Punk And The Godfather." *Melody Maker*, 11 October 1980.

Hewitt, Paulo, "The Kids Are Alright." *Melody Maker*, 17 January 1981.

Hiltbrand, David, "*The Iron Man*: The Musical (review)." *People Weekly*, 18 September 1989.

Holder, Noddy, "Blind Date." *Melody Maker*, 28 August 1971.

Hopkins, Jerry, "Keith Moon Bites Back." *Rolling Stone*, 21 December 1972.

Hopkins, Jerry, "One-man Wrecking Crew." *Rolling Stone*, 19 October 1978.

Hughes, Rob, "The Wild Bunch." *Uncut*, October 2001.

Jisi, Chris, "Mister Fantastic!" *Bass Player*, March 2004.

Johnson, Derek, "*I Can't Explain*." *NME*, 15 January 1965.

Johnson, Derek, "*Anyway, Anyhow, Anywhere*." *NME*, 21 May 1965.

Johnson, Derek, "*My Generation*." *NME*, 29 October 1965.

Johnson, Derek, "*Substitute*." *NME*, 11 March 1966.

Johnson, Derek, "*A Legal Matter*." *NME*, 18 March 1966.

Johnson, Derek, "*The Kids Are Alright*." *NME*, 19 August 1966.

Johnson, Derek, "*Ready Steady Who / La-La-La-Lies*." *NME*, 11 November 1966.

Johnson, Derek, "*The Seeker*." *NME*, 21 March 1970.

Johnson, Derek, "*See Me, Feel Me*." *NME*, 17 October 1970.

Johnson, Derek, "*Let's See Action*." *NME*, 16 October 1971.

Jones, Nick, "Well, What is Pop Art?" *Melody Maker*, 3 July 1965.

Jones, Nick, "The Price Of Pop Art." *Melody Maker*, 28 August 1965.

Jones, Nick, "Who: Where To?" *Melody Maker*, 10 September 1966.

Jones, Nick, "*Psychedelicamania* At Roundhouse." *Melody Maker*, 7 January 1967.

Jones, Nick, "Pictures Of The Who." *Melody Maker*, 29 April 1967.

Jones, Nick, "Second Thoughts On Monterey." *Melody Maker*, July 1967.

Jones, Nick, "The Last Time / Under My Thumb." *Melody Maker*, 8 July 1967.

Jones, Nick, "I Became A Hero – Smashing Guitars!" *Melody Maker*, 14 October 1967.

Jones, Nick, "Who Killed Flower Power?" *Melody Maker*, 28 October 1967.

Kaufman, Mike, "I Am Completely Unstoppable." *Mojo*, July 1996.

Kaye, Lenny, "*Quadrophenia*: Who's Essay On Mod Era." *Rolling Stone*, 26 December 1973.

Kent, Matt, "*Lifehouse* Interview." www.petetownshend.com, August 1999.

Kroll, Jack, "From The Who To The Whom." *Newsweek*, 3 May 1993.

Lappen, John, "Roger Daltrey." *Music Connection*, 15 August 1994.

Lewis, Alan, "A Happy Resting Place at Plumpton." *Melody Maker*, 16 August 1969.

Loder, Kurt, "Townshend cuts solo disc; Who set North American dates." *Rolling Stone*, 17 April 1980.

Loder, Kurt, "The Rolling Stone Interview: Pete Townshend." *Rolling Stone*, 24 June 1982.

Loder, Kurt, "*All The Best Cowboys Have Chinese Eyes* (Review)." *Musician*, August 1982.

Loder, Kurt, "Last Time Around." *Rolling Stone*, 11 November 1982.

Loder, Kurt, "*Who's Last* (review)." *Rolling Stone*, February 1985.

Logan, Nick, "Won't Get Fooled Again." *Melody Maker*, 26 June 1971.

Logan, Nick, "Who Enter Period of Self Examination," *NME* 17 July 1971.

MacFarlane, David, "Pay-TV Concert Flops As Who Wrap Up Tour." *Rolling Stone*, 3 February 1983.

Marcus, Greil, "The Who On Tour/Magic Bus." *Rolling Stone*, 9 November 1968, pg. 21.

Marcus, Greil, "*Live At Leeds* (review)." *Rolling Stone*, July 1970.

Marcus, Greil, "The Who: Who Are You (review)." *Rolling Stone*, 19 October 1978.

Marcus, Greil, "The Different Drummer." *Rolling Stone*, 19 October 1978.

Marcus, Greil, "The *Rolling Stone* Interview: Pete Townshend." *Rolling Stone*, 26 June 1980.

Marlowe, Chris, "Online Revenue G-g-generation: A Q&A With Pete Townshend." www.hollywoodreporter.com, 15 June 2001.

Marsh, Dave, "The Who: The Who By Numbers (review)." *Rolling Stone*, 20 November 1975.

Marsh, Dave, "The Who Come To A Fork In The Road." *Rolling Stone*, 5 October 1978.

Marsh, Dave, "Keith Moon 1947–1978." *Rolling Stone*, 19 October 1978.

Marsh, Dave, "Rock & Roll Religion The Hard Way." *Rolling Stone*, 26 June 1980.

Marsh, Dave, "All The Best Cowboys Have Chinese Eyes (review)." *The Record*, August 1982.

Marsh, Dave, "*Psychoderelict* (review)." *Playboy*, October 1993.

Marsh, Dave, "Betrayed By Rock'n'Roll." *Mojo*, July 1996.

Marsh, Dave, "Who Are We." *Mojo*, December 2006.

Marten, Neville, "Behind Blue Eyes." *Guitarist*, June 1990.

Martin, Gavin, "*Face Dances*." *NME*, 21 March 1981.

Masley, Ed, "Who's Return Is Awesome." www.post-gazette.com, 30 June 2000.

Mattingly, Rick, "Kenney Jones Faces The Law." *Musician*, June 1991.

McAnuff, Des, "See Me, Feel Me, Touch Me." *American Theatre*, November 1993.

McAuliffe, Kathleen, "Brain Tuner." *Omni*, January 1983.

McAuliffe, Kathleen, "The *Penthouse* Interview: Pete Townshend." *Penthouse*, August 1983.

McCormick, Neil, "Smash, Bang, Crash – The Who Are Back." www.telegraph.co.uk, 3 August, 2000.

McCormick, Neil, " 'I Look My Age – But I Certainly Don't Feel It' " www.telegraph.co.uk, 2 June 2001.

McKenna, Christine, "Free Drinking and Heavy Thinking." *Spin*, March 1986.

McKeough, Kevin, "The Who Are Just Alright In Chicago." *Rolling Stone*, November 1999.

McKnight, Connor, and Tobler, John, "Chatting With Pete Townshend, *Zigzag*, no. 43, 1974.

McNeill, Phil, "Pete Townshend & Ronnie Lane: *Rough Mix*." *NME*, 17 Sept. 1977.

Mendelsohn, John Ned, "*Who's Next*." *Rolling Stone* 90.

Miller, Debby, "The Who To Begin 'Final' US Tour." *Rolling Stone*, 30 September 1982.

Miller, Jim, "The Who: Talkin' About A Generation." *Rolling Stone*, 5 December 1974.

Milward, John, "*Join Together* (review)." *Rolling Stone*, 17 May, 1990.

Mitchum, Rob, "Interview: Pete Townshend." www.pitchforkmedia.com, 16 October 2006.

Mohan, Dominic, "Cops Can Come And Get Me." www.thesun.co.uk, 13 January 2003.

Mohan, Dominic, "My Chauffeur Used To Wait While I Slept Off The Booze In A Skip." www.thesun.co.uk, 11 February 2002.

Molenda, Michael, "British Accents." *Guitar Player*, March 1998.

Molenda, Michael, "Union Jacks." *Guitar Player*, March 1998.

Moore, John, " '60s Tommy Still Speaks To Young." www.denverpost.com, 6 January 2002.

Morley, Paul, "Laser Laser On The Wall Who Are Complacent After All." *NME*, 25 August 1979.

Morley, Paul, "Pete Townshend: The Unimportance Of Being Townshend." *NME*, 12 March 1983.

Morris, Chris, "No Takers For Classic Who Tapes On eBay." www.billboard.com, 27 July 2000.

Murray, Charles Shaar, "Townshend: The True Saga Of Clapton's Rainbow Gig." *NME*, 24 February/3 March 1973.

Murray, Charles Shaar, "Four-Way Pete." *NME*, 27 October 1973.

Murray, Charles Shaar, "Listening To You, I Forget The Story." *NME*, 29 March 1975.

Murray, Charles Shaar, "Just Who Is The World's Greatest Rock Band?" *NME*, 1 November 1975.

Murray, Charles Shaar, "*Who Are You.*" *NME*, 19 August 1978.

Murray, Charles Shaar, "In Search Of Ancient Mods." *NME*, 9 June 1979.

Murray, Charles Shaar, "Wanna Be A hero?" *NME*, 5 January 1980.

Murray, Charles Shaar, "Conversations With Pete." *New Musical Express*, 19 April 1980.

Murray, Charles Shaar, "Pete Townshend: *Empty Glass.*" *NME*, 26 April 1980.

Murray, Charles Shaar, "Townshend Talks!" *Trouser Press*, July/August 1980 (reprint of 'Conversations With Pete' above).

Murray, Charles Shaar, "Pete Townshend: *All The Best Cowboys Have Chinese Eyes.*" *NME*, 3 July 1982.

Newquist, H.P., "Pete Townshend: The Chronicles Of An Angry Guitarist." *Guitar*, August 1996.

O'Hare, Kevin, "Who's Next." *Newhouse News Service*, 10 September 2006.

Patterson, Margaret A., "Casa Filadelfia Detox Center." www.rlministries.com, 2001.

Patterson, Margaret A., "Effects Of Neuro-electric Therapy (N.E.T.) In Drug Addiction: Interim Report." www.undcp.org, 1976.

Pond, Steve, "Schlitz Sponsors The Who's US Tour." *Rolling Stone*, 11 November 1982.

Pond, Steve, "The Who Reboards The Magic Bus, But Will It Still Be Magic?" *Rolling Stone*, 13 July 1989.

Poniewozik, James, "CBS: The World Looks Just The Same, And History Ain't Changed." *Time*, 20 May 2004.

Puterbaugh, Parke, "The Who: *It's Hard* (review)." *Rolling Stone*, 30 September 1982.

Resnicoff, Matt, "Godhead Revisited: The Second Coming Of Pete Townshend." *Guitar Player*, September 1989.

Resnicoff, Matt, "Flailing Your Way To God." *Guitar Player*, October 1989.

Roberts, Chris, "Mecca for Mods?" *Melody Maker*, 25 January 1964.

Robinson, Lisa, "It's Probably The Sack!" *NME*, 30 August 1975.

Rogers, Sheila, "Random Notes." *Rolling Stone*, 17 May, 1990.

Rothman, David, "A Conversation With Pete Townshend." *Oui*, March 1980.

Rudis, Al, "When We Fight It Can Get Vicious." *Melody Maker*, 9 February 1974.

Salewicz, Chris, "Pete Townshend Stops Hurting People; Stops Hurting Himself: Action For The 80s." *Creem*, November 1982.

Scapelliti, Christopher, "To Die For." *Revolver*, Fall 2000.

Schultz, David, "Schultz By Southwest: Earvolution Goes To Austin." www.earvolution.com, 21 March 2007.

Seligmann, Jean, "Mourning Lovely Linda." *Newsweek*, 22 June 1998.

Selwood, Clive, "Muddy Hell." *Melody Maker*, 30 August 1969.

Sexton, Paul, "Ronnie Lane Benefit." www.billboard.com, April 8, 2004.

Sexton, Paul, "Winwood, Townshend Bill Capaldi Charity Concert." *Billboard*, 4 December 2006.

Sharken, Lisa, "Long Live Rock!" *Guitar Player*, September 2000.

Sharp, Ken, "*Who's Next* Revisited." *Goldmine*, 2 February, 2007.

Sheff, David, "Pete Townshend: *Playboy* Interview." *Playboy*, February 1994.

Shelden, Michael, "We'll Go On Until We Drop Dead." www.telegraph.co.uk, 15 July 2003.

Simmons, Sylvie, "Lemmy: The *Mojo* Interview." *Mojo*, July 2006.

Simon, Bruce, "Townshend and Vedder Rock NYC." www.launch.yahoo.com, 29 July 1999.

Simon, Bruce, "The Who Set For New York City Charity Gig." www.launch.com, 28 April 2000.

Simon, Bruce, "David Bowie's Heathen To Feature Pete Townshend & Dave Grohl." www.launch.yahoo.com, 5 April 2002.

Simon, Bruce, "Pete Townshend's Mother Stands By Her Son, Says She's Ignorant Of His Abuse Claim." www.launch.yahoo.com, 15 January 2003.

Simon, Bruce, "Queen Guitarist Standing With Pete Townshend, Unhappy With Media Coverage." www.launch.yahoo.com, 17 January 2003.

Simpson, Dave, "Ground control." www.guardian.co.uk, 5 June 2002.

Simpson, Janice C., "Pete, We Can Hear You." *Time*, 12 July 1993.

Sinclair, Tom, "*Psychoderelict* (review)." *Entertainment Weekly*, 18 June 1993.

Skanse, Richard, "Roger Daltrey Says Who Reunion Not Nostalgia, But Magic." www.rollingstone.com, 16 June 2000.

Smith, Alan, "The Who Use Force To Get Sound They Want!" *NME*, 18 June 1965.

Soghomonian, Talia, "L'interview de Pete Townshend en anglais." www.metrofrance.com, 6 June 2007.

Spencer, Neil, "World Class Axe In Pistols Niterie Fracas." *NME*, 29 January 1977.

Spencer, Neil, "Roddam's Mod(ern) Vision." *NME*, 18 August 1979.

Steininger, Alex, and McGovern, Sera, "Interview: Pete Townshend." www.inmusicwetrust.com, 24 February2000.

Stewart, Tony, "*Relay*." *NME*, 23 December 1972.

Stewart, Tony, "Roger And Out." *NME*, 14 April 1973.

Stewart, Tony, "Who's Last?" *NME*, 9 August 1975.

Stewart, Tony, "Daltrey Fights Back." *Creem*, November 1975.

Stewart, Tony, "Rainy Day Rock Fans." *NME*, 5 June 1976.

Stewart, Tony, "Pursey, Rotten In Line For Who Film Role." *New Musical Express*, 12 August 1978.

Stewart, Tony, "The Who & Various Artists: *Quadrophenia* Soundtrack." *NME*, 22 September 1979.

Strauss, Neil, "Toasting Townshend." *Rolling Stone*, 679, 7 April 1994.

Sullivan, Mike, and Lea, Michael, "Cops Swoop On Townshend." www.thesun.co.uk, 14 January 2003.

Sutcliffe, Phil, "Indeed, He Can Explain." www.latimes.com, 28 May 2000.

Sweeting, Adam, "Pete Townshend: *Scoop.*" *Melody Maker*, 19 March 1983.

Swenson, John, "The One-Time Guitar-Smasher Looks Back." *Guitar World*, November 1983.

Tannenbaum, Rob, "*White City: A Novel* (review)." *Rolling Stone*, 16 January 1986.

Taylor, Letta, "The Kids Are Alright." www.newsday.com, July 9, 2000.

Thigpen, David, "*Tommy* Sells Out." *Rolling Stone*, 10 June 1993.

Tickell, Paul, "Why Do They Bother?" *NME*, 21 March 1981.

Tobler, John, "Can You Believe It? Chatting With Pete Townshend." *ZigZag*, June 1974.

Townshend, Pete, "Pop Think-In." *Melody Maker*, 26 March 1966.

Townshend, Pete, "Blind Date." *Melody Maker*, 8 October 1966.

Townshend, Pete, "Pop Think – In." *Melody Maker*, 14 January 1967.

Townshend, Pete, "Dear Melody Maker." *Melody Maker*, 12 August 1967.

Townshend, Pete, "Don't Hold Me Responsible For What I Do Or Say!" *Melody Maker*, 22 August 1970.

Townshend, Pete, "Another Fight In The Playground." *Melody Maker*, 19 September 1970.

Townshend, Pete, "On The Road Again." *Melody Maker*, 17 October 1970.

Townshend, Pete, "TV Miming: Who Is Being Fooled?" *Melody Maker*, 14 November 1970.

Townshend, Pete, "In Love With Meher Baba." *Rolling Stone*, 26 November 1970.

Townshend, Pete, "Is Rock Dead?" *Melody Maker*, 12 December 1970.

Townshend, Pete, "Do You Suffer From Media Frustration?" *Melody Maker*, 16 January 1971.

Townshend, Pete, "Change – By Taking People UP." *Melody Maker*, 13 February 1971.

Townshend, Pete, "Learning To Walk – The Second Time Around." *Melody Maker*, 13 March 1971.

Townshend, Pete, "Things Are Different Across The Sea." *Melody Maker*, 17 April 1971.

Townshend, Pete, "We're Sorry!" *Melody Maker*, 24 November 1971.

Townshend, Pete, "*Meaty, Beaty, Big and Bouncy.*" *Rolling Stone*, 9 December 1971.

Townshend, Pete, "Rock Recording." *Hit Parader*, May 1974.

Townshend, Pete, "Pro's Reply." *Guitar Player*, September 1974.

Townshend, Pete, "Pete Townshend's Back Pages." *NME*, 5 November 1977.

Townshend, Pete, "The Punk Meets the Godmother." *Rolling Stone*, 17 November 1977.

Townshend, Pete, "Townshend's Rebuttal." *The Record*, December 1982.

Townshend, Pete, "Songwriting." *Making Music*, June 1989.

Townshend, Pete, "An Introduction To *Lifehouse*." *The Richmond Review*, 1999.

Townshend, Pete, "Chat Transcript." www.barnesandnoble.com, 21 May 2000.

Townshend, Pete, "The Who Sell Out." www.q4music.com, 31 January 2001.

Townshend, Pete, "*Quadrophenia* heads for theaterland." www.eelpie.com, March 2001.

Townshend, Pete, "Meher Baba – The Silent Master: My Own Silence." www.eelpie.com, July 2001.

Townshend, Pete, "Peter Blake." *Mojo*, March 2002.

Townshend, Pete, "A *Different* Bomb." www.petetownshend.com, January 2002.

Townshend, Pete, "*White City* Teleplay." www.eelpie.com, 13 March 2002.

Tracy, Dick, "*Quadrophenia*." *New Musical Express*, 12 May 1979.

Turner, Steve, "Pete Townshend: Genius Of The Simple." *Beat Instrumental*, December 1971.

Turner, Steve, "Peter Meaden [obituary]." *New Musical Express*, 12 August 1978.

Turner, Steve, "Who Said That!" *New Musical Express*, 12 August 1978.

Valentine, Penny, "*Happy Jack*." *Disc & Music Echo*, 10 December 1966.

Valentine, Penny, "The Townshend Talk-In." *Sounds*, 12 August 1972.

Van Ness, Chris, "The Who Have A Smashing Time." *NME*, 8 January 1972.

Vercammen, Paul, "Meet The New Boss." www.cnn.com, 15 May 1996.

Ward, Simon, "Lifehouse." *Record Collector*. January 2000.

Warner, Simon, "The Who Know Who They Are And From Whence They Came." www.popmatters.com, 18 July 2006.

Weales, Gerald, "The Who's *Tommy* (review)." *Commonweal*, 4 June 1993.

Watts, Michael, "It's [Still] A Mod, Mod, Mod World." *Melody Maker*, 14 October 1978.

Watts, Michael, "Townshend: Picking Up The Pieces." *Melody Maker*, 14 October 1978.

Weisbard, Eric, "Ten Past 'Ten.'" *Spin*, August 2001.

Welch, Chris, "The Who Fulfilled – And A Mini-Opera, Yet!" *Melody Maker*, 10 December 1966.

Welch, Chris, "It's A Knockout!" *Melody Maker*, 31 December 1966.

Welch, Chris, "Jimi Hendrix Versus The Who." *Melody Maker*, 4 February 1967.

Welch, Chris, "Love, Beauty, The Fuzz And The UFO." *Melody Maker*, 17 June 1967.

Welch, Chris, "I Can See For Miles." *Melody Maker*, 14 October 1967.

Welch, Chris, "Who Needs To Take Pop Seriously?" *Melody Maker*, 30 December 1967.

Welch, Chris, "Would You Let Your Daughter Marry A Venusian?" *Melody Maker*, 4 May 1968.

Welch, Chris, "Tackling The Most Serious Project Of Their Lives." *Melody Maker*, 9 September 1968.

Welch, Chris, "Bus Ride Back To Pop 30 For Who." *Melody Maker*, 21 September 1968.

Welch, Chris, "*Pinball Wizard*." *Melody Maker*, 8 March 1969.

Welch, Chris, "The Crazy World Of Thunderclap Newman, *Melody Maker*, 19 July 1969.

Welch, Chris, "Rock At Its Most Electrifying." *Melody Maker*, 6 September 1969.

Welch, Chris, "Where Now For *Tommy*?" *Melody Maker*, 10 January 1970.

Welch, Chris, "*Summertime Blues*." *Melody Maker*, 18 July 1970.

Welch, Chris, "The Life And Hard Times Of Arthur Brown." *Melody Maker*, 23 October 1971.

Welch, Chris, "Squire Daltrey." *Melody Maker*, 23 October 1971.

Welch, Chris, "5.15." *Melody Maker*, 6 October 1973.

Welch, Chris, "Townshend Tops *Tommy!*" *Melody Maker*, 20 October 1973.

Welch, Chris, "Talking 'bout My Generation." *Melody Maker*, 27 October 1973.

Welch, Chris, "The Who: Another Victory." *Melody Maker*, 3 November 1973.

Welch, Chris, and Ward, Jeff, "Who Eat Humble Pie!" *Melody Maker*, 25 May 1974.

Welch, Chris, "Odds & Sods." *Melody Maker*, 28 September 1974.

Welch, Chris, "Daltrey: Grandfather Of Punk Rock." *Melody Maker*, 30 April 1977.

Welch, Chris, "The Return of You Know Who: Pete Townshend and Ronnie Lane." *Melody Maker*, 17 Sept. 1977.

Welch, Chris, "The Who Sell In." *Melody Maker*, 27 January 1979.

Welch, Chris, "A Face In The Who." *Melody Maker*, 21 April 1979.

Welch, Chris, "Townshend: Still No Touring." *Melody Maker*, 26 May 1979.

Wells, John, "Third Time Lucky Name." *NME*, 26 February 1965.

Wells, John, "*Magic Bus*." *NME*, 12 October 1968.

Wenner, Jann, "Rock And Roll Music." *Rolling Stone*, 20 January 1968.

Wenner, Jann, "The *Rolling Stone* Interview: Pete Townshend." *Rolling Stone*, 14–18 September 1968.

Wickham, Vicki, "Ten-Dollar Seats For The Who!" *Melody Maker*, 20 June 1970.

Wild, David, "The Who Rock On." *Rolling Stone*, 2 July, 2002.

Wild, David, "Who's On Broadway?" *Rolling Stone*, 18 March 1993.

Wild, David, "*Tommy* Scores Again." *Rolling Stone*, 3 September 1992.

Williams, Mark, "Why Pete didn't need a wheelchair . . ." *New Musical Express*, 12 May 1979.

Willman, Chris, "*Endless Wire* (review)." www.ew.com, 3 November 2006.
Wilson, Tony, "Scuffles at the Proms." *Melody Maker*, 12 July 1969.
Wilson, Tony, "Now Pete's Brainchild Is Set For The Big Screen."
    Melody Maker, 19 July 1969.
Wood, Christina, "Rockin' Good Software: The PC Takes On MTV."
    PC World, July 1994.

Newspapers

7 February 1971   *New York Times*, The Who, From Tommy to Bobby.
6 November 1973   *Newcastle Evening Chronicle*, The Who – A Ridiculous
                      Display Of Unwarranted Violence. Steve Hughes.
13 September 1982   *The Times*, The Who – National Exhibition Centre,
                      Birmingham. Richard Williams.
28 June 1989   *Oakland Tribune*, Who's Townshend keeps tight focus
                      on Iron Man. Larry Kelp.
2 July 1989   *Washington Post*, Who's Laughing Now. Richard
                      Harrington.
23 July 1989   *Atlanta Journal*, Townshend Proves Mettle With Spirited
                      Iron Man. Keith L. Thomas.
23 July 1989   *Detroit Free Press*, Pete Townshend takes a stab at a rock
                      musical. Gary Graff.
23 July 1989   *Detroit Free Press*, Who Cares. Gary Graff.
11 August 1989   *Salt Lake City Deseret News*, Pete serves up treat for
                      lovers of music and stories. Ray Boren.
20 August 1989   *San Diego Union*, Who Knows its limits. George Varga.
5 July 1992   *LA Times*, The Resurrection of Tommy. Michael
                      Walker.
5 July 1992   *San Diego Union*, For pop fans, Tommy remains the one
                      and only. George Varga.
5 July 1992   *San Diego Union*, Tommy for a new generation. Michael
                      Phillips.
11 July 1992   *LA Times*, The Wizardry of High-Tech Makes It Work.
                      Sylvie Drake.
11 July 1992   *LA Times*, They've Taken a Generation's Magic Away.
                      Robert Hilburn.
12 July 1992   *Orange County Register*, Kinder, gentler 'Tommy' lacks
                      fire. Jeff Niesel.
14 July 1992   *San Jose Mercury News*, See it, hear it, feel it. Judith
                      Green.
24 July 1992   *Washington Times*, No one asks Who is most popular
                      boy of rock opera. George Vargas.
24 July 1992   *Washington Times*, Tommy plays his pinball again.
                      Michael Phillips.
15 February 1993   *New York Post*, Tommy Tunes up for B'Way. Lisa
                      Robinson.

18 April 1993	*LA Times*, Will New York Embrace the Pinball Wizard of La Jolla? Patrick Pacheco.
22 April 1993	*Philadelphia Inquirer*, See it, feel it, hear it. Ann Holson.
23 April 1993	*New York Times*, Capturing Rock-and-Roll and the Passions of 1969. Frank Rich.
23 April 1993	*New York Daily News*, Tommy Scores. Jim Farber.
23 April 1993	*New York Daily News*, We've got a Tommy ache. Howard Kissel.
23 April 1993	*New York Post*, Score's a score for pinball wizard. Dan Aquilante.
23 April 1993	*New York Post*, Tommy Terrific. Clive Barnes.
24 April 1993	*San Jose Mercury News*, A Who-less Tommy falters. Michael Kuchwara.
25 April 1993	*Philadelphia Inquirer*, Rock opera Tommy explodes on Broadway. Clifford A. Ridley.
2 May 1993	*Hartford Courant*, Tommy splendid yet preposterous, 'Brothers' drags. Malcolm Johnson.
16 May 1993	*Boston Globe*, See me, feel me, touch me, stage me. Michael Walker.
18 June 1993	*LA Times*, 'What Did We Do With the Future?' Richard Cromelin.
20 June 1993	*New York Daily News*, For Pete's Sake . . . Jim Farber.
4 July 1993	*Washington Post*, Talkin' 'Bout His Regeneration. Richard Harrington.
11 July 1993	*New York Daily News*, Full-Tilt Townshend. David Hinckley.
31 July 1993	*LA Daily News*, Townshend offers stale rock opera. Fred Shuster.
1 August 1993	*Orange County Register*, Townshend fans get who they want, and more. Mark Brown.
2 August 1993	*LA Daily News*, Pete's generation. Fred Shuster.
3 August 1993	*San Francisco Examiner*, Townshend's Dud. Barry Walters.
4 August 1993	*Oakland Tribune*, Townshend's PsychoDerelict upstaged by his older material. Dave Becker.
4 August 1993	*Orange County Register*, Townshend enjoys acting his age. Mark Brown.
4 August 1993	San Jose Mercury News, Things they do look awful cool. Harry Sumrall.
6 August 1993	*Boston Herald*, 'Wizard of the windmill' reaches out to a new generation on his first tour. Tristram Lozaw.
6 August 1993	*San Diego Union-Tribune*, Rocker's benefit concert mines musical riches. George Varga.
11 August 1993	*Boston Herald*, Townshend unleashes fury, bad-boy attitude. Dean Johnson.
10 October 1993	*Dallas Morning News*, Free at Last. William Snyder.
28 November 1993	*Boston Globe*, Tommy grows up. Matthew Gilbert.

1 December 1993	*Boston Globe*, Townshend's other musical comes to Ch. 2. Steve Morse.
7 December 1993	*Boston Herald*, Rock opera Tommy a theatrical wonder. Iris Fanger.
21 January 1994	*Detroit News*, Too-tame Tommy is flashy, but drowns in '90s need for normalcy. Reed Johnson.
25 February 1994	*New York Times*, The Who, Regrouped and Reinterpreted. Jon Pareles.
26 February 1994	*San Diego Union-Tribune*, Daltrey fest is no Who reunion. George Varga.
12 May 1994	*LA Daily News*, In keeping its energy intact, Tommy stays true to The Who. Daryl H. Miller.
12 May 1994	*LA Times*, 'The Who's Tommy': Is Wizardry Enough? Chris Willman.
20 May 1994	*Seattle Times*, Tommy terrific. Misha Berson.
2 June 1994	*Oakland Tribune*, Broadway's version falls short on vocals. David Barton.
9 June 1994	*San Francisco Examiner*, Sure plays a mean pinball. Robert Hurwitt.
5 July 1994	*San Jose Mercury News*, The Pete Principles. Harry Sumrall.
10 July 1994	*LA Daily News*, Changing Direction. Daryl H. Miller.
17 July 1994	*Detroit News and Free Press*, Daltrey, Townshend split on value of nostalgia. Gary Graff.
18 July 1994	*LA Daily News*, Images, sound make Tommy soar. Daryl H. Miller.
11 August 1994	*Houston Chronicle*, 'Lost' but not forgotten. Mike McDaniel.
15 August 1994	*Newark Star-Ledger*, TV is taking a look back. George Kanzler.
2 October 1994	*Chicago Sun-Times*, See Me, Hear Me, Touch Me: Tommy Reborn for the 90s. Hedy Weiss.
2 October 1994	*Chicago Tribune*, Pete Townshend: So Why Did a Guy Who Hates Pinball Write a Rock Opera About it? Jessica Seigel.
30 October 1994	*LA Times*, Nothing But Blue Skies. Barbara Isenberg.
29 November 1994	*Philadelphia Inquirer*, Want theatrical effect? Then Try out Tommy. Douglas J. Keating.
18 December 1994	*Washington Times*, Townshend's journey. Jeffrey Staggs.
23 December 1994	*Baltimore Sun*, 'The Who's Tommy' goes high-tech, for better or worse. J. Wynn Rousuck.
23 December 1994	*Washington Times*, Who could hate this Tommy? Unsigned.
24 December 1994	*Richmond Times-Dispatch*, 'The Who's Tommy' in D. C. proves a spectacular show. Roy Proctor.
27 December 1994	*Washington Post*, Tommy's Musical Mentor. Lisa Leff.

1 September 1995	*Owensboro Messenger-Inquirer*, Tommy Opens Thursday. Keith Lawrence.
18 December 1995	*Philadelphia Inquirer*, A Bit of Broadway will be lighting up the stage in Camden. Unsigned.
26 March 1996	*Providence Journal-Bulletin*, Two Broadway hits aim for fresh successes here. Bill Gale.
2 May 1996	*Oakland Tribune*, Townshend Rocks-When he wants to. William Friar.
2 May 1996	*San Jose Mercury News*, Townshend's greatness: Not relying solely on hits. Brad Kava.
6 May 1996	*New York Daily News*, Townshend Triumphant. Jim Farber.
16 May 1996	*Baltimore Sun*, Tommy needs shot of wizardry. J. Wynn Rousuck.
27 June 1996	*Reno Gazette-Journal*, Reno Audiences finally get a chance to see, feel and touch Tommy. Wayne Melton.
30 June 1996	*The Sunday Times*, Rock legends roll back the years. Unsigned.
17 July 1996	*Reuters*, Quadrophenia (performance review). Kevin Zimmerman.
18 July 1996	*Boston Globe*, Resurrected Quadrophenia Resounds. Jim Sullivan.
19 October 1996	*LA Times*, Blasts from Britain's Past. Richard Cromelin.
21 October 1996	*San Francisco Chronicle*, A Who's Who of music. Joel Selvin.
21 October 1996	*San Jose Mercury News*, The Who's Tommy goes to Vegas. Mark De La Vina.
25 October 1996	*San Diego Union-Tribune*, Don't get fooled: New Who a shell of old Who. Dennis Hunt.
24 November 1996	*Baltimore Sun*, Guiliano's 'Townshend': from The Who's mouth. J. D. Considine.
21 January 1997	*Oakland Tribune*, Magic of Tommy still shines through. Paul Sterman.
17 February 1997	*The Times*, Ghost of The Who's Tommy returns to win Olivier award. Helen Johnstone.
6 June 1997	*The Times*, Ronnie Lane; Obituary. Unsigned.
16 June 1997	*Arlington Heights Daily Herald*, Townshend Makes Strong, Sober Chicago comeback. Mark Guarino.
3 July 1997	*Baltimore Sun*, Feeling Tommy's Pain. Mike Guiliano.
21 July 1997	*St Louis Post-Dispatch*, The Who still plays on? Yes . . . and with pizzazz. Joe Williams.
22 July 1997	*Chicago Tribune*, The Who's Mixed Bag. Rick Reger.
23 July 1997	*Minneapolis Star Tribune*, The Who shows it's still passionate in Target Center show. Jon Bream.
25 July 1997	*Milwaukee Journal Sentinel*, Never mind their age – The Who can still rock. Dave Tianen.

26 July 1997	*Detroit Free Press*, Fans didn't see Who they expected. Brian McCollum.
1 August 1997	*Knight-Ridder/Tribune News Service*, The Who Revives Quadrophenia Album in hopes of a Broadway successor to Tommy. John Mark Eberhart
4 August 1997	*The Hartford Courant-Connecticut News*, The Who's Quadrophenia a glorious production. Roger Catlin.
5 August 1997	*The Home News & Tribune*, Who's on first with rock show: Townshend, Daltrey wow Jersey crowd. Chris Jordan.
16 August 1997	*Tampa Tribune*, The Who fulfill quest with Quadrophenia. Curtis Ross.
15 September 1997	*The Times*, Hendrix joins Handel with pop's first blue plaque. Unsigned.
9 June 1998	*The Times*, Sir Paul pays a last tribute to Linda, his diamond lady. Unsigned.
17 June 1998	*The Times*, Edwin Astley; Obituary. Unsigned.
6 November 1998	*The Times*, As Mod for it as ever. David Sinclair.
7 February 1999	*The Sunday Times*, Townshend writes a new rock opera. Nicholas Hellen.
11 July 1999	*The Times*, Ted Hughes's Iron Man wins film friends. Christopher Goodwin and Richard Brooks.
30 July 1999	*Chicago Sun-Times*, Pete and repeat. Jim DeRogatis.
30 July 1999	*New York Daily News*, Look Who's Playing. David Hinckley.
30 July 1999	*New York Post*, Townshend Live & Kickin'. Dan Aquilante.
1 October 1999	*USA Today*, Pete Townshend's Psychoderelict Broadway-bound. David Patrick Stearns.
6 October 1999	*The Times*, Who Make Comeback. Unsigned.
8 October 1999	*USA Today*, Pete Townshend gives back to the Pearl Jam generátion. Edna Gunderson.
31 October 1999	*Las Vegas Review Journal*, The Who show muscle in marvelous return. Mike Weatherford.
14 November 1999	*The Chicago Sun Times*, Who almost too good for reunion gig. Jim DeRogatis.
15 November 1999	*Chicago Tribune*, Look Who's back playing all the hits. Greg Kot.
15 November 1999	*The Times*, Who's Who on Pete. Unsigned.
23 November 1999	*The Guardian*, Dinosaurs rule the earth. Bill Borrows.
3 December 1999	*The Guardian*, Peter rabbits. Tom Cox.
6 December 1999	*The Guardian*, Lifehouse. Anne Karpf.
24 December 1999	*The Times*, The Who, Shepherds Bush Empire. Unsigned.
28 December 1999	*The Guardian*, A band that won't fade away. Caroline Sullivan.
28 February 2000	*The Guardian*, I really want to know. Keith Cameron.

29 February 2000	*The Times*, Son of Tommy Comes of Age. Nigel Williamson.
19 March 2000	*The Observer*, Schools of thought. Jonathan Jones.
11 April 2000	*USA Today*, To Online Fans, from you-know-Who. Edward C. Baig.
26 June 2000	*Chicago Sun-Times*, The Who at the New World Music Theatre. Jim DeRogatis.
8 July 2000	*The Washington Times*, You know Who still rock wizards. Christian Toto.
20 July 2000	*The Guardian*, Web life: Urban myths. John Eason.
30 July 2000	*The Sunday Times*, On Record. Dan Cairns.
24 September 2000	*The Tampa Tribune*, Connect the dots to bassist's art show. Curtis Ross.
26 September 2000	*Palm Beach Post*, The Who older, wiser, but its music still snarls, thrills. Larry Aydlette.
27 September 2000	*St Petersburg Times*, The Who in vintage form. Philip Booth.
29 September 2000	*The Cleveland Plain Dealer*, Never say never. John Soeder.
29 October 2000	*The Times*, Cornwall's most expensive view. Christian Dymond.
3 November 2000	*The Guardian, The Who: Manchester Arena.* Dave Simpson.
5 November 2000	*The Observer*, Careful with that axe, Pete. Sam Taylor.
15 November 2000	*The Times*, Who you kidding? Paul Sexton.
22 March 2001	*The Independent*, BBC's £280,000 and the dying thoughts of the last Kray. Paul Lashmar.
25 May 2001	*The Guardian*, Bob can't fix it for Dylan at music awards. Esther Addley
25 June 2001	*San Diego Union-Tribune*, Pete smashes barriers instead of instruments. George Varga.
21 October 2001	*The Times*, Driven to distraction in Richmond. Cally Law.
5 November 2001	*The Times*, The midlife rambler. Nigel Williamson.
1 January 2002	*San Diego Union-Tribune*, Rock's cycle of success. George Varga.
9 February 2002	*The Guardian*, The Who, Royal Albert Hall London. John Aizlewood.
31 March 2002	*The Observer*, Tommy, get your gun . . . Pete Townshend.
6 June 2002	*The Guardian*, Speedy Keen. Alan Clayson.
28 June 2002	*The Guardian*, John Entwistle, The Who's bass guitarist, found dead in hotel. Vikram Dodd.
29 June 2002	*The Guardian*, John Entwistle. Adam Sweeting.
2 July 2002	*The Times*, The Who rediscover their old edgy spirit. Richard Morrison.
3 July 2002	*San Jose Mercury News*, After loss, The Who wows Mtn. View crowd. Brad Kava.

References

6 July 2002	*Sacramento Bee*, The Who keeps making rock'n'roll history. David Barton.
27 July 2002	*Boston Globe*, The Who knows why its rock lives long. Steve Morse.
27 July 2002	*Boston Herald*, Who knows how to rock'n'roll. Dean Johnson.
29 July 2002	*Philadelphia Inquirer*, Who shows who's standing tall. Dan DeLuca.
2 August 2002	*New York Times*, The Song Isn't Over for The Who, Aging but Defiant. Jon Pareles.
26 August 2002	*Chicago Sun Times*, Who at the Tweeter Center. Jim DeRogatis.
26 August 2002	*Indianapolis Star*, Rock legends let loose again. David Lindquist.
28 August 2002	*The Flint Journal*, A seemingly grateful Who gets its groove back. Doug Pullen.
28 August 2002	*The Grand Rapids Press*, This is . . . What The Who Do. John Sinkevics.
16 September 2002	*Las Vegas Review*, Band takes 'then there were two' approach. Mike Weatherford.
16 September 2002	*The Las Vegas Sun*, The Who heats up The Joint with classic hits. Spencer Patterson.
16 September 2002	*The Orange County Register*, No one needs to ask who's Who. Steve Fryer.
20 September 2002	*Rocky Mountain News*, Townshend, Daltrey reign o'er Green. Mark Brown.
20 September 2002	*The Denver Post*, Who are they? An enduring pop force. G. Brown.
22 September 2002	*Star Telegram*, Who's Coup. Dave Ferman.
22 September 2002	*The Dallas Morning News*, Half a Who. Thor Christensen.
24 September 2002	*St Paul Pioneer Press*, Despite line-up changes, The Who still the real thing. Brian Lampert.
25 September 2002	*Chicago Sun-Times*, Moon, Entwistle gone, but long live The Who. Richard Roeper.
25 September 2002	*Chicago Sun-Times*, The Who try to make it all right for the kids. Jim DeRogatis.
25 September 2002	*St Paul Star Tribune*, The Who's main two show their intensity. Jon Bream.
26 September 2002	*The Chicago Tribune*, Who's next? (unsigned)
28 September 2002	*Boston Herald*, Fiery Performance shows Who still matters. Sarah Rodman.
29 September 2002	*Toronto Star*, The Who is alright. Vit Wagner.
29 September 2002	*Toronto Sun*, Two for The Who. Jane Stevenson.
30 September 2002	*The Globe and Mail*, The Who's back, and why not? Robert Everett-Green.
3 November 2002	*The Observer*, Kurt Cobain's Journals. Pete Townshend.

16 January 2003	*USA Today*, Arrest has Townshend fans searching for clues, too. Elysa Gardner.
10 July 2003	*Evening Standard*, Townshend: My life has changed. Richard Simpson.
11 July 2003	*Richmond and Twickenham Times*, Rock star hits back. Hannah Thorpe.
22 September 2003	*Knight Ridder/Tribune News Service*, Can explain: Roger Daltrey demonstrates 'Extreme History' on TV. Luaine Lee.
28 December 2003	*The Observer*, My suicide thoughts over porn – Townshend. Zoe Smith.
24 March 2004	*The Times Online*, Review. David Sinclair.
30 March 2004	*New Musical Express*, The Grown Ups Are Alright.
31 March 2004	*The Guardian*, Review. Alexis Petridis.
22 May 2004	*The Boston Globe*, Still no substitute for The Who. Tom Kielty.
24 May 2004	*Reuters, Concert Review*. Frank Scheck.
24 May 2004	*The Star Ledger*, Townshend breathes new life into The Who. Bradley Bambarger.
30 July 2004	*Sydney Morning Herald*, The Who, Entertainment Centre. Bernard Zuel.
3 July 2005	*The Sunday Times*, Child porn suspects set to be cleared in evidence 'shambles'. David Leppard.
4 July 2005	*The Daily Telegraph*, Guess who stole the show? Neil McCormick.
5 July 2005	*The Daily Mirror*, Live 8 Heroes. Cameron Robertson.
6 July 2005	*The Daily Mirror*, Give 8. Cameron Robertson.
4 June 2006	*The Independent*, Who release first single in 23 years. Anthony Barnes.
9 June 2006	*The Times*, Selling themselves short. Penny Wark.
22 June 2006	*Daily Mail*, Children's charities attack Townshend for erotic teenage fiction. Tom Bryant.
3 July 2006	*Evening Standard,* Who2 are still on fire. David Smyth.
3 July 2006	*Huddersfield Daily Examiner*, O2 Wireless Festival. Unsigned.
6 July 2006	*Liverpool Daily Post*, After 35 years, The Who are back. Mike Chapple.
7 July 2006	*The Times*, Hope I get a record out before I get old. Paddy Jansen.
8 July 2006	*The Daily Record*. Who's that on the net. John Dingwall.
10 July 2006	*The Scotsman*, At 123, veterans rock new generation. Craig Brown.
8 September 2006	*Courier-Post*, Rockers back on the road. Chuck Darrow.
11 September 2006	*Connecticut Post*, The Who preps for tour at Arena. James D. Shay.
12 September 2006	*Philadelphia Inquirer*, Let Pete explain. Dan DeLuca.

12 September 2006	*Philadelphia Inquirer*, The Who deliver ferocious, career-spanning opener of US tour. Dan DeLuca.
12 September 2006	*USA Today*, The Who hits stage, screens. Elysa Gardner.
16 September 2006	*Ottawa Citizen*, The Who prove they still have that '60s energy. Lynn Saxberg.
16 September 2006	*Ottawa Sun*, You Bet classic Who's golden. Denis Armstrong.
17 September 2006	*The Observer*, Generation Terrorists. Simon Garfield.
18 September 2006	*New York Post*, Baba O'Nasty. Dan Aquilante.
18 September 2006	*Philadelphia Inquirer*, Talkin' 'bout the generations. John Grogan.
18 September 2006	*The Republican*, The Who adds to rock legacy. Kevin O'Hare.
20 September 2006	*New York Post*, Pete is one Happy Jack at garden party. Dan Aquilante.
23 September 2006	*Home News Tribune*, The Who shows off new material at PNC. Chris Jordan.
24 September 2006	*Des Moines Register*, Pete Townshend: Who's still relevant. Kyle Munson.
24 September 2006	*Washington Post*, In the virgin fest, a bacchanal at the starting gate. J. Freedom du Lac.
25 September 2006	*Chicago Sun-Times*, Composer Fuller in loving creative loop with Townshend. Jeff Elbel.
25 September 2006	*Oakland Press*, A new Who rocks the Palace. Gary Graff.
25 September 2006	*Chicago Sun Times*, Riding nostalgia's magic bus. Jim DeRogatis.
26 September 2006	*Chicago Tribune*, Where Who is now. Greg Kot.
30 September 2006	*Oakland Press*, A new Who rocks the Palace. Gary Graff.
1 October 2006	*Detroit Free Press*, Talking 'bout all generations. James Reaney.
1 October 2006	*Flint Journal*, You bet – Aging Who still rock. Doug Pullen.
6 October 2006	*Calgary Herald*, Who still true. Heath McCoy.
7 October 2006	*Edmonton Sun*, Kids are all right. Yuri Wuensch.
7 October 2006	*The Edmonton Journal*, The Who: rock'n'roll heaven. Sandra Sperounes.
7 October 2006	*Vancouver Sun*, Touring's a little like golf to Townshend. John Mackie.
9 October 2006	*Vancouver Sun*, The Who energize new generation. Chantal Eustace.
12 October 2006	*Seattle Post-Intelligencer*, The Who thrills baby boomer fans. Gene Stout.
15 October 2006	*Tacoma News Tribune*, Who's Left: Townshend and Daltrey mix old and new rock well. Ernest A. Jasmin.
19 October 2006	*Wall Street Journal*, Who's The Who Now? Jim Fusilli.
28 October 2006	*The Daily Mirror*, Endless Wire. (unsigned)

30 October 2006	*Toronto Sun*, The Who: Endless Wire. (unsigned)
31 October 2006	*The Guardian*, The Who: Roundhouse, London. Caroline Sullivan.
6 November 2006	*Los Angeles Times*, Meet the new Who, not the same as the old Who. Richard Cromelin
6 November 2006	*San Diego Union-Tribune*, Two original members emerge triumphant. George Varga.
6 November 2006	*San Jose Mercury-News*, Who: what, where, and why. Shay Quillen
9 November 2006	*Los Angeles Time*, Gathered to make some noise. Ann Powers.
9 November 2006	*San Francisco Chronicle*, Who caught between forging ahead, debts to past. Joel Selvin.
11 November 2006	*Desert Sun*, Find Out 'Who's Next'. Bruce Fessier.
14 November 2006	*Daily Bulletin*, Can The Who still play a mean rock tune? You bet. George A. Paul.
14 November 2006	*Salt Lake Tribune*, The Who and The Pretenders: One memorable night. Dan Nailen.
15 November 2006	*Rocky Mountain News*, Energetic The Who get better? You bet. Mark Brown.
18 November 2006	*Dallas Morning News*, Review: Moves smooth but voice a bit rough during Who's show at AAC. Thor Christensen.
21 November 2006	*Palm Beach Post*, Who show no need for leeway often granted to aging rockers. Leslie Gray Streeter.
24 November 2006	*Dallas Morning News*, The Who's leftovers. Katie Menzer.
28 November 2006	*Lancaster New Era*, The Who rocks – and with sentiment. John Duffy.
29 November 2006	*Connecticut Post*, The Who rock Bridgeport. Sean Spillane.
1 December 2006	*Boston Herald*, For Pete's sake: Townshend taps Daltrey to put The Who back in action. Jed Gottlieb.
3 December 2006	*Grand Rapids Press*, Who's Who: Daltrey, Townshend in rock's elite. John Sinkevics.
4 December 2006	*Boston Globe*, More than a riff of familiar in Who's new songs. Joan Anderman.
6 December 2006	*Grand Rapids Press*, Illness cannot rob The Who of greatness. John Sinkevics.
7 December 2006	*Minneapolis Star-Tribune*, Pete Townshend: The complete interview. Jon Bream.
9 December 2006	*Minneapolis Star-Tribune*, Who show: Roger, can you hear me? Jon Bream.
11 December 2006	*Chicago Sun-Times*, Townshend unplugs to reconnect. Dave Hoekstra.
12 December 2006	*The Columbus Dispatch*, The Who prove themselves rock'n'roll troopers. Aaron Beck.

14 December 2006   *The Daily Telegraph*, On stage, I feel like the goalkeeper. Neil McCormick.

14 December 2006   *The Other Paper*, See them, feel them. John Petric.

9 February 2007   *Evening Standard*, What is in Pete Townshend's Attic? David Smyth.

9 February 2007   *Western Mail*, The mods are back in town. Karen Price.

13 February 2007   *The Independent*, Townshend sniffy over bank manager jibe. Henry Deedes.

16 February 2007   *The Guardian*, Enemy No 1. Chris Salmon.

22 February 2007   *The Independent*, In The Attic: A website with lofty musical ambitions. Pierre Perone.

25 February 2007   *LA Times*, You Can Go Home Again. Irene Lacher.

25 February 2007   *Long Beach Press-Telegram*, An interview with The Who's Pete Townshend. Ryan Ritchie.

25 February 2007   *New York Post*, See Them, Feel Them. Mary Huhn.

25 February 2007   *New York Times*, A Star is Born. Jane L. Levere.

27 February 2007   *Orange County Register*, The Who stages a replay in Long Beach. Ben Wener.

1 March 2007   *Arizona Republic*, The Who returns to the Valley. Michael Senft.

1 March 2007   *San Diego Union-Tribune*, Atlas shrugged. George Varga.

7 March 2007   *Chicagon Sun-Times*, Revived Who is more than a jukebox. Jeff Elbel.

7 March 2007   *Indianapolis Star*, The Who draws on the big picture. David Lindquist.

10 March 2007   *Washington Post*, The Who. Dave McKenna.

14 March 2007   *Tampa Tribune*, Who Abruptly Cancel Show, Citing Illness. Curtis Ross.

15 March 2007   *Chicago Daily Herald*, Pete talkin' 'bout his generation. Mark Guarino.

16 March 2007   *Austin Chronicle*, Spiritual Boys. Jody Denberg.

25 March 2007   *The Oklahoman*, The Who hit all targets. George Lang.

26 March 2007   *St Petersburg Times*, Behold the rock gods at twilight. Sean Daly.

2 April 2007   *Evening Standard*, No substitute for fire. David Smyth.

17 June 2007   *The Independent*, Pete Townshend's daughter looks back on her extraordinary childhood. Emma Townshend.

Index

Singles releases are in roman. Albums, films and plays are in italics.
Song performers' names are in parentheses.

622

Popular (Pete Townshend), 315–316
Porter, Cole, 119
Post, Mike, 567*n.*, 568
Postcard (Who), 137, 146, 227
Postle, Denis, 178–179
Power, John, 414
Praying The Game (Pete Townshend), 256
Predictable (Pete Townshend), 437
Prelude: The Right To Write (Pete
    Townshend), 340, 354*n.*, 358, 385
Presidents, The, 20
Presley, Elvis, 7, 9, 36, 531
Pretenders, The, 296–297, 300, 349*n.*,
    433*n.*
Pretty Thing (Bo Diddley), 36
Price, Bill, 300, 338, 350, 584
Pridden, Bob, 71, 80, 123*n.*, 130, 144*n.*, 148,
    193, 211–212, 240*n.*, 261, 263, 309,
    414
Prince, 406
Proby, P.J., 464
Procol Harum, 461
Psychoderelict (Pete Townshend), 68, 168,
    430–435, 437–448, 450, 467, 469, 475,
    477, 489, 494, 503, 540–541, 544
psychoderelictliveinnewyork (Pete Townshend)
    (DVD), 446
Punk And The Godfather, The (Who), 291
Purcell One Note (Quick Movement (Pete
    Townshend), 491
Purcell, Henry, 41, 324, 583
Purdom, C.B., 94*n.*, 107
Purdy, Joe, 574, 579–580, 581*n.*
Pure And Easy (Pete Townshend), 491
Pure And Easy (Who), 159, 165–166,
    168–169, 172, 183, 227, 260, 556
Purple Rain (film), 377
Pursey, Jimmy, 280
Put The Money Down (Who), 227
Puterbaugh, Parke, 348
Pynchon, Thomas, 564*n.*

Quadrophenia (film), 277, 279–280, 282–286,
    576
Quadrophenia (film soundtrack), 206, 278,
    285–286
Quadrophenia (stage production), 576–577)
Quadrophenia (stage version), 505–507
Quadrophenia (Who), 28, 190, 193, 199–201,
    203, 206–211, 213, 215–218, 221–222,
    227, 239, 317, 338, 342, 372, 373, 375,
    388, 445, 457–464, 467, 470–471, 477,
    490, 500, 505–507, 521*n.*, 527,
    539–542, 571, 576
Queen, 11, 296, 538

Quiet One, The (Who), 314, 321
Quivers, Robin, 565

R.E.M., 135, 538
Raconteurs, The, 562, 575–576
Rael 1&2 (Who), 91–92, 111, 458
RAF Dance Orchestra, 1
Rainbow (Andy Newman), 119*n,*
Rainbow In Curved Air, A (Terry Riley), 164
Rainier, Prince, 131
Raise Your Hands (Rose Hill Drive), 563
Ralphs, Mick, 219
Ramones, 426*n.*
Ravens, Jan, 442
Ray High And The Glass Household (Pete
    Townshend) (novel), 431, 540, 543
Ray, Stevie, 411
Ray, Sugar, 485
Reagan, Nancy, 422
Real Good Looking Boy (Who), 530–532,
    537, 561
Real Me, The (Pete Townshend), 578
Real Me, The (Who), 200, 204, 208, 289,
    317, 527
Real World (Can You Really Dance?) (Pete
    Townshend), 384, 386
Record Producers, The (John Tobler & Stuart
    Grundy) (book), 316
Red Hot Chili Peppers, The, 535, 558, 562
Reed, Jimmy, 13, 17, 51
Reed, Lou, 219, 222, 391, 449–450, 472,
    577–578
Reed, Oliver, 219, 223
Reeves, Jim, 184, 254–255
Reger, Rick, 468
Reizner, Lou, 190–192
Relax (Who), 90, 93
Relay (Pete Townshend), 491
Relay (Who), 185–187, 261, 279, 557
Rent (play), 463
Resnicoff, Matt, 367, 389–390, 392, 401,
    434–435, 438
Rich, Frank, 426
Richard, Cliff, 57
Richard, Cliff, & The Shadows, 9, 14
Richards, Keith, 21, 85, 279, 303, 494, 573
Richman, Stuart, 127
Ride A Rock Horse (Roger Daltrey), 239
Riggio, Melissa, 577
Riggio, Steve, 577
Righteous Brothers, The, 40
Riley, Terry, 150, 164, 484, 491, 582, 583n.
Rimmer, Dave, 361
Ring Of Fire (Johnny Cash), 487
Ring Of Fire (Who), 487